D1600876

KARL MARX
FREDERICK ENGELS
COLLECTED WORKS
VOLUME
28

KARL MARX
FREDERICK ENGELS

COLLECTED
WORKS

INTERNATIONAL PUBLISHERS

NEW YORK

KARL MARX
FREDERICK ENGELS

Volume
28

KARL MARX: 1857-61

INTERNATIONAL PUBLISHERS

NEW YORK

This volume has been prepared jointly by Lawrence & Wishart Ltd., London, International Publishers Co. Inc., New York, and Progress Publishers, Moscow, in collaboration with the Institute of Marxism-Leninism, Moscow

Editorial commissions:
GREAT BRITAIN: E. J. Hobsbawm, John Hoffman, Nicholas Jacobs, Monty Johnstone, Martin Milligan, Jeff Skelley, Ernst Wangermann.
USA: Louis Diskin, Philip S. Foner, James E. Jackson, Leonard B. Levenson, Betty Smith, Dirk J. Struik, William W. Weinstone.
USSR: for Progress Publishers — A. K. Avelichev, N. P. Karmanova, V. N. Sedikh, M. K. Shcheglova; for the Institute of Marxism-Leninism — P. N. Fedoseyev, L. I. Golman, A. I. Malysh, M. P. Mchedlov, V. N. Pospelova, A. G. Yegorov.

Library of Congress Cataloging in Publication Data

Marx, Karl, 1818-1883

    Karl Marx, Frederick Engels: collected works.

    1. Socialism—Collected works. 2. Economics—Collected works. I. Engels, Friedrich, 1820-1895. Works. English. 1975. II. Title.
HX 39.5.   A16 1975   335.4   73-84671
ISBN 0-7178-0528-X (v. 28)

Printed in the Union of Soviet Socialist Republics

Contents

KARL MARX

ECONOMIC WORKS

1857-1861

ECONOMIC MANUSCRIPTS

OF 1857-58

(FIRST VERSION OF *CAPITAL*)

NOTES AND INDEXES

ILLUSTRATIONS

Translated by

ERNST WANGERMANN

Preface

Volume 28 of the *Collected Works* of Marx and Engels opens a new section of this edition, containing Marx's main work, *Capital,* its preliminary versions and the economic writings which immediately preceded it.

The first two volumes of this section, 28 and 29, contain the *Outlines of the Critique of Political Economy*—the economic manuscripts widely known as the *Grundrisse der Kritik der politischen Oekonomie* (the editorial heading under which they were first published in the language of the original in Moscow in 1939-41)— and also Marx's work *A Contribution to the Critique of Political Economy.* The findings of research undertaken in the Soviet Union, the German Democratic Republic and other countries into the *Grundrisse* since the appearance of the first edition, particularly in connection with their publication in the second Russian edition of *Works* of Marx and Engels and in the second edition of *Marx-Engels Gesamtausgabe* (*MEGA*₂, a collection of works by Marx and Engels in the languages of the originals), have been taken into account.

In the present edition the whole range of economic works written in the period 1857-61 is divided up into two interrelated groups. The first of these is the series Economic Manuscripts of 1857-58 which strictly speaking represent the original rough version of *Capital.* Of these Volume 28 includes "Bastiat and Carey", "Introduction" and the first, larger instalment of the *Grundrisse* (the Chapter on Money and the greater part of the Chapter on Capital).

Volume 29 contains the concluding part of the Chapter on Capital and the *Index to the 7 Notebooks.* It also includes the second group of works dating from that period: *A Contribution to the Critique of Political Economy* (which came out in 1859) and preparatory material for that work—a fragment of the original text of the second and of the beginning of the third chapter, a draft plan for the third chapter, and also *References to My Own Notebooks.*

Viewed as a whole, these works represent a complete cycle, reflecting a crucial stage in the formation of Marxist political economy and in the writing of *Capital.* They immediately preceded the economic manuscript of 1861-63, which was the first systematic, although still not final, elaboration of the contents of all the volumes of *Capital.* Basing himself on the results achieved and completing yet another manuscript version of his work in 1863-65, Marx was able to start preparing for publication the first volume of *Capital,* which came out in September 1867, and continue work on the other volumes.

Capital represents the supreme achievement of Marx's theoretical thought, an outstanding scientific feat accomplished in the name of the intellectual and social emancipation of toiling mankind. This work of genius is virtually the product of Marx's whole life. As early as the 1840s, when Marx had only just embarked on research into economic problems and was working on his *Economic and Philosophic Manuscripts of 1844,* he sketched the outlines of a major economic work. His subsequent studies in political economy were subordinated to this broad plan, which he originally intended to realise in the form of a two-volume work entitled *A Critique of Politics and Political Economy.*

The 1840s were an important stage in the development of Marxist economic theory. The dialectical materialist conception of history worked out by Marx and Engels enabled them to reveal the essential features of the capitalist economy and understand its contradictory, antagonistic nature. In his works of the 1840s— *The Poverty of Philosophy, Speech on the Question of Free Trade* and *Wage Labour and Capital* (see present edition, vols. 6 and 9)—Marx took his first steps towards a detailed elaboration of his economic theory. In those works certain aspects of the future theory of value and surplus value were worked out. However, it required further elaboration to become a comprehensive economic teaching.

A new stage in Marx's economic research began after the defeat of the revolution of 1848-49, when, in the autumn of 1849, he was to move to England, where he was able to resume his studies in political economy. Not content with the results already achieved and the material he had collected during his stay in Paris in 1844 and in Brussels between 1845 and 1847, which made up many notebooks of excerpts from various economic writings, Marx, in his own words, started from scratch once more. With unflagging energy he supplemented, elaborated and developed the economic data collected in the forties, without losing sight of his long-term project for a major economic work.

Until July 1857 Marx's work consisted mainly in collecting and critically assessing an enormous wealth of material on economic problems, "a veritable Mont Blanc of factual material", to use Lenin's expression, and also in direct study of all and every development of significance in the economic life of Britain and other countries at that time. Marx turned once again to the works of Adam Smith and David Ricardo, of which he made a most thorough study. He also used voluminous material on various aspects of economics and politics from the vast collection of the British Museum library and from the current press. Between 1850 and 1853 Marx filled with excerpts 24 notebooks which he numbered I to XXIV (there are also several unnumbered notebooks). He made repeated attempts to systematise that material. Evidence of this are his notebooks in which excerpts from different authors are grouped according to subject and supplied with brief commentaries, and also his manuscript headlined "Reflections" (present edition, Vol. 10). Marx made extensive use of the notebooks in writing his works. He often refers to them by number and page number in the *Grundrisse*.

Marx set forth his first theoretical conclusions drawn from his new research in letters to Engels dated 7 January and 3 February 1851 (see present edition, Vol. 38), in which he criticised Ricardo's theory of rent, based on Malthus's law of diminishing returns, and also Ricardo's theory of money circulation, based on the quantitative theory of money.

Expecting a new rise in the revolutionary movement, he intensified his economic research. In the summer of 1857 he twice embarked on an exposition of his economic theory: made drafts on the vulgar economists Bastiat and Carey and started writing the general "Introduction" which he did not finish. Yet on both occasions he had to interrupt his work.

The first ever world economic crisis, which broke out in the autumn of 1857, made Marx set down once again to a systematic exposition of the results of his research in political economy. "I am working like mad all night and every night collating my economic studies so that I at least get the outlines clear before the déluge," he wrote to Engels on 8 December 1857 (see present edition, Vol. 40, p. 217). At the time Jenny Marx wrote to Conrad Schramm: "By day Karl works for his living and by night at the completion of his political economy" (ibid., p. 566). Physical discomfort stemming from a liver disease seriously slowed down this work, obliging Marx to modify his plans. Nevertheless between late 1857 and May 1858 he completed an extensive manuscript of over fifty printed sheets—not for the press but for "self-clarification".

The draft manuscript "Bastiat and Carey", opening this volume, shows that by that time Marx had reached a far clearer understanding of the distinctions between the classical bourgeois political economy and its vulgar school, whose rise pointed to a decline in bourgeois economic thought. Marx accurately character-ised the merits of the classical school while at the same time pointing out its limitations. Using his analysis of the views of Bastiat and Carey as an illustration, Marx singled out the main areas in which the theory of the classical political economists Smith and Ricardo was vulgarised by their imitators. He pointed out that unlike the classical economists, who did not conceal the contradic-tory character of capitalist production relations and "naively analysed their antagonism" (see this volume, p. 6), Bastiat, Carey and other vulgar economists sought to gloss over the antagonistic nature of the capitalist system, depicting it as the natural ideal of harmonious social development.

Although unfinished, Marx's draft "Introduction" to his future economic treatise is of extraordinary scientific value. It shows that by the autumn of 1857 he had already worked out in detail the methodological principles of his economic theory, which rests on the basic conclusions drawn from the materialist conception of history, above all on the proposition concerning the primacy of social production. At the same time, unlike bourgeois economists who declared capitalist production eternal and treated production as some general abstraction, Marx in his "Introduction" wrote of production as shaped by specific social conditions, singling out bourgeois production of his time as the object of his research.

Setting forth his understanding of the subject of political economy, Marx rises above the limitations of the bourgeois economists, including the classical economists, who confined the tasks of economics to the study of relations of distribution. His analysis of the dialectical unity and interaction of production, distribution, exchange and consumption leads Marx to conclude that production is not just the point of departure but also the decisive moment of this unity and that the forms of distribution are merely an expression of the forms of production. Thus the production relations between men, and the laws governing the development of a given mode of production, constitute the true subject matter of economics.

Marx worked out his ideas on various aspects of political economy in close connection with general philosophical questions of the revolutionary world outlook. Regarding production relations as the economic basis of social development, Marx went on to examine processes at work within the political and ideological superstructure, pointing out their dependence on the basis and their reaction on the basis. In the "Introduction", for example, we find statements reflecting the development and concretisation of Marx's views on certain ideological phenomena, in particular his ideas on the specific laws governing the development of art as one of the forms of social consciousness.

The conclusions drawn by Marx in the "Introduction"—that artistic creation is conditioned by specific historical social relations, although these are not reflected in works of art in a primitive, mechanical way, but in accordance with the special laws of development peculiar to art; that as a result of this periods of florescence in art do not necessarily coincide with periods of progress in the economy and other social spheres; that art plays an enormous social role and exerts a strong influence on social progress, and finally that the art of different epochs and different peoples contains inimitable and undying values of general relevance—form an essential part of the overall heritage of Marxian aesthetic ideas.

In the "Introduction" Marx thoroughly substantiated the method of political economy as a science, a method which he applied from all possible angles in his subsequent economic research. He contrasted the dialectical materialist interpretation of scientific method with Hegel's idealist dialectics, while at the same time utilising all the rational elements of Hegel's logic of scientific analysis.

Research, Marx pointed out in the "Introduction", should start out from the immediately manifest and probe down into the very heart of phenomena until finally the very simplest determinations are reached. Only after that can the researcher move on from abstract determinations to "a rich totality of many determinations and relations" (see this volume, p. 37). While the first part of this path—from the concrete to the abstract—has virtually been traversed by bourgeois political economy, the most important object of subsequent research is the "return journey", from the abstract to the concrete. This method of progression from the abstract to the concrete Marx regarded as "the correct scientific method". It presupposes that the concrete, which provides the starting point for theoretical analysis, appears in the outcome of research as the unity of diverse elements, the synthesis of many definitions. In Marx's theory, scientific abstractions are inseparably linked with concrete reality as their premiss, while the course of abstract thought moving on from the simple to the complex corresponds, on the whole, to the actual historical process.

Pointing to the need of combining the logical and historical approaches to the object of research in progressing from the abstract to the concrete, Marx regarded the logical and the historical as a dialectical unity but not an identity. He stressed that a logical appraisal of individual economic categories cannot be replaced by an historical one, for at different stages of history various economic phenomena have played roles different from the one they play in a given economic structure. However, the researcher is obliged to bear in mind that the economic categories under investigation are the product of historical development, that they came into being within a definite historical context and have undergone a definite historical evolution. In order to grasp the essence of an economic phenomenon, it is vital to study both its developed form and its embryo, its origins. Logical analysis cannot be an arbitrary mental construction divorced from actual historical development. It must be organically combined with historical analysis, for this combination provides for more detailed research and verification of conclusions.

The "Introduction" contains Marx's first outline of the structure of his future economic work (see this volume, p. 45). Amplifying it, he wrote to Lassalle on 22 February 1858: "The whole is divided into 6 books: 1. On Capital (contains a few introductory chapters). 2. On Landed Property. 3. On Wage Labour. 4. On the State. 5. International Trade. 6. World Market" (present edition, Vol. 40, p. 270). Marx gave a more detailed account of his plan to Engels in a letter dated 2 April 1858. In the framework of this overall plan Marx conducted his economic research between 1857 and 1861. It was only later that he changed the structure of his economic treatise.

The Manuscript of 1857-58 constitutes a landmark in the history of Marxism. In it Marx for the first time elaborated his theory of value and, on that basis, the theory of surplus value.

This was his second great discovery which, together with his discovery of the materialist conception of history, transformed socialism from a Utopia into a science.

The Manuscript of 1857-58 introduces the reader directly into the workings of Marx's mind, enabling him to follow step by step the creation of Marx's economic theory. Here the logic of Marx's research and the concrete aspects of the application of the scientific method described in his "Introduction" come particularly clearly to the fore.

The Manuscript of 1857-58 opens with a chapter on money, which later Marx numbered with the Roman figure II, since it was to be preceded by a chapter on value (see this volume, p. 51). Marx began this chapter with a critique of the economic views of Proudhon, in particular his theory of money. "To clear the way for critical and materialist socialism seeking to make understandable the actual historical development of social production, it was necessary to break with that brand of idealist political economy, whose last embodiment was, without himself realising it, Proudhon," Marx wrote later in an article "La 'Misère de la Philosophie'" which appeared in the French newspaper *Égalité* (No. 12, 7 April 1880).

Marx had first undertaken a critical analysis of Proudhon's sociological and economic conceptions underlying his Utopian reformist schemes for overcoming the contradictions of bourgeois society in his work *The Poverty of Philosophy* (1847). In that work, however, Marx still based his arguments to a considerable extent on the economic views of Ricardo. Now he criticised Proudhonism from the standpoint of the economic theory he had created, totally refuting the Proudhonist thesis concerning the possibility of overcoming the antagonistic character of the contradictions of capitalist society by means of a reform of the banks. These contradictions, Marx wrote, "can never be exploded by a quiet metamorphosis" (see this volume, pp. 96-97). Marx's research made it quite clear that the attempts by Proudhon and his adherents to "amend" the capitalist system and eliminate its "shortcomings", while retaining its economic foundations, were scientifically untenable and in practice could only disorient the working class and divert it from the real tasks of the proletarian struggle.

Criticising Proudhonist illusions, Marx elaborated in his manuscript all the basic elements of the genuinely scientific theory of value. He demonstrated how in the process of development of social production and of the social division of labour products are converted into commodities and commodities into money. "The real question is: does not the bourgeois system of exchange itself make a specific instrument of exchange necessary?" Marx noted, "Does it not of necessity create a special equivalent of all values?" (see this volume, p. 65). Here Marx raised the question of the essential link between commodity and money, which he had first formulated in *The Poverty of Philosophy*; however, he provided a solution to this question only in the Manuscript of 1857-58. It was based on his analysis of the two aspects of the commodity—its use value and its value—and of the dual nature of labour creating the commodity. Marx showed that the contradiction between the qualitative homogeneity of commodities as values and their natural difference as use values finds its external solution in the process of exchange, in the splitting of the commodity into commodity and money, in the fact that the value of the commodity acquires an independent existence in a special commodity, namely money. Money, which provides an external solution to the contradiction between the use value and the value of the commodity, at the same time aggravates all the contradictions of commodity production based on private exchange. Inherent in these contradictions is the possibility of economic crises.

Marx's thesis on the dual nature of labour in commodity production constitutes the basis of his theory of value. It is precisely here that we find one of the main dividing lines which set apart his theory from the labour theory of value put forward by the classical bourgeois economists. These economists did not understand the qualitative difference between concrete and abstract labour, reducing the whole question to measuring value by labour time. Actually, as Marx was later to point out, "the *whole* understanding of the facts" hinged upon the appreciation of this dual nature of labour.

As he elaborated his theory of value, Marx discovered in the commodity the "economic cell" of bourgeois society. The point of departure in his analysis of the economic structure of society is neither value nor the value relationship of commodities but the commodity itself, the material bearer of those relations. This was precisely the reason why Marx later changed the name of the first chapter of his work, calling it "The Commodity". Already in his first draft of this chapter, at the end of the manuscript (see Vol. 29) Marx wrote: "The commodity is the first category in which bourgeois wealth makes its appearance."

One of the main conclusions drawn by Marx in the Chapter on Money was that the developed form of commodity production in conditions of private property in the means of production presupposes capitalist relations. The development of commodity production and exchange value inevitably tends to "the separation of labour and property; as a result, one's labour will create someone else's property and property will command someone else's labour" (see this volume, p. 170).

The major part of the economic Manuscript of 1857-58 consists of the Chapter on Capital.

In this volume are published the first section of that chapter, examining the process of the production of capital, and a large part of the second section, which deals with the circulation of capital. The end of the chapter is included in Volume 29. Taken as a whole, the Chapter on Capital covers the main questions which Marx intended to treat in the first of the six books originally planned, namely in that which, according to the letter to Lassalle cited above (22 February 1858), was to be entitled "On Capital", and whose title is elsewhere given as "Capital in General". Later, after Marx had altered the structure of his work and started to think in terms of a three-part study (*The Process of Production of Capital, The Process of Circulation of Capital* and *The Process of Capitalist Production as a Whole*), the material contained in this chapter provided the starting-point for the whole work.

In the Chapter on Capital Marx concerned himself with the problem central to the whole of his analysis, that of explaining the mechanism of capitalist exploitation. Bourgeois economists regarded capital as the simple sum of values, vainly attempting to move on directly from value to capital and grasp the essence of the transformation of money into capital. Marx notes that "the simple movement of exchange values, as it is present in pure circulation, can never realise capital" (this volume, p. 185).

The content of capitalist production relations is the relation between worker and capitalist, between labour and capital, which stand opposed to each other and between which exchange takes place. The difficulty in analysing these relations lies in the fact that the essentially non-equivalent exchange between worker and capitalist is carried on on the basis of an exchange of equivalents.

Marx started out by dividing the exchange between capital and labour into two qualitatively different, diametrically opposed processes: (1) the actual exchange between the worker and the capitalist as a result of which the capitalist "obtains the productive power which maintains and multiplies capital" (see this volume,

p. 204); (2) the actual process of labour in which the maintenance and multiplication of capital takes place. In his analysis of the first stage Marx formulated the following thesis: "In the relationship of capital and labour ... one side (capital) faces the other above all as *exchange value* while the other side (labour) faces capital as use value" (see this volume, p. 197). From the bourgeois economists' traditional formulas "commodity labour" and "sale of labour" Marx passed on, for the first time, to an investigation of the specific properties of the commodity "labour power" (although in this manuscript he mostly uses the term "labour capacity"). Labour in Marx's analysis does not figure as a commodity, but as the use value of the commodity the worker sells to the capitalist. The peculiarity of this use value lies in the fact that it "is not materialised in a product, it does not exist in any way external to him [the worker]. Consequently, his use value does not exist in reality but only potentially, as his capacity" (see this volume, ibid.). As a result of the first stage of the exchange between labour and capital the control of the worker's living labour has passed into the hands of the capitalist. The second stage of the exchange is the actual process of the creation of exchange values, as a result of which capital is maintained and increased.

Marx demonstrated that since the worker does not own the means of production he cannot be the owner of the value which living labour creates in the production process. Part of the value created by the worker and belonging to the capitalist the latter is obliged to return to the worker in the form of wages so as to pay the value of labour power, i. e. the quantity of labour spent on the production of the worker himself. If the level of labour productivity is so high that the value created by living labour exceeds the value of labour power, surplus labour is being performed, and the capitalist receives surplus value equal to the difference between the value created by living labour and the value of labour power.

In the Chapter on Capital Marx also developed his teaching on the two forms of surplus value—absolute and relative surplus value—and in this connection formulated the ambivalent tendency of capital: towards lengthening the working day as a means of increasing absolute surplus value, and towards reducing the necessary labour time as a means of increasing relative surplus value.

Having revealed the true nature of surplus value, Marx proceeded on this basis to investigate its converted forms—profit, interest, rent—which appear on the surface of bourgeois society.

Basing himself on the theory of the two forms of capital—constant and variable—elaborated for the first time in this manuscript, Marx put forward a new theory of profit qualitatively different from that of bourgeois political economists, who constantly confused specific forms of surplus value with its general form. In a letter to Engels about his work on this manuscript Marx wrote on 16 January 1858 that he had "completely demolished the theory of profit as hitherto propounded" (see present edition, Vol. 40, p. 249).

Marx had now come very close to the discovery of the law of average profit and price of production. After establishing that the profit of the whole capitalist class could not exceed the sum of surplus value, Marx concluded that of necessity individual rates of profit varied from one branch of production to another and that these were redistributed as a result of inter-branch competition, thus forming a general rate of profit. He went on to demonstrate that this general rate was formed through the redistribution of the total sum of surplus value produced in all branches of capitalist production, in proportion to the amount of capital invested. It was a feature of this process that commodities were sold at prices that did not correspond to their values, being in some branches higher and in others lower than the values of the commodities. An exhaustive solution to the problem of average profit and price of production was to be provided by Marx later, in his Manuscript of 1861-63.

In the Manuscript of 1857-58 Marx critically analysed the theories of bourgeois economists, drawing comparisons between various bourgeois concepts and contrasting them with his own views on key questions of economics. The Manuscript of 1857-58 demonstrates graphically that Marx's elaboration of a new economic theory was combined with a critical refutation of concepts which were predominant in the economic thought of his day. Nor did Marx overlook the rational ideas expounded by his predecessors in political economy. He often came out in their defence against unjust accusations and reproaches from contemporary bourgeois political economists.

A particularly large amount of critical material is in the sub-section on bourgeois theories of surplus value and profit in Section Two of the Chapter on Capital. Although here Marx did not yet provide a comprehensive picture of the historical development of bourgeois economics, he nevertheless singled out many of the traits typical of bourgeois economic thought on this cardinal question in his critical analysis of the ideas expounded by representatives of various schools of political economy, including the classical school of Smith and Ricardo. He pointed out its incapacity to penetrate to the heart of the relations between labour and capital and grasp the character of the appropriation of the product of the worker's surplus labour by the capitalist; he showed its tendency to consider capital itself only from the point of view of its material content, ignoring its essence as an historically determined form of social relations, and indicated a number of other fundamental shortcomings. As he singled these out Marx revealed the class causes accounting for the narrow outlook of the bourgeois economists. He stressed that even as penetrating a thinker as Ricardo had failed to clarify for himself the process of capitalist production, "nor, as a bourgeois, could he" (see this volume, p. 474). Marx severely criticised the theories of capital and profit set forth in the works of Say, Senior, McCulloch and other economists as blatant example of apologetic writing that hypocritically presented capitalist exploitation in a rosy light. Malthus's interpretation of the "value of labour" and wages was characterised by Marx as "shallow fallacy", and his theory of population as a "brutal expression" of the "brutal view taken by capital" (see this volume, pp. 496, 524). Marx pointed out that his theory was false from beginning to end and that it was based on tendentious premises and completely ignored the historical changes in the conditions of production: "In this way, he [Malthus] transforms historically distinct relations into an abstract numerical relation which he simply plucks out of thin air, and which is based on neither natural nor historical laws" (see this volume, pp. 524-25).

In contrast to Malthus Marx revealed the real causes behind the formation of over-population in the pre-capitalist epoch and under capitalism. He pointed out that these causes were by no means to be found in the alleged insufficiency of natural resources and the increase of the human race, which was outgrowing them, but in the actual conditions of social production, in particular in the social contradictions, unemployment, etc., engendered by the capitalist system.

The Manuscript of 1857-58 testifies to the fact that by that time Marx was already thinking of allotting a special place in his future work to a critical survey of the history of bourgeois political economy from the viewpoint of its main problems.

While working on the Chapter on Capital Marx arrived at the conclusion—in accordance with his interpretation of the dialectical link between the logical and historical aspects of the scientific research method—that it was essential to supplement his analysis of the capitalist mode of production with a survey of the preceding social forms on the one hand, and a survey of the social form which would inevitably replace capitalism on the other.

Marx included in his Chapter on Capital an historical description of the *forms that had preceded capitalist production,* in which he traced the development of the forms of property from primitive communal society to the emergence of capitalist forms of appropriation. The investigation of the pre-capitalist modes of production undertaken here by Marx constitutes a further elaboration of his views on the principal stages of the historical process first set forth in *The German Ideology.*

While analysing the pre-capitalist forms of property Marx probed to the very heart of the question of the various types of production relations, stressing the active role of the productive forces in the process of social development, which conditioned the inevitable change of these forms. In the Manuscript of 1857-58 Marx took another important step in the development of his theory of socio-economic formations.

Profound ideas were voiced here concerning the earliest stage of human history. Marx underlined the absence of class divisions in primitive society, which was dominated by tribal ties and communal principles. The collective spirit and, at the initial stage, the "herd spirit" were the dominant traits of primitive man's whole way of life.

The Manuscript of 1857-58 also contains an analysis of the forms of pre-capitalist exploitation, in particular slave and serf labour, and the features that set them apart from wage labour.

In his analysis of pre-capitalist formations Marx concentrated on problems of the evolution of the agricultural commune. The disintegration of the commune, retained in various forms in all previous stages, was, as he stressed, one of the conditions making possible the emergence of the capitalist mode of production. This to a considerable extent serves to explain Marx's particular interest in its historical fate. The historical and typological description of the commune first provided by Marx in the Manuscript of 1857-58 to this day clarifies many of the key problems of ancient and medieval history. Marx's ideas on the universality of the commune as the most ancient social institution, on its influence on social and political structures in ancient times and the Middle Ages, on the direction and main stages of its historical evolution and modification and on the reasons for its decline and disintegration, are as valid as ever today.

His analysis of the development of pre-capitalist forms of property enabled Marx to reveal the historical conditions for the emergence of the capitalist mode of production and to demonstrate that the main precondition was the disintegration of various forms of labourers' ownership of their conditions of production or of the ownership of labourers as an objective condition of production. In the Manuscript of 1857-58 Marx provided a profound treatment of the primitive accumulation of capital, demonstrating that its essence consisted on the one hand in the formation of a class of hired workers deprived of instruments or means of production and on the other in the transformation of former means of production into a "free fund", i.e., into capital free of traditional feudal, guild and other fetters. "The same process which confronts the masses of free workers with the *objective conditions of labour,* has also put them face to face with these conditions as *capital"* (see this volume, p. 427). For the first time the epoch of primitive accumulation was singled out as a specific, transitional period of historical development. In this context, Marx pointed out that the roots of capitalism should be sought not only in the development of urban industry, but in the process of the capitalist transformation of agriculture, which began in a number of countries (Britain, Holland) at the very dawn of the capitalist era.

In the Manuscript of 1857-58 Marx elaborated in more detail the principles of the scientific periodisation of the history of capitalist society which he had originally outlined as early as the 1840s in *The German Ideology* and *The Poverty of Philosophy.* He substantiated the need to draw a distinction between the manufactory and machine stages of capitalist development, pointing out that the manufactories were still unable to create the material basis for the universal spread of capitalist relations and for the ousting of pre-capitalist social forms. Only large-scale machine production can provide the basis for the final assertion of the capitalist system, it alone really makes possible the full domination of capital and at the same time creates the material conditions for its overthrow and the emergence of a new, more progressive order.

After studying the genesis of capitalism and disclosing the laws of its emergence and development Marx went on to define its actual historical position, demonstrating the inevitability of its collapse and of the abolition of the separation between labour and property intrinsic to that society.

Surplus value, treated in Marx's theory as the necessary result of capitalist relations of production and the expression of their essence and contradictory character, shapes the law of the progress of the capitalist mode of production leading inevitably to its downfall and its replacement by communism. Since capitalist exploitation, as demonstrated by Marx, stems from the very essence of capitalist production relations, it follows on from this that the emancipation of the working class from exploitation cannot be achieved within the framework of the capitalist order.

The analysis Marx went on to provide of the new social order destined to replace capitalism contained astute ideas as to the main traits and laws of development peculiar to social relations under communism. Marx stressed the historical necessity of the transition to communism, the emergence of which presupposes a specific stage of development of material and cultural conditions. Communism, according to Marx, is a society that will be dominated by "free individuality, based on the universal development of the individuals and the subordination of their communal, social productivity, which is their social possession" (see this volume, p. 95).

The Manuscript of 1857-58 also contains significant ideas concerning the change in the character of labour in the communist society of the future. Marx pointed out that in conditions of collective production the individual's labour will, from the outset, appear as socialised labour; the contradiction between the social character of labour and the private form of the appropriation of its products which is intrinsic to capitalism will disappear. Underlining the fact that each worker will be interested in ensuring the most expedient, rational and systematic organisation of production, Marx formulated the law of time economy in communist society: "As with a single individual, the comprehensiveness of its [society's] development, its pleasures and its activities depends upon the saving of time. Ultimately, all economy is a matter of economy of time. Society must also allocate its time appropriately to achieve a production corresponding to its total needs, just as the individual must allocate his time correctly to acquire knowledge in suitable proportions or to satisfy the various demands on his activity. Economy of time, as well as the planned distribution of labour time over the various branches of production, therefore, remains the first economic law if communal production is taken as the basis. It becomes a law even to a much higher degree" (ibid., p. 109).

Unlike the Utopian socialists who dreamt of turning labour under communism from a hateful burden or curse, which it is for the vast majority of working people under capitalism, into a game or simple diversion, Marx wrote of labour in communist society as a prime necessity of life, which "is also the most damnably difficult" (see this volume, p. 530). A high level of labour organisation and discipline, a harmonic balance between the personal interests of the producer and the interests of the whole of society, wide utilisation of the results of production, of all social wealth, to satisfy the material and cultural needs of society—such was Marx's vision of communist society.

*   *   *

In the course of publishing the present *Collected Works* it was decided to expand the economic section. In particular, the whole of the Economic Manuscript of 1861-63 is to be included. This has made necessary certain modifications in the original plan of the edition. In volumes 28 and 29 the series of Marx's economic works dating from 1857 to 1861 (with the exception of his notebooks of excerpts) appears in English in a complete and systematised form.

The translation of the Economic Manuscripts of 1857-58 and the accompanying manuscripts, published in volumes 28 and 29, is based on the text: *Marx-Engels Gesamtausgabe (MEGA)*, II, 1; II, 2, Berlin, 1976-1981.

The fact that these manuscripts were rough drafts explains many of their textual features: the absence of division into sections and paragraphs over long passages, the considerable number of digressions and incomplete sentences, and a certain unevenness of style. In many places Marx put down his ideas in a cursory, fragmentary, elliptic form. The greater part of the manuscripts was written in German but Marx often made use of foreign expressions and sometimes switched over completely to English or French. He quotes sometimes in German translation, sometimes in the language of the original and sometimes in more than one language at a time with switches in the middle. There are also word forms of Marx's own invention: English and French words used with German prefixes or endings, and terms made up of elements from different language, etc. When these manuscripts were translated into English all these factors had to be taken into account and unified so that Marx's ideas expressed in different languages could be rendered unequivocally and as precisely as possible.

The indispensable elucidations in certain parts of the manuscripts, insertions, made to complete unfinished or abbreviated sentences, quotations etc. are given in square brackets, as are the numbers of Marx's notebooks (Roman numbers or Latin letters) and the page numbers in each notebook (Arabic numerals). In view of this the square brackets which are sometimes encountered in the actual manuscripts have been replaced with two oblique lines. If the text is not presented consecutively, but in a slightly rearranged way based on Marx's directions, this is pointed out in footnotes. The footnotes also point out words or passages crossed out by Marx and in certain instances reproduce the original versions.

Excessively long paragraphs have been broken up into smaller ones to make for easier reading. In certain cases where there occur particularly cumbersome phrases with incidental insertions, these insertions are given in the form of author's footnotes so as not to blur the main line of argument.

In this edition the manuscripts are printed in a new English translation. Foreign expressions including those in Greek and Latin are given in the original language. English quotations, phrases, expressions and individual words encountered in the original are set in small caps. Quotations from English sources are given according to the editions used by the author. In all cases the form of quoting used by Marx is respected. The language in which Marx quotes is indicated unless it is German.

The volume was compiled, the preface and notes written by Tatyana Vasilyeva and edited by Lev Golman and Vladimir Brushlinsky (Institute of Marxism-Leninism of the CC CPSU).

The name index and the index of periodicals were prepared by Galina Kostryukova; the index of quoted and mentioned literature and the subject index by Tatyana Vasilyeva (Institute of Marxism-Leninism of the CC CPSU).

The translation was made by Ernst Wangermann (Lawrence and Wishart) and edited by Natalia Karmanova, Margarita Lopukhina and Victor Schnittke (Progress Publishers). The volume was prepared for the press by Svetlana Gerasimenko (Progress Publishers).

Scientific editor for this volume was Larisa Miskievich (Institute of Marxism-Leninism of the CC CPSU).

KARL MARX

ECONOMIC WORKS

1857-1861

ECONOMIC MANUSCRIPTS

OF 1857-1858

(First Version of *Capital*)

5

BASTIAT AND CAREY [1]

[III-1] BASTIAT, *HARMONIES ÉCONOMIQUES*,
2-ME ÉDITION, PARIS, 1851

AVANTPROPOS

The history of modern political economy ends with Ricardo and Sismondi: antithetical figures, of whom the one speaks English, the other French—just as it begins at the end of the 17th century with Petty and Boisguillebert. The later literature of political economy ends up either in eclectic, syncretic compendia, like e.g. the work of J. St. Mill,[a] or in rather detailed elaboration of particular branches, like e.g. Tooke's *History of Prices* and in general the more recent English writings on circulation—the only branch in which really new discoveries have been made. For the writings on colonisation, landed property (in its different forms), population, etc., really go beyond the older writings only in respect of their greater abundance of material. There are some reproductions of old economic controversies for a larger public and some practical solutions for day-to-day problems, like the writings on FREE TRADE and PROTECTION. Finally, there are tendentious exaggerations of the classical theories, e.g. Chalmers exaggerates Malthus, Gülich exaggerates Sismondi, and, in their earlier writings, MacCulloch and Senior in some ways exaggerate Ricardo. This literature is altogether derivative, reproduction characterised by a greater refinement of form, a more extensive appropriation of the material, a greater emphasis, popularisation, synopsis and elaboration of detail. It lacks salient and decisive phases of development, confining itself on the one hand to stock-taking and on the other to adding detail on individual moments.

---

[a] J. St. Mill, *Principles of Political Economy with some of their Applications to Social Philosophy.*— Ed.

The only apparent exceptions are the writings of Carey, the Yankee, and Bastiat, the Frenchman, the latter acknowledging that he bases himself on the former.[a] Both understand that the opposition to political economy—socialism and communism—finds its theoretical assumptions in the works of classical political economy itself, especially in Ricardo, who must be considered as its most complete and final expression. Both therefore find it necessary to criticise the theoretical expression which bourgeois society has historically achieved in modern political economy as a misunderstanding and to demonstrate the harmony of the relations of production at the point where the classical economists naively analysed their antagonism. The entirely different, even contradictory national context from which their writings derive, nevertheless impels them in the same direction.

Carey is the only original economist among the North Americans. He belongs to a country in which bourgeois society is not developing on the basis of feudalism but in which it has originated from itself; in which it does not appear as the surviving product of the development of centuries but as the point of departure for a new development; in which the State, in contrast to all previous national forms, was from the start subordinated to bourgeois society, to its production, and could never claim to be an end in itself; in which bourgeois society itself, combining the productive forces of an old world with the immense natural terrain of a new one, is developing on an unprecedented scale and in unprecedented [conditions of] freedom of movement and far surpassing all previous achievements in [III-2] mastery of the forces of nature, and in which, finally, the contradictions of bourgeois society itself appear only as transient moments.

What could be more natural than that Carey should consider the relations of production in which this immense New World has grown so quickly, so astonishingly and so fortunately, as the eternal normal relations of social production and intercourse; that they should seem to him merely impeded and restricted in Europe and especially in England, which he really identifies with Europe, by the fetters inherited from the feudal period; that they should seem to him merely to have been regarded, depicted or generalised in a distorted, falsified way by the English economists in that they mistook accidental perversions of them for their immanent character?

---

[a] F. Bastiat, *Harmonies économiques,* 2nd ed., Paris, 1851, p. 364.— *Ed.*

American relations as opposed to English: that is what his critique of the English theory of landed property, wages, population, class antagonisms, etc., boils down to. Bourgeois society does not exist in England in its pure form, corresponding to its concept, adequate to itself. How, then, could the English economists' ideas of bourgeois society be the true, unsullied expression of a reality which they did not know?

Carey ultimately identifies the disturbing effect of traditional influences not emerging from the womb of bourgeois society itself upon that society's *natural* relations with the influence of the State on bourgeois society, with State interference and State regulation. E. g. wages [according to Carey] rise naturally with the productivity of labour. If we find that reality does not correspond to this law, we have only to abstract from the influence of government, taxes, [State] monopolies, etc., whether in Hindustan or in England. Bourgeois relations considered in themselves, i.e. after taking away the influence of the State, will in fact always confirm the harmonious laws of bourgeois political economy. To what extent these State influences (PUBLIC DEBT, TAXES, etc.) themselves arise from bourgeois relations—and thus appear in e.g. England by no means as the results of feudalism but rather of its dissolution and suppression, and to what extent even in North America the power of the central government grows with the centralisation of capital—this, naturally, Carey does not investigate.

While Carey thus seeks to confront the English economists with the higher potency of bourgeois society in North America, Bastiat seeks to confront the French socialists with the lower potency of bourgeois society in France. You think [he says to the French socialists] that you are revolting against the laws of bourgeois society in a country in which these laws have never been allowed their full realisation! You only know these laws in their stunted French form, and take as their immanent form what is only their national French distortion. Look at England. Here in France the task is to free bourgeois society from the fetters which the State lays upon it. You wish to multiply these fetters. First develop bourgeois relations in their pure form, then we shall discuss the matter again. (Bastiat is right to this extent, that in France, because of its peculiar social structure, much is taken for socialism which in England is political economy.)

Carey, however, whose starting point is the American emancipation of bourgeois society from the State, ends with the demand for State interference, lest the pure development of bourgeois relations be disturbed by external influences in the way in which this has actually happened in America. He is a PROTECTIONIST, while Bastiat is a FREE TRADER.

The harmony of economic laws appears in the whole world as disharmony, and the beginnings of this disharmony strike Carey even in the United States. How does one explain this strange phenomenon? Carey ascribes it to the destructive effect of England's striving for industrial monopoly on the world market. Originally, [economic] relations were distorted inside England by the false theories of its economists. Now, [III-3] as the dominating power on the world market, England distorts the harmony of economic relations in all countries of the world. This disharmony is real, not based merely on the subjective perception of economists.

What Russia is for Urquhart politically,[a] England is for Carey economically. The harmony of economic relations is based, according to Carey, on the harmonious cooperation of town and country, of industry and agriculture. England, having destroyed this basic harmony within itself, destroys it everywhere on the world market through its competition, and is thus the destructive element of universal harmony. The only defence against this are protective tariffs—the forcible isolation of the nation from the destructive power of English large-scale industry. Therefore the State, branded at the outset as the only disturber of the "*harmonies économiques*", becomes their last refuge.

On the one hand, Carey here once more articulates the specific national development of the United States, its opposition to and its competition with England. He does it in the naive form of proposing that the United States destroy the industrialism propagated by England by developing its own more quickly through protective tariffs. Apart from this naivety, the harmony of bourgeois relations of production ends with Carey in the total disharmony of these relations just where they appear upon the most magnificent scene, the world market, and in their most magnificent development, as the relations of producing nations. All the relations which appear to him harmonious within particular national boundaries, or also in the abstract form of general relations of bourgeois society—the concentration of capital, division of labour, wage labour, etc.—appear to him as disharmonious where they show themselves in their most developed form—in their world market form—as the internal

---

[a] An allusion to Urquhart's anti-Russia sentiments.— *Ed.*

relations which produce England's domination in the world market and which, as destructive influences, are the result of this domination.

It is harmonious, if, within a country, patriarchal production gives way to industrial production, and the process of dissolution accompanying this development is conceived only in its positive aspect. But it becomes disharmonious, if England's large-scale industry dissolves the patriarchal or petty-bourgeois or other primitive forms of another country's national production. The concentration of capital within a country and the dissolving effect of this concentration present themselves to him only in their positive aspect. But the monopoly enjoyed by concentrated English capital and its dissolving effects on the smaller national capitals of other countries, are disharmonious. Carey has not grasped that these world market disharmonies are only the ultimate adequate expression of the disharmonies which have become fixed in the economic categories as abstract relations or have a local existence on the smallest scale.

No wonder, then, that on the other side he forgets the positive content of these processes of dissolution—the only aspect which he recognises of the economic categories in their abstract form or of the real relations within particular countries from which they are abstracted—in their complete world market form. Hence, where he is confronted by economic relations in their truth, i.e. in their universal reality, he collapses from his systematic optimism into a denunciatory and irritated pessimism. This contradiction constitutes the originality of his writings and gives them their significance. He is American as much in his assertion of the harmony within bourgeois society as in his assertion of the disharmony of the same relations in their world market form.

In Bastiat nothing of all this. With him, the harmony of these relations belongs to another world which lies beyond the borders of France, in England and America. It is merely the imagined, ideal form of the un-French Anglo-American relations, not the real form which actually confronts him on his own territory. Hence, while in Bastiat harmony does not in any way arise from a wealth of living observation, but is rather the stilted product of a thin and strained, contradictory reflection, the only aspect of reality is his demand that the French state should renounce its economic limits.

Carey sees the contradictions inherent in [bourgeois] economic relations as soon as they appear as *English* relations on the world market. Bastiat, who merely imagines the harmony, begins to see its realisation only where France ends and where all the nationally separated component parts of bourgeois society compete with each other freed from State supervision. This ultimate harmony of his—and the premiss of all his earlier imagined ones—is, however, itself a mere postulate which is supposed to be realised by free trade legislation.

[III-4] Thus, if Carey, quite apart from the scientific value of his researches, has at least the merit of articulating in abstract form the magnitude of American relations and of doing so in contradistinction to those of the Old World, the only real background to Bastiat is the pettiness of French relations, whose long ears stick out of his harmonies everywhere. But this is a superfluous merit, because the relations of so old a country are sufficiently known and least of all require to be made known by such a negative circuitous route. Carey is therefore rich in so to speak *bona fide* researches into such areas of political economy as credit, rent, etc. Bastiat is only occupied with paraphrases glossing over the contradictory result of his researches; *l'hypocrisie du contentement.*

Carey's generality is Yankee universality. For him France and China are equally near. He is at all times the man who lives both on the Atlantic and the Pacific coast. Bastiat's generality is a turning away from all countries. Carey, as a true Yankee, absorbs from all directions the abundant material which the Old World offers him, not indeed to cognise the immanent soul of this material and thus to concede to it its right to its own proper life, but to work it up as lifeless pieces of evidence, as indifferent matter, for his own purposes, i.e. for the propositions derived from his Yankee point of view. Hence his traversing of all countries, his mountains of uncritical statistics, his encyclopaedic reading. Bastiat on the other hand produces fantastic history: his abstraction takes the form now of logical reasoning, now of notional events which never actually occurred anywhere. Just as the theologian discusses sin now as a law of human nature, now as the history of man's fall.

Bastiat and Carey are therefore equally unhistorical and anti-historical. But the unhistorical element in Carey is the contemporary historical principle of North America, while the unhistorical element in Bastiat is only a reminiscence of the 18th-century French mode of generalisation. Carey is therefore formless and diffuse, Bastiat affected and formally logical. The utmost that Bastiat achieves are commonplaces paradoxically expressed, polished *en facettes.* Carey's work is prefaced by a few general theses in axiomatic form. These are followed by his unshaped material—compilation serving as verification—which is not in any way worked up to sustain his theses. In Bastiat, the only material—apart from a few local examples or some ordinary English phenomena fantastically distorted—amounts to no more than the general theses of the economists.

The chief counterpart to Carey is Ricardo, in short the modern English economists; to Bastiat, the French socialists.

[III-5] XIV. DES SALAIRES[2]

The following are Bastiat's main propositions:

All men strive for fixity of income, FIXED REVENUE.

//Truly French example: (1) Everyone wants to be an official or wants his son to become an official (see p. 371).//

Wages are a fixed form of remuneration (p. 376), and thus a highly perfected form of association, in the original form of which the "aleatory element" predominates in so far as "all members of the association" are subject "to all the chances of the enterprise"[a] [p. 380].

//If capital assumes the risks by itself, the remuneration of labour becomes fixed and is called *wages*. If labour chooses to assume the risks for better or worse, the remuneration of capital detaches itself and becomes fixed as *interest* (p. 382); see further on this juxtaposition pp. 382, 383. //

However, if originally the aleatory element predominates in the worker's condition, wage stability is not yet sufficiently secured. There is an

"intermediate stage which separates the aleatory element from stability" [p. 384].

This final stage is reached by

"saving up, in days of work, the means to satisfy one's needs in days of old age and sickness" (p. 388).

The final stage develops through the "mutual aid societies" (l.c.) and in the last instance through "the workers' *pension fund*"[3] (p. 393).

(Just as man began with the desire to become an official, he ends with the satisfaction of drawing a pension.)

ad 1. Suppose everything Bastiat says about the fixity of wages is correct. Then subsuming wages under FIXED REVENUES still would not

---

[a] Here and further in this paragraph Marx quotes in French.— *Ed.*

reveal to us the *real character* of wages, their characteristic determinateness. One feature of wages—one which they have in common with other sources of income—would be emphasised; nothing more. True, this would be of some use for the advocate who wished to plead the advantages of the wage system. But it would still be of no use to the economist who wanted to understand the distinctive character of this relation in its totality. Establishing a one-sided definition of a relation, of an economic form, and exalting it in opposition to the converse definition— this common ploy of advocates and apologists is the hallmark of Bastiat's reasoning.

So let us assume instead of wages: fixity of income. Is not fixity of income a good thing? Does not everyone like to be able to count on an assured income? Especially every philistine, petty-minded Frenchman? *L'homme toujours besogneux?*[a] Serfdom has been defended on this ground, and perhaps with greater justification.

The contrary could also be asserted and has been asserted. Let us assume that wages mean non-fixity, i.e. advancement beyond a certain point. Who does not like to get ahead instead of standing still? Can a relationship be bad which makes possible a bourgeois *progressus in infinitum*? Of course, Bastiat himself argues elsewhere that wages are non-fixity. How else than by non-fixity, by fluctuations, could it become possible for the worker to stop working and to become a capitalist, as Bastiat wants him to?

Therefore wages are good because they are fixity; wages are also good because they are non-fixity. They are good because they are neither the one nor the other, but at the same time are both the one and the other. What relationship is not good, when it is reduced to a one-sided definition, which is then treated as position, not as negation? All reasoning chatter, one way or another, all apologetics, all philistine sophistry is based on this type of abstraction.

After this general preliminary consideration, we come to Bastiat's actual construction.

(Let us note in passing just one more point. His *métayer*[b] of Landes [p. 388], the poor fellow for whom the misfortune of the wage labourer is compounded by the bad luck of the small capitalist, might indeed consider himself fortunate if he were put on fixed wages.)

---

[a] The man forever in need of something?— *Ed.*
[b] Sharecropper.— *Ed.*

Proudhon's *histoire descriptive* and *philosophique*[4] does not attain the level of that of his opponent Bastiat. The original form of association, in which all *associés* share in all the risks of chance, is succeeded by a higher [III-6] form of association freely entered into by both sides, in which the remuneration of the worker is fixed. We pass over the ingenuity which first assumes a capitalist on the one side and a worker on the other, in order afterwards to derive, from the agreement between the two, the relationship between capital and wage labour.

The form of association in which the worker is exposed to all the risks of business—in which all producers are equally exposed to these risks—and which immediately precedes the wage system, in which the remuneration of labour attains fixity and becomes stable, precedes it as thesis precedes antithesis—is, as Bastiat informs us, the state in which fishing, hunting and pastoralism are the dominant forms of production and society. First the nomadic fisherman, the hunter and the herdsman—and then the wage labourer. Where and when did this *historical* transition from the half-savage to the modern condition take place? If at all, in the columns of *Charivari*.

In real history, wage labour arises from the disintegration of slavery and serfdom—or from the decay of communal property as among the Oriental and Slav peoples—and, in its adequate, epoch-making form affecting the entire social existence of labour, from the decline of the guild economy, of the feudal estates system, of labour services and income in kind, of industry carried on as a rural sideline, of small-scale feudal agriculture, etc. In all these really historical transitions, wage labour appears as the dissolution, as the destruction of relations in which labour was fixed in all respects, in respect of income, content, locality, scope, etc. *Hence as negation of the fixity of labour and its remuneration.* The direct transition from the fetish of the African to Voltaire's *être suprême*,[a][5] or from the hunting gear of a North American savage to the capital of the Bank of England, is not as absurdly anti-historical as is Bastiat's transition from the fisherman to the wage labourer.

(In all these developments, moreover, there is no evidence of changes coming about as a result of voluntary mutual agreements.)

On a level with this historical construction—in which Bastiat deceives himself by imagining his shallow abstraction in the

---

[a] Supreme being.— *Ed.*

form of an event—is the synthesis in which the English FRIENDLY
SOCIETIES and the savings banks are presented as the last word in
the wage system and as the transcendence of all social contradictions.

Historically, as we have seen, non-fixity is the character of the
wage system: the opposite of Bastiat's construction. But how could
he possibly have arrived at the construction of fixity as the
all-compensating characteristic of wages? And what prompted
him to attempt an historical presentation of the wage system
in this specific form as a higher form of the remuneration
of labour, higher than that in other forms of society or association?

All the economists, whenever they discuss the prevailing
relationship of capital and wage labour, of profit and wages, and
wish to prove to the worker that he has no right to share in the
opportunities of gain and in general to reconcile him to his
subordinate role vis-à-vis the capitalist, put great stress on the fact
that the worker, in contrast to the capitalist, enjoys a certain fixity
of income more or less independent of the great ADVENTURES of
capital. Just as Don Quixote comforts Sancho Panza with the
thought that while he does indeed get all the stick, there is at least
no need for him to be brave. In other words, Bastiat transforms a
quality which the economists attribute to wages as opposed to
profit, into a quality of wage labour as opposed to earlier forms of
labour and as a progressive development from the remuneration
of labour in these earlier relations. A commonplace put into the
prevailing relationship which consoles one side of the relationship
relative to the other, is taken out of this relationship by Mr. Bastiat
and made into the historical basis of its origin.

The economists declare that in the relationship of wages to
profit, of wage labour to capital, wages have the advantage of
fixity.

Mr. Bastiat declares that fixity, i.e. one of the aspects of the
relationship of wages to profit, is the historical foundation from
which wage labour emerged (or that fixity is the advantage of
wages, not as opposed to profit, but as opposed to the earlier
forms of the remuneration of labour), hence also the historical
foundation of profit, hence that of the whole relation.

In this way, a commonplace concerning one aspect of the
relationship of wages to profit is magically transformed in Bastiat's
treatment into the historical foundation of this entire relation.
This happens because he is constantly preoccupied with the
thought of socialism, which is then everywhere dreamed up as the

first form of association. This an example of how important a form the apologetic commonplaces which accompany the arguments in economic writings assume in Bastiat's hands.

[III-7] To return to the economists. In what does this fixity of wages consist? Are wages unalterably fixed? This would completely contradict the law of demand and supply, which is the basis of wage determination. No economist denies the fluctuation of wages, their rise and fall. Or are wages independent of crises? Or of the machines which render wage labour superfluous? Or of the divisions of labour which displace it? It would be heterodox to assert all this, and no one does so.

What is meant is that, over a period of time, wages roughly keep to an average level, i.e. there is a minimum wage for the whole [working] class, despite Bastiat's great detestation of the idea, and there is a certain average continuity of labour, e.g. wages may continue to be paid even in cases where profit declines or completely disappears for a time. Now, what does this mean other than that, assuming wage labour as the dominant form of labour and the basis of production, the working class exists by wages and the individual worker possesses on average the fixity of working for wages? In other words, a tautology. Where capital and wage labour is the dominant relation of production, average continuity of wage labour exists; to that extent there *is* fixity of wages for the worker. Where wage labour exists, it exists. And this is what Bastiat regards as the attribute of wage labour which compensates for everything else.

To state, moreover, that in the form of society in which capital has developed, social production is generally more regular, more continuous, more varied—hence also the income of those engaged in production "more fixed"—than where capital, i.e. production, has not been developed to this level, is another tautology which is inherent in the very concept of capital and of production based on capital. In other words: who denies that the general existence of wage labour presupposes a higher development of the productive forces than that which existed in the stages preceding wage labour? And how could it occur to the socialists to put forward greater demands, if they did not assume this higher development of the social productive forces brought about by wage labour? The latter is indeed the presupposition of their demands.

Note. The first form in which wages generally appear is military pay, which emerges with the decline of national armies and civic militias. First the citizens themselves are paid [for military service].

This is soon followed by mercenaries taking their place, who are no longer citizens.

2) *(It is impossible to pursue this NONSENSE any further. WE, THEREFORE, DROP MR. BASTIAT.)* [III-7]

Written in July 1857

First published in the journal *Die Neue Zeit*, Bd. 2, No. 27, 1903-04

Published according to the manuscript

[M-1] A) INTRODUCTION[6]

I. PRODUCTION, CONSUMPTION, DISTRIBUTION, EXCHANGE (CIRCULATION)[7]

1. PRODUCTION

(α) To begin with, the subject to be discussed is *material production*.

Individuals producing in a society—hence the socially determined production by individuals is of course the point of departure. The individual and isolated hunter and fisherman, who serves Adam Smith and Ricardo as a starting point,[a] is one of the unimaginative fantasies of the 18th century. Robinsonades which, contrary to the fancies of the historians of civilisation, by no means signify simply a reaction against over-refinement and a reversion to a misconceived natural life. No more is Rousseau's *contrat social*,[8] which by means of a contract establishes a relationship and connection between subjects that are by nature INDEPENDENT, based on this kind of naturalism. This is an illusion and nothing but the aesthetic illusion of the small and big Robinsonades. It is, rather, the anticipation of "bourgeois society",[9] which began to evolve in the 16th century and was making giant strides towards maturity in the 18th. In this society of free competition the individual seems to be rid of the natural, etc., ties which in earlier historical epochs made him an appurtenance of a particular, limited aggregation of human beings. The prophets of the 18th century, on whose shoulders Smith and Ricardo were still standing completely, envisaged this 18th-century individual—a product of the dissolution of the feudal forms of society on the one hand, and of the new productive forces evolved since the 16th century on the other—as an ideal whose existence belonged to the past. They saw

---

[a] See the Introduction to A. Smith's *An Inquiry into the Nature and Causes of the Wealth of Nations* (Vol. I, London, 1835, p. 2) and Section III, Chapter I of D. Ricardo's *On the Principles of Political Economy, and Taxation* (3rd ed., London, 1821, pp. 16-23).— Ed.

this individual not as an historical result, but as the starting point of history; not as something evolving in the course of history, but posited by nature, because for them this individual was the natural individual, according to their idea of human nature. This delusion has been characteristic of every new epoch hitherto. Steuart, who in many respects was in opposition to the 18th century and as an aristocrat tended rather to regard things from an historical standpoint, avoided this naive view.

The further back we go in history, the more does the individual, and accordingly also the producing individual, appear to be dependent and belonging to a larger whole. At first, he is still in a quite natural manner part of the family, and of the family expanded into the tribe [10]; later he is part of a community, of one of the different forms of community which arise from the conflict and the merging of tribes. It is not until the 18th century, in "bourgeois society", that the various forms of the social nexus confront the individual as merely a means towards his private ends, as external necessity. But the epoch which produces this standpoint, that of the isolated individual, is precisely the epoch of the hitherto most highly developed social (according to this standpoint, general) relations. Man is a ζῷον πολιτικόν [11] in the most literal sense: he is not only a social animal, but an animal that can isolate itself [M-2] only within society. Production by an isolated individual outside society—something rare, which might occur when a civilised person already dynamically in possession of the social forces is accidentally cast into the wilderness—is just as preposterous as the development of language without individuals who live *together* and speak to one another. It is unnecessary to dwell upon this point further. It need not have been mentioned at all if this inanity, which was understandable in people of the 18th century, had not been in all seriousness introduced into the most modern [political] economy by Bastiat, Carey, Proudhon,[a] etc. It is of course pleasant for Proudhon, for instance, to give a historico-philosophical explanation of the origin of an economic relationship whose historical genesis he does not know by indulging in a bit of mythology asserting that Adam or Prometheus hit upon the ready-made idea, which was then put into practice,[b] etc. Nothing is more tedious and dull than the fantasies of *locus communis*.

---

[a] See this volume, pp. 10, 13.— *Ed.*

[b] P. J. Proudhon, *Système des contradictions économiques, ou Philosophie de la misère*, Vol. I, Ch. 2, § 1, Paris, 1846, pp. 77-83.— *Ed.*

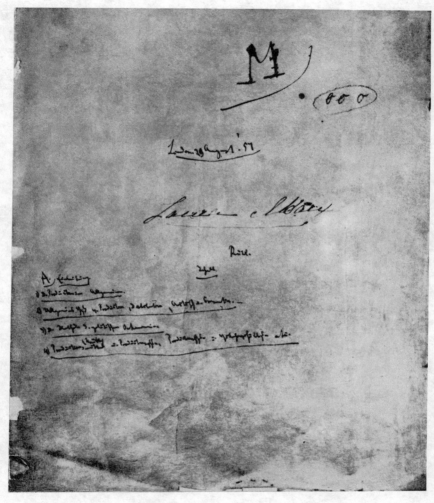

Back of the cover and page 1 of Notebook M containing the *Introduction*

Thus when we speak of production, we always have in mind production at a definite stage of social development, production by social individuals. It might therefore seem that, in order to speak of production at all, we must either trace the historical process of development in its various phases, or else declare at the very beginning that we are dealing with one particular historical epoch, for instance with modern bourgeois production, which is indeed our real subject-matter. All epochs of production, however, have certain features in common, certain common determinations. *Production in general* is an abstraction, but a reasonable abstraction in so far as it actually emphasises and defines the common aspects and thus spares us the need of repetition. Yet this *general aspect,* or the common element which is brought to light by comparison, is itself multiply divided and diverges into different determinations. Some features are found in all epochs, others are common to a few epochs. The most modern epoch and the most ancient will have [certain] determinations in common. Without them production is inconceivable. But although the most highly developed languages have laws and categories in common with the most primitive ones, it is precisely what constitutes their development that distinguishes them from this general and common element. The determinations which apply to production in general must rather be set apart in order not to allow the unity which stems from the very fact that the subject, mankind, and the object, nature, are the same—to obscure the essential difference. On failure to perceive this difference rests, for instance, the entire wisdom of modern economists who are trying to prove the eternity and harmony of the existing social relations. For example, no production is possible without an instrument of production, even if this instrument is simply the hand. None is possible without past, accumulated labour, even if this labour is merely the skill accumulated and concentrated in the hand of the savage by repeated [M-3] exercise. Capital is among other things also an instrument of production, also past, objectified labour. Consequently [modern economists say] capital is a universal and eternal relation given by nature—that is, provided one omits precisely those specific factors which turn the "instrument of production" or "accumulated labour" into capital. The whole history of the relations of production therefore appears, for instance in Carey, as a falsification maliciously brought about by the governments.

If there is no production in general, there is also no general production. Production is always a *particular* branch of production—e.g., agriculture, cattle-breeding, manufacture, etc.—or it is the *totality* [of production]. Political economy, however, is not technology. The relation of the general determinations of production at a given social stage to the particular forms of production is to be set forth elsewhere (later).

Finally, production is not only particular production, but it is invariably a definite social body, a social subject, that is active in a wider or narrower totality of branches of production. The relation of the scientific presentation to the actual movement does not yet belong here either. Production in general. Particular branches of production. Totality of production.

It is fashionable to preface economic works with a general part—and it is just this that appears under the heading "Production" (see for instance J. St. Mill[a])—which deals with the *general conditions* of all production.

This general part comprises or purports to comprise:

1. The conditions without which production is impossible. This means in fact only that the essential moments of all production are indicated. But actually this boils down, as we shall see, to a few very simple definitions, which are expanded into trivial tautologies.

2. The conditions which promote production to a larger or smaller degree, as in the case of Adam Smith's progressive and stagnant state of society.[b] In Smith's work this [proposition] has its value as an *aperçu,* but to raise it to scientific significance an inquiry into the *degree of productivity* at various periods in the development of individual nations would be necessary. Such an inquiry lies outside the actual framework of the subject, yet those aspects which are relevant to it must be dealt with in discussing competition, accumulation, etc. The answer in its general form amounts to the general statement that an industrial nation is at the height of its production when it is at all at the height of its historical development. IN FACT, a nation is at the height of its industrial development so long as gaining, not gain, is its principal aim. In this respect the Yankees are ahead of the English. Or else that for example certain racial characteristics, climates, natural conditions, such as maritime position, fertility of the soil, etc., are more favourable to production than others. This again amounts to the tautology that wealth is the easier to produce the more— subjectively and objectively—its elements are available.

---

a J. St. Mill, *Principles of Political Economy with some of their Applications to Social Philosophy,* Vol. I, London, 1848, pp. 29-236.— *Ed.*

b A. Smith, *An Inquiry into the Nature and Causes of the Wealth of Nations,* Vol. I, London, 1835, pp. 171-209 and 220-21; Vol. II, London, 1836, pp. 168-74.— *Ed.*

[M-4] But all that is not really what the economists are concerned with in this general part. It is rather—see for example Mill [a]—that production, as distinct from distribution, etc., is to be presented as governed by eternal natural laws independent of history, and then *bourgeois* relations are quietly substituted as irrefutable natural laws of society *in abstracto*. This is the more or less conscious purpose of the whole procedure. As regards distribution, however, men are said to have indeed indulged in all sorts of arbitrary action. Quite apart from the crude separation of production and distribution and from their real relation, it should be obvious from the outset that, however dissimilar [the mode of] distribution at the various stages of society may be, it must be possible, just as in the case of production, to [single out] common determinations, and it must be likewise possible to confuse or efface all historical differences in *general human* laws. For example, the slave, the serf, the wage worker, all receive an amount of food enabling them to exist as a slave, serf or wage worker. The conqueror who lives by tribute, or the official who lives by taxes, or the landowner who lives by rent, or the monk who lives by alms, or the Levite who lives by tithes, all receive a portion of the social product which is determined by laws different from those that determine the portion of the slave, etc. The two principal items which all economists include in this section are: (1) property and (2) safeguarding of property by the judiciary, police, etc.

To this, only a very brief reply is needed:

Regarding (1): All production is appropriation of nature by the individual within and by means of a definite form of society. In this sense it is a tautology to say that property (appropriation) is a condition of production. But it is ridiculous to make a leap from this to a definite form of property, e.g. private property (this is moreover an antithetical form, which presupposes *non-property* as a condition, too). History shows, on the contrary, that common property (e.g., among the Indians, Slavs, ancient Celts, etc.) is the earlier form, a form which in the shape of communal property continues to play a significant role for a long time. The question whether wealth develops better under this or under that form of property is not yet under discussion here. But it is tautological to say that where no form of property exists there can be no production and hence no society either. Appropriation which appropriates nothing is a *contradictio in subjecto*.

Regarding (2): Safeguarding of what has been acquired, etc. If

---

[a] J. St. Mill, op. cit., pp. 25-26 and 239-40.— *Ed.*

these trivialities are reduced to their real content, they say more than their preachers realise, namely, that each form of production produces its own legal relations, forms of government, etc. The crudity and lack of comprehension lies precisely in that organically [M-5] coherent factors are brought into haphazard relation with one another, i.e., into a merely speculative connection. The bourgeois economists only have in view that production proceeds more smoothly with modern police than, e.g., under club-law. They forget, however, that club-law too is law, and that the law of the stronger survives, in a different form, even in their "constitutional State".

When the social conditions corresponding to a particular stage of production are just emerging or are already in a state of dissolution, disturbances naturally occur in production, although these may be of varying degree and varying effect.

To recapitulate: there are determinations which are common to all stages of production and are fixed by reasoning as general; the so-called *general conditions* of all production, however, are nothing but these abstract moments, which do not define any of the actual historical stages of production.

2. THE GENERAL RELATION OF PRODUCTION TO DISTRIBUTION, EXCHANGE AND CONSUMPTION

Before starting upon a further analysis of production it is necessary to consider the various rubrics which economists place alongside it.

The quite obvious conception is this: in production members of society appropriate (produce, fashion) natural products in accordance with human needs; distribution determines the proportion in which the individual shares in these products; exchange supplies him with the particular products into which he wants to convert the portion accruing to him through distribution; finally, in consumption the products become objects of use, of appropriation by individuals. Production creates articles corresponding to needs; distribution allocates them according to social laws; exchange in its turn distributes what has already been allocated, according to the individual needs; finally, in consumption the product drops out of this social movement, becomes the direct object and servant of an individual need, which its use satisfies. Production thus appears as the point of departure, consumption as the final point, distribution and exchange as the middle, which has a dual aspect since distribution is determined as actuated by society, and exchange as actuated by individuals. In production the person acquires an objective aspect, in the person the object acquires a subjective aspect; in distribution, society in the form of general, dominating determinations takes over the mediation between production and consumption; in exchange, they are mediated by the chance determinateness of the individual.

Distribution determines the proportion (the quantity) of the products accruing to the individuals; exchange determines the products in which the individual claims the share [M-6] assigned to him by distribution.

Production, distribution, exchange and consumption thus form a proper syllogism; production represents the general, distribution and exchange the particular, and consumption the individual case which sums up the whole. This is indeed a connection, but a superficial one. Production [according to the political economists] is determined by general laws of nature, distribution by social chance, and it may therefore exert a more or less stimulating influence on production; exchange lies between the two as a formal social movement, and consumption, as the concluding act, which is regarded not only as the ultimate aim but as the ultimate purpose, falls properly outside the sphere of [political] economy, except in so far as it in turn reacts on the point of departure thus once again initiating the whole process.

The opponents of the political economists, whether within or without the latter's domain, who accuse them of crudely separating interconnected elements, either argue from the same standpoint or from an inferior one. Nothing is more common than the reproach that the political economists regard production too much as an end in itself. Distribution, they say, is equally important. This reproach is based on the economic conception that distribution is an independent sphere in its own right alongside production. Or [the reproach] that the different moments are not considered in their unity. As though this separation had not forced its way from real life into the textbooks, but, on the contrary, from the textbooks into real life, and as though it were a question of a dialectical reconciliation of concepts and not of comprehending actually existing relations.

(a) [Consumption and Production]

Production is directly also consumption. Two-fold consumption, subjective and objective: [firstly,] the individual, who develops his capacities while producing, expends them as well, using them up in the act of production, just as in natural procreation vital energy is consumed. Secondly, consumption of the means of production, which are used and expended and in part (as, for instance, in combustion) are broken down into the basic elements. Similarly consumption of raw material, which does not retain its natural form and condition; these are, rather, extinguished. The act of production itself is thus in all its moments also an act of consumption. But the economists concede this. Production as directly identical with consumption, consumption as directly coinciding with production, is called by them *productive consumption*. This identity of production and consumption amounts to Spinoza's proposition: *determinatio est negatio*.[12]

[M-7] But this determination of productive consumption is only advanced in order to separate consumption that is identical with production from consumption proper, which is regarded rather as the destructive antithesis of production. Let us therefore consider consumption proper.

Consumption is directly also production, just as in nature consumption of elements and chemical substances is production of a plant. It is obvious that man produces his own body, e.g., through nutrition, a form of consumption. But the same applies to any other kind of consumption which in one way or another produces man in some aspect. Consumptive production. But, says [political] economy, this [type of] production, which is identical with consumption, is a second [type, one] arising from the destruction of the first product. In the first [type] the producer objectifies himself, in the second the object created by him personifies itself. Hence this consumptive production—although it represents a direct unity of production and consumption—is essentially different from production proper. The direct unity, in which production coincides with consumption and consumption with production, allows their direct duality to persist.

Production is thus directly consumption, consumption is directly production. Each is immediately its opposite. At the same time, however, a mediating movement takes place between the two. Production mediates consumption, for which it provides the material; consumption without production would have no object. But consumption also mediates production, by providing for the products the subject for whom they are products. The product only attains its final FINISH in consumption. A railway on which no one travels, which is therefore not used up, not consumed, is only a railway δυνάμει,[a] not in reality. Without production there is no consumption, but without consumption there is no production either, since in that case production would be useless.

Consumption produces production in two ways.

(1) In that only through consumption does a product become a real product. For example, a dress becomes really a dress only by being worn, a house which is not lived in is IN FACT not really a house; in other words, a product as distinct from a mere natural object manifests itself as a product, *becomes* a product, only in consumption. It is only consumption that, by dissolving the product, gives it the FINISHING STROKE, for [the result of] production is a product not merely as objectified activity, but only as an object for the active subject.

(2) In that consumption creates the need for *new* production, and therefore the ideal, intrinsically actuating reason for production, which is the presupposition of production. Consumption furnishes the urge to produce, and also creates the object which determines the purpose of production. If it is evident that production supplies the object of consumption externally, it is [M-8] equally evident that consumption *posits* the object of production *ideally,* as an internal image, a need, an urge and a purpose. Consumption furnishes the objects of production in a form that is still subjective. No production without need. But consumption reproduces the need.

This is matched on the side of production,

(1) by the fact that it supplies the material, the object of consumption. Consumption without an object is no consumption; in this respect, therefore, production creates, produces consumption.

(2) But it is not only the object that production creates for consumption. It also gives consumption its definite form, its character, its FINISH. Just as consumption gave the product its FINISH as a product, so production gives the FINISH to consumption. *For one thing,* the object is not an object in general, but a definite object which must be consumed in a definite way, a way mediated by production itself. Hunger is hunger; but hunger that is satisfied by cooked meat eaten with knife and fork differs from hunger that devours raw meat with the help of hands, nails and teeth. Production thus produces not only the object of consumption but also the mode of consumption, not only objectively but also subjectively. Production therefore creates the consumer.

(3) Production not only provides the material to satisfy a need,

---

[a] Potentially.— *Ed.*

but it also provides a need for the material. When consumption emerges from its original natural crudeness and immediacy—and its remaining in that state would be due to the fact that production was still caught in natural crudeness—then it is itself, as an urge, mediated by the object. The need felt for the object is created by the perception of the object. An *objet d'art*—just like any other product—creates a public that has artistic taste and is capable of enjoying beauty. Production therefore produces not only an object for the subject, but also a subject for the object.

Hence production produces consumption: (1) by creating the material for consumption; (2) by determining the mode of consumption; (3) by creating in the consumer a need for the products which it first posits as objects. It therefore produces the object of consumption, the mode of consumption and the urge to consume. Similarly, consumption produces the *predisposition* of the producer by soliciting him as a purpose-determining need.

The identity of consumption and production thus appears three-fold:

(1) *Direct identity:* production is consumption; consumption is production. Consumptive production. Productive consumption. Economists call both [M-9] productive consumption, but they still make a distinction. The former figures as reproduction, the latter as productive consumption. All investigations into the former are concerned with productive and unproductive labour, those into the latter with productive and non-productive consumption.

(2) Each appears as a means of the other, is mediated by it; this is expressed as their mutual dependence; a movement through which they are brought into mutual relation and appear to be indispensable to each other, but nevertheless remain external to each other. Production creates the material as the external object for consumption, consumption creates the need as the internal object, the purpose of production. No consumption without production; no production without consumption. [This proposition] appears in political economy in many forms.

(3) Production is not only directly consumption, and consumption directly production; nor is production only a means of consumption and consumption the purpose of production, in the sense that each provides the other with its object, with production supplying the external object of consumption, and consumption the notional object of production. Each of them is not only directly the other, nor does it merely mediate the other, but each of the two, by the fact of its taking place, creates the other, creates itself as the other. It is only consumption that consummates the act

of production, since consumption completes the product as a product by dissolving it, by consuming its independent material form. Moreover, by the need for repetition consumption raises the abilities evolved during the first act of production to a skill. Consumption is therefore the concluding act which not only turns the product into a product, but also turns the producer into a producer. Production, on the other hand, produces consumption by creating the definite mode of consumption, and also by creating the incentive to consumption, the very capacity to consume, as a need. The last [kind of] identity, defined in point 3, has many times been explained by economists when discussing the relation of demand and supply, of objects and needs, of needs created by society and natural needs.

After this, nothing is simpler for a Hegelian than to posit production and consumption as identical. And this has been done not only by socialist belletrists [13] but also by prosaic economists, such as Say, in declaring that if one considers a nation—or mankind *in abstracto*—then its production is its consumption.[a] Storch has shown that this proposition of Say's is wrong,[b] since a nation, for instance, does not consume its entire product, but also creates means of production, etc., fixed capital, etc.[14] Moreover, to consider society as a single subject is wrong; a speculative approach. With regard to one subject, production and consumption appear as moments of a single act. One must only [M-9] emphasise the important point here that production and consumption, if considered as activities of one subject or of many individuals, appear in any case as moments of a process in which production is the actual point of departure and hence also the dominant moment. Consumption as a necessity, as a need, is itself an intrinsic moment of productive activity. The latter, however, is the point where the realisation begins and thus also its dominant moment, the act epitomising the entire process. An individual produces an object and by consuming it returns again to himself; he returns however as a productive individual and an individual reproducing himself. Consumption thus appears as a moment of production.

But in society, the relation of the producer to the product, once it has been completed, is extrinsic, and the return of the product

---

[a] J. B. Say, *Traité d'économie politique*, 4th ed., Vol. II, Paris, 1819, pp. 72 and 74.— *Ed.*

[b] H. Storch, *Considérations sur la nature du revenu national*, Paris, 1824, pp. 126-59.— *Ed.*

to the subject depends on his relations to other individuals. The product does not immediately come into his possession. Nor is its direct appropriation his aim, if he produces in society. *Distribution,* which on the basis of social laws determines the individual's share in the world of products, intervenes between the producer and the products, i.e. between production and consumption.

Is distribution, therefore, an independent sphere alongside and outside production?

(b) [Distribution and Production]

When looking through the ordinary run of economic works, one is struck at once by the fact that everything is posited twice in them, e.g. rent, wages, interest and profit figure under the heading of distribution, while under the heading of production we see land, labour and capital figure as agents of production. As to capital, it is evident from the outset that it is posited twice, (1) as an agent of production, and (2) as a source of income; as determining and determined forms of distribution. Interest and profit as such therefore figure in production as well, since they are forms in which capital increases and grows, and are thus moments of its very production. As forms of distribution, interest and profit presuppose capital as an agent of production. They are modes of distribution whose presupposition is capital as an agent of production. They are likewise modes of reproduction of capital.

Wages are also wage labour, which is examined in another section; the determinateness that labour has here as an agent of production appears as a determinateness of distribution. If labour were not determined as wage labour, then, as is the case, for instance, under slavery, its share in the products would not appear as wages. Finally rent—if we take the most developed form of distribution by which landed property shares [M-10] in the products—presupposes large-scale landed property (strictly speaking, large-scale agriculture) as an agent of production, and not land in general; just as wages do not presuppose labour in general. The relations and modes of distribution thus appear merely as the reverse aspect of the agents of production. An individual whose participation in production takes the form of wage labour receives a share in the products, the results of production, in the form of wages. The structure of distribution is entirely determined by the structure of production. Distribution itself is a product of production, not only with regard to the object, [in the sense] that only the results of production can be distributed, but also with regard to the form, [in the sense] that the particular mode of participation in production determines the specific forms of distribution, the form in which one shares in distribution. It is altogether an illusion to posit land in production, and rent in distribution, etc.

Economists like Ricardo, who are mainly reproached with having paid exclusive attention to production, have accordingly regarded distribution as the only subject of [political] economy,[a] for they have instinctively treated the forms of distribution as the most definite expression in which the agents of production are found in a given society.

To the single individual distribution naturally appears as a social law, which determines his position within [the system of] production in which he produces; distribution thus being antecedent to production. The individual starts out with neither capital nor landed property. He is dependent by birth on wage labour as a consequence of social distribution. But this dependence is itself the result of the existence of capital and landed property as independent agents of production.

When one considers whole societies, distribution appears in yet another way to be antecedent to production and to determine it; an ante-economic FACT, as it were. A conquering people divides the land among the conquerors and in this way imposes a definite mode of distribution and form of landed property, thus determining production. Or it turns the conquered into slaves, thus making slave labour the basis of production. Or a people breaks up the large landed estates into plots in a revolution; hence gives production a new character by this new distribution. Or legislation perpetuates land ownership in certain families, or allocates labour [as] a hereditary privilege, thus fixing it according to caste. In all these cases, and they are all historical, distribution does not seem to be regulated and determined by production but, on the contrary, production seems to be regulated and determined by distribution.

[M-11] Conceived most superficially, distribution appears as the distribution of products, and thus further removed from production and quasi-independent of it. But before distribution becomes the distribution of products, it is (1) distribution of the instruments of production, and (2) (which is another determination of the same relation) distribution of the members of society among the various types of production (the subsuming of individuals

---

[a] See D. Ricardo, op. cit., Preface, p. V.—*Ed.*

under definite relations of production). The distribution of products is obviously merely a result of this distribution, which is comprised in the production process itself and determines the structure of production. To examine production separately from this distribution, which is included in it, is obviously idle abstraction; whereas conversely the distribution of products is automatically given by that distribution, which is initially a moment of production. Ricardo, whose object was the understanding of modern production in its specific social structure, and who is the economist of production *par excellence*, for this very reason declares distribution, *not* production, the proper subject of modern [political] economy. This is added proof of the absurdity of those economists who treat production as an eternal truth, and confine history to the domain of distribution.

The question as to how this form of distribution determining production itself relates to production obviously belongs to [the sphere of] production itself. If it should be said that, since production must proceed from a specific distribution of the instruments of production, distribution is at least in this sense antecedent to and a presupposition of production, then the answer would be that production in fact has its conditions and presuppositions which constitute moments of it. At the very outset these may appear as naturally evolved. Through the process of production itself they are transformed from naturally evolved factors into historical ones, and although they appear as natural preconditions of production for one period, they were its historical result for another. They are continuously changed within production itself. For example, the employment of machinery altered the distribution of both the instruments of production and the products. Modern large-scale landed property itself is the result not only of modern trade and modern industry, but also of the application of the latter to agriculture.

The questions raised above can be ultimately resolved into this: what role do historical conditions generally play in production and how is production related to the process of history in general? This question clearly belongs to the analysis and discussion of production itself.

[M-12] In the trivial form, however, in which these questions have been raised above, they can be dealt with quite briefly. Conquests may lead to either of three results. The conquering people imposes its own mode of production upon the conquered (for example, the English in Ireland during this century, and partly in India); or it allows the old [mode of production] to continue and contents itself with tribute (e.g. the Turks and Romans); or interaction takes place, giving rise to something new, a synthesis ([this occurred] partly in the Germanic conquests). In all cases it is the mode of production—whether that of the conquering people or of the conquered or that brought about by a merging of the two—that determines the new [mode of] distribution that is established. Although the latter appears as a presupposition of the new period of production, it is itself a product of production, not only of the historical [evolution of] production in general, but of a definite historical [form of] production.

The Mongols, for example, who caused devastation in Russia, acted in accordance with their [mode of] production, cattle-breeding, for which large uninhabited tracts are a fundamental requirement. The Germanic barbarians, whose traditional [mode of] production was agriculture involving serfs and an isolated life in the countryside, could the more easily subject the Roman provinces to these conditions because the concentration of landed property carried out there had already uprooted the older agricultural relations.

It is a long-established view that at certain periods people lived exclusively by plunder. But to be able to plunder, there must be something to plunder, and this implies production. Moreover, the manner of plunder is itself determined by the manner of production, e.g. a STOCK-JOBBING NATION cannot be robbed in the same way as a nation of cowherds.

The instrument of production may be taken away by force directly in the case of slaves. But then the system of production in the country to which the slave is abducted must admit of slave labour, or (as in South America,[a] etc.) a mode of production appropriate to slave labour must be established.

Laws may perpetuate an instrument of production, e.g., land, in certain families. These laws acquire economic significance only if large-scale landed property is in harmony with the mode of social production, as for instance in England. In France, agriculture was carried on on a small scale, despite the existence of large estates, which were therefore broken up by the Revolution. But can the small plot system be perpetuated, e.g. by laws? Property concentrates itself again despite these laws. The influence of laws aimed at preserving [existing] relations of distribution, and hence their effect on production, have to be examined specially.

---

[a] Marx presumably means the Southern States of the USA.— *Ed.*

[M-13] *(c) Lastly, Exchange and Circulation*

Circulation itself is only a definite moment of exchange, or it is also exchange regarded in its totality.

Since *exchange* is only a mediating moment linking production and distribution (which is determined by production) with consumption; since consumption moreover itself appears as a moment of production, exchange is obviously also comprised in production as one of its moments.

Firstly, it is clear that the exchange of activities and capacities which takes place in production itself is a direct and essential part of production. Secondly, the same applies to the exchange of products in so far as this exchange is a means for manufacturing the finished product intended for immediate consumption. To this extent the act of exchange itself is comprised in production. Thirdly, what is called EXCHANGE between DEALERS and DEALERS[15] is by virtue of its organisation entirely determined by production and is itself a productive activity. Exchange appears to exist independently alongside production, to be indifferent to it, only in the last stage, when the product is exchanged directly for consumption. But (1) [there is] no exchange without division of labour, whether this is naturally evolved or is itself already the result of an historical process; (2) private exchange presupposes private production; (3) the intensity of exchange, its extent and nature, are determined by the development and structure of production. E.g. exchange between town and country, exchange in the countryside, in the town, etc. Thus exchange in all its moments appears either to be directly comprised in production, or else determined by it.

The result at which we arrive is, not that production, distribution, exchange and consumption are identical, but that they are all elements of a totality, differences within a unity. Production is the dominant moment, both with regard to itself in the contradictory determination of production and with regard to the other moments. The process always starts afresh with production. That exchange and consumption cannot be the dominant moments is self-evident, and the same applies to distribution as the distribution of products. As distribution of the agents of production, however, it is itself a moment of production. A definite [mode of] production thus determines a definite [mode of] consumption, distribution, exchange and *definite relations of these different moments to one another*. Production *in its one-sided form*, however, is in its turn also determined by the other moments. For example, if the market, i.e. the sphere of exchange, expands, production grows in volume, and becomes more differentiated. Changes in distribution, e.g. concentration of capital, different distribution of the population in town and country, and the like, entail changes in production. Lastly, production is determined by the needs of consumption. There is an interaction between the different moments. This is the case with any organic entity.

[M-14] 3. THE METHOD OF POLITICAL ECONOMY

When considering a given country from the standpoint of political economy, we begin with its population, the division of the population into classes, town and country, sea, the different branches of production, export and import, annual production and consumption, commodity prices, etc.

It would seem right to start with the real and concrete, with the actual presupposition, e.g. in political economy to start with the population, which forms the basis and the subject of the whole social act of production. Closer consideration shows, however, that this is wrong. Population is an abstraction if, for instance, one disregards the classes of which it is composed. These classes in turn remain an empty phrase if one does not know the elements on which they are based, e.g. wage labour, capital, etc. These presuppose exchange, division of labour, prices, etc. For example, capital is nothing without wage labour, without value, money, price, etc. If one were to start with population, it would be a chaotic conception of the whole, and through closer definition one would arrive analytically at increasingly simple concepts; from the imagined concrete, one would move to more and more tenuous abstractions until one arrived at the simplest determinations. From there it would be necessary to make a return journey until one finally arrived once more at population, which this time would be not a chaotic conception of a whole, but a rich totality of many determinations and relations.

The first course is the one taken by political economy historically at its inception. The 17th-century economists, for example, always started with the living whole, the population, the nation, the State, several States, etc., but analysis always led them in the end to the discovery of a few determining abstract, general relations, such as division of labour, money, value, etc. As soon as these individual moments were more or less clearly deduced and abstracted, economic systems were evolved which from the simple [concepts], such as labour, division of labour, need, exchange value, advanced to the State, international exchange and world market.

The latter is obviously the correct scientific method. The concrete is concrete because it is a synthesis of many determinations, thus a unity of the diverse. In thinking, it therefore appears as a process of summing-up, as a result, not as the starting point, although it is the real starting point, and thus also the starting point of perception and conception. The first procedure attenuates the comprehensive visualisation to abstract determinations, the second leads from abstract determinations by way of thinking to the reproduction of the concrete.

Hegel accordingly arrived at the illusion that the real was the result of thinking synthesising itself within itself, delving ever deeper into itself and moving by its inner motivation; actually, the method of advancing from the abstract to the concrete is simply the way in which thinking assimilates the concrete and reproduces it as a mental concrete. This is, however, by no means the process by which the concrete itself originates. For example, the simplest economic category, e.g. exchange value, presupposes population, population which produces under definite conditions, as well as [M-15] a distinct type of family, or community, or State, etc. Exchange value cannot exist except as an abstract, one-sided relation of an already existing concrete living whole.

But as a category exchange value leads an antediluvian existence. Hence to the kind of consciousness—and philosophical consciousness is precisely of this kind—which regards the comprehending mind as the real man, and only the comprehended world as such as the real world—to this consciousness, therefore, the movement of categories appears as the real act of production—which unfortunately receives an impulse from outside—whose result is the world; and this (which is however again a tautology) is true in so far as the concrete totality regarded as a conceptual totality, as a mental concretum, is IN FACT a product of thinking, of comprehension; yet it is by no means a product of the self-evolving concept whose thinking proceeds outside and above perception and conception, but of the assimilation and transformation of perceptions and images into concepts. The totality as a conceptual totality seen by the mind is a product of the thinking mind, which assimilates the world in the only way open to it, a way which differs from the artistic-, religious- and practical-intellectual assimilation of this world. The real subject remains outside the mind and independent of it—that is to say, so long as the mind adopts a purely speculative, purely theoretical attitude. Hence the subject, society, must always be envisaged as the premiss of conception even when the theoretical method is employed.

But have not these simple categories also an independent historical or natural existence preceding that of the more concrete ones? *Ça dépend.*[a] Hegel, for example, correctly takes possession, the simplest legal relation of the subject, as the point of departure of the philosophy of law.[b] No possession exists, however, before the family or the relations of lord and servant are evolved, and these are much more concrete relations. It would, on the other hand, be correct to say that families and entire tribes exist which have as yet only *possession* and not *property.* The simpler category appears thus as a relation of simpler family or tribal associations with regard to property. In a society which has reached a higher stage the category appears as the simpler relation of a developed organisation. The more concrete substratum underlying the relation of possession is, however, always presupposed. One can conceive an individual savage who has possessions; possession in this case, however, is not a legal relation. It is incorrect that historically possession develops into the family. On the contrary, possession always presupposes this "more concrete legal category". Still, one may say that the simple categories express relations in which the less developed concrete may have realised itself without as yet having posited the more complex connection or relation which is conceptually expressed in the more concrete category; whereas the more developed concrete retains the same category as a subordinate relation.

Money can exist and has existed in history before capital, banks, wage labour, etc., came into being. In this respect it can be said, therefore, that the simpler category can express relations predominating in a less developed whole or subordinate relations in a more developed whole, relations which already existed historically before the whole had developed the aspect expressed in a more concrete category. To that extent, the course of abstract thinking which advances from the elementary to the combined corresponds to the actual [M-16] historical process.

It can be said, on the other hand, that there are highly developed, and yet historically less mature, forms of society in which one finds the most advanced forms of economy, e.g. cooperation, developed division of labour, etc., but no form of

a This depends.— *Ed.*

b G. W. F. Hegel, *Grundlinien der Philosophie des Rechts*, Part 1, §§ 40, 50 and 49-52.— *Ed.*

money at all, for instance Peru.[16] In Slavonic communities too, money—and exchange, which conditions it—occurs little, or not at all, within the individual community, but is used on the borders, in the intercourse with other communities; and it is altogether wrong to posit exchange within the community as the original constituting element. On the contrary, in the beginning exchange tends to arise in the intercourse of different communities with one another, rather than among members of the same community. Moreover, although money plays a role very early and in diverse ways, it was a dominant element in antiquity only among nations determined in one particular manner, i.e. trading nations. Even in the most advanced antiquity, among the Greeks and Romans, money reaches its full development, which is presupposed in modern bourgeois society, only in the period of their disintegration. Thus this quite simple category does not emerge historically in its intensive form until the most highly developed phases of society, and it certainly does not penetrate all economic relations. For example, taxes in kind and deliveries in kind remained the basis in the Roman empire even at the height of its development. In effect, the monetary system in its fully developed form was to be encountered there only in the army,[17] and it never embraced the whole of labour.

So although the simpler category may have existed historically before the more concrete category, its complete intensive and extensive development can nevertheless occur precisely in a complex form of society, whereas the more concrete category was more fully evolved in a less developed form of society.

Labour seems to be a very simple category. The notion of labour in this universal form, as labour in general, is also as old as the hills. Nevertheless, considered economically in this simplicity, "labour" is just as modern a category as the relations which give rise to this simple abstraction. The monetary system, for example, still posits wealth quite objectively, as a thing existing independently in the form of money. Compared with this standpoint, it was a great advance when the manufacturing or mercantile system transferred the source of wealth from the object to the subjective activity—mercantile or manufacturing labour—but it still considered that only this circumscribed activity itself produced money. In contrast to this system, the Physiocrats posit one definite form of labour—agriculture—as wealth-producing, and the object itself no longer in the guise of money, but as a product in general, as the universal result of labour. In accordance with the still circumscribed activity, the product remains a naturally determined product, an agricultural product, a product of the earth *par excellence*.

[M-17] It was an immense advance when Adam Smith discarded any definiteness of the wealth-producing activity—for him it was labour as such, neither manufacturing, nor mercantile, nor agricultural labour, but all types of labour. The abstract universality of wealth-creating activity [implies] also the universality of the object determined as wealth: product in general, or once more labour in general, but as past, objectified labour. How difficult and immense a transition this was is demonstrated by the fact that Adam Smith himself still occasionally relapses into the Physiocratic system. It might seem that in this way merely an abstract expression was found for the simplest and most ancient relation in which human beings act as producers—whatever the type of society they live in. This is true in one respect, but not in another.

The fact that the specific kind of labour is irrelevant presupposes a highly developed totality of actually existing kinds of labour, none of which is any more the dominating one. Thus the most general abstractions arise on the whole only with the most profuse concrete development, when one [phenomenon] is seen to be common to many, common to all. Then it is no longer perceived solely in a particular form. On the other hand, this abstraction of labour in general is not simply the conceptual result of a concrete totality of labours. The fact that the particular kind of labour is irrelevant corresponds to a form of society in which individuals easily pass from one kind of labour to another, the particular kind of labour being accidental to them and therefore indifferent. Labour, not only as a category but in reality, has become here a means to create wealth in general, and has ceased as a determination to be tied with the individuals in any particularity. This state of affairs is most pronounced in the most modern form of bourgeois society, the United States. It is only there that the abstract category "labour", "labour as such", labour *sans phrase*, the point of departure of modern [political] economy, is first seen to be true in practice.

The simplest abstraction which plays the key role in modern [political] economy, and which expresses an ancient relation existing in all forms of society, appears to be true in practice in this abstract form only as a category of the most modern society. It might be said that what is a historical product in the United States—this indifference to the particular kind of labour—appears to be among the Russians, for instance, a natural predisposition. But in the first place, there is an enormous difference between barbarians having a predisposition to be applied to everything, and civilised people applying themselves to everything. And then, as regards the Russians, this indifference to the particular kind of labour in practice goes hand in hand with the traditional stagnation in some very definite kind of labour, from which they can only be wrenched by external influences.

[M-18] The example of labour strikingly demonstrates that even the most abstract categories, despite their being valid—precisely because they are abstractions—for all epochs, are, in the determinateness of their abstraction, just as much a product of historical conditions and retain their full validity only for and within these conditions.

Bourgeois society is the most developed and many-faceted historical organisation of production. The categories which express its relations, an understanding of its structure, therefore, provide, at the same time, an insight into the structure and the relations of production of all previous forms of society the ruins and components of which were used in the creation of bourgeois society. Some of these remains are still dragged along within bourgeois society unassimilated, while elements which previously were barely indicated have developed and attained their full significance, etc. The anatomy of man is a key to the anatomy of the ape. On the other hand, indications of higher forms in the lower species of animals can only be understood when the higher forms themselves are already known. Bourgeois economy thus provides a key to that of antiquity, etc. But by no means in the manner of those economists who obliterate all historical differences and see in all forms of society the bourgeois forms. One can understand tribute, tithe, etc., if one knows rent. But they must not be treated as identical.

Since bourgeois society is, moreover, only a contradictory form of development, it contains relations of earlier forms of society often only in very stunted shape or as mere travesties, e.g. communal property. Thus, if it is true that the categories of bourgeois economy are valid for all other forms of society, this has to be taken *cum grano salis*,[a] for they may contain them in a developed, stunted, caricatured, etc., form, always with substantial differences. What is called historical development rests, in general, on the fact that the latest form regards the earlier ones as stages leading towards itself and always conceives them in a one-sided manner, since only rarely, and under quite definite conditions, is it

_____

a With a grain of salt.— *Ed.*

capable of self-criticism (this of course does not apply to historical periods which regard themselves as times of decline). It was not until its self-criticism was to a certain extent prepared, as it were δυνάμει, that the Christian religion was able to contribute to an objective understanding of earlier mythologies. Similarly, it was not until the self-criticism of bourgeois society had begun that bourgeois [political] economy came to understand the feudal, ancient and oriental economies. In so far as bourgeois economy did not simply identify itself with the earlier economies in a mythological manner, its criticism of them—especially of the feudal economy, against which it still had to wage a direct struggle—resembled the criticism that Christianity directed against heathenism, or which Protestantism directed against Catholicism.

[M-19] Just as generally in the case of any historical, social science, so also in examining the development of economic categories it is always necessary to remember that the subject, in this context modern bourgeois society, is given, both in reality and in the mind, and that therefore the categories express forms of being, determinations of existence—and sometimes only individual aspects—of this particular society, of this subject, and that *even from the scientific standpoint* it therefore by no means begins at the moment when it is first discussed *as such*. This has to be remembered because it provides the decisive criteria for the arrangement [of the material].

For example, nothing seems more natural than to begin with rent, with landed property, since it is bound up with the earth, the source of all production and all life, and with agriculture, the first form of production in all more or less established societies. But nothing would be more erroneous. In every form of society there is a particular [branch of] production which determines the position and importance of all the others, and the relations obtaining in this branch accordingly determine those in all other branches. It is the general light tingeing all other colours and modifying them in their specific quality; it is a special ether determining the specific gravity of everything found in it.

For example, pastoral peoples (peoples living exclusively on hunting or fishing are beyond the point from which real development begins). A certain type of agriculture occurs among them, sporadically, and this determines landed property. It is common property and retains this form in a larger or smaller measure, depending on the degree to which these peoples maintain their traditions, e.g. communal property among the Slavs. Among peoples with settled agriculture—this settling is already a great advance—where agriculture predominates, as in antiquity and the feudal period, even industry, its organisation and the forms of property corresponding thereto, have more or less the character of landed property. Industry is either completely dependent on it, as with the ancient Romans, or, as in the Middle Ages, it copies in the town and in its conditions the organisation of the countryside. In the Middle Ages even capital—unless it was purely money capital—capital as traditional tools, etc., has this character of landed property.

The reverse is the case in bourgeois society. Agriculture to an increasing extent becomes merely a branch of industry and is completely dominated by capital. The same applies to rent. In all forms in which landed property rules supreme, the nature relationship still predominates; in the forms in which capital rules supreme, the social, historically evolved element predominates. Rent cannot be understood without capital, but capital can be understood without rent. Capital is the economic power that dominates everything in bourgeois society. It must form both the point of departure and the conclusion and must be analysed before landed property. After each has been considered separately, their interconnection must be examined.

[M-20] It would therefore be inexpedient and wrong to present the economic categories successively in the order in which they played the determining role in history. Their order of succession is determined rather by their mutual relation in modern bourgeois society, and this is quite the reverse of what appears to be their natural relation or corresponds to the sequence of historical development. The point at issue is not the place the economic relations took relative to each other in the succession of various forms of society in the course of history; even less is it their sequence "in the Idea" (*Proudhon*[a]) (a nebulous notion of the historical process), but their position within modern bourgeois society.

It was the predominance of agricultural peoples that made the trading peoples—Phoenicians, Carthaginians—appear in such purity (abstract determinateness) in the ancient world. For capital as merchant or money capital appears precisely in that abstract form where capital is not yet the dominant factor in society. Lombards and Jews occupied the same position in relation to mediaeval agrarian societies.

---

[a] P. J. Proudhon, op. cit., Vol. I, pp. 145-46.— *Ed.*

Another example of the different roles which the same categories play at different stages of society are JOINT-STOCK COMPANIES, one of the most recent features of bourgeois society; but they appear also in its early period in the form of large privileged commercial companies with rights of monopoly.

The concept of national wealth finds its way into the works of the economists of the 17th century as the notion that wealth is created solely for the State, whose power, on the other hand, is proportional to this wealth—a notion which to some extent survives among 18th-century economists. This was still the unintentionally hypocritical form in which wealth itself and the production of wealth was proclaimed to be the goal of the modern State, which was regarded merely as a means for producing wealth.

The arrangement has evidently to be made as follows:

(1) The general abstract determinations, which therefore appertain more or less to all forms of society, but in the sense set forth above. (2) The categories which constitute the internal structure of bourgeois society and on which the principal classes are based. Capital, wage labour, landed property. Their relation to one another. Town and country. The 3 large social classes. Exchange between them. Circulation. Credit system (private). (3) The State as the epitome of bourgeois society. Analysed in relation to itself. The "unproductive" classes. Taxes. National debt. Public credit. Population. Colonies. Emigration. (4) International character of production. International division of labour. International exchange. Export and import. Rate of exchange. (5) World market and crises.

[M-21] 4. PRODUCTION.
MEANS OF PRODUCTION AND RELATIONS OF PRODUCTION.
RELATIONS OF PRODUCTION AND CONDITIONS OF COMMUNICATION.
FORMS OF THE STATE AND OF CONSCIOUSNESS IN RELATION
TO THE RELATIONS OF PRODUCTION AND OF COMMERCE.
LEGAL RELATIONS. FAMILY RELATIONS

NB. Notes regarding points which have to be mentioned here and should not be forgotten:

(1) *War* develops [certain features] earlier than peace; the way in which as a result of war, and in the armies, etc., certain economic conditions, e.g. wage labour, machinery, etc., were evolved earlier than within civil society. The relation between productive power and conditions of communication is likewise particularly evident in the army.

(2) *The relation of the hitherto existing idealistic historiography to realistic historiography. In particular what is known as history of civilisation,* which is all a history of religion and states. (In this context something can also be said about the various kinds of historiography hitherto existing. So-called objective,[18] subjective (moral and other kinds), philosophical [historiography].)

(3) *Secondary and tertiary* [relations], in general *derived* and *transmitted,* non-original, relations of production. The influence of international relations here.

(4) *Reproaches about the materialism of this conception. Relation to naturalistic materialism.*

(5) *Dialectic of the concepts productive power* (means of production) *and relation of production,* a dialectic whose limits have to be defined and which does not abolish real difference.

(6) *The unequal development of material production and e.g. art.* In general, the concept of progress is not to be taken in the usual abstract form. With regard to art, etc., this disproportion is not so important and [not so] difficult to grasp as within practical social relations themselves, e.g. in culture. Relation of the *United States* to Europe. However, the really difficult point to be discussed here is how the relations of production as legal relations enter into uneven development. For example, the relation of Roman civil law (this applies in smaller measure to criminal and public law) to modern production.

(7) *This conception*[a] *appears to be an inevitable development.* But vindication of chance. How. (Of freedom, etc., as well.) (Influence of the means of communication. World history did not exist always; history as world history is a result).

(8) *The starting point is of course determinateness by nature;* subjectively and objectively. Tribes, races, etc.

(1) As regards art, it is known that certain periods of its florescence by no means correspond to the general development of society, or, therefore, to the material basis, the skeleton as it were of its organisation. For example, the Greeks compared with the moderns, or else Shakespeare. It is even acknowledged that certain forms of art, e.g. epos, can no longer be produced in their epoch-making, classic form after artistic production as such has begun; in other words that certain important creations within the compass of art are only possible at an early stage of its

---

[a] Marx apparently means the conception of history discussed in the preceding points.— *Ed.*

development. If this is the case with regard to the different arts within the sphere of art itself, it is not so remarkable that this should also be the case with regard to the entire sphere of art in its relation to the general development of society. The difficulty lies only in the general formulation of these contradictions. As soon as they are specified, they are already explained.

[M-22] Let us take, for example, the relation of Greek art, and that of Shakespeare, to the present time. We know that Greek mythology is not only the arsenal of Greek art, but also its basis. Is the conception of nature and of social relations which underlies Greek imagination and therefore Greek [art] possible in the age of SELFACTORS, railways, locomotives and electric telegraphs? What is Vulcan compared with Roberts and Co.,[19] Jupiter compared with the lightning conductor, and Hermes compared with the Crédit Mobilier[20]? All mythology subdues, dominates and fashions the forces of nature in the imagination and through the imagination; it therefore disappears when real domination over these forces is established. What becomes of Fama beside Printing House Square[21]? Greek art presupposes Greek mythology, in other words, nature and even the social forms have already been worked up in an unconsciously artistic manner by the popular imagination. This is the material of Greek art. Not just any mythology, i.e. not any unconsciously artistic working up of nature (here the term comprises all objective phenomena, including society). Egyptian mythology could never become the basis or material womb of Greek art. But at any rate [it presupposes] a mythology. Hence, on no account a social development which precludes any mythological, [i.e.] any mythologising, attitude towards nature, and therefore demands from the artist an imagination independent of mythology.

Regarded from another angle: is Achilles possible when powder and shot have been invented? And is the *Iliad* possible at all when the printing press and even printing machines exist? Does not the press bar inevitably spell the end of singing and reciting and the muses, that is, do not the conditions necessary for epic poetry disappear?

But the difficulty lies not in understanding that Greek art and epic poetry are bound up with certain forms of social development. The difficulty is that they still give us aesthetic pleasure and are in certain respects regarded as a standard and unattainable model.

An adult cannot become a child again, or he becomes childish. But does not the naiveté of the child give him pleasure, and must he not himself endeavour to reproduce the child's veracity on a higher level? Does not the specific character of every epoch come to life again in its natural veracity in the child's nature? Why should not the historical childhood of humanity, where it attained its most beautiful form, exert an eternal charm as a stage that will never recur? There are unbred children and precocious children. Many of the ancient peoples belong to this category. The Greeks were normal children. The charm their art has for us does not conflict with the immature stage of the society in which it originated. On the contrary, that charm is a consequence of this and is, rather, inseparably linked with the fact that the immature social conditions which gave rise, and which alone could give rise, to this art can never recur.

Written in late August 1857

First published in the journal *Die Neue Zeit*, Bd. I, Nos. 23-25, 1902-03

Printed according to the manuscript

OUTLINES OF THE CRITIQUE OF POLITICAL ECONOMY

(ROUGH DRAFT OF 1857-58) [22]

[First Instalment]

Written between late 1857 and May 1858

First published in full in Karl Marx, *Grundrisse der Kritik der politischen Oekonomie (Rohentwurf). 1857-1858*, Moscow, 1939

Printed according to the manuscript

[I-1] II. CHAPTER ON MONEY [23]

ALFRED DARIMON, *DE LA RÉFORME DES BANQUES*, PARIS, 1856

"All the trouble derives from the predominance of the precious metals which is obstinately being preserved in circulation and exchange" (pp. 1, 2).[a][24]

Begins with the measures taken by the Banque de France in October 1855

"to remedy the progressive diminution of its cash reserves" (p. 2).

Wants to give us a statistical *tableau* of the position of the Bank in the five months preceding its measures taken in October. For this purpose, he compares the size of its bullion reserves in each of these five months with the "fluctuations in its portfolio", i.e. the amount of its DISCOUNTS (the commercial papers, *bills of exchange* in its portfolio). According to Darimon, the figure expressing the value of the SECURITIES held by the Bank

"represents the greater or lesser need which the public feels for its services, *or*, which amounts to the same, the requirements of circulation" (p. 2).

Which amounts to the same? Not at all. If the amount of the BILLS presented for DISCOUNT were identical with the "requirements of circulation", strictly speaking of *money circulation*, the circulation of notes [its volume] would be determined by the amount of the bills of exchange discounted. But these movements, so far from being on average proportional to each other, often bear an inverse relationship. The amount of the bills of exchange discounted and its fluctuations express the requirements of credit, while the amount of money in circulation depends on quite different factors. In order to arrive at any conclusion about circulation, Darimon ought first to have compiled a column for the amount of

---

[a] Here and below Marx quotes from Darimon mostly in French.— *Ed.*

notes in circulation, alongside the column for the bullion reserves and that for bills discounted.

In order to discuss the requirements of circulation, it was surely necessary to establish first of all the fluctuations in actual circulation. The omission of this necessary term of the comparison betrays at once amateurish incompetence and deliberate confusion of the requirements of credit with those of money circulation—a confusion upon which the entire secret of Proudhonian wisdom is in fact based. (As if in a mortality table illnesses figured on one side and deaths on the other, while births were overlooked.)

Darimon's two columns (see p. 3), that for the bullion reserves of the Bank from April to September on the one side and that for the changes in its portfolio on the other, express nothing but the tautological fact, which needs no display of statistical illustrations, that in proportion as bills were brought to the Bank to withdraw bullion from it, its portfolio became filled with bills and its vaults emptied of bullion. And even this tautology, which Darimon seeks to demonstrate with his table, is not directly expressed in it. It shows rather that from 12 April to 13 September 1855 the bullion reserves of the Bank fell by about 144 million [francs], while the commercial papers in its portfolio rose by about 101 million.[a] The decline in the bullion reserves therefore exceeded by 43 million the increase in the commercial papers discounted. The identity of the two movements founders on this total result of the movement over five months.

A more precise comparison of the figures reveals other discrepancies.[25]

	Bullion reserves in the Bank	Bills discounted by the Bank
12 April	432,614,797 frs	322,904,313
10 May	420,914,028	310,744,925

In other words, between 12 April and 10 May, the bullion reserves fell by 11,700,769, while the volume of SECURITIES increased by 12,159,388; i.e. the increase in SECURITIES exceeded by about half a million francs (458,619 frs) the decline in the bullion reserves. An analogous discrepancy, but to a much more surprising degree,

---

a This should read "108 million". There are also other numerical inaccuracies in the section on Darimon and in the 1857-58 manuscript generally. They do not affect the substance of Marx's conclusions and are reproduced in the present edition without correction.— Ed.

Cover of Notebook VII of the manuscript *Outlines of the Critique of Political Economy*

is revealed when we compare the figures for the month of May with those for June:

	Bullion reserves in the Bank	Bills discounted by the Bank
10 May	420,914,028	310,744,925
14 June	407,769,813	310,369,439

[I-2] From 10 May until 14 June, therefore, the bullion reserves fell by 13,144,215 frs. Did the SECURITIES held by the Bank increase in the same measure? On the contrary, they decreased in the same period by 375,486 frs. Here, therefore, we have not merely a simple quantitative disproportion between the fall on the one side and the rise on the other. Even the inverse relationship between movements in the two series has disappeared. An enormous fall on the one side is accompanied by a relatively small fall on the other.

	Bullion reserves in the Bank	Bills discounted by the Bank
14 June	407,769,813	310,369,439
12 July	314,629,614	381,699,256

Comparison of the figures for June with those for July shows a decline of 93,140,199 in the reserves and an increase of 71,329,717 frs in the SECURITIES. That is, the decline of the former is 21,810,482 frs greater than the increase in the latter.

	Bullion reserves in the Bank	Bills discounted by the Bank
12 July	314,629,614	381,699,256
9 August	338,784,444	458,689,605

Here we have increases in both columns: in that for the bullion reserves by 24,154,830, in that for the portfolio by the much greater sum of 66,990,349 frs.

	Bullion reserves in the Bank	[Bills discounted by the Bank]
9 August	338,784,444	458,689,605
13 September	288,645,333	431,390,562

The fall of 50,139,111 frs in the bullion reserves was accompanied in this period by a decline of 27,299,043 frs in the SECURITIES. (In December 1855, despite the restrictions imposed by the Banque de France, its reserves were reduced by a further 24 million.)

What is sauce for the goose is sauce for the gander. The facts that emerge from successive comparison of the five-month period possess the same claim to trustworthiness as do those resulting from Mr. Darimon's comparison of the first and last figures of the columns. And what does the comparison show? Truths which devour one another. Twice there is an increase in the portfolio and a fall in the reserves, but in such a way that the decrease in the latter is smaller than the increase in the former (April-May and June-July). Twice there is a decrease in the reserves accompanied by a decrease in the portfolio, but the decrease in the latter is not as great as the decrease in the former (May-June and August-September). Finally, in one case there is an increase in the reserves and an increase in the portfolio, but the former is smaller than the latter [July-August].

A decline in one column, a rise in the other; a decline in both columns; a rise in both columns. So there is anything but a consistent pattern, above all there is not an inverse relationship [between the reserves and the portfolio], not even an interaction [between them], since a decline in the portfolio cannot be the cause of the fall in the reserves, and an increase in the portfolio cannot be the cause of the increase in the reserves. The inverse relationship and interaction is not even established by the isolated comparison between the figures for the first and the last month which Darimon makes. If the increase in the portfolio by 101 million does not make good the decline of 144 million in the reserves, there remains the possibility that the increase in the one [I-3] and the decrease in the other bear no causal relationship whatever to each other. The statistical illustration, instead of giving an answer, has only thrown up a mass of mutually intersecting questions. Instead of one riddle, three score.

In fact, the riddles would. disappear at once, if only Mr. Darimon were to set down the columns for note circulation and deposits alongside those for the reserves and the portfolio (of bills discounted). A fall in the reserves smaller than the increase in bills discounted would then be explained thus: either deposits of bullion have increased at the same time; or a part of the notes issued in discount was not exchanged for bullion but remained in circulation; or finally, the notes issued were immediately returned [to the Bank] in the form of deposits or as payment for overdue bills, thus not increasing note circulation. A decrease in the reserves accompanied by a smaller decrease in the portfolio would be explained by deposits being withdrawn from the Bank or notes being brought in and exchanged for bullion, its own discounting thus being impaired by the owners of the withdrawn deposits or of the notes converted into silver. Finally, a small decrease in the reserves accompanied by a smaller decrease in the portfolio would be explained in the same way (we omit the possibility of a drain on the reserves for the replacement of silver coinage within the country, since Darimon does not take account of it in his analysis).

But the columns which would thus have explained each other would also have proved something which it was not intended to prove: that the satisfaction of the growing requirements of trade by the Bank does not necessarily result in an expansion of the amount of its notes in circulation; that the contraction or expansion of this note circulation does not correspond to a contraction or expansion of the Bank's bullion reserves; that the Bank does not control the quantity of means of circulation, etc.—all of them conclusions which conflict with the arguments which Mr. Darimon is trying to sell. In his haste to present dramatically his preconceived opinion as to the opposition between the metallic basis of the Bank, as represented by its bullion reserves, and the requirements of circulation, represented in his view by the Bank's portfolio, he tears two columns from their necessary complementary context, which in this isolation lose all meaning, or, if they show anything at all, provide evidence against himself. We have dwelt upon this *fait*[a] to demonstrate from one example the value of the statistical and positive illustrations of the Proudhonists. Instead of the economic facts providing the test of their theories, they prove that they do not master the facts, in order to be able to play with them. Indeed their way of playing with the facts demonstrates the origins of their theoretical abstraction.

Let us follow Darimon further.

When the Bank of France saw its reserves diminished by 144 million and its portfolio increased by 101 million, it took measures on 4 and 18 October 1855 to protect its vaults against its portfolio. It raised its discount rate in successive steps from 4 to 5% and from 5 to 6%, and reduced from 90 to 75 days the time of payment of bills presented for discount. In other words: it rendered more difficult the conditions under which it placed its bullion at the disposal of commerce. What does this show? According to Darimon,

"that a bank organised on present-day principles, i.e. founded upon the predominance of gold and silver, deprives the public of its services exactly at the moment when they are most needed" [ibid., p. 3].

Did Mr. Darimon need all his statistics to show that the supplier raises the price of his services in the same measure that the demand for them rises (and exceeds them)? And do not the

---

[a] Matter.— *Ed.*

gentlemen who represent "the public" vis-à-vis the Bank follow the same "agreeable custom of life" [a]? Do the philanthropic grain dealers, who present their bills of exchange to the Bank in order to get notes to exchange for the Bank's gold, in order to exchange that gold for grain from abroad, in order to exchange that grain for the money of the French public, are they by any chance motivated by the idea that, because the public's need for grain is now at its peak, it is their duty to sell grain more cheaply? Or do they not rather rush to the Bank to exploit the rise in the price of grain, the need of the public, the imbalance between the public's demand and the available supply? And the Bank should be an exception from this general economic law? *Quelle idée!* [b]

But it may be the effect of the present-day organisation of the banks that gold must be accumulated in so large quantities that the means of purchase, which could be used most beneficially for the nation in the case of a grain shortage, are condemned to be idle, and that in general capital, which should circulate in fruitful [I-4] transformations of production, is turned into the unproductive and stagnant basis of circulation. In this case it would mean that, given the present organisation of the banks, the unproductive bullion reserves still exceed the necessary minimum, because the saving of gold and silver within circulation has not yet been pushed back to its economic limits. It would be a matter of something more or less on the same basis. But the question would have been brought down from the socialist heights to the bourgeois-practical plains in which we find it strolling in the books of most of the English bourgeois opponents of the Bank of England. *Quelle chute!* [c]

But perhaps it is not a matter of a greater or lesser economy of gold and silver by means of notes and other banking devices, but of abandoning the metallic basis of the currency altogether? But then again, the statistical fable loses its point, and so does its moral. If the Bank, under whatever conditions, is to export precious metals in case of an emergency, it must previously have accumulated them; and if foreign countries are to accept them in exchange for their commodities, these metals must have asserted their predominance.

The causes which drained from the Bank its precious metals were, according to Darimon, a bad harvest and the consequent

---

[a] An allusion to a passage in Goethe's *Egmont,* Act V.— *Ed.*
[b] What an idea! — *Ed.*
[c] What a fall! — *Ed.*

necessity of importing grain from abroad. He forgets the failure of the silk harvest and the need of extensive purchases of silk from China. Darimon also blames the many large-scale undertakings which coincided with the last months of the Paris Industrial Exhibition.[a] Again he forgets the vast speculations and ventures abroad undertaken by the Crédit Mobilier[20] and its rivals, to show, as Isaac Péreire says, that French capital distinguishes itself from that of other countries by its cosmopolitan character, just as the French language does from other languages. Add to that the unproductive expenditure occasioned by the Eastern War[b]: the loan of 750 million.

In other words, on the one hand a great and sudden shortfall in two of the most important branches of French production! On the other hand, an extraordinary use of French capital in foreign markets for undertakings which created no direct equivalent and some of which will perhaps never cover their production costs! On the one hand, the imports which made up for the decline of domestic production and, on the other hand, the increase in industrial ventures abroad, required not the tokens of circulation which serve for the exchange of equivalents, but the equivalents themselves, not money but capital. In any case, the reduction in French domestic production was not an equivalent for the investment of French capital abroad.

Now, suppose that the Bank of France had not rested upon a metallic basis, and foreign countries had been willing to accept the French equivalent or capital in any form, not only in the specific form of the precious metals. Would not the Bank have been forced just the same to raise its discount rate exactly at the time when its "public" clamoured most eagerly for its services? The notes in which the Bank discounts the bills of exchange of this public are now nothing but drafts on gold and silver. They would be, on our assumption, drafts on the nation's store of products and its immediately employable labour power. The first is limited, the second is expandable only within very definite limits and in certain periods of time. On the other hand, the paper-machine is inexhaustible, as if driven by the power of magic. Simultaneously, while the failure of the grain and silk harvest enormously diminished the immediately exchangeable wealth of the nation, the foreign investments in railways, mines, etc., immobilised immediately exchangeable wealth in a form that created no

---

[a] The Paris World Industrial Exhibition, May to November 1855.— *Ed.*
[b] The Crimean War, 1853-56.— *Ed.*

immediate equivalent and therefore swallowed it up for the moment without compensation! Thus the immediately exchangeable wealth of the nation which can circulate and can be exported, absolutely diminished! On the other hand, unrestricted growth of the issue of bank drafts. The immediate consequence: a rise in the price of manufactured goods, of raw materials and of labour. On the other hand, a fall in the price of bank drafts. The Bank would not have expanded the national wealth by the touch of a magic wand, but would only have depreciated its own paper as a result of a very ordinary operation. Would this depreciation not have led to a sudden paralysis of production?

But no, exclaims the Proudhonist. Our new bank organisation would [I-5] not be content with the negative merit of abolishing the metallic basis and leaving everything else as it was. It would create entirely new conditions of production and intercourse, and therefore intervene under entirely new circumstances. Did not the introduction of our present banks in its time revolutionise the conditions of production? Would modern large-scale industry have become possible without the concentration of credit which this effected; without the interest from the national debt which this created in opposition to rent of land, thereby creating finance in opposition to landed property, the MONEYED INTEREST in opposition to the LANDED INTEREST? Would the joint-stock companies, etc., and the thousand-fold forms of note circulation, which are as much products as they are conditions of production for modern commerce and modern industry, be possible without this new institute of circulation?

We have now arrived at the basic question, which is no longer connected with our point of departure. The general question is: is it possible to revolutionise the existing relations of production and the corresponding relations of distribution by means of changes in the instrument of circulation—changes in the organisation of circulation? A further question: can such a transformation of circulation be accomplished without touching the existing relations of production and the social relations based on them? If every such transformation of circulation were itself to presuppose changes in the other conditions of production and social upheavals, that would of course be the end of the doctrine which advocates smart gimmicks in the sphere of circulation *in order* to prevent changes from assuming a violent character on the one hand, and on the other to cast the changes themselves in the role not of the premiss but on the contrary of the gradual result of reforms in the sphere of circulation. The fallacy of this basic premiss would suffice to prove the same misunderstanding concerning the inner connection between the relations of production, distribution and circulation.

Of course, the historical example referred to above is not conclusive, since the modern institutions of credit were as much a result as a cause of the concentration of capital, representing only an aspect of this process, and the concentration of wealth may be accelerated as much by lack of circulation (as in ancient Rome) as by improved circulation.

It should further be investigated, or rather it would be relevant to the general question: whether the various civilised forms of money—metal coinage, paper money, credit notes, labour money (this last as a socialist form)—can achieve what is required of them without abolishing the production relation itself which is expressed in the category of money; and whether it is not then necessarily a self-defeating effort to seek to overcome the essential conditions of a relationship by effecting a formal modification within it. The various forms of money may correspond better to social production at various stages of its development; one form may remove certain shortcomings with which the other cannot cope. But none of them, so long as they remain forms of money, and so long as money remains an essential relation of production, can resolve the contradictions inherent in the money relationship, they can all only express these contradictions in one form or another. Though one form of wage labour may overcome the defects of another, none can overcome the defects of wage labour itself. One lever may overcome better than another the resistance of matter at rest. But all depend upon the fact that the resistance remains.

Naturally, the general question of the relationship of circulation to the other relations of production can be raised only at the conclusion. But at a first glance it is suspicious that Proudhon and his followers never once pose it in its pure form, but only occasionally declaim about it. Whenever it is touched upon, we shall have to examine it carefully.

What emerges immediately from Darimon's introduction is that he completely identifies *money circulation with credit,* which is an economic fallacy. (*Crédit gratuit,*[a] incidentally, is only a hypocritical, philistine and timid reformulation of *"La propriété c'est le vol".*[b 26] Instead of the workers *taking away* capital from the capitalists, the capitalists are to be compelled to *give* it to them.) This is another

---

[a] Free credit.— *Ed.*
[b] Property is theft.— *Ed.*

point to which we shall have to return.

In discussing the topic itself, Darimon gets no further than the point that the banks, which deal in credit, like the merchants, who deal in commodities, or the workers, who deal in labour, sell at a higher price when demand rises in relation to supply, i.e. they make it more difficult for the public to obtain their services at the very moment when the public most needs them. As we have seen, the Bank must do this, whether it issues convertible or inconvertible notes.

The policy of the Bank of France in October 1855 gave rise to an *"immense clameur"* (p. 4) and a *"grand débat"* between it and the spokesmen of the public. Darimon summarises, or rather claims to summarise, this debate. We follow him here only occasionally, because his résumé shows the weakness of both of the opposing parties—their continual desultory digressions, their blind tapping around among superficialities. Each of the opponents constantly drops his weapon in order to look for another. Neither manages to strike a blow, not only because they are constantly changing the weapons with which they should be fighting each other, but equally because they meet on one ground only to flee at once to another.

(From 1806 to 1855, the discount rate in France was never as high as 6%; for 50 years virtually *immuable à 90 jours le maximum de l'échéance des effets de commerce.*[a])

The weakness of the arguments with which Darimon lets the Bank defend itself, and his own misconception, emerge e.g. from the following passage of his fictitious [I-6] dialogue:

The opponent of the Bank says:

"Owing to your monopoly you dispense and regulate credit. When you are harsh, the private discount brokers not only emulate you, but even exceed your harshness... By your measures you have brought business to a stop" (p. 5).

The Bank replies *"humblement"*:

"What do you want me to do?... To safeguard myself against foreigners I must safeguard myself against my own nationals... Above all, I must prevent the outflow of hard cash, without which I am nothing and can do nothing" (p. 5).

A folly is here imputed to the Bank. It is made to evade the question, to take refuge in a general phrase, so that it may be answered with a general phrase. In this dialogue the Bank shares Darimon's illusion that it really regulates credit by means of its monopoly. In fact, the power of the Bank only begins where the

---

[a] For 50 years the term of bills of exchange remains virtually unchanged at 90 days.— *Ed.*

power of the private *"escompteurs"* [a] ends, that is, at a moment when its own power is already extraordinarily limited. Suppose the Bank were to allow the discount rate to remain at 5% at a time when the MONEY MARKET was in an EASY STATE, and when everyone was therefore discounting at $2\,^1/_2\%$. The *escompteurs,* instead of emulating the Bank, would discount all its business under its very nose. Nowhere is this shown more clearly than in the history of the Bank of England after the 1844 Act,[27] which made the Bank a real rival of the PRIVATE BANKERS in the discount business, etc. The Bank of England, in order to secure itself a share, and a growing share, of the discount business during the periods of EASINESS in the money market, was continually forced to lower its discount rate, not only to the level maintained by the PRIVATE BANKERS, but often below it. Its "regulation of credit" is therefore to be taken *cum grano salis,*[b] whereas Darimon makes his superstitious belief in the Bank's absolute control of the money market and of credit the starting point of his argument.

Instead of critically examining the conditions of the Bank's real power over the money market, he at once clings to the phrase that CASH is its supreme concern and that it must prevent its outflow abroad. A professor of the Collège de France [28] (Chevalier) replies:

"Gold and silver are commodities just like any other... The only use of its bullion reserves is to be sent abroad for purchases in times of need."

The Bank replies:

"Metallic money is not a commodity like any other; it is an instrument of exchange, and, by virtue of this title, it enjoys the privilege of laying down the law for all other commodities."

Here Darimon jumps in between the combatants:

"Therefore one must attribute not only the present crisis but also the periodic commercial crises to this privilege enjoyed by gold and silver of being the only authentic instruments of circulation and exchange."

To avoid all the inconveniences of crises,

"it would be sufficient for gold and silver to become commodities just like any other, or, to be precise, for all commodities to become instruments of exchange of the same rank (*au même titre*) (by virtue of the same title) as gold and silver; for products to be truly exchanged for products" (pp. 5-7).

Shallowness with which the controversy is here presented. When the Bank issues drafts on money (notes), and promissory notes on

---

[a] Discount brokers.— *Ed.*
[b] With a grain of salt.— *Ed.*

capital which are repayable in gold or silver (deposits), it is, self-evidently, only up to a point that it can look on and tolerate the diminution of its bullion reserves without taking steps against it. This has nothing to do with the theory of metallic money. We shall return to Darimon's theory of crises.

In the section entitled *Petite histoire des crises de circulation,*[a] Mr. Darimon ignores the English crisis of *1809-11*, and confines himself for *1810* to mentioning the appointment of the Bullion Committee. For 1811 he again ignores the real crisis (which began in 1809) and confines himself to mentioning the adoption by the House of Commons of the resolution that

"the depreciation of the notes against bullion resulted from the rise in the price of bullion, not from the depreciation of paper money",

and Ricardo's pamphlet[b] which asserts the opposite, and which is supposed to conclude:

"Money, in its most perfect state, is paper money" ([Darimon,] pp. 22, 23).

The crises of 1809 and 1811 were important in this respect because the Bank at that time issued inconvertible notes, hence the crises could not possibly have resulted from the convertibility of the notes into gold (metal), and hence also could not possibly have been prevented by the abolition of convertibility. Like a nimble tailor Darimon skips over these facts which refute his theory of crises. He clings to Ricardo's aphorism, which had nothing to do either with the question at issue or with the subject matter of the pamphlet—the depreciation of banknotes. He ignores the fact that Ricardo's theory of money has been totally refuted, as have been its false assumptions that the Bank controls the amount of notes in circulation, that the amount of means of circulation determines prices, whereas on the contrary prices determine the amount of means of circulation, etc. In Ricardo's time no detailed investigations into the phenomena of money circulation were yet available. This by the way.

Gold and silver are commodities like the others. Gold and silver are not commodities like the others: as universal instruments of exchange they are privileged commodities and degrade the other commodities by virtue of this very privilege. This is the final analysis to which Darimon reduces the antagonism. His final

---

[a] Darimon's title of this section is "Petite histoire des banques de circulation" (*De la réforme des banques,* p. 20).— *Ed.*

[b] *The High Price of Bullion a Proof of the Depreciation of Bank Notes.— Ed.*

decision is: abolish this privilege of gold and silver, demote them to the level of all other commodities. Then you do not abolish the specific evil of gold and silver money, or of notes convertible into gold and silver. You do away with all evils. Or rather promote all commodities to the monopoly status now possessed by gold and silver. Let the Papacy remain, but make everyone Pope. Do away with money by turning every commodity into money and endowing it with the specific properties of money.

Here the question arises whether the problem does not express its own absurdity, and hence whether the impossibility of a solution does not lie already in the conditions set by the problem. The answer can often consist only in the critique of the question, can often be provided only [I-7] by denying the question itself.

The real question is: does not the bourgeois system of exchange itself make a specific instrument of exchange necessary? Does it not of necessity create a special equivalent of all values? One form of this instrument of exchange, or of this equivalent, may be handier, more appropriate, entail fewer inconveniences than another. But the inconveniences resulting from the existence of a special instrument of exchange, of a special and yet general equivalent, are bound to reproduce themselves (if in different ways) in every form. Darimon naturally passes over this question with enthusiasm. Abolish money and do not abolish it! Abolish the exclusive privilege which gold and silver possess by virtue of their exclusive status as money, but convert all goods into money, i.e. give to all in common a property which, bereft of exclusiveness, no longer exists.

In the bullion drains there does indeed appear a contradiction which Darimon conceives and tries to resolve equally superficially. It becomes apparent that gold and silver are not commodities just like the others, and modern political economy is suddenly shocked always to find itself temporarily back among the prejudices of mercantilism. The English economists try to resolve the difficulty by making a distinction. What is required at times of such monetary crises, they say, is not gold and silver as money, gold and silver as coin, but gold and silver as capital. They forget to add: capital, but capital in the definite form of gold and silver. Why otherwise the outflow of precisely these commodities, while most others are depreciating from a lack of outflow, if capital were exportable in any form?

Let us take particular examples: a DRAIN resulting from a bad domestic harvest of some staple food (e.g. grain); or from a bad harvest abroad and therefore a rise in the price of an imported object of mass consumption (e.g. tea); a DRAIN because of a crop failure in vital industrial raw materials (cotton, wool, silk, flax); a DRAIN caused by excessive imports (through speculation, war, etc.). The replacement of a sudden or lasting shortage (of grain, tea, cotton, flax, etc.) causes the nation a double loss in case of a bad domestic harvest. A part of the country's invested capital or labour is not reproduced—a real loss of production. A part of the reproduced capital must be released to fill the gap, a part, that is, which is not simply arithmetically proportionate to the shortfall, for the price of the scarce product rises, and necessarily so, on the world market, because of the reduced supply and increased demand.

It is necessary to investigate closely what such crises would be like in the absence of the money factor, and what specific determinants money introduced within the given relationships. (*Bad grain harvests* and *excessive imports* the chief cases. War self-evidently too, since in economic terms it is the direct equivalent of a nation throwing a part of its capital into the water.)

The case of a bad grain harvest: comparing the nation affected with another, it is clear that its capital (not only its real wealth) has diminished, as clear as that the peasant who has burnt the dough for his bread and must now buy it from the baker is impoverished by the amount of his purchase. With respect to the domestic situation, the rise in the price of grain seems, so far as value is concerned, to leave everything unchanged, except that the reduced quantity of grain multiplied by the increased price in case of real bad harvests never equals the normal quantity multiplied by the lower price.

Suppose the wheat production of England were reduced to 1 quarter, and this 1 quarter fetched the same price as previously 30 million quarters of wheat. Then the nation, if we ignore the fact that it would lack the means for the reproduction of both life and grain, and if we assume that the working day needed for the reproduction of 1 quarter of wheat$=a$, would exchange $a \times 30$ million working days (production costs[29]) for $1 \times a$ working days (product). The productive power of its capital would have declined millions of times, and the sum of values owned in the country would have been reduced, for each working day would have depreciated 30 million-fold. Every item of capital would now represent only $1/30{,}000{,}000$ of its former value, of its equivalent in production costs, although in the given case the nominal value of the nation's capital would not have diminished (apart from the depreciation of land) because the diminished value of the other products would be exactly compensated for by the increased value of the 1 quarter of wheat. The 30 million-fold rise in the price of wheat would express an equal depreciation of all other products.

Incidentally, this distinction between home and abroad is quite illusory. The relationship of the nation which suffers the grain shortage to the foreign nation from which it buys, is identical to that of every individual in that nation to the farmer or grain merchant. The extra sum that he must expend for the purchase of grain is a direct diminution of his capital, of his disposable means.

In order not to confuse the issue by introducing non-essential influences, we must assume a nation with FREE TRADE in grain. Even if the imported grain were as cheap as the home-produced, the nation would be poorer to the extent of the capital not reproduced by the farmers. However, in the case we have assumed, the nation always imports as much foreign grain as may be imported at the normal price. A growth in imports thus presupposes a rise in price.

The rise in the price of grain implies a fall in the price of all other commodities. The increased production costs (represented by the price) at which a quarter of grain is obtained, imply a reduction in the productivity of the capital that exists in all other forms. The increased amount spent on the purchase of grain implies a corresponding diminution in the amount available for the purchase of all other products, and therefore an automatic fall in their prices. With or without metallic or any other kind of money, the nation would find itself in a crisis, affecting not only grain but all other branches of production, not only because their productivity would be actually diminished, and the price of their output depreciated in relation to the value determined by normal production costs, but also because all contracts, bonds, etc., are based on the average price of products. E.g. x bushels of grain must be delivered for the national debt, but the production costs of these x bushels have been increased by a definite proportion.

Quite irrespective of money, the nation [I-8] would therefore be in a general crisis. Apart not only from money, but even from the exchange value of the products, the products would have depreciated, the productivity of the nation would have declined, in so far as all its economic relations are based upon an average productivity of its labour.

Thus the crisis caused by a bad grain harvest is in no case produced by the DRAIN OF BULLION, although it can be aggravated by attempts to stem this DRAIN.

In any case, we cannot follow Proudhon in saying that the crisis is due to the fact that the precious metals alone possess authentic value in contrast to all other commodities[a]; for the rise in the price of grain means first of all only that more gold and silver must be exchanged for a given quantity of grain, i.e. that the price of gold and silver has fallen in relation to that of grain. Gold and silver therefore share in the depreciation of all other commodities relative to grain, from which no privilege protects them. The depreciation of gold and silver against grain is identical with the rise in the price of grain. (Not quite correct. A quarter of grain rises from 50 s. to 100 s., i.e. by 50%, but cotton goods fall by 100%. Silver has fallen against grain by only 50%, but cotton goods (because of slack demand, etc.) by 100%, i.e. the fall in the price of other commodities is greater than the rise in the price of grain. But the contrary may also take place. For example, in recent years when grain temporarily rose by 100%, industrial products did not depreciate in anything like the proportion in which gold had done compared to grain. This circumstance does not affect the general argument for the moment.) Nor can gold be said to possess a privilege by virtue of the fact that, as coinage, its quantity is exactly and authentically determined. A thaler (silver) remains under all circumstances a thaler. So does a bushel of wheat remain a bushel, and a yard of linen remain a yard.

The depreciation of most commodities (labour included) and the ensuing crisis in the case of a significant failure of the grain harvest cannot therefore be naively ascribed to the export of gold, since the depreciation and the crisis would occur even if no domestic gold were exported and no foreign grain imported. The crisis reduces itself simply to the law of supply and demand, which, as we all know, operates much more sharply and energetically in the sphere of primary necessities—at the national level—than in all other spheres. The export of gold is not the cause of the grain crisis, but the grain crisis is the cause of the export of gold.

Gold and silver in themselves can be said to affect the crisis and to aggravate its symptoms in only two ways: (1) In so far as the export of gold might be hindered because of the bullion-holding conditions by which the banks are bound; in so far as the measures taken by the Bank to counteract this gold export might adversely affect internal circulation. (2) In so far as the export of gold becomes necessary, because foreign nations will accept capital only in the form of gold and in no other form.

---

[a] P. J. Proudhon, *Système des contradictions économiques, ou Philosophie de la misère*, Vol. I, pp. 68-70.— *Ed.*

Difficulty No. 2 can persist even if difficulty No. 1 is removed. The Bank of England experienced it precisely during the period when it was legally authorised to issue inconvertible notes. The notes fell against gold bullion, but equally the MINT PRICE OF GOLD fell against its bullion price. Gold had become a special kind of commodity as distinct from banknotes. It can be said that the note remained dependent upon gold in so far as it nominally represented a definite quantity of gold for which IN FACT it was not redeemable. Gold remained its denominator although the note was legally no longer exchangeable for this quantity of gold at the Bank.

There is surely no doubt (?) (this is to be investigated later and is not directly relevant to the OBJECT IN QUESTION) that so long as paper money is denominated in terms of gold (i.e. so long as e.g. a £5 note is the paper representative of 5 sovereigns) the convertibility of the note into gold remains for it an economic law, whether or not it exists *politically*. Even from 1799 to 1819[30] the notes of the Bank of England continued to state that they represented the value of a definite quantity of gold. How can this assertion be put to the test other than by the fact that the banknote actually commanded such and such a quantity of bullion? From the moment that a £5 note could no longer be exchanged for bullion equal to 5 sovereigns, the note was depreciated, even though it was INCONVERTIBLE. The equality of the face value of the note with a definite value of gold immediately entered into contradiction with the actual inequality between notes and gold.

Thus the controversy in Britain among those who adhere to gold as the denominator of the note, is not really about the convertibility of the note into gold—which is only the practical equation that the face value on the note expresses theoretically—but about how this convertibility is to be secured: whether by the legal imposition of restrictions on the Bank, or by non-interference. The advocates of the latter course assert that with a bank of issue which gives advances on bills of exchange, and whose notes therefore have a secured reflux, convertibility is guaranteed ON THE AVERAGE, and that their opponents never achieve more than this average security anyhow. The latter is a FACT. The average, incidentally, is not to be despised, and calculations of the average must constitute the basis of the banks' activities no less than they do that of all insurance companies, etc. In this respect the Scottish banks above all are justly pointed to as models.

The strict bullionists for their part argue that they take [I-9] convertibility seriously—that the necessity of convertibility is imposed by the denomination of the note itself, that the obligation of the bank to convert maintains the convertibility of the note and restrains OVER-ISSUE, and that their opponents are disguised supporters of inconvertibility. Between these two positions a variety of shadings, a mass of little "*espèces*".[a]

Finally, the defenders of inconvertibility, the uncompromising anti-bullionists, are, without knowing it, disguised supporters of convertibility just as much as their opponents are of inconvertibility, because they allow the existing denomination of the note to remain and in practice therefore make the equation of a note of a particular denomination to a particular quantity of gold the measure of the full value of their notes.

In Prussia there is paper money with forced currency. (A reflux is assured for it in so far as a proportion of taxes must be paid in paper money.) These paper thalers are not drafts on silver, they are not legally exchangeable for it at any bank, etc. They are not loaned by any commercial bank against bills of exchange, but are paid out by the government to meet its expenses. But the notes are denominated in terms of silver. A paper thaler is supposed to represent the same value as a silver thaler. If either confidence in the government were seriously undermined, or this paper money were issued in greater amounts than required by the needs of circulation, the paper thaler would in practice cease to be equal to the silver thaler; it would depreciate, because it would have sunk below the value expressed by its denomination. It would even depreciate if none of the above-mentioned circumstances obtained, but if an exceptional demand for silver, e.g. for export, were to give silver a privilege over the paper thaler.

Convertibility into gold and silver is therefore in practice the measure of value of any paper currency denominated in terms of gold or silver, whether that currency is legally convertible or not. A nominal value is only a shadow running alongside its body; whether the two coincide must be proved by the actual convertibility (exchangeability) of the note. A decline of real value below nominal value is depreciation. Actual parity of nominal and real values, exchangeability, is convertibility. With [legally] inconvertible notes, convertibility shows itself not at the counter of the bank but in the day-to-day exchange between paper money and the metallic currency whose denomination it bears. Actually, the convertibility of convertible notes is already endangered when it is

---

no longer confirmed by normal business throughout the country but by special large experiments at the counter of the bank.

In the rural areas of Scotland, paper money is actually preferred to metallic currency. Before 1845, when the English Act of 1844 was imposed on it, Scotland was naturally affected by all English social crises, and in many cases to a higher degree, for in Scotland the CLEARING OF THE LAND was carried out more ruthlessly.[31] Nevertheless, Scotland did not experience a real monetary crisis (that a few banks here and there went bankrupt, because they extended credit recklessly, is not relevant here); there was no depreciation of banknotes, no complaints or investigations as to whether the quantity of CURRENCY in circulation was sufficient or not, etc.

Scotland is important in this context, because it shows on the one hand how the money system on its present basis can be completely regulated—all the evils deplored by Darimon abolished—without abandonment of the present social basis; indeed, while its contradictions, its antagonisms, the conflict of classes, etc., actually reach a higher degree than in any other country in the world.

It is significant that Darimon, as well as Émile Girardin, his protector, who writes an introduction to his book and who complements his practical swindling with theoretical utopianism, does not find the antithesis to the monopoly banks like the BANK OF ENGLAND and the BANK OF FRANCE in Scotland, but looks for it in the United States, where the banking system, because of the State charters required, is only nominally free, and where you do not have free competition among banks but a federative system of monopoly banks.

The Scottish banking and money system was indeed the most dangerous reef for the illusions of the circulation-tricksters. Gold and silver coins (where a bimetallic legal STANDARD does not exist) are not said to depreciate whenever their relative value compared to all other commodities changes. Why not? Because they are their own denominator; because their denomination is not that of a value, i.e. they are not valued in terms of a third commodity, but only express fractional parts of their own material. 1 sovereign=so much gold of such and such a weight.

Gold is therefore nominally undepreciable, not because it alone expresses *an authentic value,* but because as money it expresses *no value AT ALL,* only a certain quantity of its own material, because its own quantitative measure is stamped on its brow. (Later to be investigated more closely whether this distinctive feature of gold and silver money is ultimately an immanent property of every form of money.)

Misled by this nominal undepreciability of metallic currency, Darimon and his colleagues see only the one aspect which becomes apparent during a crisis, the appreciation of gold and silver against almost all other commodities; they fail to see the other aspect, the *depreciation* of gold and silver *or money* against all other commodities (with the possible, but not invariable, exception of labour) in periods of so-called *prosperity,* the periods of a temporary general rise in prices. As this depreciation of metallic money (and all types of money based on it) always precedes its appreciation, they should have posed their problem the other way round: how to prevent the periodic recurrence of the depreciation of money (in their language, how to abolish the privileged status of commodities as against money). Formulated in this way, the riddle would have solved itself at once: abolish the rise and fall in prices. That means, do away with prices. That, in turn, means abolishing exchange value, which, in its turn, requires the abolition of the system of exchange corresponding to the bourgeois organisation [I-10] of society. This last entails the problem of revolutionising bourgeois society economically. Then it would have become evident from the start that the evils of bourgeois society cannot be remedied by bank "transformations" or the establishment of a rational "money system".

Convertibility, legal or otherwise, therefore remains a requirement of any kind of money whose denomination makes it into a token of value, i.e. equates it quantitatively to a third commodity. This equation already implies its antithesis, the possibility of non-equivalence; just as convertibility implies its opposite, inconvertibility, and appreciation implies depreciation, δυνάμει,[a] as Aristotle would say.

Let us assume, for instance, that the sovereign was not only called "sovereign", which is a mere title of honour for the xth fraction of an ounce of gold (accounting name), as "metre" is for a particular length, but that it was called, SAY, *x hours of labour time.* $^1/_x$ ounce of gold is in fact nothing but materialised, objectified, x hours of labour time. But the gold is past labour time, defined labour time. This denomination would make a particular quantity of labour in general into its standard. A pound of gold would have to be CONVERTIBLE into x hours of labour time, would have to

---

a Potentially.— *Ed.*

be able to purchase these at any time. As soon as it could purchase more or less labour, it would appreciate or depreciate; in the latter case, its convertibility would cease to exist.

Not the labour time incorporated in [previous] output, but the currently necessary labour time determines value. Take the pound of gold itself: let it be the product of 20 hours of labour time. Suppose that for some reason it later requires only 10 hours to produce a pound of gold. The pound of gold, whose denomination asserts that it=20 hours of labour time, would now only=10 hours of labour time, since 20 hours of labour time=2 pounds of gold. Ten hours of labour in fact exchange for 1 pound of gold; therefore 1 pound of gold can no longer exchange for 20 hours of labour.

Gold money with the plebeian denomination *x hours of labour,* would be more subject to fluctuations than any other kind of money, and especially more than the present gold money; because gold cannot rise or fall against gold (being equal to itself), while the past labour time embodied in a definite quantity of gold must continually rise or fall against present living labour time. To maintain its convertibility, the productivity of an hour's labour would have to be kept constant. Indeed, according to the general economic law that production costs fall continually, that living labour becomes more and more productive, and that the labour time objectified in products therefore continually depreciates, constant depreciation would be the inevitable fate of this gold labour money. One could say that, to overcome this drawback, the denomination of labour hours should be borne not by gold but by paper money, a mere token of value, as was suggested by Weitling[32] and before him by Englishmen and after him by Frenchmen, among them Proudhon and company. The labour time embodied in the paper itself would be of as little account as the paper value of banknotes. The one would simply be a representative of labour hours, as the other is of gold or silver. If an hour of labour became more productive the token that represented it would rise in purchasing power and conversely, exactly as now a £5 note buys more or less according to the rise or fall in the relative value of gold in comparison to other commodities.

In accordance with the same law by which the gold labour money would be subject to constant depreciation, the paper labour money would enjoy constant appreciation. That is precisely what we want: the worker would be glad of the rising productivity of his labour, instead of, as now, creating proportionately more alien wealth and his own depreciation. So say the socialists.

BUT, UNFORTUNATELY, THERE ARISE SOME SMALL SCRUPLES. *D'abord,*[a] once we assume the existence of money, even if only as labour-time tickets, we must also assume accumulation of this money and contracts, obligations, interest payments, etc., which would be entered into in terms of this money. The accumulated tickets would continually appreciate, as well as the newly issued ones. Hence, on the one hand, the growing productivity of labour would benefit those who do not work, while on the other hand debts contracted earlier would keep pace with the greater productivity of labour. The rise and fall in the value of gold or silver would not matter at all if the world's business could be started anew at each instant, and obligations to pay a definite quantity of gold did not survive fluctuations in the value of gold. The same is the case with the labour-time ticket and the productivity of an hour's labour.

The point to be examined here is the convertibility of the labour-time tickets. We shall arrive at the same end if we make a digression here. Although it is still too early, we may make a few remarks about the delusions that underlie the labour-time ticket, and peer into the deepest secret that links Proudhon's theory of circulation with his general theory, his theory of the determination [I-11] of value. We find the same link, for example, in Bray and Gray. The possible elements of truth underlying it to be examined later. (Before that, INCIDENTALLY: banknotes considered simply as drafts on gold can never be issued in excess of the quantity of gold money that they purport to replace, without being depreciated. Three bank drafts of £15 each, which I issue to three separate creditors on the same £15 in gold, are in fact only drafts on $£^{15}/_3 = £5$ each. Each of these notes would therefore be depreciated to $33^1/_3\%$ from the outset.)

The *value* (the real exchange value) of all commodities (including labour) is determined by their production costs, in other words, by the labour time required for their production. Their *price* is this exchange value of theirs expressed in money. The replacement of metallic currency (and the paper or credit money denominated in terms of it) by labour money deriving its denomination from labour time itself, would therefore equate the *real value* (exchange value) of commodities and their *nominal value, price, money value*. Equation of *real value and nominal value, of value and price*. But this would be attained only on the assumption that

―――――――
[a] To begin with.— *Ed.*

value and *price* are only *nominally* distinct. But such is by no means the case. The value of commodities determined by labour time is only their *average value*. An average which appears as an external abstraction in so far as it is obtained by calculation as the average over a period of time, e.g. 1 pound of coffee, 1 shilling, if the average price of coffee is taken over a period of, say, 25 years. But this average is very real if it is recognised as both the driving force and the moving principle of the fluctuations which occur in the prices of commodities during a particular period of time.

This reality is not only of theoretical importance. It also constitutes the basis of commercial speculation, where the calculation of probability proceeds from both the mean average price, which is taken as the centre of the fluctuations, and the average heights and depths of these fluctuations above or below this centre. The *market value* of commodities is always different from this average value and always stands either below or above it.

The market value equates itself to the real value by means of its continual fluctuations, not by an equation with real value as some third thing, but precisely through continual inequality to itself (not, as Hegel would say, by abstract identity but by a continual negation of the negation,[a] i.e. of itself as the negation of the real value). I have shown in my pamphlet against Proudhon, and it need not be gone into further at this point, that the real value—independently of its dominance over the fluctuations of the market price (apart from its being the *law* of these fluctuations)—negates itself again and brings the real value of the commodities continually into contradiction with its own determination, depreciates or appreciates the real value of existing commodities.[b]

Price, therefore, differs from *value,* not only as the nominal differs from the real; not only by its denomination in gold and silver; but also in that the latter appears as the law of the movements to which the former is subject. But they are always distinct and never coincide, or only quite fortuitously and exceptionally. The price of commodities always stands above or below their value, and the value of commodities itself exists only in the UPS AND DOWNS of commodity prices. Demand and supply continually determine the prices of commodities; they never coincide or do so only accidentally; but the costs of production

---

[a] G. W. F. Hegel, *Wissenschaft der Logik,* 2. Buch, 1. Abschnitt, 2. Kapitel, A. Die Identität.— *Ed.*

[b] Karl Marx, *The Poverty of Philosophy. Answer to the "Philosophy of Poverty" by M. Proudhon* (see present edition, Vol. 6, pp. 131-37).— *Ed.*

determine for their part the fluctuations of demand and supply.

The gold or silver in which the price of a commodity, its market value, is expressed, is itself a particular quantity of stored up labour, a certain measure of materialised labour time. On the assumption that the production costs of the commodity and of the gold and silver remain constant, the rise or fall of its market price means only that a commodity equal to x labour time continually commands on the market something more or less than x labour time, stands above or below its average value determined by labour time.

The first basic illusion of the champions of labour-time tickets consists in this: that by abolishing the *nominal distinction* between real value and market value, between exchange value and price, by expressing value in labour time itself instead of in a particular objectification of labour time, SAY, gold and silver, they also remove the real distinction and contradiction between price and value. On that basis it is self-evident how the simple introduction of labour-time tickets would remove all crises, all defects of bourgeois production. The money price of commodities=their real value; demand=supply; production=consumption; money simultaneously abolished and retained; the labour time whose product the commodity is, which is materialised in the commodity, would need merely to be stated to produce its corresponding counterpart in a token of value, in money, in labour-time tickets. Each commodity would thus be directly transformed into money, and gold and silver for their part reduced to the rank of all other commodities.

We do not need to dwell on the fact that the contradiction between exchange value and price, between the average price and the prices whose average it is, the distinction between magnitudes and their average magnitude, [I-12] cannot be eliminated by abolishing the mere *difference of name* between them, i.e. by instead of saying that 1 lb. of bread costs 8d., saying that 1 lb. of bread=$^1/_x$ hour of labour. Conversely, if 8d.=$^1/_x$ hour of labour, and if the labour time materialised in one pound of bread is more or less than $^1/_x$ hour of labour, then, because the measure of value would also be the element in which the price is expressed, the difference between value and price, which is concealed in the gold or silver price, would be only too apparent. We should have an infinite equation: $^1/_x$ hour of labour (contained in 8d. or expressed by a ticket) would equal either more or less than $^1/_x$ hour of labour (contained in the pound of bread).

The labour-time ticket, which represents the *average labour time,* would never correspond to the *actual labour time* and never be convertible into it. That is, the labour time objectified in a commodity would never command a quantity of labour money equal to itself, and vice versa. It would command more or less, just as now each fluctuation of market values is expressed in a rise or fall in their gold and silver prices.

The constant depreciation of commodities—over longer periods—against the labour-time tickets, of which we spoke earlier,[a] would result from the law of the rising productivity of labour time, from the disturbances in relative value itself, which are created through its own inherent principle, labour time. The inconvertibility of the labour-time tickets, which we are now discussing, is nothing but another expression of the inconvertibility between real value and market value, exchange value and price. In contrast to all commodities, the labour-time ticket would represent an ideal labour time, which would exchange now for more, now for less, actual labour time, and which would have a separate, individual existence in this ticket corresponding to this real inequality. Once again the general equivalent, the means of circulation and measure of commodities would confront them as something individualised, following its own laws, alienated, i.e. with all the properties of our present money without performing its services. But confusion would reach quite a new peak, as the medium for comparing commodities, these objectified quantities of labour time, would not be a third commodity but their own measure of value, labour time itself.

Commodity *a,* the objectification of 3 hours of labour time,=2 hour's labour-time tickets; commodity *b,* likewise the objectification of 3 hours of labour=4 hours' labour-time tickets. This contradiction is indeed expressed in money prices, but in a concealed form. The distinction between price and value, between the commodity as measured by the labour time of which it is the product, and the product of the labour time for which it is exchanged, this distinction demands a third commodity as a measure, in which the real exchange value of the commodity is expressed. *Because price does not equal value, the element determining value, labour time, cannot be the element in which prices are expressed. For labour time would have to express itself at once as the determining and the non-determining element, as the equivalent and the non-equivalent of itself.* Because labour time as a measure of value exists only ideally, it cannot serve as the material for the comparison of prices. (This also

---

explains how and why the value relationship assumes a material and distinct existence in [the form of] money. This point to be developed further.) The distinction between price and value demands that values as prices be measured by a yardstick other than their own. Price as distinct from value is necessarily *money price*. Here it becomes clear that the *nominal* distinction between price and value is conditioned by their *real* distinction.

[THE ORIGIN AND ESSENCE OF MONEY]

Commodity $a=1$ s. (i.e. equals $1/x$ silver); commodity $b=2$ s. (i.e. $2/x$ silver). Therefore commodity $b=$twice the value of commodity a. The value relationship between a and b is expressed by the proportion in which each exchanges against a definite quantity of a third commodity, silver; not against a value relationship.

Each commodity (product or instrument of production)=the objectification of a particular [quantity of] labour time. Its value, the proportion in which it is exchanged for other commodities or other commodities are exchanged for it, is equal to the quantity of labour time realised in it. If the commodity e.g.=1 hour's labour time, it can be exchanged for all other commodities which are the product of 1 hour's labour time. (This proposition is based on the assumption that exchange value=market value; real value=price.)

The value of a commodity is different from the commodity itself. The commodity is value (exchange value) only in exchange (real or imagined). Value is not only the exchangeability of this commodity in general, but its specific exchangeability. It is at once the indicator of the ratio in which the commodity exchanges for others and the indicator of the ratio in which it has already been exchanged for others (materialised labour time) in the process of production. Value is a commodity's quantitatively determined [I-13] exchangeability. Commodities, e.g. a yard of cotton and a quart of oil, considered as cotton and oil, are of course distinct, possess different properties, are measured in different units, are incommensurable. As values, all commodities are qualitatively equal and only quantitatively different, hence they can be measured in terms of each other and are mutually replaceable (exchangeable, convertible into each other) in definite quantitative proportions.

Value is their social relationship, their economic quality. A book that has a certain value, and a loaf that has the same value, are mutually exchangeable, they represent the same value, only in different materials. As value, the commodity is at the same time an equivalent for all other commodities in a particular ratio. As value, the commodity is an equivalent; as an equivalent, all its natural properties are extinguished; it no longer bears any particular qualitative relationship to other commodities, but it is the general measure, the general representative, and the general means of exchange for all other commodities. As value it is *money*.

But because the commodity, or rather the product or instrument of production, is distinct from itself as value, it is also, as value, distinct from itself as a product. Its property as value not only can, but must, at the same time acquire an existence distinct from its natural existence. Why? Because, since commodities as values are only quantitatively different from each other, every commodity must be qualitatively distinct from its own value. Its value therefore must also have an existence qualitatively distinguishable from it, and in the actual exchange this separability must become an actual separation, because the natural distinctions between commodities must come into contradiction with their economic equivalence; the two can exist alongside one another only through the commodity acquiring a dual existence, a natural existence and alongside it a purely economic one, in which it is a mere sign, a letter for a relationship of production, a mere symbol for its own value.

As value, every commodity is uniformly divisible; in its natural existence, it is not. As value, it remains the same, no matter how many metamorphoses and forms of existence it goes through; in reality, commodities are exchanged only because they are different and correspond to different systems of needs. As value, it is general, as an actual commodity it is something particular. As value, it is always exchangeable; in actual exchange it is exchangeable only if it fulfils certain conditions. As value, the extent of its exchangeability is determined by itself: exchange value expresses precisely the ratio in which a commodity replaces other commodities; in actual exchange, it is exchangeable only in quantities related to its natural properties and corresponding to the needs of the exchangers.

(In short, all the properties that are enumerated as particular properties of money are properties of the commodity as exchange value; [properties] of the product as value as distinct from the value as product.) (The exchange value of the commodity, as a special existence alongside the commodity itself, is *money*: the form in which all commodities are equated, compared, measured; the form into which all commodities are dissolved, and which dissolves itself in all commodities; the general equivalent.)

In calculations, accountancy, etc., we are constantly transforming commodities into symbols of value, fixing them as mere exchange values, abstracting from their material composition and all their natural properties. On paper, in the head, this metamorphosis is produced by a simple process of abstraction; but in actual exchange a real *mediation* is necessary, a means by which this abstraction is effected. In its natural properties, the commodity is neither continually exchangeable, nor exchangeable with *every other commodity*; it is not exchangeable in its natural identity with itself, but only as something different from itself, only posited as exchange value. We must first convert it into itself as exchange value, in order to compare and to exchange this exchange value with others.

In the most primitive barter trade, when two commodities are exchanged for one another, each is first equated to a figure that expresses its exchange value, e.g. among certain Negro tribes on the West African coast as equal to x BARS.[a] The one commodity is equal to 1 BAR, the other to 2 BARS. In this proportion they are exchanged. The commodities are first transformed in the head and in speech into BARS before they are exchanged for one another. They are valued before they are exchanged, and in order to be valued they must be brought into a definite numerical relationship to each other. In order to bring them into such a numerical relationship and to make them commensurable, they must obtain the same denomination (unit). (The BAR possesses a merely imaginary existence, and indeed in general a relationship can obtain a specific embodiment, can itself be individualised, only through abstraction.) To cover the surplus of one value over the other, to liquidate the balance, payment in money becomes necessary in the most primitive barter trade as well as in present-day international trade.

Products (or activities) exchange only as commodities; commodities themselves exist in exchange only as values; only as such are they comparable. To determine the weight of bread that I can exchange for a yard of linen cloth, I first equate the yard of linen to its exchange value, i.e. to $1/x$ labour time. Likewise I equate the pound of bread to its exchange value, $1/\dot{x}$ or $2/x$, etc., labour time. I equate each commodity to a third, i.e. [I-14] I posit it as unequal to itself. This third thing, distinct from the other two since it ex-

---

a See W. Jacob, *An Historical Inquiry into the Production and Consumption of the Precious Metals*, Vol. II, London, 1831, pp. 326-27; D. Urquhart, *Familiar Words as Affecting England and the English*, London, 1856, p. 112.— *Ed.*

presses a ratio, exists initially in the head, in the imagination, just as in general ratios can only be *thought* if they are to be fixed, as distinct from the subjects[33] which are in that ratio to each other.

When a product (or an activity) becomes exchange value, it is not only transformed into a particular quantitative ratio, a numerical ratio—namely into a number which expresses what quantity of other commodities is equivalent to it, is its equivalent, or in what proportion it is the equivalent of other commodities—it must at the same time be qualitatively transformed, converted into another element, so that both commodities become denominated quantities, in the same units, thus becoming commensurable.

The commodity must first be transformed into labour time, that is into something qualitatively different from itself (qualitatively different (1) because it is not labour time as labour time, but materialised labour time; labour time not in the form of movement, but in that of rest; not as process, but as result; (2) because it is not the objectification of labour time in general, which exists only in the imagination (is itself only labour separated from its quality, only quantitatively different labour), but is the definite result of a definite, naturally determined labour, qualitatively different from other labours) in order then to become comparable as a definite quantity of labour time, a definite magnitude of labour, with other quantities of labour time, other magnitudes of labour.

For mere comparison, for the valuation of products, for the notional determination of their value, it is enough to make this transformation in the head (a transformation in which the product exists simply as the expression of quantitative relationships of production). For the comparison of commodities, this abstraction is sufficient; for actual exchange, this abstraction must again be objectified, symbolised, realised through a token. The necessity arises as follows: (1) As we have already said, the commodities to be exchanged are both transformed in the head into common ratios of magnitudes, exchange values, and so valued against each other. If they are now to be actually exchanged, their natural properties come into contradiction with their determination as exchange values and mere denominated numbers. They are not arbitrarily divisible, etc. (2) In actual exchange, specific commodities are always exchanged for specific commodities, and the exchangeability of each commodity, like the proportion in which it is exchangeable, depends upon circumstances of place, time, etc.

But the transformation of a commodity into exchange value does not equate it with another specific commodity, but expresses it as an equivalent, the ratio of its exchangeability to all other commodities. This comparison, which in the head is carried out at a stroke, is effected in reality only within a definite sphere, one determined by demand, and only in successive steps. (For example, I exchange little by little an income of 100 thaler, in accordance with my needs, against a whole range of commodities whose sum is equal to the exchange value of 100 thaler.)

Hence, in order to realise the commodity at a stroke as exchange value and to give it the general effect of exchange value, its exchange for a particular commodity is not sufficient. It must be exchanged for a third thing which is not itself a particular commodity but the symbol of the commodity as commodity, of the commodity's exchange value itself; *which therefore represents, say, labour time as such,* say, a piece of paper or leather which represents a certain portion of labour time. (Such a symbol presupposes general recognition; it can only be a social symbol; in fact, it only expresses a social relationship.)

This symbol represents certain portions of labour time, represents exchange value in such portions as are capable of expressing by simple arithmetic combinations all reciprocal relationships of exchange values. This symbol, this material sign of exchange value, is a product of exchange itself, not the execution of a preconceived idea. (IN FACT, the commodity which serves as the mediator of exchange is only transformed into money, into a symbol, gradually. As soon as that has happened, a symbol of the mediating commodity can in turn replace the commodity itself. It now becomes the conscious token of exchange value.)

Hence the process is simply this: the product becomes a commodity, i.e. a *mere element of exchange.* The commodity is transformed into exchange value. In order to equate it with itself as exchange value, it is exchanged for a token which represents it as exchange value as such. As such symbolised exchange value, it can then be exchanged again in certain proportions with any other commodity. Through the product becoming a commodity and the commodity becoming exchange value, it acquires, first in our mind, a dual existence. This mental duplication proceeds (and must proceed) to the point where the commodity appears dual in actual exchange: as natural product on the one hand, as exchange value on the other. I.e. its exchange value acquires an existence materially separated from it.

[I-15] The determination of the product as exchange value therefore necessarily brings it about that the exchange value acquires an existence apart from the product, detached from it.

Exchange value detached from the commodities themselves, and itself existing as a commodity alongside them, is— *money*. In *money*, all the properties of a commodity as exchange value appear as an object distinct from the commodity, as a social form of existence detached from the commodity's natural form of existence. (This is to be demonstrated further by enumerating the ordinary properties of money.) (The material used to express this symbol is a matter of some consequence, however varied it has been historically. As society develops it also evolves—along with the symbol—the material that more and more corresponds to the symbol, though it later strives to free itself from that material again; a symbol, if it is not arbitrary, requires certain conditions as regards the material in which it is presented. Thus, e.g. the signs for words possess a history; alphabetic script, etc.)

The exchange value of a product thus produces money alongside the product. Just as it is impossible to abolish complications and contradictions arising from the existence of money alongside specific commodities by changing the form of money (although difficulties inherent in a lower form of money may be avoided by a higher form), it is likewise impossible to abolish money itself, so long as exchange value remains the social form of products. It is essential to understand this clearly, so as not to set oneself impossible tasks, and to know the limits within which monetary reform and changes in circulation can remodel the relations of production and the social relations based upon them.

The properties of money (1) as measure of commodity exchange; (2) as means of exchange; (3) as representative of commodities (for that reason as the object of contracts); (4) as universal commodity existing alongside the particular ones, all follow simply from its role as objectified exchange value separated from the commodities themselves. (By virtue of its property as a universal commodity in relation to all others, as the embodiment of their exchange value, money is also the realised and always realisable form of capital, the form in which capital is always acceptable, as is demonstrated by the bullion DRAINS. It was owing to this property that capital appeared historically first only in the form of money. It explains moreover the connection of money with the rate of interest and its influence thereon.)

The more production develops in such a way that every producer becomes dependent upon the exchange value of his commodity, i.e. the more the product really becomes exchange value, and exchange value becomes the immediate object of production, the more must *money relationships* develop, and with them the contradictions immanent in *money relationships,* immanent in the relationship of the product to itself as money. The need for exchange and the transformation of the product into pure exchange value progresses in the same measure as the division of labour, i.e. with the social character of production. But with the growth of the latter grows the power of *money,* i.e. the exchange relation establishes itself as a power external to and independent of the producers. What originally appeared as a means to promote production turns into a relationship alien to the producers. In proportion as the producers become dependent upon exchange, exchange appears to become independent of them; the rift between the product as product and the product as exchange value appears to widen. Money does not create this opposition and this contradiction; on the contrary, their development creates the apparently transcendental power of money.

(To be developed: the influence of the transformation of all relationships into money relationships; of taxes in kind into taxes in money, rent in kind into money rent, feudal military service into mercenaries, in general of all personal services into monetary dues, of patriarchal, slave, serf, guild labour into pure wage labour.)

The product becomes a commodity; the commodity becomes exchange value; the exchange value of the commodity is its immanent monetary attribute; this monetary attribute detaches itself from the commodity as money, assumes a general social existence separate from all specific commodities and their natural form of existence. The relationship of the product to itself as exchange value becomes its relationship to a money existing alongside it, or the relationship of all products to money existing outside all of them. As the actual exchange of products gives rise to their exchange value, so does their exchange value give rise to money.

The next question which confronts us is this: does not the existence of money alongside commodities contain from the outset contradictions inherent in this very relationship?

Firstly: The simple fact that the commodity has a dual existence, as a specific product which contains its exchange value in its natural form of existence as idea (in latent form), and then as revealed exchange value (*money*) which has discarded all connection with the product's natural form of existence; this dual existence in two *distinct* forms must lead to *differentiation,* and the differentiation to *opposition* and [I-16] *contradiction.* The same contradiction between the particular nature of the commodity as a product and its general nature as exchange value, which necessitated its being posited as dual, on the one hand as particular commodity and on the other as money, the contradiction between its specific natural properties and its general social properties, contains from the outset the possibility that these two separate forms of existence of the commodity are not mutually convertible. The exchangeability of the commodity exists as a thing alongside it in money, as something distinct from it, no longer immediately identical with it. As soon as money is an external thing alongside the commodity, the exchangeability of the commodity for money is immediately linked to external conditions, which may or may not be present. It is subject to external circumstances.

The commodity is demanded in exchange because of its natural properties, because of the needs of which it is the object; money, on the other hand, only because of its exchange value, as exchange value. Whether therefore the commodity is convertible into money, whether it can be exchanged for it, whether its exchange value can be realised, depends upon circumstances which have no immediate connection with it as exchange value and are independent of it. The convertibility of the commodity depends upon the natural properties of the product; that of money coincides with its existence as symbolised exchange value. It therefore becomes possible that the commodity in its particular form as product can no longer be exchanged for or equated with its general form as money.

By existing outside the commodity as money, the exchangeability of the commodity has become something different from the commodity, alien to it, with which it must first be equated, to which it is therefore *d'abord* unequal; while the equating itself becomes dependent upon external circumstances, therefore a matter of chance.

Secondly: As the exchange value of a commodity has a dual form of existence, as a specific commodity and as money, so the act of exchange consists of two mutually independent acts: exchange of the commodity for money, exchange of the money for a commodity, buying and selling. Since these have now acquired a form of existence distinct from one another in space and time and indifferent to one another, their immediate identity ceases to exist. They may correspond or not; they may coincide or not; disparities may occur between them. True, they will always seek to get into balance, but the earlier direct equality has now been replaced by the continual movement towards equalisation, which of course presupposes continual inequality. It is possible that consonance between them may now be fully attained only by passing through the most extreme dissonances.

Thirdly: With the separation of buying and selling, the division of exchange into two acts independent of each other in space and time, there emerges another new relationship.

As exchange itself splits into two mutually independent acts, so the general movement of exchange is severed from the exchangers, from the producers of the commodities. Exchange for the sake of exchange is separated from exchange for the sake of commodities. An estate of merchants intervenes between the producers, an estate which buys only in order to sell, and sells only in order to buy again, aiming in this operation not at the possession of the commodities as products but merely at the acquisition of exchange value as such, of money. (A merchant estate can arise even under conditions of mere barter. But since it has at its disposal only the surplus of production on both sides, its influence on production itself remains utterly secondary, as does its whole significance.)

To the acquisition of independence by exchange value in money, divorced from the products, corresponds the acquisition of independence by exchange (trade) as a function divorced from the exchangers. Exchange value was the measure of commodity barter; but the object of the latter was the direct possession of the exchanged commodity, its consumption (whether this consumption consisted in its use as a product for the direct satisfaction of needs, or as a tool of production).

The purpose of trade is not directly consumption but the acquisition of money, of exchange values. This dual nature of exchange—exchange for the sake of consumption and exchange for the sake of exchange—results in a new disparity. The merchant in his exchange is guided merely by the difference between purchase and sale of the commodity; but the consumer must once and for all replace the exchange value of the commodity he buys. Circulation, exchange within the merchant estate, and the final stage of circulation, exchange between the merchants and the consumers, however much they must ultimately condition each other, are determined by quite different laws and motives, and the greatest contradiction can develop between them. This separation alone can be the cause of trade crises. But since production is geared directly to trade and only indirectly to [I-17] consumption, it must get caught up in this incongruity between trade and exchange for consumption just as much as, for its own part, it must produce it. (The relationships between demand and supply are completely reversed.) (The money business, in turn, becomes separated from trade in the strict sense.)

Aphorisms. (All commodities are transitory money; money is the eternal commodity. The further the division of labour develops, the more the immediate product ceases to be a means of exchange. The need arises for a general means of exchange, i.e. for a means of exchange that is independent of the specific production of any individual. In money, the value of things is separated from their substance. Money is originally the representative of all values; in practice it is the other way round, and all real products and all labour become representatives of money. In direct barter every article cannot be exchanged for every other article, and a particular activity can only be exchanged for particular products. The difficulties inherent in barter can be overcome by money only in so far as it generalises these difficulties, makes them universal. It is absolutely necessary that the forcibly separated elements which essentially belong together, should demonstrate by some violent eruption that theirs is a *separation* of what essentially belongs together., Unity is produced *by force.* As soon as the hostile separation leads to eruptions, the economists draw attention to the *essential unity* and ignore the alienation. Their apologetic wisdom consists in forgetting their own definitions at every decisive moment. The product as immediate means of exchange is still directly connected (1) with its natural properties, hence in every way limited by them; e.g. it can deteriorate, etc.; (2) with the direct need that another person has or does not have for this particular product, or might also have for his own product. Once the product of labour and labour itself are subjected to exchange, there comes a moment when they are separated from their owner. Whether they return to him from this separation in some other form becomes *a matter of chance.* In so far as money comes into the exchange, I am compelled to exchange my product for universal exchange value or universal exchangeability, and so my product becomes dependent upon general commerce and is torn out of its local, natural and individual boundaries. Precisely thereby it can cease to be a product.)

Fourthly: As exchange value in the form of money appears as the *general commodity* alongside all particular commodities, so exchange value, as money, thereby appears simultaneously as a *particular commodity* (since money has a particular existence) alongside all other commodities. Not only does this lead to the incongruity that, as it exists only in exchange, money confronts the particular exchangeability of commodities as universal exchangeability and immediately extinguishes it, while the two must nevertheless always remain convertible into one another; but money also comes into contradiction with itself and its determination because it is itself a *particular* commodity (even if only a symbol) and thus, in its exchange with other commodities, is again subject to particular conditions of exchange which contradict its universal unconditional exchangeability. (Here no mention at all yet of money as fixed in the substance of a definite product, etc.)

In addition to its existence in the commodity, exchange value acquired an existence of its own in money; it was separated from its substance precisely because the natural determinateness of this substance contradicted its general determination as exchange value. Each commodity is identical (or comparable) to another as exchange value (*qualitatively*: each represents only a *quantitative* plus or minus of exchange value). Hence this identity, this unity of commodities, differs from their natural distinctiveness, and therefore appears in money both as the element common to them and also as a third thing confronting them. But on the one hand, exchange value naturally remains an inherent quality of commodities while at the same time existing outside them. On the other hand, in so far as money no longer exists as a quality of commodities, as their general attribute, but is individualised alongside them, it becomes itself a *particular* commodity among the other commodities (subject to the determination of demand and supply; can be divided into particular types of money, etc.).

It becomes a commodity like other commodities, and at the same time is not a commodity like other commodities. In spite of its general determination it is one exchangeable among other exchangeables. It is not only the general exchange value, but at the same time a particular exchange value among other particular exchange values. Here a new source of contradictions which manifest themselves in practice. (In the separation of the money business from actual trade, the special nature of money emerges yet again.)

We see, then, how it is inherent in money to fulfil its purposes by simultaneously negating them; to make itself independent in relation to commodities; to turn itself from a means into an end; to realise the exchange value of commodities by separating them from it; to facilitate exchange by splitting it; to overcome the difficulties of the direct exchange of commodities by [I-18] generalising them; to render exchange independent of the producers to the same extent as the producers become dependent on exchange.

(It will later be necessary, before leaving this question, to correct the idealist manner of presentation which makes it appear as if it were merely a matter of the definitions of concepts and the dialectic of these concepts. Above all the phrase: the product (or activity) becomes a commodity; the commodity becomes exchange value; the exchange value becomes money.)

(*The Economist*, 24 January 1857. The following passage to be borne in mind when dealing with the BANKS[a]:

"So far as the mercantile classes share, which they now do very generally, in the profits of banks—and may to a still greater extent by the wider diffusion of joint-stock banks, the abolition of all corporate privileges, and the extension of perfect freedom to the business of banking,—they have been enriched by the increased rates of money. In truth, the mercantile classes by the extent of their deposits, are virtually their own bankers; and so far as that is the case, the rate of discount must be to them of little importance. All banking and other reserves must of course be the results of continual industry, and of savings laid by out of profits; and consequently, taking the mercantile or industrious classes as a whole, they must be their own bankers; and it requires only that the principles of free trade should be extended to all businesses, to equalise or neutralise for them the advantages and disadvantages of all the fluctuations in the money market.")

All contradictions of the *money system* and of the exchange of products under the money system lie in the development of the relationship of products as *exchange values*, of their role as *exchange value* or simply as *value*.

(*Morning Star*, 12 February 1857. "The pressure of money during last year, and the high rate of discount which was adopted in consequence, has been very beneficial to the profit account of the Bank of France. Its dividend has gone on increasing: 118 frs in 1852, 154 frs in 1853, 194 frs in 1854, 200 frs in 1855, 272 frs in 1856.")

The following passage also to be noted:

"The English silver coins [are] issued at a price higher than the value of the silver they contain. A pound silver of 60-62 sh. in intrinsic value (£3 on an average in gold) [was] coined into 66 sh. The Mint pays the market price of the day, from 5 sh. to 5 sh. 2d. the ounce, and issues at the rate of 5 sh. 6d. the ounce. There are two reasons which prevent any practical inconvenience resulting from this arrangement" (of *silver tokens*, not of intrinsic value): "first, the coin can only be procured at the Mint, and at that price; as home circulation, then, it cannot be depreciated, and it cannot be sent abroad because it circulates here for more than

---

[a] Here and further in this section, Marx quotes in English.— *Ed.*

its intrinsic value; and secondly, as it is a legal tender only up to 40 sh., it never interferes with the gold coins, nor affects their value."

Advises France likewise to

issue subordinate coins of silver tokens, not of intrinsic value, and limiting the amount to which they should be a legal tender.

But at the same time:

in fixing the quality of the coin, to take a larger margin between the intrinsic and the nominal value than we have in England, because the increasing value of silver in relation to gold may very probably, before long, rise up to our present Mint price, when we may be obliged again to alter it. Our silver coin is now little more than 5% below the intrinsic value: a short time since it was 10% (*The Economist*, 24 January 1857).

Now, it might be thought that the issue of labour-time tickets overcomes all these difficulties. (The existence of such tickets naturally presupposes conditions which are not directly given in the investigation of the relationship of exchange value and money, and without which both can and do exist: "public credit", bank, etc.; but all this not to be further discussed here; since of course the supporters of the labour-time ticket consider it as the *final* product of the "series",[34] which, if it corresponds most closely to the "pure" concept of money, "appears" last in reality.)

To begin with: if the conditions under which the price of a commodity=its exchange value are assumed as fulfilled, i.e. balance of demand and supply, of production and consumption, in the final analysis PROPORTIONATE PRODUCTION[a] (the so-called relations of distribution are themselves relations of production), then the question of money becomes quite secondary, and especially the question whether blue or green TICKETS, metal or paper ones, are issued, or in what other form social book-keeping will be done. It is then the height of absurdity to keep up the pretence that investigations of the actual money relationships should be instituted.

[I-19] The bank, ANY BANK, issues the labour-time tickets. Commodity a=exchange value x, i.e. x labour time, exchanges for money representing x labour time. The bank would have to purchase the commodity, i.e. exchange it for its monetary representative in the same way as e.g. now the Bank of England must give notes for gold. The commodity, the material and

---

[a] See J. Gray, *Lectures on the Nature and Use of Money*, Edinburgh, 1848, pp. 67, 108, 123, 125, 142-48 et al.— *Ed.*

therefore fortuitous [form of] existence of exchange value, is exchanged for the symbolic existence of exchange value as exchange value. There is thus no difficulty in converting it from the form of a commodity into that of money. The labour time it contains only needs to be authentically verified (which, incidentally, is not as easy as testing the fineness and weight of gold and silver) and produces thereby directly its *contrevaleur*[a]: its monetary existence.

However we twist and turn the matter, in the final analysis it comes to this: the bank which issues the labour-time tickets purchases the commodity at its production costs, purchases all commodities, and what is more, such purchases cost the bank nothing except the production of slips of paper, and gives to the seller, instead of the exchange value that he possessed in a particular substantial form, the symbolic exchange value of the commodity, in other words a draft upon all other commodities to the amount of the same exchange value. Exchange value as such, of course, can exist only symbolically, although this symbol, in order to be usable as a thing—not only as imaginary form— possesses an objective existence; is not only an ideal notion, but actually represented in an objective way. (A yardstick can be held in the hand; exchange value measures, but it exchanges only by the yardstick passing from one hand to another.[35])

So the bank gives money for the commodity, money which is exactly a draft upon the exchange value of the commodity, i.e. upon all commodities of the same value: the bank purchases. It is the general purchaser, the purchaser not only of this or that commodity, but of all commodities. For its specific function is to convert every commodity into its symbolic existence as exchange value. But if it is the general buyer it must also be the general seller, not only the store in which all commodities are deposited, the general warehouse, but the owner of the commodities in the same sense as every other merchant.

I have exchanged my commodity *a* for the labour-time ticket *b*, which represents the commodity's exchange value, but only so that I may now change this *b* at will into any actual commodity *c, d, e,* etc. Now can this money circulate outside the bank, otherwise than between the possessor of the ticket and the bank? How is the convertibility of this ticket secured? There are only two possible cases. Either all possessors of commodities (products or labour) wish to sell them at their exchange value, or some wish to sell and

---

others do not. If they all wish to sell them at their exchange value, then they will not wait for a buyer to turn up by chance, but will go immediately to the bank, hand over the commodity and receive for it the bank's symbol of exchange value, money: they exchange it for the bank's own money. In this case, the bank is at once general buyer and seller in one person.

Or the contrary is the case. Then the bank ticket is merely paper, it only claims to be the generally recognised symbol of exchange value, but has no value. For the distinguishing characteristic of this symbol is that it not only represents exchange value, but *is* exchange value in actual exchange. In the second case, the bank ticket would not be money, or would be money valid only by convention between the bank and its customers, not on the general market. It would be the same as a dozen meal tickets bought at a restaurant, or a dozen theatre tickets. Both represent money, but only at this particular restaurant or this particular theatre. The bank ticket would have ceased to conform to the requirements of money, for it would circulate not amongst the GENERAL PUBLIC but only between the bank and its customers. We must therefore drop the latter supposition.

The bank would therefore be the general buyer and seller. Instead of notes, it could also issue CHEQUES and instead of those run simple BOOK ACCOUNTS. Whatever the sum of commodity values which x had sold to it, he would have a claim on it for the same sum of values in other commodities. A second attribute of the bank would be necessary: to establish authentically the exchange value of all commodities, i.e. the labour time materialised in them.

But its functions could not end with that. It would have to determine the labour time in which the commodities could be produced with the average means of labour, the time in which they must be produced.

But even this would not be sufficient. It would have to determine not only the time in which a certain quantity of output must be produced, and secure for the producers such circumstances as would equalise the productivity of their labour (hence also to equalise and order the distribution of the means of labour), but also what quantities of labour time [I-20] should be expended in the different branches of production. The latter would be necessary because, in order to realise exchange value, to make its money really convertible, production in general would have to be secured, and in such proportions that the needs of the partners in exchange were satisfied.

That is still not all. The exchange that occurs on the largest scale is not that of commodities but that of labour for commodities. (More on this presently.) The workers would not sell their labour to the bank but would receive the exchange value of the whole product of their labour, etc. Strictly speaking, the bank would then be not only the general buyer and seller, but also the general producer. In fact, it would be either the despot governing production and managing distribution, or indeed nothing more than a BOARD to carry on the book-keeping and accounting for society working in common. The common ownership of the means of production is presupposed, etc., etc. The Saint-Simonians made their bank the papacy of production.

The dissolution of all products and activities into exchange values presupposes both the dissolution of all established personal (historical) relations of dependence in production, and the all-round dependence of producers upon one another. The production of each individual producer is dependent upon the production of all the others, as also the transformation of his product into means of subsistence for himself has become dependent upon the consumption of all the others. Prices are old; so is exchange; but both the increasing determination of the former by the production costs, and the increasing penetration of the latter into all relations of production only develop fully, and continue to develop ever more completely, in bourgeois society, the society of free competition. What Adam Smith in the true 18th-century manner placed in pre-history, what he assumed to have preceded history,[a][36] is rather its product.

This mutual dependence expressed in the constant need for exchange and in exchange value as the universal mediator. The economists express it thus: everyone pursues his private interest and only his private interest, and thereby unintentionally and unwittingly serves the private interests of all, the general interest. The point is not that, in pursuing his private interest, everyone serves the totality of private interests and thus the general interest is attained. This abstract statement could rather lead to the conclusion that everyone mutually hinders the assertion of the interests of everyone else, and instead of a general affirmation, a general negation results from this *bellum omnium contra omnes*.[b]

---

[a] A. Smith, *An Inquiry into the Nature and Causes of the Wealth of Nations*, Vol. I, London, 1835, p. 130.— *Ed.*

[b] War of all against all—a phrase used by Thomas Hobbes in his treatises *De cive* (Ch. I) and *Leviathan* (Ch. XVII).— *Ed.*

The point is rather that private interest is itself already a socially determined interest and can be attained only within the conditions laid down by society and with the means provided by society, and is therefore tied to the reproduction of these conditions and means. It is the interest of private persons; but its content, as well as the form and means of its realisation, are given by social conditions that are independent of them all.

The absolute mutual dependence of individuals, who are indifferent to one another, constitutes their social connection. This social connection is expressed in *exchange value,* in which alone his own activity or his product becomes an activity or product for the individual himself. He must produce a general product—*exchange value,* or exchange value isolated by itself, individualised: *money.* On the other hand, the power that each individual exercises over the activity of others or over social wealth exists in him as the owner of *exchange values,* of *money.* He carries his social power, as also his connection with society, in his pocket.

The activity, whatever its individual form of manifestation, and the product of the activity, whatever its particular nature, is *exchange value,* i.e. something general in which all individuality, all particularity, is negated and extinguished. This is indeed a condition very different from that in which the individual, or the individual extended by a natural or historical process into a family and a tribe (later community), directly reproduces himself from nature, or in which his productive activity and his share in production are dependent on a particular form of labour and of the product, and his relationship to others is determined in this particular way.

The social character of the activity, as also the social form of the product and the share of the individual in production, appear here as something alien to and existing outside the individuals; not as their relationship to each other, but as their subordination to relationships existing independently of them and arising from the collision between indifferent individuals. The general exchange of activities and products, which has become the condition of life for every single individual, their mutual connection, appears to the individuals themselves alien, independent, as a thing. In exchange value, the social relationship of persons is transformed into a social [I-21] attitude of things; personal capacity into a capacity of things. The less social power the means of exchange possesses, the more closely it is still connected with the nature of the immediate product of labour and the immediate needs of the exchangers, the greater must that power of the community still be which binds together the individuals, the patriarchal relationship, the community of antiquity, feudalism and the guild system (see my Notebook, XII, 34b [a]).

Every individual possesses social power in the form of a thing. Take away this social power from the thing, and you must give it to persons [to exercise] over persons. Relationships of personal dependence (which originally arise quite spontaneously) are the first forms of society, in which human productivity develops only to a limited extent and at isolated points. Personal independence based upon dependence *mediated by things* is the second great form, and only in it is a system of general social exchange of matter, a system of universal relations, universal requirements and universal capacities, formed. Free individuality, based on the universal development of the individuals and the subordination of their communal, social productivity, which is their social possession [Vermögen], is the third stage. The second stage creates the conditions for the third. Patriarchal conditions and those of antiquity (likewise feudal ones) therefore decline with the development of trade, luxury, *money, exchange value,* in the same measure in which modern society grows with them step by step.

Exchange and division of labour condition each other. Since each person works for himself but his product is nothing by itself, he must naturally engage in exchange, not only so as to take part in the general capacity to produce, but to transform his own product into means of subsistence for himself. (See my "Observations on Economy", p. V (13, 14).[b]) Of course, exchange as mediated by exchange value and money presupposes the absolute mutual dependence of the producers, but at the same time the complete isolation of their private interests and a division of social labour, whose unity and mutual complementarity exists as it were as a natural relationship outside the individuals, independently of them. The pressure of general demand and supply upon each other provides the connection between the mutually indifferent individuals.

The very necessity to transform the product or the activity of the individuals first into the form of *exchange value,* into *money,* and the fact that they obtain and demonstrate their social *power* only in this *objective* [*sachlichen*] form, proves two things: (1) that the individuals now only produce for and within society; (2) that their production is not *directly* social, not THE OFFSPRING OF ASSOCIATION

---

[a] This notebook has not been found.— *Ed.*

[b] This manuscript has not been found.— *Ed.*

distributing labour within itself. The individuals are subsumed under social production, which exists outside them as their fate; but social production is not subsumed under the individuals who manage it as their common wealth. There can therefore be nothing more incorrect or more absurd than to assume, on the strength of *exchange value* and *money,* control by the associated individuals of their collective production, as was done in the case of the labour-time ticket bank mentioned earlier.

The *private exchange* of all products of labour, capacities and activities, stands in contradiction to distribution based on the superordination and subordination (natural or political) of individuals to each other (*exchange* proper remaining a marginal phenomenon, or on the whole not affecting the life of entire communities, but taking place rather between different communities, by no means subjecting to itself all relationships of production and distribution) (whatever the character of this superordination and subordination: patriarchal, ancient or feudal). It also stands in contradiction to the free exchange of individuals who are associated on the basis of common appropriation and control of the means of production. (The latter association is not arbitrary: it presupposes the development of material and cultural conditions which need not be further elaborated at this point.)

Just as the division of labour produces agglomeration, combination, cooperation, the conflict of private interests, class interests, competition, concentration of capital, monopoly, joint-stock companies—all of which are antagonistic forms of the unity which calls forth the antagonism itself—so does private exchange produce world trade, private independence produces a complete dependence on the so-called world market, and the fragmented acts of exchange produce a banking and credit system whose accountancy [I-22] at least records the balancing of private exchange. However much the private interests within every nation divide it into as many nations as there are FULL-GROWN INDIVIDUALS in it, and however the interests of the EXPORTERS and the IMPORTERS of the same nation here conflict with each other—the rate of exchange creates the *semblance* of the existence of a national trade, etc., etc. No one will believe on such grounds that it is possible to abolish the *foundations* of internal or external private commerce by means of a *reform of the stock-exchange.* But within bourgeois society, based as it is upon *exchange value*, relationships of exchange and production are generated which are just so many mines to blow it to pieces. (A multitude of antagonistic forms of the social entity, whose antagonism, however, can never be exploded by a quiet metamorphosis. On the other hand, if we did not find latent in society as it is, the material conditions of production and the corresponding relationships of exchange for a classless society, all attempts to explode it would be quixotic.)

We have seen that, although exchange value=the relative labour time materialised in the products and although money=the exchange value of commodities separated from their substance, this exchange value or monetary relationship contains the contradictions between commodities and their exchange value, between commodities as exchange values and money. We have seen that a bank which directly produces the counterpart of the commodity in labour money is a utopia. Although, therefore, money is merely exchange value detached from the substance of the commodity and owes its origin only to the tendency of this exchange value to posit itself in pure form, the commodity cannot be transformed directly into money, i.e. the authentic certificate of the quantity of labour time realised in it cannot serve as its price in the world of exchange values. How is this?

(Economists see clearly that one form of money—in so far as it is a *medium* of exchange and not a *measure* of exchange value—presupposes the objectification of the social nexus, namely, to the extent that money appears as a *surety* that one person must leave behind in the hands of another in order to obtain a commodity from him. Here the economists themselves say that men put in the object (money) a trust they would not put in one another as persons. But why do they thus put their trust in the object? Clearly, only because it is the *objectified relationship* of persons to each other; as objectified exchange value, and exchange value is nothing but a mutual relation of the productive activities of persons. Any other surety may be directly of use to its possessor as such. Money is useful to him only as the "*movable surety of society*",[37] but it is such a surety only because of its social (symbolic) character; it can possess a social character only because the individuals have alienated their own social relationship in the form of an object.)

In the *current price lists*, in which all values are measured in money, it seems as though the independence of the social character of things from persons, and also the trading activity conducted on this basis of estrangement in which the general relations of production and exchange appear to the individual, to all individuals, subject the things once again to the individuals. Since the increasing autonomy of the world market, IF YOU PLEASE (which includes the activity of every individual), grows with the development of monetary relationships (exchange value) and vice versa, and since the general interconnection and absolute inter-dependence in production and consumption grows simultaneously with the independence of consumers and producers and their indifference to each other; since this contradiction leads to crises, etc., simultaneously with the development of this estrangement there are attempts to abolish it on its own ground: current price lists, exchange rates, communication between commercialists by letters, telegrams, etc. (the means of communication of course develop simultaneously), by means of which each individual provides himself with information on the activities of all others and seeks to adjust his own activity accordingly. (In other words, although the demand and supply of all proceeds independently of all, each seeks to inform himself of the general state of demand and supply; and this knowledge influences their action. Although all this does not abolish the estrangement in the context of the existing point of view, it does bring about relations and connections which entail the possibility of overcoming the old standpoint.) (The possibility of general statistics, etc.)

(Actually this is to be developed further under the heading "*Prices, Demand and Supply*". Here we need only note that this survey of total trade and total production, so far as current price lists actually represent such a survey, does indeed supply the best evidence of how their own exchange and their own production confronts individuals as an *objective* relationship *independent* of them. In the *world market* the *connection of the individual* with all others, but at the same time also the *independence* [I-23] *of this connection from the individuals*, has itself developed to such a point that its formation already contains the conditions for its being transcended.)

Comparison in place of actual community and universality.

(It has been said, and may be said, that the beauty and greatness lies precisely in this spontaneously evolved connection, in this material and spiritual exchange, which is independent of the knowledge and wishes of individuals and presupposes their mutual independence and indifference. And certainly this objective connection is to be preferred to the lack of any connection or to a purely local connection based on primitive blood ties, nature, and relationships of lordship and bondage. It is equally certain that individuals cannot subordinate their own social connections to themselves before they have created them. But it is absurd to conceive of that merely *objective connection* as a natural one, inseparable from the nature of human individuality (as opposed to knowledge and will derived from reflection) and immanent in it. It is their product. It is a product of history. It belongs to a definite phase in their development. The estrangement and isolation in which it still exists for them, show only that they are still in the process of creating the conditions of their social life instead of having started it from these conditions. It is the connection, the spontaneously evolved one, of individuals within certain narrow relationships of production.

Universally developed individuals, whose social relationships are their own communal relations and therefore subjected to their own communal control, are not products of nature but of history. The degree and the universality of development of the capacities in which *this kind* of individuality becomes possible, presupposes precisely production on the basis of exchange value, which, along with the universality of the estrangement of individuals from themselves and from others, now also produces the universality and generality of all their relations and abilities. During earlier stages of development, the single individual seems more fully developed because he has not yet worked out the fulness of his relations and has not yet set them over against himself as independent social powers and relations. It is as ridiculous to long for a return to that original fulness as it is to believe that the present complete emptiness must be permanent. The bourgeois view has never been more than the opposite of that Romantic view,[38] and so the romantic view will accompany it as a justified opposite till its blessed end.)

(Here the relationship of the individual to science can be taken as an example.)

(To compare money to blood—the word "circulation" suggested this—is about as valid as Menenius Agrippa's comparing the patricians to the stomach.[39])

(To compare money with language is no less incorrect.[40] Ideas are not transformed into language in such a way that their particular attributes are dissolved and their social character exists alongside them in language as do prices alongside commodities. Ideas do not exist apart from language. Ideas which must first be translated from their mother tongue into a foreign language in order to circulate and to become exchangeable would provide a better analogy; but then the analogy is not with the language but with its foreignness.)

(The exchangeability of all products, activities, relationships for a third, *objective* entity, which in turn can be exchanged for everything *without distinction*—in other words, the development of exchange values (and of monetary relationships) is identical with general venality, with corruption. General prostitution appears as a necessary phase in the development of the social character of personal inclinations, capacities, abilities, activities. More politely expressed: the universal relationship of utility and usefulness. Equating the incommensurate, as Shakespeare appropriately conceived of money.[a] The craving for enrichment as such is impossible without money; all other accumulation and craving for accumulation appears merely natural, restricted, conditioned on the one hand by needs and on the other by the restricted nature of the products (*sacra auri fames*[b]).)

(The money system, in its development, clearly already presupposes other general developments.)

When we consider social conditions which produce an undeveloped system of exchange, of exchange values and of money, or to which these correspond only in an undeveloped form, it is clear from the outset that individuals, although their relationships appear to be more personal, only enter into relations with each other as individuals in a particular determination, as feudal lord and vassal, lord of the manor and serf, etc., or as members of castes, etc., or as members of an estate, etc. In money relations, in a developed system of exchange (and this appearance leads democracy astray), the ties of personal dependence, distinctions of birth, education, etc. (all the personal ties at least appear as *personal* relationships), are in fact broken, abolished. The individuals *appear* to be independent (this independence, which altogether is merely an illusion and should more correctly be called unconcern, in the sense of indifference), appear to collide with each other freely, and to exchange with each other in this freedom; but they appear independent only to those who abstract from the *conditions*, the *conditions of existence*, in which those individuals come into contact with each other (and these in turn are independent of the individuals and appear, though produced by society, as it were, as *natural conditions*, i.e. beyond the control of the individuals).

The [I-24] determinateness which in the first case appears as a personal limitation of one individual by another, appears in the second case, in its developed form, as an objective limitation of the

---

a "Thou visible god, that solder'st close impossibilities" (Shakespeare, *Timon of Athens*, IV, 3).— *Ed.*

b "The accursed passion for gold" (Virgil, *Aeneid*, 3, 57).— *Ed.*

individual by relationships which are independent of him and self-sufficient. (Since the single individual cannot shed his personal determinateness but can overcome external relationships and subordinate them to himself, his freedom *appears* greater in the second case. A closer investigation of those external relationships and conditions shows, however, that it is impossible for the individuals of a class, etc., to overcome them *en masse* without abolishing them. A single individual may by chance cope with them; the mass of individuals dominated by them cannot do so, since the very existence of that mass expresses the subordination, and the necessary subordination, of the individuals to it.)

These external relationships, far from abolishing the "relationships of dependence", merely dissolve them into a general form; they are rather the elaboration of the general *foundation* of relationships of personal dependence. Here, too, individuals enter into relation with each other only as determinate individuals. These *objective* relations of dependence, in contrast to the *personal* ones, also appear in such a way that the individuals are now ruled by *abstractions* whereas previously they were dependent on one another. (The objective relationship of dependence is nothing but the social relations independently confronting the seemingly independent individuals, i.e. their own reciprocal relations of production which have acquired an existence independent of and separate from them.) Yet the abstraction or idea is nothing but the theoretical expression of those material relationships which dominate the individuals.

Relationships can naturally be expressed only in ideas, and so philosophers have seen the peculiarity of modern times in the individuals' being dominated by ideas, and have identified the birth of free individuality with the overthrow of this domination of ideas. From the ideological standpoint, this mistake was the easier to make because that domination of relationships (that objective dependence, which. incidentally is in its turn transformed into certain personal relationships of dependence, only divested of all illusion) appears in. the consciousness of individuals themselves to be the rule of ideas, and the belief in the eternal validity of these ideas, i.e. of those objective relationships of dependence, is OF COURSE in every way reinforced, sustained, drummed into people by the ruling classes.

(With regard to the illusion of the "purely personal relationships" of feudal times, etc., we must not of course for a moment forget: (1) that in a certain phase, these relationships themselves acquired within their sphere an objective character, as is shown by the development of landed property relationships, for example, out of purely military subordination. But, (2) the objective relationship in which they founder has itself a restricted, naturally determined character and thus *appears* as personal, whereas in the modern world personal relationships emerge purely as the outcome of the relationships of production and exchange.)

The product becomes a commodity. The commodity becomes exchange value. The exchange value of the commodity acquires a separate existence alongside the commodity, i.e. the commodity in the form in which (1) it is exchangeable for all other commodities; in which (2) it is therefore a general commodity and its natural particularity is extinguished; (3) in which is established the measure of its exchangeability, the particular ratio in which it equates all other commodities to itself—is the commodity as money, not indeed as money in general, but as a *particular sum of money*, for to represent exchange value in all its variability, money must be countable, quantitatively divisible.

Money, the common form into which all commodities transform themselves as exchange values, the general commodity, must itself exist as a *particular* commodity alongside the others, for they are not only mentally measured by it but must be traded and exchanged for it in actual exchange. The contradiction that arises from this is to be discussed elsewhere. Money does not originate by convention, any more than the State does. It arises from exchange, grows naturally out of exchange, is a product of exchange.

Initially that commodity will serve as money, i.e. will be acquired through exchange not as an object of need and consumption, but to be exchanged again for other commodities, which is most frequently acquired through exchange as an object of need, is therefore in general circulation; which therefore can most certainly be exchanged again for any other particular commodities; which, in other words, in a given social organisation represents wealth κατ᾽ ἐξοχήν,[a] is the object of the most general demand and supply and possesses a special use value. For example, salt, hides, cattle, slaves. Such a commodity in its particular form as commodity in fact corresponds more with itself as exchange value than do the other commodities (unfortunately it is impossible in German to render adequately the distinction between *denrée* [goods] and *marchandise* [commodities]).

---

a Par excellence.— *Ed.*

What stamps a commodity as money here is its special usefulness, whether as an object of consumption (hides), or as a direct implement of production (slaves). In the course of development, exactly the reverse will occur, i.e. the commodity which is least a direct object of consumption or implement of production will best represent precisely this aspect, that of satisfying the requirements *of exchange as such*. In the first [I-25] case a commodity becomes money because of its special use value; in the second case, it acquires its particular use value by serving as money. Durability, unalterableness, divisibility and reconstitutability, relatively easy transportability, because a large exchange value is contained in a small volume, all these properties make the precious metals particularly suitable at the later stage. At the same time they form a natural transition from the first form of money. At a somewhat higher stage of production and exchange, the instrument of production becomes *more important* than the products, and *metals* are (after stones) the first and most indispensable implements of production. In *copper*, which is so important as money in antiquity, two things are still combined: the special use value as an instrument of production, and the other properties which do not derive from the use value of the commodity but correspond to its role as exchange value (which includes means of exchange).

Later, the *precious* metals are preferred to the others, because they do not oxidise, etc., are of uniform quality, etc., and correspond better to the higher stage, in that their immediate usefulness for consumption and production becomes less important, while their very scarcity makes them more representative of value founded purely upon exchange. From the outset, they represent surplus, the form in which wealth originally appears. Metals also more readily exchanged for metals than other commodities.

The first form of money corresponds to an early stage of exchange and barter, in which money still plays a greater role as *measure* than as actual *instrument of exchange*. At this stage, the measure can still be purely imaginary (however, the BAR used by the Negro *is* composed of iron[a]) (but *cowries*, etc., fit better into the series, which reaches its final peak in gold and silver).

As a result of the transformation of the commodity into general exchange value, exchange value becomes a particular commodity. But this is possible only if one particular commodity acquires over

---

[a] See this volume, p. 80.— *Ed*.

all others the privilege of representing, of symbolising their exchange value, i.e. of becoming *money*. The appearance of a particular commodity as the money subject of the money quality of all commodities, stems from the nature of exchange value itself. In the process of development, the exchange value of money can acquire again an existence separate from its material, from its substance, as in paper money, without, however, abolishing the privilege of this particular commodity, since the separate existence must continue to receive its denomination from the particular commodity.

Because the commodity is exchange value, it can be exchanged for money, equated with money. The ratio in which it is equated with money, i.e. the determinateness of its exchange value, *antecedes* its conversion into money. The ratio in which a particular commodity is exchanged for money, i.e. the quantity of money into which a definite quantity of the commodity is convertible, is determined by the labour time objectified in the commodity. As the realisation of a *definite amount* of labour time, the commodity is exchange value; in money the amount of labour time which it represents is both measured and given its general, exchangeable form corresponding to the concept. Money is the objective medium in which exchange values are immersed, and in which they acquire a form corresponding to their general determination. Adam Smith says that labour (labour time) is the original money with which all commodities are purchased.[a] With regard to the act of production, this remains always true (and likewise with respect to the fixing of relative values). In production every commodity is constantly being exchanged for labour time.

A form of money distinct from labour time becomes necessary precisely because the amount of labour time must be expressed not in its immediate and particular product, but in a mediated and general product, in its particular product as equal to and convertible into all other products of the same labour time; labour time embodied not in one commodity, but simultaneously in all commodities, and therefore in a particular commodity which represents all others.

Labour time itself cannot be money directly (to demand this would be the same as demanding that every commodity should be directly its own money), precisely because in fact it always exists (as an object) only in the form of particular products. As a general

---

[a] *Recherches sur la nature et les causes de la richesse des nations*, Vol. I, Paris, 1802, p. 60.— *Ed.*

object it can only exist symbolically, again in a particular commodity which is posited as money. Labour time does not exist as a general object of exchange, independent of and separate (detached) from the natural particularities of commodities. It would have to exist as such if it were to fulfil the conditions of money directly. It is the objectification of the general, social character of labour (and therefore of the labour time contained in exchange value) that makes the product of labour an exchange value and gives the commodity its money quality, which, in turn, implies a money subject existing outside it and independently of it.

A definite labour time is objectified in a definite, particular commodity with particular properties and particular relations to needs. But as exchange value, it must be objectified in a commodity which expresses only its amount or quantity, is indifferent to its natural attributes, and therefore can be metamorphosed, i.e. exchanged, into any other commodity embodying the same labour time. As an object it should possess this general character, [I-26] which contradicts its natural particularity. This contradiction can be resolved only by being itself objectified, i.e. only by positing the commodity in a double form: first in its natural immediate form, then in its mediated form, as money. The latter is possible only by a particular commodity becoming, as it were, the general substance of exchange values, or by the exchange value of commodities being identified with a particular substance, a particular commodity distinct from all others; i.e. by the commodity having first to be exchanged for this general commodity, the symbolic general product or objectification of labour time, before it can, as exchange value, be exchanged indifferently for any other commodity, or be metamorphosed into it.

Money is labour time as general object, or the objectification of general labour time, labour time as a *general commodity*. Thus, if it appears very simple that labour time since it regulates exchange values, is in fact not only their inherent measure, but their very substance (for, as exchange values, commodities have no other substance, no natural characteristics), and can also serve directly as their *money*, i.e. be the element in which exchange values as such are realised, this apparent simplicity is deceptive. The truth is that the relationship of exchange values—of commodities as objectifications of labour time equal to one another and equatable—contains contradictions which are objectively expressed in a form of *money distinct* from labour time.

In Adam Smith, this contradiction still appears as two aspects set

side by side. Alongside the particular product of his labour (labour
time as particular object), the worker still has to produce a
quantity of general commodity (labour time as general object).
The two determinations of exchange value appear to him
externally *side by side*.[a] The inner essence of the whole commodity
does not yet appear gripped and penetrated by contradiction. This
corresponds to the stage of production with which Smith was
confronted, where the worker still possessed a part of his
subsistence directly in his product, and neither his entire activity
nor the whole of his product had become dependent upon
exchange, i.e. where subsistence agriculture (this or something
similar is what Steuart calls it[41]) and also patriarchal industry
(hand-weaving, domestic spinning tied to agriculture) still largely
prevailed. At that stage, only the surplus is exchanged over a wide
national area. Exchange value and determination by labour time
[have] not yet fully developed on a national scale.

(*Incidentally*: It is less true of gold and silver than of any other
commodity that their consumption can increase only in proportion
to the reduction of their production costs. It increases rather in
proportion to the increase in general wealth, since the use of gold
and silver represents specifically wealth, surplus, luxury, because
they themselves *represent* general wealth. Apart from their use as
money, more silver and gold is consumed in proportion to the
growth of general wealth. Therefore if their supply suddenly
increases, even without their production costs or their value
diminishing proportionately, they find a rapidly expanding
market, which delays their depreciation. This explains a number
of things about the *Australian-Californian* CASE,[42] which those
economists who make the general consumption of gold and silver
depend solely on a fall in their production costs cannot explain,
and where they merely move around in a circle. This results
directly from their representing wealth, therefore, from their
property as money.)

(The contrast between gold and silver as the ETERNAL commodities
and all others, which we find in Petty,[b] already hinted at in
Xenophon, *De vectigalibus*, Ch. 1, with respect to marble and
silver:

"And the pre-eminence of the land" [Attica] "is not only in the things that
bloom and wither annually; she has other good things that last for ever. Nature has

---

[a] A. Smith, *Recherches sur la nature et les causes de la richesse des nations,* Vol. I,
p. 47.— *Ed.*

[b] See this volume, p. 164.— *Ed.*

invested in her an abundance of stone", etc. (namely marble) ... "Again there is land that yields no fruit if sown, and yet, when quarried, feeds many times the number it could feed if it grew corn." [a]

(Note that exchange between different tribes or peoples—and this, not private exchange, is its first form—begins only when a surplus is purchased (obtained by trickery) from an uncivilised tribe, a surplus which is not the product of its labour but the natural product of the soil and of the region in which it dwells.)

(Analyse the ordinary economic contradictions which arise from the fact that money must be symbolised in a particular commodity, and then those which arise from the commodity itself (gold, etc.). This No. II. Then, since all commodities must be exchanged for money in order to be *priced*, whether this exchange occurs actually or only in the head, go on to determine the relation of the quantity of gold and silver to the prices of the commodities. This No. III. Clearly, as commodities are merely *measured* in gold or silver, the quantity of these metals has no influence upon the price of the commodities. The difficulty arises when exchange actually takes place, in so far as these metals actually serve as instruments of circulation; the conditions of supply and demand, etc. But whatever affects their value as an instrument of circulation obviously affects them as a measure.)

[I-27] Labour time itself exists as such only subjectively, only in the form of activity. In so far as it is exchangeable in that form (is itself a commodity), it is not only quantitatively but also qualitatively determined and differentiated, not at all general labour time equal to itself; it corresponds as subject as little to the general labour time that determines exchange value as particular commodities and products correspond to it as object.

Adam Smith asserts that the labourer must produce a general commodity alongside his particular commodity, in other words, that he must give the form of money to a part of his product, more generally that he must convert into money all that part of his commodity which is not to serve him as use value but as exchange value.[b] Subjectively expressed, this only means that his particular labour time cannot be directly exchanged for every other particular labour time; its general exchangeability must first be mediated, it must acquire an objective form distinct from itself, if it is to acquire this general exchangeability.

The labour of the individual, considered in the act of

---

[a] Marx quotes in Greek.— *Ed.*

[b] See this volume, pp. 105-06.— *Ed.*

production itself, is the money with which he immediately purchases the product, the object of his particular activity; but it is a *particular* money, which of course buys only this *particular* product. In order to be *general money* directly, it would have to be not *particular* but *general* labour from the outset, i.e. it would from the outset have to be *posited* as part of *general production*. Now, if this assumption is made, the general character of labour would not be given to it only by exchange; its assumed communal character would determine participation in the products. The communal character of production would from the outset make the product into a communal, general one. The exchange initially occurring in production, which would not be an exchange of exchange values but of activities determined by communal needs and communal purposes, would include from the beginning the individual's participation in the communal world of products. On the basis of exchange value, labour is *posited* as general labour only through *exchange*. On this basis [of the exchange of activities in production], labour would be *posited* as general labour prior to exchange, i.e. the exchange of products would not in any way be the *medium* mediating the participation of the individual in general production. Mediation has of course to take place.

In the first case, which starts from the independent production of individuals—however much these independent productions may be determined and modified *post festum* by their interrelations—the mediation takes place through the exchange of commodities, through exchange value, money, which are all expressions of one and the same relationship. In the second case the *presupposition itself is mediated*, i.e. communal production, community as the basis of production, is assumed. The labour of the individual is from the outset taken as social labour. Therefore, whatever may be the particular material form of the product that he produces or helps to produce, what he has purchased with his labour is not a definite particular product but a certain share in the communal production. Nor has he, therefore, a particular product to exchange. His product is *not exchange value*; it does not have to be first converted into a particular form to acquire a general character for the individual. Instead of a division of labour which necessarily arises from the exchange of exchange values, labour would be organised in such a way that the individual's share in common consumption would directly follow.

In the first case, the social character of production is *established* only *post festum* by the elevation of the products into exchange values and the exchange of these exchange values. In the second case, the *social character of production* is presupposed, and participation in the world of products, in consumption, is not mediated by exchange between mutually independent labours or products of labour. It is mediated by the circumstances of social production within which the individual carries on his activity.

Hence, to want to convert the labour of the individual (i.e. also his product) directly into *money*, into *realised exchange value*, means to define it *directly* as general labour, i.e. to negate the very conditions under which it must be transformed into money and exchange values and under which it depends on private exchange. This demand can only be satisfied under conditions in which it can no longer be advanced. For the fact is that labour on the basis of exchange values presupposes that neither the labour of the individual nor his product is *directly* general, but that it acquires this form only through *objective mediation* by means of a form of *money* distinct from it.

If we presuppose communal production, the time factor naturally remains essential. The less time society requires to produce corn, livestock, etc., the more time it wins for other production, material or spiritual. As with a single individual, the comprehensiveness of its development, its pleasures and its activities depends upon the saving of time. Ultimately, all economy is a matter of economy of time. Society must also allocate its time appropriately to achieve a production corresponding to its total needs, just as the individual must allocate his time correctly to acquire knowledge in suitable proportions or to satisfy the various demands on his activity. Economy of time, as well as the planned distribution of labour time over the various branches of production, therefore, remains the first economic law if communal production is taken as the basis. It becomes a law even to a much higher degree. However, this is essentially [I-28] different from the measurement of exchange values (of labours or products of labour) by labour time. The labours of individuals in the same branch of industry, and the different types of labour, are not only *quantitatively* but *qualitatively* different. What does mere *quantitative* difference between things presuppose? The sameness of their *quality*. Therefore quantitative measurement of labours [presupposes] their equivalence, the sameness of their *quality*.

(*Strabo*, Book XI, on the Albani of the Caucasus[43]:

The inhabitants of this country are unusually handsome and large. And they are frank in their dealings, and not mercenary; for they do not in general use coined money, nor do they know any number greater than one hundred, but carry on business by means of barter.[a]

He says further on:

They are also unacquainted with accurate measures and weights.)

Money made its appearance as a *measure* (oxen were used for this purpose e.g. in Homer[b]) before it became a *means of exchange*, because in barter each commodity is still its own means of exchange. But it cannot be its own measure or standard of comparison.

[THE PRECIOUS METALS
AS EXPRESSION OF THE MONEY RELATIONSHIP]

From what has been said, we may conclude that a particular product (*commodity*) (material) must become the money subject, which exists as the property of every exchange value. The subject in which this symbol is to be represented is not a matter of indifference, since the demands made on the representing subject are contained in the circumstances—conceptual definitions, determined relationships—of that which is to be represented. The analysis of the precious metals as the subjects of the money relationship, the incarnation of that relationship, does not therefore lie, as Proudhon believes, outside the sphere of political economy,[44] just as little as the physical nature of colours and of marble lies outside the sphere of painting and sculpture. The properties which the commodity has as exchange value, and which are not identical with its natural properties, express the demands to be made on the commodities which are κατ' ἐξοχήν[c] the material of money. At the stage of which alone we can speak so far, these demands are most fully realised in the precious metals. As instruments of production, metals as such are preferred to other commodities, and among the metals the one which is first found in its physical perfection and purity—gold. Next comes copper, then silver and iron. As Hegel would say, the *essence of metal* is best realised in the precious metals.

THE PRECIOUS METALS UNIFORM IN THEIR PHYSICAL QUALITIES, SO THAT EQUAL QUANTITIES OF IT SHOULD BE SO FAR IDENTICAL AS TO PRESENT NO GROUND FOR PREFERRING THE ONE FOR THE OTHER. This is not true of EQUAL NUMBERS OF CATTLE AND EQUAL QUANTITIES OF GRAIN, for example.[45]

---

[a] Strabo, *Rerum geographicarum libri XVII*, Lib. XI, Cap. IV. Marx quotes in Greek.— *Ed.*
[b] In his *Iliad.—Ed.*
[c] Pre-eminently.— *Ed.*

(a) Gold and Silver in Comparison with the Other Metals

The base metals oxidise in the atmosphere; the precious metals (mercury, silver, gold, platinum) are not changed by the atmosphere.

Aurum (Au). Density=19.5; melting point: 1200 °C.

"The glittering gold is the most splendid of all metals and therefore in antiquity was already called the sun or the king of metals. Fairly widely found, though never in great quantities; it is therefore also more valuable than the other metals. As a rule it is found pure, partly in large nuggets, partly in small grains embedded in other minerals. From the erosion of such minerals originates the gold-bearing sand which many rivers carry and from which gold can be washed because of its great density. Extraordinary ductility of gold: a grain can be drawn out into a filament 500 feet long, and beaten into a leaf of a thickness of scarcely $1/200,000$th [of an inch]. Gold resists all acids and is dissolved only by free chlorine (*aqua regia*, a mixture of nitric acid and hydrochloric acid). Gilding." [46]

Argentum. (Ag). Density=10. Melting point=1000° C. Bright appearance; the most friendly of all metals, very white and malleable; can be made into beautiful objects and drawn into fine filaments. Silver is found pure; very often alloyed with lead in silver-lead ores.

This much about the *chemical* properties of gold and silver. (The divisibility and fusibility, uniformity, etc., of pure gold and silver are well known.)

Mineralogical [properties]:

Gold. It is certainly remarkable that the more precious the metals are, the more sparsely and separated from the commonly occurring substances they appear, higher natures remote from the commonplace. Thus, as a rule gold is found pure, crystalline in various cubic forms or in the most diverse forms: irregular nuggets and grains, sand and dust, in which latter form it occurs embedded in many rocks, i.e. in granite, whose disintegration gives rise to gold-bearing sands in [I-29] rivers and in the gravel of alluvial soils. Since in this state the density of gold reaches 19.4, even those fine particles of gold can be obtained by stirring the gold-bearing sand in water. From this mixture the metal is precipitated first, because of its greater specific weight, and is, as they say, washed out. Silver is the metal most often associated with gold, and native alloys composed of both metals are encountered which contain 0.16 to 38.7% silver; this of course results in variations in colour and density.

Silver. In the considerable variety of its minerals, it occurs as one of the more abundant metals, both pure and alloyed with other metals or combined with arsenic and sulphur. (Silver chloride, silver bromide, carbonic silver oxide, bismuth-silver ore, sternbergite, polybasite, etc.)

The main *chemical* properties *of all the precious metals* are that they do not oxidise in the atmosphere; and of gold (and platinum), that they are not dissolved by acids (gold only by chlorine). Not oxidising in the atmosphere keeps them pure, free from rust; they present themselves as that which they are. Their resistance to dissolution by oxidisation: *imperishability* (so highly praised by the gold and silver fanatics of antiquity).

Physical properties: *specific gravity*, i.e. much weight in a small volume, specially important for an instrument of circulation. Gold 19.5; silver 10. *Brilliance of colour*: the lustre of gold, the whiteness of silver. Splendour, *ductility*; hence so suitable for jewellery and the embellishment of other objects. The *whiteness* of silver (which reflects all light rays in their original mixture); the red-yellow of gold (which absorbs all the colours in the light rays falling upon it and reflects only the red). [They have] *very high melting points.*

Geognostic properties: they are found *pure* (particularly in the case of gold), separate from other substances, isolated, individualised. Individual occurrence independent of the elemental.

As for the other two precious metals: (1) *Platinum*, not distinguished by its colour: grey in grey (soot of metals); too rare; unknown to the ancients; became known only after the discovery of America; in the 19th century discovered also in the Urals; only chlorine will corrode it; it is always found pure; specific gravity=21; will not melt at the highest temperatures; its value primarily scientific. (2) *Mercury*, occurs in a liquid form; vaporisable; its fumes poisonous; can be absorbed by liquid mixtures (amalgams). (Density=13.5, boiling point=360° C.)

Thus, neither platinum, still less mercury, suitable as money.

One *geognostic* property common to all the precious metals: *rarity*. Now, rarity is an element of value (leaving aside demand and supply), in so far as that which is in itself not rare, the negation of rarity, the elemental, is without value because it does not appear as the result of production. In the original determination of value, that which is most independent of conscious and willed production has the greatest value, assuming a demand for it. Pebbles are of no value, *relativement parlant*,[a] because they are available *without production* (they do not even need looking for). If a thing is to be the object of exchange, have exchange value, it must not be available to everyone without the mediation of

---

a Relatively speaking.— *Ed.*

exchange; it must not appear in so elemental a form as to be common property. To that extent rarity an element of exchange value, therefore this property of the precious metals important, even apart from the precise relationship of demand and supply.

If we look generally at the superiority of the metals as instruments of production, the advantage of gold is that it is *au fond*[a] the *first metal discovered qua metal*. And this for two reasons. *Firstly*, because of all metals, gold appears in nature as the most metallic, distinct and distinguishable metal; *secondly*, because in its preparation nature undertook the work of art, and for its first discovery only ROUGH LABOUR, neither science nor developed instruments of production, required.

"Certain it is that gold must take its place as *the earliest metal known,* and in the first record of man's progress it is indicated as a standard of man's position"[b]

(because as *surplus,* the first form in which wealth appears. The first form of value is *use value,* the everyday aspect which expresses the relationship of the individual to nature. The second form *exchange value* a l o n g s i d e use value, its command over the use values of others, its social relation: itself originally the value of things for Sunday use, over and above immediate basic necessities).

[I-30] VERY EARLY DISCOVERY OF GOLD BY MAN:

"Gold differs remarkably from the other metals, with a very few exceptions, in the fact, that it is found in nature in its metallic state. Iron and copper, tin, lead, and silver are ordinarily discovered in chemical combinations with oxygen, sulphur, arsenic, or carbon; and the few exceptional occurrences of these metals in an uncombined, or, as it was formerly called, virgin state, are to be cited rather as mineralogical curiosities than as common productions. Gold is, however, always found native or metallic... Therefore, as a metallic mass, curious by its yellow colour, it would attract the eye of the most uneducated man, whereas the other substances likely to lie in his path would offer no features of attraction to his scarcely awakened powers of observation. Again gold, from the circumstance of its having been formed in those rocks which are most exposed to atmospheric action, is found in the *débris* of the mountains. By the disintegrating influences, of the atmosphere, of changes of temperature, of the action of water, and particularly by the effects of ice, fragments of rock are continually broken off. These are borne by floods into the valleys and rolled into pebbles by the constant action of flowing water. Amongst these, pebbles, or particles, of gold are discovered. The summer heats, by drying up the waters, rendered those beds which had formed river channels and the courses of winter torrents, paths for the journeys of migratory man; and here we can imagine the early discovery of gold" [pp. 171-72].

---

[a] Basically.— *Ed.*
[b] *Lectures on Gold for the Instruction of Emigrants about to Proceed to Australia. Delivered at the Museum of Practical Geology,* London, 1852, p. 172. Here and below (see pp. 113-15) Marx quotes from this source in English.— *Ed.*

"Gold most frequently occurs pure, or, at all events, so nearly so that its metallic nature can be at once recognised", both in streams and in "quartz veins" [p. 8].

"The specific gravity of quartz, and of most other heavy compact rocks is about $2\,^1/_2$, whilst the specific gravity of gold is 18 or 19. Gold, therefore, is somewhere about 7 times as heavy as any rock or stone with which it is likely to be associated. A current of water accordingly having sufficient strength to bear along sand or pebbles of quartz or any other rock, might not be able to move the fragments of gold associated with them. Moving water, therefore, has done for the auriferous rocks formerly, just what the miner would do now, break it, namely, up into fragments, sweep away the lighter particles, and leave the gold behind it" [p. 10].

"Rivers are, indeed, great natural *cradles*, sweeping off all the lighter and finer particles at once, the heavier ones either sticking against natural impediments, or being left wherever the current slackens its force or velocity" (see *Gold (Lectures on)*, London, 1852) (pp. 12 and 13).

"In all probability, from tradition and early history, the *discovery of gold in the sand and gravel of streams would appear to have been the first step in the recognition of metals,* and in almost all, perhaps in all the countries of Europe, Africa and Asia, greater or smaller quantities of gold have from very early times been washed by simple contrivances from the auriferous deposits. Occasionally, the success of gold-streams has been great enough to produce a pulse of excitement which has vibrated for a while through a district, but has been hushed down again. In 760 the poor people turned out in numbers to wash gold from the river sands south of Prague, and three men were able in the day to extract a mark ($^1/_2$ lb.) of gold; and so great was the consequent rush to the 'diggings', that in the next year the country was visited by famine. We read of a recurrence of similar events several times within the next few centuries, although here, as elsewhere, the general attraction to surface-spread riches has subsided into regular and systematic mining" [pp. 93-95].

"Two classes of deposits in which gold is found, the *lodes* or *veins*, which intersect the solid rock in a direction more or less perpendicular to the horizon; and the *drift-beds* or *'streams'*, in which the gold mingled with gravel, sand, or clay, has been deposited by the mechanical action of water, upon the surface of those rocks, which are penetrated to unknown depths by the lodes. To the former class belongs more specially the art of *mining*; to the latter the simple operations of *digging*. Gold-mining, properly so called, is, like other mining, an art requiring the [I-31] employment of capital, and of a skill only to be acquired by years of experience. There is no art practised by civilised man which requires for its full development the application of so many sciences and collateral arts. But although so essential to the miner, scarcely any of these are necessary to the gold-washer or streamer, who must trust chiefly to the strength of his arm, or the buoyancy of his health. The apparatus which he employs must necessarily be simple, so as to be conveyed from place to place, to be easily repaired if injured, and not to require any of those niceties of manipulation which would cause him to lose time in the acquiring of small quantities" [pp. 95-97].

The difference "between the drift-deposits of gold, best exemplified at the present day in Siberia, California, and Australia; and the fine sands annually brought down by rivers, some of which are also found to contain gold in workable quantities. The latter are of course found literally at the surface, the former may be met with under a cover of from 1 to 70 feet in thickness, consisting of soil, peat, sand, gravel etc. The modes of working the 2 must be identical in principle"[p. 97].

"For the stream-workers nature has pulled down the highest, proudest and richest parts of the lodes, and so triturated and washed up the materials, that the streamer has the heaviest part of the work already done for him; whilst the miner, who attacks the poorer, but more lasting, deep-going lodes, must aid himself with all the resources of the nicest art" [p. 98].

"Gold has justly been considered the noblest of metals from various physical and chemical properties. It is unchangeable in air and does not rust." (This unchangeability precisely its resistance to the oxygen of the atmosphere.) "Of a bright reddish yellow colour when in a coherent state, and very dense. Highly malleable. Requires a strong heat to melt it. Specific gravity [19.3]" [pp. 72-73].

Thus three types of gold production: (1) In river sand. Simply found on the surface. *Washing*. (2) Deposited in BEDS. DIGGING. (3) MINING. Its production therefore does not require any development of the productive forces. Nature here does most of the work.

(For the *roots* of the words for gold, silver, etc., see *Grimm*[a]; here nothing but general concepts of *lustre* and *colour* are suggested which are soon transferred to the words. Silver is white, gold is yellow. Bronze and gold, bronze and iron interchange their names. Among the Germans, bronze in use earlier than iron. Direct relationship between *aes* and *aurum*.[b])

Copper (*brass, bronze*: tin and copper) and gold used before silver and iron.

"Gold employed long before silver, because it is found pure or only combined with a little silver; obtained by simple washing. Silver generally exists in lodes embedded in the hardest rocks of primitive formation; for its extraction machinery and complicated work are required. In South America the gold lodes are not exploited, only gold in the form of powder and grains in alluvial soils. Also at the time of Herodotus. The oldest monuments of Greece, Asia, Northern Europe and the New World show that the use of gold for utensils and jewels is possible in semi-barbaric conditions; and the use of silver for the same purpose denotes in itself fairly advanced social conditions" (cf. Dureau de la Malle, Notebook (1) [*Économie politique des Romains*, Vol. I, Paris, 1840, pp. 48-49]).[c][47]

For copper as the main instrument of war and peace ibid. 2 [p. 56] (as *money* in Italy, ibid. [p. 57]).

(b) Fluctuations in the Value Ratio of the Different Metals

If we are to examine the use of the metals as the substance of money, their use relative to each other, their earlier or later appearance, we must at the same time examine the *fluctuations in*

---

[a] J. Grimm, *Geschichte der deutschen Sprache*, Vol. I, Leipzig, 1853, pp. 9 and 7.— *Ed.*

[b] Copper and gold.— *Ed.*

[c] Here and below Marx quotes from Dureau de la Malle partly in French and partly in German translation.— *Ed.*

their relative value (see Letronne, Böckh, Jacob[a]). (In so far as this question is connected with the overall volume of the circulating metals and its relation to prices, to be considered later, as historical appendix to the chapter on the relation between money and prices.)

The *changement successif* between gold, silver and copper in different epochs inevitably depended in the first place on the nature of the deposits of these three metals and the greater or lesser purity in which they are found. Then on political changes like the invasion of Asia and part of Africa by the Persians and Macedonians, and later the Roman conquest of parts of the three continents (*orbis Romanus*, etc.) [Dureau de la Malle, op. cit., pp. 63-64].

Therefore dependent on the relative condition of purity in which they are found and the nature of the deposits.

The value ratio between the different metals can be determined without having regard to price, by means of the simple *quantitative* ratio in which they exchange for each other. We can generally adopt this procedure when we are comparing only a few commodities [I-32] that are measured in terms of the same unit, e.g. so many quarters of rye, barley, oats for so many quarters of wheat. In barter, where usually little is as yet exchanged and only a few commodities enter into commerce, this method is employed and hence money still unnecessary.

Among the *Arabs* neighbouring on the Sabaeans, according to Strabo, gold was locally so abundant that 10 lbs of gold was given for 1 lb. of iron and 2 lbs of gold for 1 lb. of silver [ibid., p. 52].

The land of the Bactrians (Bokhara, etc., in short Turkestan) and the parts of Asia SITUATED between the Paropamisus (Hundu Kush) and the Imaus (MUSTAGH MOUNTAINS), i.e. the *Desertum arenosum auro abundans*[b] (Gobi Desert), were so rich in gold that Dureau de la Malle thinks it

possible that from the 15th to the 6th century B.C. the ratio of gold to silver equalled 1:6 or 1:8, a ratio which existed in China and Japan up to the beginning of the 19th century. Herodotus puts the ratio at 1:13 for Persia under Darius Hystaspes [ibid., p. 54].

---

[a] J. A. Letronne, *Considérations générales sur l'évaluation des monnaies grecques et romaines, et sur la valeur de l'or et de l'argent avant la découverte de l'Amérique;* A. Böckh, *Die Staatshaushaltung der Athener;* W. Jacob, *An Historical Inquiry into the Production and Consumption of the Precious Metals.—Ed.*

[b] Sand desert abounding in gold.— *Ed.*

According to the code of Manu,[48] written between 1300 and 600 B.C., the gold-silver ratio=1:2 $^1/_2$. Silver mines in fact scarcely exist except in primary strata, especially in stratified rocks, and in a few lodes in secondary rocks. Silver lodes are usually embedded in the densest and hardest rocks such as quartz, etc., and not in alluvial sands. This metal is more common [than gold] in regions which are cold either due to their latitude or to their height above sea level, while gold usually prefers hot countries. Unlike gold, silver is only very rarely encountered in the pure state, etc. (most frequently combined with arsenic or sulphur) (hydrochloric acid, nitric acid). With respect to the quantity of the two metals in circulation (before the discovery of Australia and California), Humboldt (1811) estimates the ratio of gold to silver in America=1:46, in Europe (including Asiatic Russia)=1:40. The *minéralogistes* of the Académie des Sciences make the ratio nowadays (1842 [a])=1:52; yet the pound of gold is only worth 15 pounds of silver, hence the value ratio=1:15 [ibid., pp. 54-56].

Copper. Specific gravity=8.9. Beautiful colour, like the red of dawn. Fairly hard; requires a very high temperature to melt it. Not infrequently found pure; often combined with oxygen or sulphur.

Its lodes are embedded in ancient primary rocks. But is also frequently found, more than other minerals are, on the surface of the earth or at shallow depths, conglomerated in pure lumps, sometimes of considerable weight. Used before iron both in war and peace [ibid., p. 56].

(As the substance of money, gold bears the same relationship to silver as copper does to iron as an instrument of labour in historical development.)

It circulated in great quantities from the 1st to the 5th century in the part of Italy subjected by the Romans. The degree of civilisation of a people can be determined a priori simply by knowing the kind of metal—gold, copper, silver or iron—which it uses for weapons, tools and ornaments. *Hesiod* in his poem on agriculture:

"Χαλκῷ δ᾽ ε᾽ργάζοντο μέλας δ᾽οὐκ ἔσκε σιδηρος."[b]

Lucretius: "Et prior aeris erat quam ferri cognitus usus"[c] [ibid., p. 57].
Jacob refers to ancient copper mines in Nubia and Siberia (see Dureau, I, 58).
Herodotus says that the Massagetae possessed only bronze, not iron. According to the Oxford marbles, iron was not known before 1431 B.C. In *Homer,* iron is rare; by contrast, very common use of bronze (ore, bronze), this alloy of copper, zinc and tin, which for so long served both Greek and Roman society even for the manufacture of axes and razors" [ibid., p. 58].

---

[a] This should read "1840".— *Ed.*
[b] "They worked with copper. There was no black iron" (Hesiod, *Works and Days,* Verse 151).— *Ed.*
[c] "The use of bronze was known before that of iron" (Lucretius, *De rerum natura,* Book V, 1286).— *Ed.*

Italy is fairly rich in native copper; to 247 B.C. copper money formed, if not the sole currency, then the usual money, the monetary unit of middle Italy. The Greek colonies in southern Italy received silver from Greece and Asia either directly or via Tyre and Carthage, which they coined from the 5th and 6th century onwards [ibid., p. 64].

The Romans apparently possessed silver money before the expulsion of the kings, but according to Pliny, "interdictum id vetere consulto patrum, Italiae parci" (i.e. of her silver mines) "jubentium" [a] [Plinius, *Naturalis historia*, Book III, Chapter 20]. They feared the consequences of a convenient means of circulation—luxury, increase of slavery, accumulation, concentration of landed property [ibid., pp. 65-66].

Also among the Etruscans, copper was used as money earlier than gold.

Garnier is wrong in saying (see Notebook III, p. 22) that

"the material destined for accumulation was naturally sought and chosen in the realm of minerals".[b]

On the contrary, it was after the coming into use of metallic money (whether as money in the proper sense or still merely as a privileged means of exchange by weight) that accumulation began. This point to be *discussed particularly in relation to gold.*

Reitemeier [is] right [when he says] (see Notebook III, p. 33):

"Gold, silver and copper first used among the peoples of antiquity to make breaking and crushing tools, despite their *relative weakness,* earlier than iron and earlier than their use as money." (Tools improved when men learnt to harden copper by tempering it, so that it could stand up to solid rock. A very much hardened copper was used to make chisels and hammers, which served to master stone. Finally, iron discovered.)[c]

Jacob writes:

"In the patriarchal state (see Notebook IV, p. 3) when the metals from which arms were made, such as (1) BRASS and (2) IRON, were scarce and enormously expensive compared with the COMMON FOOD AND CLOTHING THEN USED, although no COINED MONEY OF THE PRECIOUS METALS was known, YET GOLD AND SILVER HAD ACQUIRED THE FACULTY to be more easily and CONVENIENTLY exchanged for the other metals than CORN and CATTLE".[d]

---

[a] "It was banned by an ancient decree of the Senate, which ruled that Italy" (i.e. her silver mines) "should be spared."— *Ed.*

[b] G. Garnier, *Histoire de la monnaie,* Vol. I, Paris, 1819, p. 7.— *Ed.*

[c] J. F. Reitemeier, *Geschichte des Bergbaues und Hüttenwesens bey den alten Völkern,* Göttingen, 1785, pp. 14-16 and 32.— *Ed.*

[d] W. Jacob, *An Historical Inquiry into the Production and Consumption of the Precious Metals.* Vol. I, London, 1831, p. 142.— *Ed.*

[I-33] Moreover, only simple washing was required to obtain the pure, or nearly pure, gold of the immense areas of alluvial land situated between the Hindu Kush and Himalayan ranges. At that time the population was abundant in these Asian countries and labour was therefore very cheap. Silver, because of the (technical) difficulty of its exploitation, relatively dearer. The opposite obtained in Asia and in Greece after Alexander's death. The gold-bearing sands became exhausted; the price of slaves and labour rose; since mechanics and geometry had made immense progress between Euclid and Archimedes, it became possible to exploit profitably the rich seams of the silver mines of Asia, Thrace and Spain, and silver being 52 times more plentiful than gold, the ratio between the values of these two metals naturally changed, and a pound of gold, which in Xenophon's time, 350 B.C., had exchanged for 10 pounds of silver, was worth 18 pounds of the latter metal in A.D. 422 [Dureau de la Malle, op. cit., Vol. I, pp. 62-63].

Hence gold had risen from 1:10 to 1:18.

At the end of the *5th century* A.D., there was an unusual decline in the quantity of coins and stagnation in mining. In the Middle Ages until the end of the 15th century, gold coins made up a relatively significant portion of the money supply. (The decline affected particularly the silver [coins], which had earlier provided the bulk of the circulating currency.) The [gold-silver] ratio in the 15th century=1:10, in the 18th century=1:14 on the Continent, 1:15 in England.

In Asia more recently, silver more as a commodity in trade; particularly in China, where copper money (*tehen,* an alloy of copper, zinc and lead) constituted the country's coinage; in China gold (and silver) reckoned by weight served as commodities for balancing external trade.[49]

Great fluctuations in the relative values of copper and silver (used as coins) in Rome.

Until the time of Servius, metal in ingots was used in exchange: the *aes rude.* The monetary unit was the as of copper,=1 lb. of the metal. At the time of Servius, the silver-copper value ratio=279:1, till the beginning of the Punic Wars[50]=400:1, at the time of the First Punic War=140:1, at the time of the Second Punic War=112:1 [ibid., pp. 66-68, 73, 76 and 82].

Gold initially very dear in Rome while silver came from Carthage (and Spain); gold used only in ingots until 547 [from the founding of Rome]. Gold to silver in trade=13.71:1, in coin 17.14:1; under Caesar=12:1 (at the outbreak of the civil war,[51] after Caesar's plundering of the *aerarium*[a] only=8.9:1); under Honorius and Arcadius ([A.D.] 397), fixed at 14.4:1; under Honorius and Theodosius Junior ([A.D.] 422)=18:1. Silver to copper=100:1; gold to silver=18:1 [ibid., pp. 85-91 and 95-96].

The first silver coin struck in Rome in 485 from the founding of Rome, the first gold coin in 547. As soon as the weight of the as was reduced to 1 ounce after the Second Punic War it was used only as small change; the sestertius (silver) became the monetary unit and all large payments were made in silver. (In everyday

[a] Treasury.— *Ed.*

dealings, copper (and later iron) continued to be the main metallic currency.)
Under the Emperors of the East and West, the *solidus* (*aureus*), i.e. gold, the
controlling money [ibid., pp. 65, 86, 81, 84 and 96].

Thus in antiquity, taking the average:

Firstly: *Relatively high value of silver compared with gold.* Apart
from individual cases (the Arabs) where gold was cheaper than
silver and even cheaper than iron, the value ratio of gold to silver
in Asia from the 15th to the 6th century B.C.=6:1 or 8:1 (the
latter *rapport*[a] in China and Japan till the beginning of the 19th
century). In the code of Manu [the ratio was] even=$2^1/_2$:1. This
low ratio arises from the same causes owing to which gold was the
first metal to be discovered. At that time gold came chiefly from
Asia and Egypt. The use of *copper* as money marks the
corresponding period in the development of Italy. In general,
copper as the main instrument of peace and war corresponds to
gold as the dominant precious metal. Even in Xenophon's time
gold to silver=10:1.

Secondly: Since the death of Alexander, relative rise in the value
of gold compared to silver, following the exhaustion of the
auriferous sands and the progress in technology and civilisation.
Consequently, opening of silver mines; now you have the
influence of the quantitatively greater occurrence of silver than
gold in the earth. But especially the Carthaginians, whose
exploitation of [silver mines in] Spain was bound to revolutionise
the relationship of gold to silver like the discovery of American
silver at the end of the 15th century. Ratio before Caesar's
time=17:1; later 14:1; and finally, since A.D. 422, it was 18:1.
(The fall in the relative value of gold under Caesar due to
accidental causes.) To the fall in the value of silver in relation to
gold corresponds the use of iron as the main instrument of
production in war and peace.

While in the first period gold came mainly from the East, in the
second period silver came from the more temperate West.

Thirdly: *In the Middle Ages,* the ratio was once again as in
Xenophon's time, 10:1. (In some places 12:1?)

Fourthly: *After the discovery of America,* the ratio was once again
ABOUT the same as at the time of Honorius and Arcadius ([A.D.] 397),
14 or 15:1. Although gold production increased from ABOUT 1815 to
1844, gold was at a premium (e.g. in France). It is probable that the
Californian and Australian discoveries,

fifthly, will bring the ratio back to that of the Roman Imperium,

---

[a] Ratio.— *Ed.*

i.e. 18:1, if not to a still higher one.[52] Both in antiquity and in modern times silver became relatively cheaper with the progress of the production of the precious metals from East to West, until the Californian and Australian discoveries reversed this process. In the short run great fluctuations, but there is a striking recurrence, if the main differences are considered.

[I-34] In ancient times, copper was three or four times more expensive than it is today (Garnier[a]).

c) The sources of supply of gold and silver, and their connection with historical development, must now be considered.

d) *Money as coinage.* A brief historical survey of coinage. Debasement and enhancement, etc.

[MONEY CIRCULATION]

The *circulation* or *turnover of money* corresponds to an opposite *circulation or turnover of commodities. A's* commodity passes into *B's* hands, while *B's* money passes into *A's* hands, etc. The circulation of money, like that of commodities, sets out from and returns to an infinite number of different points. The turnover of money at the stage at which we are discussing it here, i.e. the stage of its *direct* circulation, does not set out from one centre towards the various points of the periphery, or return from those points to one single centre. This takes place only when circulation is *mediated* by the banking system, though this first spontaneous and natural circulation does consist of a mass of turnovers. But turnover in the proper sense begins only when gold and silver cease to be commodities. No circulation in this sense takes place between countries exporting the precious metals and those importing them, for in this case we have only a simple exchange, since gold and silver figure as commodities, not as money.

In so far as money mediates the exchange of commodities, i.e. in this case their circulation, and is therefore the means of exchange, it is the *instrument of circulation, the "wheel of circulation".*[b] But in so far as it is itself circulated in this process, turned over, follows its own movement, it has itself a *circulation, money circulation, money turnover.* We must ascertain how far this circulation is governed by special laws. To begin with, it is clear

---

[a] G. Garnier, *Histoire de monnaie*, Vol. I, p. 253.— *Ed.*

[b] See A. Smith, *An Inquiry into the Nature and Causes of the Wealth of Nations*, Vol. II, London, 1836, pp. 272, 276 and 284.— *Ed.*

that if money is the wheel of circulation for commodities, commodities are likewise the wheel of circulation for money. If money circulates commodities, commodities circulate money. The circulation of commodities and the circulation of money therefore condition each other.

There are three points to consider in relation to money turnover: (1) the form of the movement itself, the line it follows (its concept); (2) the quantity of money in circulation; (3) the velocity with which it accomplishes its movement, circulates. This can only be done in relation to commodity circulation. It is clear, to begin with, that commodity circulation possesses elements which are completely independent of money circulation and which, indeed, determine the latter, either directly or e.g. because the same circumstances which govern the velocity of commodity circulation also govern that of money circulation. The character of the mode of production as a whole will govern both, and more directly the circulation of commodities.

[On it depends] the number of people carrying on exchange (the size of the population); their distribution as between town and countryside; the absolute quantity of commodities, of products and of productive agents; the relative quantity of commodities put into circulation; the development of the means of communication and transport, in the double sense that it determines both the circle of those involved in exchange with each other, entering into contact, and the speed with which the raw material gets to the producer and the product to the consumer; finally the development of industry, which concentrates different branches of production in one place, e.g. spinning, weaving, dyeing, etc., thus making superfluous a series of mediating acts of exchange. Commodity circulation is the basic premiss of money circulation. How far the latter reacts back on the circulation of commodities, to be examined.

To start with, the *general concept of circulation or turnover* must be established.

Also to be noted that it is exchange values and hence *prices* which are circulated by money. In commodity circulation, therefore, we must take into account the prices of commodities just as much as their volume. Obviously, less money is needed to circulate a large quantity of commodities of low exchange value (price) than to circulate a small quantity at double the price. The concept of price must therefore be developed *before* that of circulation. Circulation is the positing of prices, the movement in which commodities are transformed into prices, their realisation as prices. Money has a dual determination: (1) as the *measure* or element in which the commodity is realised as exchange value, and (2) as *means of exchange,* instrument of circulation; and these two determinations have effects in quite different directions. Money only circulates commodities which have already been *notionally* transformed into money, not only in the mind of the individual but in the imagination of society (directly, of the parties involved in the process of purchase and sale). The notional transformation into money and the real one are not governed by the same laws at all. The relationship between them must be investigated.

(a) [Money as Measure of Value]

An essential characteristic of circulation is that it circulates exchange values, exchange values, that is, in the form of *prices.* Hence, not every type of commodity exchange, e.g. BARTER, payments in kind, feudal services, etc., constitutes circulation. For circulation, two things above all are necessary: *firstly,* the premiss of commodities as prices; *secondly,* a circuit of exchanges, rather than isolated acts of exchange; a totality of exchanges in constant flow and taking place more or less over the whole surface of society; a system of acts of exchange.

[I-35] The commodity is cast in the role of exchange value. As such it is equivalent in a definite proportion (in proportion to the labour time contained in it) to all other values (commodities). But it does not correspond directly to itself in this role. As an exchange value it differs from itself in its natural form of existence. A mediation is required to posit the commodity as exchange value. Hence, in the form of money, exchange value confronts the commodity as something different from it. Only when posited as money is the commodity pure exchange value; or the commodity as pure exchange value is money. But at the same time, money now exists outside and alongside the commodity; its exchange value, the exchange value of all commodities, has acquired an existence independent of it, embodied in a material of its own, in a specific commodity. The exchange value of the commodity expresses the totality of the quantitative proportions in which all other commodities can be exchanged for it, as determined by the unequal quantities of the various commodities which can be produced in the same labour time. Money now exists as the exchange value of all commodities alongside and outside of them.

It is above all the general material into which they must be dipped to be gold- and silver-plated so as to acquire their free existence as exchange values. They must be translated into money, expressed in its terms. Money becomes the general denominator of exchange values, of commodities as exchange values. Exchange value expressed in money, i.e. equated to money, is *price*. Since money has been posited as something independent as against exchange values, exchange values are cast in the role of the money confronting them as subject.[33] But every exchange value is a definite quantity, is a quantitatively determined exchange value. As such it is=to a particular quantity of money. The particular quantity is determined according to the general law by the labour time realised in the exchange value. Thus, an exchange value that is the product of, SAY, a day's labour, is expressed in a quantity of gold or silver that is equal to a day's labour time, the product of a day's labour. The general measure of exchange values now becomes the measure between every exchange value and the money to which it is *equated.*

(Gold and silver are determined in the first instance by their production costs in the countries in which they are produced.

"In the MINING COUNTRIES all prices depend ultimately upon the production costs of the precious METALS; THE REMUNERATION PAID TO THE MINER AFFORDS THE SCALE upon which the REMUNERATION of all other PRODUCERS is calculated... The gold and silver value of all commodities not subject to any monopoly in a country not possessing mines depends upon the gold and silver WHICH CAN BE OBTAINED BY EXPORTING THE RESULT OF A GIVEN QUANTITY OF LABOUR, THE CURRENT RATE OF PROFIT, AND, IN EACH INDIVIDUAL CASE, THE AMOUNT OF WAGES WHICH HAVE BEEN PAID, AND THE TIME FOR WHICH THEY HAVE BEEN ADVANCED" (Senior [*Three Lectures on the Cost of Obtaining Money,* London, 1830, pp. 14-15 and 13-14]).

In other words, this value depends on the QUANTITY OF GOLD AND SILVER WHICH is DIRECTLY OR INDIRECTLY obtained from the mining countries for a certain quantity of labour (i.e. of exportable products). Money is first of all that which expresses the relation of equality of all exchange values: in money they all have the same denominator.

Exchange value posited in terms of money is *price.* In price it is expressed as a definite quantity of money. In price, money appears, firstly, as the *unity* of all exchange values; and secondly, as the unit of which they contain a particular number, so that their quantitative character, their quantitative ratio to one another, is expressed by comparison with that unit. Hence money here plays the role of the *measure* of exchange values, and prices that of exchange values measured by money. That money is the measure of prices, and hence the basis for the comparison of exchange values, is a definition that follows automatically. But more important for the purpose of this argument is that in price *exchange value is compared with money.* Once money has been cast in the role of exchange value independent of and separate from commodities, the particular commodity, the specific exchange value, is again *equated* to money, i.e. taken as equal to a certain sum of money, expressed in money, translated into it. By being equated to money, the commodities are again related to each other as they were, conceptually, as exchange values: as corresponding and comparable to each other in definite proportions.

The particular exchange value, the commodity, is expressed, subsumed, posited in the character of exchange value made independent, in money. How that happens (i.e. how the quantitative proportion between the quantitatively determined exchange value and a definite quantity of money is found), cf. above.[a] But since money has an independent existence outside commodities, the price of the commodity appears as an *external* relation of exchange values or commodities to money. The commodity *is not* price, not in the way it was exchange value in its social substance; it does not *immediately* coincide with its character as price; it acquires this character only through being compared with money. The commodity *is* exchange value, but it *has* a price. Exchange value was there in direct unity with the commodity, as its immediate character, from which it separated just as immediately so that on the one side there was the commodity, on the other its exchange value (as measured in money). But now, in its *price,* the commodity is on the one hand related to money as to something existing outside it, and on the other it is itself seen as money *notionally,* since money has a reality distinct from it. Price is an attribute of the commodity, a determination in which it is *introduced* as money. It is no longer an immediate but a reflected determinateness of the commodity. [I-36] Alongside real money there now exists the commodity as something notionally cast in the role of money.

This next determination both of money *as measure* and of the commodity as *price* is most simply illustrated by the distinction between *real money* and *money of account.* As measure, money always serves as money of account; and as price, the commodity is always transformed into money only notionally.

"The valuation of the commodity by the seller, the offer made by the buyer, the calculations, obligations, rents, inventories, etc., in short everything leading up to and preceding the material act of payment, must be expressed in money of account. Real money intervenes only in order to realise the payments and to balance" (liquidate) "the accounts. If I have 24 livres 12 sous to pay, the money of account presents 24 units of one kind and 12 of another, while I will actually pay with two pieces of material: one piece of gold worth 24 livres and one of silver worth 12 sous. The total volume of real money has necessary limits in the needs of the circulation. The money of account is an ideal measure, which has no limits other than those of the imagination. Employed *to express every kind of wealth, if only it is considered from the viewpoint of its exchange value*: the national wealth, the national income, the income of individuals; accounting values, in whatever form these values may exist, regulated according to that same form; so there is not a single article in the mass of *choses consommables*[a] that is not repeatedly transformed into money in thought, while compared with this mass, the total sum of real money is at most=1:10" (Garnier [*Histoire de la monnaie*, Vol. I, pp. 72, 73, 77, 78]).

(This ratio is wrong. 1:many millions would be more correct. But this cannot be measured at all.)

Thus, if money originally expresses exchange value, the commodity as price, as notionally posited and conceptually realised exchange value, now expresses a sum of money: money in a particular proportion. As prices, all commodities are in various forms representatives of money, while previously money as exchange value made independent was the representative of all commodities. To money really posited as a commodity succeeds the commodity notionally posited as money.

It is now clear, to start with, that in this notional transformation of commodities into money, or in the positing of commodities as *prices,* the quantity of money actually available is completely irrelevant in two respects: *Firstly,* the notional transformation of commodities into money is *prima facie*[b] independent of and unrestricted by the quantity of real money. Not a single coin is necessary for this process, just as little as a measuring rod (say, a yardstick) need actually be employed in order to express, say, the length of the Earth's Equator in yards. If e.g. the whole national wealth of England is estimated in money, i.e. expressed as price, everyone knows that there is not enough money in the whole world to realise this price. Money is necessary here only as a category, as an imagined ratio. *Secondly,* since money is taken as a unit, and the commodity is thus expressed as containing a certain sum of equal parts of money, is measured by it, it follows that the measure between the two is the general measure of exchange values—the production costs or labour time. If $1/3$ oz. of gold is the product of 1 working day, and the commodity x the product

---

a Consumable articles.— *Ed.*

b At first sight; here in the sense of "clearly".— *Ed.*

of 3 working days, that commodity=1 ounce of gold or £3 17 s. 7 d. sterling. In measuring money and commodity, the original measure of exchange values comes in again. Instead of being expressed in 3 working days, the commodity is expressed in the quantity of gold or silver which is the product of 3 working days. Obviously, the actual supply of money has no bearing on this proportion.

(*Error of James Mill*: overlooks the fact that the production costs, not their quantity, determine the value of the precious metals, and the prices of commodities MEASURED IN METALLIC VALUE.[53]

"Commodities in exchange act as each other's measure... But this procedure would require as many points of comparison as there are commodities in circulation. If one commodity were exchanged only for one, not for two commodities, it could not serve as the term of comparison... Hence the need for a *terme commun de comparaison*... This term can be a purely notional one... The determination of measure is the original one, more important than that of *gage*[a]... In the trade between Russia and China, silver is used to evaluate all commodities, yet this *commerce* is carried on by *trocs*[b]" (Storch [*Cours d'économie politique*, Vol. I, Paris, 1823, pp. 81-84, 87, 88]).

"Measuring with money is like the use of weights to compare material quantities. The same name for the two units whose function was to count the weight as well as the value of each object. *Measures of weight and measures of value have the same names.* An *étalon*[c] that is always of the same weight was easily found. With money, it was a question of the *value* of a pound of silver=its costs of production" (Sismondi [*Études sur l'économie politique*, Vol. II, Brussels, 1838, pp. 264-68]).

Not only the same names. Gold and silver originally weighed. Thus, the Roman *as*=1 lb. of copper. Wirth.[d])

[I-37] "Sheep and oxen, not gold and silver, figure as *money*, as the measure of value, in Homer and Hesiod. On the battle field of Troy, barter" (Jacob [*An Historical Inquiry into the Production and Consumption of the Precious Metals*, Vol. I, p. 109]). (Similarly *slaves* in the Middle Ages, ibid. [p. 351].)

Money can function as the measure and general element of exchange values without assuming its further determinations— hence even before it has assumed the form of metallic money, e.g. in the case of simple barter. But this presupposes that little exchange of any kind takes place, that commodities have not been developed as exchange values and consequently not as *prices* either.

---

[a] Security.— *Ed.*

[b] Barter.— *Ed.*

[c] Standard.— *Ed.*

[d] See J. G. A. Wirth, *Die Geschichte der Deutschen*, Vol. I, Stuttgart, 1846, pp. 97-99.— *Ed.*

("A COMMON STANDARD in the price of ANYTHING presumes ITS FREQUENT and FAMILIAR ALIENATION. This is not the case in simple states of society. In non-industrialised countries many things are without a definite price... SALE ALONE CAN DETERMINE PRICES, AND FREQUENT SALE ALONE CAN FIX A STANDARD. The FREQUENT SALE of articles of first NECESSITY depends on the relation of town and country", etc.[a])

Developed pricing presupposes that the individual does not directly produce his subsistence but that his immediate product is *exchange value,* and hence must first be mediated by a social process to become the *means of subsistence* for him. Between the full development of this basis of industrial society and patriarchal conditions many intermediate stages, endless nuances.

This much can be concluded from (a): if the costs of production of the precious metals rise, the prices of all commodities fall; if the costs of production of the precious metals fall, the prices of all commodities rise. This is the general principle which is, as we shall see, modified in particular cases. [I-37]

[I-38] (Note to *a*)[b] ("The term 'measure', used as an attribute of MONEY, means an *INDICATOR OF VALUE*"... Ridiculous assertion that "PRICES MUST FALL, because COMMODITIES are valued at SO MANY OUNCES OF GOLD and the AMOUNT OF GOLD IS DIMINISHED IN THIS COUNTRY."... THE EFFICIENCY OF GOLD AS AN INDICATOR OF VALUE IS UNAFFECTED BY ITS QUANTITY BEING GREATER OR SMALLER IN ANY PARTICULAR COUNTRY. If the whole paper and metallic circulation in this country were reduced by half by means of BANKING EXPEDIENTS, the relative value of gold and commodities would remain the same.[c] Examples of this: Peru in the 16th century and the transmission from France to England. Hubbard [*The Currency and the Country,* London, 1843, pp. 44-46,] VIII, 45.)

("On the African Coast, the measure of value is neither gold nor silver but a notional STANDARD, an imaginary bar", Jacob, [*An Historical Inquiry into the Production and Consumption of the Precious Metals,* Vol. II, London, 1831, pp. 326-27,] V, 15.) [I-38]

(b) [Money as a Means of Circulation]

[I-37] If exchange values are *notionally* transformed into money in prices, then in exchange, in purchase and sale, they are *really* transformed into money, exchanged for money in order, as money, to be again exchanged for commodities. The particular exchange value must first be exchanged for the *general,* so as to be again exchanged for particular ones. The commodity is realised as

---

[a] J. Steuart, *An Inquiry into the Principles of Political Oeconomy,* Vol. I, Dublin, 1770, pp. 395 and 396.— *Ed.*
[b] In the manuscript the text marked "Note to *a.*" is written on the next page, in a passage belonging to section *b.*— *Ed.*
[c] Cf. this volume, p. 111.— *Ed.*

exchange value only by means of this mediating movement in which money plays the role of mediator. Hence money circulates in the opposite direction from commodities. Money appears as mediator of commodity exchange, as means of exchange. It is the wheel of circulation, the instrument of circulation for the turnover of commodities; but as such it simultaneously has a circulation of its own—the *monetary turnover, money circulation.* The price of the commodity is only realised in its exchange for real money, or in its real exchange for money.

This much can be concluded from the foregoing. Commodities are exchanged for money in reality, transformed into real money, only after they have been previously transformed into money in idea—i.e. after they have acquired a *price determination,* as *prices. Prices* are therefore the *prerequisite* for money circulation, however much their realisation may appear as the result of that circulation. The circumstances which make the exchange value and hence the *prices* of commodities rise above or fall below their average value, are to be analysed in the section on exchange value; they precede the process of the actual *realisation* of the prices in money; consequently appear at first to be completely independent of it. The relations of numbers to one another obviously remain the same when I represent them in decimal fractions; I have merely given them another *name.*

The actual circulation of commodities requires *instruments of transport*; it cannot be effected by money. If I have bought 1,000 lbs of iron for the sum of £x, the ownership of this iron has been transferred to me. My £x has done its job as means of exchange and has circulated, just as the title of ownership has done. The seller, on the other hand, has realised the price of the iron, has realised the iron as exchange value. But money does not contribute to bringing the iron from him to me; for that wagon, horses, roads, etc., are needed. Money does not effect the actual circulation of commodities in space and time. It merely realises their *price* and in that way transfers the title of ownership to the commodities to the purchaser, to the person who has offered the means of exchange. What is circulated by money is not commodities, but the titles of ownership to them; and what is realised in return in this circulation, whether by purchase or sale, is again not the commodities, but their prices.

Thus, the quantity of money required for circulation is determined, in the first place, by the level of prices of the commodities that are put into circulation. But, the sum total of these prices is determined *firstly,* by the prices of the individual commodities; *secondly*, by the volume of commodities which enter into circulation at given prices. For example, twice as much money is needed to circulate a quarter of wheat at the price of 60 s. than at the price of 30 s. And 30,000 s. is necessary to circulate 500 quarters at 60 s. each, while only 12,000 s. is needed for the circulation of 200 quarters at the same price. Thus the amount of money required depends on the level of commodity prices and the volume of commodities to be circulated at given prices.

Secondly, however, the quantity of money required for circulation depends not only on the sum of the prices to be realised, it also depends on the velocity with which the money circulates, with which it accomplishes the business of realisation. If 1 thaler makes 10 purchases in an hour, at the price of 1 thaler each time, i.e. exchanges itself 10 times, it completes QUITE the same business as 10 thaler which effects only 1 purchase in an hour. Velocity of circulation is the negative moment; it offsets quantity; by means of it, a single coin multiplies itself.

The factors determining, on the one hand, the aggregate of commodity prices to be realised, and, on the other hand, the velocity of circulation of money are to be examined later. This much is clear, that prices are not high or low because much or little money is in circulation, but that much or little money is in circulation because prices are high or low; and further, that the velocity of the circulating money does not depend on its quantity; rather, [I-38] the quantity of the circulating medium depends on ils velocity (HEAVY PAYMENTS are not counted but weighed; this saves time).

But as already mentioned,[a] the circulation of money does not begin from one central point, nor does it return to a central point from all the points of the periphery (as is the case with the BANKS OF ISSUE and partly the case with state money); but it begins from and returns to an infinite number of points (this reflux itself, and the time in which it is completed, are fortuitous). The velocity of the means of circulation can therefore offset the quantity of the circulating medium only up to a certain point. (Factory-owners and farmers, e.g., pay the labourer; he pays the shopkeeper, etc.; and from the latter, the money returns to the factory-owners and farmers.) A given quantity of money can only effect a series of payments *successively*, whatever the velocity with which it effects them. But a certain number of payments must be made *simultaneously*. Circulation starts from a multitude of different

---

[a] See p. 121.— *Ed.*

points simultaneously. Hence a definite quantity of money is needed for circulation, a quantity which will always be in circulation, and which is determined by the total sum which sets out from the simultaneous points of departure of circulation and the velocity with which it runs its course (returns). However much this quantity of the circulating medium may be subject to ebbs and flows, there is an average level; for the permanent changes in it are only very gradual, take place only over long periods of time, and, as we shall see, are always counteracted by a mass of secondary circumstances.

In its determination as measure, money is indifferent to its quantity, or the existing quantity of money is a matter of indifference. In its determination as means of exchange, instrument of circulation, its quantity is measured. Whether these two determinations of money can come into contradiction with each other, to be examined later.

(The concept of *forced, compulsory circulation* (see Steuart[a]) does not belong here yet.[54])

It is an essential feature of *circulation* that exchange appears as a process, a fluid whole of purchases and sales. Its first premiss is the circulation of the commodities themselves, the circulation of these which continually sets out from a large number of points. The precondition of the circulation of commodities is that they are produced as *exchange values,* not as *immediate use values* but as use values mediated by exchange value. Appropriation through and by means of alienation and sale is a basic premiss. Circulation as the realisation of exchange values implies (1) that my product is a product only in so far as it is a product for others, in other words, transcended individuality, generality; (2) that it is a product for me only in so far as it has been alienated, has become a product for others; (3) that it is a product for the other person only in so far as he alienates his own product. This in turn implies (4) that production appears for me not an end in itself but a means.

Circulation is the movement in which general alienation appears as general appropriation and general appropriation as general alienation. Though the whole of this movement may well appear as a social process, and though the individual elements of this movement originate from the conscious will and particular purposes of individuals, nevertheless the totality of the process appears as an objective relationship arising spontaneously; a

---

[a] J. Steuart, *An Inquiry into the Principles of Political Oeconomy,* Vol. II, Dublin, 1770, p. 389.— *Ed.*

relationship which results from the interaction of conscious individuals, but which is neither part of their consciousness nor as a whole subsumed under them. Their own collisions give rise to an *alien* social power standing above them. Their own interaction [appears] as a process and force independent of them. Because circulation is a totality of the social process, it is also the first form in which not only the social relation appears as something independent of individuals as, say, in a coin or an exchange value, but the whole of the social movement itself. The mutual social relationship of individuals as an independent power standing over them, whether it is conceived of as a force of nature, an accident, or in any other form, is a necessary result of the fact that the starting point is not the free social individual. Circulation as the first totality among the economic categories serves well to illustrate this fact.

[I-39] At first sight, circulation appears to be *simply a never-ending process*.[55] The commodity is exchanged for money; money is exchanged for the commodity, and this is repeated *ad infinitum*. This constant renewal of an identical process does indeed constitute an essential feature of circulation. But on closer examination, it reveals other phenomena as well: the phenomena of closing the circle or the return of the point of departure into itself. The commodity is exchanged for money; money is exchanged for the commodity. So, commodity is exchanged for commodity, except that this exchange is a mediated one. The buyer becomes a seller again, and the seller again becomes a buyer. So each is placed in a dual and antithetical determination, and so we have the living unity of both determinations.

It is, however, quite incorrect to proceed as do the economists: as soon as the contradictions of the money system emerge suddenly to focus only on the end results, forgetting the process which mediates them, seeing only the unity without the difference, the affirmation without the negation. The commodity is exchanged in circulation for a commodity; but in so far as it is exchanged for money, it is also *not* exchanged for a commodity. In other words, the acts of purchase and sale appear as two acts, indifferent to each other, separated in place and time. If it is said that a seller is at the same time a buyer, in so far as he buys money, and that a buyer is at the same time a seller, in so far as he sells money, this is to ignore precisely the distinction, the specific distinction between commodity and money.

After the economists have shown us so beautifully that barter, in which sale and purchase coincide, will not suffice for a more developed form of society and mode of production, they suddenly look at barter mediated by money as if it were immediate, and ignore the *specific* character of this transaction. After having shown us that in distinction to commodities money is needed, they ALL AT ONCE assert that there is no difference between money and commodities. They take refuge in this abstraction because, in the real development of money, contradictions occur which are embarrassing for the apologetics of bourgeois COMMON SENSE and must therefore be covered up. In so far as purchase and sale, the two essential moments of circulation, are indifferent to one another, separate in space and time, they need not coincide at all. Their mutual indifference can go so far as to fortify one against the other and to make them apparently independent of each other. But in so far as they are both essential moments of a single whole, there must come a time when their independent form is violently broken up and their inner unity is outwardly established by a violent explosion. Hence, the quality of money as mediator, the separation of exchange into two acts, already contains the germ of crises, at least their possibility, which cannot be realised except where there exist the basic conditions of classically and fully developed circulation corresponding to its concept.

It has become further apparent that in circulation money only realises prices. Price appears first of all as a notional characteristic of the commodity; but the money exchanged for a commodity is its realised price, its real price. Hence price appears quite as much *external to* and independent *alongside* the commodity as attached to it in thought. If the commodity cannot be realised in money, it ceases to be capable of circulating, and its price becomes purely notional; just as originally the product transformed into exchange value ceases to be a product if it is not actually exchanged. (The rise and fall of prices not the question here.)

Considered under (a), *price* appeared as *an attribute of commodities;* but considered under (b), *money* appears *as the price outside the commodity.* A mere demand for the commodity does not suffice, it must be *backed up with cash.* If the price of the commodity cannot be realised, if the commodity cannot be converted into money, it appears *devalued, depriced.* The exchange value expressed in its price must be sacrificed as soon as this specific transformation into money is necessary. Hence, the complaints of Boisguillebert, for instance, that money is the executioner of all things, the Moloch to which everything must be sacrificed, the despot over commodities.[a] At the time of the rise of

a P. Boisguillebert, "Dissertation sur la nature des richesses, de l'argent et des absolute monarchy, when all taxes were being converted into money taxes, money does indeed appear as the Moloch to which real wealth is sacrificed. So it appears in every MONETARY PANIC, too. Boisguillebert says that money has been transformed from the servant of commerce into its despot. In fact, however, pricing itself already anticipates what is implied in the exchange for money, namely that money no longer represents the commodity, but the commodity represents money. Complaints that trading by means of money was not legitimate trade in some writers of the period of transition from feudal to modern times; as later among socialists.

(α) The more the division of labour develops, the more the product ceases to be a means of exchange. It becomes necessary to have a general means of exchange, independent of the specific production of any particular individual. In production directed towards immediate subsistence, it is not possible to exchange *every* article for *every* other, and a particular activity can only [I-40] be exchanged for a *particular* product. The more specialised, the more manifold, the less independent the products become, the greater becomes the need for a general means of exchange. Initially, the product of labour or labour itself is the general means of exchange. It gradually ceases to be such as it becomes increasingly specialised. It is a prerequisite for a fairly developed division of labour that everyone's needs have become very many-sided and his product very one-sided. The *need for exchange* and the *immediate means of exchange* develop in inverse proportion. Hence the need for a *general means of exchange,* where the particular product and the particular labour must be exchanged for *exchangeability.* The exchange value of an object is nothing but the quantitatively specified expression of its ability to serve as a *means of exchange.* In money the *means of exchange* itself becomes an object, or the exchange value of the object acquires an independent existence outside it. Since the commodity is a means of exchange of only limited power as compared with money, it may cease to be a means of exchange as against money.

(β) The separation of exchange into purchase and sale makes it possible for me to buy without selling (stockpiling of commodities) or to sell without buying (accumulation of money). It makes speculation possible. It makes exchange into a special business; i.e. it creates the *merchant estate.* This separation has made possible a multitude of transactions between the definitive exchange of

tributs"(the metaphors Marx quotes from this work occur on pp. 395, 399 and 413 of the collection *Économistes financiers du XVIIIᵉ siècle,* Paris, 1843.— Ed.

commodities, enabling a large number of persons to exploit this division. It has made possible a multitude of *pseudo-transactions*. At times it becomes clear that what appeared as an essentially divided act, is something essentially integrated; at other times, that what was thought to be an essentially integrated act is in reality essentially divided. At times in which purchase and sale assert themselves as essentially distinct acts, a general depreciation of all commodities takes place. At those in which money only functions as a means of exchange, a depreciation of money takes place. General fall or rise in prices.

Money makes possible an absolute division of labour, because it renders labour independent of its specific product, independent of the immediate use value of its product for labour.

The general rise in prices at times of speculation cannot be attributed to a general rise in the *exchange value* of commodities or their *production costs*; for if the *exchange value or the production costs* of gold rose to the same extent as those of all other commodities, their exchange values expressed in money, i.e. their *prices,* would remain the same. Just as little can it be ascribed to a fall in the price of production [56] of gold. (Here we are not dealing with credit yet.) But since money is not only the general commodity but a particular commodity *as well,* and as a particular commodity is subject to the laws of demand and supply, the general demand for particular commodities relative to money must bring money down [in price].

Hence, we see that it is in the nature of money to resolve the contradictions of both direct barter and exchange value only by making them general. It was a matter of chance whether the *particular means of exchange* was exchanged for another particular means of exchange or not. But now the commodity must be exchanged for the *general means of exchange,* to which its particularity stands in still greater contradiction. In order to secure the exchangeability of the commodity, it is confronted with exchangeability itself as an independent commodity. (It turns from a means into an end.) Previously, the question was whether the particular commodity would encounter the particular commodity. But money resolves the act of exchange itself into two acts indifferent to one another.

(Before going further into problems of circulation, its strength, weakness, etc., and especially into the contentious issue of the quantity of money in circulation and prices, money must be considered in its third determination.)

One moment of circulation is that commodity is exchanged for commodity by means of money. But there is the other moment, namely that, just as commodity exchanges for money and money for commodity, so money exchanges for commodity and commodity for money, in other words, that money is mediated with itself by means of the commodity, and appears as the unit which goes together with itself in its circulation. Thus it no longer appears as the means but as the end of circulation (as e.g. for the merchants) (in trade in general). If circulation is considered not merely as a continuous alternation, but in the circular motions which it describes in itself, this circular motion appears as a double one: commodity—money—money—commodity; on the other hand, money—commodity—commodity—money, i.e. if I can sell in order to buy, I can just as well buy in order to sell. In the first case, money is only the means of obtaining the commodity, and the commodity is the end; in the second case, the commodity is only the means of obtaining money, and money is the end. We can recognise this clearly if we consider the moments of circulation together. Considered as mere circulation, it does not matter at which point I break in to make it the point of departure.

Certainly, there is a specific difference between the commodity in circulation and money in circulation. The commodity is ejected from circulation at a certain point and fulfils its ultimate purpose only when it is definitively withdrawn from circulation, consumed, either in the act of production or [I-41] in consumption proper. The purpose of money, on the contrary, is to remain in circulation as the agent which effects it, as a *perpetuum mobile* ever renewing its circular course.

Nevertheless, that second purpose is present in circulation as much as the first. Now one can say: to exchange commodity for commodity makes sense, for although commodities are equivalents as prices, they are qualitatively different and thus their exchange ultimately satisfies qualitatively different needs. To exchange money for money is senseless, however, unless a quantitative difference occurs through the exchange of less money for more, by selling more dearly than one buys, and we are not yet concerned with the category of profit. Hence the conclusion money—commodity—commodity—money, which we derive from the analysis of circulation, might appear merely as an arbitrary and senseless abstraction, rather as if one were to describe the cycle of life as: death—life—death; though in the latter case, it could not be denied that the constant dissolution of the individual into the elemental is as much an element of the natural process as the constant individualisation of the elemental. Similarly, in circulation: the constant monetarisation of commodities no less than the constant transformation of money into commodities.[a]

Admittedly, in the real process of buying in order to sell the motive is the profit which is made in that transaction, and the ultimate aim is to exchange by means of the commodity less money for more money, since there is no qualitative difference between money and money. (We are not speaking here either of a particular metallic currency or of particular kinds of coinage.) Yet it cannot be denied that the operation can miscarry, and that, indeed, exchange of money for money without a quantitative difference repeatedly occurs in real life, and therefore can occur. But for this process, upon which trade is based and which therefore by its extent is also an important phenomenon of circulation, to be possible at all, the circuit money—commodity—commodity—money must be recognised as a special form of circulation. This form is specifically distinct from that in which money appears as a mere means of exchange of commodities; as the middle term; as a minor premiss for the conclusion. This circuit has to be distinguished in its purely qualitative form, its specific movement, alongside the quantitative determinateness which it possesses in trade.

Secondly, it already implies that money does not serve only as a measure or only as a means of exchange or only as both, but that it has yet a third determination. It appears here *firstly* as an end-in-itself, which commodity trade and exchange merely serve to realise. *Secondly,* since money is the final stage of the circuit here, it *leaves the circuit* just as the commodity exchanged for its equivalent by means of money is ejected from circulation. It is quite correct that money, in so far as it serves only as the agent of circulation, always remains included in the circuit. But now it becomes evident that money is something more than this instrument of circulation; that it also possesses an independent existence outside circulation, and in this new determination *can* be

---

[a] Here the following passage is crossed out in the manuscript: "Now on this we must remark, firstly, that the two moments of circulation are produced by the third, which we previously called its infinite process; and that by means of this process—whether we take money or the commodity as the starting point—the end point can and must lead again and again beyond the circuit. Hence: commodity—money—money—commodity—money, but equally, money—commodity—commodity—money—commodity. Therefore, although neither of the two moments ends in itself, it must nonetheless be considered in its specific character. Seen in this way, it no longer seems so curious that one moment of the movement consists in money exchanging itself for itself through the medium of the commodity, thus momentarily appearing as the ultimate object."— *Ed.*

withdrawn from it, just as the commodity *must* always definitively be withdrawn from it. Hence we must consider money in its third determination, in which it includes the previous two, namely the role of serving as measure and that of being the general means of exchange and thus the realisation of commodity prices.

(c) Money as Material Representative of Wealth.
(Accumulation of money. But first we have still to consider money as the general material of contracts, etc.)

It is implicit in the nature of the circuit that each point in it appears simultaneously as point of departure and termination, and that, indeed, it appears as the one to the extent that it appears as the other. The form $M—C—C—M$ is therefore quite as correct as the other, which appears to be the original one, $C—M—M—C$. The difficulty is that the second commodity is qualitatively different, while this is not true of the second money. It can only be quantitatively different.

When money is considered as a *measure,* its material substance is essential, although its availability and especially its quantity, the *number* of the portions of gold or silver which serves as *unit,* is completely immaterial for it in this determination in which it is used merely as an imaginary, non-existent unit. It is as a unit that it must be available in this determination, not as a number. If I say that 1 lb. of cotton is worth 8d., I am saying that 1 lb. of cotton=$^{1}/_{116}$ ounce of gold (the ounce at £3 17s. 7d. or 931d.). This equation then also expresses its determinateness as exchange value, as the equivalent of all other commodities which contain so-and-so many times the ounce of gold, since they are all likewise compared with [I-42] the ounce of gold. This initial ratio of a pound of cotton to gold, which defines the quantity of gold that is contained in a pound of cotton, is given by the quantity of labour time realised in both, the real common substance of exchange values. This to be assumed from the chapter that deals with exchange value as such.[57]

The difficulty of finding this equation is not as great as it appears. For example: in terms of the labour that directly produces gold, a particular quantity of gold appears directly as the product of, say, a day's labour. Directly or indirectly, competition equates the other labour days with this, *modificandis modificatis.* In a word, in the direct production of gold a particular quantity of gold appears directly as product and therefore as the value, the equivalent, of a particular labour time. Hence, one only has to determine the labour time that is realised in the various commodities, and relate it with the labour time that directly produces gold, to be able to say how much gold is contained in a particular commodity.

The determination of all commodities as prices—as measured exchange values—is a process that takes place only gradually, and presupposes extensive exchange and hence repeated comparison of commodities as exchange values. But once the existence of commodities as prices has become an assumption—an assumption that is itself a product of the social process, a result of the social process of production—the determination of new prices seems simple, for the elements of the production costs themselves already exist in the form of prices and thus have simply to be added together. (FREQUENT ALIENATION, SALE, FREQUENT SALE (Steuart[a]). Moreover, all this must have continuity, in order that prices may acquire a certain regularity.)

However, the point we wanted to come to is this: in so far as gold is to be established as a unit of measurement, its relation to commodities is determined by BARTER, by direct exchange, just like the relationship of all other commodities to one another. In BARTER, however, exchange value is only the product *in itself,* the first form in which exchange value appears; but the product is not yet posited as exchange value. Firstly, this determination [as exchange value] does not yet dominate production as a whole, but concerns only its surplus and is therefore itself more or less *superfluous* (like exchange itself); a fortuitous enlargement of the circle of satisfactions, of pleasures (relation to new objects). Consequently, it [exchange] takes place at only a few points (originally, at the borders of naturally evolved communities, in their contact with foreigners), is confined to a narrow area, something passing production by, incidental to it, ends as fortuitously as it comes into existence. Barter in which the surplus of one's own production is casually exchanged for that of the foreigner is only the *first occurrence* of the product as exchange value in general and is determined by accidental needs, desires, etc. But if it continues, if it becomes a continual act that contains in itself the means for its constant renewal, then—outwardly equally fortuitously—the regulation of reciprocal exchange through the regulation of reciprocal production gradually sets in, and the production costs, which in the final analysis are all reducible to labour time, would thus become the measure of exchange. This shows us how exchange and the exchange value of commodities evolve.

The circumstances in which a relationship is first encountered, however, never show us this relationship either in its purity or in its totality. A product posited as exchange value is essentially no longer determined as a simple product. It is posited in a form distinct from its natural qualities. It is posited as a *relationship,* a general relationship, not to one commodity but to every commodity, to every possible product. It therefore expresses a general relationship, the product that relates itself to itself as the realisation of a *definite quantity* of general labour, of social labour time, and to that extent it is equivalent to every other product in the ratio expressed in its exchange value. Exchange value presupposes social labour as the substance of all products, quite apart from their natural characteristics. Nothing can express a relationship unless it relates itself to a particular thing; and nothing can express a general relationship unless it relates itself to something general. Since labour is movement, time is its natural measure. BARTER in its crudest form presupposes labour as the substance and labour time as the measure of commodities; and this becomes evident as soon as barter becomes regularised, continuous, and if it is to contain in itself the reciprocal conditions for its renewal.

The commodity is *exchange value* only in so far as it is expressed in something else, in other words, as a ratio. A bushel of wheat is worth so many bushels of rye; in this case, the wheat is exchange value in so far as it is expressed in rye, and rye is exchange value in so far as it is expressed in wheat. If either of these two products is related only to itself, it is not exchange value. Now, to the extent to which money appears as measure, it is itself expressed not as a ratio, not as exchange value, but as a natural quantity of a certain material, a natural part by weight of gold or silver. In general, the commodity in which the exchange value of another is expressed, is never expressed as exchange value, never as a ratio, but as a particular quantity in its natural state. If 1 bushel of wheat is worth 3 bushels of rye, only the bushel of wheat is expressed as value, not the bushel of rye. Admittedly, the other is posited *in itself* as well; 1 bushel of rye then $= 1/3$ bushel of wheat; but this is not [I-43] *posited,* it is only a second ratio that is indeed directly implicit in the first. When one commodity is expressed in another, the first is treated as a ratio, and the second as a simple quantity of a particular material. 3 bushels of rye are in themselves not a value, but the rye occupying a definite amount of space, as measured by a standard of volume.

The same is true of money as a measure, as the unit in which the exchange values of the other commodities are measured. It is a certain weight of the natural substance in which it is represented, gold, silver, etc. If 1 bushel of wheat is priced at 77s. 7d., it is expressed as another thing to which it is equal, as 1 ounce of gold, as a ratio, as exchange value. But 1 ounce of gold in itself is not exchange value; is not expressed as exchange value, but as a definite quantity of itself, of its natural substance, of gold. If 1 bushel of wheat is priced at 77s. 7d. or 1 ounce of gold, this may represent a greater or smaller value, for 1 ounce of gold will rise or fall in value in proportion to the quantity of labour required for its production. But this is immaterial for its pricing as such, since its price of 77s. 7d. expresses exactly the ratio in which it is an equivalent for all other commodities, can buy them. The particular level of price, whether 77s. or 1,780s. the quarter, falls outside pricing in general, i.e. outside the positing of wheat as price. It has a price, whether it costs 100s. or 1s. The price of wheat merely expresses its exchange value in a unit common to all commodities, and therefore assumes that this exchange value is already settled by other relations.

Gold and wheat bear no relationship whatever to each other as natural objects; as *such,* they do not measure one another, are *indifferent* to one another. That 1 quarter of wheat has the price of 1 ounce of gold is established, because the ounce of gold in its turn is considered in relation to the labour time necessary for its production. Both wheat and gold are therefore considered in relation to a third thing, labour, and are equated in this ratio. The two are therefore compared with one another as exchange values. But this only shows us how the price of wheat is found, the quantity of gold with which it is equated. In this relationship itself, where money appears as the price of wheat, money itself is not posited as a ratio, as exchange value, but as a definite quantity of a natural material.

In exchange value, commodities (products) are posited as ratios of their social substance, of labour; but as prices they are expressed in quantities of other products in their natural properties. To be sure, it may be said that the price of money is also posited as 1 quarter of wheat, 3 quarters of rye, and all the other quantities of different commodities whose price is 1 ounce of gold. But then, in order to express the price of money, the whole range of commodities would have to be enumerated, each in the quantity in which it is equal to 1 ounce of gold. Hence money would have as many prices as there are commodities whose price it itself expresses. The chief characteristic of price, *uniformity*, would be missing. No commodity would express the price of money because none would express its relationship to all other commodities, its general exchange value. But the specific feature of price is to express exchange value itself in its generality and yet in a particular commodity. But even that is immaterial. In so far as money appears as the material in which the price of all commodities is expressed, measured, money itself is posited as a definite quantity of gold, silver, etc., in short of its natural material; a simple quantity of a particular material, not itself as exchange value, as ratio. Thus every commodity in which another is expressed as price, is not itself *posited* as exchange value but as a simple quantity of itself.

In the determination of money as the unit of exchange values, as their measure, their general basis of comparison, the natural material of money—gold, silver—appears esssential, since as the price of the commodity it is not exchange value, not a ratio, but a definite weight of gold or silver, e.g. one pound, with its subdivisions; and thus money does indeed appear originally as a pound, *aes grave.*ª It is precisely this which distinguishes price from exchange value, and we have seen that exchange value necessarily leads to pricing. Hence the folly of those who wish to make labour time as such into money, i.e. to posit and not to posit the distinction between price and exchange value.

Money as measure, as element of pricing, as the unit of measurement of exchange values, therefore displays the phenomenon (1) that it is only necessary as a notional unit, once the exchange value of an ounce of gold has been determined for any one commodity; that its actual presence and hence even more the quantity in which it is present is superfluous; the AMOUNT in which it exists in a country is irrelevant to its role as an indicator (INDICATOR of value); it is necessary only as a unit of reckoning; (2) that while it need be posited only notionally, and is in fact only notionally attached *to* the commodity as its price, it simultaneously provides the basis of comparison, the unit, the measure, as a simple quantity of the natural substance in which it represents itself, a definite weight of gold, silver, etc., adopted as unit. Exchange values (commodities) are conceptually transformed into certain units of weight of gold or silver, and posited in thought as equal to, as expressing, this imagined quantity of gold, etc.

[I-44] If we now consider money in its second determination, as

---

ª Pound weight.— *Ed.*

means of exchange and realiser of prices, we have found that it must be present in a definite *quantity*; that a particular amount of the weight of gold or silver posited as the unit is necessary to fulfil this role adequately. If the sum of prices to be realised is given, on the one hand, this depending upon the price of a particular commodity multiplied by its quantity, and the velocity of money circulation, on the other, then a certain quantity of means of circulation is required. But if we now consider more closely the original form, the immediate form in which circulation is represented, *C—M—M—C*, money appears in it purely as a means of exchange. The commodity is exchanged for a commodity, and money appears merely as the means of this exchange. The price of the first commodity is realised in money, in order to realise with that money the price of the second commodity, and thus to obtain it in exchange for the first. After the price of the first commodity is realised, the person who has now obtained its price in money does not aim to receive the price of the second commodity. Rather, he pays its price to obtain the commodity. Basically, money has therefore served him only for the purpose of exchanging the first commodity for the second. As mere means of circulation, money has no other function. The man who has sold his commodity for money wishes to buy another commodity, and the person from whom he has bought uses the money to buy another commodity, etc.

In this determination of pure means of circulation, the function of money itself exists only in this circular movement which it effects by the fact that its quantity, its amount, is determined in advance. How many times it is itself contained in the commodities as a unit is determined in advance in their prices, and as the instrument of circulation it appears simply as the number of this presupposed unit. In so far as it realises the price of the commodities, the commodity is exchanged for its real equivalent in gold and silver; its exchange value is actually expressed in money as another commodity. But in so far as this process takes place merely to reconvert money into commodity, in other words, to exchange the first commodity for the second, money appears only fleetingly, and its substance consists only in its continual appearance in this fleeting form, as this bearer of mediation. Money as a means of circulation is *only* a means of circulation. To be able to serve in this role, its one essential attribute is that of the quantity (amount) in which it circulates. (Since the amount is determined also by the velocity of circulation, this requires no special mention at this point.) In so far as it realises price, its material existence as gold and silver is essential; but in so far as this realisation is merely fleeting and is to be transcended, it is of *no consequence*. It is a mere *semblance,* as if it were [only] a question of exchanging the commodity for gold or silver as a particular commodity: a semblance that vanishes, since the process is completed as soon as the gold and silver are exchanged once more for a commodity, and thereby commodity is exchanged for commodity. Gold and silver as mere means of circulation, or the means of circulation as gold and silver, are therefore indifferent to their qualities as particular natural commodities.

Assume that the total price of the commodities in circulation is 10,000 thaler. Their measure is then 1 thaler=x weight of silver. Now suppose that 100 thaler are needed to circulate these commodities in 6 hours, i.e. each thaler pays the price of 100 thaler in 6 hours. What is now essential is that 100 thaler, the amount 100 of the metallic unit, is available, which measures the total sum of commodity prices, 100 such units. That these units consist of silver is irrelevant to the process itself. This is already evident from the fact that 1 thaler in the cycle of circulation represents a quantity of silver 100 times greater than is really contained in it, although it represents only the weight of silver of 1 thaler in each particular act of exchange.

Taking the whole circulation, therefore, 1 thaler represents 100 thaler, a weight of silver 100 times greater than it actually contains. In fact, it is merely a *symbol* of the weight of silver contained in the 100 thaler. It realises a price 100 times that which it actually realises considered as a quantity of silver.

Suppose that the £ sterling e.g.=$^1/_3$ ounce of gold (in fact, it is worth less). In so far as the price of a commodity of £1 is paid, i.e. its price of £1 is realised, the commodity being exchanged for £1, it is crucial that the £ sterling should actually contain $^1/_3$ ounce of gold. If it were a counterfeit £ sterling, consisting of a base metal, a £ sterling only in appearance, the price of the commodity would not in fact be realised. For the price to be realised, it would have to be paid in as much base metal as=$^1/_3$ ounce of gold.

Considered in the context of this isolated aspect of circulation, it is accordingly essential that the money unit should actually represent a definite quantity of gold and silver. But it is a different matter if we consider the whole of circulation, circulation as a process in which the circle completes itself: $C—M—M—C$. In the first case, the realisation of the price would be merely a semblance: only *part* of the price would be realised. The price notionally attached to the commodity would not be obtained in reality. The commodity notionally taken as=so many units by weight of gold would not in actual exchange bring in this number of units by weight of gold. Yet if a counterfeit £ sterling took the place of a genuine one in circulation, it would perform in the whole circulation absolutely the same service as if it were genuine. If commodity *a* at a price of £1 is exchanged for a counterfeit pound, and this counterfeit pound is further exchanged for commodity *b* priced at £1 sterling, the counterfeit pound has performed absolutely the same service as if it [I-45] were a genuine £ sterling.

Hence in this process the real pound sterling is in fact merely a *symbol*, in so far as we are considering not the aspect in terms of which it realises the prices, but the whole of the process in which the pound sterling serves only as the means of circulation, and in which the realisation of prices is merely a *semblance*, a fleeting mediation. Here the pound [sterling] of gold serves merely to exchange commodity *a* for commodity *b* which has the same price. The actual realisation of the price of commodity *a* is here commodity *b*, and that of the price [of] *b* is the commodity *a* or *c* or *d*, which is the same thing so far as the form of the relationship is concerned, since the particular content of the commodity is quite immaterial for it. Commodities of equal price are exchanged. Instead of commodity *a* directly exchanging for commodity *b*, the price of commodity *a* is exchanged with commodity *b*, and the price of commodity *b* with commodity *a*.

Money accordingly represents in respect of the commodity only its price. Commodities are exchanged for one another at their price. The price of the commodity itself is the notional expression attached to it that it [the commodity] is the amount of a certain natural unit (unit of weight) of gold or silver, the material in which money is embodied. In money, or the realised price of the commodity, an actual number of this unit now confronts it. But in so far as the realisation of price is not the end, and we are not concerned to obtain the price of the commodity as price but as the price of another commodity, the material of which money is composed, e.g. gold or silver, is of no consequence. Money becomes the subject as instrument of circulation, as means of exchange, and the natural material in which it is represented appears as an ACCIDENT, whose significance vanishes in the act of exchange itself, because it is not in this material that the commodity exchanged for money is eventually to be realised, but in the material of the other commodity.

For in addition to the fact that in circulation money (1) realises prices; (2) circulates titles of ownership, we now also have the fact that (3) by means of circulation something happens which could not happen directly, namely, that the exchange value of the commodity is expressed in every other commodity. If 1 yard of linen costs 2 s., and 1 lb. of sugar costs 1 s., the yard of linen is realised in 2 lbs of sugar by means of the 2 s., and the sugar is therefore converted into the material of the linen's exchange value, into the material in which the linen's exchange value is realised.

As a mere means of circulation, in its determination in the process of circulation as a continuous flow, money is neither a measure of prices, for it is already posited as such in the prices themselves, nor is it a means for the realisation of prices, for as such it exists only in the one phase of circulation but vanishes in the totality of all its phases. It is rather the mere *representative* of price in relation to all commodities, and serves only as the means by which commodities are exchanged at equal prices. Money is exchanged for the one commodity because it is the general representative of its exchange value and as such the *representative* of every other commodity of the same exchange value, the general representative, and as such it is in circulation itself. It *represents* the price of the one commodity relative to all other commodities, or the price of all commodities relative to one commodity. In this respect it is not only the *representative* of commodity prices but *symbol* of itself, i.e. in the act of circulation itself, its material, gold and silver, is of no consequence.

It *is* price; it is a definite quantity of gold or silver. But in so far as the reality of price is here merely a fleeting one, destined constantly to disappear, to be transcended, not to be accepted as a definitive realisation but always only as an intermediate, mediating one; in so far as the purpose here is not the realisation of price at all, but the realisation of the exchange value of a particular commodity in the material of another commodity, the material of money itself is of no consequence, it disappears as the realisation of price, since the realisation itself vanishes. In so far as money is in this continuous movement, it is so only as the representative of exchange value, which becomes actual only by real exchange value continually taking the place of its representative, continually changing places with it, being continually exchanged for it.

In this process, therefore, its reality is not that it is price but that it *represents* price, that it is its representative. It is the objectively present representative of price, therefore of itself, and as such of the exchange value of commodities. As means of exchange it realises commodity prices only in order to posit the exchange value of one commodity in another as its unit, in order to realise its exchange value in the other commodity, i.e. to posit the other commodity as the material of its exchange value.

As such an objective symbol, therefore, money appears only in circulation. Withdrawn from circulation it becomes realised price again; but within the process, as we have seen, the quantity, the number of these objective symbols of the monetary unit is essentially determined. Hence, while in circulation, in which money appears as objectively confronting commodities, its material substance, its basis as a definite quantity of gold or silver, is without significance, its amount, on the contrary, is essentially determined since it is merely a *symbol* for a definite number of these units. In its determination as measure, in which it was introduced only notionally, its material basis was of essential significance but its quantity and its existence in general were of no consequence. From this it follows that money as gold and silver, in so far as it serves *merely* as means of circulation, means of exchange, can be replaced by any other *symbol* [I-46] that expresses a definite quantity of its unit. Hence symbolic money can replace real money because material money as mere means of exchange is itself symbolic.

These contradictory determinations of money as measure, as realiser of prices and as mere means of exchange, explain the otherwise inexplicable phenomenon that if metallic money, gold, silver, is *debased* by the admixture of a base metal, the money is depreciated and prices rise. This occurs because in this case the measure of prices is no longer the cost of production of, say, 1 ounce of gold but of the ounce [of the alloy], $2/3$ of which is copper, etc. (Debasements of the coinage, which consist merely in falsifying or altering the names of the fractional weight units of the precious metals, by calling e.g. the eighth part of an ounce 1 sovereign, leave the standard absolutely the same and alter only its name. If $1/4$ of an ounce was previously called 1 sovereign, and it is now $1/8$ of an ounce, the price of 1 sovereign now expresses only $1/8$ of an ounce of gold; hence ABOUT 2 sovereigns are necessary to express the same price as was earlier expressed by one.) In other words, if only a falsification of the name of the fractional parts of the precious metals has occurred, the standard remains the same, but the fractional part is expressed in twice as many francs, etc., as before. On the other hand, if the basis of money—gold or silver—is entirely abolished and replaced with paper bearing the symbol of a definite amount of real money, in the quantity

required by circulation, the paper circulates as currency at the full
value of the gold and silver. In the first case, [the rise in prices
occurs] because the means of circulation is simultaneously the
material of money as a measure and the material in which price is
definitively realised. In the second case, [no rise in prices occurs]
because money is functioning only in its determination as means
of circulation.

Example of clumsy confusion of the contradictory functions of
money:

"PRICE IS EXACTLY DETERMINED BY THE QUANTITY OF MONEY THERE IS TO BUY IT
WITH. ALL THE COMMODITIES IN THE WORLD CAN FETCH NO MORE THAN ALL THE MONEY
IN THE WORLD."

Firstly, pricing has nothing to do with actual sale; in it, money
only [serves] as measure. Secondly, all the commodities present in
circulation could FETCH a thousand times more MONEY than there is
in the WORLD, if each PIECE of money circulated a thousand times
(passage from the *London Weekly Dispatch,* 8 November [1857]).

Since the total sum of prices that are to be realised in circulation
changes with the price of commodities and the volume in which
they are put into circulation; since on the other hand the velocity
of the means of circulation present in each case is determined by
circumstances which are independent of it, the quantity of the
means of circulation must be able to change, to be enlarged and
contracted— *contraction and expansion of circulation.*

It can be said of money as mere means of circulation that it
ceases to be a commodity (a *particular* commodity) in that its
material is of no consequence, and it now only satisfies the
requirements of [the act of] exchange itself, no longer any other
immediate requirements. Gold and silver cease to be commodities
as soon as they circulate as money. On the other hand, it can be
said of money that it is *just commodity* (*general* commodity),
commodity in its pure form, indifferent to its particular natural
properties and hence to all immediate requirements, without
natural relationship to a particular need as such. The adherents of
the monetary system,[58] even some of those who adhere to the
system of protection (see e.g. F. L. A. Ferrier, p. 2 [59]) have clung
to the first aspect, and the modern economists to the second; e.g.
Say, who says that money is a "particular" commodity, treats it as
a commodity like any other.[a]

As means of exchange, money appears as the necessary
mediator between production and consumption. In a system of

_____

[a] J. B. Say, *Traité d'économie politique,* 3rd ed., Vol. II, Paris, 1817, pp. 460-
61.— *Ed.*

developed money relationships, one produces only in order to exchange, or one produces only by exchanging. Hence, if money were abolished, one would either be thrown back to a lower level of production (to which corresponds barter playing a marginal role in production), or one would progress to a higher level, where exchange value would no longer be the primary attribute of the commodity, because general labour, whose representative it is, would no longer appear only as socially mediated private labour.

The question whether money as means of circulation is productive or not is answered just as readily. According to Adam Smith, money is unproductive.[a] Yet Ferrier says e.g.:

"It creates *valeurs*,[b] since they would not exist without it" [F. L. A. Ferrier, *Du gouvernement considéré dans ses rapports avec le commerce*, Paris, 1805, p. 52]. One must not only "consider its *value* as metal, but just as much its *quality* as money" [op. cit., p. 18].

A. Smith is right in so far as money is not the instrument of some particular branch of production; Ferrier is right, [I-47] since it is inherent in general production based on exchange value to posit product and agent of production in the determination of money, and this implies a money distinct from the product; because the money relationship is itself a relationship of production, if production is considered in its totality.

In so far as $C—M—M—C$ is divided up into its two moments, although the *prices* of the commodities are implied (and this makes all the difference), circulation is divided up into two acts of direct barter. $C—M$: the exchange value of the commodity is expressed in another particular commodity, the material of money, as also that of money in the commodity; equally in $M—C$. To that extent, A. Smith is correct in saying that money as means of exchange is only a more complicated kind of BARTER.[c] But when the whole of the process is considered, not the two phases as independent acts, so that the commodity is realised in money and money is realised in the commodity, the opponents of A. Smith are correct in their contention that he misunderstood the nature of money and that money circulation supplants BARTER; since money merely serves to balance the "ARITHMETICAL DIVISION" which arises from the division of labour. These "ARITHMETICAL FIGURES" need no more be of gold or silver than measures of length (see Solly,

---

[a] A. Smith, *An Inquiry into the Nature and Causes of the Wealth of Nations*, Vol. II, London, 1836, pp. 271-85; Vol. III, London, 1839, pp. 70-106.— *Ed.*

[b] Values.— *Ed.*

[c] A. Smith, *An Inquiry into the Nature and Causes of the Wealth of Nations*, Book I, Chapter IV.— *Ed.*

[*The Present Distress, in relation to the Theory of Money*, London, 1830, pp. 5-6,] p. 20).
Commodities from being *marchandises* become *denrées*, pass into consumption. Money as a means of circulation does not. *So long as it retains its role of means of circulation, it does not cease at any point to be a commodity.*

We pass now to the third determination of money, which results directly from the second form of circulation: *M—C—C—M*. Here money appears not only as a *means*, nor as a *measure*, but as an end in itself, and hence leaves circulation, in the same way as the particular commodity which completes its circuit, and which has changed from *marchandise* to *denrée*.
First still to be noted that, given the determination of money as an immanent relation of general production based upon exchange value, its service as an instrument of production can now also be demonstrated in detail.

"The advantage of gold and silver stems from the fact that it replaces labour" (Lauderdale, [*Recherches sur la nature et l'origine de la richesse publique*, Paris, 1808, p. 140,] p. 11 [60]).
Without money a large number of *trocs*[a] is necessary to obtain in exchange the object one desires. Further, [without money,] it would be necessary to ascertain the relative value of the commodities in each particular exchange. The former necessity is obviated by money as instrument of exchange (instrument of trade); the latter, by money as measure of value and representative of all commodities (idem, [pp. 142, 140 and 144,] l.c.).

The opposite assertion, that money is *not* productive,[b] amounts only to saying that it is *unproductive* outside the role in which it is productive as measure, instrument of circulation and representative of values, that its quantity is productive only in so far as it is required to fulfil these determinations. It is true to say that money becomes not merely *unproductive* but *faux frais de production*[c] as soon as more of it is employed than is necessary for its productive role. But this is equally true of every other instrument of production or exchange, of machinery as much as of means of transport. But if by this is meant that money merely exchanges already existing real wealth, then this is wrong, for money likewise exchanges and purchases labour, productive activity itself, *potential* wealth.

---

[a] Acts of barter.— *Ed.*
[b] See this volume, p. 149.— *Ed.*
[c] Overhead costs of production.— *Ed.*

The *third determination* of money in its complete development presupposes the first two determinations and constitutes their unity. Money, then, has an independent existence outside circulation; it has stepped outside it. As a *particular* commodity, it can be converted from its form as money into that of objects of luxury, gold and silver ornaments (so long as the artistic labour involved is still very simple, e.g. as in the earlier periods of English history, silver money was continually converted into PLATE and vice versa. See *Taylor*[a]). Or it can be *accumulated* as money and so constitute a *hoarded treasure*. So far as money in its independent existence derives from circulation, it appears in circulation itself as the result of circulation; it closes its own circle by means of circulation. In this aspect, its role as *capital* is already latent. It is negated as mere means of exchange. Nevertheless, since historically it can be posited as measure before it appears as means of exchange, and can conversely appear as means of exchange before it is posited as measure—in the latter case it would exist only as a preferred *commodity**—it can also appear historically in its third determination before it has been posited in the two previous ones. But gold and silver can be accumulated as *money* only if they are already present in one of the two previous determinations, and in its third determination it can appear in a developed form only if it has already been developed in the earlier two. Otherwise, its accumulation is merely accumulation of gold and silver, not of money.

[I-48] (Mention as a particularly interesting example of this the *accumulation of copper money* in the earlier period of the Roman Republic.)

In so far as money as the *universal material representative of wealth* derives from circulation and as such is itself a *product of circulation,* which is simultaneously exchange to a higher degree and a *special* form of exchange, money is also in this third determination related to circulation. It is independent of circulation, but this independence is only circulation's own process. In the same measure as it leaves circulation, it re-enters it. Devoid of all relation to circulation, money would not be money but a simple natural object, gold or silver. In this determination money is as

* [II-8] "Since the dawn of civilisation people have fixed the exchange value of the products of their labour not by comparison with the *products offered in exchange* but by comparison with a certain preferred product" (Ganilh, [*Des systèmes d'économie politique*, Vol. II, Paris, 1809, pp. 64-65] 13a[61]). [II-8]

---

[a] J. Taylor, *A View of the Money System of England, from the Conquest*, London, 1828, pp. 18-19.— *Ed.*

much the premiss as the result of circulation. Its very independence is not a cessation of the relation to circulation, but a *negative* relation to it. This is inherent in the independence of money as a result of *M—C—C—M.*

Money as *capital* implies: (1) that money is as much a premiss of circulation as its result; (2) that its independence is therefore only a *negative* relation to circulation, but always a relation to it; (3) that it is itself posited as *instrument of production* in that circulation no longer appears in its initial simplicity, as quantitative exchange, but as process of production, as the real exchange of matter. And so money itself is determined as a particular moment of this production process. Production is concerned not merely with simple pricing, i.e. with translating the exchange value of commodities into a common unit, but with the creation of exchange values, hence with the creation of *what determines* prices as well, with the creation not merely of their form, but of their content. Hence, if in simple circulation money appears in general as productive, namely in so far as circulation in general is itself a moment of the system of production, as yet it has this determination only *for us*; it has not yet been *posited* in money. (4) Consequently, as capital, money is also posited as relating to itself by means of circulation—the *relation* of *interest and capital.* But here we are not yet concerned with this. We have simply to consider here how money in its third determination has emerged as *something independent* from circulation, or, more precisely, from its two earlier determinations.

("An increase of money [is] merely an increase in the *means of reckoning*" (Sismondi [*Études sur l'économie politique..* Vol. II, Brussels, 1838, p. 278]).

This is correct only in so far as money functions as mere means of exchange. In its other role its increase is also an increase in the *means of payment.*)

"Trade has detached the shadow from the body, and introduced the possibility of possessing them separately" (Sismondi [op. cit., p. 300]).

Thus money is now exchange value become independent (as such it always appears as *means of exchange* only ephemerally) in its general form. True, it possesses its own materiality or substance, gold and silver, and it is just this which gives it its independence, for what only exists as an aspect of something else, as a determination or relation of other things, is not independent. On the other hand, in this material independence as gold and silver, it represents not only the exchange value of one commodity relative to the other but exchange value relative to all commodities; and while it itself possesses a substance, it simultaneously appears in its particular existence as gold and silver as the general exchange value of the other commodities. On the one hand it is possessed as their exchange value; on the other they exist as just so many particular substances of the latter, so that it can be converted into each of these substances by means of exchange just as much as it is indifferent to and raised above their determinateness and particularity. They are thus merely fortuitous existences. It is the "*précis de toutes les choses*",[a] in which their particular character is wiped out; general wealth as concise compendium as against its spread and fragmentation in the world of commodities. While wealth appears in particular commodities as a feature of them, or they appear as a particular element of wealth, general wealth itself appears in gold and silver as concentrated in a particular material.

Every particular commodity, in so far as it is exchange value and has a price, itself expresses only a definite quantity of money in an incomplete form. For it must first be thrown into circulation to be realised, and because of its particularity, its realisation remains fortuitous. But in so far as the commodity is not posited as price, but in its natural quality, it is a moment of wealth only through its relation to a particular need which it satisfies, and expresses in this respect (1) only the wealth of use, (2) only one very special aspect of this wealth. Money, on the contrary, apart from its particular usefulness as a valuable commodity, is (1) realised price; (2) satisfies every need, in that it can be exchanged for the object of every need [and is] quite indifferent to every particularity. The commodity possesses this property only through the mediation of money. Money possesses it directly in relation to all commodities, therefore in relation to the whole world of wealth, to wealth as such. In money, general wealth is not only a form but at the same time the content itself. The concept of wealth is so to speak realised in a particular object, *individualised.* In the particular commodity, [II-1][b] so far as it is price, wealth is present only notionally, in a form which has not yet been realised; so far as it has a definite use value, it exhibits only one quite isolated aspect of it. In money, on the other hand, the price is realised, and the substance of money is wealth itself, both in its abstraction from its

---

[a] *Summary of all things*—paraphrase of Boisguillebert's expression *précis de toutes les denrées* from his "Dissertation sur la nature des richesses, de l'argent et des tributs", in *Économistes financiers du XVIIIe siècle*, p. 399.— *Ed.*

[b] Here page 1 of Notebook II begins. The notebook is headed: "The Chapter on Money (continued)." Written in the upper right-hand corner of the page are the words "Abundance, accumulation".— *Ed.*

particular modes of existence and in its totality.

Exchange value constitutes the substance of money, and exchange value is wealth. In another way, therefore, money is also the embodiment of wealth, as against all the particular substances of which wealth is composed. If, therefore, on the one hand, the form and content of wealth are identical in money considered in itself, on the other hand, money is, in contrast to all other commodities, the general form of wealth in relation to them, while the totality of these particularities constitutes its substance. If money in the first determination is wealth itself, in the second determination it is *its general material representative.* In money itself this totality exists as the imagined quintessence of all commodities. Wealth (exchange value as totality and also as abstraction) therefore exists, to the exclusion of all other commodities, individualised as such, as a particular tangible object, only in gold and silver. Money is therefore the god among commodities.

As an isolated tangible object, money can thus be fortuitously sought, found, stolen, discovered, and general wealth can be tangibly brought into the possession of the individual. From its state of servitude, in which it appears as mere means of circulation, money suddenly becomes the ruler and god in the world of commodities. It represents the celestial existence of commodities, while they represent its earthly existence. Every form of natural wealth, before it is replaced by exchange value, implies an essential relationship of the individual to the object, so that one side of him becomes objectified in the thing and his possession of the thing also appears as a particular development of his individuality: wealth in sheep as the development of the individual as shepherd, wealth in corn as his development as farmer, etc. *Money, on the contrary, as the individuality* of general wealth, itself emerging from circulation and merely representing the general, as *mere social result,* implies no individual relation at all to its owner. Its possession is not the development of any one of the essential aspects of his individuality, but rather possession of something devoid of individuality, for this social [relationship] exists at the same time as a tangible, external object, of which possession can be taken mechanically and which can similarly be lost.

Its relationship to the individual appears therefore as a purely fortuitous one; while this relationship to a thing quite unconnected with his individuality gives him at the same time, because of the thing's character, general domination over society, over the whole world of enjoyment, labour, etc. It is the same as if e.g. my discovery of a stone, quite independent of my individuality, were to procure me mastery over all fields of learning. The possession of money relates me to (social) wealth in very much the same way as that in which the philosopher's stone would relate me to all fields of learning.

Money is therefore not only *an* object of the quest for enrichment, it is *the* object of it. It is essentially *auri sacra fames*.[a] The quest for enrichment as such, as a particular form of impulse, i.e. as distinct from the quest for particular wealth, e.g. the quest for clothes, weapons, jewellery, women, wine, etc., becomes possible only when general wealth, wealth as such, has been individualised in a particular thing, i.e. when money has assumed its third determination. Money is therefore not only the object but at the same time the source of the quest for enrichment. Avarice is possible without money, but the quest for enrichment is itself the product of a definite social development, not a *natural*, in contrast to an *historical*, development. This explains the lamentations of the ancients about money as the source of all evil. The quest for pleasure in its general form and avarice are two particular forms of greed for money. The abstract quest for pleasure implies an object that can embody the possibility of all pleasures. The abstract quest for pleasure is realised by money in the determination in which it is the *material representative of wealth*; avarice is realised in so far as money is merely the general form of wealth as against commodities as its particular substances. To hoard money as such, the individual must sacrifice all relation to the objects that satisfy particular needs, he must abstain, in order to satisfy his need or greed for money as such. The greed for money or quest for enrichment is necessarily the downfall of the ancient communities. Hence the opposition to it. It itself is the *community*, and cannot tolerate any other standing above it. But this implies the full development of exchange value, hence of a social organisation corresponding to it.

In antiquity, exchange value was not the *nexus rerum*[62]; it appears as such only among the trading nations, but they had only a CARRYING TRADE and did not themselves produce. At least production was secondary among the Phoenicians, Carthaginians, etc. They could live in the interstices of the ancient world, like the Jews in Poland or in the Middle Ages. Rather, the ancient world was itself the precondition for the existence of such trading peoples. That is why they were ruined every time they came into serious conflict with the communities of antiquity.

---

[a] See footnote [b] on p. 100.— *Ed.*

Among the Romans, Greeks, etc., money appears at first ingenuously in its two initial determinations as measure and means of circulation, in neither in very developed forms. But as soon as their trade, etc., developed or, as with the Romans, conquest supplied money to them [II-2] in abundance—then, suddenly at a certain stage of their economic development, money necessarily appears in its third determination and, the more its development in that form proceeds, the more it appears as the downfall of their community. To act productively, money in its third determination must be, as we have seen, not merely the premiss but just as much the result of circulation. And as the premiss of circulation, it must be itself a moment of circulation, something posited by it. In the case of the Romans, for instance, where money was accumulated by the plunder of the whole world, this was not the case.

It is inherent in the very nature of money itself that it can exist as a developed element of production only where *wage labour* exists, and hence far from dissolving the social order, it is indeed a condition for its development and a driving force for the development of all productive forces, material and spiritual. Today an individual person can still acquire money fortuitously, and its possession can therefore have just as destructive an effect on him as it had on the ancient communities. But the very destruction of this individual in modern society is only the enrichment of the productive part of society. The owner of money in the ancient sense is destroyed by the industrial process which he serves willy-nilly. The destruction concerns only his person. As *material representative of general wealth*, as *individualised exchange value*, money must be the *immediate* object, aim and product of general labour, of the labour of all individuals. Labour must directly produce exchange value, i.e. money. It must therefore be *wage labour*.

The quest for enrichment, being the driving force of everyone, since everyone wishes to produce money, produces general wealth. Only thus can the general quest for enrichment become the source of general wealth, wealth which continually reproduces itself anew. In that labour is wage labour and its immediate purpose is money, general wealth is *posited* as its purpose and object. (*In this context the connection with the transformation of the ancient military system into a mercenary one to be discussed.*) Here, money as an end becomes the means to general industriousness. General wealth is produced in order to seize hold of its representative. In this way, the real sources of wealth are opened up.

Since the aim of labour is not a particular product that bears a particular relation to the particular needs of the individual, but money, wealth in its general form, the industriousness of the individual firstly has no limits. It is indifferent to its particularity and assumes any form that serves the aim; it is inventive in the creation of new objects for social need, etc. It is clear, therefore, that with wage labour as its basis, the effect of money is not destructive but productive; while the ancient community by its very nature was in contradiction to wage labour as its general basis. General industry is possible only where all labour produces general wealth, not a particular form of it; where, therefore, the wage of the individual is also money. Otherwise only particular forms of industry are possible. Exchange value as immediate product of labour is money as its immediate product. The immediate labour that produces exchange value as such is therefore wage labour. Where money is not itself the community, it must dissolve the community.

The ancients could purchase labour directly, a slave; but the slave could not buy money with his labour. An increase in money could make slaves dearer, but could not make their labour more productive. *Negro slavery*—a purely industrial form of slavery which in any case is incompatible with and disappears as a result of the development of bourgeois society— *implies* wage labour; if other, free, states with wage labour did not exist alongside slavery, but it were isolated, all social conditions in the Negro states would immediately revert to pre-civilised forms.

Money as individualised exchange value and thus as incarnate wealth has been sought in alchemy; so it was determined in the monetary system. The prehistory of the development of modern industrial society opens with a general greed for money, on the part of both individuals and states. The actual development of the sources of wealth proceeds, as it were, behind its back, as a means to get possession of the representative of wealth. Where money does not originate from circulation but is physically discovered— as in Spain—the nation is impoverished, while the nations which have to work to take it away from the Spaniards develop the sources of wealth and really enrich themselves. The discoveries, the finding of gold in new parts of the world, in new countries, play such a great role in the history of the revolution because colonisation is being improvised here, forced in hot-house fashion.[42]

The hunt for gold in all countries leads to their discovery; to the foundation of new states; first of all, to the expansion of the range of commodities which enter into circulation, creating new wants, and drawing remote parts of the world into the process of exchange and interchange of matter. In this respect, money as the general representative of wealth, as individualised exchange value, was therefore also a two-fold means of expanding wealth into universality and extending the dimensions of exchange to cover the whole earth; of first creating the real *universality* of exchange value in respect to material and space. But it is inherent in the determination of money discussed here that the illusion about its nature, i.e. the preoccupation with one of its determinations in its abstraction and the neglect of the contradictions contained in it, endows money—behind the back of individuals—with this really magical significance. It is in fact by means of this self-contradictory and hence illusory determination, through this abstraction, that money becomes so potent [II-3][a] an instrument in the real development of the forces of social production.

The elementary precondition for bourgeois society is that labour directly produces exchange value, in other words, money; and equally that thereupon money directly buys labour, hence buys the labourer only in so far as he himself sells his activity in exchange. Hence *wage labour* on the one hand, and *capital* on the other, are only different forms of developed exchange value and of money as its incarnation. Money is thus directly at once the *real community*, in so far as it is the general material of existence for all, and also the communal product of all. But, as we have seen, in money the community is also a mere abstraction, a mere external, accidental thing for the individual, and at the same time only a means for his satisfaction as an isolated individual. The community of antiquity implies quite a different relation of the individual in itself. Therefore it is shattered by the development of money in its third determination. Every production is an objectification of the individual. But in money (exchange value) the objectification of the individual is not that of himself in his natural character but that of himself posited in a social determination (relationship), which is at the same time external to him.

Money *posited* in the form of medium of circulation, is *coin*. As coin, it has lost its use value; its use value is coincident with its determination as means of circulation. E.g. it must first be melted down to be able to serve as money as such. It must be

---

[a] In the upper right-hand corner of this page Marx wrote: "*BARTER, SALE, COMMERCE*—three stages of exchange (Steuart)."— *Ed.*

demonetised. That is why in the form of coin, money is merely a *symbol* and indifferent to its material. But as coin, money also loses its universal character, taking on a national, local one. It is divided up into coinage of different sorts, according to the material of which it consists, gold, copper, silver, etc. It acquires a political title, and speaks, as it were, a different language in different countries. Finally, in the same country, it acquires different denominations, etc. Money in the third determination as *independently* emerging from and confronting circulation, therefore, negates also its character as coin. It reappears as gold and silver, whether it is melted down into it, or is only valued according to the number of units by weight of gold or silver it contains. It also loses its national character again and serves as means of exchange between nations, as universal means of exchange; no longer as *symbol*, however, but as a definite quantity of gold and silver. In the most developed system of international exchange, gold and silver therefore reappear in just the form in which they played a role already in primitive barter. Gold and silver, like exchange itself, as already mentioned, do not initially appear within the sphere of a social community but at the point at which it ends, at its boundaries; at its not very numerous points of contact with foreign communities. Gold and silver now appear posited as the *commodity* as such, the universal commodity which preserves its character as a commodity at all places. In this determination of its form money is uniformly valid in all places. Only in this way is money the material representative of *general* wealth. In the mercantile system, gold and silver are therefore regarded as the measure of the power of the various communities.

"As soon as the PRECIOUS METALS become OBJECTS OF COMMERCE, A UNIVERSAL EQUIVALENT FOR EVERYTHING, they also become the MEASURE OF POWER BETWEEN NATIONS. Hence the mercantile system" (Steuart [*An Inquiry into the Principles of Political Oeconomy*, Vol. I, p. 327]).

However much the modern economists consider themselves to have advanced beyond the mercantile system, in periods of general crises gold and silver figure in precisely this determination, in the year 1857[63] as much as in 1600. In this character, gold and silver [play] an important role in the creation of the world market. Hence the circulation of American silver from West to East; the metallic link between America and Europe, on the one hand, with Asia on the other, since the beginning of the modern epoch. In primitive communities this trade in gold and silver is only incidental, like exchange as a whole, related only to the surplus. But in developed trade, posited as a moment that is essentially

connected with the whole of production, etc. Money no longer
appears for the exchange of the surplus, but to balance the
surplus in the overall process of international commodity exchange. It is now coin only as *world coin*. But as such it is
essentially indifferent to its determination as form of the means of
circulation, whereas its material is the all-important thing. As
form, in this determination, gold and silver remain the ubiquitous
accessible commodity, the *commodity* as such.

(In this first section,[64] where exchange value, money and price
are considered, commodities always appear as already in existence.
The determination of form [is] simple. We know that they express
characteristics of social production, but the latter itself is their
presupposition. But they are *not posited* in this determination. And
so in fact the first exchange appears as an exchange of the
surplus, which does not embrace and condition the whole of
production. It is the *available* surplus of a total production which
is outside the world of exchange value. Even in a developed
society, this surplus still emerges on the surface as the immediately
existing world of commodities. Through itself, however, it points
beyond itself to economic relationships which are posited as
relations of production. The internal structure of production
therefore forms the second section; its culmination in the
State the third; the international relationship [of production] the
fourth; and as the conclusion, the world market, in which production
is posited as a totality and all its moments also, but in which
simultaneously all contradictions are set in motion. Hence the world
market is likewise both the presupposition of the totality and its
bearer. Crises are then the general pointer to beyond the
presupposition, and the urge to adopt a new historical form.)

"THE QUANTITY OF GOODS AND THE QUANTITY OF MONEY MAY REMAIN THE SAME,
AND PRICES MAY RISE OR FALL NOTWITHSTANDING" (namely through greater EXPENDI-
TURE by e.g. the MONIED CAPITALISTS, landlords, State officials, etc. Malthus,
[*Principles of Political Economy,* 2nd ed., London, 1836, p. 391] X, 43).[65]

[II-4] As we have seen, money in the form in which it
independently emerges from circulation and confronts it, is the
negation (negative unity) of its determination as means of
circulation and measure.*

* In so far as money is the means of circulation, "the quantity of it that
circulates" can "never be individually employed, it must always circulate" (Storch
[*Cours d'économie politique,* Vol. II, Paris, 1823, pp. 113-14]). The individual can use
money only by divesting himself of it, by positing it as *being for others,* in its social

We have already shown:

Firstly: Money is the negation of the means of circulation as such, of *coin*. But it at the same time includes it as its determination, negatively, since it can always be converted into coin; positively as *world coin*. But as such it is indifferent to its form determination, and is essentially *commodity* as such, ubiquitous commodity, not locally determined. This indifference expresses itself in two ways: *one*, it is now money only as gold and silver, and not as a *symbol* nor in the form of coinage. Hence the *façon*[a] put on money as coinage by the State has no value; only its metallic content gives value to the coin. Even in internal trade it has only a temporary, local value,

"because it is no more useful to him who possesses it than to him who possesses the commodities to be bought" [Storch, op. cit., p. 175].

The more domestic trade is conditioned on all sides by foreign trade, the more even the value of this *façon* disappears: it does not exist in private exchange but only appears as a tax. *Then,* as such a *general commodity,* as world coin, gold and silver do not have to return to their point of departure, circulation as such is not necessary at all. *Example*: Asia and Europe. Hence the lamentation of the adherents of the monetary system that money vanishes among the heathens, and does not return (see *Misselden*[b] ABOUT 1600). The more the external circulation is conditioned and comprehended by the domestic circulation, the more world coin as such enters into circulation (rotation). We are not yet concerned here with this higher stage, and it is not part of the simple relationship which we are considering here.

Secondly: Money is the negation of itself as simple realisation of the prices of commodities, where the particular commodity always

determination. This, as Storch correctly observes, is why the material of money "must not be indispensable for the existence of man", as are e.g. hides, salt, etc., which are used as money among many nations. For the quantity of it which is in circulation is lost to consumption. Hence, firstly, metals are generally preferred to other commodities as money, and, secondly, the precious metals to those which are useful as instruments of production. It is characteristic of the economists that Storch formulates it thus: the material of money must "have a direct value but based on a *besoin factice* [artificial need]". By *besoin factice* the economist means firstly: the *besoins* that arise from the *social* existence of the individual; secondly, those that are not a consequence of his bare existence as a natural object. This illustrates the desperate internal poverty that is the basis of bourgeois wealth and its science.

---

[a] Stamp.— *Ed.*

[b] [E. Misselden,] *Free Trade. Or, the Means to Make Trade Florish,* London, 1622, pp. 19-24.— *Ed.*

remains the essential factor. Rather, money becomes price realised in itself, and as such both the *material representative of wealth* and the *general form of wealth,* relative to all commodities as merely particular substances of wealth; but

Thirdly: Money is also negated in the determination in which it is merely the *measure* of exchange values. As the general form of wealth and as its material representative, money is no longer the notional measure of something else, of exchange values. For in its metallic existence it is itself the adequate reality of exchange value. The determination of measure must here be posited in money itself. It is its own unit; and the measure of its own value, its measure as wealth, as exchange value, is the quantity of itself which it represents. The multiple of a quantity of itself which serves as unit. As a measure, its amount was of no consequence; as a means of circulation, its substance, the material of which the unit is composed, was of no consequence; but as money in this third determination its own amount as a definite material quantity is essential. Given its quality as general wealth there is no further distinction in it other than the quantitative one. It represents a greater or lesser amount of general wealth, in the proportion in which a given unit of it is possessed in a greater or lesser number.

If it is general wealth, one is the richer the more of it one possesses, and the sole important process for both the individual and the nations is its *accumulation.* In accordance with its determination, it here performed the act of stepping out of circulation. Now this withdrawal from circulation and this *accumulation* of it appear as the essential object of the drive for enrichment and as the essential process of enrichment. In gold and silver I possess general wealth in its pure form, and the more of it I hoard up, the more general wealth I appropriate to myself. If gold and silver represent general wealth, then as certain quantities they represent it only to a certain degree, which is capable of being expanded indefinitely. This accumulation of gold and silver, which takes on the appearance as their repeated withdrawal from circulation, is simultaneously the safeguarding of general wealth against circulation, in which it continually gets lost in exchange for some particular wealth which eventually disappears in consumption.

Among all ancient peoples, the accumulation of gold and silver appears initially as a priestly and royal privilege, since only gods and kings are entitled to the god and king of commodities. Only they are worthy of possessing wealth as such. This accumulation then on the one hand merely for the exhibition of the surplus, i.e.

of wealth as something extraordinary, something only for Sundays; for gifts to the temple and its gods; for public works of art; finally as a *security* for cases of extraordinary emergency, for the purchase of arms, etc. Accumulation later becomes a matter of politics among the ancient peoples. The *State treasury* as reserve fund and the temple are the original banks, in which this holy of holies is preserved. Hoarding and accumulation [attains] its ultimate development in the modern banks, but in this case [II-5] with a more developed determination. On the other hand, with private persons, accumulation as a means of safeguarding wealth in its pure form against the vicissitudes of the external world, the form in which it can be *buried,* etc., in which, in short, it enters into a *very secret* relationship to the individual. This still occurs on a great historical scale in Asia. It is repeated in all PANICS, wars, etc., in bourgeois society, which then falls back into the condition of barbarism. Likewise the hoarding up of gold, etc., for ornaments and display among semi-barbaric peoples. But a very great and continually growing part of gold, etc., withdrawn from circulation as luxury objects in the most developed bourgeois society (see Jacob,[a] etc.).

The wealth of individuals is proved precisely by their retaining possession of it as the representative of general wealth, without yielding it up to circulation and employing it for particular needs. And in the same degree as money is developed in its different determinations, i.e. as wealth as such becomes the general yardstick of the worth of individuals, there develops the impulse to exhibit wealth and hence the DISPLAY of gold and silver as representatives of wealth, just as Herr von Rothschild displays as his chosen coat of arms, I believe, two banknotes of £100,000, each in its own frame. The barbaric display of gold, etc., is only a more naive form of this modern exhibition, in that it is less related to gold as money than to gold as something which simply *glitters.* In the modern display gold makes a reflected point, the point that gold is *not* being used as money; the antithetical form to circulation is the important thing here.

The accumulation of all other commodities less original than that of gold and silver:

(1) because of their perishability. Metals as such represent durability relative to other commodities. They are also eagerly accumulated because of their greater scarcity and their exceptional

[a] W. Jacob, *An Historical Inquiry into the Production and Consumption of the Precious Metals,* Vol. II, pp. 270-323.— *Ed.*

character as instruments of production *par excellence.* The precious metals, as they are not exposed to oxidisation in the atmosphere, etc., are even less perishable than the base metals. What other commodities lose is precisely their form; but it is their form which gives them exchange value, while their use value consists in the destruction of this form, in consumption. With money, on the contrary, its substance, its materiality, is the very form in which it represents wealth. If money appears as the commodity which is general everywhere, with respect to space, it now also becomes general in respect to time. It preserves itself as wealth at all times. It has specific durability. It is the treasure which neither moth nor rust doth corrupt.[a] All commodities are merely perishable money; money is the imperishable commodity. Money is the ubiquitous commodity; the commodity is only local money. But accumulation is essentially a process which goes on in time. On this aspect *Petty* writes [66]:

"The great and ultimate effect of trade is not wealth at large, but particularly abundance of silver, gold, and jewels, which are not *perishable,* nor so *mutable* as other Commodities, but are wealth at all times, and in all places; whereas abundance of wine, corn, fowls, flesh, etc., are riches but *hic et nunc,*[b] so as the raising of such commodities, and the following of such trade, which does store the country with gold and silver, is profitable before others" ([W. Petty, *Several Essays in Political Arithmetick,* London, 1699, pp. 178-79] p. 3). "Suppose that money by way of tax be taken from one who spends the same in superfluous eating and drinking and delivered to another who employs the same in improving of land, in fishing, in working of mines, in manufacture or in the purchase of clothes; then the Commonwealth has an advantage, because even clothes do not altogether perish as soon as meats and drinks. But if the same be spent in furniture of houses, the advantage is yet a little more; if in building of houses, yet more; if in improving of lands, working of mines, fishing, yet more; but most of all, in bringing gold and silver into the country, because those things are not only *not perishable,* but are esteemed for wealth at all times, and everywhere" ([ibid., pp. 195-96] p. 5).

Thus an author of the 17th century. One can see how the conception of gold and silver as the material representative and general form of wealth supplied the real stimulus to their accumulation. The cult of money has its corresponding asceticism, its renunciation, its self-sacrifice—thrift and frugality, contempt for the worldly, temporary and transient pleasures; the pursuit of *eternal* treasure. Hence the connection of English Puritanism or also Dutch Protestantism with money-making. A writer at the beginning of the 17th century (*Misselden*) expressed the matter quite ingenuously in this way:

---

[a] Matthew 6:20.— *Ed.*
[b] Here and now.— *Ed.*

"The natural matter of commerce is merchandise, the artificial is money. Money, though it be in nature and time after merchandise, yet forasmuch as it is now in use, become the chief." He compares this to the two [grand]sons of the old Jacob, who laid his right hand upon the younger and his left hand upon the older[a] ([E. Misselden, *Free Trade. Or the Meanes to Make Trade Florish*, p. 7] p. 24).

"We consume among us a great abundance of the wines of Spain, of France, of the Rhine, of the Levant, and of the Isles; the raisins of Spain, the corinths of the Levant, the cambrics of Hannault[b] and the Netherlands, the silks of Italy, the sugars and tobacco of the West Indies, the spices of the East Indies; all which are of no necessity unto us and yet are bought with *ready* money... If it [a commonwealth] vented fewer of the foreign [commodities], and more of the native, the residue must needs return in gold and silver, as treasure" (l.c. [pp. 12, 13]).

The modern economists naturally make fun of such remarks in the general section of their treatises. But if we consider the anxiety expressed in the theory of money in particular, and the feverish anxiety with which the inflow and outflow of gold and silver are watched over in practice in times of crises, we see that to regard money in the determination in which the adherents of the monetary and mercantile system conceived of it with naive one-sidedness is still quite justified, not merely in thought but as a real economic category.

[II-6] This contrast between the actual needs of production and the supremacy of money is most strikingly depicted by *Boisguillebert* (see the striking passages excerpted in my Notebook [67]).

(2) Apart from the perishability of other commodities, their accumulation differs in two essential respects from that of gold and silver, which are here identical with money. For one, the hoarding up of other commodities does not possess the character of a hoarding up of wealth in general, but of a particular wealth, and is therefore itself a particular act of production, where simple accumulation is not sufficient. Special appliances, etc., are required for the storage of grain; the accumulation of sheep does not automatically produce a herdsman; of slaves or land requires master-servant relationships, etc. All this, therefore, requires actions and certain conditions different from simple accumulation, from the augmentation as such of wealth. Secondly, if I now wish to realise the stored-up goods as general wealth, to appropriate to myself wealth in all its particular forms, I must carry on trade with the particular commodities that I have accumulated, I must become a corn dealer, cattle dealer, etc. Money as the *general* representative of wealth relieves me of this.

The ACCUMULATION of gold and silver, of money, is the first

---

[a] Genesis 48:1, 8-20.— *Ed.*
[b] A province of the former Spanish Netherlands (now part of Belgium).— *Ed.*

historical appearance of the accumulation of capital and the first great means for this. But as such it is not the accumulation of capital. For that, the re-entry of the accumulated money into circulation itself would have to be posited as a regular feature and means of accumulation.

Money in its final perfected determination now appears in all respects as a contradiction which resolves itself, which drives itself to its own resolution. As the *general form of wealth,* it is confronted by the whole world of real riches. It is their pure abstraction— hence comprehended as such, it is mere imagination. Where wealth appears to exist as such in a quite material, tangible form, it has its existence merely in my mind, is a sheer figment of the imagination. Midas. On the other hand, as the *material representative of general wealth,* money is realised only when it is thrown back into circulation and vanishes in procuring the individual particular forms of wealth. It remains in circulation as the means of circulation; but it is lost to the accumulating individual, and this disappearance is the only possible way in which it can be secured as wealth. The dissolution of the stored-up wealth into individual enjoyments is its realisation. It can now be amassed once more by other individuals, but then the same process commences anew. I can really posit its being for myself only by giving it up as mere being for others. If I want to hold on to it, it evaporates in my hand into a mere phantom of real wealth.

Furthermore, the idea of the augmentation of money by means of its accumulation, the idea that its own quantity is the measure of its value, again proves a delusion. If the other riches are not accumulated it loses its value in the measure in which it is accumulated. What appears as its augmentation is in fact its diminution. Its independence is only a semblance; its independence of circulation exists only in relation to circulation, as dependence on it.

It pretends to be the general commodity, but because of its natural particularity it is again a particular commodity, whose value both depends on demand and supply and changes with its specific production costs. And since it is itself incarnated in gold and silver, it becomes one-sided in any actual form; so that when the one appears as money the other appears as particular commodity, and vice versa, and thus each appears in both determinations.

As absolutely secure wealth quite independent of my individuality, it is simultaneously quite external to me; it is absolutely insecure wealth, which any accidental event can separate from me.

The same is true of the quite contradictory determination of money as measure, as means of circulation, and as money as such. Finally, in the last determination it contradicts itself in yet another way, because it is supposed to represent value as such; but in fact it represents only an identical quantity of variable value. It therefore transcends itself as *perfected* exchange value.

As mere measure, money is already negated in itself as means of circulation; as means of circulation and measure it is negated in itself as money. Its negation in the last determination is thus at the same time its negation in the other two. Negated as mere *general form of wealth*, it must therefore be realised in the particular substances of real wealth; but in actually proving itself as the *material representative* of the totality of wealth, it must at the same time preserve itself as the general form. Its entry into circulation must itself be an element of its staying with itself, and its staying with itself must be an entry into circulation. That is to say, as realised exchange value it must also be posited as process in which exchange value is realised. It is at the same time the negation of itself as a purely objective form, a form of wealth which is external and fortuitous for the individuals. It must appear, rather, as the production of wealth, and this as the result of the relations of individuals to one another in production.

In other words, exchange value is now determined no longer as a simple object, for which circulation is only an external movement, or which exists individually in a particular material, but as a process, as its self-relation by means of the process of circulation. On the other hand, circulation itself is no longer merely the simple process of the exchange of commodities for money and of money for commodities, no longer the mere mediating movement that takes place in order to realise the prices of the different commodities, to equate them as exchange values for one another, where both appear external to circulation: the presumed exchange value, the final withdrawal of the commodity into consumption, and hence the annihilation of exchange value on the one hand; and on the other, the withdrawal of money, which makes it independent of its substance, and which is again another form of its annihilation.

Exchange value itself, and now no longer [II-7] exchange value in general but measured exchange value, must, as a presupposition, appear as posited by circulation and, as posited by it, preposited to it. The process of circulation must appear also as the process of the production of exchange values. It is thus, on the one hand, the return of exchange value into labour, and, on the other hand, of money into exchange value; which, however, is now posited in a more profound determination. In circulation, the *definite* price is assumed, and it is only formally posited by circulation as money. The *definiteness* of exchange value itself, or the measure of price, must now itself appear as brought about by circulation. Posited in this way, exchange value is *capital,* and circulation is simultaneously posited as an act of production.

Omission: In circulation, as it appears as circulation of money, the coincidence in time of both sides of the exchange is always assumed. But a time gap can occur in between the availability of the commodities to be exchanged. It can be the nature of the reciprocal services rendered that one service is performed today but the reciprocal service can be performed only a year later, etc.

"In the majority of contracts," says Senior, "only one of the contracting parties has the thing at its disposal and loans it; and if exchange is to take place, one must transfer it at once under the condition of receiving the equivalent only at a later time. Since the value of all things varies in a given period of time, one takes as means of payment the thing whose value varies least, which over the longest period maintains a given average capacity to purchase things. So money becomes the *expression or representative* of value" [N. W. Senior, *Principes fondamentaux de l'économie politique,* Paris, 1836, pp. 116, 117].

According to that, the latter determination of money is in no way connected with its earlier ones. But that is wrong. It is only when money is established as an independent representative of value, that contracts are no longer estimated in e.g. quantities of grain or in services to be performed. (The latter prevails e.g. in feudalism.) It is only a notion of Mr. Senior that money possesses a "long-term average capacity" to maintain its value. THE FACT is that it is made the general material of contracts (*general commodity of contracts,* says Bailey[a]) as *general commodity, representative of general wealth* (says Storch[b]), *exchange value made independent.* Money must already be highly developed in its first two determinations to appear generally in its third. Now, it turns out in fact that the value of money can vary even though its quantity remains uniformly the same; that altogether, as a definite quantity, money is subject to the variability of all values. Here its nature as a particular commodity asserts itself over its general determination. [Money] as measure is indifferent to changes in its value, for

---

[a] [S. Bailey,] *Money and Its Vicissitudes in Value,* London, 1837, p. 3.— *Ed.*
[b] H. Storch, *Cours d'économie politique,* Vol. II, p. 135.— *Ed.*

"in a variable medium, two different relations to that medium can be expressed as well as in a constant".[a]

As means of circulation it is also indifferent to changes in its value, for its quantity as such is posited by the measure. But as *money,* as it appears in contracts, it is affected [by such changes], just as, in general, its contradictions come to the fore in this determination.

To be inserted in particular sections:

(1) *Money as coin.* Coinage can be dealt with very summarily here. (2) An historical survey of the sources of supply of gold and silver. Their discoveries, etc. The history of their production. (3) Causes of VARIATIONS in the value of the precious metals and thus of metallic currency; effects of these changes on industry and the different classes. (4) *Above all* the QUANTITY of money in circulation in relation to the rise and fall of prices. (16th century; 19th century.) In this connection also to be examined how money is affected as a measure by increases in its QUANTITY, etc. (5) On circulation: velocity, necessary quantity, the effect of circulation; more, or less, developed circulation, etc. (6) The dissolving effect of money.

(*This to be inserted.*) (Include here the specifically economic investigations.)

(The specific gravity of gold and silver, its containing much weight in a relatively small volume, AS COMPARED WITH OTHER METALS, recurs in the world of value, where gold and silver contain great value (labour time) in a relatively small volume. The labour time realised in it, its exchange value, is the specific gravity of the commodity. This makes the precious metals especially suitable for use in circulation (since one can carry a considerable portion of value in one's pocket) and for accumulation, since a large value can be securely kept and stored up in a small space. Gold does [not] change while it is being accumulated, unlike iron, lead, etc. It remains what it is.)

"If Spain had never possessed the mines of Mexico and Peru, it would never have needed the corn of Poland" (Ravenstone [*Thoughts on the Funding System, and Its Effects,* London, 1824, p. 20]).

"Illi unum consilium habent et virtutem et potestatem suam bestiae tradunt. Et ne quis posset emere aut vendere, nisi qui habet characterem aut nomen bestiae, aut numerum nominis ejus" (*Apocalypse. Vulgata*).[b]

---

[a] This passage is a summary of the relevant arguments from Samuel Bailey's book, *Money and Its Vicissitudes in Value* (pp. 9-10).— *Ed.*

[b] "These have one mind, and shall give their power and strength unto the beast ... and that no man might buy or sell, save he that had the mark, or the name of the beast, or the number of his name" (Revelation 17:13, 13:17).— *Ed.*

"The correlative quantities of commodities that one gives up for one another, constitute the price of commodities" (Storch [*Cours d'économie politique*, Vol. I, p. 72]).
"Price is the *degré de la valeur échangeable*[a]" (l.c. [p. 73]).

As we have seen, in simple circulation as such (in exchange value in its movement), the action of individuals upon one another is in content only the reciprocal self-interested satisfaction of their needs; in its form, it is exchange, positing things as equal to each other (equivalents). Hence property, too, is still posited here only as the appropriation of the product of labour by labour, and of the product of someone else's labour by one's own labour, in so far as the product of one's own labour is bought by someone else's labour. Property in someone else's labour is acquired through the equivalent of one's own labour. This form of property—just like freedom and equality—is posited in this simple relationship. In the course of the further development of exchange value, this will be transformed, and ultimately it will appear that the private property in the product of one's own labour is identical with the separation of labour and property; as a result, one's labour will create someone else's property and property will command someone else's labour.

---

[a] Degree of exchange value.— *Ed.*

[III. CHAPTER ON CAPITAL[68]]

[Section One]

[THE PROCESS OF PRODUCTION OF CAPITAL]

[II-8] Chapter on Money as Capital

[TRANSFORMATION OF MONEY INTO CAPITAL]

What makes the comprehension of money in its fully developed character as money especially difficult—difficulties from which political economy seeks to escape by neglecting one of the aspects of money in favour of another, and when confronted by the one appealing to the other—is that here a social relationship, a specific relationship of individuals to one another, appears as a metal, a stone, a purely corporeal object outside individuals, something which is found as such in nature, and in which not a single aspect of its form remains to be distinguished from its natural existence. Gold and silver are not money in and for themselves. Nature no more produces money than it produces a rate of exchange or bankers. In Peru and Mexico, gold and silver were not used as money, although they can be found as jewelry and a developed system of production existed there. To be money is not a natural property of gold and silver, and is therefore entirely unknown to the physicist, chemist, etc., as such. But money is directly gold and silver. Considered as a measure, its specific form still predominates; still more as coin, where this also appears externally in the stamp on the face of the coin. But in the third determination of money, i.e. in its perfected form, in which to be measure and coin appears as merely a function of money, all specificity of form has disappeared, or it coincides directly with its metallic existence. It does not at all appear on its face that it has acquired the function of money as the mere result of the social process; it *is* money.

This is the more difficult to understand since the immediate use value of precious metal for the living individual bears no relation at all to this role, and altogether, in its role as incarnation of pure exchange value, the recollection of its use value as distinct from exchange value is completely extinguished. Consequently, the basic contradiction contained in exchange value and in the corresponding social mode of production here stands out in its purest form. The attempts to abolish this contradiction by divesting money of its metallic form and postulating it as something also externally *posited* by society, as the expression of a social relationship of which the ultimate form would be labour money, have already been criticised above[a]. It must be quite clear by now that this is mere folly so long as the basis of exchange value is maintained; and, even more, that the illusion that metallic money perverts exchange arises from a complete ignorance of the nature of money. On the other hand, it is also clear that, as the opposition to the dominant relations of production grows, and as these relations themselves push ever more insistently towards casting off the old skin, the polemic turns against metallic money or money in general as the most striking, most contradictory and harshest aspect in which the system tangibly confronts us. Contradictions, of which money is merely the palpable manifestation, are then to be transcended by means of all kinds of artificial monetary manipulations. It is no less clear that many revolutionary operations with money can be carried out, in so far as an attack on it appears only to rectify it while leaving everything else unchanged. We then beat the sack on the donkey's back, while aiming at the donkey. But so long as the donkey does not feel the blows, one actually beats only the sack, not the donkey; contrariwise, if he does feel the blows, we are beating him and not the sack. As long as the operations are directed against money as such, it is simply an attack upon the effects, while the causes remain operative; in other words, a disturbance of the productive process which the solid basis [of the process] has the strength to take and to master—by a more or less violent reaction to it—as a merely temporary *disturbance.*

On the other hand, in so far as the monetary relationship has hitherto been developed in its pure form, and without reference to more highly developed relations of production, it is inherent in its role that, in monetary relationships simply conceived, all immanent contradictions in bourgeois society appear to be extinguished. Bourgeois democracy therefore falls back on this in its apologetics for existing economic relationships. Bourgeois economists are less inclined to do so (they are at least consistent enough to go back to even simpler determination of exchange value and exchange).

Indeed, in so far as the commodity or labour is now only

---

[a] See this volume, pp. 64-67.— *Ed.*

determined as exchange value, and the relationship of the different commodities to one another is now only determined as the mutual exchange—the equating—of these exchange values, the individuals—the subjects between whom this process takes place—are only and simply determined as exchangers. There is absolutely no difference between them, so far as their specific form is concerned, and this is the economic role, the role in which they stand in a commercial relationship to each other; it is the indicator of their social function or social relationship to one another. Each of the subjects is an exchanger, i.e. each has the same social relationship to the other as the other has to him. As subjects of exchange, their relation is therefore that of *equality*. It is impossible to find any trace of a difference, let alone of a conflict between them, not even a distinction. Furthermore, the commodities which they exchange are, as exchange values, equivalents or at least count as such. (They could only make subjective mistakes in their valuation of each other's commodity; and if one individual were to cheat the other, this would *not be because of the nature of the social function in which they confront each other*, for this is *the same*; in this they are *equal*; but only because of the natural cunning, the arts of persuasion, etc., in short because of the purely individual superiority of the one individual over the other. The difference would be a natural one, having nothing to do with the nature of the relationship as such, and which, as further analysis will show, will even be weakened by competition, etc., and robbed of its original force.)

Considering the pure form, the economic aspect of the relationship, there emerge only three formally distinct moments. (The content outside this form here really does not concern political economy; or it is posited as a natural content distinct from the economic; and it can be said to be completely distinct from the economic relationship, because it still directly coincides with it.[69]) These three moments are: the subjects of the relationship, the *exchangers,* posited in the same role; the objects of their exchange, exchange values, *equivalents,* [II-9] which not only are equal but are explicitly supposed to be equal, and are posited as equal; finally, the act of exchange itself, the mediation by which the subjects are posited precisely as exchangers, equals, and their objects as equivalents, as equal. The equivalents are the objectification of the one subject for the others, i.e. they themselves are of equal worth and prove themselves in the act of exchange as of equal value and at the same time as indifferent to one another. The subjects exist for one another in exchange only through the equivalents, as individuals of equal value, and prove themselves as such by the exchange of the objectivity in which the one exists for the others. Since they only exist for one another in this way, as individuals of equal value, as possessors of equivalents who prove this equivalence in exchange, they are both equivalent and at the same time indifferent to one another. Any other individual difference between them does not concern them; they are indifferent to all other properties they may individually possess.

The act of exchange is both the positing and the confirmation of exchange values as well as of the subjects as exchangers. The content falling outside the act of exchange, outside the specific economic form, can only consist of: (1) the natural particularity of the commodities exchanged; (2) the particular natural need of the exchangers. Or, combining both aspects, the different use value of the commodities to be exchanged. So far from compromising the social equality of individuals, this content of exchange, which lies wholly outside the specifically economic form, turns their natural difference into the basis of their social equality. If individual A had the same need as individual B, and had realised his labour in the same object as individual B, no relation at all would exist between them. From the viewpoint of production, they would not be different individuals at all. Both of them must breathe; for both of them the air exists as the atmosphere; but this does not bring them into any social contact. As individuals who must breathe, they are related to one another not as persons but only as natural bodies. Only the difference of their needs and their production is the occasion for exchange and for their being socially equated in it. Hence this natural difference is the precondition of their social equality in the act of exchange and of this relationship in general, in which they relate to each other as productive agents. Regarded in the light of this natural difference, individual A exists as the possessor of a use value for B, and B exists as the possessor of a use value for A. In this respect their natural difference again places them in the relationship of mutual equality. However, this does not make them indifferent to one another, but integrate with one another, they need each other, so that individual B, objectified in his commodity, is needed by A and vice versa. Accordingly, they stand not merely in a relation of equality to one another, but also in a social relation.

More: the fact that the need of the one individual can be satisfied by the product of the other and vice versa, and that the one is able to produce the object for the other's need, and that each confronts the other as possessor of the object of the other's need, shows that as a *human being* each transcends his own particular needs, etc., that they are behaving towards each other as men, that their common species being is known by all. This is unique. Elephants do not produce for tigers, or animals for other animals. A swarm of bees, for instance, *au fond* constitutes only one bee, and all the bees produce the same thing.

Moreover, in so far as this natural difference between individuals and their commodities[a] constitutes the motivation for their integration, for their social relationship as exchangers, in which they are *presupposed* as and *prove* themselves to be equals, *freedom* comes to play a role in addition to equality. Although individual *A* may feel a need for the commodity of individual *B,* he does not seize it by force, or vice versa; *A* and *B* recognise each other as owners, as persons, whose commodities are permeated by their will. Accordingly, the juridical concept of the person comes in here, as well as that of freedom in so far as it is contained therein. Neither forcibly takes possession of the property of the other; each disposes of it voluntarily.

But this is not all. Individual *A* satisfies individual *B*'s need by means of the commodity *a* only to the extent that and because individual *B* satisfies individual *A*'s need by means of commodity *b,* and vice versa. Each serves the other in order to serve himself; and makes reciprocal use of the other as his means. Each individual is now conscious that (1) each attains his end only in so far as he serves the other as means; (2) each becomes a means for the other (being for another) only as end for himself (being for himself); (3) this reciprocity whereby each is at once means and end, and moreover attains his end only in so far as he becomes means, and only becomes means in so far as he posits himself as end for himself, in other words that each posits himself as being for another in so far as he is being for himself, and the other as being for him in so far as he is being for himself—that this reciprocity is a necessary FACT, presupposed as a natural condition of exchange, but that it is as such a matter of indifference for each of the two subjects of exchange, and is of interest to each of them

---

[a] Here Marx inserted the following passage in brackets: "Products, labour, etc., are not at all differentiated here yet[70] but exist only in the form of commodities or, as Mr. Bastiat, echoing Say, wishes to put it, *services*[71]; Bastiat imagines that by reducing the economic role of exchange value to its natural content, commodity or service, thereby showing himself unable to grasp the economic relationship of exchange value as such, he has made a great advance over the classical economists of the English school, who are able to grasp the relations of production as such in their specific characteristics, in their pure form."— *Ed.*

only in so far as it satisfies his own interest as excluding that of the other, without relation to it.

This means that the social interest which appears as the motive of the act as a whole, is certainly recognised as a FACT on both sides, but as such it is not the motive, but goes on, as it were, merely behind the back of the self-reflected[72] particular interests, behind the back of an individual's interest in contrast to that of the other. In this latter respect, the individual can at most have the consoling awareness that the satisfaction of his individual interest as opposed to that of the other is precisely the realisation of the transcended [II-10] antithesis, of the general social interest. From the act of exchange itself, the individual, each of them, is reflected in himself as the exclusive and dominant (determining) subject of the exchange. With that the complete freedom of the individual is posited: voluntary transaction; force on neither side; positing of oneself as means, or as serving, only as a means to posit oneself as end in oneself, as the dominating and transcending element; ultimately realising the selfish interest, not an interest standing above it. The other party to the exchange is also recognised and known as likewise realising his own selfish interest, so that both know that the social interest is nothing but the exchange of the selfish interest in its duality, many-sidedness and autonomy. The general interest is nothing but the generality of selfish interests.

Thus, if the economic form, exchange, in every respect posits the equality of the subjects, the content, the material, both individual and objective, which impels them to exchange, posits *freedom*. Hence equality and freedom are not only respected in exchange which is based on exchange values, but the exchange of exchange values is the real productive basis of all *equality* and *freedom*. As pure ideas, equality and freedom are merely idealised expressions of this exchange; developed in juridical, political and social relations, they are merely this basis at a higher level. And indeed this has been confirmed by history. Equality and freedom at the higher level are the exact opposite of freedom and equality in the ancient world, which were not based on developed exchange value, but which on the contrary perished through its development. They presuppose relations of production not yet realised in the ancient world, nor indeed in the Middle Ages. Direct forced labour was the foundation of the ancient world; it was on this existing basis that the community rested. Labour itself regarded as a privilege, as still particularised, not labour generally producing exchange values, was the foundation of the Middle

Ages. [Modern] labour is neither forced labour, nor, as in the second case, is it carried on with reference to something common, as something higher (corporations).

Admittedly, it is true that [the relationship of] the exchangers is also based on a certain coercion when considered from the viewpoint of their motive for carrying on exchange, i.e. their natural needs, which fall outside the economic process. But on the one hand, this relationship itself is merely the indifference of the other for my need as such, for my natural individuality; in other words, his equality with me and his freedom, which is, however, just as much the precondition of mine. On the other hand, in so far as I am conditioned, forced by my needs, it is merely my own nature as a totality of needs and impulses (or, posited in a general, reflected form, my *interest*) that does violence to me, not something alien. But it is after all also precisely this aspect of me with which I coerce the other, driving him into the system of exchange.

In Roman Law the *servus* is therefore correctly defined as one who can acquire nothing for himself by means of exchange (see *Institutiones*[73]). It is therefore clear that this *law*, although it corresponds to a state of society in which exchange was by no means developed, nevertheless, in as much as it was developed in a certain sphere, could evolve *the definitions of the legal person, i.e. the individual engaged in exchange*, and could thus (at least in basic principle) anticipate the legal system of industrial society. Above all, it could be upheld as the law of emerging bourgeois society as against the Middle Ages. It is significant that its development coincides exactly with the dissolution of the Roman community.

Since exchange value is only realised in money, and the system of exchange value has only been realised with the rise of a developed money system or conversely, the money system can in fact only be the realisation of this system of freedom and equality. As a measure, money merely gives a definite expression to the equivalent. It turns it into the equivalent also in form. In the process of circulation, it is true, a distinction in form arises: the two parties to the exchange appear in the distinct roles of buyer and seller; exchange value appears first as general in the form of money, then as particular in the natural commodity, which now has a price. However, firstly, these forms alternate; circulation itself does not establish inequality, but is an equalisation, a transcendence of the merely imagined difference. The inequality is purely formal. Finally, equality is established quite objectively in money when in circulation, appearing now in the hands of one person, now in the hands of another, and quite indifferent to where it appears. In the process of exchange, each party appears to the other as the possessor of money, as money itself. Hence the indifference and equivalence gain explicit existence in the form of the object. The particular natural difference that characterised the commodity is extinguished and is continually being extinguished by means of circulation. A worker who buys a commodity for 3s. appears to the seller in the same function, in the same equality, in the form of 3s., as the king who buys this commodity. All difference between them is extinguished. The seller qua seller appears only as the possessor of a commodity priced at 3s., so that both [buyer and seller] are perfectly equal, except that the 3s. exist once in the form of silver, the other time in the form of sugar, etc.

In the third form of money, it might appear that the subjects of the process play different roles. But in so far as money here appears as material, as the universal commodity of contracts, all distinction between the parties to the contract is in fact extinguished. In as much as money becomes the object of accumulation, the subject here [II-11] appears only to withdraw money, the universal form of wealth, from circulation, in so far as he does not withdraw from it commodities for the same price. If, therefore, one individual accumulates while the other does not, neither does so at the expense of the other. The one enjoys real wealth, the other gains possession of the universal form of wealth. If one becomes impoverished while the other enriches himself, it is by their own free will and in no way the result of economic conditions, of the economic relation in which they stand to one another. Even inheritance and similar juridical relationships, which perpetuate inequalities arising in this manner, do not impair this natural freedom and equality. If the original relationship of individual A is not in contradiction with this system, such a contradiction certainly cannot be created by individual B taking the place of individual A, thus perpetuating him. Rather, inheritance makes the social determination valid beyond the natural length of [human] life; it reinforces the social determination against the casual impact of nature, whose effect as such would indeed be tantamount to the transcendence of the freedom of the individual. Besides, since the individual in this relationship is merely the individuation of money, he is as such just as immortal as money, and his representation by his heirs is nothing but the realisation of this role.

If this way of looking at the matter is not emphasised in its historical significance, but held up in refutation of the more highly developed economic relationships in which individuals emerge no longer as mere exchangers or buyers and sellers but in specific relationships to one another, in which they no longer all have the same character—this would amount to the assertion that no difference exists between natural bodies, still less antagonism and contradiction, because they are e.g. all heavy and consequently equal in so far as defined by having weight; or that they are equal because they are all spatially three-dimensional. Also exchange value itself is here taken in its simple character as against its more developed antagonistic forms. Seen as part of the process of science these abstract roles appear as the first and most rudimentary. To some extent this is how they occur in history; what is more highly developed appears later. In the totality of existing bourgeois society, this postulation as price and its circulation, etc., appears as the superficial process, below which, in the depths, quite other processes occur in which the apparent equality and freedom of individuals disappear.

On the one hand, it is forgotten that right from the start the *premiss* of exchange value as the objective basis of the whole system of production already implies coercion of the individual, that his immediate product is not a product for himself but *becomes* such only in the social process, and *is obliged* to adopt this general and nevertheless exterior form. It is forgotten that the individual no longer exists except as a producer of exchange value. This implies the complete negation of his natural existence; hence he is wholly determined by society. It is forgotten, moreover, that this also presupposes division of labour, etc., in which the individual is already placed in relationships other than those of mere *exchangers,* etc. It is forgotten that, consequently, the premiss [of the individual as producer of exchange value] in no way arises either from the individual's will or his immediate nature, but is *historical,* and already assumes the individual as *determined* by society.

On the other hand, it is forgotten that the higher forms in which exchange or the relations of production realised in exchange now appear, certainly do not remain in this simple determinateness, where the greatest difference which develops is formal and hence insignificant.

Finally, it is overlooked that the antagonism of wages [a] and capital, etc., is already latent in the simple determination of

---

[a] The use of the word *Arbeitslohn* (wages for labour) instead of *Lohnarbeit* (wage labour) may be a slip of the pen.— *Ed.*

exchange value and money. What this wise approach therefore
amounts to is a refusal to advance beyond the simplest economic
relationships. Conceived of in isolation these are pure abstractions;
but in reality they are mediated by means of the most profound
contradictions, and present an aspect in which the expression of
these contradictions is blurred.

On the other hand, this also shows the folly of those socialists
(especially the French socialists, who wish to prove socialism to be
the realisation of the ideas of *bourgeois* society enunciated by the
French Revolution) who purport to demonstrate that exchange,
exchange value, etc., were *originally* (in time) or are *essentially* (in
their adequate form) a system of the freedom and equality of all,
but have been perverted by money, capital, etc. Or alternately,
that history has so far failed in its attempts to realise exchange and
exchange value in their real essence, and that now the socialists,
e.g. Proudhon, have discovered the genuine recipe which will
substitute the true history of these relationships for the false. The
answer to them is as follows: exchange value or, more precisely,
the money system, is indeed the system of freedom and equality,
and what disturbs them in the more recent development of the
system are disturbances immanent to the system, i.e. the very
realisation of *equality and freedom,* which turn out to be inequality
and unfreedom. It is an aspiration as pious as it is stupid to wish
that exchange value would not develop into capital, or that labour
which produces exchange value would not develop into wage
labour. What distinguishes these gentlemen from the bourgeois
apologists is, on the one hand, their awareness of the contradictions inherent in the system and, on the other, their utopianism,
manifest in their failure to grasp the inevitable difference between
the real and ideal shape of bourgeois society, and the consequent
desire to undertake the superfluous task of changing the ideal
expression itself back into reality, whereas it is in fact merely the
photographic image [Lichtbild] of this reality.

[II-12] Now behold, in opposition to these socialists, the vapid
arguments of the degenerate political economy of the most recent
times,[a] claiming to *prove* that economic relationships always
express the *same* simple determinations and hence always express

---

[a] Here Marx inserted the following passage in brackets: "Whose classical
representative, as regards tediousness, affectation of dialectics, philistine conceit,
silly, self-satisfied triviality, and complete inability to conceive of historical
processes, is *Frederick Bastiat,* for the American *Carey* at least brings out the
particular American situation as against the European."—*Ed.*

the equality and freedom of the simply determined exchange of exchange values, which amounts to nothing but infantile abstraction. For example: the relationship of capital and interest is reduced to the exchange of exchange values. No sooner is it admitted on the basis of experience that exchange value not only exists in this simple determinateness but also in the essentially different one as capital, than capital is reduced once more to the simple concept of exchange value; and, what is more, interest, which expresses a definite relationship of capital as such, is likewise divested of its specific form and equated to exchange value. The entire relationship in its specific form is turned into an abstraction and reduced to the undeveloped relationship of the exchange of commodity for commodity. If I abstract from that which distinguishes something concrete from its abstract form it [the result] is naturally the abstract and [turns out to be] in no way different from it. *According to this procedure, all economic categories are only various names given to one and the same relationship, and this crude inability to grasp the real differences between them is then supposed to represent pure* COMMON SENSE *as such. Hence the "economic harmonies" of Mr. Bastiat amount au fond to asserting that only a single economic relationship exists which adopts different names, or that difference can occur only in nomenclature.* His reductionism is not even formally scientific in the sense that everything is reduced to one real economic relationship ignoring the difference inherent in development. He merely ignores now one aspect, now another, so as to bring out now one side of the identity, now another.

For example, the wages for labour are said to be payment for the service which one individual renders to another. (Here, as already pointed out above, the economic form as such is ignored.) Profit is also defined as the payment for the service which one individual renders to another. Consequently, wages for labour and profit are identical, and it is really an aberration of language which leads us to call one payment "wages" and the other "profit". But now for profit and interest. In profit, the payment for service is exposed to risk; in interest, it is fixed. Hence, since in wages payment is relatively fixed, while in profit, in contrast to labour, it is exposed to risk, the relationship between interest and profit is the same as that between wages and profit, which, as we have seen, is a reciprocal exchange of equivalents. The opponents [of Bastiat][74] then take these trivialities literally (which arise because they go back from economic relationships in which the conflict is explicit to those in which it is still merely latent and obscured) and purport to prove that, e.g. with capital and interest, there is not a simple exchange, in that capital is not replaced by an equivalent, but that after the owner has consumed 20 times the equivalent in the form of interest, he still has it in the form of capital and can exchange it again for 20 new equivalents. Thus we get the unedifying debate in which one side asserts that there is no difference between developed and undeveloped exchange value, while the other asserts that such a difference unfortunately does exist, but in all fairness should not.

Money as capital is a determination of money that goes beyond its simple determination as money. It can be considered as a higher form of realisation just as it might be said that man is a developed ape. In this case, however, the lower form is taken as the transcending subject and set above the higher form. In any case, *money as capital* is distinct from *money as money.* We must analyse the new determination. On the other hand, *capital as money* appears to be the retrogression of capital into a lower form. But it is only the positing of capital in a particular form which as non-capital already exists prior to it, and constitutes one of its presuppositions. Money recurs in all later relationships, but then it no longer functions as mere money. If, as at this point, our first task is to follow its development up to its totality as money market, the rest of the development is presupposed, and must be brought into the argument from time to time. Thus, we consider here the general determination of capital before we go on to discuss its particular form as money.

If, like e.g. Say, I define capital as a *sum of values,*[a] I am saying nothing more than that *capital= exchange value.* Every sum of values is an exchange value, and every exchange value is a sum of values. I cannot get from exchange value to capital by simple addition. As we have seen, the mere accumulation of money does not yet imply the relationship of capitalisation.

In what is called retail trade, the daily commerce of bourgeois life, as it is carried on directly between producers and consumers, in petty trade, the aim is the exchange of the commodity for money on the one hand and the exchange of money for a commodity on the other, for the satisfaction of individual needs. And it is only in this movement, which takes place on the surface of the bourgeois world, that the movement of exchange values,

---

[a] J. B. Say, *Traité d'économie politique,* 3rd ed., Vol. II, pp. 428 and 478.— *Ed.*

their circulation, proceeds in its pure form. A worker who buys a loaf of bread, and a millionaire who does the same, appear in this transaction merely as simple purchasers, just as the shopkeeper appears to confront them merely as a seller. Here all their other characteristics are extinguished. The *content* as well as the *volume* of their purchases appear completely irrelevant [II-13] to this specific form.

In theory, the concept of value is antecedent to that of capital but, on the other hand, its pure development presupposes a mode of production based on capital. The same is true in practice. For this reason the economists necessarily view capital on the one hand as the creator and source of values, and on the other hand they presuppose value for the formation of capital and represent capital itself only as a sum of values in a particular function. The existence of value in its pure state and generality presupposes a mode of production in which the individual product has ceased to exist as such for the producer in general, and still more for the individual worker, and is nothing unless realised in circulation. For the person who produces an infinitesimal part of a yard of cotton, it is not a formal definition that it is value, exchange value. If he had not produced an exchange value, money, he would have produced nothing at all. Hence, this determination of value presupposes a given historical stage of the social mode of production and is itself a historical relationship arising out of that stage.

On the other hand, individual moments of the determination of value develop at earlier stages of society's historical process of production and appear as its result.

Within the system of bourgeois society, therefore, capital directly follows upon value. *Historically, it is preceded by other systems* which constitute the material basis for the less complete development of value. Just as exchange value here only figures incidentally alongside use value, not capital but the relation of landed property appears as the real basis. Modern landed property, by contrast, cannot be understood at all [in this context], because its existence presupposes that of capital, and historically it does in fact develop as the earlier historical version of landed property turned by capital into a form adequate to itself. Thus the development of landed property is particularly suitable for the study of the gradual victory and establishment of capital. That is why Ricardo, the economist of the modern era, with a fine sense of history chose to examine the relations of capital, wage labour and ground rent within the boundaries of landed property, in order to describe them in their specific form. The relationship of the industrial capitalist to the landlord appears to lie outside the sphere of landed property. But as the relationship of the modern farmer to the recipient of rent, it appears immanent in landed property itself, and the latter now appears to exist only in relation to capital. In fact, the history of landed property, demonstrating the gradual transformation of the feudal landlord into the recipient of rent, of the hereditary, half-tributary and often unfree tenant into the modern farmer, and of the serf and villein tied to the soil and subjected to labour-services into the agricultural day-labourer, would be the history of the formation of modern capital. It would include the relationship [of landed property] to urban capital, trade, etc. But here we are concerned with bourgeois society as it has become, developing on its own basis.

In the first instance capital emerges from circulation, and money is its point of departure. We have seen[a] that money entering into circulation, and at the same time returning from circulation into itself, is the ultimate form of money, in which money is transcended. It is simultaneously the first concept of capital and the first form in which capital appears. Money has negated itself as something merely absorbed in circulation; but it has likewise negated itself as something independently confronting circulation. This negation, taken as a whole, in its positive aspects, contains the first elements of capital. Money is the first form in which capital appears as such. *M—C—C—M*; the exchange of money for the commodity and of the commodity for money; *this movement of buying in order to sell, which constitutes the specific form of trade, capital as merchant capital,* is found in the earliest periods of economic development. It is the first movement in which exchange value as such forms the content of the exchange, is not only form but its own content. This movement can take place within peoples and between peoples for whose production exchange value has by no means yet become the prerequisite. The movement only touches the surplus of their output, which is still directed towards the satisfaction of their immediate needs, and takes place only on the boundary of production. Special trading peoples could play this mediating role between peoples whose mode of production did not yet presuppose exchange value as its basis. Thus in antiquity, and later the Lombards, thus the Jews within the old Polish society or in medieval society in general.

Commercial capital is merely circulating capital, and circulating capital is the first form of capital, a form in which it *has by no means yet become the basis of production.* A more developed form of capital is *money capital and monetary interest,* usury, whose independent appearance likewise belongs to an early stage of development. Finally, the initial appearance of merchant capital presupposes the form, *C—M—M—C,* in which money and circulation in general appear as mere means for the *circulating commodity,* which for its part leaves circulation again and directly satisfies needs. The preconditions appear to be distributed among different peoples, or within society commercial capital as such is conditioned only by this circulation directed purely towards consumption. On the other hand, the *circulating commodity,* the commodity that is realised only by adopting the form of another commodity which drops out of circulation and satisfies immediate [II-14] needs, is also an original form of capital, which is essentially *commodity capital.*

On the other side, it is equally clear that the simple movement of exchange values, as it is present in pure circulation, can never realise capital. It can lead to the withdrawal and hoarding of money, but as soon as money enters into circulation again it is dissolved in a series of exchange processes with commodities, which are consumed. It is therefore lost once its purchasing power has been exhausted. Equally, the commodity that has been exchanged for a commodity by means of money, drops out of circulation to be consumed, destroyed. But if it is made independent of circulation as money, it now represents only the non-substantial general form of wealth. Since equivalents are exchanged for one another, the form of wealth which is fixed as money disappears as soon as that money is exchanged for the commodity, and the use value existing in that commodity disappears as soon as the commodity is exchanged for money. By means of the simple act of exchange, each can only be lost in its determination for the other when it is realised in the other. Neither can maintain itself in its own determination by transforming itself into the other. The sophistries of the bourgeois economists, who whitewash capital by purporting to reduce it to pure exchange, have therefore been countered by the demand—no less sophistical but justified against them—*really* to reduce capital to pure exchange, whereby it would disappear as a [social] power and be destroyed either in the form of commodity or money.*

---

* Just as exchange value, i.e. all relations of commodities as exchange values, appears as a thing in *money,* so in *capital* all determinations of the activity producing exchange values, *labour,* [appear as a thing].

The repetition of the process from both points, money or commodity, is not implied in the conditions of exchange itself. The act can only be repeated until it is completed, i.e. until there has been exchange up to the amount of the exchange value. It cannot rekindle itself. *Circulation therefore does not contain in itself the principle of self-renewal. Its moments are presupposed in it,* not posited by it itself. New commodities must continually be thrown into it from without, like fuel into fire. Otherwise it goes out in indifference. It would be extinguished in money as the indifferent result. For in so far as it no longer related to commodities, prices, circulation, money would cease to be money and to express a relationship of production; it would now continue to exist only as a metal but not economically. Circulation therefore, which appears as that which is immediately present on the surface of bourgeois society, exists only in so far as it is continually mediated. Considered in itself, it is the mediation of presumed extremes. But it does not posit these extremes. Hence it must itself be mediated not only in each of its moments but as the totality of mediation, as a total process. Its immediate being is therefore pure semblance. *It is the image of a process occurring behind it.*

Circulation is now negated in each of its moments—as commodity—as money—and as relation between them, as simple exchange and as circulation of both commodity and money. If originally the act of social production appeared as the positing of exchange values and this, in its further development, appeared as circulation—as the fully developed reciprocal movement of exchange values—then circulation itself now goes back into the activity that posits or produces exchange values. It goes back into it as into its ground. Commodities (whether in their particular form or in the general form of money) are the premiss of circulation, and these are the realisation of a definite labour time, and as such are values. Circulation therefore presupposes both the production of commodities by labour as well as their production as exchange values. This is its point of departure and by its own movement it returns into the production which creates exchange values as its result.

Once again, therefore, we have arrived back at the point of departure: *production* which creates, which posits, exchange values. But now it *presupposes circulation as a developed moment* and appears as a constant process positing circulation and continually returning from circulation back into itself, in order to posit it anew. Hence the movement which posits exchange values now appears in a much more complex form, in that it is no longer only the movement of the presupposed exchange values or the movement which formally posits them as prices, but the movement which simultaneously creates, produces, exchange values as its own premiss. Production itself is here no longer present before its results, is no longer presupposed, but appears as something which itself simultaneously produces these results. But it no longer produces these results as merely leading to circulation, as at the first stage, but as simultaneously presupposing circulation, developed circulation, in its process. (*Au fond,* circulation only consists in the formal process of positing exchange value, now in the determination of commodity, now in that of money.)

This movement appears in different forms, both historically as giving rise to labour which produces value and also, on the other hand, within the system of bourgeois production itself, i.e. production which posits exchange values. In the case of barbarian or semi-barbarian peoples, the trading peoples at first act as intermediaries; or else tribes whose production is different in character due to natural conditions enter into contact with each other and exchange their surplus. The first case is the more classical form. Let us therefore stick to it. The exchange of surpluses is a relation which posits exchange and exchange value, but it extends only to the surplus and plays a secondary role vis-à-vis [II-15] production itself. But with the more frequent return of the traders soliciting exchange (the Lombards, Normans, etc., play this role in relation to almost all European peoples), a continuing trade is developed. In this trade the producing people now only carries on a so-called *passive* trade, in that the stimulus to the activity positing exchange value is an external one, not the internal form of its production. When this happens, the surplus product must not be a fortuitous one, only occasionally available, but must be continually reproduced. In this way domestic production itself acquires a tendency to be directed towards circulation, towards the positing of exchange values.

At first the effect is mainly material. The range of needs is enlarged; the aim is the satisfaction of new needs, and therefore greater regularity in and expansion of production. The organisation of domestic production itself has already been modified by circulation and exchange value; but it has not yet been captured by them either over its entire surface or in its full depth. This is what is called the *civilising effect* of foreign trade. To what extent the activity positing exchange value captures production as a whole then depends partly upon the intensity of this external influence, partly upon the degree to which the elements of domestic production—division of labour, etc.—have already been developed. Thus in England in the 16th century and at the beginning of the 17th, the importation of commodities from the Netherlands gave a decisive significance to the surplus of wool that England had to offer in exchange. In order to produce more wool, arable land was converted into sheep pastures, the small leaseholding system was broken up, etc., the CLEARING of ESTATES took place, etc.

Agriculture therefore lost the character of labour for use value, and the exchange of its surplus lost its character of indifference towards the internal structure of agriculture. At certain points, agriculture was exclusively determined by circulation, transformed into a production positing exchange value. Not only was the mode of production changed thereby, but all the former conditions of population and production, all the economic relations corresponding to that mode, were dissolved. Thus, here we have a case of circulation which originally presupposed a production creating exchange values only as a surplus; but this production gave way to one purely oriented towards circulation, a production whose exclusive content was the positing of exchange values.

On the other hand, in modern production, which presupposes exchange value and developed circulation, prices and production determine each other.

If it is said that capital "is accumulated (realised) labour (properly *objectified* labour) which serves as the means for new labour (production)",[a] then only the simple substance of capital is being considered, and its formal character, without which it is not capital, is ignored. It means no more than that capital is—an instrument of production, for, in the broadest sense, everything must first be appropriated by means of some kind of activity, even an object supplied purely by nature, e.g. stones, before it can serve as an instrument, a means of production. According to this, capital would have existed in all forms of society, would be something entirely unhistorical. According to this, every part of the body is capital, for each part has not only to be developed by activity, by labour, but must also be nourished, reproduced, in order to be active as an organ. The arm and especially the hand are capital according to this. Capital would only be a new name for something as old as mankind, for each type of labour, even the most undeveloped, like hunting, fishing, etc., presupposes that the

---

[a] Cf. D. Ricardo, *On the Principles of Political Economy, and Taxation*, pp. 327 and 499.— *Ed.*

product of previous labour is used as a means for immediate, living, labour.

A further implication of the definition given above is that the physical matter of the products is wholly abstracted from, and previous labour itself is considered as their only content (matter). Also abstracted from is the particular special purpose for whose fulfilment this product is intended to serve as means, and only production in general is posited as purpose. All this would appear merely as the work of abstraction, which is equally valid for all social conditions, and which only takes the analysis further and formulates it more abstractly (generally) than was usually the case.

If we abstract in this way from the specific form of capital, and emphasise only its *content with respect to which it is a necessary moment of all labour*, then of course *nothing is easier than to prove that capital is a necessary condition for all human production*. We have only to abstract from the specific characteristics of capital which make it into a moment of a particularly developed *historical* stage of human production. The irony is that if all capital is objectified labour which serves as means for new production, not all the objectified labour that serves as means for new production is capital. *Capital is conceived of as a thing, not as a relationship.*

If it is said on the other hand that capital is a sum of values employed for the production of values, then this means: capital is self-reproducing exchange value. But formally exchange value also reproduces itself in simple circulation. In this explanation, admittedly, the form is grasped wherein exchange value is the point of departure, but the relation to content (which in the case of capital, unlike in that of simple exchange value, is *not irrelevant*) is dropped.

If it is said that capital is exchange value which produces a profit, or at least is employed with the intention of producing a profit, capital is already presupposed for its own explanation, for profit is a definite relationship of capital to itself. Capital is not a simple relationship but a *process,* always remaining capital in its various moments. This process must therefore be analysed.

There is already something surreptitious about defining capital as *accumulated* labour, for [II-16] in its essential characteristic it should be merely *objectified* labour, though this admittedly embodies an already accumulated definite quantity of labour. But accumulated labour itself already comprises a quantity of objects in which labour is realised.

"In the beginning everyone was satisfied, since only objects without value to the respective exchangers were exchanged; no importance was attached to this exchange, and each was satisfied to get a useful object in exchange for a useless one. But when the division of labour had made ... everyone into a merchant and society into a commercial society, no one wished to part with one's products except in exchange for their equivalent; it was therefore necessary, in order to determine this equivalent, to know *the value* of what was being offered and what was received" (Ganilh, [*Des systèmes d'économie politique,* Vol. 2, Paris, 1809, pp. 11-12,] 12, b[75]).[a]

In other words, exchange did not remain at the stage of formally positing exchange values but necessarily went on to subject production itself to exchange value.

1. CIRCULATION AND EXCHANGE VALUE DERIVING FROM CIRCULATION AS A PREREQUISITE OF CAPITAL

In order to develop the concept of capital, we must begin not with labour but with value, or more precisely, with the exchange value already developed in the movement of circulation. It is just as impossible to pass directly from labour to capital as from the different races of men directly to the banker, or from nature to the steam-engine. We have seen that in money as such exchange value has already acquired a form independent of circulation, but only a negative, evanescent or illusory one when fixed. Money exists only in relation to circulation and as the possibility of entering into it; but it loses this determination as soon as it realises itself, and falls back into its two earlier determinations as measure of exchange values and as means of exchange. As soon as money is posited as exchange value which not merely makes itself independent of circulation but maintains itself inside it, it is no longer money, for money as such does not extend beyond the negative determination; it is *capital.*

It is an historical FACT that money is the first form in which exchange value proceeds to the character of capital, and that therefore the first *form* in which capital *appears* is confused with capital itself or is considered to be its only adequate form. And this fact, far from contradicting our analysis, actually confirms it. The first attribute of capital is this: that the exchange value deriving from circulation and thus presupposing it, maintains itself within it and by means of it; that it does not lose itself when it enters into circulation; that circulation is not the movement of its vanishing but rather the movement of its real self-positing as exchange value, its realisation as exchange value.

---

[a] Marx quotes partly in French and partly in German.— *Ed.*

It cannot be said that in simple circulation exchange value as such is realised. It is always realised only in the moment of its disappearance. If a commodity is exchanged for another commodity by means of money, its value-character disappears in the moment in which it is realised, and it steps outside the relation, becomes indifferent to it and is now only a direct object of need. If money is exchanged for a commodity, then this posits even the disappearance of the form of exchange as merely formal mediation to get hold of the natural material of the commodity. If a commodity is exchanged for money, the form of exchange value, exchange value posited as exchange value, money, persists only so long as it remains outside exchange, withdraws from it. Money is therefore a purely illusory, purely notional realisation in this form, in which the independence of exchange value palpably exists. Finally, if money is exchanged for money—the fourth form in which circulation can be analysed but *au fond* only the third form expressed in the form of exchange—there no longer appears even a formal distinction between the different things; DISTINCTION WITHOUT A DIFFERENCE; not only does exchange value disappear, but so does the formal movement of its disappearance. *Au fond,* these four specific forms of simple circulation can be reduced to two, which, however, coincide in themselves. The difference between them is a question of emphasis and depends on which of the two moments—money and commodity—is stressed, which of them is taken as the point of departure. Thus, money for commodity: the exchange value of the commodity disappears and is replaced by its material content (substance); commodity for money: its content (substance) disappears and is replaced by its form as exchange value. In the first case the form of exchange value is extinguished, in the second its substance; in both, therefore, its realisation is its disappearance.

Only in *capital* is exchange value posited as exchange value, because only there does it maintain itself in circulation, i.e. only there does it neither lose its substance, because it realises itself in ever different substances, in a totality of them; nor does it lose its specific form, because it maintains its identity with itself in each of the different substances. Hence it always remains both money and commodity. It is, at each instant, both of the moments which disappear into one another in the course of circulation. But it is this only because it is itself a constantly self-renewing circuit of exchanges. In this respect, too, the circulation of exchange value [in capital] is distinct from that of simple exchange values as such. This simple circulation is in fact circulation only from the standpoint of the observer, or circulation *in itself,* not circulation posited as such. Precisely because the substance of exchange value is a particular commodity, it is not the same exchange value which first becomes money and then commodity again; on the contrary, it is always different exchange values, different commodities, which confront money. Circulation, the circuit, consists merely of the simple repetition or alternation [II-17] of the determination of commodity and money, and not of the identity of the real point of departure and the point of return. Therefore, simple circulation as such where only money is the persistent moment, has been described as mere *circulation of money,* mere *turnover of money.*

"Capital values perpetuate themselves" (Say, [*Traité d'économie politique,* 3rd ed., Vol. II, p. 185,] 14 [76]).[a]

"Capital—permanent value" ("multiplying itself" is not yet relevant here) "which did not perish any more. This value tears itself away from the commodity which had created it; it remained equal to a metaphysical, insubstantial quality always in the possession of the same *husbandman"* (the precise term makes no difference: say "owner") "for whom it assumed different forms" (Sismondi, [*Nouveaux principes d'économie politique,* 2nd ed., Vol. I, Paris, 1827, p. 89,] VI [77]).

The immortality to which money aspired when it posited itself negatively as against, and withdrew from, circulation, is attained by capital, which maintains itself precisely by surrendering to circulation. As exchange value presupposed by or presupposing circulation and maintaining itself in it, capital is not only at each instant *ideally* each of the two moments contained in simple circulation, but alternately adopts the form of each of them. But it does so no longer merely by passing from one into the other, as in simple circulation, but by being in each of these determinations at the same time a relation to the opposite one, i.e. notionally containing it within itself.

Capital alternately becomes commodity and money. But (1) *it is itself the alternation of these two determinations;* (2) it becomes commodity, not this or that commodity, but *a totality of commodities.* It is not indifferent to the substance [of the commodity] but to its particular form. In this respect, it appears as a constant metamorphosis of this substance. In so far as capital is posited as a particular content of exchange value, this particularity is itself a totality of particularity; hence not indifferent to particularity as such, but to single or individuated particularity. The identity, the form of generality which it acquires, is that of being exchange value and as such money. Hence it is still posited as money, IN FACT

---

[a] Marx quotes in French.—*Ed.*

it exchanges as commodity for money. But being posited as money, i.e. as this antithetical form of the generality of exchange value, it is at the same time inherently bound to lose not generality, as in simple circulation, but rather the antithetical attribute of generality, or to adopt it only fleetingly, i.e. it exchanges itself again for the commodity, but as a commodity which expresses in its very particularity the generality of exchange value and therefore continually changes its particular form.

When we speak of capital here, it is still only a name. The only determinateness in which capital is posited in distinction from immediate exchange value and from money, is *that of exchange value maintaining and perpetuating itself in and by circulation.* We have so far considered only one aspect of this quality, that of self-maintenance in and by circulation. The other, equally important, aspect is that exchange value is *presupposed,* no longer as simple exchange value, as it exists as a purely notional determination in the commodity before it enters into circulation, or rather as a merely intended determination, since it fleetingly becomes exchange value only in circulation; nor as exchange value as it exists as a moment in circulation, as money. It exists here as money, as objectified exchange value, but in such a way that the relation just described is posited in it.

What distinguishes the second determination from the first is that exchange value (1) exists in an objective form; (2) comes out of circulation, hence presupposes it, but simultaneously starts from itself as a premiss as against circulation.

There are two ways of expressing the result of simple circulation:

The simple negative: The commodities thrown into circulation have fulfilled their purpose. They have been exchanged for one another; each becomes the object of need and is consumed, and circulation is thereby terminated. Only money remains as simple residue. But as such a residue, money has ceased to be money, it has lost its characteristic form. It collapses into its own matter, which remains behind as the inorganic ashes of the whole process.

The positive negative: Money is negated not as objectified exchange value existing for itself—not as exchange value merely disappearing in circulation—but what is negated is its *antithetical* independence, its merely abstract generality in which it has established itself. However:

Thirdly: Exchange value as the premiss and at the same time the result of circulation, just as it is assumed to have emerged from it, must emerge from it again. If this happens only in a formal manner, exchange value would merely become money again; if it emerges as a real commodity, as in simple circulation, it would become a simple object of need, would be consumed as such, and would also lose its characteristic form. If the emergence from circulation is to become real, exchange value must also become an object of need and be consumed as such; but it must be consumed by labour, and in this way reproduce itself anew.

Differently expressed: As regards its content, exchange value was originally an objectified quantity of labour or labour time. As such it progressed, in the process of its objectification, through circulation until it became money, palpable money. Now it must again posit the point of departure of circulation, which lay outside of, and was presupposed by, circulation, in relation to which circulation itself appeared as a movement grasping it from outside and transforming it within itself. That is, exchange value must now posit labour; but now no longer as the simple equivalent or simple objectification of labour but as objectified exchange value become independent, which yields itself up to labour as its material, only in order to renew itself and from itself to begin circulation anew. And with that it is no longer a simple equation, a maintenance of its identity, as in circulation; but a *multiplication* of itself. Exchange value posits itself as exchange value only by valorising itself, i.e. by increasing its value. *As capital, money* (having returned from circulation to itself) *has lost its rigidity, and has turned from a palpable thing into a process.* But on the other hand, labour has modified its relationship to its own objectivity: it has also returned to itself. Yet the nature of the return is such that the labour objectified in exchange value posits living labour as a means for its reproduction, while originally exchange value appeared only as a product of labour.

III. Capital as credit.
IV. Capital as share capital.
V. *Capital as money market.*
VI. Capital as source of wealth. The capitalist.
After capital, landed property would have to be dealt with.
After that wage labour. Then, assuming all three, the *movement of prices* as circulation now defined in its inner totality. On the other hand, the three classes as production posited in its three basic forms and presuppositions of circulation. Then the *State.* (State and bourgeois society.—Taxation, or the existence of the unproductive classes.—The national debt.—Population.—The State in its external relations: Colonies. Foreign trade. Rate of exchange. Money as international coin.—Finally the world market. Encroachment of bourgeois society on the State. Crises. Dissolution of the mode of production and form of society based upon exchange value. The real positing of individual labour as social and vice versa.)//

(Nothing is more erroneous than the way in which both the economists and the socialists consider *society* in relation to economic conditions. Proudhon, for example, replies to Bastiat by saying ([*Gratuité du crédit. Discussion entre M. Fr. Bastiat et M. Proudhon,* Paris, 1850, p. 250,] XVI, 29):

"*For society* the distinction between capital and product does not exist. This distinction is a purely *subjective* one, existing only for individuals." [a]

Thus it is precisely the social aspect which he calls subjective and the subjective abstraction which he calls society. The distinction between product and capital is precisely that, as capital, the product expresses a specific relation belonging to an historical form of society. This so-called consideration from the point of view of society means nothing more than to overlook precisely the *differences* which express the *social relation* (relation of civil society). Society does not consist of individuals, but expresses the sum of the relationships and conditions in which these individuals stand to one another. As if someone were to say: for society, slaves and CITIZENS do not exist: both are men. They *are* both men, if we consider them outside society. To be a slave and to be a CITIZEN are social determinations, relations between human beings A and B. Human being A as such is not a slave; he is a slave in and through society. Mr. Proudhon's remarks about capital and

---

[a] This and the subsequent quotations from *Gratuite du crédit* are in French in the manuscript.— *Ed.*

product mean that in his view there is no distinction between capitalists and workers from the point of view of society. But actually this distinction exists only from the point of view of society.)

(Proudhon's polemic against Bastiat, *Gratuité du crédit*, amounts only to his wish to reduce the exchange between capital and labour to the simple exchange of commodities as exchange values, to reduce them to moments of simple circulation, i.e. he abstracts precisely from the specific distinction upon which everything depends. He says:

"Every product becomes capital at a certain moment, because everything that is consumed is at a certain moment consumed reproductively" [ibid., p. 177].

This is profoundly mistaken, BUT NEVER MIND.

"What causes the sudden transformation of the notion of product into that of capital? It is the *idea of value*. This means that the product, in order to become capital, must have passed through an authentic valuation, must have been bought or sold, its price discussed and fixed by a kind of legal convention. Hides, for instance, coming from the butcher's shop, are the product of the butcher. Have these hides been bought by a tanner? At once he adds either them or their value to his working capital. By the work of the tanner this capital becomes a product again" [ibid., pp. 179-80].

Every capital is here "an *established value*". Money is the "*most established value*",[a] established value of the highest potency. This means (1) the product becomes capital by becoming value, or capital is nothing more than simple value. There is no difference between them. Therefore he says alternately "commodity" (the natural aspect of the commodity expressed as product) and "value" or rather "price", since he assumes the act of purchase and sale. (2) Since money appears as the perfected form of value, as value exists in simple circulation, money is also the true *established value*.)

The transition from simple exchange value and its circulation to capital may also be expressed in the following way: in circulation, exchange value appears dual—once as commodity, again as money. If it is present in one of these determinations, it is not present in the other. This is valid for every particular commodity. But the whole of circulation considered in itself consists in the same exchange value, exchange value as subject, positing itself once as commodity and again as money; it is the movement by means of which exchange value posits itself in this dual

---

[a] Marx gives the two Proudhonian terms in French: "une valeur faite" and "la valeur la plus parfaite".— *Ed.*

determination, and preserves itself in each of its roles as its opposite, in the commodity as money, and in money as the commodity. This is in itself present in simple circulation, but it is not posited in it. Exchange value posited as the unity of commodity and money is *capital,* and this positing itself appears as the circulation of capital. (But this is a spiral line, an expanding curve, not a simple circle.)

Let us first analyse the simple determinations contained in the relationship of capital and labour, in order to discover the inner connection, both of these determinations and of their further developments, to what has gone before.

[II-19] The first presupposition is that capital stands on one side and labour on the other, each as an independent entity confronting the other, and hence each also alien to the other. The labour that confronts capital is *alien* labour; the capital that confronts labour is *alien* capital. The extremes that confront each other are *specifically* distinct. In the first form in which simple exchange value was posited, labour was determined in such a way that its product was not immediately use value for the labourer, not his direct means of subsistence. This was the general condition for the production of exchange value and of exchange in general. Otherwise the worker would merely have produced a product—an immediate use value for himself—but not exchange value. However, this exchange value was materialised in a product, which as such had use value for others and as such was the object of their needs. The use value which the worker has to offer to capital, and hence which he has to offer to others in general, is not materialised in a product, it does not exist in any way external to him. Consequently, his use value does not exist in reality but only potentially, as his capacity. It becomes reality only when it is solicited by capital, set in motion, since activity without an object is nothing, or, at most, mental activity, with which we are not dealing here. As soon as this use value is set in motion by capital, it exists as the definite, productive activity of the worker; it is his vitality itself, directed towards a definite aim and hence manifesting itself in a definite form.

In the relationship of capital and labour, exchange value and use value are brought into relation to one another: one side (capital) faces the other above all as *exchange value** while the other

---

* Should not *value* be conceived as the unity of use value and exchange value? In and for itself is not *value* as such the general form as compared with use value and exchange value as *particular* forms of it? Is this not significant in political economy? Use value is also presupposed in simple exchange or pure exchange. But

side (labour) faces capital as use value. In simple circulation, every commodity can be considered alternately in one or the other determination. In both cases, provided that it is considered as a commodity as such, it steps outside circulation as an object satisfying a need, and falls entirely outside the economic relationship. In so far as the commodity is fixed as exchange value— money—it tends towards the same formlessness, but remains within the economic relationship. In any case, commodities are of interest in the exchange relationship (simple circulation) only to the extent that they have exchange values. On the other hand, their exchange value is of only passing interest, for it transcends their one-sidedness—the fact of their usefulness, their use value, being related to, and hence *immediately* existing for, only one specific individual—but does not transcend this use value itself. Rather, exchange value posits and mediates use value, namely, as

there exchange is only taking place because of the reciprocal use of the commodity; and use value, i.e. the content, the natural particularity of the commodity as such, has no existence as a characteristic economic form. Rather, its characteristic form is exchange value. The content outside this form is of no consequence; it is not the content of the relationship as a social relationship. But does not this content develop as such in a system of needs and production? Does not use value as such enter into the form itself as something determining the economic form itself, e.g. in the relationship of capital and labour? in the different forms of labour?— Agriculture, industry, etc.—Rent?—Influence of the seasons on the price of primary products? etc. If *only* exchange value as such played a role in political economy, how could there be introduced at a later stage such elements as relate purely to use value, e.g. in the case of capital considered as raw material, etc.? How does the physical quality of the soil suddenly turn up in Ricardo? etc. The [German] word *Waare* ["commodity"] implies the relation (the German *Güter* ["goods"] perhaps be taken in the sense of [the French] *denrée* as opposed to *merchandise?*). Price appears as a merely formal· determination in it. This is quite compatible with exchange value being the predominant determination. Obviously, the element of use does not cease to exist because it is *only* determined by exchange, although the direction of use is of course determined in this way. In any case, this question should be examined thoroughly in the investigation of value. One should not completely abstract from it, as does Ricardo, nor give oneself airs by merely presupposing the word "utility",[78] as does the insipid Say. Above all, it will and must be shown, in the analysis of the individual sections, to what extent use value not only remains outside political economy and its characteristic forms·as a presupposed matter but to what extent it enters into them. For Proudhon's insipidities see my *Misère*.[79] This much is certain: in exchange, we have (in circulation) the commodity—use value—as price; that apart from its price it is a commodity, the object of need, goes without saying. The two determinations do not enter into any relationship at all to each other, except in so far as the particular use [value] appears as a natural limit of the commodity, and hence posits money, i.e. the commodity's exchange value, simultaneously as existence of the commodity in money outside itself, but only formally. Money itself is a commodity, it has a use value as its substance.

use value for others, etc. But in so far as exchange value as such is fixed in money, use value confronts it merely as an abstract chaos; and it is precisely by being separated from its substance that exchange value collapses and drifts out of the sphere of simple exchange value, whose highest movement is simple circulation and whose highest perfection is money. But within the sphere of simple exchange value itself, the distinction exists IN FACT only as a superficial difference, a purely formal distinction. Money in its maximum fixation is itself commodity, and is distinguished as such from other commodities only by the fact that it expresses exchange value *more perfectly*. But precisely by doing so, by being coin, [II-20] it loses its immanent determination as *exchange value* and becomes *mere* use value, even if it be use value for the purpose of positing the price, etc., of commodities. The two determinations are still directly coincident in it and equally directly fall apart. Where they behave independently to one another, *positively,* as in the case of the commodity which becomes an object of consumption, it ceases to be a moment of the economic process; where negatively, as in money, it becomes *madness;* madness, however, as a moment of political economy, and a factor determining the practical life of peoples.

We have seen earlier[a] that exchange value cannot be said to realise itself in simple circulation. But this is so because [in simple circulation] use value as such does not confront exchange value. Use value is not here determined as such by exchange value. Conversely, use value as such stands in no relation to exchange value, but turns into a specific exchange value only by the application of the common feature of use values—their being labour time—as an external yardstick to them. As yet the unity of use value and exchange value directly falls apart, and their distinctness still fuses directly into unity. It must now be posited that use value becomes use value by virtue of its being exchange value, and that exchange value mediates itself through use value. In money circulation, we had only two different forms of exchange value (price of the commodity—money) or only different use values ($C—C$), for which money, exchange value, was merely a fleeting mediator. A real relationship between exchange value and use value did not occur. And for that reason the commodity as such—its particularity—is an irrelevant, a merely fortuitous content conceived only in general and falling outside the relation of economic form. Or else the latter is only a

---

[a] See this volume, p. 191.— *Ed.*

superficial form, a formal determination, outside whose field the real substance lies and which has no relationship at all to this real substance as such. Consequently, if this formal determination as such is to be fixed in money, it surreptitiously transforms itself into an indifferent natural product, a metal, in which whatever remained of a relationship, whether to the individual or to the intercourse of individuals, has been extinguished. Metal as such does not, of course, express any social relations; the form of coin, the last sign of life of its social significance, is also extinguished in it.

Exchange value which confronts use value posited as one side of the relationship, confronts it as money; but money confronting it in this way is no longer money in its determination as such, but money as *capital*. The *use value* or commodity confronting capital or posited *exchange value* is no longer the commodity as it appeared as against money, when its specific form was quite as irrelevant as its content, and when it merely appeared as any substance whatsoever.

(1) Firstly [the commodity now appears] as use value for capital, i.e. as an object which can be exchanged for capital without the latter losing its value dimension as e.g. money does when it is exchanged for a particular commodity. The only utility which an object in general can have for capital can only be to maintain it or to augment it. We have already seen, in the case of money, that value having become independent as such—or the general form of wealth—is incapable of any movement other than a quantitative one; it can only increase itself. According to its concept it is the essence of all use values; yet as always being merely a definite quantity of money (here capital) its quantitative limitation contradicts its quality. Hence it lies in its nature constantly to exceed its own limits. (As something to be enjoyed, wealth consequently appears as limitless prodigality, as e.g. in the time of the Roman emperors by the devouring of salads of pearls, etc. Here the attempt is made to realise a fantasy of enjoyment without limits.) That is why increase coincides with self-preservation in the case of value which adheres to its nature as value, and it preserves itself only by constantly striving to exceed its quantitative limits, which contradict its characteristic form, its inner generality.

Hence enrichment is an end in itself. The activity corresponding to the purpose of capital can only be that of enrichment, i.e. that of its own increase and multiplication. A specific sum of money (and money always exists for its owner only in a specific quantity, always as a specific sum of money) (this should already be shown in the chapter on money) may completely suffice for a specific volume of consumption, as a result of which it ceases to be money. But as the representative of general wealth, it cannot so suffice. As a quantitatively determined, limited sum it is only a limited representative of general wealth or the representative of a limited wealth which corresponds exactly to its exchange value, is exactly measured by it. Thus it does not by any means have the capacity which it should have according to its general concept: that of being able to buy all pleasures, all commodities, the totality of material substances of wealth. It is not a "précis de toutes les choses",[a] etc. Fixed as wealth, as the general form of wealth, as value which counts as value, it is therefore the constant impulse to exceed its quantitative limits: an endless process. Its own vitality consists exclusively of that; it *maintains* itself only as exchange value which is distinct from use value and valid for itself, only by *constantly multiplying* itself.

(It is damned difficult for our economists to explain theoretically how we get from the self-preservation of value in capital to its multiplication, i.e. to explain the latter as inherent in the fundamental determination of capital, and not merely as an accident or a result. See e.g. how *Storch* brings in this fundamental determination with an adverb, "actually".[80] Admittedly, the economists try to introduce this increase into the relationship of capital as an essential aspect. But if this is not done in the brutal form of defining capital as that which yields profit, in which case the very increase of capital is already posited as a particular *economic form* in profit, [II-21] it only appears surreptitiously and very feebly, as we shall later demonstrate, by a brief review of all that the economists have offered us concerning the definition of the concept of capital. The drivel to the effect that no one would employ his capital without obtaining a profit thereby, amounts either to the idiocy that the worthy capitalists would remain capitalists even *without* employing their capital; or to the very simple-minded assertion that the profit-bearing employment of capital is inherent in the very concept of capital. WELL. That is just what would then have to be demonstrated.)

Money as a sum of money is measured by its quantity. This measurableness contradicts its determination, which must be oriented towards what has no measure. Everything said about money here, is even more true of capital, in which money in its perfected determination really first develops. Only that which

---

[a] See footnote on p. 153.— *Ed.*

increases it, multiplies it, and therefore preserves it as capital, can represent use value, i.e. usefulness, to capital as such.

(2) Capital, according to its concept, is money, but money that no longer exists in the simple form of gold and silver, nor as money in opposition to circulation, but in the form of all substances—commodities. To that extent therefore it does not, as capital, stand in opposition to use value, but exists apart from money only in use values. Its substances themselves are therefore now transitory, which would have no exchange value if they had no use value; but which lose their value as use values, are dissolved simply by the natural exchange of matter, if they are not actually used; and which, if actually used, disappear all the more. In this regard, the opposite of capital cannot itself be a particular commodity; for as such it does not constitute an antithesis to capital, since the substance of capital itself is use value; since it is not this or that commodity, but every commodity. The common substance of all commodities, i.e. their substance once again not as their material stuff, as physical determination, but their common substance as *commodities* and therefore as *exchange values,* is that they are *objectified labour.*

⫽But it can only be a question of this economic (social) substance of use values, i.e. their economic determination as content in distinction from their form (but this form is *value,* because specific quantity of this *labour*), if one is looking for the antithesis to them. So far as their natural differences are concerned, none of them excludes capital from entering into it and making it capital's own body, so long as none of them excludes the character of exchange value and commodity.⫽

The only thing distinct from *objectified* labour is *non-objectified* labour, labour still objectifying itself, *labour* as subjectivity. Or *objectified* labour, i.e. *labour present in space,* can also be opposed as *past labour* to labour still *present in time.* If it is to be present in time, present alive, it can only be present as a *living subject,* in which it exists as capacity, as potentiality; therefore as *worker.* The only *use value,* therefore, which can constitute an antithesis to capital is *labour* ⫽to be exact, *value-creating, i.e. productive labour.* This is an anticipation; must first be developed; BY AND BY. Labour as mere service for the satisfaction of immediate needs has nothing at all to do with capital, which does not seek this kind of labour. If a capitalist hires a woodcutter to cut wood to roast his mutton, both his relationship to the woodcutter and that of the woodcutter to him is one of simple exchange. The woodcutter gives him a service, a use value that does not increase capital but in which it is consumed, and the capitalist gives him another commodity in exchange in the form of money. Such is the case with all services which workers exchange directly for the money of other people and which are consumed by these people. This is consumption of revenue, which as such is always part of simple circulation, not consumption of capital. Since one of the contracting parties does not confront the other as capitalist, this form of service cannot come into the category of productive labour. From the harlot to the Pope there is a mass of such rabble. But the honest and "working" Lumpenproletariat, too, belongs to this category, e.g. the large mob of casual day-labourers, etc., in ports, etc. The person representing money requires the service only for its use value, which immediately disappears for him; but the casual labourer demands the money and since in this way the person supplying money is concerned with the commodity, and the person supplying the commodity is concerned with the money, they merely represent the two sides of simple circulation to one another. It is always clear that the casual labourer, who is concerned with the money, hence directly with the general form of wealth, seeks to enrich himself at the expense of his improvised friend, which hurts the latter, a HARD CALCULATOR, all the more, as the service he now requires is to be ascribed only to his ordinary human weaknesses, but is in no way required by him *qua capitalist.*

A. Smith was *essentially* right with his distinction between *productive* and *unproductive* labour, right from the standpoint of bourgeois political economy.[a] The arguments advanced against it by other economists are either rot (e.g. Storch, Senior still more pitiable,[81] etc.), namely that any action after all acts upon something, thus confusion of the product in its natural and economic sense. According to this a criminal is also a productive worker, since he [II-22] indirectly produces books on criminal law (at least this reasoning as sound as if a judge is called a productive worker because he protects *from* theft). Or the modern economists have become such sycophants of the bourgeois, that they wish to make him believe that it is productive labour if someone picks the lice out of his hair, or strokes his tail, because the latter activity might make his fat head—BLOCKHEAD—clearer the next day for the office. It is therefore quite correct—but at the same time also characteristic—that for the consistent economists the workers in e.g. luxury shops are productive, although the fellows who consume such objects are

---

[a] A. Smith, *An Inquiry into the Nature and Causes of the Wealth of Nations,* Book 2, Ch. III.— *Ed.*

explicitly castigated as unproductive wastrels. The FACT is that these
workers are INDEED productive AS FAR AS THEY INCREASE THE CAPITAL OF THEIR
MASTER; UNPRODUCTIVE AS TO THE MATERIAL RESULT OF THEIR LABOUR. In fact, this
"productive" worker is just as interested in the shit which he must
make as the capitalist who employs him, and who does not give a
damn about the junk. But looked at more precisely, it turns out in
fact that the true definition of a productive worker consists
in this: a man who requires and demands absolutely no more
than is necessary to enable him to bring to his capitalist the
greatest possible advantage. ALL THIS NONSENSE. Digression. But
have to return to the productive and unproductive in more
detail later.[82] //

EXCHANGE BETWEEN CAPITAL AND LABOUR

Use value confronting capital as posited exchange value is *labour.*
Capital exchanges itself, or exists in this specific form only in
relation to *non-capital,* the negation of capital, in respect to which
alone it is capital; the real non-capital is *labour.*

If we consider the exchange between capital and labour, we find
that it is divided into two processes which are not only formally
but qualitatively distinct and even contradictory:

(1) The worker exchanges his commodity, labour, the use value
which as a commodity also has a *price* like all other commodities,
for a specific sum of exchange values, specific sum of money,
which capital cedes to him.

(2) The capitalist obtains, in exchange, labour itself, labour as
value-positing activity, as productive labour; i.e. he obtains the
productive power which maintains and multiplies capital and
which therefore becomes the productive power and reproducing
power of capital, a power belonging to capital itself.

The separation of these two processes is so evident that they can
fall asunder in time and need in no way coincide. The first process
can be completed, and in most cases is to a certain extent
completed, before the second has even begun. The completion of
the second act implies the completion of the product. The
payment of wages cannot wait for this. We shall even find it an
essential characteristic of the relationship [between worker and
capitalist] that it does not do so.

In simple exchange, circulation, this two-fold process does
not occur. If commodity *a* is exchanged for money *b*, and this
then for commodity *c* which is destined for consumption—the
original object of the exchange for *a*—the use of commodity *c,* its

consumption, falls quite outside circulation; does not concern the form of the [economic] relationship; lies beyond circulation itself, and is a purely physical interest which now only expresses a relationship of individual *A* in his natural quality to an object of his individual need. What he does with commodity *c* is a question that lies outside the economic relationship.

Here, on the contrary, the *use value of what is exchanged for money* appears *as a particular economic relationship,* and the *specific utilisation of what is exchanged for money constitutes the ultimate purpose of both processes. Thus there is already a distinction of form between the exchange of capital and labour and simple exchange — two distinct processes.*

If we now investigate further how the exchange between capital and labour differs in content from simple exchange (circulation), we find that this distinction does not arise from an external relation or comparison, but that in the totality of the latter process the second form distinguishes itself from the first, that the comparison itself is included. The difference of the second act from the first — the particular process of appropriation of labour on the part of capital is the second act — is EXACTLY the distinction between the exchange of capital and labour and the exchange of commodities as mediated by money. *In the exchange between capital and labour, the first act is an exchange and falls wholly within ordinary circulation; the second is a process qualitatively different from exchange and it is only BY MISUSE that it* could have been called *exchange* of any kind *at all.* It stands directly opposed to exchange; essentially different category.

// Capital.

I. *Generality:* (1) (a) Evolution of capital from money. (b) Capital and labour (mediating itself by *alien* labour). (c) The elements of capital, distinguished according to their relationship to labour (product, raw material, instrument of labour). (2) *Particularisation of capital*: (a) Circulating capital, fixed capital. Turnover of capital. (3) *Singularity of capital*: Capital and profit. Capital and interest. Capital as *value*, distinct from itself as interest and profit.

II. *Particularity:* (1) Accumulation of capitals. (2) Competition of capitals. (3) Concentration of capitals (quantitative difference of capital as at the same time qualitative, as *measure* of its volume and effect).[a]

---

[a] Here the following passage is crossed out in the manuscript: "(b) Capital as credit. (c) Share capital. (d) The money market. (e) Capital as determining price." — *Ed.*

[II-23] III. *Singularity*: (1) Capital as credit. (2) Capital as share capital. (3) Capital as money market.

In the money market, capital is posited in its totality; there it *determines price, provides work, regulates production,* in a word, *source of production*; but capital, not only as something producing itself (materially by means of industry, etc., positing price, developing the productive forces), but at the same time as creator of values, must posit a value or form of wealth specifically distinct from capital. This is *rent*. It is the only value created by capital as value distinct from itself, and from its own production. Both by its nature and historically, capital is the *creator* of modern landed property, of rent; just as its action therefore appears also as the dissolution of the old form of landed property. The new form arises from the action of capital on the old. Capital is this—in one respect—as creator of modern agriculture. In the economic relationships of modern landed property which appears as a process: rent—capital—wage labour (the form of the series can also be otherwise conceived as: wage labour—capital—rent; but capital must always be the active middle element), the inner structure of modern society, or capital in the totality of its relations, is therefore posited.

The question now is: how does the transition from landed property to wage labour come about? (The transition from wage labour to capital comes about of itself; for capital here has returned into its active ground.) Historically, the transition is indisputable. It is already implied in the fact that [modern] landed property is the product of capital. We thus always find that wherever the reaction of capital on the older forms of landed property converts the latter into money rent (the same thing occurs in other ways, where the modern farmer is created) and agriculture therefore, carried on by capital, is converted into industrial agronomy, the COTTIERS, serfs, villeins, copyholders, cottagers, etc., necessarily become day-labourers, wage labourers. Thus *wage labour* in its totality is first created by the action of capital upon landed property, and later, as soon as this has been elaborated as a form, by the landowner himself. The landowner himself then CLEARS the land, as Steuart says,[a] of its superfluous mouths, rips the children of the earth away from the breast on which they were raised, and so converts even labour on the land, which appears by its nature as immediate source of subsistence,

---

[a] J. Steuart, *An Inquiry into the Principles of Political Oeconomy,* Vol. I, Book 1, pp. 50, 153, 156 and 157.— *Ed.*

into a mediated source of subsistence, purely dependent on social relations. (The mutual dependence must first have developed into its pure form, before there can be any question of a real social communality [Gemeinschaftlichkeit]. All relations as posited by society, not as determined by nature.) This alone makes possible the application of science and the full development of productive power.

There can therefore be no doubt that *wage labour* in its *classical* form, as permeating the whole extent of society, and making itself in lieu of the soil the ground on which society rests, is first created by modern landed property, i.e. by landed property as a value created by capital itself. This is why landed property leads back to wage labour. It is in one respect nothing but the transference of wage labour from the towns to the countryside, therefore wage labour spread over the whole surface of society. The old landowner, if he is rich, does not require a capitalist to become a modern landowner. He only has to convert his labourers into wage labourers and to begin producing for profit instead of revenue. Then the modern tenant farmer and the modern landowner are presumed in his person. But it is not a formal distinction, that the form in which he receives his revenue or the form in which the labourer is paid, is changed; it implies, rather, *a total transformation of the mode of production* (of agriculture) itself; it therefore presupposes a particular level of development of industry, of trade and of science, in short of the productive forces.

In general, production based upon capital and wage labour is not only formally different from other modes of production, but also presupposes a total revolution and development of material production. Although capital as merchant capital can develop itself fully (only not to the same extent quantitatively) without this transformation of landed property, it cannot do so as industrial capital. Even the development of manufacture presupposes an incipient-dissolution of the old economic relationships of landed property. On the other hand, it is not until modern industry is developed to a high degree that this dissolution at individual points becomes the new form in its totality and full extent; but this development itself always proceeds the more quickly, the higher the development of modern agriculture, of the form of property, of the economic relationships corresponding to it. Thus England in this respect the model country for other, continental countries.

Equally: if the first form of industry, large-scale manufacture, already presupposes the dissolution of landed property, this dissolution, in turn, is determined by the subordinate development of capital in its still undeveloped (medieval) forms, which has taken place in the towns, and at the same time by the effect of manufacture flourishing together with trade in other countries (thus Holland's influence upon England in the 16th and the first half of the 17th centuries). In these countries themselves the process already gone through and agriculture sacrificed to stock-raising, and grain imported from backward countries, like Poland, etc. (Holland AGAIN).

It must be kept in mind that the new productive forces and relations of production do not develop out of *nothing,* or out of thin air, or from the womb of the Idea positing itself, but within and in contradiction to the existing development of production and inherited, traditional property relations. If in the fully developed bourgeois system each economic relationship presupposes the other in a bourgeois-economic form, and everything posited is thus also a premiss, that is the case with every [II-24] organic system. This organic system itself has its premisses as a totality, and its development into a totality consists precisely in subordinating all elements of society to itself, or in creating out of it the organs it still lacks. This is historically how it becomes a totality. Its becoming this totality constitutes a moment of its process, of its development.

On the other hand, if, within a society, the modern relations of production, i.e. capital, are developed in their totality, and this society now takes possession of a new terrain, as e.g. in the colonies, it finds, more especially its representative the capitalist finds, that his capital ceases to be capital without wage labour, and that one of the premisses of wage labour is not only landed property in general but modern landed property; landed property which, as capitalised rent, is expensive and as such excludes the direct utilisation of the soil by individuals. Therefore *Wakefield's* theory of colonisation, followed in practice by the English government in Australia. Landed property is here artificially raised in price in order to transform the workers into wage workers, to make capital act as capital, and thus to make the new colony *productive*; to develop wealth in it, instead of, as in America, using it for the direct provision of wage workers. *Wakefield's* theory is immensely important for a correct understanding of modern landed property.[83]

Capital, as a producer of rent, thus returns to the production of wage labour as its general creative ground. Capital arises from circulation and posits labour as wage labour; thus it takes form, and developed as a whole it posits landed property both as its condition and as its antithesis. But it turns out that in doing this, it has only created wage labour as its general premiss. This, therefore, must now be considered for itself. On the other hand, modern landed property itself appears at its most powerful in the process of the CLEARING OF ESTATES and the transformation of the rural labourers into wage labourers.

Thus two-fold transition to wage labour. This the positive side. Negatively, after capital has posited landed property and thereby achieved its two-fold aim: (1) industrial agriculture and thereby development of the productivity of the soil and (2) wage labour, therefore the general domination of capital on the land, it considers the existence of landed property itself as a purely transitory development, which is necessary as the action of capital on the old relationships of landed property, and is a *product of their decomposition*; but which as such—once this aim has been achieved—is merely a restriction on profit, not a necessity for production. Capital therefore seeks to dissolve landed property as private property and to transfer it to the State. This the negative side. Thus to transform the whole internal society into capitalists and wage labourers.

When capital has reached this point, wage labour has as well, and tries, like the bourgeois, to get rid of the landlords as supererogatory in order to simplify the relationship, to moderate taxes, etc., on the one hand; and on the other, in order to escape from wage labour and to become independent producer—for direct use—it demands the break-up of the great landed estates. Landed property is here negated from two directions; the negation from the direction of capital is only a change of form, to its undivided rule. (Rent as the general State rent (State tax), so that bourgeois society reproduces the medieval system in another way, but as the complete negation of it.) The negation from the direction of wage labour is only a hidden negation of capital, and therefore also of wage labour itself. It is now to be considered as independently confronting capital.

Thus the transition two-fold: (1) *positive transition* from modern landed property or transition of capital by means of modern landed property to general wage labour; (2) *negative transition*: negation of landed property by capital, i.e. negation of independent value by capital, i.e. precisely negation of capital by itself. But their negation is *wage labour*. Then negation of landed property and by means of it negation of capital from the direction of wage labour, i.e. wage labour that wishes to posit itself as independent.//

//The *market,* which at the beginning in political economy appears as abstract determination, assumes total forms. First the *money market.* This includes the bill of exchange market; in general the loan market; therefore dealings in money, bullion market. As *money-lending market,* it appears both in the banks, FOR INSTANCE in the rate of discount: LOAN-MARKET, BILL-BROKERS, etc.; but then also as the market for all *interest-bearing bills:* state bonds and the SHARE MARKET. The latter fall into larger groups. Firstly the SHARES *of the monetary institutes* themselves; BANK SHARES; JOINTSTOCK BANK SHARES; *means of communication* SHARES (RAILWAY SHARES the most important; CANAL SHARES; STEAM NAVIGATION SHARES; TELEGRAPH SHARES; OMNIBUS SHARES); SHARES *of general industrial* ENTERPRISES (MINING SHARES the main ones). Then for the supply of the general elements (GAS SHARES, SHARES in water-works). MISCELLANEOUS going into thousands. For the *storing of commodities* (DOCK SHARES, etc.). MISCELLANEOUS in infinite variety, such as ENTERPRISES of industrial or commercial companies based on shares. Finally for securing the whole, INSURANCE SHARES of all kinds.

Just as the market by and large divides itself into the HOME MARKET and the FOREIGN MARKET, so the domestic market itself divides further into MARKET OF HOME SHARES, NATIONAL FUNDS, etc., and FOREIGN FUNDS, FOREIGN [II-25] SHARES, etc. But this development really belongs to the world market, which is not only the domestic market in relation to all the FOREIGN MARKETS existing outside it, but at the same time the domestic market of all FOREIGN MARKETS, as, in turn, components of the HOME MARKET.

The *concentration of the money market* in one main place within a country, whereas the other markets distribute themselves more according to the division of labour; although here also great concentration in the capital city, if this is also the port for its exports.

The markets distinct from the money market are in the first place as different as are the products and branches of production, and likewise constitute markets in their own right. The main markets for these different products establish themselves in centres which are such either in relation to import or export, or because they are either themselves centres of a particular production or the direct points of supply for such centres. But from this simple distinction, the markets proceed further to a more or less organic separation into large groups, which them-selves necessarily divide up according to the basic elements of capital into: markets for products and markets for raw materials. The instrument of production as such constitutes no particular market; it exists as such mainly, first, in the raw materials themselves, which are sold as means of production; but then in particular in the metals, since these exclude all thought of direct consumption, and then in products such as coal, oil, chemical materials, which are destined to disappear as accessory means of production. Likewise dyestuffs, timber, DRUGS, etc.

Accordingly:

I. *Products.* (1) *Grain market,* with its different subdivisions, e.g. SEED market: rice, sago, potatoes, etc. This economically very important; at the same time market for production and for direct consumption. (2) COLONIAL-PRODUCE MARKET. Coffee, tea, cocoa, sugar; tobacco; SPICES (pepper, all-spice, CINNAMON, cassia lignea, CLOVES, GINGER, MACE, NUTMEGS, etc.). (3) *Fruits.* ALMONDS, CURRANTS, FIGS, PLUMS, PRUNES, RAISINS, ORANGES, LEMONS, etc. *MOLASSES* (for production, etc.). (4) *Provisions.* Butter; CHEESE; BACON; HAMS; LARD; PORK; BEEF (smoked); fish, etc. (5) *SPIRITS.* Wine, rum, beer, etc.

II. *Raw produce.* (1) *Raw materials of the mechanised industry.* Flax; hemp; cotton; silk; wool; hides; leather; gutta percha, etc. (2) *Raw materials of the chemical industry.* Potash, SALTPETRE; turpentine; nitrate OF soda, etc.

III. *Raw materials which are at the same time instruments of production: Metals* (copper, iron, tin, zinc, lead, steel, etc.). *Wood.* [Fire] WOOD. TIMBER. Dyer's wood. Timber for ship-building, etc. *Accessory means of production* and *raw materials.* DRUGS and DYES (cochineal, indigo, etc.). Tar. Tallow. Oils. Coal, etc.[84]

Each product must naturally enter the market; but really large markets, as distinct from retail trade, are formed only by the important products for consumption (economically important only the market for grain, tea, sugar and COFFEE; wine-market to some extent and the market for spirits in general) or those which are the raw materials of industry (wool, silk, wood, metal-market, etc.). At which point the abstract category of the market has to be brought in, will become clear later.//

The exchange between the worker and the capitalist is a simple exchange; each obtains an equivalent; the one money, the other a commodity whose *price* is exactly equal to the money paid for it. What the capitalist receives in this simple exchange is a use value: disposition over alien labour. From the worker's side—and this is the exchange in which he appears as seller—it is evident that for him, as for the seller of any other commodity, of a use value, the use the buyer makes of the purchased commodity does not concern the characteristic form of the relationship. What the worker sells is the disposition over his labour, which is a specific labour, specific skill, etc.

It is quite immaterial what the capitalist does with his labour, although he can naturally employ it only according to its specific characteristics and his disposition itself is limited to only a *specific* labour and is *restricted in time* (so much labour time). The system of piece-rate payment, it is true, makes it appear that the worker receives a certain share in the product. But this is only another form of measuring time. (Instead of saying, you will work for 12 hours, it is said, you will receive so much per piece; i.e. we measure the time you have worked by the quantity of the products.) This does not at all concern us here, where we are considering the general relationship.

If the capitalist were to content himself with the mere right of disposing, without actually setting the worker to work, e.g. in order to have his labour as a reserve, etc.,or to take away the right of disposing over that labour from his competitors (as e.g. theatre directors purchase singers for a SEASON, not to let them sing but so that they do not sing in a rival theatre), the exchange would have taken place in full. The worker receives the exchange value in money, the general form of wealth in a definite quantity, and the more or less he receives procures for him a greater or smaller share in general wealth. How this more or less is determined, how the quantity of money he obtains is measured, concerns the general relationship so little that it cannot be deduced from it as such. In general, the exchange value of his commodity can only be determined not by the way in which the buyer *uses* his commodity but only by the quantity of objectified labour present in the commodity itself; here, therefore, by the quantity of labour required to produce the worker himself. For the use value which [II-26] he offers exists only as ability, as his bodily capacity; it has no existence outside of that. The objectified labour necessary both to maintain the general substance in which his labour capacity[85] exists, i.e. bodily to maintain the worker himself, as well as to modify this general substance for the development of the particular capacity—that is the labour objectified in this substance. This, in general terms, is the measure of the quantity of value, the sum of money, which he receives in exchange. This is not yet the place for the further development of the argument as to how the wages of labour are determined like [the value of] all other commodities by the labour time necessary to produce the worker as such.

In circulation, when I exchange a commodity for money and for that money purchase a commodity and satisfy my need, the act is at an end. So it is with the worker. But he has the possibility to start again from the beginning, because his life is the source constantly renewing his own use value for a certain time, until it is used up, and constantly confronts capital again, in order to begin the same exchange anew. As in the case of every individual standing in circulation as subject, the worker is the owner of a use value; he disposes of it for money, the general form of wealth, but only in order to dispose of this money in turn for commodities as objects of his immediate consumption, as the means for the satisfaction of his needs. Since he exchanges his use value for the general form of wealth, he shares in the enjoyment of general wealth up to the limit of his equivalent—a quantitative limit which, of course, changes into a qualitative one, as in every exchange. But he is not restricted to particular objects, nor to a particular kind of satisfaction. The range of his enjoyments is not limited qualitatively, but only quantitatively. This distinguishes him from the slave, serf, etc.

Consumption CERTAINLY reacts back upon production; but this reaction concerns the worker in his exchange as little as it does every other seller of a commodity; rather, from the standpoint of simple circulation—and as yet we have no other developed relationship before us—it falls outside the economic relationship. This much, however, can already be said in passing: that the relative limitation of the range of the workers' consumption, which is only quantitative, not qualitative, or rather qualitative only as posited by quantity, gives them as consumers (in the course of the further analysis of capital, the relationship of consumption and production must, in general, be considered more closely) a quite different importance as agents of production from that which they possess and possessed in e.g. ancient world, in the Middle Ages or in Asia. But all this does not belong here, as we have already said.

Equally, while the worker receives his equivalent in the form of money, in the form of general wealth, he figures in this exchange as the equal of the capitalist, like every other exchanger; at least, *in appearance.* In FACT, this equality is already disturbed in that his relationship as worker to the capitalist, as use value in the form specifically distinct from exchange value, in contrast to the value posited as value, is presupposed for this apparently simple exchange. He therefore already stands in a differently determined economic relationship—outside that of exchange, in which the nature of the use value, the particular use value of the commodity as such, is immaterial.

This appearance, however, exists as an illusion on his part and to a certain extent on the other side, and therefore essentially modifies his relationship by comparison to that of labourers in other social modes of production. But, what is essential is that the aim of the exchange for him is the satisfaction of his need. The object of his exchange is the immediate object of need, not exchange value as such. True, he receives money, but only in its determination as coin; i.e. only as a self-transcending and vanishing mediator. What he gets in exchange is therefore not exchange value, not wealth, but means of subsistence, objects to sustain his life, satisfaction of his needs in general, of his physical, social, etc., needs. It is a specific equivalent in means of subsistence, objectified labour, measured by the production costs of his labour.

What he gives up is the right of disposition over his labour. On the other hand, it is true that even within simple circulation, coin may develop into money and that, therefore, in so far as he receives coin in exchange, he can convert it into money, by accumulating it, etc., withdrawing it from circulation; fixing it as general form of wealth, instead of as vanishing means of exchange. In this respect it could thus be said that, in the exchange of the worker with capital, his object—and therefore also the product of the exchange for him—is not means of subsistence but wealth, not a particular use value, but exchange value as such. According to this, the worker could make exchange value into his own *product* in the only way wealth can *appear* at all as *product of simple circulation* in which equivalents are exchanged, namely by sacrificing substantial satisfaction to the *form* of wealth, i.e. by *self-denial,* saving, cutting down his consumption, and thus withdrawing less from circulation than he puts into it in *goods.* This is the only possible form for enriching oneself which is posited by circulation itself.

Self-denial could then also appear in the more active form, not posited in simple circulation, of denying himself more and more rest, thus sacrificing altogether his existence as distinct from his existence as worker, and being as much as possible only a worker; thus renewing the act of exchange more often, or extending it quantitatively further, in other words, by *industriousness.* Thus in present-day society, the demand for industriousness and especially also for *saving,* for *self-denial,* is addressed not to the capitalists but to the workers, and especially by the [II-27] capitalists. Present-day society makes the paradoxical demand that he for whom the object of exchange is means of subsistence should deny himself, not he for whom it is enrichment. The illusion as if the capitalists in fact practised "self-denial"—and thereby became capitalists—a demand and a notion which made any sense at all only in the early period when capital was emerging from feudal, etc., relationships—has been abandoned by all serious modern economists. The worker is told to save, and much fuss has been made with savings banks, etc.

(As regards the latter, even the economists concede that their real purpose is not wealth, but only a more appropriate distribution of expenditure, so that in old age, or in sickness, crises, etc., the workers do not become a burden on the poorhouses, on the State, or go begging (in a word, so that they become a burden on the working class itself and not by any means on the capitalists, vegetating on the latter's pocket); i.e. so that they save for the capitalists and reduce the costs of production for them.)

Still, not a single economist will deny that, if the workers acted on this demand *in general,* that is as *workers* (what the individual worker, in distinction from his *genus,* does or can do, can only exist as an *exception,* not as the *rule,* because it is not determined by the relationship itself), hence if they acted on this demand as a *rule* (apart from the damage they would do to general consumption— the loss would be enormous—therefore also to production, therefore also to the number and volume of exchanges that they could make with capital, therefore to themselves as workers), they would employ means which would absolutely negate their own end, and which would inevitably degrade them to the level of the Irish, to that level of wage labourers where the merest animal minimum of needs and means of subsistence appears as the sole object and purpose of their exchange with capital.

In aspiring to wealth instead of use value, the worker would not only not enrich himself but also lose the use value into the bargain. For as a rule the maximum of industriousness and of labour, and the minimum of consumption—and this amounts to the maximum of his self-denial and his money-making—could lead to nothing else than that he would receive a minimum of wages for a maximum of labour. By his exertion he would only have diminished the general *level* of the costs of production of his own labour and thereby its general price. It is only as an exception that the worker, by means of will-power, physical strength and endurance, parsimoniousness, etc., can convert his coin into money, as an exception from his class and from the general conditions of his existence.

If all or the majority are over-industrious (in so far as industriousness is left to their own discretion at all in modern industry, which is not the case in the most important and most developed branches of production), they do not increase the value of their commodity, but only its quantity; that is, the demands which would be imposed on them as use value. If they all save, a general reduction of wages will soon put them back on the right foot. For such general saving would show the capitalist that their wages were in general too high, that they were receiving more than the equivalent for their commodity, the right to dispose over their labour; for it is precisely the essence of simple exchange— and they stand in this relation towards the capitalist—that no one throws more into circulation than he withdraws from it, but also that no one can withdraw more than he has thrown in.

An individual worker can be *industrious* above the necessary level, more industrious than is necessary to live as a worker, only because another is below the level, is lazier. He can save only because and if another squanders. The most he can attain on average with his frugality is to be better able to endure the adjustment of prices—high and low, their circuit; that is only to distribute his enjoyments more appropriately, not to acquire wealth. And that is actually what the capitalists demand. The workers should save enough in times of good business to be able to more or less live in bad times, to endure SHORT TIME or the reduction of wages, etc. (The wage would then fall still lower.) It really amounts to the demand that they should always make do with a minimum of pleasures of life and make crises easier, etc., for the capitalists; that they should consider themselves as pure labouring machines, and pay as much as possible of their WEAR AND TEAR themselves. Apart from the sheer brutalisation to which this would lead—and this brutalisation would itself make it impossible even to strive for wealth in its general form, as money, as accumulated money—(and the worker's participation in higher, including spiritual, pleasures, agitation for his own interests, subscription to newspapers, attending lectures, educating his children, developing his taste, etc., his only share in civilisation, which distinguishes him from the slave, is economically possible only by his extension of the range of his enjoyments in times of good business, that is at the times when saving is possible to a certain degree)—apart from this, if he truly saved in this ascetic fashion, and so accumulated premiums for the Lumpenproletariat, the rogues, etc., whose number would grow in proportion to demand, he would merely be able to preserve his savings—if they went beyond the saving-boxes of the official savings banks, which pay him a minimum of interest so that the capitalists make a large interest on them or the State consumes them, whereby he only increases the power of his opponents and his own dependence—he would be able to preserve and gain from his savings only if he put them into banks, etc., so that he afterwards loses his deposits in times of crises, while in times of prosperity he has abstained from all the pleasures of life in order to expand the power of capital. Thus he has in every way saved *for* capital, not [II-28] for himself.

Moreover—in so far as the whole thing is not a hypocritical pretence of bourgeois "philanthropy", which in general consists in fobbing the workers off with "pious wishes"—each capitalist certainly demands that his workers should save, but only *his* own, because they confront him as workers; but by no means the remaining *world of workers,* because they confront him as consumers. IN SPITE of all "pious" phrases, he therefore tries to find all kinds of means to spur them on to consumption, to endow his commodities with new attractions, to talk the workers into feeling new needs, etc. It is precisely this aspect of the relationship between capital and labour which is an essential moment of civilisation, and upon which rests the historical justification but also the present power of capital. (This relationship between production and consumption is only to be developed later, under capital and profit, etc., or also under accumulation and competition of capitals.)

These are nevertheless all exoteric considerations, relevant here in so far as the demands of hypocritical bourgeois philanthropy are shown to be self-negating and therefore to prove precisely what they are meant to refute: that in the exchange between the worker and capital, the worker finds himself in the relationship of simple circulation, therefore does not obtain wealth, but only subsistence, use values for immediate consumption. That the demand contradicts the relationship itself, emerges from the simple reflection (We shall deal with the demand, recently advanced occasionally with self-complacency, to give the workers a certain share in profit, in the section on the *wages of labour*; except as *special bonus* which can fulfil its purpose only as an exception to the rule, and which is IN FACT virtually restricted to the buying of individual OVERLOOKERS, etc., in the interest of the employer *against* that of their own class; or to [the employment of] salesmen, etc., in short no longer *common workers,* in which case it no longer affects the general relationship. Or it is a special way of cheating the workers and *withholding part of their wages* in the more precarious form of a profit depending on the state of the business.) that if the saving of the worker is not to remain a simple product of circulation—saved-up money which can only be realised by being converted sooner or later into the substantial content of wealth, enjoyments—the accumulated money itself would have to become capital, i.e. would have to buy labour, to relate to labour as use value. It thus again presupposes labour which is not capital, and presupposes that labour has turned into its opposite—non-labour. The worker's saving, in order to become capital, implies labour as non-capital in contrast to capital. Therefore the contradiction which was supposed to have been overcome at one point, would reappear at another point.

If, then, in the original relation itself the object and the *product* of the exchange of the worker—as product of simple exchange it cannot be any other product—were not use value, subsistence, satisfaction of immediate needs, withdrawal from circulation of the equivalent put into it, in order to be destroyed by consumption—labour would confront capital not as labour, not as non-capital, but as capital. But capital, too, cannot confront capital, if it is not confronted by labour, for capital is capital only as non-labour, in this antithetical relation. Therefore the concept and relation of capital itself would be destroyed.

That there are conditions in which owners who themselves work exchange with one another is CERTAINLY not denied. But such conditions are not conditions of a society in which capital developed as such exists; they are everywhere destroyed, therefore, by its development. Capital can posit itself as capital only by positing labour as non-capital, as pure use value.

(As a slave, the labourer has *exchange value,* a *value*; as a free worker, he has *no value*; only the right to dispose over his labour, acquired by exchange with him, has value. He does not confront the capitalist as exchange value, but the capitalist confronts him as exchange value. His *valuelessness* and *devaluation* is the prerequisite of capital and the condition for *free* labour in general. Linguet considers it a retrogression[a]; he forgets that the worker is thereby formally posited as a person who is something for himself *apart from his labour,* and who alienates what expresses his life [Lebensäusserung] only as a means for his own life.[86] So long as the worker as such has *exchange value, industrial capital* as such cannot exist, therefore developed capital in general cannot exist. Labour must confront capital as *pure use value,* which is offered as a commodity by its owner himself in exchange for capital, in

---

[a] [S. N. H. Linguet,] *Théorie des loix civiles, ou Principes fondamentaux de la société,* Vol. II, London, 1767, pp. 462-513.— *Ed.*

exchange for its *exchange value* [coin], which, of course, becomes real in the hands of the worker only in its determination as general means of exchange; otherwise disappears.) WELL.

The worker, then, is only in the relation of simple circulation, of simple exchange, and obtains only *coin* for his use value; subsistence; but mediated. This form of mediation is, as we have seen, essential for and characteristic of the relationship.[a] That he can proceed to the conversion of his coin into money—savings— only proves that his relationship is that of simple circulation; he can save more or less; but beyond that he cannot go. He can realise his savings only by temporarily enlarging the range of his enjoyments. It is important—and it affects the determination of the relationship itself—that, as money is the product of his exchange, general wealth drives him on as an illusion; makes him industrious. At the same time, this not only formally provides scope for arbitrariness for the realisation [II-29][b]...

[In this exchange, the worker indeed receives money only as *coin*, i.e. only in the vanishing form of subsistence for which he exchanges it. Subsistence, not wealth, the purpose of the exchange for him.

The *capacity to work* has been called the capital of the worker, in so far as it is the fund which he does not consume in an individual exchange, since he can constantly repeat the exchange for the duration of his *life as a worker*. According to this, everything would be capital which is a fund of repeated[c]]

[III-8] [87] processes of the same subject; e.g. the substance of the eye is the capital of sight, etc. Such belletristic phrases, which by means of some sort of analogy relate everything to everything else, may even appear profound when are said for the first time, and the more so the more they identify the most disparate things. If repeated, and especially if repeated complacently, as statements of

---

a See this volume, pp. 211-14.— *Ed.*

b The last, 29th, page of Notebook II of the manuscript is missing. The contents of this page can be judged by reference to the following passage in the *References* Marx made in the summer of 1861 as a guide to the notebooks of his 1857-58 manuscript (see present edition, Vol. 29): "Capital confronts the worker only as power of things. Without personal worth. Distinction from service-rendering. The worker's aim in exchange with capital—consumption. Must keep starting afresh. *Labour as the worker's capital.*"— *Ed.*

c The end of the missing page is restored according to the Economic Manuscript of 1861-63 (Notebook II-A), where Marx reproduced it. Further as on page 8 of Notebook III of the 1857-58 manuscript.

Page 8 of Notebook III of the manuscript is marked: *Chapter on Capital (continuation)* (from Notebook II) (Last day of November) "*29, 30 November* and *December*".— *Ed.*

scientific value, they are *tout bonnement*[a] foolish. Suitable only for belletristic story-tellers and empty chatterboxes who besmear all sciences with their liquorice-sweet rubbish.

The fact that labour is always a new source of exchange for the worker so long as he is able to work—that is to say, not of any exchange but of exchange with capital—is inherent in the nature of the concept itself, namely that he sells only the temporary right to dispose over his labour capacity, hence can always begin the exchange anew as soon as he has absorbed the required amount of substances to be able to reproduce his life-activity. Instead of making this the object of their amazement—and telling the worker it is a great merit of capital he can live at all, that he can repeat certain life processes every day, as soon as he has slept and eaten sufficiently—these whitewashing sycophants of bourgeois political economy should rather have noted that after constantly repeated labour, the worker has *only* his living immediate labour to exchange. The repetition itself is IN FACT only apparent. *What he exchanges with capital is his entire labour capacity which he spends in, SAY, 20 years.* Instead of paying him for this at once, capital pays for it in instalments, as he puts it at the disposal of capital, say, in weekly instalments. This alters absolutely nothing in the nature of the matter and does not at all justify the conclusion that, because the worker must sleep for 10-12 hours before he is able to repeat his labour and his exchange with capital, labour constitutes *his capital.* What is IN FACT conceived of as capital here, is the limit on, the interruption of, his labour, the fact that he is not a *perpetuum mobile.* The struggle for the Ten Hours Bill,[88] etc., proves that the capitalist desires nothing more than that the worker should *expend his dosages of life power as much as possible without interruption.*

We come now to the second process, which constitutes the relation between labour and capital *after* this exchange. We want to add here only that the political economists themselves express the above statement thus: *wages are not productive.* Productive for them, OF COURSE, means productive of wealth. Now, since wages are the product of exchange between worker and capital—and the only product that is posited *in* this act itself—they admit that the worker produces *no wealth* in this exchange, either for the capitalist, for whom the payment of money for a use value—and this *payment* forms the only function of capital in this relationship—is the giving up of wealth, not its creation, which is why he tries to pay as little as possible; or for the worker, because it

---

[a] Simply.— *Ed.*

produces for him only means of subsistence, satisfaction of individual needs, more or less— *never* the general form of wealth, never wealth. Nor can it, for the content of the commodity which he sells does not in any way place it above the general laws of circulation, under which the value he throws into circulation obtains him, by means of coin, an equivalent in another use value, which he consumes. Such an operation can OF COURSE never enrich, but must at the end of the process bring the operator back exactly to the point at which he was at its beginning. This does not, as we have seen,[a] exclude but rather includes the possibility that the range of his immediate satisfactions may contract or expand to a certain extent. On the other hand, if the capitalist—who in this exchange is not even posited yet as capitalist but only as *money*—repeated this act again and again, his money would soon have been eaten up by the worker and he [III-9] would have squandered it in a series of other satisfactions, patched trousers, polished boots,—in short, services received. In any case, the repetition of this operation would be measured exactly by the limit of his purse. It would not enrich him any more than the expenditure of money for other use values for his own beloved self, all of which, as is well known, do not bring in but cost money.

Seeing that in the relationship of labour and capital, and also in this first relationship of exchange between the two, the worker buys exchange value and the capitalist use value, in that labour confronts capital not as *a* use value but as use value *pure and simple*, it may seem peculiar that the capitalist should obtain wealth, and the worker only a use value which is extinguished in consumption. //In so far as this concerns the capitalist, this is only to be developed in relation to the second process.// This appears as a dialectic, which turns into the reverse of what would be expected. But looked at more closely, it becomes clear that the worker, who exchanges his commodity, goes through the form C—M—M—C in the process of exchange. If in circulation we start from the commodity, from use value as the principle of exchange, we necessarily arrive back at the commodity, in that money appears only as coin, and as means of exchange is only a vanishing mediator; but the commodity as such, after it has traversed its circuit, is consumed as a direct object of need. On the other hand, capital represents M—C—C—M; the antithetical moment.

The *separation of property from labour* appears as a necessary law

---

[a] See this volume, pp. 211-17.— *Ed.*

of this exchange between capital and labour. Labour as *non-capital*, posited as such, is:

(1) *Not objectified labour, negatively conceived* (itself still objective; the not-objective itself in objective [objectiver][a] form). As such it is non-raw material, non-instrument of labour, non-raw product: labour separated from all means of labour and all objects of labour, from its whole objectivity [Objektivität]. Living labour existing as *abstraction* from these moments of its actual reality (likewise, non-value); this complete denudation, the purely subjective existence of labour lacking all objectivity [Objektivität]. Labour as *absolute poverty*: poverty, not as shortage, but as a complete exclusion of objective wealth. Or also as *the* existing *non-value* and hence purely objective use value, existing without mediation, this objectivity can only be one not separated from the person; only one coincident with his immediate corporality. Since the objectivity is purely immediate, it is also immediately non-objectivity. In other words: not an objectivity falling outside the immediate existence of the individual himself.

(2) *Not-objectified labour, non-value, positively* conceived; or negativity relating itself to itself. As such it is not-*objectified*, therefore non-objective, i.e. subjective existence of labour itself. Labour not as object but as activity; not as itself *value*, but as the *living source* of value. General wealth, in contrast to capital, in which wealth exists objectively, as reality—general wealth as its *general possibility*, which [possibility] proves itself as such in activity. It is therefore no contradiction at all that labour is on the one hand *absolute poverty as object*, and on the other the *general possibility* of wealth as subject and activity, or rather these mutually wholly contradictory statements condition each other and follow from the essence of labour, as it is *presupposed* by capital as its opposite, as the antithetical existence of capital, and as, on the other hand, it, in its turn, presupposes capital.

The last point, to which attention still has to be paid concerning the relationship of labour to capital, is this: as use value *as such* confronting money posited as capital, it is not this or that labour, but *labour pure and simple*, abstract labour; absolutely indifferent to its particular *determinateness*, but capable of assuming any determinateness. Labour must of course correspond to the particular

---

[a] Except for the cases where the German words *objectiv* or *Objektivität* (objective, objectivity as against subjective, subjectivity) is given in brackets, the English *objective* and its derivatives stand for words derived from the German *Gegenstand* (object, thing).— *Ed.*

substance of which a particular capital consists as a particular labour; but since capital *as such* is indifferent to every particularity of its substance, and is both the totality of all its particularities as well as the abstraction from all of them, labour confronting capital has subjectively this same totality and abstraction in itself. E.g. in guild and craft labour, where capital itself still has an undeveloped form, is still completely immersed in a specific substance, hence is not yet *capital as such*, labour, too, appears as still immersed in its particular specificity; [appears] not in the totality and abstraction of labour *as such* as it confronts capital. That is to say, though labour is in every individual case a specific kind of labour, capital can confront any *specific* labour; the *totality* of all labour confronts it δυνάμει[a] and it is fortuitous which particular one confronts it at any particular time.

On the other hand, the worker himself is absolutely indifferent to the specificity of his labour; it has as such no interest for him, but only in so far as it is, in general, *labour* and is as such use value for capital. [III-10] To be the bearer of labour as such, i.e. of labour as *use value* for capital, is therefore the sum total of his economic character; he is *worker* in contrast to the capitalist. This is not the character of the artisan, guild-member, etc., whose economic character lies precisely in the *specificity* of their labour and their relation to a *specific master*, etc.

This economic relation—the character which capitalist and worker bear as the extremes of a relation of production—is therefore developed the more purely and adequately, the more labour loses all craft-like character, the more its particular skill becomes something abstract, irrelevant, and the more it becomes *purely abstract*, purely mechanical *activity*, hence irrelevant, indifferent to its particular form; the more it becomes merely *formal* activity or, what is the same, merely *physical* [*stoffliche*] activity, activity pure and simple, indifferent to its form. Here we have another example of how the particular specificity of the relation of production, of the category—here capital and labour—becomes real only with the development of a particular *material mode of production* and a particular stage of development of the industrial *productive forces*. (This point in general to be particularly developed in the context of this relation later, as it is already *posited* here in the relation itself, while in the case of the abstract determinations, exchange value, circulation, money, it is still more relevant to our subjective reflection.)

---

[a] Potentially.— *Ed.*

(2) We come now to the second aspect of the process. The exchange between capital or capitalist and the *worker* is now complete, in so far as it is a question of the process of *exchange* at all. It now proceeds to the relation of capital to labour as its use value. Labour is not only the *use value* confronting capital, it is *the use value* of capital itself. As the non-being of values in so far as they are objectified, labour is their being in so far as they are not objectified, their ideal being; the possibility of values, and as activity the positing of value. Opposed to capital it is the mere abstract form, the mere possibility of value-positing activity which exists only as ability, capacity in the bodily existence of the worker. But brought into real activity by contact with capital—by itself it cannot enter upon such activity, since it is without object—it becomes a real value-positing, productive activity. With respect to capital, the activity can, in general, only consist in the reproduction of capital—the preservation and increase of it as *real* and *effective* value, not of only notional value, as in money as such. By the exchange with the worker, capital has appropriated labour itself, which has become one of the moments of capital, and which now acts as a fructifying vitality upon its merely present and hence dead objectivity.

Capital is money (exchange value posited for itself), but no longer money as in a particular substance and therefore excluded from the other substances of the exchange values existing alongside it, but obtaining its ideal determination in all substances, in exchange values representing every form and mode of existence of objectified labour. In so far as capital, as money existing in all particular forms of objectified labour, now enters the process with labour, not objectified labour but living labour, labour existing as process and action, it is initially in this qualitative difference of the substance in which it exists from the form, in which it now *also* exists as labour. It is in the process of this distinction and the transcendence of this distinction that capital itself becomes a process.

Labour is the yeast thrown into capital, bringing it now into fermentation. On the one hand, the objectivity in which capital exists must be processed, i.e. consumed by labour. On the other hand, the mere subjectivity of labour as pure form must be transcended, and it must be objectified in the material of capital. The relation of capital in accordance with its content to labour, of objectified labour to living labour—in this relation where capital appears as passive towards labour, it is its passive being, as a particular substance, that enters into relation with labour as creative activity—can in general only be the relation of labour to its objectivity, its physical matter—(which must be dealt with already in the first chapter which must precede that on exchange value and must treat of production in general)—and with regard to labour as activity the physical matter, the objectified labour, has only two relations: that of the *raw material*, i.e. of the formless physical matter, of mere material for the form-giving, purposive activity of labour; and that of the *instrument of labour*, of the means, itself objective, by which the subjective activity inserts an object as its conductor between itself and the object.

The determination as *product*, which the economists bring in here, does not yet belong here at all, as a determination *distinct* from raw material and instrument of labour. It appears as *result*, not as *premiss* of the process between the passive content of capital and labour as activity. As *premiss*, the product is not a relation of the object to labour different from raw material and instrument of labour, because raw material and instrument of labour, as they are the substance of values, are themselves *objectified labour, products.* The substance of value is in general not the particular natural substance, but objectified labour. This itself, [III-11] in turn, appears in relation to *living labour* as *raw material* and *instrument of labour.* Considering the simple act of production in itself, the instrument of labour and the raw material may appear as already existing in nature, so that they only need to be *appropriated*, i.e. made into object and means of labour, which is not itself a process of labour. In relation to them, therefore, the *product* appears as something qualitatively different, and is a product not only as the result of labour applied by means of the instrument to the physical matter, but as the first *objectification of labour* alongside them. But as component parts of capital, raw material and instrument of labour are themselves already objectified labour, that is *product.*

This still does not exhaust the relationship. For, e.g. in production in which no exchange value at all exists, no capital therefore exists, the product of labour can become the means and object of new labour. For example, in agriculture producing purely for use value. The bow of the hunter, the net of the fisherman, in short the simplest conditions already presuppose the product which ceases to count as product and becomes *raw material*, or in particular *instrument of production*, for this is really the first specific form in which the product appears as means of reproduction. This relation therefore by no means exhausts the relationship in which *raw material* and *instrument of labour* make their appearance as moments of capital itself.

The economists, incidentally, bring in the *product* as the third element of the substance of capital in quite a different connection as well. It is the product, in so far as it is destined to step outside both the process of production and circulation, and to be immediate object of individual consumption, *approvisionnement*, as Cherbuliez calls it.[a] That is to say, the products which are presupposed so that the worker lives as worker and is capable of living during production, before a new product is produced. That the capitalist possesses this capacity is posited in that each element of capital is money and as such can be transformed from itself as the general form of wealth into the physical matter of wealth, objects of consumption. The *approvisionnement* of the economists, therefore, applies only to the workers; i.e. it is the money expressed in the form of consumable objects, use value, which they receive from the capitalist in the act of exchange between the two [parties]. But this belongs in the first act [of the exchange]. How far this first act is related to the second, is not yet at issue here. The only diremption posited by the process of production itself is the original diremption, that posited by the distinction between objectified labour and living labour itself, i.e. that between *raw material* and *instrument of labour*. That the economists confuse these determinations is quite in order, since they must confuse the two moments of the relation between capital and labour and dare not fix the specific difference between them.

Thus: the raw material is consumed by being changed, formed by labour, and the instrument of labour is consumed by being used up in this process, worn out. On the other hand, labour is likewise consumed by being employed, set in motion and so a definite quantity of the muscular strength, etc., of the worker is spent, whereby he exhausts himself. But it is not merely consumed; at the same time, it is converted from the form of activity and fixed, materialised, into that of object, of rest; as change of object, it changes its own form and from activity becomes being. The end of the process is the *product*, in which the raw material appears as combined with labour, and in which the instrument of labour has likewise translated itself from mere possibility into reality, in that it has become the real conductor of labour, but thereby it has been consumed in its static form through its mechanical or chemical relation to the material of labour.

---

[a] Cherbuliez used "approvisionnement" in the sense of "means of subsistence" (*Richesse ou pauvreté*, Paris, 1841, p. 16).— *Ed.*

All three moments of the process: material, instrument, labour, coincide in a neutral result: *the product*. In the product are at once reproduced the moments of the process of production which were consumed in it. The whole process therefore appears as *productive consumption*, i.e. as consumption which neither ends in *nothing* nor in the mere subjectification of the objective, but which, in turn, is itself posited as an *object*. The consumption is not a simple consumption of the physical matter, but consumption of consumption itself; in the transcendence of the physical matter, it is the transcendence of this transcendence, and hence the *positing* of the physical matter. The *form-giving* activity consumes the object and consumes itself, but it consumes the given form of the object only in order to posit it in a new objective form, and it consumes itself only in its subjective form as activity. It consumes the objectivity [das Gegenständliche] of the object—the indifference to form— and the subjectivity [das Subjektive] of the activity; forms the one, materialises the other. As *product*, however, the result of the process of production is *use value*.

[III-12] If we now consider the result so far obtained, we find:

Firstly: By the appropriation, incorporation of labour into capital—money, i.e. the act of purchase of the right to dispose over the worker, appears here only as a means of bringing about this process, not as a moment of the process itself—capital begins to ferment and becomes a process, the *process of production*, in which it, as totality, as living labour, relates to itself not only as objectified, but—because objectified—as *mere object* of labour.

Secondly: In simple circulation, the substance of the commodity and of money was itself of no consequence for their formal character, i.e. in so far as commodity and money remained moments of circulation. The commodity, so far as its substance was concerned, fell outside the economic relationship as object of consumption (of need). Money, in so far as its form made itself independent, still related itself to circulation, but only negatively, and was only this negative relation. Fixed for itself, it was likewise extinguished in dead materiality, ceased to be money. Commodity and money were both expressions of exchange value and different only as general and particular exchange value. This difference itself was, in turn, only a notional one, in that both in real circulation the two determinations were exchanged, and each considered for itself changed its determination: money itself was a particular commodity and the commodity as price was itself general money. The difference was only formal. Each was posited in the one determination only because, and in so far as, it was not posited in the other. Now, however, in the process of production, capital distinguishes itself as a form from itself as a substance. It is both aspects at once, and at the same time the relation of the two to one another. But:

Thirdly: It appeared as this relation still only *in itself*. The relation is not yet *posited*, or is initially posited only in the character of one of the two moments, that of the *physical matter*, which is in itself different as material (raw material and instrument) and form (labour), and as the relation of both, as real process, is itself again only a relation of physical matter—relation of the two physical elements which make up the content of capital distinct from its formal relation as capital.

If we consider capital from the aspect in which it originally appears distinct from labour, it is in the process only passive being, only objective being, in which the formal character which makes it capital—i.e. a social relationship existing for itself[89]—is completely extinguished. It enters the process only as content—as objectified labour in general; but the fact that it is objectified labour is completely indifferent to labour, and it is the relation of labour to capital which constitutes the process. Indeed, it is only as object, not as *objectified labour*, that it enters the process, that it is worked on. Cotton which becomes yarn, or yarn which is woven into cloth, or the cloth which becomes material for printing and dyeing, exist for labour only as already available cotton, yarn, cloth. In so far as they themselves are products of labour, are objectified labour, they do not enter into any process at all; they do so only as material existences with particular natural properties. *How* these have been posited in them does not concern the relation of living labour to them; for living labour they exist only in so far as they exist in distinction from it, i.e. as material for labour.

This, in so far as the point of departure is capital in its objective form as a prerequisite for labour. On the other hand, in so far as labour itself has become one of capital's objective elements through the exchange with the worker, its distinction from the objective elements of capital is itself only an objective one; the objective elements are in the form of rest, labour is in the form of activity. The relation is the physical one of one of its elements to the other; but not *its own* relation to both.

Capital appears therefore on the one hand only as *passive object*, in which all relation of form has been extinguished; it appears on the other hand only as simple *process of production*, in which capital as such, as distinct from its substance, does not enter. It does not even appear in the substance appropriate to it—as objectified labour, for this is the substance of exchange value—but only in the natural form of being of this substance, in which all relation to exchange value, objectified labour, to labour itself as use value of capital—and therefore all relation to capital itself—has been extinguished.

Looked at from this side, [III-13] the process of capital coincides with the simple process of production as such, in which its character as capital is quite as extinguished in the form of the process, as money was extinguished as money in the form of value. So far as we have considered this process up to this point, capital existing for itself, i.e. the capitalist, does not enter at all. It is not the capitalist who is consumed by labour as raw material and instrument of labour. Nor is it the capitalist who consumes, but labour. The process of production of capital thus does not appear as the process of production of capital but as the process of production pure and simple, and, in *distinction from labour*, capital appears only in its physical determination of *raw material* and *instrument of labour*. It is this aspect—which is not merely an arbitrary abstraction but an abstraction vanishing in the process itself—which the economists seize upon in order to represent capital as a necessary element of every process of production. Of course, they only do this by forgetting to pay attention to its behaviour as capital during this process.

Here is the place to draw attention to a moment which here, for the first time, arises not only from the standpoint of observation but is posited in the economic relationship itself. In the first act, in the exchange between capital and labour, labour as such, existing *for itself*, necessarily appeared as the *worker*. Similarly here in the second process: capital in general is posited as value existing for itself, as *egotistic* value, so to speak (something which was only aspired to in money). But capital existing for itself is the *capitalist*. Of course, socialists say: we need capital, but not the capitalist.[90] Capital then appears as a pure thing, not as relationship of production, which, reflected in itself, is precisely the capitalist. I can indeed separate capital from this individual capitalist and it can pass on to another one. But when the former loses his capital, he loses the quality of being a capitalist. Capital is therefore quite separable from an individual capitalist, but not from *the* capitalist who as such confronts *the* worker. In the same way the individual worker can cease to be the being-for-itself of labour; he can inherit money, steal, etc. But then he ceases to be a *worker*. As worker he is only labour existing for itself. (This to be further developed later.)

[LABOUR PROCESS AND PROCESS OF VALORISATION]

Nothing can emerge at the end of the process which did not appear at its beginning as its premiss and condition. On the other hand, however, all this must indeed emerge. If, therefore, at the end of the process of production which began with capital as its premiss, capital seems to have finally disappeared as a formal relation, this can only be the case because the invisible threads which it draws through the process, have been overlooked. Let us therefore consider this aspect.

The first result, then, is:

α) By the incorporation of labour into capital, capital becomes process of production; but initially *material* process of production; process of production in general, so that the process of production of capital is not distinct from the material process of production in general. Its determinateness of form is completely extinguished. Since capital has exchanged a part of its objective being for labour, that objective being itself is internally divided into object and labour; the relation of the two constitutes the process of production, or more precisely the *labour process.* Thus the *labour process, posited as point of departure before value,*—a process which because of its abstractness, its pure materiality, is equally common to all forms of production—here reappears *again within capital,* as a process which proceeds within its physical matter, forms its content.

(It will become evident that also within the process of production itself, this *extinction of the determinateness of form* is only a semblance.)

In so far as capital is value, but as a process initially appears under the form of the simple process of production, the process of production not posited in any particular *economic* determinateness, but the process of production in general, it can be said—depending on which particular aspect of the simple process of production (which as such, as we have seen, does not presuppose capital at all but is common to all modes of production) is fixed on—that capital becomes product, or that it is instrument of labour, or also the raw material of labour. Further, if it is conceived as one of those aspects which confronts labour as physical matter or mere means, then it is correct to say that capital is not productive [91] because it is then considered merely as the object, the material confronting labour; as merely passive. What is correct, however, is that it does not appear as one of these aspects, nor as the distinction of one aspect in itself, nor as mere result (product), but as the simple process of production itself; that this process now appears as the self-moving *content* of capital.

[III-14] β) Now to consider the aspect of formal determinateness, as it preserves and modifies itself in the process of production.

//What is *productive labour* or what is *not*, a point about which there has been much contention since *Adam Smith* made this distinction,[a] must emerge from the dissection of the different aspects of capital itself. *Productive labour* is only that which produces *capital*. Is it not crazy, asks e.g. (at least something like that) Mr. Senior, that the piano-maker should be a *productive worker* but not the *piano-player*, although surely the piano would be a NONSENSE without the piano-player[b]? But this is exactly the case. The piano-maker reproduces *capital*; the pianist only exchanges his labour for revenue.[92] But doesn't the pianist produce music and satisfy our musical ear; doesn't he also produce the latter to a certain degree? IN FACT, he does so; his labour produces something; but it is not thereby *productive labour* in the *economic* sense; as little productive as is the labour of the madman who produces delusions. *Labour is productive only when it produces its own opposite.* Other economists therefore allow the so-called unproductive worker to be indirectly productive. For example, the pianist stimulates production; partly because he gives a more positive, vital tuning to our individuality, or also in the ordinary sense that he awakens a new need for whose satisfaction more industry is applied in immediate material production. But this already implies the admission that only labour which produces capital is productive; that therefore labour which does not do that, however *useful* it may be—it may just as well be harmful—is not productive for capitalisation, HENCE is unproductive labour.

Other economists say that the distinction between productive and unproductive labour should be related not to production but to consumption. QUITE THE CONTRARY. The tobacco-producer is productive, although the consumption of tobacco is unproductive.

---

[a] A. Smith, *An Inquiry into the Nature and Causes of the Wealth of Nations,* Vol. II, London, 1836, pp. 335-85.— *Ed.*

[b] N. W. Senior, *Principes fondamentaux de l'économie politique,* Paris, 1836, pp. 195-206.— *Ed.*

Production for unproductive consumption is QUITE AS PRODUCTIVE AS THAT FOR PRODUCTIVE CONSUMPTION; ALWAYS SUPPOSED THAT IT PRODUCES OR REPRO- DUCES CAPITAL.

"*PRODUCTIVE LABOURER* HE THAT *DIRECTLY* AUGMENTS HIS *MASTER'S WEALTH*," says Malthus therefore quite correctly ([*Principles of Political Economy*, 2nd ed., London, 1836, p. 47] IX,[a] 40).[65]

Correct at least in one aspect. The expression is too abstract, since, formulated like this, it is equally true of the slave. The MASTER'S WEALTH in relation to the worker is the form of wealth itself in its relation to labour, i.e. capital. PRODUCTIVE LABOURER HE THAT DIRECTLY AUGMENTS CAPITAL.//

As *use value* labour exists only *for capital*, and it is the use value of capital itself, i.e. the mediating activity by which capital *valorises* itself. Capital reproducing and increasing its value is independent exchange value (money) as process, as *process of valorisation*. Labour does not therefore exist as use value for the worker; it does not exist *for* him, therefore, as *power productive* of wealth, as means or as activity of enrichment. He brings it as use value into the exchange with capital, which thus confronts him not as capital but as *money*. It is only capital as capital in relation to the worker through the consumption of labour, which initially falls outside this exchange and is independent of it. Whereas it is *use value* for capital, labour is *mere exchange value* for the worker; available *exchange value*. As such it is posited in the act of exchange with capital, by means of its sale for money.

The use value of a thing does not concern its seller as such, only its buyer. The property of saltpetre—that it can be used to make gun-powder—does not determine the price of saltpetre. This price is determined by the production costs of the saltpetre itself, the quantity of labour objectified in it. In circulation, into which use values enter as prices, their value does nor result from circulation, although it is realised only in circulation; it is *presupposed* to it, and is realised only by means of exchange for money.

Similarly, the labour which is sold by the worker as *use value* to capital, is for the worker his *exchange value* which he wants to realise, but which has already been *determined* before this act of exchange, is presupposed as condition for it, determined like the value of every other commodity by demand and supply or, in general—and we are concerned here only with the general

---

[a] This should be X.— *Ed.*

level—by the costs of production, the quantity of objectified labour, by which the worker's labour capacity has been produced and which it therefore receives as equivalent. The [III-15] exchange value of labour, whose realisation takes place in the process of exchange with the capitalist, is therefore *presupposed*, predetermined, and merely undergoes the formal modification which every price posited only notionally receives through its realisation. It is not determined by the use value of labour. For the worker himself, labour has use value only in so far as it i s *exchange value*, not in so far as it produces exchange values. For capital, it has exchange value only in so far as it is use value. It is use value as distinct from its exchange value not for the worker himself, but only for capital. The worker therefore exchanges labour as a simple exchange value which has been predetermined, determined by a previous process. He exchanges labour itself as *objectified labour*, i.e. only in so far as it already objectifies a definite quantity of labour and hence its equivalent is already measured, given. Capital obtains it through exchange as living labour, as the general power productive of wealth; as wealth-augmenting activity. It is clear, therefore, that the worker cannot *enrich* himself through this exchange, since, in exchange for his labour capacity as a given magnitude, he surrenders its *creative power*, like Esau who gave up his birthright for a mess of pottage.[a] Rather, he necessarily impoverishes himself, as we shall see later on, in that the creative power of his labour establishes itself as the power of capital, and confronts him as an *alien power*. He *divests* himself of labour as power productive of wealth; capital appropriates it as such. The separation of labour and property in the product of labour, the separation of labour and wealth, is therefore posited in this very act of exchange. What appears as paradoxical *result*, is already contained in the premiss itself. The economists have expressed this more or less empirically.

Thus the productivity of his labour, his labour altogether, in so far as it is not a *capacity* but movement, *real* labour, *becomes* an *alien power* relative to the worker. Capital, on the contrary, valorises itself through the *appropriation of alien labour*. (At least valorisation is thereby made possible; as a result of the exchange between labour and capital. The relationship is realised only in the act of production itself, where capital actually consumes alien labour.)

Just as labour as *presupposed* exchange value is exchanged by the

---

[a] Genesis 25:31-34.— *Ed.*

worker for an equivalent in money, this is, in turn, exchanged for
an equivalent in *commodities* which are consumed. In this process
of exchange, labour is not productive; it only becomes so for
capital; it can withdraw from circulation only what it has thrown
into it, a *predetermined* quantity of commodities which is no more
its own product than it is its own value.

> The workers, says *Sismondi,* exchange their labour for grain and consume it,
> while their labour "has become *capital* for their master" (Sismondi, [*Nouveaux
> principes d'économie politique,* Vol. I, p. 90,] VI).
> "Giving their labour in exchange, the workers *convert* it into capital" (idem,
> [p. 105,] VIII).
> By selling his labour to the capitalist, the worker receives a right only to the
> *price of labour,* not to the *product of this labour* nor to the value *he has added to it*
> (Cherbuliez, [*Richesse ou pauvreté,* pp. 55-56,] XXVIII).
> "*Sale of labour = renunciation of all the fruits of labour*" (l.c. [p. 64]).

All advances of civilisation, therefore, or in other words all
expansion of the *social productive forces,* or, IF YOU WANT, of the
productive forces of labour itself—as they result from science,
inventions, division and combination of labour, improved means
of communication, creation of the world market, machinery,
etc.—do not enrich the worker but *capital*; hence they only
further enlarge the power dominating over labour; enlarge only
the productive power of capital. Since capital is the antithesis of
the worker, they augment only the *objective power* standing over
labour.

The *transformation of labour* (as living, purposive activity) into
capital is, *in itself,* the result of the exchange between capital and
labour, in so far as that transformation gives the capitalist the
right of ownership over the product of labour (and command over
labour). *This transformation* is *posited* only in the *process of
production* itself. The question whether or not capital is productive
is therefore absurd. Labour itself is *productive only* as absorbed into
capital, only where capital constitutes the basis of production and
the capitalist is therefore the commander of production. The
productivity of labour becomes the productive power of capital in
the same way as the general exchange value of commodities fixes
itself in money. Labour, as it exists in contrast to capital, *for itself,*
in the worker, labour therefore in its *immediate being,* separated
from capital, is *not productive.* As activity of the worker, moreover,
it never becomes *productive,* because it enters only into the simple
process of circulation, which effects only formal transformations.
Those writers, therefore, who demonstrate that all [III-16] the
productive power ascribed to capital is a *misplacement,* a *transposi-*

tion of the productive power of labour, forget precisely that capital is itself essentially this *misplacement, this transposition,* and that wage labour as such presupposes capital, which is, therefore, this TRANSUBSTANTIATION also from the viewpoint of wage labour; the necessary process for wage labour to posit its own powers as *alien* to the worker. To leave wage labour and at the same time to abolish capital is therefore a self-contradictory and self-negating demand.

Others, even economists, e.g. Ricardo, Sismondi, etc., say that *only labour,* not capital, is productive.[a] But then they do not conceive capital in its *specific determinateness of form,* as a *relation of production,* reflected in itself, and think only of its physical substance, raw material, etc. But these physical elements do not make capital into capital. On the other hand, it then again occurs to them that capital is in one respect *value,* i.e. something *immaterial,* indifferent to its physical consistency. Thus *Say:*

"*Capital is always immaterial by nature,* since it is not matter which makes capital, but the *value* of that matter, value which has nothing corporeal about it" (Say, [*Traité d'économie politique,* 3rd ed., Vol. II, p. 429,] 21).

Or *Sismondi:*

"Capital is a commercial *idea*" (J. C. L. Simonde de Sismondi, [*Études sur l'économie politique,* Vol. II, p. 273,] LX).[b]

But then again it occurs to them that capital is also another economic determination than *value,* for otherwise it would not be possible at all to speak of capital *in distinction from value,* and, that even if all capitals are values, values as such are not capital. Then they take refuge again in its physical form within the process of production, e.g. when Ricardo explains capital as ACCUMULATED LABOUR EMPLOYED IN THE PRODUCTION OF NEW LABOUR, i.e. as mere *instrument of labour* or *material for labour.*[c] In this sense, *Say* even speaks of the *productive service of capital,*[d] upon which its remuneration is supposed to be based, as if the instrument of labour as such had a claim upon the gratitude of the worker, and as if it were not

---

[a] D. Ricardo, *On the Principles of Political Economy, and Taxation,* pp. 334-37; J. C. L. Simonde de Sismondi, *Études sur l'économie politique,* Brussels, 1837-38, Vol. I, p. 22 and Vol. II, p. 273.— *Ed.*

[b] The quotations from Say and Sismondi are in French in the manuscript.— *Ed.*

[c] D. Ricardo, *On the Principles of Political Economy, and Taxation,* pp. 327 and 499.— *Ed.*

[d] J. B. Say, *Traité d'économie politique,* 3rd ed., Vol. II, pp. 425 and 429. Marx quotes in French.— *Ed.*

precisely and only through him that it can function as instrument of labour and become *productive*. The independence of the instrument of labour, i.e. a *social* determination of the instrument of labour, i.e. its determination as capital, is thus presupposed in order to deduce the claims of capital. *Proudhon's* phrase "capital is value, labour produces"[a] means absolutely nothing but: capital is value, and as nothing is said about capital here other than that it is value, value is value (the subject of the judgement is here simply another name for the predicate); and labour produces, is productive activity, means labour is labour, since it is nothing apart from the "produces".

That these identical judgements do not contain any great fund of wisdom must be obvious; and especially that they cannot express a relationship such as that between value and labour in which they themselves relate to one another and distinguish themselves from each other, and do not just lie side by side in mutual indifference. Already the fact that it is *labour* which appears confronting capital as subject, i.e. the worker only in the determination of *labour,* and this is not *he himself,* should open one's eyes. This already implies, quite apart from capital, a relationship of the worker to his own activity which is in no way the *"natural"* relationship, but itself already contains a specific *economic* determination.

Capital, so far as we consider it here, as a relationship of value and money, which must be distinguished, is *capital in general,* i.e. the quintessence of the characteristics which distinguish value as capital from value as simple value or money. Value, money, circulation, etc., prices, etc., are all presupposed, as well as labour, etc. But we are concerned neither as yet with a *particular* form of capital, nor with *one individual capital* as distinct from other individual capitals, etc. We are present at the process of its becoming. This dialectical process of becoming is only the ideal expression of the real movement through which capital comes into being. The later relations are to be considered as a development coming out of this germ. But it is necessary to fix the specific form in which capital exists at a *certain* point. Otherwise, confusion results.

[III-17] Capital has so far been considered under the aspect of its physical matter as *simple process of production*. But this process is,

---

[a] P. J. Proudhon, *Système des contradictions économiques, ou Philosophie de la misère,* Vol. I, p. 61. Marx quotes in French.— *Ed.*

under the aspect of its formal determination, a *process of self-valorisation.* Self-valorisation includes both the preservation of the original value and its multiplication.

Value enters as subject. Labour is purposive activity, and so, as far as the physical aspect is concerned, it is presupposed that in the process of production the instrument of labour has really been used as a means to an end, and that the raw material has obtained a higher use value as product than it had before, whether as a result of a chemical change of matter or of a mechanical transformation. But this side of the process, as it concerns only use value, still belongs to the simple process of production. It is not the issue here—this is indeed included, presupposed—that a higher use value has been produced (this is itself very relative; if corn is transformed into brandy, the higher use value itself is already posited with respect to circulation). Also no higher use value is produced for the individual, for the producer. At least this is fortuitous and does not concern the relationship as such. But a higher use value is produced *for others.* The point is that a *higher exchange value* has resulted.

In simple circulation, the process ended for the individual commodity when it reached its destination as use value and was consumed. It thereby went out of circulation, lost its exchange value, and its economic determination in general. Capital has consumed its material by means of labour and labour by means of its material; it has consumed itself as use value, but only as *use value for it itself,* as capital. Its consumption as use value itself, therefore, here falls within circulation, or rather it itself posits the *beginning of circulation,* or its end, whichever one wishes. The consumption itself of use value falls here within the economic process, because the use value itself is here determined by exchange value. At no moment of the process of production does capital cease to be capital or value to be value, and as such *exchange value.* Nothing is more stupid than to say, as Mr. Proudhon does,[a] that capital changes from product into exchange value by the act of exchange, i.e. by the fact that it re-enters simple circulation. We would thereby have been flung right back to the beginning, even to direct barter, where the genesis of exchange value from the product is observed.

---

[a] *Gratuité du crédit. Discussion entre M. Fr. Bastiat et M. Proudhon,* pp. 177-81. See this volume, pp. 195-96.— *Ed.*

That capital can and does re-enter circulation as commodity after the conclusion of the process of production, after its consumption as use value, is already implied in the fact that it was presupposed as self-preserving exchange value. But in so far as it now becomes commodity again only as product, and as commodity becomes exchange value, gets a price and as such is realised in money, it is a simple commodity, exchange value in general. As such it is in circulation exposed to the even chance that it may or may not be realised in money, i.e. that its exchange value may or may not become money. It is therefore much truer to say that its exchange value has become problematical—previously it was notionally posited—than that it has *come into existence*. And what is more, the fact that it is *really* posited as a higher exchange value in circulation cannot have arisen from circulation itself, in which in its simple determination only equivalents are exchanged. If it comes out of circulation as a higher exchange value, it must have entered it as such.

Capital as a form consists not of objects of labour and labour, but of *values* and still more definitely of *prices*. That its value elements have assumed different substances during the process of production, does not concern their determination as values; they are not thereby changed. If out of the form of unrest—of the process—they again condense themselves at the end of the process into resting, objective form in the product, this is likewise a mere change of physical matter in relation to value which does not affect it. True, the substances as such have been destroyed, but they have not been made into nothing but into a differently formed substance. Earlier, they appeared as elementary, indifferent conditions of the product. Now they are the product. The value of the product can therefore only=the sum of values which were materialised in the particular physical elements of the process, as raw material, instrument of labour (to this category belong also the purely instrumental commodities) and as labour itself. The raw material has been entirely consumed, so has the labour; the instrument only partly so; it therefore continues to possess part of the value of the capital in its particular mode of existence before the process began. This part therefore does not enter at all into consideration here, since it suffered no alteration. The different modes of existence of value were mere semblance, value itself constituted the essence which remained identical to itself in their disappearance. The product considered as value is from this aspect not a *product*, but rather identical, unchanged value, only existing in a different mode, which is, however, also irrelevant to it and can be exchanged for money.

The value of the product=the value of the raw material+the value of the destroyed part of the instrument of labour (i.e. the part which has been transferred to the product and transcended in its original form)+the value of the labour. Or the price of the product is equal to its costs of production, i.e.=the sum of the prices of the commodities which have been consumed in the process of production. In other words, this means nothing more than that with respect to its physical matter the process of production was of no consequence for value; [III-18] that it has therefore remained identical with itself and has only adopted another physical mode of existence, has been materialised in another substance and form. (The form of the substance does not concern the economic *form*, i.e. value as such.)

If the capital was originally=to 100 thaler, then afterwards, as before, it is 100 thaler, although the 100 thaler existed in the process of production as 50 thaler of raw cotton, 40 thaler of wages+10 thaler of the spinning machine; and now exists as spun cotton yarn to the price of 100 thaler. This reproduction of the 100 thaler is a simple retention of self-identity, it is only mediated by the material process of production. This must therefore proceed to the product or else the cotton loses its value, the instrument of labour has been consumed in vain and wages paid to labour in vain. The only condition for the self-preservation of value is that the process of production is really a total process, i.e. proceeds to the product. The totality of the process of production, i.e. that it proceeds to the product, is here in fact the condition for the self-preservation, retention of self-identity of value; but this is already implied in the first condition, that capital really becomes use value, real process of production; it is therefore at this point *presupposed*.

On the other hand, the process of production is a process of production for capital *only* in so far as it preserves itself as value in this process, i.e. in the product. The statement that the necessary price=the sum of the prices of the costs of production, is therefore purely analytical.[93] It is the premiss of the production of capital itself. First, the capital is posited as 100 thaler, as simple value; then it is posited in this process as the sum of the prices of specific value elements of itself, determined by the very process of production. The price of capital, its value expressed in money=the price of its product. That is, the value of capital as result of the process of production is the same as it was as the premiss of the process.

During the process, however, it does not subsist in the simplicity it had at the beginning, or the one which it takes on again at the end as result, but divides itself into what are initially completely indifferent quantitative components, namely value of labour (wages), value of instrument of labour and value of raw material. As yet, no other relation is posited than that in the process of production simple value divides itself numerically as several values which fuse again in the product in their simplicity, but which exist now as a *sum*. But the sum=the original unity. With respect to value, there is apart from the quantitative division absolutely no distinction in the relation between the different value quantities. 100 thaler was the original capital, 100 thaler is the product, but the 100 thaler now as the sum of 50+40+10 thaler. I could also have taken the 100 thaler originally as a sum of 50+40+10 thaler, but just as well as a sum of 60+30+10 thaler, etc. That it now appears as a sum of specific numbers of units is posited by the fact that each of the different physical elements into which the capital divided itself in the process of production represented a part, but a specific part, of its value.

It will become clear later that these numbers into which the original unity is divided, themselves have certain relations to one another, but that does not concern us here yet. In so far as a movement is posited in value itself during the process of production, it is a purely formal movement consisting in the following simple act: that value first exists as a unity, a definite number of units, which is itself regarded as a unity, as a whole: capital of 100 thaler; second, that during the process of production this unity is divided into 50 thaler, 40 thaler, and 10 thaler, a division which is essential in so far as material of labour, instrument and labour are required in specific quantities, but here, in relation to the 100 thaler themselves, this division is merely an indifferent breaking down into different amounts of the same unit; finally, that the 100 thaler reappear in the product as sum. The only process in relation to value, that at one time it appears as a whole, a unity; then as division of this unity into specific amounts; finally as sum. The 100 thaler which appear at the end as sum are equally and precisely the sum which appeared at the beginning as a unity. The determination of the sum, of the adding together, came about only through the division occurring in the act of production; but does not exist in the product as such. The statement thus says nothing more than that the price of the product=the price of the production costs, or that the value of the capital=the value of the product, i.e. that the value of the capital has preserved itself in the act of production and now appears as sum.

With this simple identity of capital or reproduction of its value through and throughout the process of production, we would not yet have got any farther than we were at the beginning. What was there at the beginning as premiss is now [III-19] there as result and indeed in unaltered form. It is clear that this is not what the economists in fact mean when they speak of the determination of price by the production costs. Otherwise, a value greater than was originally present could never be created; no greater exchange value, although a greater use value, which is not the point at all here. The point is the *use value of capital* as such, not of the use value of a commodity.

If one says that the production costs or the necessary price of a commodity is=to 110, the calculation is as follows: original capital=100 (thus e.g. raw material=50; labour=40; instrument=10)+5% interest +5% profit. Therefore the production costs=110, not=100; the production costs [Produktionskosten][29] are therefore greater than the costs of production [Kosten der Produktion].

It is of absolutely no avail to flee from the exchange value of commodities to their use value, as some economists like to do. Whether this use value is higher or lower does not as such determine exchange value. Commodities often fall below their price of production,[94] though they doubtless have obtained a higher use value than they had in the period *before* production.

It is just as useless to take refuge in circulation. I produce for 100 but sell for 110.

"PROFIT IS NOT MADE BY EXCHANGING. HAD IT NOT EXISTED BEFORE, NEITHER COULD IT AFTER THAT TRANSACTION" (Ramsay, [*An Essay on the Distribution of Wealth*, Edinburgh, 1836, p. 184] IX, 88).

That amounts to trying to explain from simple circulation the augmentation of value, whereas, on the contrary, circulation *expressly* posits value only as an equivalent. It is also clear empirically that if everyone sells 10% too dear, this is the same if they all sold for the production costs. Surplus value[95] would thereby be purely nominal, fictitious, conventional, a mere phrase. And since money is itself a commodity, a product, it would also be sold 10% too dear, i.e. the seller who received 110 thaler would IN FACT receive only 100.

(See *Ricardo* on foreign trade which he conceives of as simple circulation and therefore says:

"Foreign trade can never increase the exchange values of a country" (Ricardo, [*On the Principles of Political Economy, and Taxation*, p. 131,] 39, 40 [96]).

The reasons he advances for this are absolutely the same as those which "prove" that exchange as such, simple circulation, that is trade in general, so far as it is conceived of as circulation, can never raise *exchange values*, can never produce *exchange value*.)

The statement that price=production costs, would otherwise have to be read as: the price of a commodity is always greater than its production costs.

Apart from the simple numerical division and adding together, the process of production also adds the formal element to value, namely that its elements now appear as *production costs*, i.e. precisely that the elements of the process of production itself are not preserved in their physical qualities but rather as *values,* which are consumed in the form of being they had *prior* to the process of production.

On the other hand, it is clear that, if the act of production is only the reproduction of the value of capital, only a change of physical matter, not an economic one, would have occurred in it, and that such a mere preservation of its value contradicts its concept. True, it would remain outside circulation, like autonomous money, it would adopt the form of various commodities, but to no purpose. This would be a pointless process, since it would ultimately represent only the identical sum of money, and would merely have run the risk of being damaged in the act of production, which can miscarry, and in which money gives up its imperishable form.

WELL. The process of production is now at en end. The product has also been realised in money again, and has adopted once more the original form of the 100 thaler. But the capitalist must also eat and drink; he cannot live on this change in the form of money. A part of the 100 thaler would therefore have to be exchanged not as capital, but as coin for commodities as use values and consumed in this form. The 100 thaler would have become 90, and since he always ultimately reproduces capital in the form of money, more precisely, in the form of the quantity of money with which he began production, in the end the 100 thaler would be eaten up and the capital would have gone. But the capitalist is paid for the *labour* of throwing the 100 thaler as capital into the process of production instead of consuming them. But with what is he to be paid? And does not his labour appear absolutely useless, since capital includes wages, which means that the workers could live by the simple reproduction of the production costs, which the capitalist cannot do? He would therefore appear among the *faux frais de production*.[a] But whatever the service he renders may be—reproduction would be possible without him, since the workers in the process of production demand only the value they bring into it, therefore do not need the whole relation of capital in order to begin the process of production always anew. Secondly, there would be no fund from which the capitalist's service could be paid for, since the price of the commodity=the production costs. But if his labour were conceived of as a special labour, alongside and apart from that of the workers, perhaps as the labour of SUPERINTENDENCE, etc., then he would receive like them a definite wage, therefore he would fall into their category, and his relationship to labour would not at all be that of a capitalist; neither would he ever enrich himself, he would only receive an exchange value which he would have to consume through circulation.

The existence of capital as against labour requires that capital in its being-for-itself, the capitalist as *not-worker,* should be able to exist and live. On the other hand, it is equally clear that capital, even from the standpoint of [III-20] its ordinary economic characteristics, if it could only preserve its *value* would *not* in fact do so. *The risks of production must be compensated for.* Capital must preserve itself in the fluctuations of prices. The depreciation of capital which goes on constantly through rising productivity must be compensated for, etc. Therefore the economists flatly assert that if no proceeds, no profit, resulted from the process of production, every capitalist would consume his money instead of throwing it into production and employing it as capital. In short, if this *non-valorisation,* i.e. non-multiplication of the value of capital is presupposed, it is presupposed that capital is not a real element of production, not a *particular relation of production*; a condition is presupposed in which the production costs do not have the form of capital, and capital is not posited as a condition of production.

It is easy to understand how labour can augment use value; the difficulty lies in understanding how it can create higher exchange values than those with which it began.

---

a Overhead costs of production.— *Ed.*

Suppose the exchange value which capital pays to the worker were an exact equivalent for the value which labour produces in the process of production. In this case, an increase in the exchange value of the product would be impossible. What labour as such would have brought into the process of production over and above the original value of the raw material and instrument of labour would be paid to the worker. The value of the product itself, in so far as it is a surplus over and above the value of the raw material and instrument, would go to the worker; only the capitalist pays this value to the worker in wages and the worker gives it back to the capitalist in the product.

//The fact that the term *production costs* does not mean the sum of values entering production—even by the economists who assert that it does—is clearly illustrated by interest on borrowed capital. For the industrial capitalist this belongs directly to his outgoings, to his *real* production costs. But the very existence of interest already implies that capital emerges from production as surplus value, since interest is itself only *one form* of this surplus value. Therefore, since interest constitutes for the borrower already a part of his *direct production costs,* it is apparent that capital as such enters into the production costs, but capital as such is not a mere addition of its value components.

In interest, capital itself reappears in the character of a *commodity,* but as a commodity *specifically* distinct from all other commodities; *capital as such*—not as a simple sum of exchange values—enters into circulation and becomes *commodity.* Here the character of the commodity itself is present as *economic, specific* determination, not indifferent as in simple circulation, nor directly related to labour as its [capital's] opposite, as its use value, as in industrial capital; that is, in capital as it is in its more immediate determinations resulting from production and circulation. The commodity as capital or capital as *commodity* is not, therefore, exchanged in circulation for an equivalent. By entering into circulation, it *maintains its being-for-itself;* it therefore maintains its original relation to its owner even when it passes into the possession of another. It is therefore merely *loaned.* Its use value as such for its owner is its *valorisation,* money as money, not as means of circulation; its *use value as capital.*

The demand put forward by Mr. Proudhon that capital should not be loaned and bear interest, but should be sold as a commodity for its equivalent, like every other commodity,[a] is

---

[a] *Gratuité du crédit. Discussion entre M. Fr. Bastiat et M. Proudhon,* pp. 65-74.— *Ed.*

nothing but the demand that exchange value should never become capital but remain mere exchange value, i.e. that *capital should not exist as capital*.[97] This demand, together with the other one, namely that wage labour should remain the general basis of production, displays a delightful confusion about the simplest economic concepts. Hence the miserable role which he played in the polemic with Bastiat, about which later.[a] His chatter about considerations of fairness and justice only amounts to this: he wants to apply the property or legal relationships corresponding to simple exchange, as a standard for the property and legal relationships of a higher stage of exchange value. Therefore Bastiat himself, unconsciously, re-emphasises the moments in simple circulation which tend to give rise to capital.

Capital itself as commodity is *money as capital* or *capital as money.*//

//The third moment to be developed in the formation of the concept of capital, is *primitive accumulation* as against labour, therefore also objectless labour as against accumulation.

The *first moment* took its point of departure from value, as emerging from circulation and presupposing it. It was the *simple concept* of capital: money on the direct path to becoming capital. The *second moment* proceeded from capital as the premiss of production and the result of it. The *third moment* posits capital as a *specific unity* of circulation and production.

It must be distinguished from the accumulation [III-21] of capitals; this presupposes capitals, presumes the relationship of capital as *present,* and therefore also implies its relations to labour, prices (*capital fixe* and *circulant*), interest and profit. But capital, in order to become capital, presupposes a certain accumulation which is already contained in the independent antithesis of objectified labour to living labour; in the independent existence of this antithesis. This accumulation, which is necessary for the genesis of capital, and is therefore already contained in its concept as premiss—as a moment—is to be distinguished essentially from the accumulation of capital which has already become capital, where *capitals* must already be available.//

//We have already seen so far[b] that capital presupposes: (1) the process of production in general, as it is common to all social

---

[a] Cf. Appendix to Chapters on Money and Capital in the 1857-58 manuscript, present edition, Vol. 29.— *Ed.*

[b] See this volume, pp. 167-68, 186-87 and 189-95.— *Ed.*

conditions, that is without historical character, *human* IF YOU PLEASE; (2) *circulation,* which is already a specific *historical* product in each of its moments, and still more in its totality; (3) *capital* as the *specific* unity of both.

Now, how far the general process of production is itself modified historically, as soon as it appears only as an element of capital, must emerge in the course of its analysis; just as capital's historical premisses in general must emerge from the simple conception of its distinctive characteristics.//

//Everything else is empty chatter. Which determinations belong to the first section, *On Production in General,* and in the first part of the second section, *On Exchange Value in General,* can only emerge at the end of and as a result of the whole analysis. For example, we have already seen[a] that the distinction between use value and exchange value belongs within political economy itself, and use value should not be passed over in silence as a simple premiss as in Ricardo. The chapter on production ends objectively with the product as result; that on circulation begins with the *commodity,* which is itself *use value* and *exchange value* (therefore also *value* distinct from both), circulation as the unity of both—which, however, is only formal, and therefore collapses in the commodity as mere object of consumption, extra-economic, and in exchange value as money become independent.//

The *surplus value of capital at the end of the production process*—a surplus value which is realised in the higher price of the product only in circulation, but realised in it as all prices are, by already being *presupposed* to it in thought, laid down, before they enter into it—signifies, if expressed according to the general concept of exchange value, that the labour time objectified in the product—or the quantity of labour (expressed in terms of rest, the magnitude of labour appears as a spatial quantity, but expressed in terms of motion it is measurable only by time)—is greater than that present in the original components of capital. Now this is possible only if the labour objectified in the price of labour is less than the living labour time which has been bought with it.

The labour time objectified in capital appears, as we have seen,

---

[a] See this volume, pp. 197-98.— *Ed.*

as a sum made up of three parts: (a) the labour time objectified in the raw material; (b) the labour time objectified in the instrument; (c) the labour time objectified in the price of labour. Now, parts (a) and (b) remain unchanged as components of capital; even if they alter their form in the process, their physical modes of being, they remain unchanged as values. It is only (c) which capital exchanges for something qualitatively different: a given quantity of objectified labour for a quantity of living labour. If the living labour time were to reproduce only the labour time objectified in the price of labour, this exchange would also be purely formal, and in general with respect to value, there would only have been an exchange for living labour as another form of being of the same value, just as with respect to the value of the material and instrument of labour, only a change in its physical form of being has occurred. If the capitalist has paid the worker a price=one day's labour and the day's labour of the worker adds only one day's labour to the raw material and instrument, the capitalist would simply have exchanged exchange value in one form for exchange value in another. He would not have acted as capital. On the other hand, the worker would not have remained in the simple process of exchange: he would in fact have received the product of his labour in payment, except that the capitalist would have done him the favour of paying him the price of the product in advance before its realisation. The capitalist would have given him credit and gratis at that, *pour le roi de Prusse.*[a] *Voilá tout.*[b]

The exchange between capital and labour, the result of which is the price of labour, even though for the worker it is a simple exchange, must for the capitalist be not-exchange. He must receive more value than he has given. From the point of view of capital, the exchange must be merely *apparent,* i.e. an economic category other than exchange, or else capital as capital and labour as labour in antithesis to it would be impossible. They would exchange for each other only as equal exchange values, which exist physically in different forms of being.

In order to vindicate capital, to defend it, the economists therefore take refuge in this simple [III-22] process; they explain capital by the very process which makes impossible its existence. In order to demonstrate it, they demonstrate it away. You pay me for my labour, exchange it for its own product, and deduct the value

[a] For the King of Prussia, i.e. for nothing.— *Ed.*
[b] That's all.— *Ed.*

of the raw and other materials with which you have supplied me. That is to say, we are *associates* who bring different elements into the production process and exchange them according to their value. Thus the product is turned into money, and the money is divided up in such a way that you, the capitalist, obtain the price of your raw material and instrument, and I, the worker, get the price which labour has added to them. The benefit for you is that you now possess the raw material and the instrument in a consumable form; for me, that my labour has been valorised. Of course, you would soon be in the position of having consumed your capital in the form of money, while I as worker would get possession of both.

What the worker exchanges for capital is his labour itself (in the exchange, the right of disposing over it); he *alienates* it. What he receives as price is the *value* of this alienation. He exchanges the value-positing activity for a predetermined value, regardless of the result of his activity.

//Mr. Bastiat displays immense wisdom when he claims that the *wage* is an inessential, merely outward form; a form of association which *as such* has nothing to do with the economic relation of labour and capital.[a] If the workers were so well off, he says, as to be able to wait for the completion and sale of the product, the wage system, wage labour, would not hinder them from concluding a contract with the capitalist just as advantageous as that which one capitalist makes with another. Therefore the evil does not lie in the form of the wage system but in conditions independent of it. It does not occur to him, of course, that these conditions themselves are the *conditions of the wage system*. If the workers were also capitalists, they would in fact be related to non-labouring capital as labouring capitalists, not as labouring workers, i.e. not in the form of wage workers. Hence for Bastiat wages and profit are *essentially* the same as *profit* and *interest*. He calls this the *harmony of economic relationships,* meaning that economic relationships only *seem* to exist, while in essence, only one relationship exists—that of simple exchange. Hence the *essential* forms appear to him as in themselves *without content,* i.e. not as real forms.//

Now, how is the worker's value determined? By the objectified labour contained in his commodity. This commodity exists in his

---

a See this volume, pp. 11-16 and 180-82.— *Ed.*

vitality. In order to maintain it from day to day (we are not yet dealing with the working class, i.e. not with compensation for WEAR and TEAR by which it can maintain itself as a class, since here the worker faces capital as *worker,* as the presupposed perennial subject in antithesis to capital, not yet as a transient individual of the type "worker") he must consume a certain quantity of provisions, replace the consumed blood, etc. He receives only an equivalent. Hence tomorrow, after the conclusion of the exchange—and it is only after he has formally concluded the exchange that he carries it out in the process of production—his labour capacity will exist in the same way as before; he has received an exact equivalent, as the price he has received leaves him in possession of the same exchange value as he had before. Capital has paid him the quantity of objectified labour contained in his vitality. He has consumed it, and since it did not exist as a thing but as a capacity in a living being, he can renew the exchange in view of the *specific* nature of his commodity—the specific nature of the life process. Since we are not dealing here with *specially* skilled labour, but with labour pure and simple, we are not yet concerned with the fact that in addition to the labour time objectified in his vitality—i.e. to the labour time necessary to pay for the products required for the maintenance of his vitality—more labour is objectified in his immediate being, namely the values he has consumed in order to produce a specific *labour capacity,* a particular *skill,* the value of which is given by the costs of production of a similar specific skill.

If a whole working day were required in order to keep a worker alive for a working day, capital would not exist, because one working day would exchange for its own product. As a result, capital could not valorise itself as capital and thus could not preserve itself. The self-preservation of capital is its self-valorisation. If capital had to work in order to live, it would not preserve itself as capital but as labour. The ownership of raw materials and the instruments of labour would be purely *nominal*; [III-23] economically, they would belong just as much to the worker as to the capitalist, since they would produce *value* for the capitalist only in so far as he was himself a worker. He would therefore not treat them as capital but as mere physical matter and means of labour, just as the worker himself does in the process of production.

If, on the contrary, e.g. only half a working day is needed to keep a worker alive for a whole working day, a surplus value of the product is the automatic result, because the capitalist has paid in the price [of labour] only half a working day and he has received a whole working day objectified in the product; therefore has exchanged *nothing* for the second half of the working day. It is not exchange but a process in which he obtains without exchange *objectified labour time,* i.e. *value,* which alone can make him into a capitalist. Half the working day costs capital *nothing*; it therefore receives a value for which it has given no equivalent. And the augmentation of values can occur only because a value over and above the equivalent is obtained, hence *created.*

Speaking generally, surplus value is value over and above the equivalent. The equivalent, by definition, is only the identity of value with itself. Surplus value can never, therefore, spring from the equivalent; nor, therefore, can it spring originally from circulation. It must spring from the process of production of capital itself. The matter can also be expressed thus: if the worker requires only half a working day to live for a whole day, he needs to work only half a day to eke out his existence as a worker. The second half of the working day is forced labour; surplus labour.[98] What appears on the side of capital as surplus value, appears on the worker's side precisely as surplus labour over and above his requirements as worker, hence over and above his immediate requirements to sustain his vitality.

The great historical aspect of capital is the *creation* of this *surplus labour,* superfluous from the point of view of mere use value, of mere subsistence, and its historical mission is fulfilled when, on the one hand, needs are developed to the point where surplus labour beyond what is necessary has itself become a general need and arises from the individual needs themselves; and on the other, when, by the strict discipline of capital to which successive generations have been subjected, general industriousness has been developed as the universal asset of the new generation; and, lastly, when the productive forces of labour, constantly whipped on by capital in its unbounded lust for enrichment, and in the conditions in which alone it can satisfy this lust, have been developed to the stage where the possession and preservation of general wealth requires from the whole of society only comparatively little labour time on the one hand, and on the other labouring society takes a scientific attitude towards the process of its continuing reproduction, its reproduction in ever greater abundance; so that labour in which man does what he can make things do for him has ceased.

Accordingly, capital and labour relate to each other here like money and commodity: if the one is the general form of wealth, the other is merely the substance seeking immediate consumption. As the ceaseless striving for the general form of wealth, however, capital forces labour beyond the limits of natural need and thus creates the material elements for the development of the rich individuality, which is as varied and comprehensive in its production as it is in its consumption, and whose labour therefore no longer appears as labour but as the full development of activity itself, in which natural necessity has disappeared in its immediate form; because natural need has been replaced by historically produced need. This is why *capital is productive,* i.e. an *essential relationship for the development of the productive forces of society.* It ceases to be such only where the development of these productive forces themselves encounters a barrier in capital itself.

The Times of November [21,] 1857 contains a most endearing scream of rage from a West Indian planter.[a] With great moral indignation this advocate—by way of plea for the reintroduction of Negro slavery—explains how the *Quashees* (the free blacks of Jamaica) content themselves to produce only what is strictly necessary for their own consumption and apart from this "use value", regard loafing itself (INDULGENCE and IDLENESS) as the real luxury article; how they don't give a damn about sugar and the fixed capital invested in the PLANTATIONS, but rather react with malicious pleasure and sardonic smiles when a planter goes to ruin, and even exploit their acquired Christianity as a cover for this sardonic mood and indolence.

They have ceased to be slaves, not in order to become wage workers, but SELF-SUSTAINING PEASANTS, working for their own meagre consumption. Capital as capital does not exist for them, because wealth made independent in general exists *only* either through *direct* forced labour, slavery, or through *mediated* forced labour, *wage labour.* Wealth confronts direct forced labour not as capital but as *relationship of domination.* On the basis of direct forced labour, therefore, only the relationship of domination is reproduced, for which wealth itself has value only as gratification, not as wealth as such, and which [III-24] can therefore never create *general industriousness.* (We shall come back later to this relationship between slavery and wage labour.)

The difficulty in grasping the genesis of [surplus] value is illustrated by (1) the modern English economists, who accuse

---

[a] "Negroes and the Slave Trade. To the Editor of *The Times*", *The Times,* No. 22844, 21 November 1857.— *Ed.*

Ricardo of failing to understand surplus [the excess of the value produced over the production costs], *surplus value*[99] (see *Malthus on value,*[100] who at least tries to proceed scientifically[a]), yet of all economists, Ricardo alone has grasped it, as his polemic against A. Smith's confusion of the determination of value by wages and by the labour time objectified in the commodity shows.[b]

The new economists are nothing but shallow simpletons. True, Ricardo himself often gets into confusion, because, although he understands the emergence of surplus value as the prerequisite of capital, he often falters in the attempt to understand on this basis[c] the multiplication of values except by the investment of *more objectified labour time* in the same product, in other words only by production becoming *more difficult.* Hence the absolute contradiction between *value* and *wealth* in his theory.[d] Hence the one-sidedness of his theory of rent; his false theory of international trade, which is supposed to produce only use value (which he calls wealth), not exchange value.[e] The only remaining path leading to the multiplication of values as such, other than the *growing difficulty of production* (theory of rent), is the increase in *population* (the natural increase in the number of workers through the growth of capital), although he himself has nowhere coherently analysed this relation. His fundamental error, that he nowhere examines what actually gives rise to the distinction between the determination of value by wages and its determination by objectified labour. Money and exchange itself (circulation) thus appear only as a purely formal element in his political economy; and although political economy according to him deals *only* with exchange value, profit, etc., appear *only* as a percentage share of the product, which is equally the case on the basis of slavery. He nowhere investigates the form of the mediation.

(2) *The Physiocrats.* Here the difficulty of understanding capital, the self-valorisation of value, hence the surplus value which capital creates in the act of production, stands out palpably, as it was bound to do with the fathers of modern political economy, just as at its ultimate classical conclusion with Ricardo, who [...] the creation of surplus value in the form of rent...[f]

---

[a] Th. R. Malthus, *The Measure of Value Stated and Illustrated.—Ed.*

[b] See D. Ricardo, *On the Principles of Political Economy, and Taxation,* pp. 1-12.— *Ed.*

[c] On that of the labour theory of value.— *Ed.*

[d] D. Ricardo, op. cit., pp. 60-61, 131-32.— *Ed.*

[e] Ibid., pp. 320-37.— *Ed.*

[f] The sentence is unfinished in the manuscript.— *Ed.*

It is *au fond* the question of the concept of capital and wage labour, and hence the fundamental question which arises at the threshold of the system of modern society. The money system grasped the independence of value only in the form in which it emerges from simple circulation—as *money*; the monetarists therefore made this *abstract form* of wealth into the exclusive target of the nations, which were just then entering the period when *enrichment as such* appeared as the aim of society itself.

Then came the *mercantile system,* coinciding with the epoch in which industrial capital and therefore wage labour appeared in manufacture and developed in opposition to and at the cost of non-industrial wealth, feudal landed property. The mercantilists already dimly conceived money as capital, but really again only in the form of money, of the circulation of *merchant* capital, of capital *turning itself into money*. Industrial capital had for them a value, indeed the highest value—as means, not as wealth itself in its productive process—because it created merchant capital and this became money in the process of circulation. Manufacturing labour—i.e. *au fond* industrial labour. But agricultural labour, on the other hand, was and appeared to them as mainly productive of use value; raw produce processed is more valuable, because in this clear form, a form more suitable for circulation, for COMMERCE, a mercantile form, it produces more money (in this context, the historically evolved view of the wealth of non-agricultural nations, notably Holland, in contrast to the agricultural, feudal ones; agriculture did not appear at all in industrial but in feudal form, therefore as source of feudal, not bourgeois, wealth). One form of wage labour, industrial wage labour, and one form of capital, industrial capital, were thus recognised as a source of wealth, but only in so far as they created money. Exchange value itself was therefore not yet conceived of in the form of capital.

Now the *Physiocrats*. They distinguish capital from money and conceive it in its general form as exchange value made independent, preserving itself in and augmented by production. Hence they also consider the relation for itself, not as itself a moment of simple circulation but rather as its premiss, and as it continually reproduces itself in circulation as its premiss. The Physiocrats are therefore the fathers of modern political economy.[101]

They also understand that the positing of surplus value by wage labour is the self-valorisation of capital, i.e. its realisation. But how is surplus value created through capital, i.e. through existing values, by means of labour? Here they disregard the form altogether and consider only the simple process of production.

Hence only such labour can be productive which is carried on in a field where the natural power of the instrument of labour palpably allows the worker to produce more values than he consumes. Surplus value thus originates not from labour as such, but from the natural power used and directed by labour—[III-25] i.e. agriculture. Agricultural labour is thus the only *productive labour*, for this much the Physiocrats understand that *only labour which creates surplus value is productive*. (That surplus value must express itself in the form of a material product, is a primitive view still to be encountered in A. Smith.[a] Actors are productive workers, not by virtue of the fact that they produce plays, but in so far as they INCREASE THEIR EMPLOYER'S WEALTH. But what sort of labour is performed, in what form labour is materialised, is a matter of absolute indifference for *this relationship*. On the other hand, it is not indifferent from later points of view.) But this surplus value is imperceptibly transformed into a greater quantum of use value arising from production than that which was consumed in it. This multiplication of use values, the excess of the product above the component part of it which must be used for new production—of which a part can therefore be unproductively consumed, appears palpably only in the relationship of the natural seed to its product. Only a part of the harvest has to be directly returned to the soil as seed. In products themselves occurring naturally, in the elements, in air, water, soil, light, and in substances supplied through manure and otherwise, the seeds then reproduce that part in a multiplied quantity as grain, etc. In short, human labour has only to guide the chemical exchange of matter (in agriculture), partly also to promote it mechanically or to promote the reproduction of life itself (stock-raising) to obtain a surplus, i.e. to convert these same natural substances from a useless into a valuable form. The true form of general wealth is therefore the surplus of the products of the soil (grain, cattle, raw materials). From the economic viewpoint, therefore, only *rent* is a form of wealth. This is why the first prophets of capital recognise only the non-capitalist, the *feudal landowner* as the representative of *bourgeois* wealth. But then the consequence, the levying of all taxes on rent, is entirely to the advantage of bourgeois capital. The theory accords a bourgeois accolade to feudalism in principle—which misled many a feudal gentleman, like the elder Mirabeau—only in order to ruin it in the practical application.

---

[a] A. Smith, *An Inquiry into the Nature and Causes of the Wealth of Nations*, Vol. II, London, 1836. p. 356.— *Ed.*

All other values represent only raw material+labour; labour itself represents grain or other products of the soil which the worker consumes. Therefore the factory worker, etc., adds to the raw material no more than he consumes in raw materials. Neither he, by his labour, nor his employer, therefore, add anything to wealth—for wealth is the surplus above the commodities consumed in production—but only impart to it agreeable forms useful for consumption.

At that time the utilisation of the powers of nature in industry had not been developed, nor had the division of labour, etc., which increases the natural power of labour itself. But by Adam Smith's time this was the case. For him, therefore, labour in general is the source of value, as it is the source of wealth. But actually even labour posits surplus value only in so far as in the division of labour the surplus appears likewise as a gift of nature, as the natural power of society, just as with the Physiocrats it appeared as a gift of the soil. Hence the importance A. Smith attaches to the division of labour.

On the other hand, *capital* appears to him originally not as containing within itself the moment of wage labour, antagonistically, but as it emerges from circulation, as money, and hence as it is created out of circulation through *saving*.[a] Initially, therefore, capital does not valorise itself—precisely because the appropriation of another's labour has not been assimilated into its concept. It appears only *subsequently*, after it has already been presupposed as *capital—mauvais cercle*[b]—as *command over alien labour*. Thus labour should really receive its own product as wage according to A. Smith, the wage should be=to the product, therefore labour should not be wage labour, and capital not capital. Therefore, in order to introduce profit and rent as original elements of the production costs, i.e. to make a surplus value result from the process of production of capital, he presupposes them in the crudest form. The capitalist does not want his capital to be used for nothing; similarly, the landowner does not want to make his land available for production for nothing. They demand something in return. In this way, they and their demands are brought

---

[a] Here Marx inserted the following passage in brackets: "For, although he conceives of labour as creating value and itself being use value, productivity existing for itself, *human* natural power in general (this distinguishes him from the Physiocrats), he does not conceive of it as wage labour, not in its *specifically* determined form in opposition to capital".— *Ed.*

[b] Vicious circle.— *Ed.*

in as historical FACTS, not explained. Wages are really the *only economically* justified, because necessary, element of the production costs. Profit and rent are merely *deductions* from wages, arbitrarily enforced in the historical process by capital and landed property, and *legally,* not economically, justified.

But since on the other hand Smith opposes to labour the means and materials of production in the form of landed property and capital as independent elements, he has virtually posited labour as wage labour. Hence contradictions. Hence his vacillations in the determination of value; his placing of profit and rent at the same level; his false [III-26] views on the influence of wages upon prices, etc.

Now *Ricardo* (see 1 [a]). He again understands wage labour and capital as a natural, not specific historical, social form of the production of wealth as use value, i.e. its form as such, precisely because it is conceived of as natural, is *indifferent,* and is not conceived in its *specific* relation to the form of wealth, just as wealth itself, in its form as exchange value, appears as a purely formal mediation of its physical existence. Therefore he does not understand the specific character of bourgeois wealth—just because it appears [to him] as the adequate form of wealth in general. Although his point of departure is *exchange value,* the *specific economic forms of exchange* themselves play *economically* no role at all in his political economy. Instead he only speaks about the distribution of the general product of labour and the soil among the three classes, as though wealth based on *exchange value* were only a matter of *use value,* and as though exchange value were only a ceremonial form, which in Ricardo disappears in quite the same manner as does money as means of circulation in exchange. To bring out the true laws of political economy, he therefore likes to refer also to this relation of money as a merely formal one. Therefore also his weaknesses in the basic theory of money proper.

The exact development of the concept of capital necessary, because it is the basic concept of modern political economy, just as capital itself, of which it is the abstract reflected image, is the basis of bourgeois society. The clear understanding of the basic premiss of the [capitalist] relationship must reveal all the contradictions of bourgeois production, as well as the limits at which this relationship outgrows itself.

---

[a] See this volume, pp. 251-52.— *Ed.*

//It is important to note that wealth as such, i.e. bourgeois wealth, is always expressed to the highest power in exchange value, where it is posited as *mediator,* as mediation between the extremes of exchange value and use value themselves. This middle term always appears as the completed *economic* relation, because it comprises the opposites, and always ultimately appears as a higher power than the extremes themselves, but in a one-sided way; because the movement or the relationship which *originally* appears as mediating between the extremes, must dialectically come to appear as mediation with it itself, as the subject of which the extremes are merely the elements. It transcends their autonomous premises, and by doing so posits itself as that which alone is autonomous. An example in the religious sphere is Christ the mediator between God and man—mere instrument of circulation between them—becomes their unity, God-man, and as such becomes more important than God; the saints more important than Christ; the priests more important than the saints.

The total economic expression, itself one-sided as against the extremes, is always exchange value, where it is posited as middle link; e.g. money in simple circulation; capital itself as mediator between production and circulation. Within capital itself, one of its forms resumes the position of use value as against the other form as exchange value. Industrial capital, for example, appears as producer in relation to the merchant, who appears as circulation. So the former represents the physical aspect, and the latter the formal aspect, hence wealth as wealth. At the same time, merchant capital itself, in turn, mediates between production (industrial capital) and circulation (the consuming public) or between exchange value and use value, where both sides are posited alternately, production as money, circulation as use value (consuming public), or the first as use value (product) and the second as exchange value (money).

Likewise within trade itself: the wholesaler as mediator between manufacturer and retailer, or between manufacturer and farmer, or between different manufacturers, represents this same higher middle link. And again, the commodity brokers in relation to the wholesaler. Then the banker in relation to the industrialists and merchants; the joint-stock company in relation to simple production; the financier as mediator between the State and bourgeois society at the highest level.

Wealth as such represents itself the more distinctly and broadly the further it is removed from immediate production and itself mediates between aspects each of which, considered by itself, is

already posited as a characteristic economic form. [This is due to
the fact] that^a money turns from means into an end, and the
higher form of mediation as capital itself posits everywhere the
lower form as labour, as merely source of surplus value. For
example, the BILL-BROKER, banker, etc., in relation to the manufacturers and FARMERS, who for him are posited in the determination
of labour (of use value), while he posits himself in relation to them
as capital, production of surplus value; in the most extravagant
form in the FINANCIER.//

Capital is the *immediate unity* of product and money, or, better,
of production and circulation. So it is in turn itself something
immediate, and its development consists in positing and transcending itself as this unity, which is posited as a specific and therefore
simple relation. The unity initially appears in capital as something
simple.

[III-27] //Ricardo's reasoning is simply this:

Products are exchanged for each other—hence capital for
capital—in the ratio of the quanta of objectified labour contained
in them. A day's labour always exchanges for a day's labour. This
is the assumption. Exchange itself can therefore be ignored
altogether. The product—capital posited as product—is *in itself*
exchange value, to which the act of exchange merely adds form, in
Ricardo, formal form.

The only question now is: in what *ratios* the product is to be
shared. These *ratios* are the same, whether they are regarded as
specific quotas of the presupposed exchange value or of its
content, material wealth. Indeed, since exchange as such is mere
circulation—money as circulation—it is better to abstract from it
altogether, and to consider only the proportions of material wealth
which are distributed to the various agents within the process of
production or as the result of that process. In the form of
exchange, all value, etc., is purely *nominal;* it is real only in the
form of the *ratio.* The entire exchange, in so far as it does not
produce a greater *material variety,* is *nominal.* Since a whole day's
labour is always exchanged for a whole day's labour, the sum of
values remains the same—the growth of the productive forces
affects only the content of wealth, not its form. Augmentation of
value can therefore originate only in increased difficulty of
production—and this can only occur in agriculture where the
natural power of equal quantities of human labour no longer

---

^a In the manuscript the sentence begins with the conjunction *dass* (that).— *Ed.*

renders the same service, therefore the fertility of the natural elements declines. The fall of profits is therefore caused by rent.

Firstly the false assumption that a *whole day's labour* is always worked in all conditions of society; etc., etc. (see above[a]).⫽

We have seen[b]: the worker needs to work for only (e.g.) half a working day to live a whole day, and thus be able to begin the same process on the following day. In his labour capacity—so far as it exists in him as a *living being*, or in him as a *living* instrument of labour—only half a working day is objectified. One whole living day (day of life) of the worker is the static result, the objectification of half a working day. The capitalist, by appropriating the whole working day in exchange for the labour objectified in the worker, i.e. in exchange for half a working day, and then consuming it in the production process by applying it to the materials of which his capital consists, in this way creates the surplus value of his capital—in the case assumed here, half a day of objectified labour.

Let us now assume that the productivity of labour doubles, i.e. a given amount of labour produces twice as much *use value* in the same time. (In the relation we are discussing here, use value is defined for the time being as that which the worker consumes to keep alive as a worker; the quantum of provisions for which, through the mediation of money, he exchanges the labour objectified in his living labour capacity.) The worker would then have to work for only $1/4$ of a day to live a whole day; the capitalist then has to give only $1/4$ of a day's objectified labour in exchange to the worker to increase his surplus value in the process of production from $1/2$ to $3/4$; because he would gain, instead of $1/2$ day's objectified labour, $3/4$ of a day of it. The value of the capital, as it emerges from the process of production, would have increased by $3/4$ instead of by $2/4$.[c] The capitalist thus would need to require only $3/4$ of a day's work to add to his capital the same surplus value—$1/2$ or $2/4$ of objectified labour.

But since capital represents the general form of wealth—money—it has a boundless and measureless urge to exceed its own limits. Every boundary is and must be a barrier for it. Otherwise it would cease to be capital, money reproducing itself. If a particular boundary were not to be a barrier for it, but one to which it could

---

[a] See this volume, p. 252.— *Ed.*
[b] See this volume, pp. 249-50.— *Ed.*
[c] Marx abstracts from the value of the constant capital.— *Ed.*

confine itself without difficulty, capital would itself have declined from exchange value to use value, from the general form of wealth to a particular substance of it. Capital as such creates a particular surplus value, because it cannot create an infinite one AT ONCE; but it is the constant drive to create more of it. The quantitative border to surplus value appears to it only as a natural barrier, as a necessity, which it constantly tries to overcome and beyond which it constantly tries to go.

//The limitation appears as an accidental phenomenon which must be overcome. This is obvious even on the most superficial examination. If capital grows from 100 to 1,000, then 1,000 becomes the new point of departure from which further expansion must proceed; the ten-fold increase, by 1,000%, counts for nothing; profit and interest, in turn, become capital. *What appeared as surplus value now appears as a simple premiss,* etc., as comprised in the *simple composition* [of capital] *itself.*//

Hence (quite apart from the factors entering in later, competition, prices, etc.) the capitalist will not make the worker work only $3/4$ of a day, because $3/4$ of a day creates *the same surplus value* as did a whole day previously, he will make him work the full day; and the increased productive power, which enables the worker to live for a whole day on the basis of $1/4$ of a working day, now expresses itself simply in the fact that he must now work $3/4$ of a day [III-28] for capital, whereas he previously worked for it only $2/4$ of a day. The increased productivity of his labour, in so far as it means shortening of the time necessary for the replacement of the labour objectified in him (for the use value, for the subsistence), appears as a lengthening of his labour time for the valorisation of capital (for the exchange value).

From the worker's point of view, he must now perform a surplus labour of $3/4$ of a day to live a full day, while previously he had only to perform a surplus labour of $2/4$ of a day. The increase, the doubling of his productive power has increased his surplus labour by $1/4$ [of a day]. One thing should be noted here: productivity has doubled, the surplus labour performed by the worker has not; it has grown by only $1/4$ [of a day]. Nor has the surplus value of capital doubled, it too has increased by only $1/4$ [of a day, i.e. by 50%]. This shows that surplus labour (from the worker's point of view) or surplus value (from the point of view of capital) does not grow in the same numerical proportion as does productivity. How does this come about?

The doubling of productivity is the reduction of necessary labour [102] (for the worker) by $1/4$ [of a day]; hence also the production of surplus value is [greater] by $^1/_4$, because the original ratio assumed was $^1/_2$. If the worker had to work, originally, $^2/_3$ of a day to live one full day, the surplus value (as well as the surplus labour) would have been $^1/_3$. A doubling of the productivity of labour would then have enabled the worker to reduce the amount of necessary labour to one-half of $^2/_3$, or $\frac{2}{3 \times 2}$, $^2/_6$ or $^1/_3$ of a day, and the capitalist would have gained $^1/_3$ of [a day's surplus] value. The total surplus labour would amount to $^2/_3$ [of a day]. The doubling of productivity, which in the first example resulted in an [extra] $^1/_4$ of a day's surplus value and surplus labour, would now result in an [extra] $^1/_3$ of a day's surplus value and surplus labour. The multiplier of productivity—the factor by which it is multiplied—is, therefore, [as a rule] not the multiplier of surplus labour or surplus value; if the original ratio of labour objectified in the price of labour was $^1/_2$ of the labour objectified in one day's labour—and a day is always the limit^a—then the doubling of productivity is tantamount to the division of $^1/_2$ (the original ratio) by 2, or $^1/_4$. If the original ratio was $^2/_3$, then the doubling is tantamount to the division of $^2/_3$ by $2=^2/_6$ or $^1/_3$.

The multiplier of productivity is thus never the multiplier but always the divisor of the original ratio, not the multiplier of its numerator but of its denominator. If the former were the case, the multiplication of productivity would result in a corresponding multiplication of surplus value. But the [growth of] surplus value is always equal to a division of the original ratio by the multiplier of productivity. If the original ratio was $^8/_9$, i.e. the worker needed $^8/_9$ of the working day to live, and capital therefore gained only $^1/_9$ of a day in the exchange with living labour, and surplus labour equalled $^1/_9$, then, if productivity were doubled, the worker could earn his subsistence in one-half of $^8/_9$ of the working day, i.e. with $^8/_{18}=^4/_9$ (it is the same whether we divide the numerator or multiply the denominator), and the capitalist, who orders a full day's work, would have a total surplus value of $^5/_9$ of the working day; subtract from that the original surplus value of $^1/_9$, and $^4/_9$ remains. The doubling of productivity in this case is thus tantamount to a growth of surplus value or surplus labour time by $^4/_9$.

This is simply because surplus value always depends on the ratio between the whole working day and that part of it which is

---

^{a} Here Marx inserted the following passage in brackets: "though the worthy manufacturers have extended it into the night. *Ten Hours' Bill*. See the report of Leonard Horner. The working day itself is not limited by the natural day; it can be extended *deep into the night*; this belongs in the Chapter on *Wages*".[103]— *Ed.*

necessary for the worker to keep himself alive. The unit by which surplus value is calculated is always a fraction, i.e. the particular part of a day which exactly represents the price of labour. If this fraction$=^1/_2$, the growth[a] of [III-29] productivity=reduction of necessary labour to $^1/_4$; if it$=^1/_3$, necessary labour is reduced to $^1/_6$; hence in the first [case] the total surplus value$=^3/_4$, in the second$=^5/_6$. Relative surplus value,[104] i.e. [the increase] in relation to that previously obtained, in the first case$=^1/_4$, in the second$=^1/_6$.

The value of capital therefore does not grow in the same proportion as productivity grows, but in the proportion in which the increase of productivity, the multiplier of productivity, divides the fraction of the working day expressing the part of the day belonging to the worker. By how much [the growth of] the productivity of labour increases the value of capital thus depends on the original ratio of the part of labour which is objectified in the worker to his living labour. This part always expresses itself as a fraction of the whole working day, $^1/_3$, $^2/_3$, etc. The increase in productivity, i.e. its multiplication by a certain number, is tantamount to a division of the numerator, or a multiplication of the denominator of this fraction by the same number. How large or small the increase in the value of capital is, depends therefore not only on the number expressing the multiplication of productivity, but equally on the previously given proportion expressing the part of the working day pertaining to the price of labour. If that proportion is $^1/_3$, a doubling of the productivity of the working day means a reduction of the proportion to $^1/_6$; if the proportion is $^2/_3$, a reduction to $^2/_6$.

The objectified labour contained in the price of labour is always equal to a fraction of the whole working day; always arithmetically expressed by a fraction; always a numerical ratio, never a simple number. If productivity doubles, is multiplied by 2, the worker needs to work only $^1/_2$ the former time to cover the price of labour; but it depends on the initially given ratio, namely on the time he required before the increase in productivity, how much labour time he now still requires for this purpose. The multiplier of productivity is the divisor of the original fraction. [Surplus] value or surplus labour, therefore, does not grow in the same numerical proportion as does productivity. If the original ratio is $^1/_2$ and productivity doubles, the *necessary* labour time (for the worker) is accordingly reduced to $^1/_4$ [of the working day] and surplus value grows by only $^1/_4$ [of the working day]. If

---

[a] Should be "doubling".— *Ed.*

productivity is multiplied four-fold, the original ratio changes to $^1/_8$ and [surplus] value grows by only $^3/_8$.

[Surplus] value can never be equal to the whole working day, i.e. a definite part of the working day must always be exchanged for the labour objectified in the worker. Altogether, surplus value is always determined by the ratio of living labour to that objectified in the worker; *this* [the latter] *part of the ratio must therefore always remain.* By the very fact that the ratio is constant as a ratio, although its factors vary, a definite correlation is already given between an increase in productivity and an increase in [surplus] value. On the one side, we thus see that the relative surplus value is exactly equal to the relative surplus labour. If the [necessary] working day was $^1/_2$ and productivity doubled, then the part of the working day belonging to the worker, *necessary labour,* is reduced to $^1/_4$ [of the working day] and the newly created [surplus] value is also exactly $^1/_4$; but total [surplus] value is now $^3/_4$. While surplus value has risen by $^1/_4$, i.e. in the ratio of 1:4, the total [surplus] value$=^3/_4$ of the working day, i.e. the ratio=3:4.

If we now assume $^1/_4$ to have been the originally *necessary* working day, and a doubling of productivity to have occurred, then necessary labour is reduced to $^1/_8$, and [the increase in] surplus labour or surplus value exactly$=^1/_8=1:8$. On the other hand, total surplus value=7:8. In the first example, total surplus value was originally$=1:2$ ($^1/_2$) and then rose to 3:4; in the second case it was originally $^3/_4$ and has now risen to 7:8 ($^7/_8$). In the first case it grew from $^1/_2$ or $^2/_4$ to $^3/_4$; in the second, from $^3/_4$ or $^6/_8$ to $^7/_8$; in the first case by $^1/_4$, in the second by $^1/_8$; i.e. in the first case the increase was twice as big as in the second; [III-30] but in the first case total surplus value [after the doubling of productivity] is only $^3/_4$ or $^6/_8$, while in the second it is $^7/_8$, therefore $^1/_8$ more.

Let us assume the *necessary labour* to be $^1/_{16}$: then total surplus value$=^{15}/_{16}$ which is $^3/_{16}$ higher than in the previous case, where total surplus value was taken to be $^6/_8=^{12}/_{16}$. Let us assume now a doubling of productivity: necessary labour now$=^1/_{32}$; previously it was$=^2/_{32}$ ($^1/_{16}$); therefore surplus [labour] time has risen by $^1/_{32}$, hence also surplus value. Let us consider total surplus value, which was $^{15}/_{16}$ or $^{30}/_{32}$; it is now $^{31}/_{32}$. As compared to the earlier relation (where *necessary labour* was $^1/_4$ or $^8/_{32}$), total surplus value is now $^{31}/_{32}$, while in the earlier example it was only $^{28}/_{32}$, so the difference equals $^3/_{32}$. But considered relatively, the increase in surplus value resulting from the doubling of productivity equalled in the former case $^1/_8$ or $^4/_{32}$, whereas now it equals only $^1/_{32}$, i.e. it is less by $^3/_{32}$.

If *necessary labour* had already been reduced to $^1/_{1,000}$, total surplus value would be $^{999}/_{1,000}$. Now, if productivity increased a thousand-fold, *necessary labour* would decline to $^1/_{1,000,000}$ of a working day and total surplus value would amount to $^{999,999}/_{1,000,000}$ of a working day; while before this increase in productivity it amounted only to $^{999}/_{1,000}$ or $^{999,000}/_{1,000,000}$ of a working day; it would thus have grown by $^{999}/_{1,000,000}=^1/_{1,001}$ (with the addition of $\frac{1}{1,001+^1/_{999}}$), i.e. the thousand-fold increase in productivity would not have raised total surplus [value] by even $^1/_{1,001}$, i.e. not even by $^3/_{3,003}$, while in the previous case surplus value rose by $^1/_{32}$ as a result of a mere doubling in productivity. If necessary labour declines from $^1/_{1,000}$ to $^1/_{1,000,000}$, it declines by exactly $^{999}/_{1,000,000}$ (for $^1/_{1,000}=^{1,000}/_{1,000,000}$), i.e., by as much as surplus value rose.

If we summarise all this, we find:

Firstly: The increase in the productivity of living labour increases the *value* of capital (or diminishes the value of the worker), not because it increases the quantity of products or use values produced with a given amount of labour—productivity of labour is its natural power—but because it reduces *necessary* labour and thus in the same proportion creates *surplus labour,* or, what amounts to the same thing, surplus value; because the surplus value of capital, which it obtains by means of the process of production, consists solely in the excess of surplus labour over *necessary labour.* The increase in productivity can only increase surplus labour, i.e., the excess of labour objectified in capital as a product over that objectified in the exchange value of the working day, in so far as it reduces the ratio of *necessary labour* to *surplus labour,* and only in the proportion to which it reduces this ratio. Surplus value is exactly equal to surplus labour; its increase is measured exactly by the reduction of *necessary labour.*

Secondly: The surplus value of capital does not increase in the same way as the multiplier of productivity, i.e. by the number by which productivity (posited as a unity, as multiplicant) is increased; but by the surplus of the fraction of the living working day which originally represents necessary labour over and above the same fraction divided by the multiplier of productivity. Thus if *necessary labour*$=^1/_4$ of the living working day, and productivity doubles, the [surplus] value of capital does not double but [III-31] grows by $^1/_8$; which is equal to $^1/_4$ or $^2/_8$ (the original fraction of the working day which represents necessary labour)$-^1/_4$ divided by 2, or$=^2/_8-^1/_8=^1/_8$. (Value doubles, which can also be expressed thus: it grows $^4/_2$-fold or $^{16}/_8$-fold. If in the above example,[105] therefore, productivity grew by $^{16}/_8$, profit[a] would rise by only $^1/_8$. Its growth would relate to that of productivity as $^1/_{16}$.[b] (THAT IS IT!) If the fraction was $^1/_{1,000}$ and productivity increased a thousand-fold, the value of capital would grow not a thousand-fold but by less than $^1/_{1,001}$; it would grow by $^1/_{1,000} - ^1/_{1,000,000}$, i.e. by $^{1,000}/_{1,000,000} - ^1/_{1,000,000} = ^{999}/_{1,000,000}$).

The *absolute sum* by which capital increases its value because of a certain increase in productivity depends, therefore, on the *given fraction* of the working day, on the fractional part of the working day, which represents *necessary* labour, and which therefore expresses the original ratio of necessary labour to the living working day. The expansion of productivity in a given proportion, therefore, may increase the value of capital differently e.g. in the *different countries.* A general increase in productivity in the same proportion may increase the value of capital differently in different branches of industry, and will do so according to the different ratios of *necessary labour* to the living working day in these branches. This ratio would of course be the same in all branches of business in a system of free competition, if labour were in all cases simple labour, and hence *necessary labour* were the same. (If it represented the same amounts of objectified labour.)

Thirdly: The greater the surplus value of capital *before the increase in productivity,* i.e. the greater the quantum of surplus labour or surplus value of capital presupposed, or the smaller the fraction of the working day which constitutes the equivalent of the worker and expresses necessary labour, the smaller is the growth of surplus value accruing to capital from increased productivity. The surplus value of capital rises, but in an ever diminishing ratio to the development of productivity. Thus the more developed capital already is, the more surplus labour it has already created, the more tremendously must it develop productivity if it is to valorise itself, i.e. to add surplus value even in a small proportion—because its barrier always remains the ratio between that fractional part of the working day which expresses *necessary labour* and the whole working day. It can move only within these limits. The smaller the fractional part already which represents *necessary* labour, the greater the *surplus labour,* the less can any increase in productivity perceptibly diminish necessary labour; for the denominator [of the fraction] has grown enormously. The

---

[a] This should read "surplus value".— *Ed.*
[b] Instead of "... as $^1/_{16}$" it should read "... as $16^2/_3$:100 or 1:6".— *Ed.*

self-valorisation of capital becomes more difficult to the extent to which it is already valorised. The increase in productivity could become a matter of indifference to capital; its valorisation itself could cease to matter, because its proportions have become minimal; and it would have ceased to be capital.

If necessary labour were $1/_{1,000}$ and productivity tripled, necessary labour would fall only to $1/_{3,000}$ or surplus labour would have grown by only $2/_{3,000}$. But this happens not because wages or the share of labour in the product have increased, but because they have *already* fallen so low, considered in relation to the product of labour or the living working day.

⫽The labour objectified in the worker here shows itself as a fractional part of *his own living working day*; for this is the same ratio as that between the objectified labour he receives from capital as his wage and the whole working day.⫽

(All these propositions correct in this degree of abstraction only for the relation at this particular stage of the analysis. Further relations will come in later which modify them significantly. All this, in so far as it does not [present] itself in the most general form, *really belongs in the doctrine of profit.*)

So much in general for the time being: the development of the productivity of labour—in the first place the positing of surplus labour—is a necessary condition for the growth of the value or the valorisation of capital. As an infinite drive for enrichment, capital strives for an infinite enlargement of the productive forces of labour and calls them into being. But on the other hand, every enlargement of the productivity of labour—apart from the fact that it increases use values for the capitalist—is an increase in the *productivity of capital* and is, from the present standpoint, only a productive force of labour in so far as it is a productive force of capital.[a]

---

[a] Here the following passage is crossed out in the manuscript: "If after the doubling of productivity and the resultant fall of *necessary labour*—which was $1/_2$—to $1/_4$, and the consequent rise of the surplus labour at the disposal of the capitalist, from $2/_4$ to $3/_4$, capital only commanded $3/_4$ of a day's labour, then, as Ricardo says,[106] the increase in productivity would not, in fact, increase values, the *value of capital*. It would remain the same; if originally it represented the $2/_4$ of the working day objectified in capital that remained over and above the part of the working day belonging to the worker, it still would do so. The same [III-32] surplus of objectified labour would have been created. But as we have seen, it lies in the nature of capital to consume the whole surplus labour at its disposal, for it is the creation of surplus labour that is its concept."— *Ed.*

[ABSOLUTE AND RELATIVE SURPLUS VALUE]

[III-32] This much is already clear and can at least be mentioned in anticipation: the increase in productivity does not in and by itself raise prices.[a] For example, the bushel of wheat. If half a working day were objectified in a bushel of wheat, and this was the price of the worker, the surplus labour can only produce 1 bushel of wheat. 2 bushels of wheat therefore the value of one working day and, if this in money=26s., then 2 bushels of wheat=26s. The bushel=13s.

If productivity now doubles, the bushel of wheat now only=$^1/_4$ of a working day;=$6^1/_2$s. The price of this fractional part of the commodity has fallen because of the [doubling of] productivity. But the total price has remained the same; but now surplus of $^3/_4$ of a working day. Every quarter=1 bushel of wheat=$6^1/_2$s. Therefore the total product=26s.=4 bushels. The same as before. The value of capital increased from 13 to $18^3/_2$s. The value of labour diminished from 13s. to $6^1/_2$; material production up from 2 bushels to 4. [The surplus value of capital] now $18^3/_2$.

If productivity also doubled in gold production, so that if 13s. was previously the product of half a working day, and half a working day the *necessary labour;* now of $^1/_4$ [of a working day], so produces 52s., or 52−13, or 39s. more. 1 bushel of wheat now=13s.; now, as before, the same fractional price; but the total product=52s.; earlier only=26s. But on the other hand, the 52s. now buy 4 bushels, while the 26 earlier bought only 2.

WELL. *D'abord,* it is clear that, if capital has already raised the surplus labour so far that the whole living working day is consumed in the process of production (and here we take the working day to be the natural quantum of labour time which the worker can place at the disposal [of capital]; he always puts his capacity to work at the disposal of capital only for a *specific time,* i.e. *a specific labour time),* then an increase in productivity cannot increase labour time, nor, therefore, objectified labour time. One working day is objectified in the product, WHETHER THE NECESSARY TIME OF LABOUR BE REPRESENTED BY 6 OR 3 HOURS, BY $^1/_2$ OR $^1/_4$ of the working day. The surplus value of capital has grown, i.e. its value relative to the worker—for if previously it was only=$^2/_4$, it is now=$^3/_4$ of the objectified labour time; but its value has grown, not because the *absolute* but because the *relative amount of labour* has grown, i.e. the

---

[a] Crossed out in the manuscript: "because we always take a fractional part of the product as a unit".— *Ed.*

total amount of labour has not grown. Now, as before, one day's work is done; hence no absolute increase in surplus time (surplus labour time), but the *amount of necessary labour has diminished,* and thereby the relative surplus labour has increased.

Previously, the worker IN FACT worked the whole day, but only $^1/_2$ day surplus time; now, as before, he works the whole day, but $^3/_4$ of the working day is surplus time. To that extent, therefore, the price (assuming the value of gold and silver to remain the same) or the exchange value of capital has not increased as a result of the doubling of productivity. This therefore affects *the rate of profit,* not the price of the product nor the value of the capital which has been changed back into a commodity in the form of the product. But IN FACT the absolute values also increase in this way, because the part of wealth posited as capital increases—as self-valorising value. *(Accumulation of capitals.)*

Take our earlier example.[a] Let *capital* be=100 thaler, and let it split itself up in the process of production into the following component parts: 50 thaler cotton, 40 thaler wages, 10 thaler the instrument. Assume also, to simplify the calculation, that the whole of the instrument of labour is consumed in one act of production (and this assumption here as yet quite insignificant), its value would therefore reappear completely, in the form of the product. Let us assume, in this case, that labour gives 8 hours to capital in exchange for 40 thaler, which expresses the labour time objectified in its living labour capacity, say, a labour time of 4 hours. The instrument and raw material assumed, the total product would amount to 100 thaler if the worker worked for only 4 hours, i.e. if the raw material and instrument belonged to him and he worked for only 4 hours. He would increase the 60 thaler by 40, which he could consume, since he firstly replaces the 60 thaler—the raw material and instrument required for production—and [secondly] adds to them a surplus value of 40 thaler, as reproduction of his own living labour capacity, or of the time objectified in him. He could recommence labour again and again, since he has reproduced in the process of production both the [III-33] value of the raw material and the instrument and of his labour capacity; the latter by constantly increasing the value of the former by 4 hours of objectified labour. But now let him receive the wages of 40 thaler only if he worked for 8 hours, i.e. if he added to the material and instrument of labour now confronting him as capital a surplus value of 80 thaler; while the former

---

[a] See this volume, pp. 239-44.— *Ed.*

surplus value of 40 thaler that he added was exactly equal to only the value of his labour. He would thus add [to the value of the raw material, the instrument and his labour capacity] a surplus value exactly=the surplus labour or surplus time.

//It is not in the least necessary at this point to assume that the material and instrument must also increase along with surplus labour or surplus time. For how mere surplus labour increases the raw material, see *Babbage,* e.g. the working of gold filament [in Venice], etc.[a]//

The value of the capital would therefore have increased from 100 thaler to 140 thaler.

//Suppose further that the raw material doubles and the instrument of labour increases (for simplicity of calculation) [proportionally]. The outlays of capital would now amount to 100 thaler cotton, 20 thaler instrument, therefore 120 thaler, and for labour now, as before, 40 thaler; ALTOGETHER 160 thaler. If the surplus labour of 4 hours increases 100 thaler by 40% it increases 160 thaler by 64 thaler. Therefore the total product=224 thaler. Here it is assumed that the rate of profit remains the same with the magnitude of capital, and the material and instrument of labour are not considered as already being themselves realisations of surplus labour, capitalisation of surplus time; as we have seen,[b] the greater the surplus time already posited, i.e. the greater the size of capital as such, the more it is assumed that the *absolute increase in labour time* impossible and that relative increase DECLINING in geometrical proportion, because of increased productivity.//

Now, capital considered as simple exchange value would be absolutely greater, 140 thaler instead of 100; but IN FACT only a new value would be produced, i.e. a value which is not necessary just to replace the outlays of 60 thaler for the material and instrument of labour and 40 thaler for labour, a new value of 40 thaler. The values present in the circulation would be increased by 40 thaler, by 40 thaler more objectified labour time.

Now make the same assumption as before. 100 thaler capital; namely 50 for cotton, 40 thaler for labour, 10 for the instrument of production; let surplus labour time remain the same as in the previous case, namely 4 hours, and the total labour time 8 hours. Hence the product in all cases only=8 hours labour time=140 thaler. Suppose now that the productivity of labour doubles, i.e. 2

---

[a] Ch. Babbage, *Traité sur l'économie des machines et des manufactures,* Paris, 1833, pp. 216-19.— *Ed.*

[b] See this volume, pp. 265-66.— *Ed.*

hours would be sufficient for the worker to utilise the raw material and instrument to the extent necessary for the maintenance of his labour capacity. If 40 thaler were the labour time of 4 hours objectified in silver, then 20 thaler would be the objectified labour time of 2 hours. These 20 thaler now express the same use value as earlier the 40 thaler did. The exchange value of labour capacity has diminished by half, because half the original labour time creates the same use value, while the exchange value of the use value is measured only by the labour time objectified in it.

But the capitalist makes the worker work 8 hours as before, and his product therefore represents as before a labour time of 8 hours=80 thaler labour time, while the value of raw material and instrument has remained the same, namely 60 thaler; ALTOGETHER, as before, 140 thaler.

(The worker himself to live would only have had to add to the 60 thaler present as raw material and instrument a value of 20 thaler, he would therefore have produced a value of 80 thaler. Because of the doubling of productivity the total value of his product would have diminished from 100 to 80, by 20 thaler, i.e. by $^{1}/_{5}$ of 100=20%.)

But the surplus time or surplus value of capital is now 6 hours instead of 4, or 60 thaler instead of 40. Its increase is 2 hours, 20 thaler. The capitalist's calculation would now run thus: for raw material 50, for labour 20, for instrument 10; total outlay=80 thaler. Gain=60 thaler. The capitalist would sell the product for 140 thaler as before, but make a gain of 60 thaler instead of the previous 40. In one respect he throws into circulation only the same exchange value as before, 140 thaler, but the surplus value of his capital has grown by 20 thaler. Accordingly, only his share in the 140 thaler [is] the rate of his profit. The worker has IN FACT worked gratis for him for 2 more hours; namely 6 hours instead of 4, and for him it is· the same as if he had worked 10 instead of 8 hours, i.e. increased his *absolute labour time,* under the earlier condition.

But in fact, a *new value* has emerged, too, namely, 20 thaler more are posited as *independent* value, as objectified labour, which has become free, relieved of the necessity merely to serve for the exchange of the previous labour power [Arbeitskraft]. This can occur in two forms. Either the 20 thaler are used to set as much additional labour in motion as corresponds to their becoming *capital* and creating increased exchange value, i.e. to their making a greater quantity of objectified labour into the starting point of the new production process. Or the capitalist exchanges the 20 thaler as money for commodities other than those he requires in his production as industrial [III-34] capital; in that case all commodities other than labour and money itself exchange for 20 thaler more, for 2 more hours of objectified labour time. Their *exchange value,* therefore, has risen by precisely this *sum which has been set free.*

I<small>N FACT</small>, 140 thaler are 140 thaler, as the very "astute" French publisher[a] of the Physiocrats observes in opposition to *Boisguil-lebert.* But it is false that these 140 thaler represent only more use value; they represent a greater part of *independent exchange value,* of *money,* of *latent capital;* therefore of wealth posited as *wealth.* This the economists themselves concede when they later allow the accumulation of capitals to comprise not only the increase in the mass of use values but that in *exchange values* too; for according to Ricardo himself,[b] the element of the accumulation of capitals is posited just as completely by relative surplus labour—and indeed it cannot be otherwise—as it is by absolute surplus labour.

On the other hand, it is already implicit in the thesis best developed by Ricardo himself [107] that these excess 20 thaler which are created purely by the increase in productivity, can again become capital. Of the 140 thaler, only 40 could earlier have become new capital (leaving aside the consumption of capital for the moment); 100 thaler did not become but remained capital. Now 60 thaler can become new capital, therefore a capital of an exchange value of 20 thaler more is now available. Exchange values, *wealth as such,* have therefore increased, although now, as before, the total sum of wealth has *not* directly increased. Why has wealth increased? Because there has been an increase in that part of its total sum which is not merely means of circulation but money, or which is not merely an equivalent but *exchange value existing for itself.*

The 20 thaler set free would either be accumulated as money, i.e. added to the existing exchange values in the abstract form of exchange value, or they all pass into circulation, and then the prices of the commodities purchased with them rise. They all represent more gold, and, since the cost of production of gold has not fallen (rather it has risen relative to the commodity produced with the capital which has become more productive), more objectified labour. (As a result, the surplus, which initially

---

   [a] E. Daire, "Commentaires et des notes explicatives", *Économistes financiers du XVIIIe siècle,* p. 419, Note 1.— *Ed.*
   [b] D. Ricardo, *On the Principles of Political Economy, and Taxation,* p. 89.— *Ed.*

appeared on the side of one producing capital, now appears on the side of the other capitals which produce the commodities that have become dearer.) Or the 20 thaler are directly utilised by the original circulating capital itself as capital. In this way a new capital of 20 thaler—a sum of self-preserving and self-valorising wealth—is posited. Capital has risen by the exchange value of 20 thaler.

(We are not really concerned yet with circulation, for we are dealing here with capital in general, and circulation can only mediate between the form of capital as money and its form as capital; capital as money may realise money as such, i.e. exchange it for commodities, which it consumes in greater quantity than before; in the hands of the producer of these commodities, however, this money is converted into capital. It thus becomes capital either directly in the hands of the first capital, or by a detour, in those of another capital. But the other capital is always once more capital as such; and we are dealing here with *capital as such*, SAY THE CAPITAL OF THE WHOLE SOCIETY. We are not yet dealing with the difference, etc., between capitals.)

In general, these 20 thaler can appear only in two forms: [(1)] as money, so that capital itself once more adopts the determination of money which has not yet become capital—its point of departure; the abstract-autonomous form of exchange value or general wealth; or [(2)] again as capital, as a new domination of objectified labour over living. As general wealth materialised in the form of money (of the thing where it is merely abstract), or as *new* living labour.

//In the example given productivity has doubled, has risen by 100%, the [surplus] value of capital has risen by 50%.//

(Every expansion of the mass of capital employed can increase *productive power* not only in an arithmetic but in a geometric proportion, while—precisely as the multiplier of productive power—it can increase profit only at a much lower rate. The effect of the increase of capital upon the increase in productive power is therefore infinitely greater than that of the increase of productive power upon the growth of capital.)

Of the 140 thaler, the capitalist consumes (say) 20 as use values for himself by means of money as the medium of circulation. Thus, under the first assumption, he could begin the process of self-valorisation only with a greater capital, with a greater exchange value of 120 thaler (as against 100). After the doubling of productivity, he can do it with 140 thaler, without restricting his consumption. A greater part of the exchange values fixes itself as exchange value, instead of disappearing in use value (whether it directly fixes itself in this way or indirectly through production). To create a larger capital means to create a larger exchange value: although exchange value in its *direct* form as simple exchange value has not been increased by the growth of productivity, it has been increased in its intensified form as *capital*.

This larger capital of 140 thaler[a] represents absolutely more objectified labour than did the earlier capital of 120 thaler. [III-35] It thus sets in motion, at least relatively, more living labour, and thus also ultimately reproduces a greater simple exchange value. The capital of 120 thaler at [a rate of profit of] 40% produced a product or simple exchange value of 60 thaler at 40%; the capital of 140 thaler, a simple exchange value of 64 thaler.[b] Here then the augmentation of exchange value in the form of capital is also directly posited as an increase of exchange value in its simple form.

It is of the highest importance to grasp this. It is not enough to say, as Ricardo does, that [with increased productivity] exchange value, i.e. the abstract form of wealth, does not increase, but only exchange value as capital.[c] In saying this, he only means the original process of production. But when relative surplus labour increases—and thus capital increases absolutely—the *relative* e x c h a n g e v a l u e *existing as exchange value*, money as such, necessarily increases within circulation, and thereby, through the mediation of the production process, also *absolute exchange value*. In other words: a part of this same amount of exchange value (or money)—and it is in this simple form that the product of the process of valorisation appears—(the product is surplus value only in relation to capital, to value as it existed prior to the production process; for itself, considered as independent existence, it is merely *quantitatively determined exchange value*)—has been set free which does not exist as equivalent for existing exchange values nor for existing labour time. If it is exchanged for the existing exchange values, it gives them not an equivalent but more than an equivalent, and therefore sets free a part of the exchange value on their side. In a state of rest, this released exchange value, by which society has enriched itself, can only be money; and then only the abstract form of wealth is increased; when in motion, it can only realise itself in *new* living labour (it may be that previously

---

a See this volume, p. 269.— *Ed.*

b Figures in this paragraph do not correspond to previous calculations.— *Ed.*

c D. Ricardo, *On the Principles of Political Economy, and Taxation*, pp. 325-26.— *Ed.*

unemployed labour is set in motion or that *new workers* are created
(population [growth] is accelerated); or again that a new circle of
exchange values is created, that the circle of exchange values in
circulation is enlarged, which can occur on the production side, if
the released exchange value opens up a *new branch of production,*
therefore [creates] a new object of exchange, objectified labour in
the form of a new use value; or finally that the same is achieved
by the introduction of objectified labour into the sphere of
circulation in a new country by means of the expansion of trade).
This [new living labour] must therefore be created [by raising
productivity].

The form in which Ricardo tries to clarify the matter for himself
(and he is very unclear in this respect), *au fond* amounts to
nothing more than that he at once brings in a certain relationship,
instead of simply saying that of the same sum of simple exchange
values a smaller part is posited in the form of simple exchange
value (equivalent) and a larger part in the form of money (of
money as the original, antediluvian form, which constantly gives
rise to capital; of money in its determination as money, not as
coin, etc.); that therefore the part posited *as* exchange value for
itself, i.e. as *value,* increases, *wealth in its form as wealth*[a] (whereas
he comes to exactly the wrong conclusion that wealth increases
only in its *material, physical* form as use value). The origin of *wealth
as such,* in so far as it does not proceed from *rent,* i.e. according to
him not from the *increase* of productivity but, on the contrary,
from *its diminution,* is therefore *totally incomprehensible* to him, and
he gets entangled in the craziest contradictions.

Let us take the matter in his form. Capital 1,000 sets in motion
50 workers; or 50 living working days. By a doubling of
productivity, it could set 100 working days in motion. But these
latter do not exist in his premiss and are arbitrarily brought in,
because otherwise—if no *more real working days* are brought
in—he does not understand the increase of exchange value arising
from increased productivity. On the other hand, the *growth of
population* is nowhere *analysed* by him as an *element in the increase of
exchange values*; he doesn't even clearly and definitely mention it.

Let the given assumption be capital 1,000 and workers 50. The
correct deduction—and he *draws* it (see Notebook [108]): 500 capital
with 25 workers can [with productivity doubling] produce the

---

[a] The following note relating to this passage is written in the upper margin of
the next, 36th page of Notebook III: "(*Money* for itself should be designated
neither as use value nor as exchange value, but as *value.*)"—*Ed.*

same use value as before; the other 500 with the other 25 workers starts a new business and also produces exchange value of 500. Profit remains the same, since it arises not from the exchange of the 500 for the 500, but from the proportions in which profit and the wages of labour originally share in the 500, and the exchange is, rather, that of equivalents, which can increase value here no more than it can in *foreign trade*, in relation to which Ricardo explicitly demonstrates this.[a] For exchange of equivalents implies nothing more than that the value which existed in the hand of *A* before the exchange with *B*, still exists in his hand after the exchange with *B*.

Total value or wealth has remained the same [after the doubling of productivity]. But the use value or the *physical substance of wealth* has doubled. Now, there is absolutely no reason why *wealth as wealth, exchange value as such*, should grow at all—so far as the *increase in the productive forces* is concerned. If the productive forces are doubled in both [III-36] branches again, capital *a* can again be divided into two of 250 with $12^1/_2$ days labour each, and capital *b* can do the same. There are now four capitals, with the same exchange value of £1,000, consuming, as before, altogether 50 living working days //it is *au fond wrong to say* that living labour consumes capital; capital (objectified labour) consumes living labour in the production process// and producing four times as much use value [as] before the doubling of consumption value.

Ricardo is too classical to commit the absurdities of those who claim to improve him, who ascribe the increase in value resulting from the growth of productivity to the fact that one party sells more dearly in circulation. Instead of exchanging the capital of 500, so soon as it has become commodity, simple exchange value, for 500, he exchanges it for 550 (at 10%), but obviously the other obtains in exchange only 450 instead of 500, and the total sum remains 1,000 as before. This occurs quite frequently in trade, but it explains the profit of one capital only by the loss of the other capital, hence not the profit as such of capital as such, and without this premiss, there can be profit neither on one side nor the other.

Ricardo's process [the growth of the mass of use values] can therefore continue without coming up against any other limitation than that of the *increase in productivity* (and this is again physical, initially located outside the *economic relation* itself) which is possible with a capital of 1,000 and 50 workers. See the following passage:

---

[a] *On the Principles of Political Economy, and Taxation*, Chapter VII.— *Ed.*

"Capital is that part of the wealth of a country which IS EMPLOYED WITH A VIEW TO FUTURE PRODUCTION, *AND MAY BE INCREASED IN THE SAME MANNER AS WEALTH*" [*On the Principles of Political Economy, and Taxation*, p. 327].

(*WEALTH* is for him here the abundance of use values, and considered from the standpoint of simple exchange, the same objectified labour can express itself in unlimited use values and always remain *the same exchange value*, so long as it remains the same amount of objectified labour, since its *equivalent* is measured not by the mass of use values in which it exists but by its own amount.)

"AN *ADDITIONAL CAPITAL* WILL BE EQUALLY EFFICACIOUS IN THE FORMATION [109] OF FUTURE WEALTH, WHETHER IT BE OBTAINED FROM IMPROVEMENTS OF SKILL OR MACHINERY, OR FROM USING MORE REVENUE PRODUCTIVELY; FOR WEALTH" (use value) "ALWAYS DEPENDS ON THE *QUANTITY* OF COMMODITIES PRODUCED" (also to some extent on their VARIETY, IT SEEMS), "WITHOUT REGARD TO THE FACILITY WITH WHICH THE INSTRUMENTS EMPLOYED IN PRODUCTION MAY HAVE BEEN PRODUCED" (i.e. the labour time objectified in them). "A CERTAIN QUANTITY OF CLOTHES AND PROVISIONS WILL MAINTAIN AND EMPLOY THE SAME NUMBER OF MEN; BUT THEY WILL BE OF TWICE THE VALUE" *(exchange value)* "IF 200 HAVE BEEN EMPLOYED ON THEIR PRODUCTION" [ibid., pp. 327-28].

If by means of the increase in productivity 100 produce as much in use values as 200 did earlier, then:

"half of the 200 are dismissed, thus the remaining 100 produce as much as did the previous 200. One-half of the capital can therefore be withdrawn from the branch of industry; just as much capital has been released as labour. And since half the capital performs exactly the same service as previously the entire capital did, two capitals are now formed, etc." (cf. ibid., pp. 39, 40 on international trade,[110] to which we must return).

Ricardo does not speak here about the working day; that, if the capitalist previously exchanged half a day's objectified labour for the entire living working day of the worker, he gained, *au fond,* only half a living working day, since he gives the other half to the worker in objectified form and gets it back from him in the form of living labour, i.e. pays the worker half a working day, [he presents it] rather in the form of simultaneous working days, i.e. of the working days of different workers. This changes nothing in the substance of the matter, only in its expression. [As a result of the increase in productive power] each of these working days provides so much more surplus time. If formerly the capitalist's limit was *the* working day, he now has 50 days, etc. As has been said, in this form the increase in the number of capitals arising from the increase in productivity, does not posit any increase in exchange values; and, according to Ricardo, the population could also decline from say 10,000,000 to 10,000 without a decrease in exchange value or in the quantity of use values (see the conclusion of his book[a]).

We are the last to deny that contradictions are contained in *capital*. Indeed, it is our aim to analyse them fully. But Ricardo *does not analyse them*. He SHIFTS THEM OFF BY CONSIDERING THE VALUE IN EXCHANGE AS INDIFFERENT FOR THE FORMATION OF WEALTH. THAT IS TO SAY, HE CONTENDS THAT IN A SOCIETY BASED UPON THE VALUE OF EXCHANGE, AND WEALTH RESULTING FROM SUCH VALUE, THE CONTRADICTIONS WHICH THIS FORM OF WEALTH IS DRIVEN TO WITH THE DEVELOPMENT OF PRODUCTIVE POWERS ETC. DO NOT EXIST, AND THAT A PROGRESS OF VALUE IS NOT NECESSARY IN SUCH A SOCIETY TO SECURE THE PROGRESS OF WEALTH, [III-37] CONSEQUENTLY THAT VALUE AS THE FORM OF WEALTH DOES NOT AT ALL AFFECT THAT WEALTH ITSELF AND ITS DEVELOPMENT, i.e. he considers exchange value as merely *formal*.

But then he suddenly remembers that (1) capitalists are concerned with VALUE; (2) historically, the progress of the productive forces (just as of international trade—he *should* have thought of this) has been accompanied by the growth of *wealth as such*, i.e. of the sum of values. How does he explain this? Capitals accumulate more quickly than the population; therefore wages rise; therefore population; therefore the price of grain; therefore the difficulty of production and therefore *exchange values*. Thus, the latter are finally reached by a detour.

We still here omit altogether the element of rent for at this stage we are concerned not with greater difficulty of production but on the contrary with the growth of the productive forces. With the accumulation of capitals, wages rise, unless population grows simultaneously; the worker marries, stimulus is given to propagation or his children live better, do not die prematurely, etc. In short, the population grows. But its growth leads to competition among the workers, and thus compels the worker once again to sell his labour capacity to the capitalist at, or even for a time below, its *value*. Now the accumulated capital, which in the meantime has grown more slowly, disposes over the surplus—once more as money—which it laid out before in the form of wages, that is as coin, to buy the use value of labour; as money, the surplus can be utilised as capital in exchange for [new] living labour, and since it now also disposes over greater quantities of working days, its *exchange value* grows again.

---

[a] *On the Principles of Political Economy, and Taxation*, pp. 416-17.— Ed.

(Even this not properly analysed by Ricardo, but mixed up with the theory of rent; for the growth of population now deprives capital of the surplus in the form of rent, which it lost before in the form of wages.) But even the growth of population is not really comprehensible in his theory. Nowhere does he show that there is an *immanent* relationship between the whole of the labour objectified in capital and the living working day (whether this is represented as a working day of 50×12 hours or as 12 hours' work by 50 workers, is the same as far as the relationship is concerned), and that this immanent relationship is precisely the *proportion of the fractional part of the living working day*, or of the equivalent for the objectified labour, with which the worker is paid, to the [whole] living working day; where the whole is the day itself and the immanent relationship is the variable proportion (the day itself is a constant magnitude) of the *fraction of the necessary hours of labour* to that of the *hours of surplus labour*. And just because he has not analysed this relationship, he has not demonstrated (and we have not as yet been concerned with this, for we were dealing with *capital as such*, and the development of the productive forces was introduced as an extraneous factor) that the development of productive power itself presupposes both the augmentation of capital and that of the simultaneous working days, but that within the given limits of the capital which sets in motion one working day (even if it be one of 50×12 hours, 600 hours) this development is itself the barrier to the development of its productive power.

Wages include not only the worker, but also his reproduction— so that when this specimen of the working class dies, another replaces him; when the 50 workers are dead, there are 50 new ones to replace them. The 50 workers themselves—as living labour capacities—represent not only the costs of their own production, but the costs that had to be paid to their parents over and above their own wages as individuals in order to replace themselves in 50 new individuals. Therefore the population grows even without a rise in wages. Now, why does it not grow quickly enough? Why must it receive a special stimulus? Surely only because it is of no use to capital merely to obtain more "WEALTH" in Ricardo's sense, it wants to command more VALUE, more objectified labour. But, according to him, it can do so in fact only if wages fall, i.e. more living working days are exchanged for the same capital with objectified labour and therefore a greater VALUE is produced. To make wages fall, he presupposes an increase in population. And in order to prove increase in population here, he presupposes that the demand for working days increases, in other words, that capital can buy more *objectified labour* (objectified in labour capacity), hence that its VALUE has grown. But originally, he proceeded from precisely the opposite assumption, and made the detour only *because* he started from that assumption. If £1,000 could buy 500 working days and productivity grows, then it can either continue to employ the 500 in the same branch of labour, or split itself up into 2 capitals of 500 and employ 250 in one branch of labour and 250 in another. But it can never command more than 500 working days, for otherwise, according to Ricardo, not only the use values produced by it, but their *exchange value* must have been multiplied, the *objectified labour time* over which it has command. Therefore, if one proceeds from Ricardo's assumption, there can be no greater demand for labour. And if there [III-38] is, then the *exchange value* of capital has grown. Cf. *Malthus on value*,[a] who *senses* the contradictions, but comes a cropper when he himself tries to analyse them.[111]

We have always spoken only of the two elements of capital, of the two parts of the living working day, of which the one represents wages and the other profit, the one necessary labour and the other surplus labour. Where, then, are the two other parts of capital, which are realised in the material and instrument of labour? As regards the simple production process, labour implies the existence of an instrument which facilitates labour and of material in which it represents itself, which it forms. This form gives it its use value. In exchange, this use value becomes exchange value to the extent that it contains objectified labour. But as components of capital, are the material and instrument values which labour must replace?

Thus in the above example[b] (and such objections are frequently made to Ricardo: he considers only profit and wages as components of the production costs, it is said, not machinery and material) it would seem that, if the capital of 100—splitting itself up into 50 for cotton, 40 for wages, 10 for instrument, and wages of 40 thaler=4 hours of objectified labour—orders a working day of 8 hours, then the worker who would have to reproduce 40 thaler for wages, 40 thaler surplus time (profit), 10 thaler for the instrument, 50 thaler cotton=140 thaler, reproduces only 80 thaler. For 40 thaler [wages] is the product of half a working day,

---

[a] Th. R. Malthus, *The Measure of Value Stated and Illustrated.—Ed.*
[b] See this volume, pp. 268-70.—*Ed.*

40 of the other, surplus half. But 60 thaler is the value of the two other components of capital. Since the real product of the worker is 80 thaler, he can reproduce only 80, not 140. Rather, he would have diminished the value of the 60 [instrument and material], since, of the 80, 40 is replacement of his wages; and the remaining 40 surplus labour is smaller than 60 by 20. Instead of a profit of 40, the capitalist would have suffered a loss of 20 on the original part of his capital consisting of instrument and material.

How is the worker to produce another 60 thaler value in addition to the 80, seeing that one-half of his working day, as his wages show, produces only 40 thaler with the instrument and material; the other half only produces the same amount; and he disposes of only one working day, as he cannot work two days in one?

Let us assume that the 50 thaler material=x pounds of cotton yarn; the 10 thaler instrument=the loom. Now, first as regards the *use value,* it is clear that, if the cotton were not already in the form of yarn and the wood and iron already in that of the loom, the worker could not produce any *cloth,* any higher use value. For the worker himself in the production process, the 50 thaler and the 10 thaler are *nothing more than yarn and loom, not exchange values.* His labour has given them a higher use value, and added to them an amount of objectified labour of 80 thaler, namely 40 thaler in which he reproduces his wages and 40 surplus time. The use value—the cloth—contains one working day more, one-half of which, however, replaces only that part of capital in return for which the right to dispose over the labour capacity is exchanged. The worker did not produce the objectified labour time contained in the yarn and loom and constituting part of the value of the product; for him they were and remain material to which he has given a new form and in which he has incorporated new labour. The only condition is that he must not WASTE them, and he has not done so, to the extent that his product has a use value, indeed a higher use value than before. It now contains two parts of objectified labour—his working day, and the labour already present in his material, yarn and loom, independently of him and prior to his labour.

The labour previously objectified was the condition of *his* labour; it alone made it into labour but cost him no labour. Assume that they [yarn and loom] were not already presupposed as components of capital, as *values,* and had not cost *him* anything. Then the value of the product, if he had worked for a whole day, would be 80 thaler, if for half a day, 40 thaler. It would just=an objectified working day. They did not, in fact, cost him anything in production. But that does not cancel out the labour time objectified in them, which remains and only receives another form. If the worker had to produce during the same working day the yarn and loom as well as the cloth, the process would IN FACT be impossible. It is precisely the fact that they do not require his labour either as use values in their original form or as exchange values, but are already *present,* which makes it possible to create with the addition of a day's labour a product of a value higher than that of a day's labour. But he succeeds in this in so far as he does not have to produce this surplus over and above a day's labour but *finds* it already *available* as material, as premiss.

It can therefore only be said that he reproduces these values in so far as they would go to waste, would be useless, *without* labour; but *labour* would be equally useless *without them.* So far as the worker reproduces these values, he does not do so by giving them a higher exchange value or entering into any process with their exchange value, but just by subjecting them to the simple process of production, merely by *working.* [III-39] But it costs him no more labour time *besides* that which he requires for their working-up and their higher valorisation. It is a condition under which capital has set him to work. He reproduces the value of material and instrument only by giving them a higher value, and this process of giving them a higher value=his day's labour. In other respects he leaves them as they are. The preservation of their old value derives from the addition of a new one, not from the production or *reproduction* of the old value itself. In so far as they are products of previous labour, a product of previous labour, i.e. a sum of previously objectified labour, remains an element of his *product*; the product contains the previous value as well as the new.

In fact, therefore, he produces in this product only the working day which he adds to it, and the preservation of the old value costs him absolutely nothing apart from what it costs him to add the new. For him the old value is only material and remains such, no matter how it changes its form; therefore it is something present *independently* of his labour. It does not concern him, it concerns capital, that this material which remains, as it only receives another form, itself already contains labour time; it is also *independent* of his labour and continues on *after* it as it existed before it. This so-called reproduction does not cost him any labour time but is the condition for his labour time, for it is nothing but the positing of the substance on hand as the material of his labour, relating to it as material.

282 Outlines of the Critique of Political Economy

He therefore replaces the old labour time by the *act* of labouring itself, not by the application of particular labour time for this purpose. He replaces it simply by the addition of *new* labour time, whereby the old is preserved in the product and becomes an element of a new product. The worker therefore does not replace with his working day the raw material and instrument, in so far as they are values. *The capitalist thus obtains this preservation of the old value just as free of charge as he obtains surplus labour.* But he obtains it free of charge [not] because it costs the worker nothing, but because the material and instrument of labour are already in his hands as *presupposition* and the worker thus cannot *work* without making the labour already present in objectified form in the hands of capital into the material of his labour, and thereby also conserving the labour objectified in this material. The capitalist, then, pays the worker nothing for the fact that the yarn and the loom—to wit their value—reappears in the cloth, and has thus maintained itself as value. This preservation results simply from the addition of new labour, which adds higher value.

From the original relationship between capital and labour, it therefore emerges that the same service which living labour renders to the objectified labour by means of its relation to it as living, does not cost capital anything, any more than it does the worker, but merely expresses the fact that the material and the instrument of labour confront him as capital, as premisses *independent* of him. The preservation of the old value is not an act separate from the addition of the new, but occurs of itself; appears as the natural result of it. But the fact that this preservation costs capital nothing, and costs the worker nothing either, is already posited in the relationship of *capital and labour,* which in itself is already the profit of the one and the wages of the other.

The individual capitalist can imagine (and for his calculation it serves the same purpose) that, if he owns a capital of 100 thaler, 50 thaler cotton, 40 thaler provisions with which to buy labour, 10 thaler instrument; plus a profit of 10% counted on his production costs, then labour has to replace his 50 thaler in respect of raw cotton, 40 thaler provisions, 10 thaler instrument, and 10% of 50, 40 and 10 respectively; so that in his imagination labour creates for him 55 thaler raw material, 44 thaler provisions, 11 thaler instrument, ALTOGETHER=110. But for economists[112] this is a peculiar notion, although asserted with great pomp as an innovation against Ricardo.

If the working day of the worker=10 hours, and he can produce 40 thaler in 8 hours, i.e. produce his wages or, what is the same thing, maintain and replace his labour capacity, he requires $^4/_5$ of a day to compensate capital for his wages and gives capital $^1/_5$ of a day surplus labour or 10 thaler. Capital therefore receives in exchange for the 40 thaler wages, for 8 hours of objectified labour, 10 hours of living labour, and this surplus constitutes its entire profit. The total objectified labour which the worker has created, then, is 50 thaler, and whatever may be the costs of instrument and raw material, he cannot add any more to them, for his day cannot objectify itself in more labour. So now, by the fact that he has added to the 60 thaler raw material and instrument the 50 thaler—10 hours labour (of which 8 are merely the replacement of his wages)—he has at the same time preserved the material and the instrument—they are preserved just by again coming into contact with living labour and being utilised as instrument and material. This costs him no labour (and he would have no time available for it), nor is he paid for it by the capitalist. Like every natural or social power of labour which is not the product of earlier labour or is not the product of such earlier labour as must be repeated (e.g. the historical development of the worker, etc.), this animating natural power of labour—namely that while it utilises material and instrument it preserves them in one form or another, and thus preserves also the labour objectified in them, their exchange value—this power becomes the *power of capital*, not of labour. Hence also not paid for by capital, any more than the worker is paid for his ability to think, etc.

[III-40] We have seen that originally the prerequisite for the appearance of *capital* is the *value* which has become independent of and *opposed to* circulation—i.e. the commodity for which the character of exchange value is not a purely formal, vanishing character facilitating its exchange for other use values and ultimately leading to its disappearance as an object of consumption—*money as money,* that is money withdrawn from circulation and *negatively* asserting itself as opposed to it.[a] On the other side, *money* (in its third, adequate form[b])—as value which no longer enters circulation as an equivalent, but is not yet potentiated to the level of capital, i.e. *negative* value independent of and opposed to circulation—again results from the product of capital, in so far as that product is not merely the *reproduction* of the capital (but this

---

[a] See this volume, pp. 182-204.— *Ed.*

[b] Ibid., pp. 151-52.— *Ed.*

reproduction is purely formal, since of the three parts of the value of capital only one is really consumed, therefore reproduced, that replacing wages; but profit is not reproduction, it is addition of value, surplus value). Just as money first appeared as the prerequisite of capital, as cause of it, so it now appears as its effect. In the first movement, money arose from simple circulation; in the second it arises from the production process of capital. In the first it *makes a transition* to capital; in the second it appears as a prerequisite of capital posited by capital itself, and is already *in itself* therefore posited as capital; already contains within itself ideally the relation to capital. [In the second movement] money no longer simply makes a transition to capital, but its potential transformation into capital is already inherent in it as *money.*

The augmentation of values is therefore the result of the self-valorisation of capital; [regardless of] whether this self-valorisation is the result of absolute *surplus time* or *relative,* i.e. of an actual increase of absolute labour time or of an increase in relative surplus labour, i.e. of the diminution of the fractional part of the working day representing necessary labour time for the maintenance of labour capacity, *necessary* labour in general.

Living labour time reproduces nothing more than the part of the objectified labour time (of capital) which appears as payment for the right to dispose over the living labour capacity, and which, therefore, as an equivalent, must replace the labour time objectified in this labour capacity, i.e. replace the production costs of the living labour capacity, in other words, keep the worker alive as a worker. What it produces in addition to that is not reproduction, but new creation, and indeed new creation of values, because objectification of new labour time in a use value. That the labour time contained in the raw material and instrument is preserved at the same time, is the result *not of the quantity of labour,* but of its *quality* of being labour as such; and there is no special payment for this general quality—which does not qualify it as any specifically determined labour, but consists in *labour as labour being labour*—since capital has purchased *this quality* in the exchange with the worker.

But the equivalent of this quality (the specific use value of labour) is measured simply by the *quantity* of labour time which has produced it. To start with, the worker's use of the instrument as instrument and his shaping of the raw material adds to the value of the raw material and instrument as much new

form[a] as is=to the labour time contained in his own wages; anything more he adds is surplus labour time, surplus value. But by
virtue of the simple relationship, that the instrument is used as an
instrument and the raw material is posited as the raw material for
labour, by virtue of the simple fact that they are brought into
contact with labour, that they are posited as its means and object
and thus as objectification of living labour, as moments of labour
itself, they are preserved not in their form but in their substance;
and, viewed economically, objectified labour time is their substance.
The labour time objectified [in raw material and instrument] ceases
to exist in a merely one-sided objective form—in which as a mere
thing, it is liable to dissolution by chemical processes, etc.—for
it is now posited as the material mode of existence, means and
object, of living labour.

Out of merely objectified labour time, in whose physical being
labour exists only as vanished, *external form* of its natural
substance, a form exterior to this substance itself (e.g. to wood the
form of the table, or to iron the form of the cylinder), as merely
existing in the external form of the physical matter, develops the
indifference of physical matter to its form. Objectified labour time
maintains that form not through any living immanent law of
reproduction, as e.g. the tree maintains its form as tree (wood
maintains itself in a particular form as tree, because this form is
a form of wood; whereas the form as table is accidental to wood,
not the immanent form of its substance); that form exists only as
a form external to the physical matter, or it exists itself only
physically. The dissolution to which its matter is subject, therefore
dissolves the form as well. But posited as conditions for living
labour, the instrument and raw material are themselves reani-
mated. Objectified labour is no longer attached to the physical
matter as a dead, external, indifferent form, since it is itself,
in turn, posited as an element of living labour, as a relation of
living labour to itself as objective material, as *objectivity* of living
labour (as means and object) (the *objective* conditions of living
labour).

While living labour by its realisation in the material transforms
the material itself, a transformation determined by the purpose of
labour, its purposive activity—(a transformation which does not,
as in the inanimate object, posit the form as external to the
physical matter, as a mere vanishing semblance of its existence)—

---

[a] Probably a slip of the pen; "labour" would seem to be the right word
here.— *Ed.*

it preserves the material in a definite form, and subjects the change of form of the physical matter to the purpose of labour. Labour is the living, form-giving fire; it is the transience of things, their temporality, [III-41] as the process of their formation by living time. In the simple production process—leaving aside the valorisation process—the transience of the form of things is used to posit their usefulness.

When raw cotton becomes yarn, the yarn becomes fabric, the fabric becomes printed or dyed fabric, etc., and this, say, becomes a dress, (1) the substance of the cotton has been preserved in all these forms. (In the chemical process, the reactions regulated by labour have throughout consisted in an exchange of (natural) equivalents, etc.); (2) in all these successive processes, the substance has obtained a more useful form, one making it more suitable for consumption, until it has finally obtained the form in which it can be direct object of consumption; in which, therefore, the consumption of the substance and the transcendence of its form constitutes human satisfaction, and its transformation is its use. The substance of raw cotton is preserved in all these processes; it perishes in one form of use value in order to *make way for a higher one, until the object is in being as the object of direct consumption.*

But when the raw cotton is converted into twist, it is posited in a definite relation to a further type of labour. If this labour did not take place, not only has the form been imposed on it uselessly, i.e. the earlier labour is not endorsed by the new, the substance is also spoilt, for it has use value in the form of twist only if it is worked on further: it is use value only in respect of the use which further labour makes of it; it is use value only if its form as twist is transcended into that of cloth, whereas the raw cotton in its being as raw cotton is capable of an infinite number of useful applications.

Thus, without further labour, the use value of raw cotton and twist, material and form, would be wrecked; it would be destroyed, instead of being produced. The material as well as the form, substance like the form, are preserved by further labour—preserved as use values, until they assume the form of use value as such, whose use is consumption. It is therefore inherent in the simple production process that the earlier stage of production is preserved by the later, and that the creation of a higher use value preserves the old, or transforms it only in so far as it is raised as use value. It is living labour which preserves the use value of the un-finished product of labour by making it into the material of further labour. But it only preserves it, i.e. only protects it from uselessness and decay, by working on it in accordance with its purpose, by making it, in general, the object of new living labour.

This *preservation of the old use value* is not a process taking place alongside the augmentation of the old use value or its completion by new labour; it is the result of this new labour of raising the use value itself. When the work of weaving transforms twist into cloth, i.e. treats it as the raw material of weaving—a particular kind of living labour—(and the twist has use value only if it is woven into fabric), it preserves the use value which the raw cotton as such possessed and that which it obtained specifically as twist. It preserves the product of [earlier] labour by making it into the raw material of new labour. But it does not (1) add new labour and (2) besides that preserve the use value of the raw material by means of another labour. *It preserves the utility of the raw cotton as yarn by weaving the yarn into fabric.* (All this belongs already to the first chapter, *on production in general.*) *Preserves it by weaving it.* This preservation of labour as a product, or of the use value of the product of labour, by its becoming the raw material for new labour, by again being posited as material objectivity of purposive living labour, is given in the simple production process. In relation to use value, labour possesses the property that it preserves the existing use value by raising it to a higher one, and raises it by making it the object of a new labour determined by a final aim; by transforming it again from the form of indifferent consistency into that of the objective material of labour, of the body of labour.

(*The same is true of the instrument.* A spindle preserves itself as use value only when it is used for spinning. Otherwise, the particular form imparted here to the iron and wood would make unusable both the labour which produced that form and the material in which it produced it. Only if it is posited as the means of living labour, as an objective moment of being of its living existence, only then are the use value of the wood and iron, as well as their form, preserved. To be used up is the specific role of the spindle as an instrument of labour, but to be used up in the process of spinning. The greater productivity which it confers on labour creates more use values and thereby replaces the use value used up in the consumption of the instrument. This appears most clearly in agriculture, since here [the product] as an immediate means of life and use value appears most readily, because earliest historically, as use value in distinction to exchange value. If, by using a hoe, the cultivator produces twice as much grain as he could otherwise produce, he needs to use less time on the production of the hoe itself; he has enough food [for the time required] to make a new hoe.)

Now in the process of valorisation, the value components of capital—one existing in the form of material, the other in the form of instrument—do not appear as values in respect of the worker, i.e. of living labour (for the worker exists only as such in this process), but as simple moments of the production process; as use values for labour, as the objective conditions for its taking place, or as its objective moments. That the worker preserves them when he uses the instrument as instrument and gives to the raw material [III-42] a higher form of use value, is inherent in the nature of labour itself. But the use values of labour thus preserved are, as components of capital, exchange values. As such they are determined by the production costs contained in them, the amount of labour objectified in them. (For use value, only the *quality* of the labour already objectified is relevant.) The amount of *objectified labour* is preserved by the preservation of its *quality as use values for further labour* through contact with living labour.

The use value of raw cotton, like its use value as yarn, is preserved by the cotton—as yarn—being woven into fabric, by its existing as one of the objective moments (along with the loom) in weaving. *The amount of labour time contained in the raw cotton and the yarn is thereby also preserved.* What appears *in the simple production process as the preservation of the quality of previous labour—and consequently* also of the material in which it is embodied—appears in the process of valorisation as the preservation of the amount of labour already objectified. *For capital,* this preservation is the preservation of the amount of objectified labour *through* the production process; for *living labour* itself, it is only the preservation of the already present use value, present for labour to use.

Living labour adds a *new amount of labour;* but it is not by virtue of this *quantitative addition* that it preserves the quantity of labour already objectified, but by virtue of its *quality* as *living labour,* or by relating itself as labour to the use values in which the previous labour exists. Living labour, however, is not paid for this quality it possesses as living labour—it would not be bought at all, were it not living labour—but for the *quantity* of labour contained in it. What is paid for is only the *price* of its use value, as is the case with all other commodities. The specific quality it possesses, its ability by adding a new amount of labour to the amount previously objectified to preserve the objectified labour in its quality as objectified labour, is not paid for, nor does it cost the worker anything, since it is the natural property of his labour capacity.

In the production process, the separation of labour from the objective moments of its existence—instrument and material—is *transcended. The existence of capital and wage labour rests on this separation. The transcendence of the separation, which really takes place in the production process*—for otherwise no work could be carried on at all—*is not paid for by capital.* (The transcendence is effected not by the exchange with the worker, but *by labour itself in the production process.* But as such *ongoing labour,* it is itself already incorporated into capital, is one of its moments. This preserving power of labour therefore appears as the *self-preserving power* of capital. The worker has only added new labour; previous labour—by virtue of the existence of capital—has eternal exist- ence as value, completely independent of its physical form of being. This is how the matter appears to capital and to the worker.) If capital also had to pay for the transcendence, it would simply cease to be capital. For this is simply part of the physical role which labour plays in the production process by virtue of its nature; part of its use value.

But as use value, labour belongs to the capitalist; as merely exchange value, it belongs to the worker. Its living quality in the production process itself, its quality of preserving objectified labour time by making it into the objective mode of being of living labour, is not the worker's concern. *This appropriation, by which living labour* transforms *the instrument and material in the production process itself* into the body of its soul, and thereby raises them from the dead, is indeed an antithesis to the fact that labour is without an object or is a reality in the worker only as immediately living labour—and that the material and instrument of labour exist in capital as beings-for-themselves. (To this we must return.)

The valorisation process of capital is carried on through and in the simple production process by putting living labour in its natural relation to its material elements of being. But in so far as living labour enters into this relation, this relation does not exist for labour itself but for capital; it is itself already an element of capital.

It is evident, then, that the capitalist, by means of the process of exchange with the worker—by actually paying the worker an equivalent for the production costs contained in his labour capacity, i.e. by giving him the means to preserve his labour capacity but appropriating living labour for himself—obtains two things free of charge: firstly, the surplus labour which increases the value of his capital, but at the same time, secondly, the quality of living labour which preserves the previous labour materialised in the component parts of capital and thus preserves the previously existing value of the capital. Yet this preservation is not due to living labour *increasing the amount of objectified labour* and thus creating value, but simply to the fact that in adding a new quantity of labour it exists as *living* labour, in the immanent relationship to the material and instrument of labour posited by the production process; i.e. it is due to its *quality* as living labour. But as this quality, living labour is itself a moment of the simple production process, and the capitalist does not have to pay for it, just as the yarn and the loom do not cost him anything over and above their price for being likewise moments of the production process.

If, e.g. in time of STAGNATION OF TRADE, etc., the MILLS are shut down, then it can indeed be seen that the machinery rusts and the yarn is useless ballast, and rots, as soon as their relation to living labour ceases. If the capitalist merely [III-43] orders work so as to produce surplus value—to produce value not yet existing—it can be seen that as soon as he ceases to order work, his already existing capital, too, is depreciated; i.e. that living labour not merely adds new value, but by the VERY ACT OF ADDING A NEW VALUE TO THE OLD ONE, MAINTAINS, ETERNALISES IT.

(This shows clearly the stupidity of the accusation levelled against Ricardo, that he conceives *only* of profit and wages as necessary components of production costs, and not also of the part of capital contained in the raw material and instrument. In so far as the value existing in them is merely preserved, no new production costs are incurred. But as far as these existing values themselves are concerned, they all dissolve themselves once more into objectified labour—necessary labour and surplus labour— wages and profit. The purely natural material, in so far as *no* human labour is objectified in it, in so far as it is thus merely matter, exists independently of human labour, has no *value,* since value is only objectified labour; any more than the basic elements in general have any value.)

The preservation of the existing capital by the labour which valorises it, thus costs capital nothing, and therefore does not belong to the production costs, although the existing values are preserved in the product, and in exchange, therefore, equivalents must be given for them. But the *preservation of these values* in the product costs capital nothing, so capital cannot rank it among the production costs. Nor are they replaced by labour, since they are not consumed, except in so far as they are consumed in an aspect of their mode of being which is indifferent to labour and exists outside it, i.e. in so far as their *transience is consumed* (transcended) through labour. Only wages are really consumed.

[SURPLUS VALUE AND PROFIT]

Let us return once more to our example[a]: 100 thaler capital, i.e. 50 thaler raw material, 40 thaler labour, 10 thaler instrument of production. The worker needs 4 hours to produce the 40 thaler, the means required for his subsistence, or the part of production necessary for his maintenance; let his working day be 8 hours. The capitalist then obtains a surplus of 4 hours free of charge; his surplus value equals 4 objectified hours, 40 thaler; therefore his product=50+10 (the values preserved, not reproduced; values which have remained *constant, unaltered,* as values)+40 thaler (wages, reproduced because consumed in the form of wages)+40 thaler surplus value. *Sum total*: 140 thaler.

Of these 140 thaler, 40 are now surplus. Now, the capitalist must live during production and before he begins to produce; say, 20 thaler. He must have these 20 thaler apart from his capital of 100 thaler; equivalents for them must therefore be present in circulation. (How these originate does not concern us here.) Capital presupposes circulation as a constant magnitude. These equivalents are present once again. He therefore consumes 20 thaler of his profit. These enter into simple circulation. The 100 thaler also enter into simple circulation, but only to be transformed again into conditions of new production: 50 thaler raw material, 40 subsistence for worker, 10 instrument. Remains a surplus value added as such, newly produced, of 20 thaler. This is *money*, value made negatively independent in opposition to circulation. It cannot enter into circulation as simple equivalent, for the exchange of objects of simple consumption, since circulation is presupposed as constant. But the independent illusory existence of money has been transcended; it exists now only to valorise itself, i.e. to become capital.

In order to do so, however, it would have to be exchanged once more for the moments of the production process: subsistence for the worker, raw material and instrument. These are all reducible to objectified labour; can only be posited by living labour. *Money,* so far as it already exists *in itself* as capital, is thus merely a *draft*

---

[a] See this volume, pp. 268-70 and 279.— *Ed.*

on future (new) labour. In objective form it exists only as *money*. The surplus value, the increase of *objectified labour*, so far as it exists for itself, is *money*; but money is now *in itself* already capital, and as such a *draft on new labour*. Here capital no longer enters into relation only with existing labour but with future labour as well. Nor does it any longer appear dissolved into its simple elements in the production process, but dissolved into these as money; but no longer as money which is merely the abstract form of general wealth, but as money which is a draft on the real possibility of general wealth—on labour capacity, and, more precisely, on *labour capacity coming into being*. As such a draft, its material existence as money is of no consequence and can be replaced by any other title. Just like the State creditor, every capitalist possesses in his newly acquired value a draft on future labour, and has already appropriated future labour by the very appropriation of current labour. (This aspect of capital to be developed later. It already reveals here its characteristic feature: that as value it exists separately from its substance. This already contains the basis of credit.) The accumulation of capital in the form of money is therefore in no way a material accumulation of the material conditions of labour, but the accumulation of property titles to labour. It posits future labour as *wage labour*, as use value of capital. No *equivalent* exists for the newly created value; its possibility [exists] only in new [III-44] labour.

In this example, then, by means of absolute surplus labour time—labour of 8 hours instead of 4—a new value of 20 thaler money is produced, and this is money already related to its form as capital (money already as *posited possibility* of capital, not, as earlier, when this possibility arose only as the result of money ceasing to be money as such). This new value is added to the old values, to the existing world of wealth.

Now, if productivity doubles, so that the worker needs to put in only 2 hours' *necessary labour* instead of 4, and the capitalist CONSEQUENTLY makes him work 8 hours as before, then the account is as follows: 50 thaler material, 20 wages, 10 instrument of labour, 60 surplus value (6 hours, previously 4). Increment of absolute surplus value: 2 hours or 20 thaler. *Sum total*: 140 thaler (in the product).

A sum of 140 thaler as before, but 60 of it is surplus value, and of that 60, 40 as before is accounted for by the absolute increase of surplus time [beyond the necessary labour time], 20 by its relative increase. But the simple exchange value contains only 140 thaler, as before. Now [that productivity has doubled] is it only the use values which have increased, or has a new value been created? Previously, capital had to recommence the process with 100 thaler in order to expand anew by 40%. What becomes of the 20 [relative] surplus value? Previously, capital consumed 20; it was left with a value of 20. Now it consumes 20, and is left with 40. On the other hand, the capital entering into production previously remained 100; now it has become 80. What has been gained on one side as value in one form, has been lost on the other as value in the other form.

The previous capital re-enters the production process, and again produces 20 surplus value (after its consumption has been deducted). At the end of this second operation newly created value exists for which there is no equivalent: 20 thaler together with the first 40. Let us now take the second capital [whose productivity is twice as high]. 50 material, 20 wages (=2 hours), 10 instrument of labour. But with the 2 hours [spent on wages], it produces a value of 8, namely 80 thaler (of which 20 are for production costs [wages]). 60 thaler are left over, since only 20 reproduce wages (therefore vanish as wages). [If the second capital re-enters the production process, at the end of this second operation it will have produced, together with the first 60 thaler, a surplus value of] 60+60=120. At the end of this second operation, 20 thaler for consumption, remainder 20 [a] surplus value; together with the first 60.

In the third operation with the first [capital], 60 [surplus value], with the second, 80; with the fourth [operation] with the first [capital], 80, with the second [capital], 100. The first capital has increased as *value* by as much as its exchange value as productive capital has diminished.[b]

Suppose that both capitals together with their surplus can be used as capital, i.e. the surplus can be exchanged for new living labour. We then get the following account (omitting the [capitalist's own] consumption): the *first capital* produces [at a rate of profit of] 40%; the second 60%. 40% of 140 is 56; 60% of 140 (i.e. 80 capital, 60 surplus value) is 84. The total product in the first instance [if surplus value is used productively] is 140+56=196; in the second, 140+84=224. In the second instance, the absolute exchange value [of the product] is thus 28 thaler greater.

---

[a] Should be 40.— *Ed.*

[b] In the manuscript there follows at this point Marx's first draft of the comparison of the first and second capitals, with corresponding calculations. However Marx crossed it out, probably because he was dissatisfied with it.— *Ed.*

The first capital has 40 thaler to purchase new labour time; the value of one working hour was assumed to be 10 thaler, so it buys another 4 working hours with the 40 thaler which produce for it 80 (of which 40 for replacement of wages) (i.e. give it 8 hours' labour time).[113] The first capital was at the end [of the production process] 140+80 (namely, reproduction of the capital of 100; surplus value 40 or reproduction of 140; the first 100 thaler [of advanced capital] reproduce themselves as 140; the second 40 (since they are spent only on the purchase of new labour, hence do not *simply* replace a value—incidentally, an impossible assumption) produce 80). 140+80=220.

The second capital [on completion of the first production cycle equals] 140; the 80 produce 40; or the 80 thaler reproduce themselves as 120. But the remaining 60 [surplus value added to capital] (as they are spent *only* on the purchase of *labour*, and are therefore not used for the simple replacement of value but reproduce themselves from themselves and posit the surplus) reproduce themselves as 180; therefore 120+120=240 (40 thaler more produced than by the first capital, a surplus time of 2 hours, for the first is a surplus time of 2 hours as assumed also in the first capital). Therefore a greater exchange value as a result because more labour objectified, 2 hours more surplus labour.

[III-45] Something else to be noted here as well: 140 thaler at 40% yield 56; capital and interest[a] together=140+56=196. But in our calculations we have obtained [for the first capital] 220, according to which the interest on 140 would not be 56 but 84, which would be 60% on 140. ($140:84=100:x$; $x=^{8,400}/_{140}=60$). Likewise in the second instance: 140 at 60%=84; capital and interest together=140+84=224. But we obtain [for the second capital] 240; according to which the interest on 140 is not 84 but 100 ($140+100=240$); i.e. % ($140:100=100:x$; $x=^{10,000}/_{140}$) $71^3/_7$%.

How does this come about? (In the first instance 60% instead of 40%; in the second instance $71^3/_7$% instead of 60%). In the first instance, where it was 60 instead of 40, 20% too much came out; in the second $71^3/_7$ instead of 60, i.e. $11^3/_7$% too much. Why, firstly, the difference in both cases, and secondly, the difference in each case?

In the first case the original capital of 100=60 (material and instrument of labour) and 40 labour, i.e. $^3/_5$ material [and instrument], $^2/_5$ labour. The first $^3/_5$ yields no interest at all; the

―――――――――
a By interest (Zins) Marx means here the whole profit made on the advanced capital.— *Ed.*

latter $^2/_5$ yields 100% interest. But computed on the basis of the whole capital, the capital has increased by only 40%; $^2/_5$ of 100=40. But 100% on 40 yields only 40% on the whole 100, i.e. growth of the whole capital by $^2/_5$. Now, if, similarly, only $^2/_5$ of the newly added capital of 40 had increased by 100%, the total would have increased by 16. 40+16=56. This added to the 140=196, which is in fact an addition of 40% to the 156, if capital and interest are taken together.

40 [the newly added capital] has grown by 100%, has doubled, is 80; an expansion of $^2/_5$ of 40 by 100% adds 16. 40 of the 80 replaces the capital [spent on wages]. 40 is profit.

The account then is [for the first case]:

100 C^a+40 interest^b+40 C+40 interest=220;

or capital of 140 with interest of 80; but had we calculated it as:

100 C+40 interest+40 C+16 interest=196;

or capital of 140 with interest of 56.

[In our initial calculation,] we added too much in interest; the extra interest on 40 thaler of capital is 24 thaler. But 24=$^3/_5$ of 40 (3×8=24); i.e. alongside the capital [of 100 thaler] a mere $^2/_5$ of the [newly added] capital [of 40 thaler] has grown by 100%, so the total [newly added] capital has grown by only $^2/_5$, i.e. 16 thaler.

The interest we calculated for the 40 thaler was 24 thaler too high (this 24 represents 100% increase of $^3/_5$ of the capital of 40); 24 on 24 is 100% on 3×8 ($^3/_5$ of 40). But on the whole sum of 140, it is 60% [extra profit] instead of [the initial] 40%, i.e. on 40 thaler 24 too much has been calculated ($^3/_5$), 24 on 40 is 60%. On the capital of 40, therefore, 60% too much has been calculated (60=$^3/_5$ of 100). But on the total capital of 140, 24 too much has been calculated (and this is the difference between 220 and 196), thus together 28 $^1/_3$% too much.[114] Hence on the total [capital of 140 thaler], not 60% too much [has been calculated], as on the 40 [thaler] capital, but only 28 $^1/_3$ too much; which makes a difference of 31 $^2/_3$%, depending on whether we calculate 24 too much on the 40 [thaler] of the capital of 140.

Similarly in the other example.[115]

Of the 80 thaler advanced, which produces a value of 120, 50+10 [expended on the raw material and instrument] was merely replaced; but the 20 [expended on wages] reproduced itself three-fold, 60 (20 reproduction, 40 surplus). If 20 thaler

---

^{a} Capital. Here: advanced capital.— *Ed.*
^{b} In the sense of the total profit obtained on the advanced capital.— *Ed.*

[expended on wages] produces 60 thaler, i.e. three times its value, then 60 thaler [of newly expended capital] produces [a surplus value of] 180.

[IV-1][a] We need not concern ourselves any longer with this most tedious calculation. The point is simply this: if, as in our first example, material and instrument amount to $^3/_5$ [of the advanced capital] (60 out of 100), wages $^2/_5$ (40) and the capital yields 40% profit, then it equals 140 at the conclusion [of the production process] (this 40% profit is equivalent to the capitalist ordering 12 hours' labour when the necessary labour time is 6 hours, thus gaining 100% of the necessary labour time). Now, if the 40 thaler profit were employed once more as capital under the same assumptions—and at the point we have reached, the assumptions have not altered—then $^3/_5$ of the 40 thaler, i.e. 24 thaler, must again be expended on the material and instrument, and $^2/_5$ on labour. So only the wages of 16 are doubled, becoming 32, of which 16 are for reproduction of the wages and 16 are surplus labour; at the end of the process of production the profit is therefore 40+16, ALTOGETHER=56 or 40%. Thus the total capital of 140 would have produced 196. under the same conditions. It is not permissible to assume, as most political economists do, that the 40 thaler are spent wholly on wages, to buy living labour, and thus at the conclusion of the process of production yield 80 thaler.

If it is said: a capital of 100 yields 10% in a certain period, 5% in another, nothing could be more mistaken than to conclude, as do Carey[b] and his associates,[116] that in the first case the share of capital in the output was $^1/_{10}$, therefore that of labour only $^9/_{10}$; and that in the second case the share of capital was only $^1/_{20}$, therefore that of labour was $^{19}/_{20}$; to conclude, in other words, that because the rate of profit falls, the share of labour rises. Of course, from the standpoint of capital, which has no awareness of the nature of its valorisation process, and has an interest in having one only at times of *crises,* the profit of 10% on a capital of 100 looks like a flat increase of 10% on each of the value components of the capital—material, instrument, wages—as though the capital as a sum of 100 thaler value, as that number of a certain unit of values, has increased by 10%.

------

[a] Here Notebook IV of the manuscript begins. Written on page 1 are the words "Notebook IV. December 1857. Chapter on Capital (continued)."— *Ed.*

[b] H. C. Carey, *Principles of Political Economy,* Part I, Philadelphia, 1837, pp. 338-39.— *Ed.*

But in fact the question is: (1) how did the components of capital relate to each other, and (2) how much surplus labour did it buy with the wages—with the hours of labour objectified in the wages? If I know the total sum of capital, the relationship of its value components to each other (in practice I should also have to know what fractional part of the instrument of production is used up in the process, therefore actually enters into the process), and if I know the profit, I know how much surplus labour has been produced.

If $^3/_5$ of the capital consisted of material [and instrument of production], therefore 60 thaler (for the sake of convenience we assume that all the material [and the instrument] is consumed productively), and [$^2/_5$] of wages, 40, and if the profit on the 100 thaler is 10, then the labour bought with the 40 thaler of objectified labour time has produced 50 thaler of objectified labour in the production process. It has therefore worked a surplus time or produced a surplus value of $25\%=^1/_4$ of the necessary labour time. If, therefore, the worker works a 12-hour day, he has worked 3 hours of surplus time, and the labour time necessary to obtain his subsistence for one day was 9 hours' labour.[a]

The new value produced in production is indeed only 10 thaler, but according to the real rate these 10 thaler are to be taken as a percentage of the 40, not of the 100. The 60 thaler value has created no new value, only the working day has. The worker has therefore increased the capital exchanged for his labour capacity by 25%, not by 10%. The total capital has been increased by 10%. 10 is 25% of 40; it is only 10% of 100. The rate of profit of capital therefore by no means expresses the rate at which living labour increases objectified labour; for this increase is simply=to the surplus with which the worker reproduces his wages, i.e.=the time which he works over and above that which he would have to work to produce his wages.

If in the above example the worker were not a [wage] worker set to work by the capitalist, and if he treated the use values contained in the 100 thaler not as capital, but merely as objective conditions of his labour, he would possess, before starting on the production process anew, 40 thaler subsistence (which he would consume during the working day) and 60 thaler instrument and material. He would work only $^3/_4$ of a day, 9 hours, and his

---

[a] Here and below it should be "$2^2/_5$ hours of surplus time" and "$9^3/_5$ hours' labour".— Ed.

product at the end of the day would not be 110 thaler but 100, which he would then exchange [for the objective conditions of his labour] in the above proportions and recommence the process again and again. But on the other hand he would work 3 hours less, i.e. save the 25% surplus labour=25% surplus value on the exchange he would have made between 40 thaler subsistence and his labour time. And if on some occasion he worked 3 hours extra, because he had extra material to hand and also the instrument, it would not occur to him to argue that he had made an additional gain of 10%, but one of 25%; because he could buy $^1/_4$ more means of subsistence, for 50 thaler instead of for 40, and the means of subsistence alone would have value to him, since he is concerned with use value.

This illusion that the new gain is not [IV-2] produced by the exchange of the 9 hours of labour objectified in the 40 thaler for 12 hours of living labour, thus producing a surplus value of 25% on this portion, but that the total capital has grown over the board by an even 10%—10% of 60 [constant capital] is 6 and of 40 [variable capital] is 4; this illusion is the basis of *compound interest calculation* made by the notorious Dr. Price,[a] which prompted the HEAVEN-BORN Pitt to commit the folly of his SINKING FUND.[117] The identity of surplus gain [Mehrgewinn] with surplus labour time—absolute and relative—sets a qualitative limit[118] to the accumulation of capital, the *working day* (the time during which the worker's labour capacity can be active within any given 24 hours), the degree of development of productive power, and the size of the population, which represents the sum of simultaneous working days, etc. If, on the contrary, surplus gain is conceived of merely as interest—i.e. as the rate at which capital grows by means of some imaginary SLEIGHT OF HAND—the limit [to the accumulation of capital] would only be quantitative. Then it would be absolutely incomprehensible why capital should not add the accrued interest to itself as capital every other morning, and so create interest on its interest in endless geometric progression. Experience has shown the economists the *impossibility* of the Priceian augmentation of interest, but they have never revealed the BLUNDER contained in it.

Of the 110 thaler which come out at the end of the process of production, 60 thaler (material and instrument), so far as they are

---

a R. Price, *An Appeal to the Public, on the Subject of the National Debt*, 2nd ed. London, 1772, and *Observations on Reversionary Payments; on schemes for providing annuities for widows, and for persons in old age; on the method of calculating the values o assurances on lives; and on the national debt*, 2nd ed., London, 1772.— Ed.

values, have remained absolutely unaltered. The worker has taken nothing from them nor added anything to them. Although he maintains objectified labour for capital free of charge, by the VERY FACT OF HIS LABOUR BEING LIVING LABOUR, it nevertheless seems, from the capitalist's standpoint, that the worker must pay him even for the capitalist's permission to enter as labour into the adequate relation to the objectified elements, the objective conditions [of labour]. Now as regards the remaining 50 thaler, 40 thaler of them represent not mere preservation but *real reproduction,* since capital has divested itself of them in the form of wages and the worker has consumed them. 10 thaler represent the production over and above the reproduction, namely $^1/_4$ surplus labour (of 3 hours).

The product of the production process is only these 50 thaler. Hence if the worker, as is wrongly maintained, shared the product [of the newly added labour] with the capitalist [at a rate of profit of 10%] in such a way as to obtain $^9/_{10}$ of it, he would have to get not 40 thaler which is only $^8/_{10}$ [of the newly added labour] (and he has received it in advance and reproduced it in return; in fact, he has fully repaid it to capital and has, moreover, maintained the already existing value for it free of charge), but 45 thaler, leaving capital only 5. Therefore the capitalist would only possess 65 thaler at the end as the product of the production process which he began with 100 thaler.

But the worker gets none of the reproduced 40 thaler, nor any of the 10 thaler surplus value. If the reproduced 40 thaler should be conceived of as destined to serve once more as wages, therefore to be used by capital for a new purchase of living labour, one can only say, as far as the ratio is concerned, that the objectified labour of 9 hours (40 thaler) purchases a living [labour] of 12 hours (50 thaler), and thus produces a surplus value of 25% of the real product of the valorisation process (partly reproduced as wage fund, partly newly produced as surplus value).

Just now the original capital was 100:

Conditions of labour	Instrument	Wage labour
50	10	40

Produced a surplus gain of 10 thaler (25% surplus time). *Altogether* 110 thaler.

Suppose that it has now become:

[Conditions of labour]	[Instrument]	[Wage labour]
60	20	20

Let the result be 110 thaler. The commonplace economist, and the even more commonplace capitalist, will argue that [the profit of] 10% has been produced in equal proportions by all parts of the capital. Once again 80 thaler of the capital would merely have been preserved; no change in its value would have taken place. The 20 thaler would have been exchanged for 30, that is all; therefore the surplus labour would have increased to 50% [of necessary labour time] from the previous 25%.

Take the third case:

[Capital]	[Conditions of labour]	[Instrument]	[Wage labour]
100	70	20	10

Result 110. In this case, the unchanging value [is] 90. The new product 20; therefore surplus value or surplus time 100%.

We thus have three cases in which the profit on the whole capital is 10 in each case; but in the first case, the new [surplus] value produced equals 25% of the objectified labour expended in the purchase of the living labour, in the second case 50%, in the third 100%.[a]

The devil take these damned wrong calculations. But NEVER MIND. *Commençons de nouveau.*[b]

In the first case we had:

Unchanging value	Wage labour	Surplus value	Total
60	40	10	110

We assume throughout the working day=12 hours. (We could also assume it as growing, e.g. that it was previously only x hours but is now $x+b$ hours, and productive power as remaining the same; or assume both factors as varying.)

	Hours	Thaler
[IV-3] The worker produces in	12	50
so in	1	$4\,^1/_6$
so in	$9\,^3/_5$	40 } In 12 hours,
so in	$2\,^2/_5$	10 } 50 thaler.

The worker's necessary labour amounts therefore to $9^3/_5$ hours (40 thaler); the surplus labour thus to $2^2/_5$ hours ([produces] value

---

[a] Several lines of calculations relating to the three cases considered above were crossed out by Marx here.— *Ed.*

[b] Let's begin anew.— *Ed.*

of 10 thaler). $2^2/_5$ hours is a fifth of the working day. The surplus labour of the worker amounts to $^1/_5$ of a day, therefore=the value of 10 thaler. Let us now consider these $2^2/_5$ hours as a percentage which capital has gained on the labour time objectified in $9^3/_5$ hours in exchange for living labour, $2^2/_5 : 9^3/_5 = {}^{12}/_5 : {}^{48}/_5$, i.e. 12:48=1:4. Hence [$2^2/_5$ hours=] $^1/_4$ of the capital [advanced for wages]=25% on it. Similarly 10 thaler : 40 thaler=1 : 4=25%.

If we now summarise the whole result:

No. I

Original capital	Unchanging value	Value reproduced for wages	Surplus value of production	Total sum	Surplus time and surplus value	% [of surplus time] to the exchanged objectified labour
					$2^2/_5$ hrs or	
100 tlr.	60 tlr.	40 tlr.	10tlr.	110 tlr.	10 tlr.	25%

(One could say that the *instrument of labour,* i.e. its value, must be reproduced, not merely replaced, since it is in fact used up, is consumed in production. This is to be considered under *capital fixe.* In fact, the value of the instrument passes over into that of the material; in so far as it is objectified labour, it alters only its form. If in the above example the value of the material was 50 and that of the instrument of labour 10, so now, where 5 of the instrument's value is used up, that of the material [together with that of the used-up part of the instrument] is 55 and that of the instrument 5. If it is completely used up, the value of the material [together with that of the used-up instrument] has gone up to 60. This is an element of the simple production process. The instrument has not, like wages, been consumed *outside the production process.*)

We come now to the second case assumed:

Original capital	Unchanging value	Value reproduced for wages	Surplus value of production	Total sum
100	80	20	10 tlr.	110 tlr.

If the worker produces 30 thaler in 12 hours, so in 1 hour $2^2/_4$ thaler, in 8 hours 20 thaler, and in 4 hours 10 thaler. 10 thaler is 50% of 20 thaler; as are 4 hours on 8; surplus value=4 hours, $^1/_3$ of a day or 10 thaler.

Therefore:

No. II

Original capital	Unchanging value	Value reproduced for wages	Surplus value of production	Total sum	Surplus time and surplus value 4 hrs.	% on [variable] capital
100	80	20 8 hours	10 tlr.	110	10 tlr.	50%

In the first case as in the second, the profit on the total capital 100=10%; but in the first case the real surplus value which capital obtains in the production process is 25%, in the second 50%.

The assumptions in No. II are in themselves quite as plausible as those in No. I. But related to each other, those in No. II appear to be absurd. The material and the instrument have been raised in value from 60 to 80 thaler, the productivity of labour has fallen from $4^1/_6$ thaler [newly created value] per hour to $2^2/_4$ thaler, and [the rate of] surplus value has increased by 100%. (But if we assume that the greater outlay for wages in the first case represents more working days, in the second fewer, then the assumption is correct.)

The fact that the necessary wages, therefore the value of labour expressed in thaler, have fallen, would in itself be of no consequence. Whether the value of one hour's labour is expressed in 2 or 4 thaler, both in the first case as well as in the second the product of 12 hours' labour exchanges (in circulation) for 12 hours' labour, and in both cases the surplus labour appears as surplus value. The absurdity of the assumption [in No. II] arises from the fact that (1) we have presupposed the maximum of labour time as 12 hours; hence cannot bring in more or fewer working days; (2) the more we allow capital to grow on one side [that of constant value], the more we cause not only the *necessary* labour *time* to diminish but its *value* as well; although the value is the same. In the second case the price would actually have to rise. The fact that the worker can live with less labour, i.e. produce more in the same number of hours, would have to make itself evident not in the [IV-4] decline in [the number of] thaler [paid] for one necessary working hour, but in the number of the necessary working hours itself.

If, e.g. as in the first example, he obtained $4^1/_6 \times 9^3/_5$ thaler, but the use value of this value, which must be *constant* in order to express *value* (not price), had so increased that he no longer required (as in the first case) $9^3/_5$ but only 4 hours for the

Page 3 of Notebook IV of *Outlines of the Critique of Political Economy*

production of his living labour capacity, then this would be bound to manifest itself in the surplus of the value. But in this case we have, in accordance with the conditions we have set ourselves, varied the "unchanging value" and have not changed the 10% which is constant here as the addition to reproductive labour, although it expresses different percentage parts of the same.

In the first case the unchanging value is smaller than in the second, the total product of [newly added] labour is greater; since if one component part of [the advanced capital of] 100 is smaller, the other must be greater; and since absolute labour time has also been fixed at the same amount; and since, finally, the total product of [newly added] labour diminishes as the "unchanging value" increases, and increases as this diminishes, we obtain less product of [newly added] labour (in absolute terms) for the same [newly added] labour time in proportion as more [constant] capital is employed. Now, this would be quite correct, since, if out of a given sum like 100, more is laid out in "unchanging value", less can be laid out in [newly added] labour time, and hence in general less new value can be produced *relatively* to the capital employed. But then [if capital is to make a profit] the *labour time* must not be fixed, as it is here, or, if it is fixed, the *value of one hour's labour* must not become smaller as it does here, which is impossible if the "unchanging value" and [the rate of] *surplus value increase*; the *number* of working hours would have to become smaller. But this is presupposed in our example. We assumed, in the first case, that in 12 hours' labour 50 thaler [of new value] is produced; in the second case, only 30 thaler. In the first case, we assumed that the worker worked for $9^3/_5$ hours [to reproduce the equivalent of his wages]; in the second case, for only 6, although he produced less in one hour. *C'est absurde.*[a]

And yet, is there not something correct about these figures, if they are looked at differently? Does not the absolute new value diminish, although the relative new value grows, when more material and instrument, relative to labour, enters into the elements of capital? Relative to a given capital, less living labour is employed. Therefore, even if the excess of [the product of] this living labour over its cost is greater, and thus the percentage increases specifically relative to wages, i.e. the percentage relative to the [variable] capital really consumed, does not the absolute new value necessarily become relatively smaller than in the case of the capital which employs less material and instrument of labour

---

[a] That's absurd.— *Ed.*

(precisely this is the main point in the change of the unchanging value, i.e. of the value unchanging as value in the production process) and more living labour, for the very reason that relatively more living labour is employed?

An increase in productive power then corresponds to the increase of the instrument of labour, since the surplus value [produced by Capital II], as in the previous mode of production [Capital I], is not proportional to its use value, its productive power, and since any increase in productive power produces surplus value, even though it does not do so in the same numerical proportion.

The increase in productive power which must manifest itself in an increase in the value of the instrument, in the relative share it accounts for in the expenses of capital, is necessarily accompanied by an increase in the [amount of] material, since more material must be worked on so that more product can be produced. (But the increase in productive power is also related to quality. It is related to quantity only, if a given product is of defined quality; it is related only to quality, if a specific quantity is given for the product; it can relate to both.)

Although [when the share of the material and instrument of labour in the advanced capital increases] less (necessary) labour exists relative to surplus labour, as in general less living labour necessarily exists relative to capital, can its surplus value not increase, though relative to total capital it declines, i.e. the so-called rate of profit declines?

For example, take a capital of 100, made up originally of material 30, instrument 30 (together 60 of unchanging value), wages 40 (4 working days), profit 10. In this case the profit [is] 25% new value relative to the labour objectified in the wages and 10% relative to capital.

Now assume that the material is 40, and the instrument 40. Assume that productivity doubles, so that only 2 working days are now necessary [for wages]=20. Suppose that absolute profit is now less than 10, i.e. the profit relative to the total capital. Can not the profit relative to the labour employed amount to more than 25%, i.e. in the given case to more than a quarter of 20? IN FACT, a third of 20 is $6^2/_3$; i.e. less than 10, [IV-5] but this is $33^1/_3\%$ of the labour employed, while in the previous case it was only 25%. Here we would have had at the end of the process only $106^2/_3$, whereas previously we had 110, and yet starting with the same sum [of advanced capital] (100), the surplus labour, the surplus gain would be greater relative to the labour employed than in the first case.

But since in absolute terms 50% less labour was employed, while the greater profit on the labour employed amounts to only $8\,^1/_3$% [$33^1/_3$%-25%] more than in the first case, the absolute quantity which results must be smaller, hence the profit on the total [advanced] capital as well. For $20\times33\,^1/_3$ [$=6^2/_3$] is smaller than 40×25% [$=10$].

This entire case is improbable and cannot be taken as a general example in political economy, for an increase both in [the cost of] the instrument of labour and in the amount of material worked up are presupposed here, although not only the relative but also the absolute number of workers has declined. (Of course, if two factors=a third, the one must become smaller as the other grows larger.) But an increase in the instrument of labour in value terms relative to capital, and an increase in the material of labour in value terms with relatively less labour, presuppose a [growing] division of labour in the whole [of society], therefore an increase in the number of workers at least in absolute terms, even though not relatively to the volume of capital employed.

However, take the example of the lithographic machine, which everyone can use himself to make lithographs. Assume the *value* of the instrument when newly invented was greater than that [of the equipment] which previously 4 workers used before these handy things were invented; assume that it only requires 2 workers for its use (here, as in the case of many machines which are a kind of instrument, one cannot speak of any further division of labour; it is rather the qualitative division which disappears). Assume that originally the instruments were of the value of only 30, but that the necessary labour (i.e. necessary for the capitalist to make a profit) [was] 4 working days.

(There are machines, e.g. forced air heating ducts, which completely eliminate labour as such, except at one point; the ducts are opened at one point; to convey the heated air to the other points no workers at all are required. This is generally the case (see Babbage[a]) with power [energy] transmission: where previously power [energy] [was conveyed] in material form from one point to another by many workers, the former stokers, the transmission of that power [energy] from one room to another, which is now a physical process, appeared as the labour of so many workers.)

If the lithographer employs his machine as a source of profit, as

---

[a] Ch. Babbage, *Traité sur l'économie des machines et des manufactures*, pp. 20-21.— *Ed.*

capital, not as use value, the material necessarily increases, since he can print more lithographs in a given period of time [than before], and it is precisely from this that his profit arises. Assume that this lithographer employs instrument of 40, material of 40, 2 working days (20), that [yields] him $33^1/_3\%$, i.e. $6^2/_3$ on 20 objectified labour time. If his capital consists, like that of the other one, of 100, it yields him only $6^2/_3\%$ profit, but he gains $33^1/_3\%$ relative to the labour employed; the other capitalist gains 10% on the capital, but only 25% on the labour employed.

The value obtained from the labour employed may be smaller, but the profit on total capital is greater, if the other component parts of the capital are proportionately smaller. Nevertheless, the business with the $6^2/_3\%$ on the total capital and $33^1/_3\%$ on the labour employed could become more profitable than that originally based on a 25% profit on the labour and 10% profit on the total capital.

Suppose e.g. grain, etc., to have risen in value so much that the subsistence of the worker rises in value by 25%. The 4 working days would now cost the first lithographer 50 instead of 40. His instruments and material remain the same: 60 thaler. He would therefore have to invest a capital of 110. His profit, with a capital of 110, on the 50 thaler for 4 working days would be 12 (25%). Therefore 12 thaler on 110 (i.e. $9^1/_6\%$ on the total capital of 110).

The other lithographer: machine 40, and material 40. But the 2 working days would cost him 25% more, i.e. 25, instead of 20. He would therefore have to invest 105; his surplus value relative to the labour would be $33^1/_3\%$, i.e. $^1/_3$, therefore $8^1/_3$. He would therefore gain $8^1/_3$ on 105; or $13^1/_8\%$.[119]

Now suppose that, over a cycle of 10 years, there are 5 good harvests and 5 bad harvests, with the AVERAGE proportions as indicated above: the first lithographer would gain, as compared to the second, 50 thaler interest [profit] in the first [good] 5 years; in the second [bad] 5 years $45^5/_6$; over the whole period, $95^5/_6$ thaler. His AVERAGE interest [average profit] over the 10 years [would be] $9^7/_{12}$ thaler. The other capitalist would have gained $31^1/_3$ in the first [good] 5 years; in the second [bad] 5 years, $65^5/_8$; over the whole period, $96^{23}/_{24}$ thaler. AVERAGE [profit] over the 10 years would be $9^{87}/_{120}$.

Since [capitalist] No. II worked up more material at the same price, he sells the product more cheaply. One could say in reply that, since he used up more instrument, he sells his product more dearly; particularly since he uses up more of the machine's value in proportion as he uses up more material. However, in practice it is [IV-6] not true that machines are used up proportionately the more quickly, i.e. that they must be replaced the sooner, the more material they work up. But all this does not belong here. We assume in both cases that the ratio of the value of the machine to that of the material is constant.

This example becomes significant only if we assume a smaller capital which employs more labour and less material and machinery but earns a higher percentage on the total capital employed; and a larger capital which employs more machinery, more material, proportionately less but in absolute terms just as many working days and makes a smaller percentage profit on the total capital employed, because less on labour, which is more productive because division of labour, etc., applied. Here, it must be assumed (and this was not assumed above) that the use value of the machine is significantly greater than its value, i.e. that its depreciation in the service of production is not proportional to its effect in increasing production.

So, assume, as above, a printing press: the first a printing press operated manually and the second a SELF-ACTING printing press.

Capital I of 100 invests 30 in material; 30 in the manually operated press; and in labour 4 working days=40 thaler. Profit is 10%, therefore 25% on the living labour (surplus time $^1/_4$ [of necessary time]).

Capital II of 200 invests 100 in material; 60 in the *press*; 4 working days (40 thaler). Profit relative to the 4 working days is $13\,^1/_3$ thaler=$1\,^1/_3$ working days, whereas in the first case it was only 1 working day. Sum total: $413\,^1/_3$, i.e. [rate of profit] $3\,^1/_3\%$, whereas in the first case it was 10%. Nevertheless, the surplus value of the labour employed is $13\,^1/_3$ thaler in this second case, while in the first it is only 10. In the first case, 4 working days produce in 4 days 1 surplus day; in the second case, 4 [days] produce $^1/_3$ surplus day. But the rate of profit on the total capital employed is smaller by $^1/_3$ or $33^1/_3\%$ in the second case than in the first; the total sum of profit is $^1/_3$ greater.

Now let us assume that the 30 and the 100 invested in material [by the two capitals respectively] consist of sheets of print, and that the instrument is used up in the same time [in both cases], in 10 years or by $^1/_{10}$ [of its value] each year. No. I then has to replace [annually] $^1/_{10}$ of the 30 invested in the instrument, i.e. 3; No. II, $^1/_{10}$ of 60, i.e. 6. As assumed above, the instrument does not enter into the annual production in either case to a greater extent [than

$^1/_{10}$ of its value] (the 4 working days can count as days of 3 months each).[a]

Capital I sells 30 sheets of print at 30 material+3 instrument+50 (objectified [newly added] labour time) [production time]=83 thaler.

Capital II sells 100 sheets of print at 100 material+6 instrument+53$^1/_3$ [objectified (newly added) labour time]=159$^1/_3$ thaler.

Capital I sells 30 sheets for 83 thaler; 1 sheet for $^{83}/_{30}$ thaler=2 thaler 23 silver groschen.[b]

Capital II sells 100 sheets for 159 thaler 10 silver groschen; 1 sheet for $\dfrac{159 \text{ thaler } 10 \text{ silver groshen}}{100}$, i.e. for 1 thaler 9 silver groschen 10 pfennigs.

Clearly, then, Capital I has had it, because it sells its product infinitely too high. Although in the first case the profit relative to total capital was 10% and only 3$^1/_3$% in the second, yet the first capital has taken in only 25% relative to [paid] labour time, while the second has taken in 33$^1/_3$%. With Capital I, the ratio of necessary labour to the total capital invested is greater, and thus the surplus labour appears, though less in absolute terms than in Capital II, as a greater rate of profit upon the smaller total capital. 4 working days at 60 [produce a] greater [relative surplus value] than 4 at 160: in the first, 1 working day corresponds to an available [constant] capital of 15, in the second, 1 working day corresponds to 40. But with the second capital, labour is more productive. (This follows both from the *greater* amount of machinery and thus from its larger share in the value components of the capital; and hence from the greater amount of material, in which the working day including [IV-7] more surplus time and hence using up more material in the same time is expressed.) It produces more surplus time (relative surplus time, i.e. surplus time resulting from the development of productivity). In the first case the surplus time is $^1/_4$ [of the necessary time], in the second $^1/_3$. [In the case of the second capital] surplus time thus produces more use values as well as a greater exchange value in the same time. But the latter not in the same proportion as the former,

---

[a] Here Marx crossed out a passage discussing an example of how the two capitals can sell their product. At its end he stated that "the example chosen is wrong, the prices being incorrect". Instead, he proceeded to give other calculations.— *Ed.*

[b] The (Prussian and Saxon) thaler equalled 30 silver groschen, the silver groschen equalled 12 pfennigs.— *Ed.*

since, as we have seen, exchange value does not grow in the same numerical proportion as does the productivity of labour. The fractional price of the product is thus smaller than the total price of production—i.e. the fractional price multiplied by the amount of fractional prices produced [is] greater [than it was before—despite the decrease of the fractional price].

If we had assumed an *absolutely greater* total number of working days than in No. I, though relatively smaller, the matter would have been even more striking. The profit of the larger capital, working with a greater amount of machinery, appears smaller than that of the smaller capital working with relatively or absolutely more living labour, precisely because the *greater profit on the living labour* appears smaller when calculated on a total capital in which the living labour employed makes up a lesser proportion of the total capital, than the *smaller profit on the living labour* which represents a greater proportion of the smaller total capital. But the fact that the proportion [of the value expended on material and instrument and that expended on living labour] in No. II is such that more material can be worked up, and a greater part of value is invested in the instrument of labour, is only the manifestation of the [increased] productivity of labour.

This, then, is the famous point of the hapless Bastiat, who had firmly convinced himself—and Mr. Proudhon did not know what to reply[a]—that, because the rate of profit seems less on the greater and more productive total capital, the worker's share had become larger, whereas in fact precisely *the opposite* is the case: his surplus labour had become greater.

Nor does Ricardo seem to have understood the matter, since OTHERWISE he would not have explained the periodical decline of profit itself only by the rise of wages caused by the rise in the price of grain (and thus of rent). But *au fond* surplus value—in so far as it is indeed the basis of profit but at the same time distinct from profit COMMONLY so-called—has never been analysed.

The hapless Bastiat would have said, in the above case, that since in the first example the profit is 10% (i.e. $\frac{1}{10}$), and in the second it is only $3\frac{1}{3}\%$, i.e. (roughly) $\frac{1}{33}$, the worker receives $\frac{9}{10}$ of the product in the first case and $\frac{32}{33}$ in the second. The ratio [of profit and wages] is wrong in each of the two CASES, as is the ratio of the one to the other.

The further relation of the new value of capital to capital as

---

[a] This refers to *Gratuité du crédit. Discussion entre M. Fr. Bastiat et M. Proudhon*, pp. 127-31, 133-57 and 288.— *Ed.*

indifferent total value (altogether, this is how capital appeared to us before we proceeded to the discussion of the production process and this is how it must appear again at the end of the process) is to be developed partly under the heading of *profit,* where the new value assumes a new determination, partly under the heading of *accumulation.* Here we are concerned above all else to analyse the nature of surplus value as the equivalent of the absolute or relative labour time over and above the necessary labour time set in motion by capital.

The consumption, in the production process, of the value component in the instrument cannot in the least distinguish the instrument of production from the material, especially in the present context, where only the creation of surplus value, self-valorisation, is still to be explained. This is simply because that consumption is part of the simple production process itself, i.e. the value of the consumed instrument (whether it be the *simple use value* or the exchange value, if production has developed to the stage of division of labour and at least the surplus is exchanged) has to be recovered in the value (exchange value or use value) of the product already in the production process, so that it can start anew from itself. The instrument loses its use value in the same measure in which it helps to raise the exchange value of raw material and serves as means of labour. This point, INDEED, must be investigated, since it is fundamentally important to draw the distinction between the unchanging value as a part of capital which is maintained, the other part which is reproduced (*reproduced* for capital; from the standpoint of the real production of labour, *produced*), and that which is newly produced.

I⸏T IS NOW TIME TO *finir avec la question regardant la valeur résultant de l'accroissement des forces productives.*[a] We have seen that a *surplus value* (not merely a greater use value) is created, as in the case of an absolute increase of surplus labour.[b] If a definite limit is given [to necessary labour as against surplus labour], say e.g. that the worker requires only half a day in order to produce his subsistence for a *whole* day, if the natural limit of surplus labour the worker can provide with a given quantity of labour is reached, then an increase in the absolute labour time is possible only if more workers are employed *simultaneously,* if the real working day

---

[a] Finish with the question of value resulting from the growth of the productive forces.— *Ed.*

[b] See this volume, pp. 267-71.— *Ed.*

is SIMULTANEOUSLY multiplied, rather than merely lengthened. (Under the assumption made here, one worker can work for only 12 hours. If the surplus time provided by 24 hours [of labour] is to be gained, 2 workers must be employed.) In this case, the capital, before it enters upon the process of self-valorisation, must buy an extra 6 hours' labour in the act of exchange with the worker, in other words, it has to lay out a greater part of itself. On the other hand, the capital on average has to spend more on the material to be worked up (apart from the fact that the extra worker has to be *available,* i.e. that the working population must have grown). Hence the possibility of the further process of [IV-8] valorisation depends here on a previous accumulation of capital (considered in terms of its physical substance).

If, on the contrary, productivity, and thus relative surplus time, grow—from the present standpoint capital can still be regarded as directly producing means of subsistence, raw material, etc.—a smaller outlay for wages is necessary and the increase in the material is created by the valorisation process itself. But this question is related RATHER to the *accumulation* of capitals.

We return to the point where we last broke off.[a] Growing productivity increases *surplus value,* though it does not increase the absolute sum of exchange values. It increases values because it produces a new *value as value,* i.e. a value which is not intended simply to be exchanged as an equivalent but to maintain itself; in a word, more money. The question is: does the growth in productivity eventually increase the sum of exchange values as well? *Au fond,* this may be conceded, since even Ricardo admits that with the accumulation of capitals, savings, HENCE the amount of exchange values produced, also grow. The growth of savings implies nothing but the growth of autonomous values—of money. But Ricardo's demonstration of this fact contradicts his own assertion.

Take our old example.[b] 100 thaler capital: 60 unchanging value; 40 wages, produces 80; hence product=140.

⫫Here we see again that the surplus value on the whole capital =half of the newly produced value, since a half of it=necessary labour. The proportion accounted for by surplus value, which is always equal to surplus time, therefore=the total product of the worker minus the part which constitutes his wages, depends on (1) the ratio of the unchanging part of capital to the productive part; (2) the ratio of necessary labour time to surplus time. In the above

a Ibid., pp. 272-79.— *Ed.*
b Ibid., pp. 268-70, 279 and 291-96.— *Ed.*

example, the ratio of surplus time to necessary labour time is 100%; which gives 40% on the capital of 100; hence (3) it depends not only on the ratio specified in (2), but also on the absolute volume of necessary labour time.

If 80 of the capital of 100 were the unchanging part, the part exchanged for necessary labour would be=to 20; and if this produced 100% surplus time, the profit of the capital would be 20%.

But if the capital were=to 200 with the same proportion of constant and variable parts [120] (namely $^3/_5$ to $^2/_5$), the sum would be 280, which is 40 [thaler profit] on [each] 100 [thaler of the capital employed]. In this case the absolute amount of profit would grow from 40 to 80, but the ratio would remain 40%.

However, if the constant element in the capital of 200 were 120, and the amount of necessary labour 80, but this increased by only 10%, i.e. by 8, the sum total would be equal to 208, therefore profit would be 4%. If necessary labour increased by only 5, then the sum total 205, i.e. [profit] $2^1/_2$%.//

Let this 40 in surplus value be absolute labour time.

Suppose now that productivity doubles. If the worker could provide for 40 thaler [wages] 8 hours of necessary labour, he now produces in 4 hours a whole day of living labour. Surplus time would then grow (previously $^2/_3$ of a working day was necessary to produce a whole day, now only $^1/_3$ of a day is necessary) by $^1/_3$. Of the product of a working day, $^2/_3$ would be surplus value, and if the hour of necessary labour=5 thaler ($5 \times 8 = 40$), he would now need only $5 \times 4 = 20$ thaler. Consequently, there is a surplus profit of 20 on the capital, namely 60 instead of 40. At the end of the process, the total sum is 140, of which 60=constant value, 20=wages and 60=surplus profit; altogether 140. With 80 thaler capital, the capitalist may now begin production anew:

Let capitalist A at the same stage of the old production invest his capital of 140 in new production. According to the original proportions, he uses $^3/_5$ [of that 140] for the invariable part of capital, therefore $3 \times {}^{140}/_5 = 3 \times 28 = 84$. 56 remains for the necessary labour. He previously expended 40 for labour, he now expends 56, i.e. $^2/_5$ of 40 more. Then at the end his capital $=84+56+56=196$.

Capitalist B at the higher stage of production would similarly invest the 140 thaler in new production. If out of a capital of 80, he needs 60 for invariable value and only 20 for labour, then out of 60 he needs 45 for invariable value and 15 for labour. Hence the sum would be, firstly, $=60+20+20=100$ and, secondly, $=45+15+15=75$.

His total product is therefore 175, while that of the first capitalist=196.

An increase in the productivity of labour means only that the same capital produces the same value with less labour; or that less labour produces the same product with a greater capital; that a decrease in necessary labour results in an increase in surplus labour. Necessary labour [IV-9] being smaller relative to capital, for its valorisation process, is obviously the same as capital being greater relative to the necessary labour which it sets in motion; for the same capital sets more surplus labour in motion, therefore less necessary labour.

//If it is assumed, as in our example, that the capital remains the same, i.e. that both capitalists recommence [the process of production] with 140 thaler, then in the case of the more productive capital, a larger part has to go to capital (that is to say, to its invariable part), and in the case of the less productive capital, a larger part to labour. Thus the first capital of 140 sets in motion necessary labour of 56, and this necessary labour assumes for its process an invariable part of the capital, 84. The second capital sets in motion labour of 20+15=35; and [operates with] an invariable capital of 60+45=105 (and it also follows from our previous argument that the increase in productivity does not increase value in the same proportion as it increases itself).//

//In the first case, as already shown,[a] the absolute new value [surplus value] is greater than in the second, because the amount of labour employed is greater in relation to the invariable part of capital [labour is less productive], while in the second case the amount of labour is smaller precisely because labour is more productive. But (1) the difference, that the [total] new value [surplus value] in the first case was only 40 while it was 60 in the second, excludes [given equality of the initial capitals] the possibility of the first capitalist recommencing production with the same capital as the second. For a part of the new value in both cases must go into circulation as an equivalent, so that the capitalist may live, and indeed live by means of his capital. If both consume 20 thaler of their capital, the first would begin the new labour [after the first production cycle] with 120 capital, the other also with 120 [owing to the fact that the first capitalist entered the first production cycle with 100 thaler and the second with 80], etc. See above.[b] We must return to all this again; but the question of the

---

[a] See this volume, pp. 291-93.— Ed.
[b] Ibid., pp. 293-94.— Ed.

relationship of the new value produced by greater productivity to the new value produced by an absolute increase in labour, belongs to the chapter on *accumulation and profit.//*

This is why it is said of machinery that it *saves labour* [by helping reduce necessary labour and increase surplus labour]. But the *mere* saving of labour is not, as *Lauderdale*[a] correctly observed, the characteristic thing, since with the help of machinery human labour performs actions and creates things which it absolutely could not do and create without it. The latter concerns the use value of machinery. The *saving* of necessary labour and the production of *surplus labour* is the characteristic thing. The greater productivity of labour expresses itself in the fact that capital has to buy less necessary labour to produce the same value and a greater mass of use values, or that less necessary labour produces the same exchange value, valorises more material, and creates a greater mass of use values.

The growth of productivity therefore implies that, if the *total value of capital remains the same,* the constant part of it (consisting of material and machinery) grows relative to the variable, i.e. to that part of the capital which is exchanged for living labour, the part which constitutes the wages fund. This means at the same time that a smaller amount of labour sets in motion a greater amount of capital. If the *total value of capital* entering into the production process grows, the wages fund (the variable part of capital) must decline *relatively* to what it would be, if the productivity of labour, i.e. the ratio of necessary labour to surplus labour, had remained the same.

Let us suppose the 100 capital in the above case is agricultural capital, then 40 thaler seeds, fertilisers, etc., 20 thaler instrument of labour and 40 thaler wages, at the old level of production. (Assume that these 40 thaler=4 days' necessary labour.) These produce a sum of 140 at the old level of production. Suppose that fertility doubles, perhaps by improvement of the instrument or by the application of improved fertilisers, etc. In this case, the product must be [as before]=to 140 thaler (assuming the instrument to be totally used up in the process). Let fertility double, so that the price of a necessary working day falls by one-half; or so that only 4 necessary half-days of work (i.e. 2 whole days) are required in order to produce 8. 2 working days being necessary to produce 8 is the same as $1/4$ (3 hours) of a

---

[a] J. Lauderdale, *Recherches sur la nature et l'origine de la richesse publique*, Paris, 1808, pp. 119-20.— *Ed.*

[12-hour] working day being necessary labour. Instead of 40 thaler, the farmer now has to spend only 20 on labour.

Thus, at the end of the process, the components of capital have changed: it now consists of the original 40 on seeds, etc., which has doubled in use value; 20 instrument of labour; and 20 labour (2 whole working days). Previously the ratio of the constant part of capital to the variable=60:40=3:2, now=80:20 or=4:1. If we consider the whole capital, the necessary labour was previously $^2/_5$ of it; now it is $^1/_5$. If the farmer wants to continue to employ labour in the earlier proportion, by how much must his capital grow? But let us avoid the *malicious assumption* that he continued to operate with 60 constant capital and 40 wages fund after the doubling of productivity, which would bring in false ratios; // although in the case of the farmer this is quite correct, if favourable SEASONAL conditions doubled fertility. It would be equally correct for every industrialist, if productivity doubled not in his branch of industry, but in the branches whose output he uses, e.g. if cotton cost him 50% less, and grain (i.e. wages), and finally the instrument; he would then continue as before to spend 40 thaler on raw cotton, which would now buy double the amount; 20 on machinery; and 40 on labour// because this assumes that, despite the doubled productivity, capital continued to operate with the same component parts, to employ the same amount of necessary labour, without spending more on raw material and instrument of labour. //Suppose that only the cotton doubled in productivity, while that of the machinery remained the same—this is to be examined further.// Hence productivity doubles, so that, if he had to spend 40 thaler for labour before, he now needs only 20.

(If it is assumed that 4 whole working days—each=10 thaler—were necessary to produce for the capitalist a surplus of 4 whole working days, and that this surplus was produced for him by [e.g.] the 40 thaler raw cotton being converted into yarn, then he now requires only 2 whole working days [IV-10] to produce the same value—i.e. that of 8 working days; the value of the yarn previously expressed a surplus time of 4 working days, now of 6. Or each worker previously required 6 hours' necessary labour time to produce 12; *now* 3. The necessary labour time amounted to 12×4=48 [hours] or 4 days. In each of these days the surplus time=$^1/_2$ day (6 hours). The necessary labour time now amounts to only 12×2=24 [hours] or 2 days; 3 hours [per working day].

To produce the surplus value, each of the 4 workers had previously to work 6×2 hours, i.e. 1 day; now he needs to work for only 3×2, i.e. $^1/_2$ day. Now, it comes to the same thing whether

4 workers work for $^1/_2$ day each, or 2 for a whole day. The capitalist could now dismiss 2 of the workers. Indeed, he would have to do so, because he can make only a definite quantity of yarn from a definite quantity of cotton. Consequently, he can no longer provide work for 4 whole days, but only for 4 half-days.

Yet, if the worker must work 12 hours to obtain 3 hours, i.e. his *necessary* wages, he will receive only $1^1/_2$ hours' exchange value if he works 6 hours. And if he can maintain himself for 12 hours with 3 hours of necessary labour, he can maintain himself for only 6 hours with $1^1/_2$ hours' necessary labour. Each of the 4 workers therefore, if all 4 continue to be employed, could only live for half a day, i.e. all 4 of them could not be kept alive as *workers* by the same capital, but only 2 of them. The capitalist could pay 4 workers from the former [wages] fund for 4 half working days; but he would then pay them 2 days' too much, and would be making them a gift out of productivity, since he can use only 4 half-days of living labour. Such "possibilities" neither occur in practice nor can we deal with them here, where we are concerned with the relation of capital as such.)

20 thaler of the capital of 100 are now [after the doubling of productivity] not utilised directly in production. The capitalist, as before, invests 40 thaler in raw material, 20 in the instrument, therefore 60, but now only 20 thaler in labour (2 working days). Of the total capital of 80, he uses $^3/_4$ (60) for the constant part and only $^1/_4$ for labour. Therefore, if he invests the remaining 20 in the same way, it is $^3/_4$ in constant capital, $^1/_4$ in labour; i.e. 15 for the first, 5 for the second. Now, since a working day is assumed to be=to 10 thaler, 5 thaler would=6 hours=$^1/_2$ working day. With the new value of 20 gained through [the increase in] productivity, the capital could buy only half a working day more, to valorise itself in the same proportion. The capital would have to grow three-fold (i.e. to 60) (together with the 20,=80) to be able to employ fully the 2 dismissed workers, to utilise fully the previously utilised 2 working days. According to the new ratio [between the constant and variable parts after productivity doubled], capital invests $^3/_4$ of itself in constant capital in order to invest $^1/_4$ in the wages fund.

With a total capital of 20, $^3/_4$, i.e. 15, are thus used for constant capital, and $^1/_4$ for labour (i.e. 5)=$^1/_2$ working day.

With a total capital of 4×20, therefore, 4×15=60 constant and 4×5 wages=$^4/_2$ working days=2 working days.

If, therefore, the productivity of labour doubles, so that a capital of 60 thaler raw cotton and instrument requires only 20 thaler labour (2 working days) for its valorisation, when previously this [a valorisation process on this scale] required [a total capital of] 100 thaler, the total capital would have to grow from 100 to 160, or the capital of 80, on which we now base our calculation, would have to double, if the whole of the labour put out of work is to be kept in employment. But the doubling of productive power creates a new capital of only 20 thaler=$^1/_2$ the previously employed labour time; and this is only sufficient to utilise $^1/_2$ working day more. The capital, which before the doubling of productivity was 100 and employed 4 working days (under the assumption that $^2/_5$=40 wages fund), now, when the wages fund has fallen to $^1/_5$ of 100, to 20=2 working days (but to $^1/_4$ of 80, the capital newly entering into the valorisation process), would have to rise to 160, by 60%, to be able to utilise the previous 4 working days. It can only employ $^1/_2$ new working day with the 20 thaler withdrawn from the wages fund because of the increase in productivity, if the whole of the former capital is to continue to be invested. Previously, it utilised, with a sum of 100, $^{16}/_4$ (4) working days; now it could employ only $^{10}/_4$ days.

Consequently, if productivity doubles, capital does not have to double to set in motion the same necessary labour (4 working days), hence it does not have to grow to 200, but only to twice the whole minus the part withdrawn from the wages fund. (100−20=80)×2=160. (In contrast, the first capital which, before the increase in productivity, out of a sum of 100 expended 60 on constant capital, and 40 for wages (4 working days), needed to grow from 100 to only 150 to utilise 2 extra working days; i.e. $^3/_5$ constant capital (30) and $^2/_5$ wages fund (20). Assuming that in both cases the [total] working day increased by 2 days, the second capital would amount to 160 at the end of the process [IV-11], whereas the first to only 150.)

Of the part of capital withdrawn from the wages fund as a result of the growth in productivity, a part must again be converted into raw material and instrument, and another part exchanged for living labour. This can only happen in the proportions between the different components as posited by the new productivity. It can no longer happen in the old proportions, for the ratio of the wages fund to the fund for constant capital has fallen. If a capital of 100 invested $^2/_5$ in the wages fund (40), and as a result of the doubling of productivity only $^1/_5$ (20), then $^1/_5$ of the capital (20 thaler) has been released. The employed part, 80 thaler, now invests only $^1/_4$ in the wages fund. Thus of the [released] 20 thaler only 5 thaler ($^1/_2$ working day) is used for wages. The whole capital of 100 therefore now utilises $2^1/_2$ working days; or it would have to grow to 160 to utilise 4 again.

If the original capital had been 1,000 and had been divided up in the same way: $^3/_5$ constant capital and $^2/_5$ wages fund, we would have 600+400 (let 400 be equal to 40 working days; 1 working day=10 thaler). Doubling of the productivity of labour, i.e. only 20 working days (=200 thaler [wages]) required for the same product, and the capital needed to begin production anew would =800; namely 600+200; 200 thaler would have been released. This is invested in the same proportions as formerly, $^3/_4$ in constant capital=150 and $^1/_4$ wages fund=50. Hence, if the whole of the 1,000 thaler is invested, 750 would be constant capital+250 wages fund=1,000 thaler. But 250 wages fund would=25 working days (i.e. the new fund can utilise labour time only in the new proportions, i.e. $^1/_4$ [of the advanced capital]; to utilise all of the previous labour time, it would have to *quadruple*).

The released capital of 200 employed a wages fund of 50=5 working days ($^1/_4$ of the released labour time). (The part of the wages fund detached from capital, when itself invested as capital, is now only $^1/_4$ wages fund, which is exactly the same proportion as that between the part of the new capital which is wages fund and the total sum of the capital.) To utilise 20 working days (4×5 working days), therefore, this fund would have to grow from 50 to 4×50=200, hence the released part would have to increase from 200 to 600, i.e. grow three-fold; so that the total new capital would have to be 800. Hence the total capital 1,600. If so, 1,200 would be the constant part and 400 wages fund.

If, then, the capital of 1,000 originally contained a wages fund of 400 (40 working days), and, as a result of a doubling of productivity, required a wages fund of only 200 in order to purchase the *necessary labour,* i.e. only $^1/_2$ of the previous labour, the capital would have to grow by 600 to employ all the previous labour (and gain the same surplus time). It would have to be able to employ double the wages fund, namely 2×200=400; but since the ratio of the wages fund to the total capital is now 1:4, this would require a total capital of 4×400=1,600.

//The total capital which would be necessary to utilise the previous labour time therefore=the *previous wages fund×the denominator* of the fraction expressing the ratio of the wages fund to the new total capital. If the doubling of productivity has reduced this to $^1/_4$, then multiplied by 4; if reduced to $^1/_3$, then multiplied by 3. If productivity doubles, the necessary labour and thus the wages fund is reduced to $^1/_2$ its former value; but this amounts to $^1/_4$ of the new total capital of 800 or $^1/_5$ of the former total capital of 1,000. *Or the new total capital* [required to employ the previous labour time]= *2×the previous capital minus the released part of the wages fund*; $(1,000-200)\times2=(800)\times2=1,600$.

The new total capital expresses exactly the total sum of constant and variable capital necessary to employ half the former labour time ($^1/_3$, $^1/_4$, etc., $^1/_x$, depending on whether productivity has increased by 3×, 4×, x×). 2× therefore is the capital needed to utilise the whole of the previous labour time (or 3×, 4×, x×, etc., depending on the proportion in which productivity has grown). The original ratio between the [constant and variable] components of capital must always be given here (*technologically*); for on that depend e.g. the fractions in which the multiplication of productivity is expressed as the division of the *necessary labour.*//

Or, which is the same thing, [IV-12] it=2× *the new capital* which replaces the old capital in the production process as a result of the new productivity (*800×2*) (therefore, if productivity had quadrupled, increased five-fold, etc.=4×, 5× *the new* capital, etc. If productivity has doubled, *necessary labour* is reduced by $^1/_2$, and so is the wages fund. If necessary labour, therefore, amounted to 400 as in the above case of the former capital 1,000, i.e. $^2/_5$ of the total capital, it now amounts to $^1/_5$ or 200. This proportion, by which it is reduced, is the released part of the wages fund=$^1/_5$ of the previous capital=200. $^1/_5$ of the previous capital=$^1/_4$ of the new. The new capital is=to the old capital $+^3/_5$ of it. These trivia in more detail later, etc.).

Given the same initial ratios between the components of capital and the same increase in productivity, the particular magnitude of the capital does not in the least affect the general propositions. Quite another question is whether, when capital *grows,* the ratios actually remain the same (but this really belongs in the section on accumulation). But, given this, we see how the increase in productivity changes the ratios between the components of capital. For a capital of 1,000, as for one of 100, a doubling of productivity has the same effect, if in both cases [e.g.] $^3/_5$ of the capital was originally invested in constant capital and $^2/_5$ in the wages fund. (The term *wages fund* [*Arbeitsfonds*] is used here merely for the sake of convenience; we have not yet analysed this *specific characteristic* of capital. So far 2 parts: the one exchanged for commodities (material and instrument), the other for labour capacity.)

(The *new capital,* i.e. that part of the old capital which performs its *function*, is=to the old capital minus the released part of the wages fund; but this released part is=to the fraction expressing necessary labour (or, which is the same, the wages fund) divided by the multiplier of productivity. Hence if the old capital was 1,000, the fraction expressing necessary labour or the wages fund=$^2/_5$; and if productivity doubles, the new capital performing the same function as the old,=800: namely $^2/_5$ of the previous capital=400; this divided by 2, the multiplier of productivity, =$^2/_{10}$=$^1/_5$=200. Therefore the new capital=800 and the released part of the wages fund=200.)

We have seen that, given these conditions, a capital of 100 thaler must grow to 160, and one of 1,000 to 1,600, to maintain the same labour time (of 4 or 40 working days), etc. Both must grow by 60%, i.e. by $^3/_5$ of themselves (of the old capital), to be able to re-employ the released $^1/_5$ (in the first case 20 thaler, in the second 200)—to reinvest the released wages fund as such.

// *N.B.* We saw earlier how the same percentage yield on total capital can express very different proportions in which capital creates its surplus value, i.e. in which it posits surplus labour, relative or absolute.[a] If the ratio of the unchanging value part of capital and the variable part (exchanged for labour) were such that the latter=$^1/_2$ of the total capital (therefore capital of 100=50 (constant)+50 (variable)), the part exchanged for labour would have to increase by only 50% in order to yield 25% on the capital, i.e. 50+50 (+25)=125; whereas in the above example it was 75+25 (+25)=125; therefore the part exchanged for living labour increased by 100% to yield 25% on the capital. Here we see how, if the proportions [between the components of capital] remain the same, the percentage yield on the total capital also remains the same, however large or small it may be, i.e. if the proportion of the wages fund to total capital remains the same, hence $^1/_4$ as above. Thus: 100 yields 125, 80 yields 100, 1,000 yields 1,250, 800 yields 1,000, 1,600 yields 2,000, etc., always=25%. If capitals with different ratios between their component parts, and therefore with different levels of productivity, [nevertheless] yield the same percentages on the total capital, then the real surplus value must be very different in the different branches of industry.[b]

---

a See this volume, pp. 296-311.— *Ed.*
b The following table occurs on the next, 13th page in Notebook IV, but belongs here contextually.— *Ed.*

[Total capital]	Constant capital		Variable capital	[Surplus value]		[Value of product]	[Rate of profit]
100	60	+	40	(Original proportion)			
100	75	+	25	(+25)	=	125	(25%)
160	120	+	40	(+40)	=	200	(25%)

//Thus the example is correct, productivity compared under the same conditions with the same capital *before* the rise in productivity.

Let a capital of 100 invest 50 in constant value, 50 in wages. Let the wages fund increase [in the course of production] by 50%, i.e. by $^1/_2$; then the total product=125. Let the wages fund of 50 thaler utilise 10 working days, paying 5 thaler per day. Since the new value=$^1/_2$ the wages fund, the surplus time must be=to 5 working days, i.e. the worker, who needed to work only 10 days to live for 15, must work 15 for the capitalist in order to live for 15, and his surplus labour of 5 days constitutes the surplus value of capital. Expressed in hours, if the working day=12 hours, the surplus labour=6 hours per day. So in 10 days or 120 hours he works 60 hours too much=5 days.

Now, with the doubling of [IV-13] productivity, the ratio of the components of the 100 thaler would be 75 and 25, i.e. the same capital would only need to employ 5 workers to produce the same value of 125. Thus the 5 working days=10, it doubles itself, i.e. 5 working days are paid for, 10 are produced. The worker would need to work only 5 days to live for 10 (before the increase of productivity he had to work 10 days to live for 15: therefore he could live for only $7^1/_2$ days if he worked for 5); but he must work 10 days for the capitalist in order to live for 10. The capitalist accordingly profits to the extent of 5 days; a day per day; or, expressed by the day, before he had to work for $^1/_2$ day to live for 1 (i.e. 6 hours to live for 12); now he would need to work only $^1/_4$ day to live for 1 day (i.e. 3 hours). Previously, if he worked for a whole day, he could live for 2 days; if he worked 12 hours, he could live for 24 hours; if he worked 6 hours, 12 hours. But now he must work 12 hours to live for 12 hours. He would need to work only $^1/_2$ day to live for 1; but he must work $2 \times ^1/_2 = 1$, to live for 1. At the previous level of productivity, he had to work 10 days to live for 15, or 12 hours to live for 18; or 1 hour to live for $1^1/_2$ hours, or 8 hours to live for 12, i.e. $^2/_3$ of a day to live for $^3/_3$ of a day. But he has to work $^3/_3$ to live for $^3/_3$, i.e. $^1/_3$ too much.

The doubling of productivity raises the proportion of surplus time from $1:1^1/_2$ (i.e. 50%) to 1:2 (i.e. 100%). In comparison with the previous labour time: he had to work 8 hours in order to live for 12, i.e. the necessary time was $^2/_3$ of the whole working day; he now has to work only $^1/_2$ day, i.e. 6 hours to live for 12 hours. As a consequence, capital now employs 5 workers instead of 10. If previously the 10 workers (cost 50) produced 75, now the 5 ([cost] 25) produce 50, i.e. the former only 50% [surplus value], the second 100%. The workers work as before 12 hours, but in the first case capital bought 10 working days, now it buys only 5; because productivity has doubled, the 5 [working days now produce] 5 surplus working days; because in the first case 10 working days only produced 5 surplus working days, whereas now that productivity has doubled, [the ratio of surplus value to variable capital] having risen from 50% to 100%, 5 [working days produce] 5 [surplus working days]. In the first case, 120 hours of work (=10 working days) produce 180 hours [total time in terms of value], in the second 60 [hours of work] produce 60 [surplus hours], i.e. in the first case, the surplus time amounts to $^1/_3$ of the whole day (50% of necessary labour time) (i.e. 4 hours out of 12; necessary time 8); in the second case, the surplus time amounts to $^1/_2$ of the whole day (100% of necessary labour time) (i.e. 6 hours out of 12; necessary time 6). Hence the 10 days in the first case produced 5 days' surplus time (surplus labour), and in the second the 5 produce 5. The relative surplus time has therefore doubled; relative to the previous proportion it has grown by only $^1/_2$ compared to $^1/_3$, i.e. by $^1/_6$, i.e. by $16^4/_6$%.//

Since surplus labour or surplus time is the prerequisite of capital, it consequently rests on the basic presupposition that there exists a surplus over and above the labour time necessary for the maintenance and propagation of the individual, so that e.g. the individual has to work only 6 hours in order to live for a day, or 1 day to live for 2, etc. With the development of the productive forces, necessary labour time diminishes and as a result surplus time increases. Or, to put it another way, one individual can work for two, etc.

("*WEALTH IS DISPOSABLE TIME* AND NOTHING MORE. If the whole labour of a country were merely sufficient TO RAISE THE SUPPORT OF THE WHOLE POPULATION, THERE WOULD BE NO *SURPLUS LABOUR,* and consequently NOTHING THAT CAN BE ALLOWED TO ACCUMULATE AS CAPITAL... A nation is truly rich if *no interest* exists or if the working day is 6 hours rather than twelve... WHATEVER MAY BE *DUE* TO THE CAPITALIST, HE CAN ONLY RECEIVE THE *SURPLUS LABOUR* OF THE LABOURER; FOR THE LABOURER MUST LIVE" (*The Source and Remedy of the National Difficulties* [London, 1821, pp. 6, 4, 6 and 23]) (pp. 27, 28 [121])).

Property. Origin in the productivity of labour. "If one can produce only for one, everyone is a worker; THERE CAN BE NO PROPERTY. WHEN ONE MAN'S LABOUR CAN

MAINTAIN FIVE, THERE WILL BE FOUR IDLE MEN FOR ONE EMPLOYED IN PRODUCTION. PROPERTY GROWS FROM THE IMPROVEMENTS IN THE MODE OF PRODUCTION... THE GROWTH OF PROPERTY, THIS GREATER ABILITY TO MAINTAIN IDLE MEN AND UNPRODUC- TIVE INDUSTRY=CAPITAL... MACHINERY itself CAN SELDOM BE APPLIED WITH SUCCESS TO ABRIDGE THE LABOURS OF AN INDIVIDUAL: *MORE TIME WOULD BE LOST IN ITS CONSTRUC- TION THAN COULD BE SAVED BY ITS APPLICATION. IT IS ONLY REALLY USEFUL WHEN IT ACTS ON GREAT MASSES, WHEN A SINGLE MACHINE CAN ASSIST THE LABOURS OF THOUSANDS.* IT IS ACCORDINGLY IN THE MOST POPULOUS COUNTRIES WHERE THERE ARE MOST IDLE MEN THAT IT IS ALWAYS MOST ABUNDANT. IT IS NOT CALLED INTO ACTION BY A SCARCITY OF MEN, BUT BY THE FACILITY WITH WHICH THEY ARE BROUGHT TOGETHER... Less than one-quarter OF THE ENGLISH POPULATION PROVIDES [IV-14] EVERYTHING THAT IS CONSUMED BY ALL. Under William the Conqueror e.g., the number directly participating in production was much greater in proportion to the IDLE MEN" (Ravenstone, [*Thoughts on the Funding System, and Its Effects,* London, 1824, pp. 11, 13, 45 and 46,] IX, 32).[122]

If it is true that capital produces surplus labour, it is equally true that surplus labour is the prerequisite for the existence of capital. The entire development of wealth rests upon the creation of disposable time. The ratio of the *necessary* labour time to the *superfluous* (such it is initially from the standpoint of necessary labour) changes at the different stages of development of the productive forces. At the more primitive stages of exchange, men exchange nothing but *their superfluous labour time*; it is the measure of their exchange, which is therefore confined also to their superfluous products. In production based on capital, the exis- tence of *necessary* labour time is conditioned by the production of *superfluous* labour time. At the lowest stages of production, firstly, few human needs have as yet been produced, hence there are few to be satisfied. Necessary labour time is therefore restricted, not because labour is productive but because little is necessary. Secondly, there exists at all stages of production a certain common quality [Gemeinsamkeit] of labour, it has a *social* character, etc. Later, social productive power, etc., develops. (Return to this.)

Surplus time exists [firstly] as the excess of the working day over and above that part of it which we call *necessary* labour time. It exists secondly as the multiplication of *simultaneous working days,* i.e. of the *working population.*

(It can also be produced—but this to be mentioned here only allusively, as this point belongs to the chapter on wage labour—by a forcible extension of the working day beyond its natural limits; or by the addition of wives and children to the working population.)

The first ratio of the surplus time to the necessary time in the working day can be and is modified by development of the productive forces, so that necessary labour is restricted to an ever smaller fractional part. The same is then true relative to the population. A working population of, say, 6 million can be considered as one working day of 6×12, i.e. 72 million hours; so that the same laws are applicable here.

It is the law of capital, as we have seen, to produce surplus labour, disposable time. It can do this only by setting in motion *necessary labour*, i.e. by entering into exchange with the worker. It is therefore the tendency of capital to produce as much labour as possible, just as it is its tendency to reduce necessary labour to a minimum. It is therefore as much the tendency of capital to enlarge the working population, as well as constantly to make a part of that population surplus—that is useless, until such time as capital can utilise it. (Hence the correctness of the theory of surplus population and surplus capital.)

It is as much the tendency of capital to render human labour (relatively) superfluous, as to drive it on without limit. Value is only objectified labour, and surplus value (valorisation of capital) is only the excess over and above that part of objectified labour which is necessary for the reproduction of labour capacity. But labour as such is and remains the prerequisite, and surplus labour exists only in relation to necessary labour, therefore only in so far as necessary labour exists. Capital must therefore constantly posit necessary labour in order to posit surplus labour; it must increase it (i.e. the *simultaneous* working days), in order to increase the surplus; but, equally, it must transcend it as necessary labour in order to posit it as surplus labour.

With respect to the single working day, the process is, of course, simple: (1) to lengthen it to its natural limits; (2) to shorten more and more the necessary part of it (i.e. to increase the productive forces without limit). But, the working day regarded spatially—time itself regarded spatially—is the *existence of many working days alongside one another.* The greater the number of working days with which capital can enter into exchange AT ONCE, in which it exchanges *objectified labour for living,* the greater is its valorisation AT ONCE. It can go beyond the *natural* limit imposed by the living working day of the individual, *at a given stage of the development of the productive forces* (and this is not affected by the fact that this stage is CHANGING), only by setting *alongside* the one working day *another* one—by the spatial addition *of more simultaneous working days.*

E.g. I can extend the surplus labour of *A* only to 3 hours; but if I add the working days of *B, C, D,* etc., I have created surplus labour of 12 hours. Instead of a surplus time of 3, I have created one of 12. As a result, capital solicits the increase of population, and the VERY PROCESS by which necessary labour is reduced, makes it possible to set to work new necessary labour (and hence surplus labour). (That is to say, the *production of workers* becomes cheaper, more workers can be produced in the same time, in the same measure as *necessary labour time* becomes less, or the time required for the *production of the living labour capacity* becomes relatively less. These are identical propositions.)

(This still irrespective of the fact that the increase in population increases the productive power of labour, by making possible greater division and greater combination of labour, etc. Increase in population is a *natural power* [IV-15] of labour for which nothing is paid. From the present standpoint, we use the term *natural power* to refer to *social power*. All *natural powers of social labour* are themselves historical products).

On the other hand, it is the tendency of capital—just as previously in the case of the single working day—to reduce to a minimum the many simultaneous necessary working days (which, so far as value alone is concerned, may be considered as *one* working day), i.e. to posit as many of them as possible as *not necessary*. As previously in the case of the single working day, it was the tendency of capital to reduce the hours of necessary labour, so now it tends to reduce the necessary working days in relation to the total of objectified labour time. (If 6 are necessary to produce 12 superfluous working hours, then capital works towards the reduction of these 6 to 4. Or the 6 working days can be considered as a single working day of 72 hours; if capital succeeds in reducing necessary labour time by 24 hours, 2 days of necessary labour are eliminated, i.e. 2 workers.)

On the other hand, the newly created surplus capital can be valorised as such only by being exchanged for living labour. Hence the tendency of capital just as much to increase the *working population* as constantly to diminish the *necessary* part of it (constantly to reallocate a part of it as a reserve). And the increase in population is itself the chief means for the reduction of the necessary part.

Au fond this is only the application of the ratio [between necessary and surplus labour] *to the single working day.* Here we thus already have all the contradictions which have been expressed as such, although not understood, in modern population theory. Capital, in positing surplus labour, equally and simultaneously posits and does not posit necessary labour; it exists only in so far as necessary labour both exists and does not exist.

*//*It does not belong here yet, but can already be mentioned here, that the creation of surplus labour on the one side corresponds to a creation of minus-labour, relative IDLENESS (or at best *non-productive* labour) on the other. This goes without saying, to start with, as regards capital itself; but it applies equally to the classes with which it shares, i.e. to the PAUPERS living on the surplus product, FLUNKEYS, JENKINSES, etc., in short the whole TRAIN of RETAINERS; the part of the *serving* class which does not live on capital but on revenue.

Essential distinction between this *serving* class and the *working* class. In relation to the whole of society, the production of *disposable time* [can] also [be considered] as the creation of time for the production of science, art, etc. It is by no means the course of social development that an individual, having satisfied his needs, goes on to produce his surplus, but that an individual or class of individuals are compelled to work more than is necessary for the satisfaction of their own needs; and because *surplus labour* is thus posited on the one side, non-labour and surplus wealth are posited on the other.

In reality, the development of wealth exists only in these contradictions; in potentiality, it is this very development of wealth which makes it possible to transcend these contradictions. Or, because an individual can satisfy *his own* needs only by simultaneously satisfying the needs of, and producing a surplus over and above that for, *another* individual. Under slavery, this merely brutal, only under the conditions of wage labour does it lead to *industry, industrial* labour.

Hence Malthus was quite consistent when, along with surplus labour and surplus capital, he demands SURPLUS IDLERS, CONSUMING WITHOUT PRODUCING, postulating the necessity of waste, luxury, extravagant spending, etc.[a]*//*

If the ratio of the necessary working days to the total of the objectified working days=9:12 (i.e. surplus labour=$1/4$), capital strives to reduce it to 6:9 (i.e. $2/3$, hence surplus labour=$1/3$). (This to be developed in more detail later; but the basic outlines here, where we are dealing with the general concept of capital.)

---

[a] Th. R. Malthus, *Principles of Political Economy*, 2nd ed., London, 1836, pp. 314-30.— *Ed.*

329

[Section Two]

[CIRCULATION PROCESS OF CAPITAL]

[REPRODUCTION AND ACCUMULATION OF CAPITAL]

We have now seen how, by means of the *valorisation process,* capital has (1) maintained its value by means of exchange (i.e. exchange with living labour); (2) increased, produced surplus value. There now appears, as the result of this unity of the production and valorisation process, the product of the process, i.e. capital itself, as it emerges as the product of the process whose precondition it was—as a product which is value. Or *value* itself appears as the product of this process, but a *higher value,* because more objectified labour is contained in it than in that from which the process originally set out. This value as such is *money.* However, this is the case only *in itself*; it is not posited as such. What is initially *posited,* what is actually there, is a commodity of a certain (ideal) price, i.e. a commodity which exists only in idea in the form of a certain sum of money, and which can be *realised* as such only in exchange, i.e. it must first re-enter the process of simple circulation in order to be posited as *money.* Hence we arrive at *the third side of the process* in which capital is posited as such.

(3) Strictly considered, the valorisation *process* of capital—and it is only by means of the valorisation process that money becomes capital—appears at the same time as its *devaluation process,* ITS DEMONETISATION. And this in two respects. Firstly, in so far as capital does not increase absolute labour time, but reduces relative necessary labour time by increasing productive power, it reduces its own cost of production, i.e. in so far as it was presupposed as a definite sum of commodities, it reduces its exchange value. A part of the existing capital is continually devalued by the reduction of the costs of production at which it can be *reproduced*; by the

reduction not of the labour objectified in it, but of the living labour which it is now necessary to objectify in this specific product.

This constant [IV-16] devaluation of *existing* capital does not belong here, because it presupposes capital as completed. It is to be noted here only in order to indicate how later developments are already contained in the general concept of capital. Belongs to the doctrine of concentration and competition of capitals.

The *devaluation* being dealt with here, is that capital has made the transition from the form of money to that of a *commodity,* of a product which has a certain price, which is to be *realised.* As money, it existed as *value.* Now it *exists* as product and only in idea as price; but not as *value as such.* In order to *valorise* itself, i.e. to preserve and to multiply itself as value, it would first have to make the transition from the form of money into that of use values (raw material—instrument—wages). But in doing so it would lose its *form* as value. It now has to re-enter circulation in order to posit this form of general wealth anew. No longer does the capitalist enter into the circulation process merely as an exchanger; he does so now as a *producer* confronting the other exchangers as *consumers.* They are to exchange money to obtain his commodity for their consumption, while he exchanges his product in order to obtain their money. If this process miscarries—and the very separation [of producers and consumers] entails the possibility of miscarriage in the individual case—the money of the capitalist has been transformed into a worthless product; not only has it not gained any new value, it has lost its original value.

But whether this is so or not, the devaluation of capital constitutes a moment of its valorisation process. This is already inherent in the simple fact that the product of the process in its immediate form is not *value,* but must first re-enter circulation to be realised as such. Hence, if capital is reproduced as value and new value by means of the production process, it is simultaneously posited as *non-value,* something still to be *valorised by means of exchange.*

The three processes [maintenance of the value of the capital employed, valorisation, realisation of the value of the product] whose unity is formed by capital are external to one another, separate in time and space. As such, the transition from one to the other, i.e. their unity in relation to the individual capitalists, is fortuitous. They exist *independently* alongside one another, despite their *inner unity,* and each exists as the precondition of the other. Over the whole range of production it must assert itself, in so far as the whole of production is based on capital, and capital must therefore realise all the necessary moments of its self-formation and contain the conditions for the realisation of these moments. At the point which we have reached so far, capital does not yet appear as determining circulation (exchange) itself, but merely as a moment of circulation and ceasing to be capital precisely at the point where it enters into circulation. As *commodity* in general, capital now shares the fate of commodities in general; it becomes a matter of chance, whether or not it is exchanged for money, whether or not its *price* is realised.

In the production process itself—where capital always remained presupposed as value—its *valorisation* appeared to be entirely dependent upon its relationship as objectified labour to living labour, i.e. upon the relationship of capital to wage labour. But now as product, as commodity, it appears dependent on circulation, which lies outside the production process. (In fact, as we have seen,[a] it returns into that process as its ground, but just as much re-emerges from it.) As a commodity, it must be (1) use value, and as such object of need, object of consumption; (2) exchanged for its equivalent—in money. Only through a sale can the new value be realised.

If the capital previously contained objectified labour at a price of 100 thaler, and now does so at a price of 110 (the price merely expressing in money the volume of objectified labour), this has to come out in the fact that the objectified labour now contained in the produced commodity exchanges for 110 thaler. To start with, the product is devalued in so far as it must be exchanged for money at all in order to regain its form as value.

Within the production process the valorisation appeared to be completely identical with the production of surplus labour (the objectification of surplus time), and thus without any *limits* other than those which are partly presupposed and partly posited within this process itself, but always posited within it as *barriers* to be overcome.

But now barriers appear which lie *outside* the process. To start with, considered quite superficially, the commodity is exchange value only in so far as it is simultaneously *use value,* i.e. object of consumption (what kind of consumption, still quite irrelevant here). It ceases to be exchange value if it ceases to be use value (since it does not as yet exist again as money but in a specific mode of being coinciding with its natural quality).

---

[a] See this volume, pp. 150-52, 167-68 and 186-87.— *Ed.*

The first barrier [it runs up against] is therefore *consumption* itself—the *demand for it.* (Within the assumptions so far made, there can be no question of an *ineffective* demand, i.e. a demand not backed up by a commodity or money to be given in exchange [IV-17] for the commodity demanded.) Secondly, however, an equivalent for the commodity must be available, and since circulation was originally presupposed as a fixed magnitude, as having a given volume, while capital has produced a new value in the production process, it appears that there can in fact be no equivalent available for it.

Hence, when capital emerges from the production process and returns into circulation, it appears

(a) that as *production* it has come up against the barrier of the given volume of *consumption,* or of the *consumption capacity.* As a specific use value, its quantity is to some extent irrelevant. But at a certain level it ceases to be required for consumption—since it satisfies only a specific need. As a *particular, one-sided, qualitative* use value, e.g. as grain, its quantity itself is irrelevant only to a certain degree; it is required only in a specific quantity, i.e. in a certain measure. But this measure is given partly by the quality of the commodity as use value—its *specific* utility, usability—and partly by the number of exchangers who have a need for this particular object of consumption. The number of consumers multiplied by the size of their demand for this *specific* product. Use value in itself does not possess the boundlessness of value as such. Certain objects can be consumed and are the objects of demand only to a certain degree. E.g. only a definite quantity of grain, etc., is consumed. As *use value,* the product accordingly has a barrier within itself—precisely that of the demand for it—but this barrier is now measured not by the need of the producer but by the aggregate demand of the exchangers. At the point where the demand for a certain use value ceases, it ceases to be use value. As use value it is measured by the demand for it. As soon as it ceases to be use value, it ceases to be an object of circulation (in so far as it is not money).

(b) As *new value* and *value* as such, capital appears to come up against the barrier of the volume of *available equivalents,* in the first place of money—money not as means of circulation but as money. Surplus value (the surplus over and above the original value) requires a surplus equivalent. This now appears as the second barrier.

(c) Originally, money—i.e. wealth as such, wealth existing in and through exchange for *alien objectified labour*—appeared to collapse into itself, in so far as it did not proceed to the exchange for *alien living labour,* i.e. to the production process. Circulation was incapable of renewing itself from within itself. On the other hand, the production process now appears to be IN A FIX, if it cannot make the transition into the process of circulation. Capital as production based on wage labour presupposes circulation as a necessary condition and moment of the entire movement. This specific form of production presupposes the specific form of exchange which finds its expression in money circulation. If the process is to be renewed, the whole product must be converted into money; not as in earlier stages of production, where exchange embraces only superfluous production and superfluous products, but not production in its totality.

These are the contradictions which cannot escape a simple, objective, impartial examination. How they are constantly transcended in production based on capital, yet constantly reproduced, and only forcibly transcended (although up to a certain point this transcendence appears merely as a smooth adjustment), is another question. For the moment, the important thing is to take note of the existence of these contradictions. All the contradictions of [simple commodity] circulation come to life again in a new form. The product as use value is in contradiction to itself as value; i.e. in so far as it exists in a specific quality, as a specific thing, as a product possessing specific natural properties, as a substance of need in contradiction with the substance which as value it possesses exclusively in the *labour objectified in it.* But this time the contradiction is no longer posited as *a purely formal difference,* as in [simple] circulation. Being measured by use value is here tantamount to being measured by the aggregate demand of the exchangers for this product, i.e. by the amount of total consumption.

This appears here as the *measure* for the product as use value and therefore also as *exchange value.* In simple circulation the product simply had to be transposed from the form of the particular use value to that of exchange value. Its barrier was merely that, as use value, it existed in a particular form because of its *natural properties,* rather than in the value form in which it was directly exchangeable for all other commodities. But now it is posited that the *measure* of its availability is actually given in its *natural properties.* If it is to be transposed into the general form, the use value must be present only in a specific quantity; a *quantity* the measure of which does not lie in *the labour objectified in it,* but arises from *its nature as use value,* that is to say *as use value for others.*

At the same time, the previous contradiction that the money
existing for itself [IV-18] had to proceed to its exchange for living
labour, appears even greater now, because the surplus money, in
order to exist as such, or the surplus value, has to be exchanged
for surplus value. Hence, as value, it comes up against a barrier in
the production of others, just as, as use value, it comes up against
a barrier in the consumption of others. As use value, its measure is
the size of the demand for the specific product; as value, its
measure is the *amount of objectified labour* existing in circulation.
The indifference of value as such towards use value is thereby
brought into just as false a position as are, on the other side, the
substance and measure of value as objectified labour in general.

// As yet we cannot go on to the relationship of demand, supply,
prices, for they presuppose capital in their characteristic development. In so far as demand and supply are abstract categories, not
as yet expressing any particular economic relationships, they
should perhaps be considered along with simple circulation or
production? //

The main point here, where we are concerned with the general
concept of capital, is that capital is *this unity of production and
valorisation* not *immediately* but only as a *process* tied to certain
conditions, and, as it appeared, *external* conditions.

// We have already seen how the valorisation process of capital
presupposes the prior development of the *simple production process.*[a]
This will be the case with *demand and supply* in so far as in simple
exchange a need for the product is presupposed. The (immediate)
producer's *own* need as a need for the demand of others. In the
course of this development it will appear of itself what has to be
presupposed to this demand, and all this is then to be thrown into
the first chapters. //

Capital's creation of *absolute surplus value*—more objectified
labour—is conditional upon the expansion, indeed the constant
expansion, of the periphery of circulation. The *surplus value*
produced at one point requires the production of surplus value at
another point, for which it may be exchanged. Initially the
production of more gold and silver, more money, will suffice so
that, if the surplus value cannot directly become capital again, it
can exist in the form of money as the possibility of new capital. A
condition of production based on capital is therefore *the production
of a constantly expanding periphery of circulation,* whether the sphere

---

[a] See this volume, pp. 230-66.— *Ed.*

is directly expanded, *or whether* more points within it *become points of production.*

If circulation initially appeared as a given magnitude, it appears here as a moving one, expanding through production itself. In the light of this, it already appears itself as a moment of production. Hence, just as capital has the tendency to produce ever more surplus labour, it has the complementary tendency to produce more points of exchange. With respect to *absolute* surplus value or surplus labour, this means that capital tends to generate more surplus labour as complement to itself; *au fond,* that it tends to propagate production based on capital or the mode of production corresponding to it. The tendency to create the *world market* is inherent directly in the concept of capital itself. Every limit appears as a barrier to be overcome. At first [capital strives] to subject each moment of production itself to exchange, and to transcend the production of immediate use values which do not enter into exchange, i.e. to replace the earlier and from its standpoint naturally evolved modes of production by production based on capital. *Trade* appears no longer as an activity carried on between independent productions for the exchange of their surplus product, but as the essential, all-embracing prerequisite for and moment of production itself.

OF COURSE, all production directed towards the creation of immediate use values reduces the number of exchangers just as much as it does the sum of exchange values thrown into circulation, and above all the production of surplus values. HENCE THE TENDENCY OF CAPITAL (1) TO CONTINUALLY ENLARGE THE PERIPHERY OF CIRCULATION; (2) TO TRANSFORM IT AT ALL POINTS INTO PRODUCTION CARRIED ON BY CAPITAL.

On the other side, the production of *relative surplus value,* i.e. the production of surplus value based upon the increase and development of the productive forces, requires production of new consumption, so that the sphere of consumption within circulation is enlarged, as that of production [of absolute surplus value] was enlarged before. Firstly, quantitative increase in existing consumption; secondly, the creation of new needs by the propagation of existing ones over a wider area; *thirdly,* production of *new* needs and discovery and creation of new use values. In other words, it requires that the surplus labour obtained does not remain a merely quantitative surplus, but that at the same time the range of qualitatively distinct types of labour (including surplus labour) must be constantly extended, rendered more diverse, and internally differentiated.

E.g. if because of a doubling of productivity, a capital of only 50

needs to be invested where 100 was needed before, and a capital
of 50 and the necessary labour corresponding to it are released,
[IV-19] a new, qualitatively different branch of production
satisfying and generating a new need, must be created for the
released capital and labour. The value of the old industry is
preserved [by] the creation of a FUND for a new industry, in which
the relation of capital and LABOUR establishes itself in a *new* form.

Hence the exploration of the whole of nature in order to
discover new useful properties of things; the universal exchange
of the products coming from the most diverse climates and lands;
new (artificial) modes of processing natural objects to give them
new use values. //The role played by *luxury* in antiquity in
contrast to its role in modern times, TO BE ALLUDED TO later.// The
all-round exploration of the earth to discover both new useful
objects and new uses for old objects, such as their use as raw
materials, etc.; hence the development of the natural sciences to
their highest point; the discovery, creation and satisfaction of new
needs arising from society itself; cultivating all the qualities of
social man and producing him in a form as rich as possible in
needs because rich in qualities and relations—producing man as
the most total and universal social product possible (for in order to
enjoy many different kinds of things he must be capable of
enjoyment, that is he must be cultivated to a high degree)—all
these are also conditions of production based on capital. This
creation of new branches of production, i.e. qualitatively new
surplus time, is not only the division of labour, but also the
separation of a definite kind of production from itself as labour of
a new use value; the development of a constantly expanding
comprehensive system of different kinds of labour, different kinds
of production, with a corresponding system of ever more
extended and ever more varied needs.

Thus, just as production based on capital produces universal
industry, i.e. surplus labour, value-creating labour, on the one
hand, so does it on the other produce a system of universal
exploitation of natural and human qualities, a system of universal
utility, whose bearer is science itself as much as all the physical and
spiritual qualities, and under these conditions nothing appears as
something *higher-in-itself,* as an end in itself, outside this circle of
social production and exchange. Thus it is only capital which
creates bourgeois society and the universal appropriation of nature
and of the social nexus itself by the members of society. HENCE THE
GREAT CIVILISING INFLUENCE OF CAPITAL; hence its production of a stage of
society compared to which all previous stages seem merely *local*

developments of humanity and *idolatry of nature.* For the first time, nature becomes purely an object for men, nothing more than a matter of utility. It ceases to be acknowledged as a power for itself, and even the theoretical cognition of its autonomous laws appears merely as a stratagem for its subjection to human needs, whether as object of consumption or as means of production. It is this same tendency which makes capital drive beyond national boundaries and prejudices and, equally, beyond nature worship, as well as beyond the traditional satisfaction of existing needs and the reproduction of old ways of life confined within long-established and complacently accepted limits. Capital is destructive towards, and constantly revolutionises, all this, tearing down all barriers which impede the development of the productive forces, the extension of the range of needs, the differentiation of production, and the exploitation and exchange of all natural and spiritual powers.

But from the fact that capital posits every such limit as a barrier which it has *ideally* already overcome, it does not at all follow that capital has *really* overcome it; and since every such limit contradicts the determination of capital, its production is subject to contradictions which are constantly overcome but just as constantly posited. Moreover, the universality for which capital ceaselessly strives, comes up against barriers in capital's own nature, barriers which at a certain stage of its development will allow it to be recognised as being itself the greatest barrier in the way of this tendency, and will therefore drive towards its transcendence through itself.

The economists who, like Ricardo, conceive production as directly identical with the self-valorisation of capital, who therefore ignore the barriers of consumption or the existing barriers of circulation itself, so far as circulation must represent counter-values at all points, and who are only concerned with the development of the productive forces and the growth of the industrial population—i.e. with supply, regardless of demand— have therefore grasped the positive essence of capital more correctly and profoundly than those who, like Sismondi, emphasise the barriers of consumption and of the existing circle of counter-values, although the latter has better grasped the limitations of production based on capital, its negative one-sidedness. Ricardo has better grasped its universal tendency, Sismondi its particular restrictedness.

The whole controversy as to whether *overproduction* is possible and necessary in production based on capital, is about whether the valorisation of capital in production directly posits its valorisation in circulation; whether its [IV-20] valorisation posited in the *production process* is its *real* valorisation. Ricardo of course also has A SUSPICION that *exchange value* is not value outside exchange, and that it proves itself as value only through exchange. But he considers the barriers which production encounters in this direction as accidental, as barriers which are simply overcome. He therefore conceives the overcoming of such barriers as implied in the very essence of capital, although his exposition of this is often absurd. *Sismondi,* by contrast, emphasises not only the encountering of the barrier but its creation by capital itself, which thus gets itself into contradictions, contradictions in which he glimpses the impending BREAKDOWN of capital. He therefore wants to impose barriers on production from outside, by means of custom, laws, etc., which, as merely external and artificial constraints, would necessarily be demolished by capital. On the other hand, Ricardo and his entire school have never comprehended the real *modern crises* in which this contradiction of capital discharges itself in violent thunderstorms, which more and more threaten capital itself as the basis of society and production.

The attempts made from the orthodox economic standpoint to deny the fact of *general overproduction* at a given moment are indeed childish. To rescue production *based on capital,* the orthodox economists (see e.g. MacCulloch[a]) either ignore all its specific characteristics, all its conceptual definitions, and rather conceive of it as simple production for *immediate use value.* [They] entirely abstract from its essential relations. IN FACT, to purify it of contradictions, they simply drop it and negate it. Or, like e.g. *Mill,*[b] they adopt a more perceptive procedure (insipidly imitated by Say): *supply* and *demand* are identical, hence they must correspond to each other. For supply is really a demand, measured by its [supply's] own amount.[123]

Here a great confusion: (1) the identity of supply, i.e. being a demand which is measured by its [supply's] own amount, is true only to the extent that it is *exchange value*=a certain amount of objectified labour. To that extent, supply is the measure of its own demand as far as *value* is concerned. But as such a value, it is realised only through exchange for *money*; and as an object of exchange for money it depends upon (2) its *use value*; and as use

---

[a] J. R. MacCulloch, *The Principles of Political Economy,* Edinburgh, 1825, p. 190.— *Ed.*

[b] J. Mill, *Éléments d'économie politique*, Paris, 1823, pp. 250-60.— *Ed.*

value, in turn, it depends upon the mass of existing needs for it, the demand for it. However, as use value it is absolutely not measured by the labour time objectified in it, but by a standard quite unconnected with its nature as exchange value.

Or else it is asserted that *supply itself is a demand for a certain product* of *a certain value* (which is expressed in terms of the required amount of the product). If, therefore, the product supplied cannot be sold, this proves only that too much of the commodity supplied and too little of some other commodity, demanded by the supplier, has been produced. Thus, allegedly, there is no general overproduction, only overproduction of one or some articles, but underproduction of others. What is forgotten here is the fact that producing capital demands not a particular use value but *value* for itself, i.e. money—money not in its role as means of circulation but as the general form of wealth, or as the form of the realisation of capital in one respect, and return to its original dormant state in the other.

The assertion that too *little money* is being produced is tantamount to the assertion that production does not coincide with valorisation, hence is *overproduction*; or, which is the same thing, that it is production which cannot be converted into money, hence into *value,* production which does not pass the test of circulation. HENCE THE ILLUSION of the money-conjurers (also Proudhon, etc.) that there is a shortage of *means of circulation* because of the dearness of money, and that more money has to be created artificially. (See also the Birmingham School, e.g. the *Gemini.*[124])

Or it is said that, *considered from the social standpoint, production and consumption* are identical; therefore an excess of one in relation to the other or a disproportion between them can never occur. The "social standpoint" here referred to is precisely the abstraction which *ignores* the specific social structure and relations and hence also the contradictions arising from them. Already *Storch,* for example, argued very correctly against Say[a] that a large part of consumption is not consumption for immediate use but consumption within the production process, e.g. consumption of machines, coal, oil, necessary buildings, etc.[14] This type of consumption [IV-21] is not at all identical with the consumption which is being discussed here. Similarly, *Malthus* and *Sismondi* have correctly observed that e.g. the consumption of the workers

---

[a] H. Storch, *Considérations sur la nature du revenu national,* pp. 126-59.— *Ed.*

is by no means in itself a *sufficient* consumption for the capitalist.[a] The moment of valorisation is here completely excluded, and production and consumption simply counterposed to each other, i.e. a production based directly on *use value,* and hence not on capital, is presupposed.

Or in *socialist* jargon: let labour and the exchange of labour, i.e. production and exchange of the product (circulation), be the whole process. How could a disproportion then arise, except by an oversight or a miscalculation? Labour is not conceived here as wage labour, nor capital as capital. On the one hand, the consequences of production based on capital are taken for granted; on the other hand, the requisite and condition of these consequences is denied—necessary labour as labour posited by and for surplus labour.

Or—e.g. *Ricardo*[b]—since production is itself regulated by the costs of production, it regulates itself. And if a particular branch of production does not valorise itself, capital withdraws from it to a certain degree and moves into other branches in which it is necessary. But, quite apart from the fact that the very necessity of evening-up *presupposes* the imbalance, the disharmony and hence the contradiction, in a general crisis of overproduction the contradiction is not between different types of productive capital, but between industrial and loan capital, between capital as it is directly involved in the production process and capital as it appears as money independently *(relativement)* outside that process.

Finally, PROPORTIONATE PRODUCTION[c] (this also already in Ricardo, etc.). But if it is the tendency of capital to distribute itself in the correct proportions, it is just as much its necessary tendency to drive beyond the correct proportion, because it strives boundlessly for surplus labour, surplus productivity, surplus consumption, etc.

(In *competition,* this immanent tendency of capital appears as a compulsion imposed upon it by *other* capital and driving it beyond the correct proportion with a constant *March, march!* As Mr. *Wakefield* correctly sniffs out in his commentary on Smith,[d] free

    [a] Th. R. Malthus, *Principles of Political Economy*, 2nd ed., London, 1836, p. 405 (publisher's note), and J. Ch. L. Simonde de Sismondi, *Études sur l'économie politique*, Vol. I, p. 61.— *Ed.*

    [b] D. Ricardo, *On the Principles of Political Economy, and Taxation*, pp. 80-85.— *Ed.*

    [c] See J. Gray, *Lectures on the Nature and Use of Money*, pp. 67, 108, 123, 125 and 142-48.— *Ed.*

    [d] A. Smith, *An Inquiry into the Nature and Causes of the Wealth of Nations*. With a Commentary, by the Author of *England and America* [E. G. Wakefield], Vol. I, London, 1835, pp. 244-46.— *Ed.*

competition has *never* been analysed *at all* by political economists, however much they may chatter about it, even though it is the basis of the entire bourgeois production based on capital. It has only been understood negatively, i.e. as the negation of monopolies, corporations, legal regulations, etc., and as the negation of feudal production. But, after all, it must also be something *for itself,* since a mere 0 is an empty negation, an abstraction from a barrier which is immediately resurrected e.g. in the form of monopoly, natural monopolies, etc. Conceptually, *competition* is nothing but the *inner nature of capital,* its essential character, manifested and realised as the reciprocal action of many capitals upon each other; immanent tendency realised as external necessity.) (Capital exists and can only exist as many capitals; hence its own character appears as their reciprocal action on each other.)

Capital is just as much the constant positing of, as it is the constant transcendence of PROPORTIONATE PRODUCTION. The existing proportions must constantly be transcended through the creation of surplus values and the increase of productive forces. But to demand that production should be expanded *instantaneously,* SIMULTANEOUSLY and in *the same proportions,* is to impose external demands on capital, which in no way correspond to anything arising from capital itself. In fact, the departure from the given proportion in one branch of production drives all the other branches out of that proportion, and at unequal rates. So far (for we have not yet reached capital in its character as *capital circulant*; we still have circulation on one side and capital on the other, or production as the premiss of circulation or the ground from which it arises), even from the standpoint of production, circulation has the relation to consumption and production, in other words, surplus labour as counter-value, and differentiation of labour in ever richer variety.

The simple concept of capital must contain *in itself* its civilising tendencies, etc. They must not be presented, as they are up to now in political economy, as merely external consequences. Similarly, the contradictions which are later released, must be demonstrated as already latent within it.

So far, we have in the valorisation process only the indifference of the individual moments to each other, that they determine each other internally and search for each other externally, but that they may or may not find each other, balance each other, correspond to each other. The necessary inner connection of moments belonging together and their mutually indifferent, independent existence are already a foundation [IV-22] of contradictions.

However, we have by no means finished yet. The contradiction between production and valorisation—of which capital, according to its concept, is the unity—has to be grasped more intrinsically than merely as the mutually indifferent and apparently independent appearance of the individual moments of the process or, rather, of the totality of processes.

To get closer to the point: *d'abord* THERE IS A LIMIT, NOT INHERENT TO PRODUCTION GENERALLY, BUT TO PRODUCTION FOUNDED ON CAPITAL. This LIMIT is two-fold, or rather it is the same limit considered from two different aspects. Here it is sufficient to demonstrate that capital contains a *particular* restriction on production—which contradicts its general tendency to drive beyond every barrier to production—to have uncovered the foundation of *overproduction,* the basic contradiction of developed capital; or, to put it more generally, to have uncovered that capital is not, as the economists believe, the *absolute* form for the development of the productive forces—not the absolute form for that, nor the form of wealth which absolutely coincides with the development of the productive forces.

The stages of production which precede capital appear, when looked at from the standpoint of capital, as just so many fetters upon the productive forces. But capital itself, correctly understood, appears as the condition for the development of the productive forces only so long as they require an external spur, a spur which at the same time appears as their bridle. It is a discipline over them, which at a certain level of their development becomes quite as superfluous and burdensome as [previously] the corporations, etc. These inherent limits must coincide with the nature of capital, with the essential character of its very concept. These necessary LIMITS are:

(1) *necessary labour* as the limit on the exchange value of living labour capacity or on the wages of the industrial population;

(2) *surplus value* as the limit on surplus labour time; and, with respect to relative surplus labour time, as the limit on the development of the productive forces;

(3) what is the same, *transformation into money,* exchange value in general as the limit on production; or exchange based on value, or value based on exchange, as the limit on production. It is:

(4) again identical as the *restriction of the production of use values* by exchange value; or that real wealth has to assume a *specific* form distinct from itself, i.e. a form not absolutely identical with itself, if it is to become an object of production at all.

On the other hand, it arises from the *general tendency of capital* (and this is what in simple circulation was manifest in the fact that money as a means of circulation appeared only fleetingly, devoid of independent necessity, and hence not as a limit and barrier) that it forgets and abstracts from:

(1) necessary labour as the limit on the exchange value of living labour capacity; (2) surplus value as the limit on surplus labour and the development of the productive forces; (3) money as the limit on production; (4) the restriction of the production of use values by exchange value.

Hinc overproduction, i.e. a sudden *reminder* of all these necessary moments of production based on capital; hence general devaluation in consequence of forgetting them. This immediately faces capital with the task of trying again from a higher level of development of the productive forces, etc., resulting in an ever greater COLLAPSE *as capital.* Therefore clear that the higher the level to which capital has developed, the more it appears as a barrier to production—hence also to consumption—quite apart from the other contradictions which make it appear as a burdensome barrier on production and commerce.

//The whole *credit system,* and the OVER-TRADING, OVER-SPECULATION, etc., connected with it, rest upon the necessity to extend the range of, and to overcome the barrier to, circulation and exchange. This appears more colossal, more classical, in the relationship between peoples than in the relationship between individuals. Thus e.g. Englishmen compelled to *lend* to foreign nations to have them as their CUSTOMERS. *Au fond,* the English capitalist carries on a two-fold exchange with *productive* English capital: (1) as himself, (2) as Yankee, etc., or in whatever other form he has placed his money.//

//Capital as a *barrier to production* is hinted at in e.g. *Hodgskin*:

"IN THE PRESENT STATE, EVERY ACCUMULATION OF CAPITAL ADDS TO THE AMOUNT OF PROFIT DEMANDED FROM THE LABOURER, AND EXTINGUISHES ALL THAT LABOUR WHICH WOULD ONLY PROCURE THE LABOURER HIS COMFORTABLE EXISTENCE... *PROFIT* THE LIMITATION OF PRODUCTION" [Th. Hodgskin, *Popular Political Economy*, London, 1827, pp. 245, 246] (IX, p. 46).[125]

By means of FOREIGN TRADE the limit on the sphere of exchange is extended and capitalists are enabled to consume more surplus labour:

"IN A SERIES OF YEARS THE WORLD CAN TAKE NO MORE FROM US, THAN WE CAN TAKE FROM THE WORLD. EVEN THE PROFITS MADE BY OUR MERCHANTS IN THEIR FOREIGN TRADE ARE PAID BY THE CONSUMER OF THE RETURN GOODS HERE. FOREIGN TRADE MERE BARTER, AND AS SUCH EXCHANGE FOR THE CONVENIENCE AND ENJOYMENT OF THE

CAPITALIST. [IV-23] BUT HE CAN CONSUME COMMODITIES TO A CERTAIN DEGREE ONLY. HE EXCHANGES COTTONS ETC. FOR THE WINES AND SILKS OF FOREIGN COUNTRIES. BUT THESE *REPRESENT ONLY THE SURPLUS LABOUR OF OUR OWN POPULATION* AS MUCH AS THE CLOTHES AND COTTONS, AND IN THIS WAY THE *DESTRUCTIVE POWER OF THE CAPITALIST IS INCREASED BEYOND ALL BOUNDS.* THUS NATURE IS *OUTWITTED*" ([*The*] *Source and Remedy* [*of the National Difficulties*, pp. 17-18,] pp. 27, 28).

To what extent GLUT is connected with the *barrier* of necessary labour:

"THE VERY MEANING OF AN INCREASED DEMAND [for work] BY THE LABOURERS IS A DISPOSITION TO TAKE LESS THEMSELVES, AND LEAVE A LARGER SHARE FOR THEIR EMPLOYERS; AND IF IT BE SAID THAT THIS, BY *DIMINISHING CONSUMPTION, INCREASES GLUT,* I CAN ONLY SAY THAT *GLUT THEN IS SYNONYMOUS WITH HIGH PROFITS*" (*Enquiry,* etc., [*An Inquiry into those Principles, respecting the Nature of Demand and the Necessity of Consumption, lately advocated by Mr. Malthus,*] London, 1821, [p. 59] p. 12 [126]).

Herein the one aspect of the contradiction fully expressed.

"THE PRACTICE OF STOPPING LABOUR AT THAT POINT WHERE IT CAN PRODUCE, IN ADDITION TO THE SUBSISTENCE OF THE LABOURER, A PROFIT FOR THE CAPITALIST, OPPOSED TO THE NATURAL LAW WHICH REGULATES PRODUCTION" (Hodgskin, [op. cit., p. 238,] 41,[127] IX).

"THE MORE THE CAPITAL ACCUMULATES, THE *WHOLE AMOUNT OF PROFIT DEMANDED* DOES SO; SO THERE ARISES AN *ARTIFICIAL CHECK* TO PRODUCTION AND POPULATION" (Hodgskin, [op. cit., p. 246,] 46).

The contradictions between capital as instrument of production in general and instrument of production of VALUE are developed by *Malthus* thus (IX, 40 ff):

"PROFITS ARE INVARIABLY MEASURED BY *VALUE* AND NEVER BY *QUANTITY*... THE WEALTH OF A COUNTRY DEPENDS PARTLY UPON THE *QUANTITY OF PRODUCE* OBTAINED BY ITS LABOUR, AND PARTLY UPON *SUCH AN ADAPTATION OF THIS QUANTITY TO THE WANTS AND POWERS OF THE EXISTING POPULATION* AS IS CALCULATED TO GIVE IT VALUE. NOTHING CAN BE MORE CERTAIN THAN THAT IT IS NOT DETERMINED BY EITHER OF THEM ALONE. BUT WHERE WEALTH AND VALUE ARE PERHAPS THE MOST NEARLY CONNECTED, IS IN *THE NECESSITY OF THE LATTER TO THE PRODUCTION OF THE FORMER.* THE VALUE SET UPON COMMODITIES, THAT IS THE SACRIFICE OF LABOUR WHICH PEOPLE ARE WILLING TO MAKE IN ORDER TO OBTAIN THEM, IN THE ACTUAL STATE OF THINGS MAY BE SAID TO BE *ALMOST THE SOLE CAUSE* OF THE EXISTENCE OF WEALTH... THE CONSUMPTION AND DEMAND OCCASIONED ONLY BY THE WORKMEN EMPLOYED IN PRODUCTIVE LABOUR CAN NEVER *ALONE* FURNISH A MOTIVE TO THE ACCUMULATION AND EMPLOYMENT OF CAPITAL ... THE *POWERS OF PRODUCTION ALONE DO NOT SECURE THE CREATION OF A PROPORTION-ATE DEGREE OF WEALTH,* AS LITTLE AS THE *INCREASE OF POPULATION.* What it requires in addition IS SUCH A *DISTRIBUTION OF PRODUCE,* AND SUCH AN ADAPTATION OF THIS PRODUCE TO THE WANTS OF THOSE WHO ARE TO CONSUME IT, AS CONSTANTLY TO INCREASE THE *EXCHANGEABLE VALUE OF THE WHOLE MASS,* I.E. THE POWERS OF PRODUCTION ARE ONLY CALLED FULLY INTO ACTION BY THE UNCHECKED DEMAND FOR ALL THAT IS PRODUCED..." [*Principles of Political Economy,* 2nd ed., London, 1836, pp. 266, 301, 302, 315, 361, 311 and 361].

True, this is brought about on the one hand by constant establishment of new branches of industry (and *reciprocal* expansion of the old), by means of which the old obtain new MARKETS, etc. Production does indeed create DEMAND in that it employs more labourers in the same branch of business and creates new branches of business, in which new capitalists employ new labourers and at the same time reciprocally become a market for the old; but

"THE DEMAND CREATED BY THE PRODUCTIVE LABOURER HIMSELF CAN NEVER BE AN *ADEQUATE* DEMAND, BECAUSE IT DOES NOT GO TO THE FULL EXTENT OF WHAT HE PRODUCES. IF IT DID, THERE WOULD BE NO PROFIT, CONSEQUENTLY NO MOTIVE TO EMPLOY HIM. THE VERY EXISTENCE OF A PROFIT UPON ANY COMMODITY PRESUPPOSES *A DEMAND EXTERIOR TO THAT OF THE LABOUR WHICH HAS PRODUCED* IT" [ibid., p. 405, publisher's note]. "BOTH LABOURERS AND CAPITAL MAY BE REDUNDANT COMPARED WITH THE MEANS OF EMPLOYING THEM PROFITABLY" [ibid., p. 414, note].//

//To be noted for (3),[a] to which we shall soon proceed, that the preliminary accumulation, which is the form in which capital appears in relation to labour, and by means of which it is COMMAND over it, is initially nothing but SURPLUS LABOUR itself in the form of SURPLUS PRODUCE, and on the other hand a *draft on the* CO-EXISTING LABOUR[b] *of others.*//

OF COURSE, the point here is not yet to analyse overproduction in all its specific characteristics, but only the predisposition to it as it is posited in primitive form in the relation of capital itself. We must therefore also omit the other possessing and consuming classes, etc., which do not produce but live from their revenue, and therefore exchange with capital, constitute centres of exchange for it. We can take them partly into account only in so far as they play a MOST IMPORTANT role in the historical formation of capital (but they are better dealt with in connection with *accumulation*).

In production based on slavery, and similarly in patriarchal rural-industrial production, where the great majority of the population satisfies most of its needs directly by its labour, the sphere of circulation and exchange is very narrow; and particularly in the first, the slave does not come into consideration at all as an *exchanger.* But in production based on capital, consumption is at all points mediated by exchange, and labour never has direct use value for those who perform it. Its [IV-24] whole basis is labour as exchange value and as producer of exchange value.

WELL. *D'abord*

the wage worker, as distinct from the slave, is himself an independent centre of circulation, someone who exchanges, posits

---

[a] See this volume, pp. 245-46.— *Ed.*

[b] An expression from Hodgskin's anonymously published book *Labour Defended against the Claims of Capital*, London, 1825.— *Ed.*

exchange value and maintains exchange value by means of exchange. *Firstly*: Through the exchange between the part of capital which is determined as wages and his living labour capacity, the *exchange value* of this part of capital is directly posited before capital again steps out of the production process to enter into circulation; or this may itself be conceived of as an act of circulation. *Secondly*: In relation to each capitalist the total mass of all workers except his own appears not as workers but as consumers, possessors of exchange values (wages), of money, which they exchange for his commodities. They are so many centres of circulation, from which the act of exchange begins and by means of which the exchange value of capital is preserved. They constitute a very large proportion of consumers, although NOT QUITE SO GREAT AS IS GENERALLY IMAGINED if one thinks only of the industrial workers proper. The greater their number—the greater the size of the industrial population—and the greater the amount of money over which they dispose, the greater the sphere of exchange for capital. We have seen that it is the tendency of capital to increase the industrial population as much as possible.[a]

Actually, we are not at all concerned here yet with the relationship of one capitalist to the workers of *other* capitalists. It only shows the illusion of each capitalist, but does not alter the relationship of capital in general to labour. Each capitalist knows that he does not confront his own worker as a producer confronts a consumer, and so he wants to restrict his consumption, i.e. his ability to exchange, his wages, as much as possible. But of course, he wants the workers of *other* capitalists to be the greatest possible consumers of *his* commodity. Yet the relationship of *each* capitalist to *his* workers is the *general relationship* of *capital and labour,* the essential relation. It is precisely this which gives rise to the illusion—true for each individual capitalist as distinct from all the others—that *apart from his own* workers, the rest of the working class confronts him not as workers, but as *consumers* and *exchangers*—as moneyspenders. It is forgotten that, as *Malthus* says,

"THE VERY EXISTENCE OF A PROFIT UPON ANY COMMODITY PRESUPPOSES A *DEMAND EXTERIOR TO THAT OF THE LABOURER WHO HAS PRODUCED IT*", and hence the "*DEMAND OF THE LABOURER HIMSELF CAN NEVER BE AN ADEQUATE DEMAND*" [*Principles of Political Economy*, 2nd ed., London, 1836, p. 405, publisher's note].

Since one production sets another production in motion and hence creates consumers for itself in the *alien* capital's workers,

---

[a] Here Marx wrote, in a separate line, "*JANUARY (1858)*".— *Ed.*

(1858)

Page 24 of Notebook IV of *Outlines of the Critique of Political Economy*

the demand of the working class posited by production itself *appears* to each individual capital as an "ADEQUATE DEMAND". On the one hand, this demand posited by production itself drives on production beyond the *proportion* in which it would have to produce with regard to the [effective demand of] workers, and must do so. On the other hand, the demand EXTERIOR TO THE DEMAND OF THE LABOURER HIMSELF disappears or shrinks, hence the COLLAPSE occurs. Capital itself then regards the *demand of the labourer,* i.e. the payment of wages upon which this demand is based, not as gain but as loss, i.e. the *immanent relationship of capital and labour* asserts itself.

Here again, it is owing to the competition of capitals, their indifference to and independence of one another, that the individual capital does · *not* relate to the workers of the entire remaining capital *as workers*: *hinc* is driven beyond the right proportion. It is precisely this which distinguishes capital from the [feudal] relationship of domination—that the *worker* confronts the capitalist as consumer and one who posits exchange value, in the form of a *possessor of money*, of money, of a simple centre of circulation—that he becomes one of the innumerable centres of circulation, in which his specific character as worker is extinguished.

//Exactly the same is true of the demand created by production itself for raw materials, semi-finished products, machinery, means of communication, and for the accessory materials used in production, such as dyes, coal, tallow, soap, etc. This demand, being effective and positing exchange value, is adequate and sufficient as long as the producers exchange among themselves. Its inadequacy becomes evident as soon as the final product encounters its limit in immediate and final consumption. This *semblance* [of adequate demand], which drives [production] beyond the right proportion, also arises from the essence of capital, which, as will have to be shown in more detail in the analysis of competition, *is* that of a number of capitals entirely indifferent to one another, repelling one another. In so far as one capitalist *buys* from others, buys or sells commodities, they stand in the relationship of simple exchange and do not relate to one another as capital. The *correct* (imaginary) proportion in which they must exchange with one another in order to be able to valorise themselves at the end as capital, lies *outside* their relation to one another.//

To begin with: capital compels the workers beyond necessary labour to surplus labour. Only thus does it valorise itself and create surplus value. But on the other hand capital posits necessary labour only *in so far as* and *to the extent to which* it is surplus labour, and is *realisable* as *surplus value*. It therefore posits surplus labour as a condition of necessary labour, and surplus value as the limit to objectified labour, to value in general. When it can no longer posit the former, it no longer posits the latter, and on the basis of capital only capital can posit necessary labour. Consequently, it restricts labour and the creation of value—by an ARTIFICIAL CHECK, as the English put it[a]—and it does so for the same reason and to the same extent that it posits surplus labour and surplus value. By its very nature, therefore, capital sets [IV-25] a *limit* for labour and the creation of value, which stands in contradiction to its tendency to expand them boundlessly. And by both positing a limit *specific* to itself and on the other hand driving beyond *any* limit, it is the very embodiment of contradiction.

//Since value constitutes the basis of capital, and capital thus necessarily exists only through exchange for a *counter-value*, it necessarily repels itself from itself. A *universal capital*, not confronted by alien capitals with which it exchanges—and from our present standpoint nothing confronts it but wage labour or itself—is consequently an impossibility. The mutual repulsion of capitals is already inherent in capital as realised exchange value.//

While capital thus on the one hand makes surplus labour and its *exchange* for [other] *surplus labour*[b] the precondition of necessary labour and therefore of positing the *capacity to labour* as a centre of exchange—hence already restricting and qualifying the sphere of exchange in this direction—it is just as essential for capital, on the other hand, to limit the consumption of the worker to what is necessary for the reproduction of his labour capacity, i.e. to make the *value* which expresses *necessary labour* the limit of the utilisation of the worker's labour capacity and hence of his *capacity to exchange*, and to try to reduce to a minimum the ratio of this necessary labour to surplus labour. [This is] a new limit on the sphere of exchange which, however, like the first, is identical with the tendency of capital to treat every limit on its self-valorisation as a barrier [which must be overcome]. The boundless enlargement of its value—the boundless positing of value—is thus absolutely identical here with the setting of limits to the sphere of exchange, i.e. to the possibility of valorisation, to the realisation of the value posited in the production process.

---

[a] Th. Hodgskin, *Popular Political Economy*, p. 246.— *Ed.*
[b] I.e. its realisation in the process of exchange.— *Ed.*

The same is true of the *productive power*. On the one hand, the tendency of capital necessarily to raise it to the utmost in order to increase relative *surplus time*. On the other hand, *necessary labour time*, i.e. the workers' capacity to exchange, thereby diminished. Moreover, as we have seen,[a] relative *surplus value* grows much less relative to the productive power and indeed the proportion [between the increase in surplus value and that in productive power] declines the higher the level of productivity already attained. *But the volume of products grows in similar proportion*—if it did not, new capital and labour would be set free which would not enter into circulation. But in proportion to the growing volume of products, the difficulty of utilising the labour time contained in them also grows, because the demands made on consumption rise.

(Here, we are still only concerned with the way in which the *process of the valorisation* of capital is simultaneously its *process of devaluation*. We are not discussing the extent to which, while it has the tendency *boundlessly to expand the productive forces*, it also makes one-sided, limits, etc., the *main force of production, man* himself, and tends in general to restrict the productive forces.)

Capital thus posits *necessary labour time* as the limit on the exchange value of living labour capacity; posits *surplus labour time* as the limit on necessary labour time, and posits *surplus value* as the limit on surplus labour time. At the same time, it pushes all these limits aside, in so far as it looks to *labour capacity* as simply a participant in exchange, as money, and posits surplus labour time as the only limit, because it is the creator of surplus value. (Or, from the first aspect, capital posits the exchange of surplus values as a limit on the exchange of necessary values.)

Capital simultaneously ·posits the *values already present* in circulation—or, what amounts to the same thing, the ratio of the value created by capital to the value *presupposed* in capital itself and in circulation—as the limit, the necessary limit, to its creation of value. On the other hand, it posits its productivity as the only limit on, and as the sole creator of, values. Hence it constantly drives towards its own devaluation on the one hand, and towards the restriction of the productive forces and of the labour which objectifies itself in values on the other.

//The nonsense about the impossibility of overproduction (in other words, the assertion of the immediate identity of the production process of capital and its process of valorisation) was at

---

a See this volume, pp. 259-66.— *Ed.*

least sophistically, i.e. ingeniously, expressed by James Mill, as mentioned above,[a] in the formula: supply=its own demand, hence demand and supply are identical, which, put differently, means only that value is determined by labour time, and consequently *exchange adds nothing to value*. The only thing which is forgotten here is that exchange must take place, and whether it does or does not depends upon *use value* (in the final analysis). Therefore, as Mill says, if demand and supply are not identical, this is the result of too much being produced of one particular product (which is supplied) and too little of another (for which there is a demand). This too much and too little concerns not exchange value, but use value. More of the product is supplied than can be "used"; that is the essence of the matter; hence overproduction derives from use value and therefore from exchange itself.

Say expresses this proposition in stultified form: products are exchanged only for products[b]; therefore all that can happen is that too much is produced of one product and too little of another. He forgets (1) that values are exchanged for values, and one product is exchanged for another only in so far as it is value, i.e. only in so far as it is or becomes money; and (2) is exchanged for labour. The good fellow adopts the standpoint of *simple exchange*, in which indeed no overproduction is possible because it really is concerned with use value, not with exchange value. Overproduction takes place in relation to valorisation, NOTHING ELSE.//

[IV-26] Proudhon, who certainly hears the bells ringing, but never knows where, derives overproduction from the fact that "the worker cannot buy back his product".[c] By this he means that interest and profit are charged on it, or that the price charged for the product is in excess of its actual value. This proves *d'abord* that he understands nothing of value determination, which, GENERALLY SPEAKING, cannot possibly include an item like OVERCHARGE. In actual commerce, capitalist *A* can cheat capitalist *B*. One profits by the amount the other loses. If we add them both together, the sum of their exchange=the sum of the labour time objectified in their products, of which capitalist *A* merely pocketed more than his due in relation to *B*. From the entire profits that capital, i.e. the total number of capitalists, makes, there are deducted (1) the constant

---

[a] See this volume, p. 338.— *Ed.*

[b] J. B. Say, *Traité d'économie politique*, 3rd ed., Vol. II, p. 441.— *Ed.*

[c] P. J. Proudhon, *Qu'est-ce que la propriété?*, Ch. IV, § 5, Paris, 1841, p. 202; *Gratuité du crédit. Discussion entre M. Fr. Bastiat et M. Proudhon*, pp. 207-08. — *Ed.*

part of capital; (2) the wages, or the objectified labour time necessary to reproduce the living labour capacity. They can therefore divide among themselves only surplus value. The proportions—just or otherwise—in which they share out this surplus value among themselves, make absolutely no difference to the exchange and to the relation of exchange between capital and labour.

It might be said that *necessary labour time* (i.e. wages), which therefore does not include profit but is RATHER to be subtracted from it, is itself in turn determined by the *prices* of the products, which already include profit. Where else could the profit come from, which the capitalist not directly employing this worker makes in the exchange with him? E.g. the worker employed by the SPINNER exchanges his wages for so many bushels of grain. But the profit of the farmer, i.e. of capital, is already included in the price of each bushel, so that the *price* of the means of subsistence which necessary labour time itself buys, already includes surplus labour time. *D'abord,* it is clear that the wages paid by the SPINNER to his WORKINGMEN must be sufficient to buy the necessary bushels of corn, whatever the farmer's profit entering into the *price* of the bushel of corn, but that equally, on the other side, the wages paid by the farmer to his labourers must be sufficient to enable them to obtain the necessary quantity of clothing, whatever may be the profit of the SPINNER and WEAVER entering into the *price* of this clothing.[a]

[IV-27] The point is simply that in this argument (1) *price* and *value* are confused; (2) relations are brought in which are irrelevant to the determination of value as such.

Assume, initially—and this is the conceptual relation—that capitalist A himself produces all the means of subsistence which the worker requires, or which represent the sum of use values in which his necessary labour objectifies itself. The worker would therefore have to buy back from the capitalist, with the money he received from him—money appears in this transaction merely as means of circulation—that fractional part of the product which represents his necessary labour. The *price* of a fractional part of the product of capitalist A is OF COURSE the same for the worker as it is for any other exchanger. From the moment he buys from the capitalist, his specific quality as worker is extinguished; in his money, every trace of the relationship and of the operation by

---

[a] Here Marx crossed out a series of calculations illustrating the above proposition. He gives these calculations, in somewhat changed form, below (see pp. 354-55).— *Ed.*

means of which it was obtained has disappeared. He confronts the capitalist in circulation simply as *M* [money], and the capitalist confronts him as *C* [commodity]; he confronts the capitalist as realiser of the *price* of *C,* which is therefore presupposed for him just as it is for every other representative of *M*, i.e. for every other buyer.

WELL. But in the price of the fractional parts of the commodity which he buys there is included the profit in which the surplus value falling to the capitalist appears. If, therefore, his necessary labour time represents 20 thaler=a particular fractional part of the product, and if profit is 10%, the capitalist sells him the commodity for 22 thaler.

This is what Proudhon thinks, and he therefore concludes that the worker cannot buy back his product, i.e. the fractional part of the total product which objectifies his *necessary labour*.[a] (We shall come back directly to his other CONCLUSION: that *therefore* capital is unable to exchange adequately, *hence* overproduction.) To clarify the matter, suppose that the 20 thaler received by the worker=4 bushels of grain. If 20 thaler was the value of the 4 bushels expressed in money, and the capitalist sold it for 22, the worker could not then buy back the 4 bushels; he could buy only $3^7/_{11}$ bushels. In other words, he [Proudhon] imagines that the monetary transaction falsifies the relationship. The price of necessary labour is 20 thaler=4 bushels, and this the capitalist hands over to the worker. But as soon as the latter wants to obtain the 4 bushels for his 20 thaler, he finds that he only gets $3^7/_{11}$. But since he would then not be getting his *necessary* wages he could not live at all, and thus Mr. Proudhon proves too much.

//The fact that in practice, capital both in its general tendency and directly via the *price,* as e.g. in the TRUCK-SYSTEM, tries to cheat *necessary* labour and to depress it below the standard set by nature as well as by a particular state of society, is irrelevant here. Here we must assume throughout that the wages being paid are *economically* just, i.e. determined by the general laws of political economy. The contradictions here must follow from the general relations themselves, not from the fraudulent tricks of individual capitalists. How all this develops in reality belongs to the theory of wages.//

But the presupposition, if you please, is wrong. If 5 thaler express the *value* of a bushel, i.e. the labour time objectified in it,

---

a *Gratuité du crédit. Discussion entre M. Fr. Bastiat et M. Proudhon,* pp. 191-208.— Ed.

and 4 bushels the necessary wages, capitalist A does not sell these 4 bushels for 22 thaler, as Proudhon believes, but for 20 thaler. The point is this: let total product (including necessary and surplus labour time) be 110 thaler=22 bushels; of these 16 bushels=80 thaler represent the capital laid out on seed, machinery, etc.; 4 bushels=20 thaler represent the necessary labour time; and 2 bushels=10 thaler represent surplus labour time. The capitalist sells each bushel for 5 thaler, the necessary value of the bushel, and yet he gains 10% on each bushel, or $^5/_{10}$ thaler, $^1/_2$ thaler=15 silver groschen. Where does this come from? From the fact that he sells 22×5 instead of 20×5. We can here let the additional capital he must lay out to produce 2 more bushels=0, since they can be reduced to pure surplus labour, such as more thorough ploughing, weeding, spreading-on of animal manure, etc., which cost him nothing at all.

[IV-28] The value contained in the 2 surplus bushels has cost *him nothing,* and therefore constitutes a surplus above his expenses. If he sells 20 of the 22 bushels for what they have cost him, 100 thaler, and 2, which have cost him nothing—but whose value=the labour contained in them—for 10 thaler, this is the same for him as if he [having 20 bushels to sell] had sold each bushel for 15 silver groschen more than it cost him. (For $^1/_2$ thaler or 10% on 5 thaler=$^5/_{10}$.) Thus, although he makes a profit of 2 thaler on the 4 bushels sold to the worker, the worker gets the bushel for its necessary value. The capitalist only makes a profit of 2 thaler on the 4 bushels, because in addition to these he sells another 18 at the same price. If he sold only 16 additional ones, he would make no profit; for he would then sell a total of 5×20=100, his capital outlay.

In manufacture, in fact, the outlays of capital need not necessarily grow for a surplus value to be realised; i.e. it is not necessary for the outlay on raw material and machinery to grow. Suppose that a given product acquires a higher FINISH and a higher use value merely through labour by hand—the volume of necessary raw material and instrument is assumed to be constant—and thus its use value is increased, not because its quantity but because its quality has been raised due to the increased handiwork employed on it. Its exchange value—the labour objectified in it—simply grows in proportion to this labour. If the capitalist then sells the product 10% more dearly, the fractional part of the product (expressed in terms of money) which represents necessary labour is paid to the worker, and if the product were divisible, the worker could purchase this fractional part. The capitalist's profit would not originate from his overcharging the worker for this fractional part, but from the fact that with the whole he sells a fractional part for which he has not paid, and which represents precisely *surplus labour time.*

As value, the product is always divisible; in its natural form it need not be so. Profit here always comes from the fact that the total value contains a fractional part which is not paid for, and therefore a fractional part of surplus labour is paid for in each fractional part of the whole. Take the example given above: if the capitalist sells 22 bushels, i.e. 2 representing the surplus labour, it is the same thing as if [with only 20 bushels to sell] he sold each bushel for $^1/_{10}$ too much, i.e. $^1/_{10}$ surplus value. If e.g. only 1 clock has been produced, with the same ratio of labour, capital and surplus value, the quality of the clock has been raised by $^1/_{10}$ of the labour time, a rise of $^1/_{10}$ in value which costs the capitalist nothing.

Assume a third example in which the capitalist, as is often the case in manufacture (though not in the extractive industries), requires more raw material, in which surplus labour time is objectified (we assume that [the value of] the instrument remains constant; but it would make no difference if it were assumed to be variable).

(Really, this does not belong here yet, for capital can or must just as well be presumed to have produced the raw material, e.g. cotton, and surplus production at any particular point must be reducible to *mere* surplus labour; or, what is rather the *reality,* capital presupposes the *simultaneous* existence of surplus labour at all points in circulation.)

Let the capitalist spin 25 lbs of cotton, costing him 50 thaler, for which he needs machinery (which we shall assume to be completely used up in the production process) to a value of 30 thaler and let wages be 20 thaler; all this for 25 lbs of twist which he sells for 110 thaler. He then sells each pound of twist for $4^2/_5$ thaler or 4 thaler 12 silver groschen. The worker consequently obtains $4^6/_{11}$ lbs of twist, if he wishes to buy back his product. If the worker worked for himself, he would likewise sell the pound for 4 thaler 12 silver groschen and make no profit—assuming that he merely performs the necessary labour; but he will spin less cotton into twist.[a]

[IV-29] As we know, the value of a pound of twist consists exclusively of the amount of labour time objectified in it. Now

---

[a] In the manuscript, there follows a passage, crossed out by Marx, containing a series of calculations which must have dissatisfied him.— *Ed.*

suppose the value of the pound of twist is 5 thaler. Suppose, $^4/_5$ [of that 5 thaler], i.e. 4 thaler, represent cotton, instrument, etc.; then 1 thaler represents the labour realised in the cotton by means of the instrument. If the worker needs 20 thaler to subsist for say a month as a spinner, he would have to spin 20 lbs of twist, since he earns 1 thaler for spinning 1 lb. of twist, but needs to earn 20. If he himself owned the cotton, instrument, etc., and worked for himself, i.e. if he were his own master, he would have to sell 20 lbs of twist; for he would only earn on each lb. $^1/_5$ [of its value], a thaler, and 1×20=20. If he works for the capitalist, the labour which spins the 20 lbs of cotton only represents necessary labour; for, by presupposition, of the 20 lbs of twist or 20×5=100 thaler, 80 thaler represent only the raw cotton and instrument already purchased, and the newly reproduced value represents nothing but *necessary labour*.

4 of the 20 lbs of twist=20 thaler would represent necessary labour and 16 nothing but the constant part of capital. 16×5=80 thaler. Every lb. in excess of 20 which the capitalist orders to be produced would contain $^1/_5$ surplus labour, surplus value for him. (Objectified labour which he sells without having paid for it.) If he orders one more pound of twist spun, he makes a profit of 1 thaler; if 10 pounds more, 10 thaler. Out of 10 pounds or 50 thaler [obtained for surplus product] the capitalist would have 40 thaler to replace his outlays and 10 thaler of surplus labour; or 8 lbs of twist to buy the material for 10 (machinery and cotton), and 2 lbs of twist or their value which cost him nothing.

If we now summarise the capitalist's accounts, we find that he has invested

Thaler [Constant capital]	Thaler Wages	Thaler Surplus value	Thaler [Value of the product]
80+40=120 (raw material, instrument, etc.)	20	10	
120	20	10 =	150

The capitalist has produced a total of 30 lbs of twist (30×5=150); the pound at 5 thaler, its precise *value,* i.e. the value determined purely by the labour objectified in it and derived from it alone. Of these 30 lbs, 24 represent constant capital, 4 lbs are expended on wages, and 2 constitute *surplus value.* This surplus value, if we calculate it—as the capitalist himself does—on the basis of his total outlay, i.e. 140 thaler (or 28 pounds), is $^1/_{14}=7^1/_7\%$ (although in the present example the rate of surplus value on the [necessary] labour is 50%).

[IV-30] Suppose that there is an increase in the productivity of labour, so that the capitalist can spin 40 lbs with the same outlay on labour. According to our assumption, he would sell these 40 lbs at their real value, i.e. for 5 thaler per pound, 4 thaler representing the labour objectified in cotton, etc., and 1 thaler the labour newly added. He would therefore sell:

Thaler		Thaler	
40 lbs—the lb. for 5=40×5= 20 lbs are expended for necessary labour, etc.	=	200; of these 40 lbs	
		100	
		100. On the first 20 lbs he would not have earned a farthing; from the remaining hundred, take off $^4/_5=4×20=80$. 80 for material, etc. Leaves	
		20 thaler.	

On an outlay of 200 thaler, the capitalist would have gained 20, or 10% on the total outlay. In fact, however, his gain would be derived from the 20 thaler profit on the second 100 thaler, or from the second 20 lbs, for he has not paid for the labour objectified in them. Assume now that he can double his output, say:

Lbs		Thaler
80 20 for necessary labour, etc.	=	400. Of these take away 100. Leaves
		300. Of these, take away $^4/_5$ for material, etc.
		240. Leaves
		60; a profit of 60 on 400 =6 on 40=15%

IN FACT, in the above example, the outlay of the capitalist is only 180, and on this he gains 20, or $11^1/_9$%.

The smaller the proportion of the outlay representing necessary labour, the larger will be his profit, though it bears no obvious relation to the real surplus value, i.e. surplus labour. For example, for the capitalist to make a profit of 10%, he must have 40 lbs of twist spun; the worker needs to spin only 20=necessary labour.

Surplus labour=necessary labour, hence 100% surplus value. This is our old-established law. But this is not what is at issue here.

In the above example of the 40 lbs, the *real value* of the pound is 5 thaler, and, like the capitalist, the worker, if he carried on his own business, *as a worker* who could advance to himself the funds to enable him to utilise the raw material, etc., to the extent required to enable him to subsist as a worker, would sell the pound at 5 thaler. But he would produce only 20 pounds; from the proceeds he would employ $^4/_5$ for the purchase of new raw materials and $^1/_5$ for his subsistence. His yield from the 100 thaler would only be his wages. The profit of the capitalist does not arise from selling the pound of twist too dearly—he sells it for its *exact value*—but from selling it for more than its *production costs him* (not for what its production costs in general; for the $^1/_5$ [of the value of twist which constitutes the capitalist's profit] costs the worker his surplus labour). If he sold it for less than 5 thaler, he would sell it for *less* than its value, and the buyer would get the $^1/_5$ labour contained in each pound of twist over and above the outlays, etc., free of charge. But the capitalist reckons in this way:

Value of 1 lb.   =   5 thaler
        of 40 lbs =   200   thaler; of which take away costs
                         180
                        ─────
                         20. Leaves 20.

He does not calculate that he [IV-31] gains 20 on the second 100 thaler, but that his profit is 20 on his total outlay of 180. This gives him a profit of $11^1/_9$%, instead of 20. Furthermore, he calculates that in order to make this profit he must sell 40 lbs. 40 lbs at 5 thaler per lb. do not yield him $^1/_5$, or 20%, but 20 thaler distributed over 40 lbs or $^1/_2$ thaler per pound. At the price for which he sells the pound, he gains $^1/_2$ thaler on 5 thaler; or 1 thaler on 10, 10% on the selling price.

The price [of the total product] is determined by the price of the fractional unit (1 lb.) multiplied by the number of these units sold; in this case, 1 lb. at 5 thaler ×40. Appropriate as this way of determining the price may be with regard to the wallet of the capitalist, it is liable to mislead theoretically, since it seems as if there were an overcharge above the *real* value of each individual pound, and the creation of surplus value in the individual pound has disappeared from sight. This *price determination by means of the multiplication of the value of the unit (measure) of use value (pound, yard, hundredweight, etc.) by the number of units produced,* is important later on in the theory of prices. There follows from it among other things that the fall in the unit-price and the rise in the number of units, which occurs as the productive forces grow, demonstrates that profit rises in relation to labour or that the ratio of necessary labour to surplus labour falls—not the opposite, as maintained by Mr. Bastiat,[a] etc.

E.g. if labour increased because of an increase in productivity, so that the worker produced twice as much twist as before in the same time—presupposing that e.g. 1 lb. of twist renders him the same service whatever it costs, and that he needs only twist, clothing to live—then the value added by labour to 20 lbs of twist would no longer amount to $\frac{1}{5}$ but only to $\frac{1}{10}$, because he would now convert 20 lbs of cotton into twist in half the time. Hence a value of only 10 thaler, not 20, would be added to the 80 the raw material cost. The cost of the 20 lbs would be 90 thaler, and that of each pound $\frac{90}{20}$ or $\frac{49}{20}$ thaler.[128]

But if total labour time remained the same, labour would now convert 80 lbs, not 40, of cotton into twist. 80 lbs of twist, at $\frac{49}{20}$ thaler per lb.=356 thaler. The capitalist's calculation would be:

Total revenue	356 thaler;
	90 deducted for labour, etc., leaving
	266. From this take away for outlays, etc.,
	$239 \frac{17}{89}$
	————
	$26 \frac{72}{89}$.
	The profit of the capitalist is therefore $26 \frac{72}{89}$ now, instead of 20. Say 27, which is somewhat more ($\frac{17}{89}$ more). His total outlays are 330; more than 12%, although he would make a smaller profit on each pound.

The profit of the capitalist calculated in relation to the value of the measure (unit) of use value—pound, yard, quarter, etc.—declines in proportion to the decline in the ratio of living labour to raw material, etc.—newly added labour, i.e. in proportion to the decline in the quantity of labour time necessary to give the raw material the form expressed by the unit of use value, a yard of cloth, etc. But on the other hand—since this is identical with the increasing productivity of labour, or the growth of surplus labour time—there is an increase in the number of these units in which

---

[a] See *Gratuité du crédit. Discussion entre M. Fr. Bastiat et M. Proudhon,* pp. 130-31 and 133-57.— *Ed.*

surplus labour time is contained, i.e. labour time not paid for by the capitalist.[129]

It further follows from the above that capital can still make a profit even if the price falls *below* the value. The capitalist has only to sell a number multiplied by the unit which constitutes a surplus, over and above the number multiplied by the unit constituting the necessary price of labour [and constant capital]. If the proportion of [surplus] labour to raw material, etc., is $1/_5$, he can e.g. sell at a price of only $1/_{10}$ [IV-32] above constant value, since surplus labour *costs him nothing*. He then makes a present of $1/_{10}$ of the surplus labour to the consumer and realises only $1/_{10}$ for himself. This is a very important factor in competition, which Ricardo in particular overlooked.

The determination of price is based on the determination of value; but new elements are added. The price, which originally appears merely as value expressed in money, is further determined as itself a specific magnitude. If 5 thaler is the *value* of a pound of twist, i.e. if the same labour time is contained in 5 thaler as in a pound of twist, the determination of value is the same whether 4 or 4 million pounds of twist are valued. The factor of the n u m b e r   o f   p o u n d s becomes decisively significant in the *determination of price,* because it expresses the ratio of surplus to necessary labour in another form. This point illustrated in simple terms by the question of the *Ten Hours Bill,*[88] etc.

It also follows from the above:

The worker would spin only 20 lbs of twist, utilise raw materials, machinery, etc., to the value of only 80 thaler per month, if he confined himself to *necessary* labour. Apart from the raw materials, machinery, etc., which are necessary for the *reproduction,* self-maintenance, of the worker, the capitalist must lay out *necessary* capital in raw materials (and in machinery, even if not in the same proportion) for the objectification of surplus labour. (In the case of agriculture, fishing, and the extractive industries in general, this is not absolutely necessary; but it is always necessary even in these industries as soon as they are carried on on a large scale, i.e. *industrially.* The additional outlay then does not appear to be for the raw materials themselves but for the instruments to procure them.) These surplus outlays, i.e. making available the material for surplus labour, the objective elements for its realisation, are in fact what constitutes the specific so-called *preliminary accumulation* of capital; the accumulation of stock (let us say for the time being), *specifically* for capital. For it is absurd, as we shall see in more detail later, to regard it as a condition specific only to capital that the objective conditions of living labour must be present at all, whether they are supplied by nature or historically produced. These *specific* ADVANCES which capital makes signify nothing more than that it *valorises* surplus labour—surplus product—in new living surplus labour, instead of investing (spending) it on the building of pyramids, etc., like, say, the Egyptian Pharaohs or the Etruscan priestly nobles.

So far as *price determination* is concerned (and this will also be apparent in connection with profit), *fraud, mutual cheating,* also comes in. One party can gain through exchange what the other party loses; they, capital as a class, can only divide surplus value among themselves. It is the proportions [of exchange] which open up a whole field of individual trickery, etc. (quite apart from the effect of supply and demand), and this has nothing to do with the determination of value as such.

This, then, puts paid to Mr. Proudhon's discovery that the worker cannot buy back his product. It arises from his (Proudhon's) failure to understand either value determination or price determination. But even apart from that, his CONCLUSION that *this is the cause* of overproduction is false at this level of abstraction. Under the slave system, masters are not troubled by the fact that the labourers do not compete with them as consumers. (However, *luxury production,* as it appeared in antiquity, is a necessary result of the slave system. Not overproduction but *overconsumption* and *absurd consumption,* which in their degeneration to the level of the monstrous and the bizarre mark the downfall of the ancient state system.)

After capital steps out of the production process as a *product,* it must be reconverted into money. Money, which before appeared only as realised commodity, etc., now appears as *realised capital,* or realised capital as *money.* This is a new determination of *money* (and also of capital). It is already evident from the previous argument that the volume of money as means of circulation has nothing to do with the difficulty of realising capital, i.e. *valorising* it.

[IV-33] In the above example, where the capitalist sells the pound of twist for 5 thaler—i.e. 40 lbs at 5 thaler per pound—he sells the pound for its *real value* and thereby gains $1/2$ thaler on 5 (the sale price), 10% on the sale price, or $1/2$ on $4^1/2$, i.e. $11^1/9\%$ on his outlay. Assume that he sells it for only a 10% overall profit—that he takes only $9/20$ thaler profit on $4^1/2$ thaler (this differs by $^1/_{20}$ from $^1/_2$ thaler on $4^1/_2$; a difference of precisely $1^1/_9\%$).

Let him then sell the pound for $4^1/_2$ thaler$+^9/_{20}$ thaler, i.e. $4^{19}/_{20}$ thaler, or the 40 lbs for 198 thaler. There are now various possibilities. Suppose that the capitalist with whom he exchanges— to whom he sells his 40 lbs—is the owner of a silver-mine, therefore a silver producer, and pays him only 198 thaler, hence gives him 2 thaler too little objectified labour in silver for the labour objectified in 40 lbs of twist. Suppose the proportions [of the component parts] of the outlay, etc., to be exactly the same for this capitalist B [as for capitalist A]. If capitalist B also takes only 10% profit instead of $11^1/_9\%$, he could not demand 40 lbs of twist for 200 thaler but only $39^3/_5$ lbs. Hence it is impossible for both capitalists at the same time to sell for $1^1/_9\%$ too little, or for the one to offer 40 lbs for 198 thaler and the other to bid 200 thaler for $39^3/_5$ lbs; this situation cannot occur. Hence, in the case assumed, capitalist B would have paid $1^1/_9\%$ too little in purchasing the 40 lbs of twist; i.e. he would have gained $1^1/_9\%$ by the other capitalist incurring a loss, in addition to the profit of $11^1/_9\%$ which he does not obtain in exchange but which is merely confirmed in exchange, or a total profit of $12^2/_9\%$. He would have profited $11^1/_9\%$ from his own workers—the labour set in motion with his own capital; the extra $1^1/_9\%$ is surplus labour performed by the workers of capitalist A and appropriated by capitalist B.

Consequently, the *general rate of profit* can fall in one or another branch of business, because competition, etc., forces the capitalist to sell below *value*, i.e. to realise a part of surplus labour not for himself but for the buyers of his product. But the general rate [of profit] cannot fall in this way; it can fall only because of a *relative* fall in the ratio of surplus labour to necessary labour [and constant capital]. And this, as we have seen earlier, occurs if the ratio [of constant to variable capital] is already very large or, otherwise expressed, the proportion of living labour set in motion by capital is very small—if the part of capital exchanged for living labour is very small relative to that which is exchanged for machinery and raw materials. In that case the general rate of profit may fall, even though absolute surplus labour rises.

This brings us to another point. A *general rate of profit* becomes possible only if the rate of profit in one branch of business is too great and in another too small, i.e. if a part of surplus value—which corresponds to surplus labour—is transferred from one capitalist to another. If, for example, in 5 branches of business, the rate of profit is respectively

a   b   c   d   e

15% 12% 10% 8% 5%, the average rate of profit is 10%. But for this rate to exist in reality, capitalists A and B must give up 7% to D and E, i.e. 2% to D and 5% to E, while in the case of C things remain as they are.

Equality of the rate of profit on the same capital of 100 [in the cases considered] is impossible, since the proportions of surplus labour [to the outlays of capital] are completely different [in them], depending on the productivity of labour and the proportions between raw materials, machinery and wages, and the scale on which the product must generally be produced. But assume that branch e is necessary, e.g. that of BAKERS, then the average 10% must be paid to it. But this can only happen, if a and b transfer part of their surplus labour to the credit of e. The capitalist class to a certain extent distributes total surplus value among its members in such a way that, TO A CERTAIN DEGREE, the capitalists [share in it] in proportion to the *size* of their capital, instead of to the surplus values actually created by the capitals in the particular branches. The larger profit which arises from actual surplus labour within one branch, from surplus value really created in that branch, is forced down to the general level by competition, and the minus of surplus value in the other branch is forced up to the general level by withdrawal of capital from that branch and the resulting favourable relationship between demand and supply. Competition cannot depress the general level itself, but only tends to create such a level. Further analysis [of this problem] belongs to the section on competition.

The general level is realised by the relationship of prices in the different branches, which in the one branch fall *below value,* in the other *rise* above it. This creates the appearance that an equal sum of capital in different branches creates *equal surplus labour or surplus value.*

[IV-34] In the above example, where capitalist A is forced, say by competition, to sell at a profit of 10% instead of $11^1/_9$%, and therefore sells the pound of twist $^1/_{20}$ thaler too cheaply, the worker would continue, as assumed, to receive 20 thaler in money as before, his necessary wages; but in twist he would receive $4^4/_{99}$ lbs instead of 4. In terms of twist, he would get [a little over] $^4/_{20}$ thaler=$^1/_5$ thaler or 6 silver groschen, i.e. 1% more than his necessary wages.[130]

If the worker works in a branch of business whose product is completely outside the sphere of his consumption, he gains not a farthing from this operation, but for him it is a question of performing a part of his surplus labour indirectly for capitalist *B* instead of directly for capitalist *A*, i.e. through the mediation of capitalist *A*. The worker can only gain from the fact that capitalist *A* lets go of a part of the labour objectified in his product free of charge, if he is himself a consumer of this product and only to the extent to which he is such a consumer. Consequently, if his consumption of twist amounts to $^1/_{10}$ of his outlay, he gains EXACTLY $^1/_{50}$ thaler by means of the operation ($^2/_{100}$ thaler on 2 thaler, $^1/_{100}$ on 1, exactly 1% on the 2 thaler), i.e. $^1/_{10}$% on his total wages of 20 thaler, or $7^1/_5$ pfennigs.[a] This would be the proportion—$7^1/_5$ pfennigs—in which he would share in his own surplus labour of 20 thaler. This is the order of magnitude which the worker's surplus wage can reach in the most favourable case as the result of a fall in the *price* of the product below necessary value in the branch of business in which he is employed. In the *most favourable* case—and that is impossible—the LIMIT is (in the given case) 6 silver groschen or 1%, i.e. if he could live exclusively on twist. This means that in the most favourable case, his surplus wage is determined by the ratio of necessary labour time to surplus labour time. In the luxury-goods industries proper, from whose consumption he is himself excluded, it always=0.

Now let us assume that the capitalists *A, B, C* exchange [their products] among one another; for each of them, the total product=200 thaler. *A* produces twist, *B* grain and *C* silver. Let us assume that the ratio of surplus labour and necessary labour, and of outlay and profit, are exactly the same. *A* sells 40 lbs of twist for 198 thaler instead of for 200 thaler and loses $1^1/_9$% profit; ditto, *B* his (say) 40 bushels of grain for 198 instead of for 200; but *C* exchanges all of his labour objectified in 200 thaler. The relationship between *A* and *B* is such that if each exchanged all of his product with the other, neither would lose. *A* would obtain 40 bushels of grain, *B* 40 lbs of twist; but each would obtain a value of only 198. *C* obtains for 198 thaler 40 lbs of twist or 40 bushels of grain, and in both cases pays 2 thaler too little, or obtains $^2/_5$ lb. of twist or $^2/_5$ of a bushel of grain too much.

But let us assume that the relationship was such that *A* sold his 40 lbs of twist to the silver producer *C* for 200 thaler, but the silver producer in turn must pay 202 thaler to the grain producer

---

[a] The (Prussian and Saxon) thaler equalled 30 silver groschen, the silver groschen equalled 12 pfennigs.— *Ed.*

B, i.e. *B* receives 2 thaler more than the value of his product. In the relationship between the twist producer *A* and the silver producer *C*, everything is ALL RIGHT; both exchange [equal] values with one another. But because for *B*, price has risen above the value of his product, the 40 lbs of twist and the 200 thaler of silver expressed in terms of grain have fallen by $1^1/_9\%$, or both can in fact no longer purchase 40 bushels of grain with the 200 thaler but only $39^{61}/_{101}$ bushels. $39^{61}/_{101}$ bushels of wheat would cost 200 thaler, or one bushel of wheat $5^1/_{20}$ thaler, 5 thaler $1^1/_2$ silver groschen, instead of 5 thaler.

Assume now in the latter relationship that the worker's consumption consists $^1/_2$ of wheat. His consumption of twist amounted to $^1/_{10}$ of his income, his consumption of wheat to $^5/_{10}$. On the $^1/_{10}$ he gained $^1/_{10}\%$ on his total wages; on the wheat he loses $^5/_{10}\%$; hence he loses $^4/_{10}\%$ in all instead of gaining. Although the capitalist would have paid him his necessary labour, his wages would fall below the necessary wages because of grain producer *B*'s overcharging. If this persisted, his necessary *wages* would have to *rise*.

Thus, if the sale of twist [at a lower price] by capitalist *A* is due to a rise above their value in the price of *grain* or other use values which form the greater part of the worker's consumption, capitalist *A*'s worker loses in the same proportion in which his consumption of the dearer product is greater than that of the cheaper one produced by himself. But had *A* sold his twist $1^1/_9\%$ above its value, and had *B* sold his grain $1^1/_9\%$ below its value, the worker could at best, if he consumed only grain, have gained no more than 6 silver groschen. Or, since we have assumed that he [consumes] half his income in grain, he would gain only 3 silver groschen or $^1/_2\%$ [IV-35] on his wages of 20 thaler.

For the worker, therefore, all three cases are possible: his gain or loss by the operation [the evening-up of profits] could=zero; the operation could depreciate his necessary wage so that it no longer suffices, hence depress it below the necessary minimum; lastly, it could create for him a surplus wage, which would amount to an EXTREMELY SMALL share of his own surplus labour.

We have seen above that if the proportion of necessary labour to the other conditions of production [needed to perform necessary labour]=$^1/_4$ (20 of the total outlay of 100) or=20% of the total value (4 lbs of the 20 lbs of twist produced) (or the 100 thaler capital would be divided up into 80 raw materials and instrument, 20 labour), and the proportion of surplus labour to necessary labour is 100% (i.e. the same quantity), the capitalist makes $11\frac{1}{9}\%$ on his outlay.

If he took only 10% and made a present of $1\frac{1}{9}\%$ or 2 thaler [of the 20 thaler] to the consumers (transferred surplus value to them), the worker would also gain in so far as he is a consumer, and in the best (impossible) case, if he lived only on the product produced by his MASTER, the following would take place, as we have seen:

	$1\frac{1}{9}\%$ (=2 thaler) loss on the part of the capitalist	1%=6 silver groschen on 20 thaler ($\frac{1}{5}$ thaler on 20) gain on wages for the worker

Assume that the capitalist sold the pound of twist for $4^{15}/_{20}$ $(4^3/_4)$ thaler instead of 5; then the worker would gain $^5/_{20}$ on the pound, and $^{20}/_{20}=1$ on 4 lbs; but 1 on 20 is $^1/_{20}$, i.e. 5%; (1 thaler on 20); the capitalist would sell the 40 lbs at $4^{15}/_{20}$ thaler or $^{95}/_{20}$ thaler×40=190 thaler; his outlay 180, his profit of 10 is $5^5/_9[\%]$. His loss [or] minus-profit=$5^5/_9$. If the capitalist sold the twist for $4^{12}/_{20}$, the worker would gain $^8/_{20}$ thaler on the pound, $^{32}/_{20}$ on 4 lbs, $1^{12}/_{20}$ thaler or $1^3/_5$ thaler on his total wages, i.e. 8%, but the capitalist would lose 16 thaler in surplus profit, or keep a total of only 184 thaler or 4 thaler profit on 180, i.e. $^1/_{45}$ of 180 or $2^2/_9\%$; he would then lose $8^8/_9\%$. Finally, assume the capitalist sold the pound of twist for $4^1/_2$ thaler; the 40 lbs for 180; his profit is then 0; he makes the consumer a present of the surplus value or [surplus] labour time [of the worker], so the worker gains $^1/_2$ thaler per lb.=$^4/_2$ thaler=2 thaler, or 2 thaler on 20=10%.

Right-column figures:

=1 thaler

$5^5/_9$ (=10 thaler) =5% (1 thaler on 20)

=$8^8/_9\%$ (=16) =8% (1 thaler 18 sgr.)

Profit=0 (Loss=$11\frac{1}{9}\%$)

=10% (2 thaler) (not quite $^1/_2$ lb.)

[IV-36] If, on the contrary, the capitalist had raised wages by 10%, from 20 to 22 thaler, perhaps because in his branch the demand for labour had risen above supply, while selling the pound of twist as before at its value, i.e. for 5 thaler, his profit would have fallen by only 2 thaler, from 20 to 18, i.e. by $1\frac{1}{9}\%$, and would still have been 10%.[131]

Consequently, if the capitalist, perhaps out of consideration for Mr. Proudhon, sold his commodities at the production costs they cost *him*, and his total profit=0, this would merely constitute a transfer of surplus value or surplus labour time from capitalist A to B, C, D, etc.; and with respect to his worker, in the best case the gain—i.e. his share in his own surplus labour—would be restricted to the part of his wages which he consumes in the depreciated commodity. And even if he spent his entire wages on it, his gain could not be any greater than in the proportion of necessary labour to the total product (in the above example, $20:200=\,^1/_{10}$, [his maximum share] $^1/_{10}$ of $20=2$ thaler).

With respect to the workers of other capitalists, the case is exactly the same: they gain from the depreciated commodity only (1) in proportion to their consumption of it; (2) in proportion to the size of their wages, which are determined by necessary labour. If the depreciated commodity were e.g. grain, ONE OF THE STUFFS OF LIFE, then first its producer, the farmer, and afterwards all the other capitalists would discover that the [hitherto] necessary wage of the worker is no longer the necessary wage, but stands above its level; it would therefore be lowered. Hence, in the end, only the surplus value of capitals a, b, c, etc., and the surplus labour of those employed by them would be increased.

Assume 5 capitalists, A, B, C, D and E. E produces a commodity which is consumed only by workers. E would then realise his profit exclusively by exchanging his commodity with wages. But, as always, his profit would not derive from the exchange of his commodity for the money of the workers, but from the exchange of his capital with living labour. Assume necessary labour in all 5 branches as $^1/_5$; let surplus labour in all be $^1/_5$; let constant capital in all$=\,^3/_5$ [of the value of the product]. Capitalist E then exchanges [$^4/_5$ of] his product for $^1/_5$ of capital a, $^1/_5$ of capital b, $^1/_5$ of capital c, $^1/_5$ of capital d, and $^1/_5$ constitutes his own workers' wages. He would make no profit on this last $^1/_5$, as we have seen, or RATHER, his profit would not derive from his giving the workers $^1/_5$ of his capital in money and from their buying back this $^1/_5$ from him as product. In other words, it would not derive from the exchange with the workers as *consumers* or centres of circulation. His whole transaction with them as consumers of his product consists in his giving it to them in the form of money and in their returning to him this same money for exactly the same fractional part of the product. His relationship to the workers of A, B, C, D is not that of capitalist to worker, but that of C to M, of seller to buyer.

According to our assumption, the workers of A, B, C and D do not consume anything of the latters' own products; E certainly exchanges $^1/_5$ of the product of A, B, C and D, i.e. $^4/_5$ of their product.[a] But this exchange is only a roundabout way in which A, B, C and D pay the wages to their own workers. They give their workers money, each to the amount of $^1/_5$ of their product, or $^1/_5$ of their product as payment for necessary labour, and with this, i.e. with $^4/_5$ of the value of their product or [commodity] capital, the workers buy the commodity of E.[b] This exchange with E is therefore only an indirect form in which they advance that part of their capital which represents necessary labour—it is a *deduction* from their capital. Clearly, they cannot make a profit by this transaction. The profit derives from the valorisation of the remaining $^4/_5$ of the capitals a, b, c and d, which is effected by each one getting back in the exchange the labour objectified in his product in another form. As division of labour exists among them, $^3/_5$ replaces for each his constant capital—raw material and instrument of labour. The profit derives from the mutual valorisation of the last $^1/_5$—the valorisation of surplus labour time, which posits it as surplus value.

It is not necessary for capitals a, b, c and d to exchange the $^4/_5$ [remaining after the deduction of wages] entirely among one another. Since as capitalists they are at the same time significant consumers, and cannot live on air; and since likewise as capitalists they do not live by their own labour, it follows that they have nothing to exchange or consume but the product of alien labour. I.e. for their consumption, they exchange precisely the $^1/_5$ which represents surplus labour time, the labour created by capital. Assume that each [of the capitalists A, B, C and D] consumes $^1/_5$ of this $^1/_5$, i.e. $^1/_{25}$, in the form of his [IV-37] own product. $^4/_{25}$ then still remain to be either valorised or converted into use value for the capitalist's own consumption by means of exchange. Let A exchange $^2/_{25}$ [of his product] with B, $^1/_{25}$ with C, and $^1/_{25}$ with E, and similarly on the part of B, C and E.[c]

The case we have assumed, where capital e realises its entire profit in exchange for wages, is the most favourable one—or rather it expresses the only correct relation in which it is possible

---

[a] This should read "... of A, B, C and D, giving $^4/_5$ of his own product for it".— *Ed.*

[b] This should read "... and with this the workers buy the commodity of E to the amount of $^4/_5$ of the value of his product or [commodity] capital".— *Ed.*

[c] Here Marx crossed out several lines representing an unfinished outline of the exchange of products between capitals belonging to different branches.— *Ed.*

for capital to realise in *exchange* its surplus value produced in *production,* by means of the workers' consumption. But in this case, capitals *a, b, c* and *d* can realise their value only by means of exchange with one another, i.e. by exchange of the capitalists among themselves. Capitalist *E* does not consume any of his own commodity, since he has paid $\frac{1}{5}$ of it to his own workers, exchanged $\frac{1}{5}$ for $\frac{1}{5}$ of capital *a,* $\frac{1}{5}$ for $\frac{1}{5}$ of capital *b,* $\frac{1}{5}$ for $\frac{1}{5}$ of capital *c,* $\frac{1}{5}$ for $\frac{1}{5}$ of capital *d. A, B, C* and *D* make no profit from this exchange, since it merely realises the $\frac{1}{5}$ with which they have respectively paid their own workers.

Given the proportions we have assumed, $\frac{2}{5}$ raw materials, $\frac{1}{5}$ machinery, $\frac{1}{5}$ workers' NECESSARIES, $\frac{1}{5}$ surplus produce of which Messrs. the capitalists both live and realise their surplus value, then, if the total product of each of the capitalists *A, B, C, D* and *E* = 100, we need a producer *E* for workers' NECESSARIES, 2 capitalists *A* and *B* who produce raw materials for [themselves and] all the others, 1 capitalist *C* who produces machinery, and one capitalist *D* who makes the surplus produce.

The calculation [for the different capitalists] would be as follows (the machine producer, etc., must each produce part of his commodity for himself):

	For labour	Raw material	Machinery	Surplus produce		
A. *Raw material producer*	20 —	40 —	20 —	20	= 100	2 $\frac{1}{2}$
B. *Ditto*	20 —	40 —	20 —	20	= 100	2 $\frac{1}{2}$
C. *Machine producer*	20 —	40 —	20 —	20	= 100	2 $\frac{1}{2}$
E. *Workers' NECES-SARIES*	20 —	40 —	20 —	20	= 100	2 $\frac{1}{2}$
D. *Surplus producer*	20 —	40 —	20 —	20	= 100	
	10	20	10	10	= 50	

E therefore exchanges his total product of 100 for 20 in his own workers' wages, 20 for the workers of the raw material producer *A,* 20 for the workers of the raw material producer *B,* 20 for the workers of the machine producer *C,* 20 for the workers of the surplus producer *D.* Hence he exchanges 40 for raw material, 20 for machinery, gets back 20 for [his own] workers' NECESSARIES, and 20 remain with him for the purchase of surplus produce, on which he himself subsists. Likewise in proportion the other capitalists. What constitutes their surplus value is the $\frac{1}{5}$ or 20 which they can all exchange for surplus produce. If they consumed the entire surplus, they would have got no further at the end than they were at the beginning, and the surplus value of their capital would not grow.

Suppose that they consume only 10, or $^1/_{10}$ [of the value of the product], half the surplus value. As a result, the surplus producer D would himself consume 10 less, and each of the others 10 less. In total, therefore, D would sell only half his commodity=50, and could not recommence his business.

So assume that he produces only 50 in consumables [for the capitalists].[a] Of the 400 thaler which exist in the form of raw materials, machinery, workers' NECESSARIES, only 50 become available in the form of consumables for the capitalists. But each of the capitalists now possesses a surplus of 10, 4 of which he lays out in raw materials, 2 in machinery and 2 in workers' NECESSARIES, on which he should get a profit of 2 (as previously with 80, 100). D has gained 10 on his 40 and can therefore increase his production in the same proportion [as the other capitalists], viz. by 5. In the next year he will increase his production by $7^1/_2$ [the total then being]=$57^1/_2$.

[IV-38] This example may or may not be developed later. Does not really belong here. This much is clear that valorisation occurs here in the exchange of the capitalists among one another. For although E produces only for workers' consumption, he obtains by means of exchange in the form of wages $^1/_5$ of A, $^1/_5$ of B, $^1/_5$ of C, and $^1/_5$ of D. In the same way, A, B, C and D exchange with E: not directly but indirectly, since each one of them must get $^1/_5$ from E as workers' NECESSARIES. The valorisation consists in each capitalist exchanging his own product for a fractional part of the products of the other four, and this in such a way that a part of the surplus product is destined for the consumption of the capitalist, and a part is converted into surplus capital with which to set new labour in motion. The valorisation consists in the *real possibility* of greater valorisation—the production of new and larger values.

It is clear here that if D and E (E representing commodities entirely consumed by workers and D commodities entirely consumed by capitalists) had produced too much—i.e. too much

---

[a] Crossed out in the manuscript: "In money likewise 50; thus each of the capitalists A, B, C, D, E would accumulate in money 10 thaler. This would represent the unconsumed surplus value. The 10 thaler or TOGETHER 50, however, could only be valorised if invested in new labour. A and B, in order to produce more raw material, need 4 thaler more living labour and, since they have no new machinery for that, 6 thaler more manual labour."— *Ed.*

relative to the proportion of the part of capital destined for the workers, or too much relative to the part of capital consumable by the capitalists //too much relative to the rate at which they must expand capital; and this rate later becomes subject to a minimum limit in the form of interest//— *general overproduction* would occur, not because relatively *too little* of the commodities to be consumed by the workers, or relatively too little of those to be consumed by the capitalists, [would have been consumed,] but because too much of *both* would have been produced—too much *not for consumption, but too much to maintain the correct ratio between consumption and valorisation; too much for valorisation.*

In other words: at a given point in the development of the productive forces—(for this will determine the ratio of necessary to surplus labour)—there exists a fixed relationship in which the product is divided into several parts—corresponding to raw materials, machinery, necessary labour, and surplus labour; and ultimately surplus labour is divided itself into one part which falls to consumption, and another which becomes capital again. In exchange, this inner conceptual division of capital expresses itself in the particular and delimited (though in the production process constantly varying) proportions in which capitals exchange with one another. A proportional division within a capital of e.g. $^2/_5$ raw material, $^1/_5$ machinery, $^1/_5$ wages and $^1/_5$ surplus product, of which in turn $^1/_{10}$ is destined for [the capitalist's] consumption and $^1/_{10}$ for new production, will appear in exchange as the division [of the total product] between (SAY) 5 capitals. In any case, both the sum of the exchange which can take place, and the proportions in which each of these capitals must both exchange and produce, are thereby given. If the ratio of necessary labour to the constant part of capital, as e.g. in the above example, $=^1/_5:^3/_5$, then, as we have seen, the total capital which works for the consumption of both capitalists and workers [i.e. capitals D and E] cannot be greater than $^1/_5+^1/_{10}$ of the 5 capitals, each of which represents $1=1^1/_2$ capitals.

Given also is the proportion in which each capital must exchange with the other which represents one of its own particular moments. Given, finally, is the proportion in which each capital must generally exchange.

If the proportion of e.g. the raw material is $^2/_5$, then the capitals which produce raw materials can at any final point only exchange $^3/_5$, while $^2/_5$ have to be considered as fixed (e.g. seeds, etc., in agriculture). *Exchange* in and for itself gives these conceptually distinct moments a being indifferent to one another. They exist independently of one another; their inner necessity becomes *manifest* in crises, which make short shrift of the semblance of their mutual indifference.

A revolution in the productive forces further alters these relations, *transforms* these relationships themselves, whose basis— from the viewpoint of capital and thus also of valorisation by means of exchange—always *remains the ratio of necessary labour to surplus labour*, or, IF YOU PLEASE, of the different moments of objectified labour to living labour. It is possible, as we have already indicated earlier,[a] that the capital as well as the living labour capacity set free by the increase in the productive forces must both remain unused, because they are not present in the proportions required by production on the basis of the newly developed productive forces. If production proceeds regardless of this, then ultimately a minus on the one side or the other, a negative magnitude, must result from the exchange.

The limit always remains the fact that exchange—hence also production—takes place in such a way that the ratio of surplus labour to necessary labour remains the same, for this=the constancy of the valorisation of capital. The second relationship— the ratio of the part of the surplus product consumed by capital to the part converted anew into capital—is determined by the first ratio. In the first place, *the magnitude of the sum to be divided into these two parts depends on this original ratio.* Secondly, just as the creation of the surplus value of capital is based on the creation of surplus labour, so the increase of capital as capital (i.e. accumulation, without which capital cannot constitute the basis of production, since it [IV-39] would remain stagnant and would not be an element of progress, which it must needs become if only because of the growth of population, etc.) depends on the conversion of part of this surplus product into new capital. If surplus value were merely consumed, capital would *not* have valorised itself and not produced itself as *capital,* i.e. as value which produces value.

We have seen that, if 40 lbs of twist with a value of 200 thaler—because they contain the labour time objectified in 200 thaler—are exchanged for 198, not only does the twist manufacturer lose $1^1/_9\%$ profit but his product is also depreciated, is sold *below* its real value, although it is sold at a *price* which STILL LEAVES HIM A PROFIT OF 10%. On the other hand, the silver producer gains 2 thaler; he retains 2 thaler as released capital. Nevertheless, a

---

[a] See this volume, p. 351.— *Ed.*

depreciation has occurred if the total sum is considered. For the sum is now 398 thaler instead of 400. For, in the hands of the silver producer, the 200 thaler of twist are now also worth only 198; for him it is the same as if the productivity of his labour had increased in such a way that the same objectified labour as before is contained in 200 thaler, but 2 thaler of it had been transferred from the account of necessary outlay to that of surplus value; as if he had paid 2 thaler less for necessary labour.

The opposite could be the case only if the silver producer were able to resell for 200 thaler the 40 lbs of twist he had bought for 198 thaler. He would then have 202 thaler. Let us say he sold the twist to a silk manufacturer who gave him silk to the value of 200 thaler for the 40 lbs of twist. The 40 lbs of twist would then have been sold at their true value, if not at first hand by their producer, at least at second hand by their buyer. The overall calculation would then look thus: 3 products, each containing objectified labour to the value of 200, have been exchanged; hence the *sum* of values of the capitals: 600. *A* is the twist manufacturer, *B* the silver producer, *C* the silk manufacturer: [as a result of the exchange] *A* has 198, *B* 202 (namely 2 excess from the first exchange and 200 in silk), *C* 200. *Total* 600. In this case the total value of the capitals has remained the same, and there has merely been a *déplacement*, since *B* would have pocketed an excessive part of the value of which *A* received too little.

If *A*, the twist manufacturer, could only sell 180 [thaler's worth of twist] (what it cost *him*), and was absolutely unable to dispose of 20 [in] twist, objectified labour of 20 thaler would have become valueless. The same would be the case, if he sold a value of 200 for 180 thaler. *B*, the silver producer—in so far as this necessity [to reduce the price of twist] had arisen for *A* because of overproduction of twist, *B* too would be unable to dispose of the value contained in the 40 lbs of twist for more than 180—[*B*] would have 20 thaler of his capital set free for him. He would have in hand a relative surplus value of 20 thaler, but in absolute value—objectified labour time in so far as it is exchangeable— only 200 as before, viz. 40 lbs of twist for 180 and 20 thaler of released capital. For him it would be the same as if the costs of production of twist had declined, i.e. as if, as a result of a rise in the productivity of labour, 20 thaler less labour time were contained in 40 lbs of twist; or, as if the value of the working day=4 thaler; as if 5 days less labour were necessary to transform *x* lbs of cotton into 40 lbs of twist; as if he would therefore have to exchange less labour time objectified in silver for the labour time objectified in twist. But the total sum of existing values would be 380 instead of 400. Thus a *general devaluation* of 20 thaler, or a destruction of capital to the extent of 20 thaler, would have taken place.

Hence a *general devaluation* takes place, although the *depreciation* resulting from the twist manufacturer's sale of 40 lbs for 180 thaler instead of 200 necessarily appears as an appreciation on the side of silver, a depreciation of twist relative to silver, and a general depreciation of prices in any case always includes an appreciation of money, i.e. of the commodity in terms of which all others are valued. Thus in a crisis—with a general depreciation of prices—there also occurs up to a certain moment a *general devaluation* or *destruction of capital*. The devaluation can be *general, absolute*, and not just relative, as with a *depreciation*, because value does not, like price, merely express the relationship of one commodity to another, but the relationship between the price of the commodity to the labour objectified in it, or the relationship of one amount of objectified labour of the same quality to another. If these amounts are not equal, a *devaluation* occurs which is not compensated for by an appreciation on the other side, since the other side expresses a fixed amount of objectified labour which cannot be altered by exchange. In general crises, this devaluation extends even to living labour capacity.

According to what has been indicated above, [IV-40] the destruction of value and capital which occurs in a crisis coincides with—or means the same as—a *general growth of the productive forces*, which, however, does not take place through a real increase in the productivity of labour (in so far as this results from crises, it does not belong here) but through a diminution of the existing value of raw materials, machinery and labour capacity. E.g. the cotton manufacturer loses capital on his products (e.g. twist), but he buys the same value in cotton, labour, etc., at a lower price. It is the same for him as if the *real value* of labour, of cotton, etc., had diminished, i.e. as if they had been more cheaply produced through an increase in the productivity of labour.

Likewise, on the other hand, a sudden general growth of the productive forces would devalue relatively all *existing values*, labour objectified at a lower level of the productive forces, and therefore destroy existing capital just as it would destroy existing labour capacity. The other aspect of the crisis resolves itself into a real fall in production, in living labour, in order to restore the correct proportion of necessary to surplus labour, on which, in the last analysis, everything rests. (Thus it is by no means the case, as Lord

Overstone thinks[a]—as a true usurer—that crises simply resolve themselves into ENORMOUS PROFITS FOR THE ONE, AND TREMENDOUS LOSSES FOR THE OTHER.)

Exchange does not alter the inner conditions of valorisation, but it projects them outwards, gives them a form independent of one another, and thus lets their inner unity exist only as an inner necessity which is therefore given violent external expression in crises. Both are therefore posited in the essence of capital: its devaluation in the production process, as well as the transcendence of this devaluation and the restoration of the conditions for the valorisation of capital. The movement in which this really takes place can only be considered when we consider *real* capital, i.e. competition, etc.; the real, existing conditions. It does not belong here yet. On the other hand, *without* exchange, the production of capital as such would not exist, since *valorisation* as such does not exist without exchange. Without exchange, we should be concerned only with the measurement, etc., of the *use value* produced, with absolutely nothing but use value.

After capital, by means of the production process, has (1) valorised itself, i.e. created a new value; (2) devalued itself, i.e. passed from the form of money into that of a particular commodity; it (3) valorises itself together with its new value, in that the product is thrown into circulation again and exchanged as *C* for *M*. At the point which we have now reached, where capital is only being considered in general, the real difficulties of this third process exist only as *possibilities*, and are therefore likewise transcended as *possibilities*. Hence the product is now posited as having been transformed back into money.

Consequently, capital is now again posited as money, and money thus posited in its *new* determination as *realised capital*, not merely as the realised price of the commodity. In other words, the commodity realised as price is now realised capital. This new determination of money, or rather of capital as money, will be considered later. In the first place, according to the nature of money—when capital is converted into money—only the new value which it has created appears to be measured by it, i.e. the first determination of money as the general measure of commodities is reiterated, now as the measure of surplus value—of

---

    a This presumably refers to the speech on the economic crisis by Lord Overstone (Loyd) at the opening session of the House of Lords on 3 December 1857.— *Ed.*

the valorisation of capital. In the form of money, this valorisation appears measured in terms of itself, as being its own measure.

The capital was originally 100 thaler; since it is now 110, the measure of its valorisation is posited in its own form—as a proportion of the capital returned (reverted to its form as money) from the production process and from exchange, to the original capital. It is no longer posited as the relation of two qualitatively different things—objectified and living labour—or of necessary labour and the surplus labour produced. In as much as capital is posited as money, it is posited in the first determination of money, i.e. as the measure of value. But this value is here its own value, or the measure of its own valorisation. We shall return to this (in the section on profit).

The second form of money was that of means of circulation, and in this regard the money form of capital appears as a merely transitory moment, a form which capital assumes merely to be re-exchanged, but not, as in the case of money as means of circulation in general, to be exchanged for commodities—use values—for consumption, but for the particular use values of raw materials and instrument on the one hand, and living labour capacity on the other, in which it can recommence its turnover as capital.

[IV-41] In this determination it is *capital circulant,* which we shall discuss later. However, the end product of capital as money in its determination as means of circulation is the starting point of the act of production originating from *posited* capital. This is the point which we shall consider, before going any further.

(In the first determination [of capital as money], that of *measure,* the *new value* does indeed appear to be measured. But the distinction is purely formal: instead of surplus labour, money—i.e. surplus labour objectified in a particular commodity. But the *qualitative* nature of this new value, i.e. of the magnitude of the measure itself, also undergoes a change, which we shall discuss later.

Secondly, as means of circulation, the disappearance of the money form is now also only *formal.* It does not become *essential* until not only the first circuit but also the second has been completed. Thus, initially it results only in our standing at the beginning of the *valorisation process* once more. Consequently, it is at *this point* that we shall take up the development to start with.)

The third form of money as independent value maintaining itself negatively as against circulation, is capital which does not emerge from the production process as a commodity that re-enters exchange to become money, but which becomes a commodity in the form of self-relating value, and enters into circulation in this form. (*Capital and interest.*) This third form presupposes capital in the previous forms and simultaneously constitutes the transition from *capital* to *particular capitals,* the real capitals. For in this third form capital in its very concept is divided into two capitals with an independent existence. With this duality, plurality in general is then given. Such is the march of this development.

⫽Before we go any further, one more observation: *capital in general,* as distinct from particular capitals, does indeed appear (1) *only as an abstraction*; not an arbitrary abstraction but one which grasps the *differentia specifica* which distinguishes capital from all other forms of wealth or modes in which (social) production develops. These are determinations which are common to every capital as such, or which make any particular sum of values into capital. And the distinctions within this abstraction are likewise abstract particularities which characterise every type of capital, in that it is their position or negation (e.g. *capital fixe* or *capital circulant*).

But (2) capital in general is itself a *real* existence *distinct* from particular real capitals. This is recognised, even if it is not *understood,* by current political economy, and constitutes a very important element for its doctrine of evening up [of profits], etc. For instance, capital in this *general form,* although belonging to individual capitalists, in its *elemental form* as capital, constitutes capital which accumulates in banks or is distributed by them, and, as Ricardo puts it, is distributed most admirably in proportion to the needs of production.[a] Similarly, through loans, etc., it forms a level between the different countries. Therefore, if e.g. it is a law of capital in general that, in order to valorise itself, it must posit itself doubly, and must be valorised in this dual form, then e.g. the capital of a particular nation which represents capital *par excellence* in opposition to another, must be loaned to a third nation to be able to valorise itself. This double-positing, this relating itself to itself as to something alien, becomes damn real in this case. While on the one hand the general is therefore only a set of *differentia specifica in thought,* it is at the same time a *particular* real form alongside the form of the particular and individual.

(*Nous reviendrons plus tard sur ce point qui, quoique d'un caractère*

---

a D. Ricardo, *On the Principles of Political Economy, and Taxation,* pp. 81-82.— *Ed.*

plus logique[132] *qu'économiste, prouvera néanmoins d'une grande impor-*
tance dans le progrès de notre recherche.[a]

The same also in algebra. E.g. *a, b, c* are numbers as such; in
general; but they are also whole numbers as opposed to $^a/_b$, $^b/_c$, $^c/_b$,
$^c/_a$, $^b/_a$, etc., which, however, presuppose them as their general
elements.)//

[IV-42] The new value[b] is thus posited once more as capital, as
objectified labour entering into the process of exchange with living
labour, therefore dividing itself into a constant part—the objective
conditions of labour, material and instrument—and the conditions
for the subjective condition of labour, the existence of living
labour capacity, the NECESSARIES, means of subsistence for the
worker. At this second appearance of capital in this form, some
points appear clarified which were altogether unclear in its first
appearance—as money in its transition from its determination as
value to its determination as capital. Now they are explained by the
process of valorisation and production itself. In its first appearance,
the *presuppositions* themselves appeared outwardly to emerge from
circulation; as external presuppositions of the origin of capital,
and not therefore emerging from and explained by its inner
essence. These *external* presuppositions will now appear as
moments of the movement of capital itself, so that it has itself
presupposed them as its own moments—however they may have
arisen historically.

Within the production process itself, the surplus value, the
surplus value solicited by the compulsion of capital, appeared as
surplus labour; even in the form of living labour, which, however,
since it cannot produce something out of nothing, finds its
objective conditions already in existence. Now this *surplus labour*
appears objectified as *surplus product*, which in turn, to be
valorised as capital, must divide itself into two forms: the *objective
condition of labour*—material and instrument—and the subjective
condition—means of subsistence for the living labour now to be
set to work.

The general form of value—objectified labour, and objectified
labour emerging from circulation—is of course the general,

_____

[a] We shall return to this point, which, although it possesses a logical rather than
an economic character, will nevertheless prove to be of great importance in the
progress of our investigation.— *Ed.*

[b] Newly created surplus value.— *Ed.*

self-evident presupposition. Furthermore: the surplus product in its totality—objectifying the totality of surplus labour—now appears as *surplus capital* (as compared to the initial capital, before it had traversed this circuit), i.e. as exchange value become independent and confronting the living labour capacity as its *specific use value*. All the moments which confronted living labour capacity as *alien, external* powers, consuming and using it under *certain conditions independent of it,* are now posited as *its own product and result.*

Firstly: *Surplus value* or *surplus product* is nothing but a certain sum of objectified living labour—the sum of surplus labour. This new *value,* which confronts living labour as value independent of and exchanging itself with it, i.e. as capital, is the *product of labour.* It is itself nothing but the *surplus of labour in general over necessary labour*—in objective form and hence as *value.*

Secondly: The particular forms which this value must adopt to be valorised anew, i.e. to be posited as capital—on the one hand as raw material and instrument, on the other hand as means of subsistence for labour during the act of production—are likewise, therefore, merely *particular* forms of surplus labour itself. It is surplus labour which produces raw material and instrument in such a ratio—or it is itself objectively posited as raw material and instrument in such a proportion—that not only can a definite sum of necessary labour, i.e. living labour which reproduces the means of subsistence (their value), objectify itself in it and indeed do so continuously, i.e. can always begin anew the diremption into the objective and subjective conditions of its self-preservation and self-reproduction, but that living labour, by carrying out this process of reproducing its objective conditions, simultaneously posits raw material and instrument in such proportions that it can realise itself in them as *surplus labour, labour over and above necessary labour,* and can thus convert them into the material for the creation of *new* value. The objective conditions of *surplus labour* are limited to the proportion of raw materials and instrument over and above the requirements of necessary labour, while the objective conditions of necessary labour are divided within their objectivity into objective and subjective moments of labour, physical moments and subjective ones (means of subsistence for living labour). They therefore appear now, are now posited, as the product, the result, the objective form, the external existence, of surplus labour itself. Originally, by contrast, it appeared alien to living labour itself, appeared as an act of capital, that instrument and means of subsistence were available to an extent which made it possible to realise living labour not only as *necessary labour* but as *surplus labour* as well.

Thirdly: The independent being-for-itself of value vis-à-vis living labour capacity, hence its being as capital; the objective self-sufficient indifference, the *separateness* of the objective conditions of labour vis-à-vis living [IV-43] labour capacity, which goes so far that these conditions confront the person of the worker in the person of the capitalist—as a personification with its own will and interest; this absolute *divorce* and *separation* of property, i.e. of the physical conditions of labour, from living labour capacity—that they confront it as *alien property,* as the reality of another juridical person, as the absolute realm of *his* will; that on the other hand, therefore, labour appears as *alien labour* vis-à-vis the value personified in the capitalist, or vis-à-vis the conditions of labour—this absolute separation between property and labour, between living labour capacity and the conditions for its realisation, between objectified labour and living labour, between value and value-creating activity, hence also the fact that the content of labour is alien to the worker himself—this separation now also appears as the product of labour itself, as the objectification of its own moments. For through the very act of new production—which only confirmed the exchange between capital and living labour that preceded it—surplus labour and hence surplus value, the surplus product, the total result of labour altogether (of both surplus and necessary labour) are posited as capital, as exchange value confronting living labour capacity independently and indifferently, in other words as its mere use value.

Labour capacity has appropriated only the subjective conditions of necessary labour—the means of subsistence for productive labour capacity, i.e. for its reproduction as mere labour capacity separated from the conditions of its realisation—and it has posited these conditions themselves as *objects, values,* which confront it in an alien, commanding personification. It emerges from the process not only no richer but actually poorer than it entered into it. For not only has it created the conditions of necessary labour as conditions belonging to capital; but the valorisation inherent in it as a potentiality, the value-creating potentiality, now also exists as surplus value, surplus product, in a word, as capital, as domination over living labour capacity, as value endowed with its own power and will confronting it in its abstract, object-less, purely subjective poverty. Not only has it produced alien wealth and its own poverty, but also the relationship of this wealth as self-sufficient wealth to itself as poverty, which this wealth consumes to draw new life and spirit to itself and to valorise itself anew.

All this arose from the act of exchange in which the worker exchanged his living labour capacity for an amount of objectified labour, except that this objectified labour, these conditions for his being which are external to him, and the independent externality (to him) of these physical conditions, now appear as posited by himself, as *his own product*, as his own self-objectification as well as the objectification of himself as a power independent of himself, indeed dominating him, dominating him as a result of his own actions.

All the moments of *surplus capital* are the product of *alien labour — alien surplus labour* converted into capital: means of subsistence for necessary labour; the objective conditions — material and instrument — so that necessary labour can reproduce the value exchanged for it in means of subsistence; finally, the necessary amount of material and instrument so that new surplus labour can realise itself in them or new surplus value can be created.

It no longer seems here, as it still did in the first consideration of the production process, as if capital, for its part, brought with it some sort of value from circulation. The objective conditions of labour now appear as labour's product—both in so far as they are value in general, and as use values for production. But if capital thus appears as the product of labour, the product of labour for its part appears as capital—no longer as mere product nor exchangeable commodity, but as *capital*; objectified labour as dominion, command over living labour. It likewise appears as the product of labour that its product appears as *alien property*, as a mode of existence independently confronting living labour, equally as a *value*-for-itself; that the product of labour, objectified labour, is endowed with a soul of its own by living labour itself and establishes itself as an *alien power* confronting its creator.[a]

Considered from the standpoint of labour, the result of its activity in the production process thus appears to be that it rejects its realisation in objective conditions as an alien reality, and therefore posits itself as an insubstantial, merely necessitous labour capacity in face of this reality alienated from it, a reality not belonging to it but to others; that it posits its own reality not as a being-for-itself but as a mere being for something else, and hence

----
[a] See present edition, Vol. 3, pp. 270-82.— *Ed.*

also as a mere other-being or as the being of something else confronting itself.

The process of the realisation of labour is at the same time the process of its de-realisation. It posits itself objectively, but it posits this its objectivity as its own non-being, or as the being of its non-being—the being of capital. It returns back into itself as the mere potentiality of positing value or of valorisation, because the totality of real wealth, the world of real value, and equally the real conditions for its own [IV-44] realisation, are posited as independent existences facing it. It is the potentialities resting in living labour's own womb which come to exist as realities outside it as a result of the production process—but as *realities alien* to it, which constitute wealth in opposition to it.

In so far as the surplus product is valorised anew as surplus capital, enters anew the production process and the process of self-valorisation, it divides itself into (1) means of subsistence for the workers to be exchanged for living labour capacity. Let us define this part of *capital* as the *wages fund.* This wages fund, the part destined for the maintenance of labour capacity—and for its progressive maintenance, since surplus capital grows continuously—now appears as the product of *alien* labour, of labour alien to *capital,* just as much as do (2) the other components of [surplus] capital—the physical conditions for the reproduction of a value=these means of subsistence+a surplus value.

Furthermore, when we consider this surplus capital, the division of capital into a constant part—a part primevally existing before labour, namely raw materials and instruments of labour—and a variable part, i.e. the means of subsistence exchangeable for living labour capacity, appears to be a purely formal division in so far as both parts are equally *posited* by labour and equally posited by it as its own *presuppositions.* Now, however, this internal division of capital appears in such a way that labour's own product—objectified surplus labour—is divided into two components: (1) objective conditions for new utilisation of labour, and (2) a wages fund for maintaining the possibility of this living labour, i.e. for keeping living labour capacity alive, but in such a way that labour capacity can only reappropriate that part of its own result—of its own being in objective form—which is determined as wages fund, can only extract that part from the form of alien wealth confronting it, by not only reproducing its value but also by valorising the part of new capital which represents the objective conditions for the realisation of new surplus labour and surplus production or production of surplus values. Labour has itself created a new fund for the employment of new necessary labour, or, which is the same, a fund for the maintenance of new living labour capacities, of workers; but at the same time it has created the condition that this fund can be appropriated only if new surplus labour is employed on the extra part of surplus capital. Hence, by producing surplus capital, surplus value, labour has simultaneously created the real necessity for new surplus labour, surplus capital thus itself being the real possibility of both new surplus labour and new surplus capital.

It becomes evident here how progressively the objective world of wealth is enlarged through labour even as an alien power confronting it, and how it gains an ever wider and fuller existence, so that relatively, in relation to the values created or to the real conditions for the creation of value, the necessitous subjectivity of living labour capacity stands out in ever more glaring contrast. The more labour capacity—labour—objectifies itself, the greater becomes the objective world of values which confronts it as alien—as alien property. By creating surplus capital, labour imposes on itself the compulsion to create yet further surplus capital, etc., etc.

With regard to the original, not-surplus, capital the relation has changed for labour capacity in so far as (1) the part exchanged for necessary labour is reproduced by this labour itself, i.e. it no longer comes to labour out of circulation but is its own product; and (2) the part of value which represents the real conditions for the utilisation of living labour, in the form of raw material and instrument, has been maintained by living labour itself in the production process. And since every use value by its nature consists of transitory material, and exchange value is present, exists, only within use value, this maintenance=protection from destruction, or the negation of the transitory nature of the values owned by the capitalists. In this way, these values are posited as values-for-themselves, as *imperishable wealth*. Hence only in the production process has living labour posited this original sum of values as capital.

Now from the standpoint of capital: so far as *surplus capital* is considered, the capitalist represents value-for-itself, money in its third moment, wealth obtained by simple *appropriation of alien labour*. For each moment of surplus capital (material, instrument, means of subsistence) resolves into *alien labour,* which the capitalist has not appropriated by means of *exchange* for already existing values but which he has appropriated *without exchange*. True, the exchange of a *part of the values belonging to him,* or of *objectified labour* possessed by him, for alien living labour capacity, appears as the *original condition* for [the production of] this *surplus capital.*

The possession of *values* by the capitalist, part of which he *formally* exchanges for living labour capacity, appears to be the condition for the formation of *surplus capital I,* if that is what we call the surplus capital arising from the original production process, i.e. the condition for the *appropriation of alien labour, of objectified alien labour.* We say "formally", because living labour has to replace and return to the capitalist these *exchanged* values as well. Be that as it may. In any case, it appears as a condition for the formation of *surplus capital I,* i.e. for the appropriation of alien labour or of the values in which it has objectified itself, that there be an exchange of values belonging to the capitalist, thrown into circulation by him, and supplied to living labour capacity by him—of values which do *not* derive from his [IV-45] *exchange* with living labour, or from his relation as *capital* to *labour.*

But now let us think of this surplus capital being thrown again into the production process, realising its surplus value in exchange once more, and appearing once more as new surplus capital at the beginning of a third production process. This *surplus capital II* has different presuppositions from those of surplus capital I. The presupposition of surplus capital I was the existence of values belonging to the capitalist and thrown by him into circulation, or more precisely into the exchange with living labour capacity. The presupposition of surplus capital II is nothing but the existence of surplus capital I; i.e. in other words, the presupposition that the capitalist has already appropriated alien labour without exchange. This enables him to begin the process again and again. True, in order to create surplus capital II, he had to exchange a part of the value of surplus capital I in the form of means of subsistence for living labour capacity. But what he thus exchanged were values which he did not originally put into circulation from his own funds, but alien objectified labour which he appropriated without giving any equivalent for it, and which he now exchanges again for alien living labour, just as the material, etc., in which this new labour is realised and produces surplus value has come into his possession without exchange, by means of simple appropriation.

Past appropriation of alien labour now appears as the simple condition for new appropriation of alien labour. In other words, his possession of alien labour in objective [physical] form, in the form of values already in existence, appears to be the condition for his appropriation of new alien *living* labour capacity, hence of surplus labour, labour without equivalent. That he should already be confronting living labour as capital, this appears to be the sole condition not only for him maintaining himself as capital, but for him as growing capital *appropriating* alien labour without equivalent on an increasing scale, or extending his power, his existence as capital vis-à-vis living labour capacity, while constantly positing and repositing living labour capacity as living labour capacity in its subjective, insubstantial necessitousness.

Property in past or objectified alien labour appears as the sole condition for further appropriation of present or living alien labour. In so far as a surplus capital I was created by means of simple exchange between objectified labour and living labour capacity—an exchange wholly based on the laws of exchange of equivalents as estimated by the quantity of labour or labour time contained in them—and *in so far as* this exchange, speaking juridically, presupposed nothing but the right of property of each person in his own products and his right to freely dispose of them—but in so far as the relationship of surplus capital II to I is therefore a consequence of this first relationship [between labour and capital]—we see that by a peculiar logic the right of property on the side of capital is dialectically transformed into the right to an alien product or into the right of property in alien labour, the right to appropriate alien labour without equivalent; on the side of labour capacity it is transformed into the duty to relate itself towards its own labour or its own product as *alien property.* The right to property is inverted into the right on the one side to appropriate alien labour and the duty on the other side to respect the product of one's own labour and one's own labour itself as values belonging to others.

But the exchange of equivalents which appeared as the initial operation, and which juridically expressed the right to property, has been reversed in such a way that on the one side only an apparent exchange takes place, in that the part of capital exchanged for living labour capacity is, in the first place, itself *alien labour* appropriated without equivalent, and in that, secondly, it *must be replaced by labour capacity with a surplus,* i.e. it is not IN FACT given away but only transformed from one form into another. The relationship of exchange has therefore completely disappeared, or it has become a *mere semblance.*

Furthermore, the right to property originally appeared to be based on one's own labour. Now property appears as the right to alien labour and as the impossibility for labour to appropriate its own product. The complete separation of property, and even more of wealth, from labour now appears as a consequence of the law which arose from their identity.

Finally, the result of the process of production and valorisation now appears to be above all the reproduction and new production of the *very relationship of capital and labour, of capitalist and worker.* IN FACT, this social relationship, this relationship of production, appears to be an even more important result of the process than its material results. And more particularly, within this process the worker produces himself as labour capacity and produces the capital confronting him, while at the same time the capitalist produces himself as capital and produces the living labour capacity confronting him. Each reproduces himself by reproducing his other, his negation. The capitalist produces labour as alien; labour produces the product as alien. The capitalist produces the worker and the worker the capitalist, etc.

As soon as production based on capital is presupposed—actually money has been transformed into capital only *at the end of the first production* process, which resulted in its reproduction and the new production of surplus capital I; but surplus capital I is itself only *posited,* realised, as surplus capital once it has produced surplus capital II, i.e. once the presuppositions of money in the process of becoming capital which still lie outside the movement of *real* capital have disappeared, and capital therefore has IN FACT itself and in accordance with its immanent essence posited the very conditions from which it sets out in production—the condition that the capitalist must bring into circulation values [IV-46] created by his own labour or in some other way—excepting only values created by already existing, past wage labour—in order to posit himself as capital, belongs to the antediluvian conditions of capital; to its *historical presuppositions,* which, precisely as such *historical* presuppositions, have vanished and therefore belong to the *history of its formation* but by no means to its *contemporary* history, i.e. do not belong to the real system of the mode of production dominated by it.

If e.g. the flight of serfs into the cities is one of the *historical* conditions and presuppositions for the development of cities, it is not a *condition,* a moment, of the reality of fully developed city life, but belongs to its *past* presuppositions, to the presuppositions of its becoming, which are transcended in its being. The conditions and presuppositions of the *becoming,* the *emergence,* of capital imply precisely that it is not yet in being but is only *becoming.* Hence they disappear with the development of real capital, the capital which, setting out from its own reality, itself posits the conditions for its realisation. Thus e.g., while the process in which money or value-for-itself originally becomes capital presupposes an accumulation by the capitalist—perhaps by savings made on the products and values created by his own work, etc.—which he has achieved as *non-capitalist*; while, therefore, the presuppositions for the transformation of money into capital appear as the given, external *presuppositions* for the emergence of capital; as soon as capital has become capital, it creates its own presuppositions, namely the possession of the real conditions for the creation of new values *without exchange*—by means of its own production process.

These presuppositions which originally appeared as prerequisites of its becoming—and therefore could not arise from its action *as capital*—now appear as results of its own realisation, reality, as *posited* by it—*not as conditions of its emergence, but as results of its being.* It no longer sets out from presuppositions in order to become, but is itself presupposed, and, setting out from itself, it itself creates the presuppositions for its maintenance and growth. The conditions, therefore, which preceded the creation of surplus capital I, or which express the becoming of capital, do not fall within the sphere of the mode of production for which capital serves as the presupposition. They lie behind it as preliminary historical stages of its becoming, just as the processes through which the Earth was transformed from a fluid sea of fire and vapour into its present form, lie beyond its life as finished Earth. This means that individual capitals can still emerge e.g. by HOARDING. But the HOARD is transformed into capital only by the exploitation of labour.

The bourgeois economists, who consider capital to be an eternal and *natural* (not historical) form of production, nevertheless try to justify it by declaring the conditions of its becoming as the conditions of its present realisation, i.e. they present the moments in which the capitalist still appropriates as non-capitalist—because he is only in the process of becoming—as the VERY CONDITIONS in which he appropriates *as capitalist.* These attempts at apologetics demonstrate a bad conscience and the inability to bring the mode of appropriation of capital as capital into harmony with the *general laws of property* proclaimed by capitalist society itself.

On the other hand—and this is much more important for us—our method indicates the points at which historical analysis must be introduced, or at which bourgeois economy as a mere historical form of the production process points beyond itself towards earlier historical modes of production. To present the laws of the bourgeois economy, it is not necessary therefore to write the *real history of the production relations.* But the correct analysis and deduction of these relations as relations which have themselves arisen historically, always leads to primary equations— like e.g. empirical numbers in natural science—which point to a past lying behind this system. These indications, together with the correct grasp of the present, then also offer the key to the understanding of the past—a work in its own right, which we hope to be able to undertake as well. This correct approach, moreover, leads to points which indicate the transcendence of the present form of production relations, the movement coming into being, thus FORESHADOWING the future. If, on the one hand, the pre-bourgeois phases appear as *merely historical,* i.e. transcended premisses, so [on the other hand] the present conditions of production appear as conditions which *transcend themselves* and thus posit themselves as *historical premisses* for a new state of society.

If we consider first of all the relationship as it has become, value which has become capital, and living labour as mere use value confronting it, so that living labour appears as mere means for the utilisation of objectified, dead labour, for its permeation with a life-giving soul while losing its own soul to it—and having produced as a result alien wealth on the one hand, but on the other, as its own property, only the necessitousness of living labour capacity—then we can see clearly that the physical conditions of living labour (the material in which it is utilised, the instrument by means of which it is utilised, [IV-47] and the means of subsistence which kindle the flame of living labour capacity into activity and prevent its being extinguished, and supply the necessary matter for its life process) are posited in and through the process itself as alien, independent existences; in other words as the mode of existence of an *alien person,* as self-sufficient values-for-themselves, and thus as values which form wealth alien to the subjective labour capacity standing in isolation from them, the wealth of the capitalist.

The objective conditions of living labour appear as *separate* values, *become independent* as against living labour capacity as subjective being, which therefore appears, as against them, only as value of *another kind* (distinct from them not as value, but as use value). Once this separation is presupposed, the production process can only produce it anew, reproduce it, and that on a larger scale. How it does this, we have already seen. The objective conditions of living labour capacity are presupposed as an independent existence confronting it, as the objectivity of a subject distinct from living labour capacity and independently confronting it. The reproduction and *valorisation*, i.e. the expansion, of these *objective conditions* is therefore simultaneously their reproduction and their new production as the wealth of an alien subject, indifferent to and independently confronting labour capacity. What is reproduced and newly produced is not only the *being* of these objective conditions of living labour but *their being as independent values, i.e. values belonging to an alien subject, confronting this living labour capacity.*

The objective conditions of labour gain a subjective existence as against the living labour capacity—capital gives rise to the capitalist. On the other hand, the purely subjective being of labour capacity vis-à-vis its own conditions gives it a merely indifferent objective form as against these conditions—it is only a *value* of a particular use value *alongside* the conditions of its own utilisation as *values* of a different use value. Instead of being realised in the production process as conditions for its realisation, living labour capacity on the contrary emerges from the process as a mere condition for *their* valorisation and preservation as values-for-themselves over against it.

The material on which it works is *alien* material; just as the instrument is an *alien* instrument; its labour appears as a mere accessory to them as substance and therefore objectifies itself in things not belonging to *it*. Indeed, living labour itself appears as *alien* vis-à-vis living labour capacity whose labour it is, whose life it expresses, for it is surrendered to capital in return for objectified labour, for the product of labour itself. Labour capacity relates to it as to something alien, and if capital wanted to pay it *without* setting it to work, it would make the bargain with pleasure. Its own labour is therefore just as alien to it—and it really *is* alien, as regards its direction, etc.—as the material and instrument. Therefore, naturally, the product appears to it as a combination of alien material, alien instrument and alien labour—as *alien property*, and after production it has only become poorer by the life force expended; but begins the DRUDGERY anew of itself as a merely subjective labour capacity separated from the condition of its life.

The recognition of the products as its own, and its awareness that its separation from the conditions of its realisation is improper and imposed by force, is an enormous consciousness, and is itself the product of the mode of production based on capital, and just as much the KNELL TO ITS DOOM as the consciousness of the slave that he cannot be the *property of another,* his consciousness of being a person, reduced slavery to an artificial lingering existence, and made it impossible for it to continue to provide the basis of production.

However, if we consider the original relation, before money entered into the process of self-valorisation, we come up against various conditions which must have arisen, or been given, historically, for money to become capital and for labour to become labour positing, producing capital, i.e. wage labour. (*Wage labour,* here in the strict economic sense, which is the only one we need—and we shall later have to distinguish it from other forms of labour for day-wages, etc.—is labour which posits, produces capital, i.e. living labour which produces the objective conditions for its realisation as activity, as well as the objective moments of its being as labour *capacity,* as alien powers confronting itself, as *values-for-themselves independent of it.*)

The essential conditions are posited in the relationship itself as it originally appeared: (1) On the one side, the existence of living labour capacity as a purely *subjective* existence, separated from the moments of its objective reality; therefore separated just as much from the *conditions* of living labour as from the *means of existence, the means of subsistence,* the means of self-maintenance of living *labour capacity*; the living possibility of labour on one side in this complete abstraction. (2) On the other side, the value or objectified labour must be an accumulation of use values, sufficiently large to provide the objective conditions not merely for the production of the products or values necessary to reproduce or maintain living labour capacity, but also to absorb surplus labour, to [IV-48] supply the objective material for it. (3) A system of free exchange—money circulation—between the two sides; a relationship between the two extremes which is based upon exchange values, not on the lord-subject relationship, i.e. production which does not directly supply the means of subsistence to the producers but is mediated by exchange, and which cannot therefore usurp alien labour directly but must buy it from the worker himself by means of exchange. Finally (4) the one side—which represents the objective conditions of labour in the form of independent values-for-themselves—must present itself as *value* and regard as its ultimate aim the positing of value, self-valorisation, the creation of money—not immediate enjoyment or creation of use value.

So long as *both* sides exchange their labour with one another only in the form of *objectified* labour, the relation is impossible. It is equally impossible if *living labour capacity* itself appears as the property of the other side and not, therefore, as exchanger. (That slavery can exist at individual points within the bourgeois system of production, does not contradict this. But slavery is then possible only because it does not exist at other points, and represents an anomaly in relation to the bourgeois system itself.)

The conditions under which the relationship originally appears, or which appear as historical presuppositions for its becoming, exhibit at first glance a dual character—on the one side dissolution of lower forms of living labour, on the other side dissolution of happier forms of it.[a]

To start with, the first presupposition is the transcendence of the relation of slavery or serfdom. Living labour capacity belongs to itself and disposes by means of exchange over the application of its own energy. The two sides confront each other as persons. *Formally,* their relation is that of equal and free exchangers.

That this form is mere *appearance,* and *deceptive appearance* at that, appears, as far as the juridical relationship is concerned, as an *external* matter. What the free worker sells is always only a particular, specific measure of the application of his energy. Above every specific application of energy stands labour capacity as a totality. The worker sells the specific application of his energy to a specific capitalist, whom he confronts independently as a *single individual.* Clearly, this is not his [real] relationship to the existence of capital as capital, i.e. to the class of capitalists. Nevertheless, as far as the individual, real person is concerned, a wide field of choice, caprice and therefore of formal freedom is left to him. In the relation of slavery, he belongs to the *individual, specific* owner, and is his labouring machine. As the totality of the application of his energy, as labour capacity, he is a thing belonging to another, and hence does not relate as a subject to the specific application of his energy, or to the living act of labour. In the relation of serfdom, he appears as an integral element of landed property itself; he is an appurtenance of the soil, just like draught-cattle. In the relation of slavery, the worker is nothing but a living labouring

---

[a] In reproducing this passage in his 1861-63 manuscript (Notebook XXII, p. 1397) Marx added here: "for the immediate producer. On the one hand, dissolution of slavery and serfdom. On the other, dissolution of the form under which the means of production are immediately available as the property of the immediate producer, whether his work is *predominantly* directed at use value (agriculture) or exchange value (urban work). Dissolution of the form of *community* in which the worker as organ of this naturally evolved community is, at the same time, posited as owner or possessor of his means of production." — *Ed.*

machine, which therefore has a value for others, or rather is a value. Labour capacity in its totality appears to the free worker as his own property, one of his own moments, over which he as subject exercises control, and which he maintains by selling it. This to be developed later under wage labour.

The exchange of objectified labour for living labour does not [as such] constitute either capital on the one hand or wage labour on the other. The entire class of so-called *services,* from boot-black up to King, falls into this category. The same is true of the free day-labourer, whom we encounter sporadically wherever either the Oriental community or the Western commune of free landowners has broken up into its individual elements—as a result of an increase in population, release of prisoners of war, chance occurrences through which individuals were impoverished and deprived of the objective conditions for their SELF-SUSTAINING LABOUR, as a result of the division of labour, etc.

If *A* exchanges a value or money, i.e. objectified labour, in order to obtain a service from *B,* i.e. living labour, this can belong:

(1) within the relation of simple circulation. Both parties in fact exchange only use values with each other; the one means of subsistence, the other labour, a service, which the former wishes to consume either directly—a personal service—or he supplies the latter with the material, etc., in which that other person supplies him, through his labour, by the objectification of his labour, a use value designed for *A*'s consumption. E.g. when the peasant takes into his house a tramping tailor, such as existed in the past, and gives him the material to make clothes with. Or if I give money to a doctor to patch up my health. What is important in these cases is the service which the two perform for each other. *Do ut facias* appears here on quite the same level as *facio ut des* or *do ut des.*[a]

The man who uses material which I gave him to make clothes for me, gives me a use value. But instead of giving it to me directly in objectified form, he gives it in the form of activity. I give him a finished use value; he produces another one for me. The distinction between past objectified labour and living present labour appears here as a merely formal distinction between the different tenses of labour, which is in the perfect tense at one time and in the present at another. It appears in fact merely as a

a "I give that you may make", "I make that you may give", "I give that you may give" (contractual formulas in Roman law), *Corpus iuris civilis, Digesta* XIX, 5.5.— Ed.

formal distinction mediated by division of labour and exchange, whether *B* himself produces his own means of subsistence, or whether he obtains them from *A* and, instead of producing the means of subsistence directly, produces clothes for which he obtains his subsistence from *A* in exchange. In both cases, he can take possession of the use value owned by *A* only by giving him an equivalent for it, an equivalent which is ultimately always reducible to his own living labour, whatever the objective form it may assume, either before the exchange has been agreed, or as a result of it. Now, the clothes contain not only a particular form-giving labour—a particular utility bestowed upon the material by the act of labour—but also a certain quantity of labour; therefore not only use value but *value* in general, *value* as such. But this value does not exist for *A*, because he consumes the clothes and is not a clothes merchant. Therefore he has obtained the labour in exchange as an activity which creates utility, use value, not as *labour* which *posits value*.

[IV-49] In the case of personal services, this use value is consumed as such, without passing from the form of movement into that of a thing. If, as is frequently the case in simple relationships, the person performing the service does not receive *money* but direct use values, even the semblance disappears that either party to the exchange is concerned with *values* as distinct from use values. But even assuming that *A* pays money for the service, *A*'s money has not thereby been converted into capital. Rather, it is posited as mere means of circulation in order to obtain an object of consumption, a particular use value. Consequently, this act is not one which produces wealth but, on the contrary, one which consumes it. What concerns *A* is not at all that labour as such, a certain labour time, i.e. *value*, is objectified in the cloth, but that a certain need is satisfied. *A* sees his money not *valorised* but *devalued* by converting [it] from the form of value into that of use value. Labour here is not obtained in exchange as use value for value, but as itself a specific use value, as a value for use. The more frequently *A* repeats the exchange, the poorer he becomes. This exchange is not an *act by which he enriches himself*, not an act which *creates value*, but one by which he *devalues* existing values in his possession. The money which *A* exchanges here for living labour—service in kind or a service which is objectified in a thing—is not *capital* but *revenue*; money as means of circulation in order to obtain use value; money in which value is posited in a merely transient form; not money which seeks to preserve and valorise itself as such through the purchase of labour. The exchange of *money as revenue,* as mere means of circulation, for living labour, can never posit money as capital, nor, therefore, labour as wage labour in the economic sense.

It needs no elaborate explanation to show that the consumption of money is not the same as its production. In conditions where most surplus labour takes the form of agricultural labour, and where the landowner is therefore the owner of both surplus labour and surplus product, it is the revenue of the landowner which makes up the wages fund for the free workers, for the workers in manufacture (here artisans) as against the agricultural labourers.

His exchange with them is a form of the landowner's consumption—he divides another part of his revenue directly, for personal services, often for only the semblance of service, with a horde of RETAINERS. In Asiatic societies, where the monarch is the exclusive owner of the surplus produce of the land, the exchange of his revenue with the "FREE HANDS", as Steuart calls them,[a] gives rise to whole cities which are *au fond* nothing but migratory camps. In this relationship there is nothing of wage labour, although it *can* stand in contradiction to slavery and serfdom; it *need* not do so, however, for it constantly recurs under different forms of overall organisation of labour. In so far as *money* mediates this exchange, price determination will become important for both parties, but for *A* only in so far as he does not wish to pay too much for the *use value* of labour; not in so far as he is concerned about its *value.* The essence of the relationship is not affected by the fact that this price, originally largely conventional and traditional, is gradually determined economically, at first by the condition of demand and supply and eventually by the production costs at which the vendors themselves of these living services can be produced; for the determination of price remains only a formal moment for the exchange of mere use values. This determination itself, however, arises from other relationships, from the general laws and self-determination of the dominant mode of production, acting, as it were, behind the back of this particular act of exchange.

One of the forms in which this type of payment first occurs in ancient communities is the *standing army.* The pay of the common soldier is also reduced to a minimum, is determined purely by the production costs for which he can be procured. But what he

---

[a] J. Steuart, *An Inquiry into the Principles of Political Oeconomy,* Vol. I, pp. 30-31, 40, 48, 151, 153, 176, 178, 179 and 396.— *Ed.*

receives in exchange for his service is the revenue of the State, not *capital*.[17]

In bourgeois society itself all kinds of exchange of personal services for revenue belong in this category—including labour for personal consumption, cooking, sewing, etc., gardening, etc., right up to all the unproductive classes, civil servants, doctors, lawyers, scholars, etc. All MENIAL SERVANTS, etc. By means of the services they perform—often forced [upon the client]—all these workers, from the lowest to the highest, obtain for themselves a share of the surplus product, of the *revenue* of the capitalist. But it does not occur to anyone to think that through the exchange of his revenue for such services, i.e. by his private consumption, the capitalist posits himself as capital. Rather, he thereby spends the fruits of his capital. The nature of the relationship is not affected by the fact that the proportions in which revenue is exchanged for this type of living labour are themselves determined by the general laws of production.

As we have already mentioned in the section on *money*,[a] it is the person performing a service who here essentially posits *value*; who converts a use value—a certain type of labour, service, etc.—into *value, money*. In the Middle Ages, therefore, those who are orientated towards the production and accumulation of money proceed partly not from the side of the consuming landed nobility, but from the side of living labour; they accumulate and thus become δυνάμει[b] capitalists for a later period. Capitalists partly derive from emancipated serfs.

It therefore does not depend on the relation in general but on the natural, specific quality of the service performed, whether the recipient of payment obtains a day-wage, or a fee, or a Civil List—and whether he appears superior or inferior in rank to the person paying him for his service.

True, under the rule of capital, all these relationships will become more or less *dishonoured*. But this does not belong here yet, this *de-sanctification* of personal services, however exalted a character tradition, etc., may have attributed to them.

Capital and therefore wage labour are not, then, constituted simply by an exchange of *objectified labour* for *living labour*—which from this viewpoint appear as two different determinations, as use values in different form; the one as determination in objective

---

[a] See this volume, pp. 202-03. (The passage is in the section on capital, not in that on money.)— *Ed.*

[b] Potentially.— *Ed.*

form, the other in subjective form. They are constituted by the exchange of objectified labour as *value*, as self-sufficient value, for living labour as *its* use value, as use value not for a certain specific use or consumption, but as use value for *value*.

[IV-50] In the exchange of money for labour or service for immediate consumption, a real exchange always takes place; that *amounts of labour* are exchanged on both sides is merely of *formal* interest, for measuring the *particular* forms of the utility of labour in relation to one another. This concerns only the *form* of the exchange; it does not constitute its *content*. When capital is exchanged for labour, *value* is not the measure for the exchange of two use values but the *content of the exchange* itself.

(2) In periods of the dissolution of *pre-bourgeois* relationships, we sporadically find free workers whose service is bought not for the purpose of consumption but for that of *production*. But, *firstly*, even on a large scale only for the production of *direct* use values, not of *values*. *Secondly*, if the nobleman e.g. employs the free worker alongside his serf, and moreover resells part of his product, and the free worker thus produces *value* for him, this exchange takes place only for the superfluous product and only in the interest of superfluity, of *luxury consumption*; is thus *au fond* only a disguised purchase of alien labour for direct consumption or as use value. Incidentally, where these free workers increase in number and this relationship becomes more extensive, the old mode of production—commune, patriarchal, feudal, etc.—is in a state of dissolution and the elements for real wage labour are coming into being. But these free servants [Knechte] can also appear and then disappear again, as e.g. in Poland, without the mode of production being thereby changed.

//In order to express the relations into which capital and wage labour enter as *property relationships* or *laws*, we have only to express the conduct of both sides in the *process of valorisation* as a *process of appropriation*. For instance, the fact that surplus labour is posited as surplus value of capital means that the worker does not appropriate the product of his own labour; that it appears to him as *alien property*; and, conversely, that *alien labour* appears as the property of capital. This second law of bourgeois property, which is the inversion of the first [the law that the product of labour is the property of the labourer]—and which through the right of inheritance, etc., obtains an existence independent of the chance transitory existence of individual capitalists—is just as much established as a law as the first. The first law is the identity of labour with property; the second is labour as negated property or property as the negation of the alien quality of alien labour.

IN FACT, in the production process of capital, as will become more evident in the further analysis of that process, labour is a totality—a combination of labours—the individual components of which are alien to one another, so that the aggregate of labour, as a totality, is *not* the *work* of the individual worker, and, moreover, it is the work of the different workers taken together only in so far as they are combined [by an external force]—not entering into [voluntary] combination with each other. In combination, this labour likewise appears subservient to an alien will and an alien intelligence, and directed by the latter—having *its animate unity* outside itself, and subordinated in its material unity to the *objective unity* of *machinery*, of *capital fixe*, which as an *animated monster* objectifies the scientific idea, and is in fact the concentrating element, which in no way relates to the individual worker as instrument, but to which, on the contrary, he is affixed as an animated individual spot [of labour], a living isolated accessory to it.

Combined labour is thus in two ways a combination *in itself*; for it is neither combination as the relationship of individuals working together to one another, nor as their going beyond their specific individualised task or beyond [the activity proper to] their instrument of labour. Hence, if the worker relates to the product of his labour as alien, he no less relates to combined labour as alien, and to his own labour as an expression of his life which, though it certainly belongs to him, is alien to him and brought out under duress, and which Adam Smith, etc., therefore conceived as a *burden, sacrifice,* etc.[a] Labour itself, like its product, is *negated in its form as the labour of the particular, individualised worker.* The negated individualised labour is now in fact posited as social or combined labour. However, *social or combined labour* thus posited—both as activity and as having passed over into the inert form of the object—is simultaneously posited directly as an other in relation to really existing individual labour—both as *alien objectivity* (alien property) and *alien subjectivity* (that of capital). Thus capital represents both labour and its product as negated individualised labour, and hence as the negated property of the individualised worker. It is therefore the existence of social labour—its combination as subject and also as object—but it is this existence as itself existing independently as against its real

―――――――
[a] A. Smith, *An Inquiry into the Nature and Causes of the Wealth of Nations*, Vol. I, London, 1835, pp. 104-05.— *Ed.*

moments—i.e. as a *separate* existence beside them. Capital for its part therefore appears as the trespassing subject and as the owner of *alien labour,* and its own relation is as complete a contradiction as is that of wage labour.//

[FORMS PRECEDING CAPITALIST PRODUCTION][133]

One of the prerequisites of wage labour and one of the historical conditions for capital is free labour and the exchange of free labour for money, in order to reproduce money and to valorise it, in order to be consumed by money, not as use value for enjoyment, but as use value for money. Another prerequisite is the separation of free labour from the objective conditions of its realisation—from the means and material of labour. This means above all separation of the worker from the land, which functions as his natural workshop, hence the dissolution both of free small holdings and of communal landed property, based on the Oriental commune.

In both these forms the labourer relates to the objective conditions of his labour as to his property; this is the natural unity of labour with its physical prerequisites. Hence the labourer has an objective existence independent of his labour. The individual relates to himself as proprietor, as master [IV-51] of the conditions of his reality. He relates in the same way to the others, and—depending on whether this *prerequisite* derives from the community or from the individual families constituting the community—he relates to the others as co-proprietors, as so many incarnations of the common property, or as independent proprietors coexisting with him, independent private proprietors, beside whom the common property which formerly absorbed everything and embraced them all subsists as a special *ager publicus*ᵃ separate from the numerous private landed proprietors.

In both forms, the individuals relate not as workers but as proprietors—as members of a community who also work. The purpose of this labour is not the *creation of value,* although they may perform surplus labour in order to exchange it for *alien,* i.e. surplus, products. Its purpose is the maintenance of the individual proprietor and his family as well as of the community as a whole. The positing of the individual as a *worker,* who is stripped of all qualities except this one, is itself a *historical* product.

ᵃ Common land, state-owned land in ancient Rome.— *Ed.*

In the earliest form of this landed property, a naturally evolved community is the first prerequisite: the family, and the family expanded into a tribe,[134] or [formed] through INTERMARRIAGE between families, or a combination of tribes. Since we may assume that *pastoralism,* or more generally a *nomadic way of life,* is the first form of existence; that the tribe does not settle on a certain site but that it grazes off what it finds there and moves on—men are not settled by nature (unless perhaps in such an exceptionally fertile region that they settle on a tree like the monkeys; otherwise, they are ROAMING like the wild animals)—the *tribal community,* the natural community, is not the *result* but the *precondition of the common* (temporary) *appropriation* and *use of the soil.*

When men finally do settle down, the degree of change which this original community will undergo, will depend partly on various external, climatic, geographical, physical, etc., conditions and partly on their particular natural disposition, etc.—their tribal character. The naturally evolved tribal community, or, if you wish, the herd—common ties of blood, language, custom, etc.—is the first precondition for the *appropriation of the objective conditions* of their life, and of the life activity reproducing and objectifying itself (activity as herdsmen, hunters, agriculturalists, etc.).

The earth is the great workshop, the arsenal which provides both the means and the materials of labour, as well as the location, the *basis* of the community. Men relate naively to it as the *property of the community,* and of the community which produces and reproduces itself in living labour. Each individual regards himself as a *proprietor* or *owner* only qua MEMBER of such a community.

The real *appropriation* through the process of labour takes place under these *preconditions,* which are not themselves the *product* of labour but appear as its natural or *divine* preconditions. This form, where the fundamental relationship is the same [common property in land], may realise itself in a variety of ways. It does not contradict it at all, for instance, that, as in most *Asiatic* fundamental forms, the *all-embracing unity* which stands above all these small communities may appear as the *higher* or as the *sole proprietor,* and the real communities, therefore, merely as *hereditary* occupiers. Since the *unity* is the real proprietor, and the real precondition of common property, it is quite possible for it to appear as something *distinct* over and above the many real, particular communities. The individual is then IN FACT propertyless, or property—i.e. the relation of the individual to the *natural* conditions of labour and reproduction as belonging to him, as the objective body of his subjectivity present in the form of inorganic nature—appears to be mediated for him through a concession from the total unity—a unity realised in the despot as the father of the many communities—to the individual via the particular commune. It therefore follows that the surplus product (which, incidentally, is legally determined in consequence of the real appropriation through labour) belongs to this highest unity.

Hence, in the midst of Oriental despotism and the absence of property which it juridically appears to imply, there in fact exists as its foundation this tribal or communal property, mostly produced through a combination of manufacture and agriculture within the small community, which thereby becomes completely SELF-SUSTAINING and comes to contain within itself all the conditions necessary for reproduction and extended production. Part of its surplus labour belongs to the higher community, which ultimately exists as a *person,* and this surplus labour is expressed both in tribute, etc., and in common labours performed for the glorification of the unity, which is in part the real despot and in part the imagined tribal being, the god.

In so far as it is actually realised in labour, this type of communal property can appear in two ways: either the small communities vegetate independently side by side, and within each the individual labours independently with his family on the plot assigned to him. (A certain amount of labour will also be performed for the *communal reserve*—for INSURANCE, so to speak—on the one hand; and [on the other] for *defraying the costs of the community as such*, i.e. for war, religious worship, etc.; lordly dominion, in its most original sense, emerges only at this point, e.g. in the Slavonic and Romanian communities, etc. Herein lies the transition to labour services, etc.) Or the unity can extend to the communality of labour itself, which may be systematically organised, as in Mexico and especially Peru, among the ancient Celts, and among some tribes in India.

Furthermore, the communality within the tribal body may appear either in such a way that its unity is represented in one head of the tribal kinship group, or else as a relationship between the heads of families. The former will produce a more despotic, the latter a more democratic form of this community. The communal conditions for real appropriation through labour, such as *irrigation systems* (very important among the Asian peoples), means of communication, etc., then appear as the work of the higher unity—of the despotic government poised above the lesser communities. Cities in the proper sense arise alongside these villages only where the location is especially favourable to foreign trade, or where the head of State and his satraps exchange their revenue (the surplus product) for labour, spend it as LABOUR funds.

[IV-52] The second form [of property] has, like the first, given rise to substantial local, historical, etc., variations. It is the product of a more dynamic historical life, of the fate and modification of the original tribes. It also assumes the *communal system* as the first presupposition, but not, as in the first case, as the substance of which the individuals are mere accidental factors, or of which they are only naturally evolved parts. It does not presuppose land as its basis, but the city as already constructed seat [centre] of the rural population (landowners). The cultivated fields are the territory of the city, whereas [in the first form of property] the village was a mere appendage to the land.

However great the obstacles the land may put in the way of those who till it and really appropriate it, it offers no resistance to the people relating to it as the inorganic nature of the living individual, as his workshop, his means of labour, the object of his labour, and the means of subsistence of the subject. The difficulties encountered by the organised community can arise only from other communities which either have already occupied the territory or disturb the community in its occupation of it. War is therefore the great all-embracing task, the great communal labour, which is required either for the occupation of the objective conditions for being alive, or for the protection and perpetuation of this occupation. The community consisting of families is therefore organised above all on military lines, for purposes of war, and this is one of the conditions of its being there as a proprietor. Concentration of settlement in the city is the foundation of this warlike organisation.

The nature of the tribal system leads to the differentiation of kinship groups into higher and lower, and this differentiation is developed further through intermixture with subjugated tribes, etc.

Communal property—as State property, *ager publicus*—is here separate from private property. The property of the individual is here not itself direct communal property, as in our first case, where the individual is not a proprietor in separation from the community, but rather merely the occupier [of the plot of communal land allotted to him].

The less it is the case that individual property can be utilised only through communal labour (such as e.g. the irrigation systems of the Orient); the more the purely naturally evolved character of the tribe breaks down through the movement of history or migration; the more the tribe moves away from its original place of settlement and occupies *foreign* territory, thus entering into essentially new conditions of labour and stimulating the development of the energies of the individual; and the more the communal character of the tribe appears, and must appear, rather as a negative unity as against the outside world—the more are the conditions given under which the individual can become a *private proprietor* of land—of a particular plot—whose particular cultivation falls to him and his family.

The community as a State is on the one hand the relationship of these free and equal private proprietors to each other, their combination against the outside world—and it is at the same time their safeguard. Communal life is here based as much on the fact that its members are working landed proprietors, smallholding peasants, as the peasants' independence is based on their mutual relation as members of the community, on safeguarding the *ager publicus* for the communal needs and the communal glory, etc. To be a member of the community remains the precondition for the appropriation of land, but as a member of the community the individual is a private proprietor. He relates to his private property as to land but at the same time as to his being as a member of the community, and his maintenance as such is just as much the maintenance of the community, and vice versa, etc. Since the community, though here already a *product of history,* not only *de facto,* but also in its own consciousness, is therefore conceived as *having come into being,* we have here the precondition for *property* in land—i.e. for the relation of the working subject to the natural preconditions of labour as belonging to him. But this belonging is mediated through his being as a member of the State, through the existence of the State—i.e. through a *presupposition* which is regarded as divine, etc.

Concentration in the city, with the land as its territory; small-scale agriculture producing for direct consumption; manufacture as the domestic sideline of wives and daughters (spinning and weaving), or made independent only in a few individual branches (*fabri,*[a] etc.).

The precondition for the survival of this community is the maintenance of equality among its free SELF-SUSTAINING PEASANTS, and their own labour as the condition for the continued existence of their property. They relate as proprietors to the natural conditions

---

[a] Artisans (in ancient Rome).— *Ed.*

Outlines of the Critique of Political Economy

of labour; but their personal labour must constantly posit these conditions as real conditions and objective elements of the personality of the individual, of his personal labour.

On the other hand, the tendency of this small warlike community drives it beyond these limits, etc. (Rome, Greece, the Jews, etc.).

As Niebuhr says:

"When the auguries had assured Numa of the divine approval for his election, the first concern of the pious monarch was not the worship of the gods, but a human one. He distributed the land that Romulus had conquered in war and left to be occupied; he founded the worship of Terminus. All the ancient law-givers, and above all Moses, founded the success of their arrangements for virtue, justice and good morals upon landed property, or at least secure hereditary possession of land, for the greatest possible number of citizens" ([B. G. Niebuhr,] *Römische Geschichte*, Vol. I, 2nd edition, [Berlin,] 1827, p. 245).

The individual is PLACED IN SUCH CONDITIONS OF GAINING HIS LIFE AS TO MAKE NOT THE ACQUIRING OF WEALTH HIS OBJECT, BUT SELF-SUSTENANCE, HIS OWN REPRODUCTION AS A MEMBER OF THE COMMUNITY; THE REPRODUCTION OF HIMSELF AS PROPRIETOR OF THE PARCEL OF GROUND AND, IN THAT QUALITY, AS A MEMBER OF THE COMMUNE.

The continuation of the COMMUNE is the reproduction of all its MEMBERS as SELF-SUSTAINING PEASANTS, whose surplus time belongs precisely to the COMMUNE, to the labour of war, etc. Property in one's own labour is mediated through property in the conditions of labour—the hide of land, which is itself guaranteed by the existence of the community, which in turn is safeguarded by the surplus labour of its members in the form of military service, etc. The member of the community reproduces himself not by cooperation in WEALTH-PRODUCING labour, but by cooperation in labour for the (real or imaginary) communal interests aimed at maintaining the union against external and internal stress [nach aussen und innen]. Property is *quiritarium*,[a] property of the Romans; the private owner of land is such only by virtue of being a Roman, but as Roman he *is* a private landowner.

[IV-53] A third form of the property of working individuals, SELF-SUSTAINING MEMBERS OF THE COMMUNITY, in the natural conditions of their labour, is the *Germanic*. Here it is not the case, as in the specifically Oriental form, that the member of the community is as such co-holder of the communal property.[b] The Germanic

---

[a] I.e. the property of the *quirites*, citizens of ancient Rome in their civil capacity.— *Ed.*

[b] Here Marx inserted the following passage in brackets: "Where property exists *only* as communal property, the individual member is as such only the *occupier* of a

form also differs from the Roman, Greek (in short, the ancient classical) form, where the land is occupied by the community, Roman land; where part of the land remains with the community as such, as distinct from its members, *ager publicus* in its various forms; and where the remainder is distributed, and each plot is Roman by virtue of the fact that it is the private property, the domain, of a Roman, the part of the workshop which belongs to him, but he is a Roman only by virtue of the fact that he enjoys this sovereign right over part of the Roman soil.

//"In antiquity, urban crafts and trade looked down on, but agriculture held in high esteem; in the Middle Ages the contrary appraisal" [B. G. Niebuhr, op. cit., p. 418].//

//"The right to *use* communal land through *occupation* originally belonged to the patricians, who later enfeoffed their clients; the *assignment of property* out of the *ager publicus* belonged exclusively to the plebeians; all assignments in favour of plebeians as compensation for a share in the communal land. *Landed property in the strict sense,* if we except the area adjacent to the city wall, was originally in the hands only of the plebeians" (rural communities admitted at a later stage) [ibid., pp. 435-36].//

//"Essence of the Roman plebs as a totality of agriculturalists, as indicated in their quiritary property. The ancients were unanimous in regarding agriculture as the *proper occupation* of the free man, the school for soldiers. In it the ancient stock of the nation is maintained; it changes in the cities, where foreign merchants and artisans settle, as the indigenous inhabitants migrate there, enticed by the hope of gain. Wherever there is slavery, the freedman seeks his subsistence in such activities, through which he often accumulates wealth; and indeed in antiquity such occupations were mostly in their hands, and were therefore regarded as unsuitable for citizens; hence the view that the admission of craftsmen to full citizenship was risky (the early Greeks, as a rule, excluded them from it). οὐδενὶ ἐξῆν Ῥωμαίων οὔτε κάπηλον οὔτε χειροτέχνην βίον ἔχειν.[a] The ancients had no conception of the guild pride and dignity of medieval urban history; and even here the military spirit declined as the guilds overcame the noble families, and was finally extinguished; and consequently, with it, the respect and freedom the cities enjoyed in the outside world" [ibid., pp. 614-15].//

//"The tribes of the ancient states were constituted in one of two ways, either by *kinship* or by *locality*. *Kinship tribes* historically precede locality tribes, and were almost everywhere supplanted by them. Their extreme and most rigid form is the

---

particular part of it, hereditary or not, since any fraction of property does not belong to a member of the community for himself, but only as the direct part of the community, i.e. as someone in direct unity with the community and not as distinct from it. The individual is therefore merely an occupier. There is only *communal* property and *private occupation.* How this occupation relates to communal property may vary widely historically, locally, etc., depending on whether labour is performed in isolation by the private occupier or is itself determined by the community, or by the unity standing above the particular community." — *Ed.*

[a] "No Roman was permitted to lead the life of a petty trader or craftsman." Niebuhr quotes from *Roman Archaeology* by Dionysius of Halicarnassus.— *Ed.*

caste system where one caste is separated from another, without the right of intermarriage, with quite different status; each with its exclusive, unchangeable occupation.

"The *locality tribes* originally corresponded to a division of the area into districts and villages; so that someone residing in a village at the time of this division, in Attica under Cleisthenes, was registered as a *demotes* of that village, and as a member of the *phyle*[135] of the area to which that village belonged. However, as a rule his descendants, regardless of place of domicile, remained in the same *phyle* and the same *deme*, whereby this division assumed an appearance of ancestral descent."

The Roman *kin groups* did not consist of blood-relatives; to the common name, Cicero adds descent from free men as a criterion. The members of the Roman *gens* had common shrines, but this had already disappeared by the time of Cicero. The joint inheritance from fellow-kinsmen who died without dependants and intestate survived longest of all. In the earliest period, members of the *gens* obliged to assist fellow-kinsmen in need of help to bear unusual burdens. (This originally universal among the Germans, and persisted longest among the Dithmarschen.[136]) The *gentes* were guilds. "A more general organisation than that of kin groups did not exist in the ancient world. Thus among the Gaels[137] the aristocratic Campbells and their vassals constituted a single clan" [ibid., pp. 317-35].//

Since the patrician represents the community to a higher degree, he is the POSSESSOR of the *ager publicus,* and uses it through his clients, etc. (also, gradually appropriates it).

The Germanic commune is not concentrated in the city; by means of such a concentration—the city as centre of rural life, residence of the agricultural labourers, as also the centre of warfare—the commune as such gains an outward existence, distinct from that of the individual. Ancient classical history is the history of cities, but cities based on landed property and agriculture; Asiatic history is a kind of indifferent unity of town and country (the really large cities must be regarded here merely as royal camps, as an artificial excrescence on the actual economic structure); the Middle Ages (Germanic period) begins with the land as the locus of history, whose further development then proceeds through the contradiction between town and country; modern [history] is the urbanisation of the countryside, not, as in ancient times, the ruralisation of the city.

[V-1][a] With its coming together in the city, the commune as such acquires an economic existence; the very *presence* of the city as such distinguishes it from a mere multiplicity of separate houses. The whole here is not merely a collection of its separate

[a] Here Notebook V of the manuscript begins. The cover bears the words: "Notebook V. January 1858. London (Begun on 22 January)." An inscription on page 1 reads: "Notebook V. Chapter on Capital (Continued)." — *Ed.*

parts. It is a kind of independent organism. Among the Germanic peoples where the individual family chiefs settled in forests, separated by long distances, the commune exists even *outwardly* merely by virtue of the periodic gatherings of its members, although their unity *in-itself* is posited in descent, language, common past and history, etc.

The *commune* therefore appears as an *assembly*, not an *association*, as a unification whose independent subjects are the landed proprietors, and not as a unity. IN FACT, the community therefore does not exist as a *State*, as a *State system*, as among the ancients, because it does not exist as a *city*. For the community to come into real existence, the free landed proprietors must hold an *assembly*, whereas, e.g. in Rome, it *exists* apart from such assemblies, in the presence of the *city itself* and in the persons of the officials put in charge of it, etc.

True, the *ager publicus,* the communal land or people's land, occurs among the Germanic peoples also, as distinct from the property of the individual. It consists of hunting grounds, pastures, woodlands, etc., that part of the land which cannot be partitioned, if it is to serve as a means of production in this specific form. However, the *ager publicus* does not, as among e.g. the Romans, embody the specific economic being of the State, as against the private owners—so that they were *private* owners properly speaking in so far as they were *excluded* from, i.e. deprived of the use of, the *ager publicus,* like the plebeians.

The *ager publicus* is rather a mere supplement to individual property among the Germanic peoples, and figures as property only in so far as it is defended against hostile tribes as the common property of one particular tribe. The property of the individual is not mediated through the community, but the existence of the community and of communal property is mediated, i.e. it appears as a relation of the independent subjects to one another. *Au fond,* each individual household contains an entire economy, forming as it does an independent centre of production (manufacture merely the domestic sideline of the women, etc.).

In the ancient world, it is the city with its attached territory that forms the economic totality, in the Germanic world, it is the individual home, which itself appears merely as a small dot in the land belonging to it; which is not a concentration of many proprietors, but the family as an independent unit. In the Asiatic form (at least in its predominant variant), there is no property, but only occupation by individuals; the commune is properly speaking

Outlines of the Critique of Political Economy

the real proprietor—hence property only as *communal property* in land.

Among the ancients (Romans as the classical example, the thing in its purest, most fully developed form), there is a contradiction between the form of State landed property and private landed property, so that the latter is mediated through the former, or the former itself exists in this dual form. The private landed proprietor is thus simultaneously an urban citizen. Economically, citizenship may be expressed in the simple statement that the tiller of the soil is a city dweller.

In the Germanic form, the tiller of the soil is not a citizen, i.e. not a city dweller; the foundation of this form is the isolated, independent family settlement, guaranteed by its bond with the other family settlements of the same tribe, and their occasional assembly for purposes of war, religion, adjudication, etc., which establishes their mutual surety. Individual landed property does not here appear as a contradictory form as against communal landed property, nor as mediated by the community, but the other way round. The community exists only in the mutual relation of the individual landed proprietors as such. Communal property as such appears only as a communal appendage to the individual kin settlements and land appropriations.

The [Germanic] community is neither the substance, of which the individual appears merely as the accident [as in the Oriental community], nor is it the general, which exists as such and has a *unified being* [as with the ancients] either in the mind or in the reality of the city and its urban requirements as distinct from those of the individual, or in the urban territory as its separate being as distinct from the particular economic being of the member of the community. The community is, rather, on the one hand, presupposed in itself to the individual proprietor as the common element in language, blood, etc.; but on the other hand it has being only in its *real assembly* for communal purposes. In so far as it has a separate economic existence in the communally used hunting grounds, pastures, etc., it is used in these ways by every individual proprietor as such, and not in his capacity as a representative of the State (as in Rome). It is therefore genuinely the common property of the individual proprietors, and not of the union of these proprietors as an entity endowed with an existence of its own in the city, distinct from themselves as individuals.

The crucial point here is this: in all these forms, in which landed property and agriculture constitute the basis of the economic order, and hence the economic object is the production of use values, i.e. the *reproduction of the individual* in his particular relationships to his community, in which he forms its basis, we find the following elements:

(1) Appropriation of the natural condition of labour, of the *earth* as the original instrument of labour, both as workshop and repository of raw materials; however, appropriation not by means of labour but as the prerequisite for labour. The individual relates simply to the objective conditions of labour as his own, as the inorganic nature of his subjectivity, which realises itself through them. The chief objective condition of labour does not itself appear as the *product* of labour, but is already there as *nature*. [V-2] On the one hand the living individual, on the other the earth, as the objective condition of his reproduction.

(2) However, this *relation* to the land, to the soil, as the property of the working individual, who therefore right from the outset does not appear merely as a working individual in this abstraction, but who has an *objective mode of existence* in his ownership of the land, an existence which is *presupposed* to his activity and is not a mere result of it, and which is as much a precondition of his activity as his skin, his sense organs, which, though he also reproduces and develops these in his life process, are nevertheless presupposed to this reproduction process—this relation is instantly mediated by the naturally evolved and more or less historically developed and modified being of the individual as a *member of a community*—his naturally evolved being as part of a tribe, etc.

An isolated individual could no more have property in land than he could speak. True, he could live off the land, as animals do. But the relation to the soil as property always arises from the peaceful or violent occupation of the land by the tribe, the community in a form more or less naturally evolved or already historically developed. The individual here can never appear so thoroughly isolated as he does as mere free worker. If the objective conditions of his labour are presupposed as belonging to him, he himself is subjectively presupposed as belonging to a community, through which his relationship to the land is mediated. His relation to the objective conditions of labour is mediated by his being as a member of a community. Conversely, the real being of the community is determined by the particular form of his ownership of the objective conditions of labour. Whether this property mediated by his being within a community is *communal property,* where the individual is merely occupier and where there is no private property in land,—or whether property has the dual form of State and private property, but in such a way that the latter appears as posited by the former, so that only the citizen is and has to be a private proprietor, while on the other hand his property as a citizen also has a separate existence,—or whether, finally, communal property appears as merely supplementary to individual property, the latter, however, as the basis, and the community does not exist for itself at all outside the *assembly* of its members and their association for common purposes—these different forms of relation of the members of the commune or tribe to the tribal land—to the territory on which it has settled—depend partly upon the natural character of the tribe, partly on the economic conditions under which it now actually relates itself to the soil as proprietor, i.e. appropriates its fruits by means of labour, and this, in turn, depends on the climate, the physical properties of the soil, the physically conditioned mode of its utilisation, the relationship to hostile or neighbouring tribes, and the modifications brought about by migrations, historical events, etc.

For the commune to continue to exist as such in the old way, the reproduction of its members under the objective conditions presupposed is necessary. In time, production itself, the increase in population (which also belongs to production) necessarily transcends these conditions, destroys them instead of reproducing them, etc., and as a result of this the communal system decays and dies along with the property relations on which it was based.

The Asiatic form necessarily survives longest and most stubbornly. This is inherent in its presupposition, namely that the individual does not become independent vis-à-vis the commune; that there is a SELF-SUSTAINING circle of production, a unity of agriculture and handicrafts, etc.

If the individual changes his relationship to the community, he thereby changes and undermines the community and its economic premiss. On the other hand, the modification of this economic premiss, which is brought about by its own dialectic, impoverishment, etc., particularly the impact of war and conquest, which, e.g. in Rome, belongs essentially to the economic conditions of the community itself, transcends the real bond on which the community rests.

In all these forms, the basis of development is the *reproduction of presupposed* relationships between the individual and his commune —relationships more or less naturally evolved or else historically developed, but become traditional—and a *specific objective* existence, *predetermined* for the individual, both as regards his relation to the conditions of labour and his relation to his co-workers, fellow-tribesmen, etc. The development therefore is from the outset a *limited* one, but once the limit is transcended, decay and ruin ensue. The development of slavery, the concentration of landed property, exchange, a monetary economy, conquest, etc., had this effect among the Romans, though all these elements seemed up to a certain point compatible with the basis, in part a mere harmless extension of it, in part mere abuses flowing out of it. Considerable developments are possible here within a particular sphere. Individuals may appear great. But free and full development, either of the individual or of society, is inconceivable here, since such a development stands in contradiction to the original relation.

[V-3] Among the ancients, we never come across an investigation into which form of landed property, etc., is the most productive, creates the greatest wealth. Wealth does not appear as the purpose of production, although Cato may well investigate which way of field cultivation is the most profitable, or even Brutus may lend his money at the highest rate of interest. The enquiry is always about which form of property creates the best citizens. Wealth as an end-in-itself appears only among a few trading peoples— monopolists of the CARRYING TRADE—who live in the pores of the ancient world like the Jews in medieval society. Now, wealth is on the one hand a thing, embodied in things, in material products, which man confronts as subject. On the other hand, wealth as value is simply command over alien labour, not for the purpose of domination but of private consumption, etc. In all its forms it appears in physical shape, whether as a thing or as a relationship mediated by a thing, located outside the individual, somewhere near him.

In this way, the old view according to which man always appears in however narrowly national, religious or political a determination as the end of production, seems very exalted when set against the modern world, in which production is the end of man, and wealth the end of production. IN FACT, however, if the narrow bourgeois form is peeled off, what is wealth if not the universality of the individual's needs, capacities, enjoyments, productive forces, etc., produced in universal exchange; what is it if not the full development of human control over the forces of nature—over the forces of so-called Nature, as well as those of his own nature? What is wealth if not the absolute unfolding of man's creative abilities, without any precondition other than the preceding historical development, which makes the totality of this development—i.e. the development of all human powers as such, not measured by any *previously given* yardstick—an end-in-itself, through which he does not reproduce himself in any specific character, but produces his totality, and does not seek to remain something he has already become, but is in the absolute movement of becoming?

In the bourgeois economy—and in the epoch of production to which it corresponds—this complete unfolding of man's inner potentiality turns into his total emptying-out. His universal objectification becomes his total alienation, and the demolition of all determined one-sided aims becomes the sacrifice of the [human] end-in-itself to a wholly external purpose. That is why, on the one hand, the childish world of antiquity appears as something superior. On the other hand, it *is* superior, wherever fixed shape, form and established limits are being looked for. It is satisfaction from a narrow standpoint; while the modern world leaves us unsatisfied or, where it does appear to be satisfied with itself, is merely *vulgar*.

What Mr. Proudhon calls the *extra-economic* origin of property—by which he means precisely landed property[a]—is the *pre-bourgeois* relation of the individual to the objective conditions of labour, and initially to the *natural,* objective, conditions of labour. For, just as the working subject is a natural individual, a natural being, so the first objective condition of his labour appears as nature, earth, as his inorganic body. He himself is not only the organic body, but also this inorganic nature as a subject. This condition is not something he has produced, but something he finds to hand; as the natural world outside himself and presupposed to him.

Before proceeding in our analysis, one further point: the worthy Proudhon would not only be able to, he would have to, accuse *capital* and *wage labour*—as forms of property—of having an *extra-economic* origin. For the worker's encounter of the objective conditions of his labour as something separate from him, as *capital,* and the capitalist's encounter of the propertyless *worker,* as an abstract worker—the exchange as it takes place between value and living labour—presupposes an *historical process,* however much capital and wage labour themselves reproduce this relation and elaborate it in its objective scope, as well as in depth. And this

---

[a] See P. J. Proudhon, *Système des contradictions économiques, ou Philosophie de la misère,* Vol. II, Paris, 1846, p. 269; also Karl Marx, *The Poverty of Philosophy. Answer to the "Philosophy of Poverty" by M. Proudhon,* present edition, Vol. 6, p. 197.— *Ed.*

historical process, as we have seen, is the history of the emergence of both capital and wage labour.

In other words, the *extra-economic origin* of property means nothing but the *historical origin* of the bourgeois economy, of the forms of production to which the categories of political economy give theoretical or conceptual expression. The statement that pre-bourgeois history, and each phase of it, has its own *economy* and an *economic basis* of its movement, is *au fond* merely the tautology that human life has from the beginning rested on production, and, *d'une manière ou d'une autre*,[a] on *social* production, whose relations are precisely what we call economic relations.

The original conditions of production cannot initially be *themselves produced,* cannot be the results of production. (Instead of original conditions of production we might also say: the conditions for the reproduction of an increasing number of human beings by means of the natural process of the two sexes. For if this reproduction appears on one side as the appropriation of the objects by the subjects, it equally appears on the other as the shaping and the subjection of the objects by and to a subjective purpose; the transformation of the objects into results and repositories of subjective activity.) What requires explanation is not the *unity* of living and active human beings with the natural, inorganic conditions of their exchange of matter with nature, and therefore their appropriation of nature; nor of course is this the result of an [V-4] historical process. What we must explain is the *separation* between these inorganic conditions of human existence and this active being, a separation which is posited in its complete form only in the relationship between wage labour and capital.

In the relation of slavery and serfdom there is no such separation; rather, one part of society is treated by another as the mere *inorganic and natural* condition of its own reproduction. The slave stands in no relation whatsoever to the objective conditions of his labour; rather, *labour* itself, both in the form of the slave and of the serf, is placed along with the other natural beings such as cattle *as an inorganic condition* of production, as an appendage of the soil.

In other words: the original conditions of production appear as natural presuppositions, *natural conditions of the existence of the producer,* just as his living body, even though he reproduces and develops it, is not originally posited by himself, but appears as his own *presupposition;* his own (corporeal) being is a natural

---

[a] In one way or another.— *Ed.*

presupposition not posited by himself. These *natural conditions of existence,* to which he relates as to his own inorganic body, have a dual character: they are (1) subjective and (2) objective. The producer becomes aware of himself as member of a family, a tribe, a clan, etc.—which then, in the process of intermixture and conflict with others, assume historically different shapes; and, as such a member, he relates to a specific nature (we can still call it earth, land, soil) as his own inorganic being, as the condition of his production and reproduction. As the natural member of the community, he participates in the communal property and takes a particular share of it into his own possession; just so, as a native Roman citizen, he has (AT LEAST) a notional claim to the *ager publicus* and a real claim to a specified number of *jugera* of land, etc.

His *property,* i.e. his relation to the natural presuppositions of his production as belonging to himself, as *his own,* is mediated by his natural membership of a community. (The abstraction of a community whose members have nothing in common but e.g. language, etc., and barely even that, is plainly the product of much later historical circumstances.) With regard to the individual, for instance, it is evident that he himself relates to his language as *his own* only as the natural member of a human community. Language as the product of an individual is an absurdity. But this is equally true of property.

Language itself is just as much the product of a community as in another respect it is the being of the community, its articulate being, as it were.

//Communal production and communal property, as found e.g. in Peru, is evidently a *secondary* form, introduced and transmitted by conquering tribes, who had been familiar at home with communal property and communal production in the older and simpler form, as it occurs in India and among the Slavs. Similarly, the form found e.g. among the Celts in Wales appears to have been transmitted to them, a *secondary* form, introduced by conquerors among the less developed conquered tribes. The perfection and systematic elaboration of these systems by *supreme central authority* indicate their later origins. Just as the feudalism introduced into England was formally more complete than the feudalism which had evolved naturally in France.//

//Among nomadic pastoral tribes—and all pastoral peoples are originally nomadic—the land, like all other conditions of nature, appears in its elemental boundlessness, e.g. in the Asian steppes and the Asian high plateau. But it is grazed, etc., consumed by the herds, off which the nomadic peoples live. They relate to it as their property, though they never stabilise that property. This is the case with the hunting grounds of the wild Indian tribes of America; the tribe considers a certain region as its hunting territory, and maintains it by force against other tribes, or seeks to expel other tribes from the territory they claim. Among the nomadic pastoral tribes, the community is in fact always united, a travelling party, caravan, horde, and the forms of hierarchy evolve from the conditions of this mode of life. In fact, only the herd and not the soil is here *appropriated* and *reproduced,* but the soil is always temporarily used *in common* at each and every halting place.//

Let us now turn to the consideration of settled peoples. The only barrier which the community can encounter in relating itself to the natural conditions of production—to the land—as its *own,* is some *other community* which has already laid claim to them as its inorganic body. *Warfare* is therefore one of the earliest types of labour for every naturally evolved community of this kind, both for the defence of property and for its acquisition.

(It will actually be sufficient here to speak of original property in land, for among pastoral peoples property in natural products of the earth, e.g. sheep, is at the same time property in the pastures they pass through. In general, property in land includes property in its organic products.)

//If [V-5] man himself is captured together with the land as an organic appendage of it, he is captured as one of the conditions of production, and this is the origin of slavery and serfdom, which soon debase and modify the original forms of all communities, and then themselves become their basis. The simple structure is thereby negatively determined.//

Thus originally *property* means nothing more than man's relating to his natural conditions of production as belonging to him, as his own, as *presupposed along with his own being*; his relating to them as *natural presuppositions* of himself, which constitute, as it were, only an extension of his body. Actually, he does not relate to his conditions of production, but has a dual being, both subjectively as himself, and objectively in these natural inorganic conditions of his existence.

The forms of these *natural conditions of production* are dual: (1) his being as member of a community, hence the being of this community which in its original form is a *tribal community,* more or less modified; (2) his relation to the *land* by means of the community, as to *his own*; communal landed property, at the same time *individual occupation* for the individual, or in such a manner that the soil itself and its cultivation remain communal, and only its fruits are divided. (Yet, *dwellings*, etc., even if only the waggons of the Scythians, appear nevertheless to be always in the possession of individuals.) Membership of a *naturally evolved society*, a tribe, etc., is a natural condition of production for the living individual. Such membership is e.g. already a condition of his language, etc. His own productive being can only have existence under this condition. His subjective being as such is conditioned by it as much as it is conditioned by his relating to the land as to his workshop.

(True, property is originally *mobile*, for *d'abord* man takes possession of the ready-made fruits of the earth, to which, among others, belong the animals and especially those he can domesticate. However, even this situation—hunting, fishing, pastoralism, subsistence by collecting the fruits of the trees, etc.—always presupposes the appropriation of the land, whether as a place of fixed residence or a territory for ROAMING, a pasture for his animals, etc.)

Property therefore means *belonging to a tribe* (community) (having one's subjective/objective existence within it), and, mediated by the relation of this community to the land, to the earth as its inorganic body, [it also means] the relation of the individual to the land, to the external primary condition of production—since the earth is at the same time raw material, tool and fruit—as the preconditions belonging to his individuality, as its modes of being. We *reduce this property to the relation to the conditions of production*. Why not to those of consumption, since originally the act of producing by the individual is confined to the reproduction of his own body through the appropriation of ready-made objects prepared by nature for consumption? But even where the task is only to *find* and *discover*, effort, labour—as in hunting, fishing, the care of herds—and the production (i.e. the development) of certain skills are soon required on the part of the subject. This means that conditions in which man need merely reach for what is already available, without any tools (i.e. products of labour already designed for production), without alteration of form (which takes place even in herding), etc., are very transitory, and can nowhere be regarded as normal; not even as normal at the earliest stage. Of course, it has to be remembered that the original conditions of production include substances directly consumable without labour, such as some fruit, animals, etc.; thus the consumption fund is itself part of the *original production fund*.

The fundamental condition of property based on tribalism (which is what communalism originally amounts to) is to be a member of the tribe. This makes a tribe conquered and subjugated by another *propertyless* and places it among the *inorganic conditions* of the conquering tribe's reproduction, to which that community relates as to its own. Slavery and serfdom are therefore only further developments of property based on tribalism. They necessarily modify all its forms. They are least able to do this in the Asiatic form. In the SELF-SUSTAINING unity of manufacture and agriculture on which this form is based, conquest is not so essential a condition as where *landed property, agriculture,* predominate exclusively. On the other hand, since the individual in this form never becomes a proprietor but only an occupier, he is *au fond* himself the property, the slave of that [in] which the unity of the community exists. Here slavery neither puts an end to the conditions of labour, nor does it modify the essential relation.

[V-6] It is now further evident that:

In so far as property is only a conscious relation to the conditions of production as to one's *own*—and, with respect to the individual, a relation posited by the community and proclaimed and guaranteed as law, the being of the producer thus appearing as a being within the objective conditions *belonging to him*—it is realised only through production. Real appropriation does not occur through the establishment of a notional relationship to these conditions, but takes place in the active, real relationship to them, when they are really posited as the conditions of man's subjective activity.

In the light of this it is also clear that *these conditions change.* Only when a tribe hunts, does a particular region of the earth become a hunting ground; only when the soil is tilled, is the land posited as the extension of the body of the individual. Once the *city of Rome* was built, and its surrounding land cultivated by its citizens, the conditions of the community were different from what they had been before. The object of all these communities is preservation, i.e. *the reproduction of their individual members as proprietors, i.e. in the same objective mode of existence,* which *also constitutes the relationship of the members to each other, and therefore constitutes the community itself. But this reproduction is at the same time necessarily new production and the destruction of the old form.* For instance, where each individual is supposed to possess a certain amount of land, the increase in population already presents a problem. If it is to be coped with, colonisation and with it wars of conquest have to be undertaken. Hence slaves, etc., also e.g. the enlargement of the *ager publicus,* and hence more patricians, who represent the community, etc.

Thus the preservation of the old community implies the destruction of the conditions on which it rests, and turns into its opposite. For instance, if it were to be argued that productivity could be increased within the same territory, through a development of the productive forces, etc. (which in traditional agriculture is precisely what develops more slowly than anything else), this would imply new methods and combinations of labour, a high proportion of the day being devoted to agriculture, etc., and, once again, the old economic conditions of the community would be transcended. In the act of reproduction itself are changed not only the objective conditions—e.g. village becomes city, the wilderness becomes cultivated clearings, etc.—but also the producers, who transform themselves in that they evolve new qualities from within themselves, develop through production new powers and new ideas, new modes of intercourse, new needs, and new speech.

The more traditional the mode of production itself—and it persists for a long time in agriculture and even longer in the Oriental mutual complementation of agriculture and manufacture—i.e. the more the *real process* of appropriation remains the same, the more unchanging will be the old forms of property and therefore also the community as a whole.

Where the members of the community have already developed a separate entity as private proprietors from their collective entity as an urban community and owners of the urban territory, conditions already arise in which the individual may *lose* his property, i.e. the dual relationship which makes him both a citizen with equal status, belonging to the community, and a *proprietor*. In the Oriental form, this *loss* is hardly possible, except as a result of wholly external influences, since the individual member of the commune never enters into so independent a relation to it that he could lose his (objective, economic) tie with it. He is firmly rooted. This is also inherent in the union of manufacture and agriculture, of town (in this instance the village) and country.

Among the ancients [Greeks and Romans], manufacture already appears as degeneration (an occupation fit only for freedmen, clients and foreigners), etc. This development of productive labour (its emancipation from total subordination to agriculture, as domestic labour, labour of freedmen, manufacture devoted only to agricultural purposes and war, or to religious observances and communal requirements such as the construction of houses, roads or temples), this development, which necessarily arises from intercourse with foreigners, from slaves, from the desire to exchange the surplus product, etc., destroys the mode of production on which the community rests, and with it the *objective individual*—i.e. the individual Greek, Roman, etc. Exchange has the same effect, and so has indebtedness, etc.

The original unity between a specific form of communal or tribal entity and the property in nature corresponding to it, or relation to the objective conditions of production as natural, as the objective being of the individual mediated by the community—this unity, which in one sense appears as the particular form of property, has its living reality in a specific *mode of production* itself, and this mode is as much the relationship of the individuals to one another as it is their specific active relationship [V-7] towards inorganic nature, a specific mode of working (which is always family labour and often communal labour). The community itself appears as the first great force of production; particular conditions of production ([favouring] e.g. stock-breeding or agriculture) give rise to particular modes of production and particular forces of production, both subjective ones, i.e. those which appear as qualities of the individuals, and objective ones.

In the final analysis the community, as well as the property based upon it, comes down to a certain stage in the development of the productive forces of the working subjects, to which correspond certain relations of these subjects to each other and to nature. Up to a certain point, reproduction. Then this turns into dissolution.

Property—and this applies to its Asiatic, Slavonic, ancient [classical] and Germanic forms—therefore originally means the relation of the working (producing) subject (or the subject reproducing himself) to the conditions of his production or reproduction as his own. Hence it will take different forms depending on the conditions of production. The object of production itself is to reproduce the producer in and together with these objective conditions of his being. This relation as a proprietor—not as the result but as the presupposition of labour, i.e. of production—presupposes in turn a particular existence of the individual as member of a tribal or communal entity (whose property he himself is up to a certain point).

Slavery, serfdom, etc., where the labourer himself appears among the natural conditions of production for a third individual or community (this does *not* apply e.g. to the general slavery of the Orient, [or does] *only* from the European POINT OF VIEW)—and where property therefore is no longer the relation of the independently working individual to the objective conditions of labour—is always secondary, never original, although it is the necessary and logical result of property based on the community and on labour in the community.

It is of course very simple to imagine a powerful, physically superior individual, who starts by catching animals and proceeds to capture men in order to make them catch animals for him; in other words, uses man as a naturally occurring condition for his reproduction as he uses any other natural living being. His own labour then is reduced to domination, etc. But such a view is absurd, even though it may be correct from the standpoint of some particular tribal or communal entity, because it starts from the development of *isolated* individuals.

Man becomes individualised only through the process of history. Originally he is a *species being, a tribal being, a herd animal*—though by no means as a ζῶον πολιτικόν[11] in the political sense. Exchange itself is a major agent of this individuation. It makes herd-like existence superfluous and dissolves it. This occurs when matters have changed in such a way that man as an isolated individual relates only to himself, but that the means of positing himself as an isolated individual have become precisely what gives him his general and communal character. It is in the community that the objective being of the individual as a proprietor (e.g. a landed proprietor) is presupposed, and is so, moreover, under certain conditions which chain him to the community, or rather constitute a link in his chain. In bourgeois society, e.g., the worker stands there purely subjectively, without object; but the thing which *confronts* him has now become the *true community,* which he tries to make a meal of and which makes a meal of him.

All forms (more or less naturally evolved, but all at the same time results of historical processes) in which the community presupposes its subjects in a specific objective unity with the conditions of their production, or in which a specific subjective mode of being presupposes the communities themselves as condition of production, necessarily correspond only to a development of the productive forces which is limited, and indeed limited in principle. The development of the productive forces dissolves them, and their dissolution is itself a development of the human productive forces. Labour is only undertaken on a certain basis—first naturally evolved—then an historical presupposition. Later, however, this basis or presupposition is itself transcended, or posited as a transient one, which has become too narrow for the unfolding of the progressive human pack.

In so far as the landed property of [classical] antiquity reappears in modern smallholding property, it belongs to political economy

and we shall deal with it in the section on landed property.
[V-8] (We have to return to all this for a deeper and more
detailed analysis.)

What concerns us for the moment here is this: the relation of
labour to capital or to the objective conditions of labour as capital,
presupposes an historical process that dissolves the different forms
in which the labourer is a proprietor or the proprietor works.
This means first and foremost:

(1) *Dissolution* of the relation to the earth—to land or soil—as a
natural condition of production to which man relates as his own
inorganic being, the workshop of his forces and the domain of his
will. All forms in which this property is found presuppose a
communal entity whose members, whatever the formal distinctions
between them, are *proprietors* by virtue of being its members. The
original form of this property is therefore *direct communal property*
(the *Oriental form* modified among the Slavs; developed to the
point of contradiction in the property of [classical] antiquity and in
Germanic property, though still constituting its hidden, if antagonistic, foundation).

(2) *Dissolution of the relations* in which he appears as the *proprietor
of the instrument*. Just as the above form of landed property
presupposes a *real community*, so this ownership of the instrument
by the labourer presupposes a particular form of development of
manufacture—namely *handicraft labour.* Guild and corporative
institutions, etc., bound up with this. (The manufacture system of
the ancient Orient can already be considered under heading (1)
above.) Here labour itself is still half the expression of artistic
creation, half an end-in-itself, etc. Craft mastery. The
capitalist himself still a master craftsman. Special craft skill ensures
the ownership of the instrument, etc., etc. Then, in a sense, the
mode of labour becomes hereditary together with the organisation
of labour and its instrument. Medieval city organisation. Labour
still belongs to the labourer; a certain self-sufficient development
of limited specialised capacities, etc.

(3) Included in both is the fact that man possesses the means of
consumption prior to production; this necessary to enable him to
keep alive as producer—i.e. during production, *before* its completion. As landed proprietor, he is directly provided with the
necessary consumption fund. As a master craftsman he has
inherited it, earned it or saved it up, and as a youth he is first an
apprentice, i.e. not yet an independent worker properly speaking,
but living in the master's household in the patriarchal manner.

The (real) journeyman enjoys a certain communality with regard to the consumption fund owned by the master. Even if this is not the journeyman's *own property*, it is, under the laws and customs, etc., of the guild, at least his co-possession. (To be gone into further.)

(4) On the other hand, *dissolution*, also, of the relations under which the *workers themselves*, the *living labour capacities*, are still a *direct part of the objective conditions of production* and are appropriated as such—are therefore slaves or serfs. For capital, the worker does not represent a condition of production, but only labour. If capital can get it performed by machinery, or even by water or air, *tant mieux*.[a] And what capital appropriates is not the worker, but his labour—and not directly, but by means of exchange.

These, then, on the one hand, are historical preconditions for the worker to be found as a free worker, as purely subjective labour capacity, devoid of objectivity, confronting the objective conditions of production as his *non-property*, as *alien property*, as *value*-for-itself, as capital. On the other hand, the question arises, what are the conditions in which he can find himself confronting *capital*?

//The formula of capital in which living labour relates to raw material, as well as to the instrument and the means of subsistence required during work, negatively, as non-property, *d'abord includes non-property in land*. In other words, the condition is negated in which the working individual relates to land, to the soil, as his own, i.e. in which he works, produces as the proprietor of the land. In the best case, the working individual relates to the land not only as worker, but as proprietor of the land to himself as working subject. Potentially, land ownership includes property both in raw material and in the primordial instrument of labour, the soil itself, as well as in its spontaneous fruits. Within the earliest form, this means that the individual relates to the soil as its owner, finds in it raw material, instrument and means of subsistence created not through labour but springing from the soil itself. Then, reproducing this relation, secondary instruments and fruits of the earth produced by labour are taken as included in land ownership in its primitive forms. This historical situation is thus *d'abord* negated as the fuller relating-as-property in the worker's relation to the conditions of labour as capital. This is historical situation No. I, which is negated or presupposed as historically dissolved in this relation.

---

[a] So much the better.— *Ed.*

Secondly, [V-9] however, the situation where the worker has a *property in the instrument,* where the worker relates to the instrument as his own, where he works as owner of the instrument (which necessarily presupposes that the instrument is subsumed in his individual labour, i.e. presupposes a particular limited stage in the development of the productive power of labour), where this form of the *worker as proprietor* or the *working proprietor* is already posited as an independent form, separate from and alongside *land ownership*—the urban development of labour in its artisan forms; not as in the first case, as accidental to land ownership and subsumed under it. Raw material and means of subsistence are only *mediated* here as the property of the artisan, mediated by his craft, by his property in the instrument. This situation already presupposes a second historical stage, separate from and alongside the first, which must itself have been considerably modified by the fact that this *second type of property* or of *working proprietor* has established an *independent existence.*

Since the instrument itself is already the product of labour, i.e. the element which constitutes property is already posited by labour, the community can here no longer appear, as it can in the first case, in its naturally evolved form, as the community on which this form of property is based, but rather as a community which is itself already produced, which has come into being, as secondary, as a community produced by the worker himself. It is clear that where property in the instrument is the relation to the production conditions of labour as property, the instrument appears in real labour *only* as a *means* of individual labour; the art of really appropriating the instrument, of employing it as a means of labour, here appears as a special skill of the worker, which posits him as the proprietor of the instrument. In short, the essential character of the guild and corporative system, where craftwork constitutes its subject as proprietor, can be reduced to the distinction between the relation to the instrument of production— the instrument of labour—as property, and the relation to the soil, to the land (to the raw material as such), as one's own. Thus historical situation No. II, which is characterised by the fact that the relation to this single element of the conditions of production constitutes the working subject as a proprietor, a working proprietor, and which by its nature can exist only as contradiction, or, if you like, as complement, to the modified first situation, is also negated in the first formula of capital.

There is a *third possible form,* which is to relate as proprietor neither to the land nor to the instrument, hence not even to labour itself, but only to the means of subsistence, which are found as the natural condition of the working subject. This is *au fond* the formula of slavery and serfdom, which is also negated, i.e. posited as an historically superseded condition, in the relation of the worker to the conditions of production as capital.

The primitive forms of property necessarily dissolve into one's relation to the different objective elements conditioning production as to one's own; they both constitute the economic basis of different forms of community and presuppose specific forms of community. These forms are significantly modified once labour itself becomes one of the *objective conditions of production* (as in slavery and serfdom), as a result of which the simple affirmative character of all forms of property referred to in No. I is lost and modified. They all potentially include slavery, and therefore their own transcendence. So far as No. II is concerned, where labour has become particularised—where craft mastery and consequently property in the instrument of labour=property in the conditions of production—this admittedly excludes slavery and serfdom, but it may undergo an analogous negative development in the form of the caste system.//

//The third form of property, in the means of subsistence, unless it is dissolved into slavery and serfdom, cannot contain any relation of the *working* individual to the conditions of production, and therefore of existence. It can therefore only be the relation of the member of the primitive community founded upon landed property who has lost his landed property and has not yet advanced to property No. II, as in the case of the Roman plebs at the time of the *panes et circenses.*[138]//

//The relation of RETAINERS to their lords, or that of personal service, is essentially different. For personal service constitutes *au fond* merely the mode of existence of the landowner who no longer works himself but whose property includes the workers themselves as serfs, etc., among the conditions of production. Here the *relationship of dominion* exists as an essential relation of appropriation. *Au fond* there can be no relationship of dominion to animals, to the soil, etc., by virtue of appropriation, even though the animal serves. The appropriation of another's *will* is presupposed in the relationship of dominion. Creatures without will, like animals for instance, may indeed render services, but this doesn't make the owner their *lord.* However, what we see here is how the *relationships of dominion and servitude* also belong to this formula of the appropriation of the instruments of production; and they constitute a necessary ferment in the development and decay of all primitive relations of property and production, just as they express their limitations. To be sure, they are reproduced in capital, in a mediated form, and hence they also constitute a ferment in its dissolution, and are the emblems of its limitations.//

[V-10] //"The right to sell oneself and one's dependants in times of distress, was a grievous general right; it prevailed in the North, as well as among the Greeks and in Asia. The right of the creditor to take the defaulting debtor into servitude, and to redeem the debt as far as possible either by his labour or by the sale of his person, was almost equally widespread" (Niebuhr, [*Römische Geschichte*, Vol.] I, p. 600).//

//Elsewhere *Niebuhr* attributes the difficulties and misunderstandings of Greek writers of the Augustan period concerning the relationship between patricians and plebeians and their confusion of this relationship with that between patrons and clients, to the fact that they

"were writing at a time when *rich and poor constituted the only real classes of citizens*; when the man in need, no matter how noble his origins, required a patron, and the millionaire, even though only a freedman, was sought after as a patron. They could find scarcely a trace of inherited relations of attachment" (I, 620).//

//"Artisans were to be found in both classes" (*metoikos*[a] *and freedmen together with their descendants*), "and plebeians who abandoned agriculture passed into the limited citizen status enjoyed by these. Nor did they lack the honour of *legally recognised guilds*, and these were so highly respected that Numa was supposed to have been their founder. There were nine such guilds: pipers, goldsmiths, carpenters, dyers, harness-makers, tanners, coppersmiths and potters, the ninth guild embracing the rest of the crafts... Those among them who were independent citizens living outside the city limits, or who enjoyed isopolity[b] and were independent of any patron (supposing such status was recognised), or those who were descendants of dependent men whose bond had lapsed with the extinction of their patrons' families: these undoubtedly remained as remote from the quarrels of ancient citizens and the commons [der Gemeinde] as the Florentine guilds remained outside the feuds of the Guelf and Ghibelline families. It is probable that the dependent men were still as a whole at the disposal of the patricians" (I, 623).//

On the one hand, historical processes are presupposed which transform a mass of individuals of a nation, etc., if not immediately into genuine free workers, at any rate into workers who are free δυνάμει,[c] whose only property is their labour capacity and the possibility of exchanging it for existing values. Such individuals confront all objective conditions of production as *alien property*, as their *non-property*, but at the same time as *values*

---

[a] Resident aliens.— *Ed.*
[b] A status equivalent to citizenship.— *Ed.*
[c] Potentially.— *Ed.*

which can be exchanged and therefore to a CERTAIN DEGREE appropriated by living labour. Such historical processes of dissolution can take the form of the dissolution of the dependent relationship which binds the worker to the soil and to the lord but which actually presupposes his ownership of the means of subsistence (which amounts in truth to the process of his "emancipation" from the soil). They can also take the form of the dissolution of those relations of landed property which constitute him as YEOMAN, as a free working petty landowner or tenant (*colonus*), i.e. as a free peasant. //The dissolution of the even more ancient forms of communal property and of real community needs no special mention.// Or they can take the form of the dissolution of guild relations, which presuppose the worker's property in the instrument of labour and labour itself, determined as a certain form of artisanal skill, not merely as the source of property but as property itself. Lastly, they can take the form of the dissolution of the various client relationships, in which *non-proprietors* appear as co-consumers of the surplus produce in the retinue of their lord, and in return wear his livery, participate in his feuds, perform real or imaginary acts of personal service, etc.

Closer examination of all these processes of dissolution will show that relations of production are dissolved in which use value, i.e. production for immediate use, predominates and in which exchange value and its production presuppose the predominance of the other form. Thus in all the above relationships, deliveries in kind and labour services predominate over money payments and services remunerated by money. All this by the way. Closer examination will also reveal that all the relations dissolved were possible only at a certain level of development of the material (and therefore also of the mental) forces of production.

What immediately concerns us here is the following. The process of dissolution which turns a mass of individuals in a nation, etc., into δυνάμει[a] free wage workers—that is into individuals obliged to work and to sell their labour merely by their lack of property—does *not* presuppose the *disappearance* of these individuals' previous sources of income and (in part) of their previous conditions of property. On the contrary, it presupposes that *only* their use has changed, that their mode of being has been transformed, that they have passed into other hands as a *free fund,* or perhaps that they have partly remained in *the same* hands. But

---

[a] Potentially.— *Ed.*

this much is clear. The same process which has *d'une manière* OR *d'une autre* separated a mass of individuals from their previous affirmative relations to the *objective conditions of labour,* which has negated these relations and thereby transformed these individuals into *free workers,* that same process has liberated δυνάμει these *objective conditions of labour* (land, raw material, means of subsistence, instruments of labour, money, or all of these) from their *previous ties* to the individuals who are now separated from them. They are still *present,* but present in a different form, as a *free fund,* one in which all the old political, etc., RELATIONS are obliterated, and which now confront those separated, propertyless individuals merely in the form of *values,* of values maintaining themselves and each other.

The same process which confronts the masses of free workers with the *objective conditions of labour,* has also put them face to face with these conditions as [V-11] *capital.* The historical process was one of the separation of hitherto combined elements; its result is therefore not the disappearance of one of these elements, but that each of them appears negatively related to the other: the (potentially) free worker on the one hand, (potential) capital on the other. The separation of the objective conditions on the part of the classes which have been transformed into free workers, must appear just as much at the opposite pole as the attainment of independence by these same conditions.

If we consider the relationship of capital and wage labour not as something which is already of decisive importance, determining the character of production as a whole (for in this case capital, presupposed as the condition of wage labour, is the product of wage labour, and presupposed by wage labour itself as its condition, created by wage labour as its own presupposition), but as still in the stage of historical evolution—i.e. if we consider the original transformation of money into capital, the process of exchange between capital still existing only δυνάμει on the one hand, and the free workers existing δυνάμει on the other—then of course one cannot help making the simple observation, about which the economists make a great fuss—namely that the side which appears as capital must possess enough raw materials, instruments of labour and means of subsistence to enable the worker to live while producing, before production is completed.

This, moreover, takes the form that accumulation—an accumulation prior to labour and not arising from labour—must have taken place on the part of the capitalist, which enables him to set the worker to work and to maintain him in activity, as living labour capacity.* This action of capital, which is independent of and not posited by labour, is then further transferred from this history of its origin into the present, and transformed into a factor of its reality and effectiveness, of its self-formation. Ultimately it is from this that the eternal right of capital to the fruit of other men's labour is derived, or rather the mode of appropriation of capital is deduced from the simple and "just" laws of the exchange of equivalents.

Wealth present in the form of money can only be exchanged for the objective conditions of labour, because and if these have been separated from labour itself. We have seen that money can in part be accumulated by the simple exchange of equivalents; however, this is so insignificant a source that historically it is not worth mention—assuming, that is, that this money has been gained by the exchange of one's own labour. It is rather money accumulated by usury—especially usury inflicted on landed property—and mobile (monetary) wealth accumulated through mercantile profits, that turns into capital in the proper sense, into industrial capital. We will have occasion to say more about both forms below—that is, in so far as they themselves appear, not as forms of capital, but as prior forms of wealth which are the prerequisites for capital.

As we have seen, it is inherent in the concept of capital—in its origin—that it begins with *money*, and therefore with wealth in the form of money. It is likewise inherent in it that it appears as emerging from circulation, as the *product* of circulation. Capital formation does not therefore arise from landed property (it could only arise from a *tenant farmer* in so far as he is also a trader in farm produce), nor from the guild (though the latter also provides a possibility), but from merchants' and usurers' wealth. But this wealth only encounters the conditions which permit the purchase

---

* Once capital and wage labour are posited as their own presupposition, as the basis presupposed to production itself, then what appears initially is that the capitalist, in addition to the fund of raw material and means of labour required for the worker to reproduce himself, to produce the necessary means of subsistence, i.e. to realise *necessary labour,* must possess a fund of raw material and means of labour in which the worker realises his surplus labour, i.e. the capitalist's profit. Further analysis reveals that the worker is constantly creating a double fund for the capitalist, or in the form of capital, one part of which constantly fulfils the conditions of his own existence, and the other, the conditions of the existence of capital. As we have seen, in surplus capital—and surplus capital in its relation to labour in its antediluvian relation to labour—all *real, present capital,* each of its elements, has been uniformly *appropriated* as objectified *alien labour,* appropriated by capital, without exchange, without an equivalent being given in return.

of free labour, once free labour has been detached from its objective conditions of existence as a result of an historical process. Only then does it also become possible to buy these *conditions* themselves. Under the guild system, for instance, mere money (unless it is guild money, money of the masters) cannot purchase looms in order to put men to work on them. There are regulations determining how many looms one man may operate, etc. In short, the instrument itself is still so intimately linked to living labour, of which it appears as the domain, that it does not truly circulate.

What enables monetary wealth to turn into capital is, on the one hand, the availability of free workers, and on the other, the availability of means of subsistence, materials, etc., which were hitherto *d'une manière ou d'une autre* the *property* of the now objectiveless masses, but are now likewise *free* and for sale.

However, the other condition of labour—a certain craft skill, the existence of the instrument as a means of labour, etc.—is *already available* to capital in this, its preliminary or first period. This is partly the result of the urban guild system, partly of domestic industry, or of such industry as exists as an accessory to agriculture. The historical process is not the result of capital, but its prerequisite. By means of this process, the capitalist then insinuates himself as a (historical) middleman between landed property, or between property generally, and labour. History knows nothing of the cosy legend according to which the capitalist and the worker form an association, etc.; [V-12] nor is there a trace of it in the development of the concept of capital. *Manufacture* may develop sporadically in a context belonging to quite a different period, as e.g. in the Italian cities where it developed *side by side* with the guilds. But if capital is to be the generally dominant form of an epoch, its conditions must be developed not merely locally, but on a large scale. (It is no contradiction of this that during the dissolution of the guilds, individual guild masters may turn into industrial capitalists; however, in the nature of the phenomenon, the case is rare. All in all, the entire guild system—both master and journeyman—dies out, where the capitalist and the worker arise.)

It goes without saying, and is borne out by closer analysis of the historical epoch which we are now discussing, that *the period of dissolution* of the earlier modes of production and the older relations of the worker to the objective conditions of labour, is *at the same time a period* in which *monetary wealth has* already developed to a certain extent, and also one in which it is rapidly growing and expanding, through the same circumstances which accelerate this dissolution. Monetary wealth is itself one of the agents of that dissolution, just as that dissolution is the condition of its transformation into capital. But the *mere existence of monetary wealth,* even its conquest of a sort of SUPREMACY, is not sufficient for this *dissolution into capital* to occur. Otherwise ancient Rome, Byzantium, etc., would have concluded their history with free labour and capital, or rather, they would have begun a new [stage of] history. There the dissolution of the old relations of property was also linked to the development of monetary wealth—of commerce, etc. But IN FACT this dissolution did not result in industry but in the domination of the countryside over the city.

The *original formation of capital* does not, as is often supposed, occur in the form that capital *amasses* means of subsistence, instruments of labour and raw materials, in short, the *objective* conditions of labour detached from the soil and already fused with human labour.* Capital does not create the objective conditions of labour.

Its *original formation* occurs simply because the historical process of the dissolution of the old mode of production enables value, existing in the form of *monetary wealth,* to *buy* the objective conditions of labour on the one hand, and to exchange the *living* labour of the now free workers for money on the other.

All these moments are already present. Their separation is itself an historical process, a process of dissolution, and it is *this* which enables money to turn into *capital.* In so far as money itself plays a part in the process, it is only to the extent that it is itself a highly energetic agent of separation, and to that extent contributes to the creation of the *plucked,* objectiveless, *free workers.* It is certainly not by *creating* the objective conditions for their existence, but by helping to accelerate their separation from them, their property-lessness.

* Nothing would be more obviously and nonsensically circular than the argument that, on the one hand, the *workers* whom capital must set to work if it is to posit itself as capital, must first be *created* and called into life by *its* accumulation (waiting, as it were, for its "*Let* there be workers!"), while, on the other hand, capital could not *accumulate* without alien labour, could at most accumulate *its own labour,* i.e. that capital could itself exist in the form of *non-capital* and *non-money;* for prior to the existence of capital, labour can only realise itself in the form of handicraft work, of small-scale agriculture, etc., in short, only in forms in which *no* or only little *accumulation* is possible, which allow for only a small SURPLUS PRODUCE, and *consume* the greater part of that. In general, we shall have to look more closely at this concept of *accumulation* later.

For instance, when the great English landowners dismissed their RETAINERS, who had consumed with them the SURPLUS PRODUCE of their land; when their tenant farmers drove out the small cottagers, etc., then a mass of living labour power was thrown on to the *labour market,* a mass which was free in a double sense: free from the old client or bondage relationships and any obligatory services, and free also from all goods and chattels, from every objective and material form of being, *free from all property.* It was reduced either to the sale of its labour capacity or to beggary, vagabondage or robbery as its only source of income. History records that it tried the latter first, but was driven off this road and on to the narrow path which led to the labour market, by means of gallows, pillory and whip. In this way the *governments,* e.g. Henry VII, VIII, etc.,[139] appear as conditions of the historical process of dissolution and as creators of the conditions for the existence of capital.

On the other side, the means of subsistence, etc., formerly consumed by the lords with their RETAINERS, could now be obtained by money, and money wanted to purchase them in order THROUGH THEIR INSTRUMENTALITY to purchase labour. Money had neither *created* nor *accumulated* these means of subsistence. They were already present, were consumed and reproduced, before they were consumed and reproduced through the mediation of money. The only difference was, that these means of subsistence were now thrown on to the *exchange market.* They had now been released from their immediate connection with the mouths of the RETAINERS, etc., and transformed from use values into exchange values, thus falling into the domain and under the [V-13] sovereignty of monetary wealth.

It was the same with the instruments of labour. Monetary wealth neither invented nor manufactured spinning wheel and loom. But once they had been separated from their land, spinners and weavers with their wheels and looms came under the sway of monetary wealth, etc. *The only characteristic of capital is that it brings together the masses of hands and the instruments which are already there. It agglomerates them under its sway.* This is its *real accumulation*; the accumulation of workers along with their instruments at particular points. We shall have to go into this more deeply when we come to the so-called accumulation of capital.

Admittedly, monetary wealth in the form of merchants' wealth had helped to accelerate the dissolution of the old relations of production, and had e.g. enabled the landowner (as A. Smith has already nicely demonstrated) to exchange his corn, cattle, etc., for imported use values, instead of squandering his own production with his RETAINERS, and measuring his wealth largely by their number.[a] Monetary wealth had increased for him the significance of the *exchange value* of his revenue. It did the same for his tenant farmers, who were already semi-capitalists, though in a rather disguised manner.

The evolution of exchange value, which is favoured by the existence of *money* in the form of the merchant estate, dissolves the production which is orientated mainly towards immediate use value and the forms of property which correspond to it—relations of labour to its objective conditions—thus giving an impetus to the creation of the *labour market* (not to be identified with the slave market). However, even this effect of money is possible only on the basis of an *urban industriousness,* which rests *not* on capital and wage labour, but on the organisation of labour in guilds, etc. Urban labour itself had created means of production for which the guilds became as great an encumbrance as were the old relations of landed property for agricultural improvement, which was in turn partly the result of the greater sale of agricultural products to the cities, etc. The other circumstances which e.g. in the 16th century increased the mass of circulating commodities as well as of money, created new needs and therefore raised the exchange value of native products, etc., increased prices, etc.—all these fostered the dissolution of the old relations of production, accelerated the separation of the worker or the able-bodied non-worker from the objective conditions of his reproduction, and thus hastened the transformation of money into capital.

Nothing is therefore more foolish than to conceive of the *original formation* of capital as having created and accumulated the *objective conditions of production*—means of subsistence, raw materials, instruments—and then having offered them to workers *stripped* of them. For it was monetary wealth which had partly helped to *strip* of these conditions the labour power of the individuals capable of work. In part this process of separation proceeded without the intervention of monetary wealth. Once the formation of capital had reached a certain level, monetary wealth could insinuate itself as mediator between the objective conditions of life thus become free and the freed but also *uprooted and dispossessed* living labour powers, and buy the one with the other. As regards the *formation of monetary wealth* itself, prior to its transformation into capital, this belongs to the prehistory of the

---

[a] A. Smith, *An Inquiry into the Nature and Causes of the Wealth of Nations,* Book III, Chapter IV.— *Ed.*

bourgeois economy. Usury, trade, urbanisation and the development of government finance which these made possible, play the main role here. Also *hoarding* by tenant farmers, peasants, etc., though to a smaller extent.

Here we can see at the same time how trade everywhere mediates exchange and exchange value, a mediation which we can call trade—money acquires an independent existence in the merchant estate, as does circulation in trade—and how the development of exchange and exchange value brings about both the dissolution of *labour's relations of property in its* conditions of existence, and of *labour* itself *as one of the objective conditions of production.* All the relations [thus dissolved] express a predominance of use value and of production orientated towards immediate use as well as of a real community which is still in being as an immediate prerequisite of production.

Production based on exchange value and a community based on the exchange of these exchange values, however much they may appear (cf. the previous chapter on money) to posit property as the result only of *labour,* and to posit private property in the product of one's own labour as a condition [of labour], and thus to posit labour as a general precondition of wealth, actually presuppose and produce the separation of labour from its objective conditions. An exchange of equivalents occurs, [but it] is merely the surface layer of a [system of] production which rests on the appropriation of alien labour *without exchange,* but under the *guise of exchange.* This system of exchange has *capital* as its basis. If we consider it in isolation from capital, as it presents itself on the surface, as an *independent* system, we are subject to a mere *illusion,* though a *necessary one.*

It is therefore no longer surprising to find that the system of exchange values—the exchange of equivalents measured by labour—turns into, or rather reveals as its concealed background, the *appropriation of alien labour without exchange,* the total separation of labour and property. For the domination of exchange value and of production producing exchange values *presupposes* [V-14] alien labour capacity as itself an exchange value. I.e. it presupposes the separation of living labour capacity from its objective conditions. It presupposes relating to these—or to its own objectivity—as to alien property; in a word, relating to them as *capital.* The golden age of labour emancipating itself is confined to those periods when feudalism was in decay, but still engaged in internecine conflict, as in England in the 14th and the first half of the 15th centuries. If labour is once again to relate to its objective conditions as to its property, another system must replace that of private exchange. For, as we have seen,[a] private exchange posits the exchange of objectified labour against labour capacity, and therefore the appropriation of living labour without exchange.

Historically, the transformation of money into capital often assumes quite simple and concrete forms. Thus, for instance, the merchant sets to work a number of spinners and weavers, who up to then carried on these activities as a rural secondary occupation, and turns their secondary into their principal occupation, whereby he has brought them under his sway as wage workers. The next step is to remove them from their homes and to assemble them in a work place. In this simple process it is evident that the merchant has prepared neither raw material nor instrument, nor means of subsistence for the spinner or the weaver. All he has done is gradually to confine them to one sort of labour, in which they become dependent on selling, on the *buyer,* on the *merchant,* and in which they eventually produce only *for* and *through* him. Originally he has bought their labour only by the purchase of their product. As soon as they confine themselves to the production of this exchange value, and must thus directly produce *exchange values* and exchange their labour wholly for money in order to survive, they come under his sway. In the end, even the illusion that they are *selling* him products disappears. He purchases their labour and takes away first their property in the product, before long in the instrument as well, unless he lets them have it as their *sham property* in order to diminish his own production costs.

Manufacture in the strict sense of the term (not yet the factory) is one of the original historical forms in which capital appears at first sporadically or *locally, alongside* the old modes of production, but gradually destroying them everywhere. Manufacture arises where there is mass production for export, i.e. on the *basis of large-scale maritime and overland trade,* in its emporia, such as the Italian cities, Constantinople, the Flemish and Dutch cities, a few Spanish ones like Barcelona, etc. It does not initially embrace the so-called *urban trades,* but the *rural secondary occupations,* spinning and weaving, the sort of work which requires the least craft skill and technical training. Outside these great emporia, in which it finds the basis of an *export* market, and where production is, as it were, *spontaneously* orientated towards exchange value—i.e. man-

a See this volume, pp. 384-87.— *Ed.*

ufactures directly connected with shipping, shipbuilding itself, etc.— manufacture first establishes itself not in the cities but in the countryside, in villages beyond the range of guild restrictions, etc. The rural secondary occupations provide the broad basis of manufacture, while urban trades require a high degree of progress in production before they can be organised on a factory basis. Likewise such branches of production as glassworks, metal factories, sawmills, etc., which right from the start require more concentration of labour power, utilise more natural power, and demand both mass production and a concentration of the means of labour, etc. Likewise papermills, etc.

On the other hand, the emergence of the tenant farmer and the transformation of the agricultural population into free day-labourers. Though this transformation in the country is the last to develop to its ultimate consequences and in its purest form, its origins are among the earliest.

The ancients, who never progressed beyond specifically urban craft industry, could therefore never evolve large-scale industries. For the first prerequisite of the latter is the involvement of the entire countryside in the production, not of use values, but of exchange values. Glassworks, papermills, ironworks, etc., cannot be organised on guild principles. They require mass production, sales on a general market, *monetary wealth* on the part of the entrepreneur. He does not create these conditions, whether subjective or objective; but under the old property and production relations these conditions cannot be brought together.

Gradually the dissolution of the relations of serfdom and the rise of manufacture transform all branches of production into branches operated by capital. Actually, the cities themselves contain one element for the formation of genuine wage labour— the day-labourers outside the guild system, the porters, etc.

[V-15] We have thus seen that the transformation of money into capital presupposes an historical process which has separated the objective conditions of labour from, and made them independent of, the worker. Once capital has come into being, the effect of its process is to subject all production to itself, and everywhere to develop and complete the separation between labour and property, between labour and the objective conditions of labour. In the course of the argument it will become clear how capital destroys craft labour, the smallholder working for himself, etc., and even itself in all those forms in which it does *not* appear in contradiction to labour: in *small-scale capital,* and the intermediate hybrid types between the old modes of production, which may have renewed themselves on the basis of capital, and the classical, adequate modes of capitalist production.

The only accumulation which is a prerequisite for the rise of capital is that of *monetary wealth,* which, when considered in and for itself, is entirely unproductive, arising only from and belonging only to circulation. Capital rapidly creates for itself an internal market by destroying all rural secondary industries, i.e. by spinning and weaving for all, providing clothing for all, etc.; in short by turning the commodities formerly produced as immediate use values into the form of exchange values. This process arises of itself from the separation of the workers from the land and from property (perhaps only servile property) in the conditions of production.

Though the urban trades are essentially based on exchange and the creation of exchange values, the immediate, principal object of this production is not *enrichment* or *exchange value as exchange value,* but the *subsistence* [of the producer] as an *artisan,* as a *master craftsman,* i.e. use value. Production is therefore everywhere subordinate to a presupposed consumption, supply to demand, and it expands only slowly.

The *production of capitalists and wage workers is therefore a major product of the valorisation process of capital.* Ordinary political economy, which considers only the objects produced, entirely forgets this. In as much as this process posits objectified labour as simultaneously the *non-objectification* of the worker, as the objectification of a subjectivity confronting the worker, as the *property* of someone else's will, capital is necessarily also a *capitalist.* The idea of some socialists that we need capital but not capitalists,[90] is therefore completely false. It is inherent in the concept of capital that the objective conditions of labour—and these are its own product—acquire a *personality* confronting labour, or, and this amounts to the same thing, that they are posited as the property of a personality alien to the worker. The concept of capital contains the capitalist.

Still, this error is in no way greater than that of e.g. all those classicists who speak of the existence of *capital* in antiquity, and of Roman or Greek capitalists. This is merely another way of saying that in Rome and Greece labour was *free,* an assertion which these gentlemen would hardly wish to make. That we now not only describe the plantation-owners in America as capitalists, but that they *are* capitalists, is due to the fact that they exist as anomalies within a world market based upon free labour.

If our concern were with the word "capital", which does not occur in antiquity (though corresponding to the *principalis summa rei creditae*,[a] the Greek ἀρχαῖα),[b] then the still nomadic hordes with their flocks on the steppes of Central Asia would be the greatest capitalists, for the original meaning of the word "capital" is cattle. Hence the *métairie* contract[c] still common in the South of France because of the shortage of capital, is paradoxically called *bail de bestes à Chaptel.*[d] If one wants to indulge in a little bad Latin, then our capitalist or *Capitales Homines*[e] would be those "qui debent *censum de capite*".[f]

The conceptual analysis of capital entails difficulties which do not arise in that of money. Capital is essentially a *capitalist*; but at the same time it is *capital* as an element in the existence of the capitalist distinct from him, or as production in general. Thus we shall further find that in the term *capital* much is subsumed that does not appear to belong to the concept. E.g. capital is loaned. It is accumulated, etc. In all these relations it appears to be a mere thing, and entirely to coincide with the matter of which it consists. However, this and other problems will be clarified as the argument proceeds.

(Incidentally let us note for the sake of amusement: the good Adam Müller, who takes all figurative phrases very mystically, has also heard of *living capital* in ordinary life, as opposed to *dead capital*, and rationalises this theosophically.[g] King Athelstan could have enlightened him about this: "Reddam de meo proprio decimas Deo tam in *Vivente Capitali,* quam in *mortuis fructibus terrae.*"[h])

Money always retains the same form in the same substratum, and is therefore more readily conceived as a mere thing. But one and the same thing, a commodity, money, etc., can represent capital or income, etc. Thus even the economists recognise that money is nothing tangible, but that the same thing can be

---

[a] The principal of a loan.— *Ed.*

[b] See Ch. D. Du Cange, *Glossarium mediae et infimae latinitatis* ..., Vol. II, Paris, 1842, pp. 139-42.— *Ed.*

[c] Crop-sharing.— *Ed.*

[d] Contract of leasing cattle.— *Ed.*

[e] Headmen.— *Ed.*

[f] Who have to pay a *head tax.— Ed.*

[g] A. H. Müller, *Die Elemente der Staatskunst*, Part I, Berlin, 1809, pp. 226-41.— *Ed.*

[h] "I shall give a tithe of my property to God, both in *living cattle* and in the *dead fruits of the soil.*" Marx quotes from Du Cange's *Glossarium etc.— Ed.*

subsumed now under the determination of capital, now under some other and quite contrary determination, and accordingly that it *is* capital, or *is not* capital. It is thus evidently a *relation* and *can only* be *a relation of production.*

[V-16]ᵃ//One further remark on the above:
The exchange of equivalents, which appears to imply property in the product of one's own labour—and therefore also to imply that one must posit as identical *appropriation by means of labour,* the real economic process of appropriating, and *property in objectified* labour (what previously appeared as a real process here appears as legal relation, i.e. is recognised as a general condition of production, and hence legally recognised as such, posited as expression of the general will)—is reversed, manifests itself by a necessary dialectic as the absolute separation of labour and property and the appropriation of alien labour without exchange, without equivalent. Production based on exchange value, on the surface of which that free and equal exchange of equivalents takes place, is basically the exchange of *objectified labour* as exchange value for living labour as use value; or, as it may also be expressed, labour relating to its objective conditions—and hence to the objectivity created by labour itself—as to alien property: *the alienation of labour.* On the other hand, the condition of exchange value is that it is measured by labour time, and thus living labour—not its value—is the measure of values. It is a DELUSION to believe that production in all its forms and hence society rests upon the *exchange of mere labour for labour.* In the various forms in which labour relates itself to its conditions of production as to its property, the reproduction of the worker is in no way posited *merely by labour,* for his property relationship is not the result but the presupposition of his labour. In the case of landed property this is clearly the case. It must also become clear in the case of the guild system that the particular type of property which labour creates is not based merely upon labour or the exchange of labour, but upon the objective connection of the worker with a community and with conditions which he finds already in existence, from which he proceeds as his basis. They are also products of a labour, of world-historical labour, of the labour of the community. They are products of its historical development, which does not proceed from the labour of individuals or from

ᵃ Page 16 of Notebook V begins with a passage relating to the next section of the Chapter on Capital (see this volume, p. 439).— *Ed.*

the exchange of their labours. Therefore mere labour is not the presupposition of the realisation [of the product]. A condition in which labour is simply exchanged for labour—whether in the form of immediate activity or in that of product—implies the separation of labour from its original intertwinement with its objective conditions. As a result, labour appears on the one hand as mere labour, and on the other its product as objectified labour acquires a completely independent existence as value confronting [living] labour. *The exchange of labour for labour—apparently the condition for the property of the worker—is based on his propertylessness.*//

(The *most extreme form of estrangement* in which—in the relationship of capital to wage labour—labour, productive activity, appears to its own conditions and its own product, is a necessary transitional stage. This form therefore already contains *in itself*, but as yet only in inverted form, the dissolution of all *conditions restricting production,* and creates and produces the unconditional premisses for production, and hence all the material conditions for the total, universal development of the productive powers of the individual. This will be considered later.)

[CIRCUIT AND TURNOVER OF CAPITAL]

We have seen how the true nature of capital only emerges *at the end of its circulation.*[a]

We must now consider *circulation* itself or the *turnover of capital.* Initially, production appeared to lie beyond circulation and circulation beyond production. The circulation of capital—circulation posited as circulation of capital—embraces both moments. In that circulation, production appears both as the end point of circulation and as its point of departure and vice versa. Now both the independence of circulation and the remote isolation of production from it are reduced to a mere semblance.[b]

The circulation of money set out from an infinite number of points and returned at an infinite number of points. The point of return was in no way posited as the point of departure. In the circulation of capital, the point of departure is posited as the point of return, and the point of return as the point of departure. The capitalist himself is the point of departure and the point of return. He exchanges money for the conditions of production, produces

---

[a] See this volume, pp. 384-87.— *Ed.*
[b] The above two paragraphs are on page 16 of Notebook V.— *Ed.*

the product, and valorises it, i.e. converts it into money and recommences the process. The circulation of money considered for itself is necessarily extinguished in money as a static thing. The circulation of capital is a continuously self-igniting process, divides itself into its different moments, and is a perpetuum mobile. On the side of the circulation of money price is posited purely formally, in so far as *value* is presupposed independently of that circulation. The circulation of capital *posits price*, not only formally but really, in so far as it posits value.

If value itself appears within it as presupposition, it can only be as *value posited* by another capital. The circulation of money follows a path whose width has been measured in advance, and the circumstances which accelerate or retard it are external impulses. Capital in its circulation expands both itself and [V-17] its path, and the rapidity or slowness with which it circulates is one of the intrinsic moments of that path. It is qualitatively changed in circulation, and the totality of the moments of its circulation are themselves the moments of its production—of its reproduction as well as of its new production.

//We have seen how, at the end of the second curcuit, i.e. [at the stage] of surplus value which is employed as surplus capital, the illusion disappears that the capitalist exchanges with the worker anything other than a part of the latter's own, objectified labour. Within the mode of production already founded on capital itself, the part of the individual capital which represents raw material and instrument of course appears for that capital as a value *presupposed* to it and similarly presupposed to the *living labour* which it purchases. These two items turn out to be posited by *alien capital,* hence again by *capital,* but by another one. One capitalist's raw material is the other's product. One capitalist's product is the other's raw material. One capitalist's *instrument* is the other's product, and may even serve as raw material for the production of another instrument. Thus what appears as a presupposition in the individual capital, what we have called constant value, is nothing but the presupposition of capital by capital, i.e. the capitals in the different branches of industry posit one another as presupposition and condition. Each capital considered for itself can be resolved into dead labour as *value become independent* vis-à-vis living labour. In the last analysis, none of them contains anything other than labour—apart from the natural substances, which do not possess value. The discussion at this point must not be diverted by the introduction of *many* capitals. Indeed, the relationship of the *many* capitals will become clear when what they all have in common, their quality of being capital, has been analysed.//

The circulation of capital is simultaneously its becoming, its growth, its life-process. If anything can be compared to the circulation of blood, it was not the formal circulation of money, but the circulation of capital, which really has a content of its own.

If circulation presupposes production at all points, and is the circulation of products, whether money or commodity—and products everywhere emerge from the process of production, which is itself the process of capital—it follows that the circulation of money itself is determined by the circulation of capital, while it previously appeared to run *alongside* the process of production. We shall return to this point.

If we now consider circulation or the turnover of capital as a whole, the process of production and circulation itself appear as the two great distinctions within that process, both as moments of capital's circulation. How long capital remains within the sphere of the process of production depends upon the technological conditions of the process; and the time capital stays in this phase directly coincides with the development of the productive forces— however much its length must vary according to the type of production, its object, etc. The duration here is simply the labour time necessary for the manufacture of the product. (Wrong!) [140] The shorter the labour time necessary, the greater is relative surplus value, as we have seen. It is the same if less labour time is required for a given quantity of products, or if in a given labour time more finished products are supplied. The reduction of the time during which a certain amount of capital remains in the process of production and is thus taken out of circulation proper, EMBARGOED as it were,[a] coincides with the reduction of the labour time necessary for the manufacture of a product, [which comes] with the development of the productive forces, both through the application of natural forces and machinery, and through the natural powers of social labour—the agglomeration of workers, combination and division of labour. Hence in this respect, no new moment seems to enter the process. However, if we remember that the part of the individual capital which constitutes raw material and instrument (means of labour) is the product of an alien capital, it becomes clear that the speed with which it can renew the process of production is at the same time determined by

---

[a] Marx has "embarked".— *Ed.*

the development of the productive forces in all other branches of industry. This becomes quite clear if one supposes the same capital to produce its raw materials, its instruments and its final products. The length of time during which capital remains in the phase of the production process, itself becomes a moment of circulation, if we presuppose *various* capitals. But we are not yet concerned with the *many* capitals. This moment therefore does not belong here.

The second moment is the time which elapses between the completed transformation of capital into the product and its transformation into money. Obviously, the frequency with which capital can recommence the process of production, of self-valorisation, in a given period of time depends upon the speed at which this phase is run through, or on its duration.

If a capital of originally, say, 100 thaler turns over four times a year, and each time it is turned over at a profit of 5% of its value without the re-capitalisation of the new value, it is the same as if a capital 4 times as large, 400, at the same percentage, were to turn over *once* in one year. [The profit] in each case 20 thaler.

The velocity of the turnover—assuming that the other conditions of production remain the same—therefore compensates for the [smaller] *volume* of capital. In other words, if [V-18] a value 4 times smaller is realised as capital 4 times in the same period in which a 4 times greater value is realised as capital only once, the profit—the production of surplus value—on the part of the smaller capital is as great—*at least as great*—as on the part of the larger one. We say "at least", although it may actually be greater, because the surplus value itself can be employed as surplus capital.

E.g. assume that the profit on a capital of 100 is 10% each time it is turned over (for the sake of the calculation *this form* of surplus value is anticipated). Then [with 4 turnovers a year] at the end of the first three months the capital of 100 would be 110; at the end of the second three months 121; at the end of the third three months $133^1/_{10}$; and at the end of the fourth three months $146^{41}/_{100}$. Yet a capital of 400 turned over once a year [at the same rate of profit] would only be 440. In the first case the profit=$46^{41}/_{100}$, in the second case only=40. (The presupposition is incorrect in so far as the rate of profit *changes* with each increase in the volume of capital. But the issue here is not to show how much more than 40 it brings in, but the fact that in the first case it brings in more than 40—and it does.)

In our discussion of the circulation of money[a] we have already

---

encountered the law of the compensation of speed by mass and vice versa. It applies as much to production as it does to mechanics. We shall have to return to it when we come to discuss the equalisation of profit rates, prices, etc. The question which concerns us here is this: does not a moment of value determination come in here which is independent of labour, a moment which does not directly take its origin from labour but from circulation itself?

//The role of *credit* in ironing-out differences in the turnover of capital does not belong here yet. But the question itself does belong here, because it arises from the simple concept of capital—considered in general.//

The greater frequency of the turnover of capital in a given period of time resembles the more frequent repetition of the harvest in the more southerly countries compared to the more northerly ones in the course of the natural year. As already pointed out above,[a] we are here completely abstracting from the difference in the time during which capital must remain in the phase of production—in the process of productive valorisation. Just as the corn put as seed into the soil loses its immediate use value, is *devalued* as immediate use value, capital is *devalued* during the period between the completion of the process of production and its reconversion into money and thence back into capital.//The speed with which a particular capital can reconvert itself from its form as money into the conditions of production— the worker himself is not subsumed under these conditions of production, as in slavery, but rather the exchange with him— depends both on the speed and continuity of the production sustained by the other capitals which supply this particular capital with its raw material and instrument, as well as on the availability of workers. With regard to the latter, a relative surplus population is the most favourable condition for capital.//

//Quite apart from capital *a*'s production process, the speed and continuity of production process *b* appears as a moment which conditions the reconversion of capital *a* from the form of money into that of industrial capital. The duration of the *process of production* of capital *b* thus appears as a moment *of the rapidity of the process of circulation* of capital *a*. The duration of the production phase of the one determines the speed of the circulation phase of the other. Their *simultaneity* is a condition for the circulation of *a* not to be obstructed—its own elements for

---

[a] See this volume, p. 442.— *Ed.*

which it must be exchanged must simultaneously be thrown into production and circulation.

E.g. in the last third of the 18th century, hand-spinning could not supply the required volume of raw material for weaving—or, which is the same thing, spinning could not put flax or cotton through the process of production, convert them into yarn, with the required simultaneity or simultaneous speed. The result was the invention of spinning machinery which supplied an incomparably greater output in the same labour time or, which is the same thing, required an incomparably shorter labour time to produce the same output, required an incomparably shorter stay [of the raw material] in the spinning process. All the moments of capital which appear involved in it, if it is considered according to its general concept, acquire an independent reality, and moreover become manifest only when it appears in its reality as many capitals. Only then does its internal living structure, which is created within and through competition, develop on a broader scale.//

If we consider the turnover of capital in its entirety, there appear to be four moments of it; or the two major moments of the process of production and the process of circulation considered as two moments, each of which contains a duality. We can begin our discussion with either circulation or production. This much has already been said that circulation itself is a moment of production, since only through circulation does capital become capital; and production is merely a moment of circulation, in so far as circulation itself is considered as the totality of the process of production.

The moments are: (I) The real process of production and its duration. [V-19] (II) Conversion of the product into money. Duration of this operation. (III) Conversion of the money into the appropriate proportions of raw material, means of labour and labour, in short into the elements of capital as productive capital. (IV) The exchange of a part of capital for the living labour capacity can and must be considered a special moment of the process, since the labour market is regulated by other laws than the PRODUCE MARKET, etc. In the labour market, population is the main factor, not absolute but relative population. Moment (I) does not come into consideration here, as already stated, since it coincides with the conditions of valorisation in general. Moment (III) can only be considered when we are dealing not with capital in general but with many capitals. Moment (IV) belongs to the section on wages, etc.

Here we are only concerned with moment II. In the circulation of money, there was only a formal alternation of exchange value as money and commodity. Here, *money and the commodity are a condition of production*; in the final analysis, the process of production. The very contents of the moments [of circulation] are different here. The difference in capital turnover, as it is posited in II, since it depends neither on greater difficulty in the exchange with labour, nor on delays resulting from the non-simultaneous presence of raw material and means of labour in circulation, nor on the different duration of the production process, could only be due to greater difficulties in valorisation. This is obviously not an immanent case arising from the relationship itself, but coincides here, where we are considering capital in general, with what we have said about devaluation as a concomitant of valorisation.[a]

No business is founded on the principle that it can sell its products *with greater difficulty* than another business. If this [difficulty] resulted from a smaller market [for the product], a smaller capital—not a larger, as assumed—would be invested in it than in the business with a larger market. It could be connected, however, with the *greater geographical distance of the market* and hence the later RETURN. The longer time required by capital *a* for its valorisation is due here to the greater geographical distance it must travel after the process of production in order to be exchanged as *C* for *M*.

But suppose we have a product which is produced for export to China: is it not reasonable to argue that the product is only finished, only emerges from its process of production, when it has actually reached the Chinese market? The costs of valorisation would rise by the costs of transporting it from England to China. (We cannot yet discuss here the compensation for the longer fallow period of the capital, because this presupposes the secondary and derived forms of surplus value, i.e. interest.) In this case the production costs would resolve into the labour time objectified in the immediate process of production+the labour time contained in transport.

The first question which now arises is this: according to the principles we have so far established, can a surplus value be extracted from the transport costs? Let us deduct the constant part of capital used up in transporting [the commodity], i.e. ship, wagon, etc., and everything that pertains to their application, since

---

[a] See this volume, pp. 329-30.— *Ed.*

these elements are not relevant to the question and it is immaterial whether we posit them as=0 or=x. Now, is it possible that surplus labour is embodied in the transport costs, and that capital can extract surplus value from them? The question may be simply answered by another question: what is the necessary labour or the value in which it is objectified?

The product must pay for (1) its own exchange value, which is the labour objectified in it; (2) the surplus time which the sailor, the carrier, etc., employs in transportation. Whether or not he can extract this depends on the wealth of the country to which he exports the product and on the need for it, i.e. on the use value which the product has in that country. In direct production it is clear that all the surplus labour which the manufacturer compels the worker to perform is surplus value for him, for it is labour objectified in new use values which costs him nothing. But clearly he cannot stretch the time used for transporting [the product] beyond the time actually required. If he did so, he would throw labour time away, not valorise it, i.e. he would not objectify it in a use value. If the sailor, the carrier, etc., needs to work for only half a year to obtain a year's subsistence (assuming that this is GENERALLY the ratio of necessary [to total] labour), the capitalist employs him for a whole year and only pays him for half a year. By adding a whole year's labour time to the value of the transported products but paying only for half a year, he gains a surplus value of 100% on the necessary labour. It is the same as in direct production, and the original surplus value on the transported product can only derive from the fact that a part of the transport time worked by the workers *is not paid for,* because it is surplus time, time *over and above* that which is necessary for them to live.

That a single product could be made so dear by transport costs that it could not be exchanged—because of the disproportion between the value of the product and its additional value as a transported product, the latter being a quality which is extinguished in it as soon as it has reached its destination—does not affect the matter. If a manufacturer set the whole of his machinery into operation to spin 1 lb. of TWIST, the value of this lb. would likewise rise to such an extent that it would hardly find a ready sale. The rise in the price of foreign products and their limited consumption in the Middle Ages, etc., stem precisely from this cause.

Whether I extract metals from the mines or take commodities to the places where they are consumed, both equally represent a spatial [V-20] movement. Improvements in the means of transport and communication likewise fall into the category of the development of the productive forces in general. This is not the place to discuss the fact that the extent to which products can bear transport costs may depend on their value; or that, moreover, commercial traffic on a massive scale is necessary if transport costs are to be reduced—a ship of 100 tons capacity can carry 2 or 100 tons of freight at the same production costs, etc.—and if means of communication are to be commercially profitable, etc. (Nevertheless, it will be necessary to devote a separate section to the means of communication, since they constitute a form of *capital fixe*, which has its own laws of valorisation.)

If we assume that the same capital performs the functions of both production and transportation, both would be subsumed under immediate production, and circulation as we have considered it so far, i.e. conversion of the product into money as soon as the product has acquired its final form for use, the form in which it is suitable for circulation, would begin only when the product had been brought to its place of destination. This capitalist's delayed RETURN as compared to that of another, who sold his product locally, would resolve into another form of greater use of *capital fixe*, with which we are not as yet concerned. Whether capitalist *A* needs 100 thaler more for his instrument than *B* or whether he must spend 100 thaler more on bringing his product to its place of destination, to its market, is the same thing. In both cases greater *capital fixe* is required [by *A*], more *means* of production which are consumed in direct production. Thus from this aspect no immanent CASE [belonging to circulation proper] would be posited here; it would have to be considered in connection with the distinction between *capital fixe* and *capital circulant*.

Nevertheless, one additional moment does enter here: the *costs of circulation* which are not contained in the simple concept of circulation and do not as yet concern us. The *costs of circulation* which derive from circulation as an economic act—as a relation of production, not as directly a moment of production as is the case of the *means of transport and communication,* can be properly discussed only when we come to interest and especially to credit. Circulation, in the sense in which we are considering it, is a process of transformation, a qualitative process of value, as it appears in the different forms of money, production process, product, reconversion into money and surplus capital. This process of transformation as such concerns us here in so far as this transition from one determination into the other produces new determinations. The costs of circulation are not necessarily included e.g. in the transition from product to money. They could be=0.

However, in so far as circulation itself involves costs, requires surplus labour, it appears as itself included in the process of production. In this respect circulation appears as a moment of the direct production process. In the case of production directed towards immediate use, and exchanging only the surplus, the costs of circulation are incurred only in relation to that surplus, not to the main product. The more production comes to be based on exchange value, and thus on exchange, the more important for production do the physical conditions of exchange become—the means of communication and transport. By its very nature, capital strives to go beyond every spatial limitation. Hence the creation of the physical conditions of exchange—of the means of communication and transport—becomes a necessity for it to an incomparably greater degree: space must be annihilated by time. In so far as the immediate product can be valorised on a mass scale in distant markets only to the extent that transport costs decline, and in so far as, on the other hand, means of transport and communication themselves can only function as spheres of valorisation, of labour organised by capital, to the extent that commercial traffic takes place on a massive scale—whereby more than the necessary labour is replaced—the production of cheap means of transport and communication is a condition of production based on capital, and *therefore* they are produced by it. All the labour which is required to put the finished product into circulation—it is in economic circulation only when it is on the market—is regarded by capital as a barrier to be overcome. Likewise all labour required as *condition* for the process of production (such as e.g. costs incurred to ensure the security of the exchange, etc.).

Water transport, along a self-propelling route, is the means of transportation κατ' ἐξοχήν[a] of all trading peoples. On the other hand, roads for communication were originally the responsibility of the community; later, for a long time, they became the responsibility of the government. They represented pure deductions from production, coming out of the common surplus product of the country but not constituting a source of its wealth, i.e. they did not cover their production costs. In the original Asiatic SELF-SUSTAINING

---

[a] Par excellence.— Ed.

communities there was on the one hand no need for roads; on the other hand, their lack kept the communities totally isolated, and hence constituted an essential moment of their unchanging survival (as in India). The building of roads by means of forced labour or through taxation, which is another form of forced labour, amounts to the compulsory conversion of a part of surplus labour or the surplus product of the country into roads. If an individual capital is to assume that function, i.e. to produce the conditions of the process of *production* which do not fall immediately within that process, it must be possible for the labour [involved in road building] to be valorised.

A definite road between points *A* and *B* (assuming that the land [on which it is constructed] does not cost anything) contains [V-21] a definite quantity of labour, and hence of value. It is immaterial whether the capitalist or the State has organised its construction. Does the capitalist therefore derive a profit from it by creating surplus labour and therefore surplus value?[a] First strip off what is PUZZLING about the road and arises from its nature as *capital fixe.* Imagine that the road could be sold AT ONCE, like a coat or a ton of iron. If it takes, say, 12 months to produce the road, its value=12 months. If the GENERAL STANDARD OF LABOUR is such that the worker can live [for a year] on, say, six months' objectified labour, then, if the worker built the entire road, he would produce surplus value to the amount of 6 months of labour for himself. Or if the community built the road, and the worker wished to work only for the necessary time, another worker would have to be engaged for six months. But the capitalist compels the one worker to work for 12 months and pays him 6. The part of the road's value which contains the worker's surplus labour constitutes the profit of the capitalist. The specific form in which the product appears need in no way upset the foundation of the theory of value through objectified labour time.

But the question is precisely: can the capitalist valorise the road, can he realise its value by means of exchange? This question can of course be asked about any product, but it assumes a special form in relation to the general conditions of production. Let us assume that the road is not valorised. But it is built because it represents a necessary use value. How does the matter stand then?

---

[a] Here Marx crossed out the following passage: "Certainly not! Where then does his profit come from? The public pays him interest and profit. So far as the road facilitates production and exchange, it is a productive force, not value—use value for the act of production."— *Ed.*

It must be built and paid for—in so far as its production costs must be given in exchange for it. It only comes into existence through the consumption of a certain amount of labour, means of labour, raw materials, etc. It makes no difference whether it is built by means of forced labour or taxes. It is built only because it is a necessary use value for the community, because it needs it *à tout prix*.[a]

This is certainly a surplus labour which the individual must perform over and above the labour directly necessary for his own subsistence, whether it takes the form of forced labour or the mediated form of taxes. But in so far as the road is necessary for the community and for each individual *as a member* of it, it is not surplus labour which he performs but a part of his *necessary* labour, of the labour which is necessary for him to reproduce himself as a *member of the community* and hence to reproduce the community, which is itself a general condition of his productive activity.

If the labour time were wholly consumed in direct production (or, indirectly expressed, if it were impossible to levy surplus taxes for this particular purpose), the road would have to remain unbuilt. If the whole society were considered as a single individual, necessary labour would consist of the sum of all the particular functions of labour which are made independent by the division of labour. The single individual would have to spend e.g. so much time for agriculture, so much for industry, so much for trade, so much for the production of instruments, and so much, to return to our bugbear, for road construction and means of communication. All these necessary activities resolve into certain quantities of labour time which must be directed to different purposes and spent on particular activities. How much labour time can be employed depends on the amount of labour capacity (=the mass of able-bodied individuals who constitute the society) and on the development of the productive power of labour (on the quantity of products which it can produce in a given time).

Exchange value, which presupposes a more or less developed division of labour, depending on the level of exchange itself, also presupposes that, instead of the single individual (the society) performing different kinds of labour, spending his labour time in different forms, the labour time of every individual is devoted solely to the necessary particular functions. When we speak of *necessary labour time,* the particular separate branches of labour

---

[a] At any cost.— *Ed.*

appear as *necessary* [for one another]. This reciprocal necessity is mediated by exchange on the basis of exchange value, and is manifested precisely by the fact that each particular objectified labour, each particular specified and materialised labour time is exchanged for the product and symbol of general labour time, of objectified labour time pure and simple, i.e. for money, and can then be exchanged again for any particular labour. This necessity is itself subject to change, in that needs are produced just as much as products and the various craft skills. The scope of these needs and necessary labours may expand or contract.

The more the needs which are themselves historically produced, the needs produced by production itself, the social needs which are themselves the OFFSPRING of SOCIAL PRODUCTION and INTERCOURSE—the more these needs are posited as *necessary,* the higher the development of real wealth. Considered as *physical matter,* wealth consists merely in the multiplicity of needs. The crafts themselves do not appear *necessary* a l o n g s i d e SELF-SUSTAINING AGRICULTURE, where spinning, weaving, etc., are carried on as domestic sidelines. But if e.g. agriculture itself [V-22] is based upon scientific cultivation; if it requires machines, chemical fertilisers available through trade, seeds imported from distant countries, etc.; if—as all this implies—rural patriarchal manufacture has disappeared, then the machine-making factory, foreign trade, crafts, etc., appear as ' *needs* for agriculture. Perhaps guano can be obtained for it only by exporting silks. Thus silk manufacture no longer appears as a luxury industry, but as an industry necessary for agriculture. In this case, agriculture no longer finds the conditions for its own production within itself, provided by nature. These now exist outside it as independent industries, and with this outside existence, the whole complex set of interconnections in which these alien industries exist is drawn into the sphere of the conditions of agricultural production. It is chiefly and essentially owing to this that what earlier appeared as luxury is now necessary, and that so-called luxury needs appear e.g. as a necessity for the most natural industry rooted in the most basic natural need.

It is the tendency of capital to remove the natural ground from the foundation of every industry, and to transfer the conditions of its production outside it to a general context. Hence the conversion of what previously appeared superfluous into necessities, things whose necessity is a product of history. Universal exchange itself, i.e. the world market and hence the totality of activity, intercourse, needs, etc., of which it consists, becomes the universal foundation of all industries. *Luxury* is the opposite of *natural necessities.* Necessary needs are those of the individual reduced to a natural subject. The development of industry abolishes both natural necessity and luxury—though in bourgeois society it does so only in *antithetical form,* in that it itself only posits a particular social standard as the measure of what is necessary as against what is luxury.

At what point are these questions of the *system of needs* and *system of labours* to be discussed? Will emerge in due course.

Let us return to our [example of the] road. If it can be built at all, it proves that society possesses the labour time (living and objectified labour) required for that purpose.

⫽It is of course assumed here that society follows a correct instinct. It could consume its seed and let its agricultural land lie fallow, in order to construct roads. But then it would not have accomplished the *necessary labour,* because by this labour it would not *reproduce* itself, not maintain itself as living labour capacity. Or living labour capacity could also be directly murdered, as Peter I did in order to build St. Petersburg. This sort of thing does not belong here.⫽

Why is it then that, when production based on exchange value and the division of labour develops, road construction does not immediately become the private business of individuals? And it is not private business when it is carried on by the State by means of taxes. *D'abord,* society, the associated individuals, may possess surplus time with which to construct the road, but only in association. The association is always the aggregation of that part of labour capacity which the individual can employ on road construction apart from his particular work. But it is *not merely* its aggregation. The unification of their forces increases their *productive power.* But this does not mean at all that the labour capacity of the individuals numerically added together, but not employed in *working together,* would be the same. For to the sum of individual labour capacities is added that *surplus* which only exists in and through their *associated, combined labour.* Hence the forcible herding together of the people in Egypt, Etruria, India, etc., for compulsory labour on buildings and public works. Capital brings about the same concentration in *another* way, by the manner of its exchange with free labour.

⫽That capital is not concerned with isolated but with combined labour, just as it is in and for itself a social, combined force, is a point which can perhaps already be discussed here, in the general history of the emergence of capital.⫽

Secondly: The population may have developed to a sufficiently high level on the one hand, and on the other the aid given to it by the application of machinery, etc., may have been developed to such an extent that the productive power arising simply from material *concentration on a mass scale*—and in ancient times it was always this *massive* effect of the compulsory concentration of labour [which counted]—is now superfluous, and a *relatively* smaller *mass of living labour* is necessary.

//The greater the extent to which production is still based on mere manual labour, on the use of muscle power, etc., in short on the physical exertion and labour of individuals, the more does any increase in *productive power* consist in their working together *on a mass scale*. In the semi-artistic crafts, the opposite aspects become important, particularisation and individualisation, the skilfulness of individual, uncombined labour. Capital in its true development combines [V-23] mass labour with skill, but in such a way that the former loses its physical power, and skill resides not in the worker, but in the machine and in the scientific combination of both in the FACTORY operating as a single whole. The social mind of labour acquires an objective existence outside the individual workers.//

A particular class of road workers which is employed by the State can emerge.[a] Or a part of the population who happen to be unemployed at the moment can be used for that purpose, working under a number of master-builders, etc. The latter, however, do not work as capitalists but as more highly educated MENIALS. (About the relation of this skilled labour, etc., later.) The workers are wage workers in this situation, although they are not employed as such by the State, but as MENIAL SERVANTS.

Now, for the capitalist to undertake road construction as a business, at his expense, different conditions are necessary, which all amount to this, that the mode of production based on capital must have already been developed to its highest level. //If the

---

[a] Here Marx has the following digression in brackets: "*In Rome, the army constituted a mass* [of individuals]—but already divorced from the rest of the people—disciplined for labour whose surplus time belonged to the State. They sold the whole of their labour time to the State for a wage, they exchanged the whole of their labour capacity for a wage necessary for the maintenance of their life, in precisely the same way as the worker does with the capitalist. This was true of the time when the Roman army was no longer a citizens' army but an army of mercenaries. In this case the soldiers likewise freely sold their labour. But the State does not buy it for the purpose of producing values. Thus, although it may appear that the form of wage labour initially came into existence in armies, this mercenary system is essentially different from wage labour. There is a certain similarity in the fact that the State uses up the army to increase its power and wealth."—*Ed.*

State organises such projects through *State contractors,* then it is still indirectly effected through forced labour or taxes.//

Firstly: Large-scale capital is presupposed, capital concentrated in the hands of the capitalist, for him to be able to undertake projects of such dimension and where turnover, and therefore valorisation, are going to be so slow. Hence mostly *joint-stock capital,* the form in which capital has worked itself through to its ultimate form, in which it is capital not only *in itself,* in its substance, but in which it is posited in its *form* as social power and product.

Secondly: It must yield *interest,* not *profit.* (It can yield more than interest, but that is not necessary.) This point need not be further discussed here.

Thirdly: The presupposition of a sufficient volume of traffic—above all, commercial and industrial traffic—for the road to be profitable, i.e. for the price demanded for the use of the road to be *worth* that much exchange value to the producers [using the road], or for the road to supply a productive force for which they can pay so much.

Fourthly: A part of the wealth consumed as income must be available for investment in these means of locomotion.

But the two most important presuppositions are: (1) the availability of capital which can be employed for this object in the required quantity and which contents itself with receiving interest; (2) it must be worth it for the productive capitals, for industrial capital, to pay the price of passage. Hence e.g. the first railway between Liverpool and Manchester.[141] It had become a necessity of production for the Liverpool COTTON-BROKERS and even more for the Manchester MANUFACTURERS.

//*Competition* may easily create the necessity for e.g. a railway in a country where the existing level of development of the productive forces would not otherwise make it urgent. The effect of *competition among nations* belongs to the section on *international trade.* The civilising effects of capital become especially evident here.//

Capital as such—assuming its availability on the necessary scale—will only construct a road when its construction has become a necessity for the producers, especially for productive capital itself; when it has become a prerequisite for the capitalist *making a profit.* Then the road will also be profitable. But in these cases a large volume of traffic is already presupposed. It is the same presupposition become *dual:* on the one hand, the wealth of the country sufficiently concentrated and converted into the form of capital to undertake such operations as processes of the valorisation of capital; and on the other hand, the volume of traffic sufficient, and the barrier imposed on capital by the lack of means of communication sufficiently felt as such, to enable the capitalist to realise the value of the road as a road (in a piecemeal fashion, as it is used over a period of time).

All *general conditions* of *production* like roads, canals, etc., whether they facilitate circulation, perhaps even make it possible for the first time, or whether they also increase productive power (like the irrigation systems, etc., constructed in Asia and, incidentally, in Europe as well, by governments), will only be undertaken by capital rather than by the government, which represents the commonality as such, where the highest level of development of production based on capital has been attained. The separation of *travaux publics*[a] from the State and their migration into the domain of works undertaken by capital itself indicates the degree in which the real commonality has constituted itself in the form of capital. A particular country, e.g. the UNITED STATES, may sense the importance of railways for production. Yet, the immediate advantage [V-24] accruing to production may be too small for the outlay to appear as anything but *à fonds perdu.*[b] In that case capital shifts the burden onto the shoulders of the State; or, where the State still traditionally occupies a position *supérieure* to capital, the State still has the privilege and the will to force the generality of capitalists [to put] a part of their *income,* not of their capital, into such generally useful works, which at the same time appear as *general* conditions of production, and therefore not as the *particular* conditions for any particular capitalist. And so long as capital has not assumed the form of joint-stock capital, it seeks only the *particular* conditions of its valorisation, while shifting the burden of the *communal* conditions onto the whole country as national requirements. Capital only undertakes projects which are *profitable,* profitable, that is, from its own point of view.

Admittedly, it also speculates unsoundly, and *is bound,* as we shall see, to do so. In such cases, it undertakes *investments* which are not profitable and only yield a return once they have been *depreciated* to a certain degree. Hence the many undertakings where the first *mise de capital* is *à fonds perdu*[c] and the first

---

[a] Public works.— *Ed.*
[b] A waste of money.— *Ed.*
[c] Investment is lost.— *Ed.*

investors go bankrupt. The advanced capital yields a profit only at second or third hand, when it has been reduced by *depreciation.* Incidentally, the State itself and all that pertains to it belongs to these deductions from *revenue,* is part, as it were, of the *costs of consumption* for individuals, part of the social production costs. A road may itself so increase the productive forces that it creates a traffic through which it becomes profitable. There are works and investments which may be necessary without being productive in the sense of capital, i.e. without the *surplus labour* contained in them being realised as *surplus value* by means of circulation and exchange.

If a worker works on a road e.g. for 12 hours per day in a year, and if the generally necessary labour time on average=6 hours, he has worked a surplus labour of 6 hours. But if the road cannot be sold at [the value of] 12 hours [of objectified labour time], perhaps only at 6, its construction is not a suitable undertaking for capital, and road construction is not productive work for it. Capital must be able to sell the road (the type of sale and the length of time required for it are irrelevant here) in such a way that the necessary labour as well as the surplus labour is realised, or in such a way that it receives out of the general fund of profits, of surplus values, a sufficient share to make it the same as if this capital had [actually] created surplus value. *This relation* to be analysed *later, in connection with profit and necessary labour.*

Capital has attained the highest level of development when the production of the general conditions of the social process of production is not financed by *deductions from the social revenue,* i.e. out of taxation, where revenue and not capital appears as the LABOUR fund, and where the worker, though a free wage worker like all the others, stands economically in a different relation, but by *capital as capital.* This demonstrates, on the one hand, the degree to which capital has subjected to itself all the conditions of social production, and hence, on the other hand, the extent to which social reproductive wealth is *capitalised* and all needs are satisfied by means of exchange, even the *socially posited* needs of the individual, i.e. the needs which he feels and satisfies, not as an isolated individual in society, but socially, together with others— which by their very nature can only be satisfied socially—the extent to which even these are not only satisfied but also produced by exchange and individual exchange at that.

In the case of the above-mentioned road, its construction must be sufficiently profitable for a certain amount of labour time transformed into road to reproduce the worker's labour capacity in exactly the same way as if he had converted it into agriculture. Value is determined by objectified labour time, whatever the form it takes. But whether this *value* can be realised depends on the use value in which it is embodied. Here it is assumed that the road meets a need of the community, its use value is therefore presupposed. On the other hand, for capital to undertake the construction of the road, it is a prerequisite that not only the *necessary labour time* will be paid for [by the users], but also the *surplus labour time* put in by the worker—for that is the source of capital's profit. (The capitalist often enforces this payment by means of protective tariffs, monopoly, State compulsion, while under conditions of free exchange the individual exchangers would pay *at most* for the necessary labour.)

It is quite possible for surplus labour time to have been put in without being paid for (after all, this can also happen to any individual capitalist). *Where capital is dominant* (just as where slavery and serfdom or compulsory labour of any kind is dominant) *the absolute labour time of the worker is posited as the condition which he must meet, if he is to be allowed to perform necessary labour time, i.e. if he is to be allowed to realise the labour time necessary for the maintenance of his labour capacity in use values for himself.* In every type of labour, competition then brings it about that he must work the full time—i.e. surplus labour time. But it may happen that this surplus labour time is not exchangeable, even though it is embodied in the product. Now for the worker himself—as compared with the other wage workers—it is [still] surplus labour. But for the employer it is labour which has, to be sure, a use value for him, like e.g. his cook, but no exchange value. Hence the entire distinction [V-25] between *necessary and surplus labour time* does not exist.

Labour may be necessary without being productive. All *general, social* conditions of production—as long as they cannot as yet be produced by capital as such and under its conditions—are consequently paid for out of a part of the revenue of the country, by the government's treasury, and the workers do not appear as productive workers even though they increase the productive power of capital.

The result of our digression is, incidentally, that the production of the means of communication, the physical conditions of circulation, are put into the category of the production of *capital fixe,* and hence do not constitute a special CASE. But a prospect has thereby incidentally opened before us, a prospect which at this point cannot yet be clearly depicted, of a *specific relation of capital to the communal, general conditions of social production,* as distinct from the conditions of a *particular capital* and its *particular process of production.*

Circulation proceeds in space and time. The spatial condition, the conveyance of the product to the market, belongs, economically considered, to the process of production itself. The product is not really finished until it is on the market. The movement by which it gets there, represents a part of its costs of production. It does not constitute a necessary moment of circulation conceived as a particular process of value, for a product may be purchased and even consumed where it is produced. But this spatial moment is significant in so far as the expansion of the market, the exchangeability of the product, are connected with it. The reduction of the costs of this *real* circulation (in space) belongs to the development of the productive forces by capital, the diminution of the costs of its valorisation. In certain respects, as an external condition for the existence of the economic process of circulation, this moment can also be reckoned among the *production costs* of circulation, so that, with respect to this moment, circulation appears as a moment not merely of the production process in general, but of the direct production process as well. In any case, what appears here is the determination of this moment by the general degree of development of the productive forces and of production based upon capital in general.

This spatial moment, the conveyance of the product to the market, could be more precisely viewed as the conversion of the product into a *commodity,* for it is a necessary condition for its circulation, except where the place of its production is itself the market. It is a commodity only when put on the market. (WHETHER OR NOT this constitutes a particular moment is a matter of chance. If capital works to order, neither this moment nor the transformation into money exist as a particular moment for it. But *working to order,* i.e. supply which corresponds to a previously stated demand, is not a *general or dominant* situation, does not correspond to large-scale industry, and in no way arises as a condition [of the production process] from the nature of capital.)

Secondly, the temporal moment. This is an essential part of the concept of circulation. Suppose the act of converting the commodity into money is fixed by contract, this costs time—time involved in counting, weighing, measuring. The abridgement of this moment similarly constitutes an increase in productive power. This is time conceived only as the *external* condition for the transition from the form of commodity into that of money. The transition itself is presupposed. We are concerned with the time which *elapses during this presupposed act.* This belongs to the *costs of circulation.* There is also another thing: the time which elapses before the commodity is transformed into money; or the time during which it remains a *commodity,* only potential, not real, value. This is pure loss.

The conclusion from all that has been said is that circulation appears as an essential process of capital. The process of production cannot be recommenced until the commodity has been transformed into money. The *uninterrupted continuity* of that process, the unhindered and fluent transition of value from one form into the other, or from one phase of the process into the other, appears as a basic condition for production based on capital to a much greater degree than for all earlier forms of production.

On the other hand, while the necessity of this continuity is posited, the phases [of the process] fall asunder in time and space as particular processes indifferent to one another. Thus it appears to be a matter of chance for production based on capital, whether or not its essential condition, the continuity of the various processes which constitute the totality of its process, is fulfilled. The transcendence of this element of chance through capital itself is *credit.* (It has other aspects as well; but this one arises directly from the nature of the process of production and is therefore the basis of the necessity of credit.) That is why *credit* in any developed form does not appear in any earlier mode of production. There was borrowing and lending in earlier situations too; indeed, usury is the most ancient of the antediluvian forms of capital. But borrowing and lending no more constitute *credit* than working constitutes *industrial labour* or *free wage labour.* As an essential, developed relation of production, credit appears *historically* only in circulation based on capital or wage labour. (*Money* itself is a form to transcend the inequality of the time required in different branches of production in so far as this inequality obstructs [V-26] exchange.) *Usury* in its *bourgeois form, adapted to capital,* is itself a form of credit, but in its pre-bourgeois form it is rather an *expression of the lack of credit.*

(The reconversion of money into the objective moments or conditions of production presupposes their *availability.* It constitutes the various *markets* in which the producer encounters them as commodities—in the hands of the merchant—markets (alongside the LABOUR MARKET) which are essentially different from the markets for direct individual, final consumption.)

In its circulation, money was converted into a commodity, and in the exchange of *M* for *C,* consumption completed the process. Or the commodity was exchanged for money—and in the exchange of *C* for *M, M* was either a vanishing moment to be itself exchanged again for *C,* where the process again ended in consumption; or the money was withdrawn from circulation and became dead treasure, a merely symbolic wealth. At no point did the process ignite from a spark within itself, for the presuppositions of the circulation of money lay outside it and it constantly required new stimulus from without.

In so far as the two moments [*C*—*M*] exchanged for one another, the change in their form within circulation was merely formal. But in so far as content was involved in the change, it fell outside the economic process; the content did not belong within it. Neither did the commodity maintain itself as money nor the money as commodity; each was the one or the other. Value as such did not maintain itself in and through circulation as embracing its process of transformation, its change of form; nor was *use value* itself produced by *exchange value* (which is the case in the production process of capital).

With capital, the consumption of the commodity itself is not a final act; it falls within the production process and appears as itself a moment of production, i.e. of the process of *positing value.* Capital is now posited, but posited in each of the moments in which it appears now as money, now as commodity, now as exchange value, now as use value, posited as value which not only formally maintains itself throughout these changes in its form, but which *valorises* itself as well, i.e. it is posited as value relating to itself as value. The transition from one moment to the other appears as a particular process, but each of these processes is the transition into the other. In this way capital is posited as value-in-process, which is capital in every one of the moments. It is therefore posited as *capital circulant;* in each of the moments it is capital and circulating from one determination to the other. The point of return is simultaneously the point of departure and vice versa—i.e. the *capitalist.* All capital is originally *capital circulant,* both produced by and producing circulation, tracing its orbit as its own.

The circulation of money now, from the present standpoint, appears only as a moment of the circulation of capital, and its independence is posited as a mere *semblance.* It appears as determined on all sides by the circulation of capital, a point to which we shall return. In so far as it constitutes an independent movement alongside that of capital, this independence is only posited by the *continuity* of the circulation of capital, so that this one moment can be fixed and considered for itself.

//"Capital permanent *value multiplying itself,* which no longer becomes extinct. This value detaches itself from the commodity which has produced it; equivalent to a *metaphysical, insubstantial quality* always in the possession of the same cultivator" (e.g.) "for whom it assumes various forms" (Sismondi, [*Nouveaux principes d'économie politique,* Vol. I, pp. 88-89,] VI).

"In the exchange of labour for capital, the worker demands subsistence *pour vivre*[a]; the capitalist demands *du travail pour gagner*[b]" (Sismondi, l.c. [p. 91]).

"The *chef d'atelier*[c] gains, profits *de tout l'accroissement des pouvoirs productifs qu'avait opéré la division du travail*[d]" (1.c. [p. 92]).

"The sale of labour=renunciation of all the fruits of labour" (Cherbuliez, [*Richesse ou pauvreté,* p. 64,] Ch. XXVIII [142]).

"The three component parts of capital" (i.e. *matière première, instrument, approvisionnement*[e]) "do not grow in the same proportion, nor are they in *the same relation* at different stages of society. The *approvisionnement* remains the same for a definite time, however quickly the *rapidité de la production* and in consequence the quantity of products may grow. Hence the increase in *productive capital* does not necessarily entail an increase in the *approvisionnement,* which should determine the price of labour. It may actually be accompanied by its diminution" (1.c. [pp. 61-63]).//

//In as much as the continuous renewal of production depends on the sale of the finished products, on the conversion, that is, of the commodity into money and the reconversion of money into the conditions of production—raw material, instrument, wages—; and in as much as the path capital must follow in passing from one of these determinations to the other constitutes sections of circulation, and these sections are traversed in certain *periods of time*; (note that even spatial distance resolves itself into time; e.g. in the case of the market, it is not its spatial distance which really matters, but the speed, the amount of time, in which it is reached) by the same token it depends on the speed of circulation, on the *time* taken by it, how many products can be produced in a given period of time, how often capital can valorise itself in a given period of time, how often it can *reproduce* and *multiply* its value in that time.

Thus there really does enter here a moment of *value determina-*

---

[a] *In order to be able to live.— Ed.*

[b] *Labour in order to be able to make a profit.— Ed.*

[c] Factory owner.— *Ed.*

[d] By all *the growth* in the *productive forces* brought about by *the division of labour.— Ed.*

[e] Raw material, instrument, means of subsistence.— *Ed.*

tion which [V-27] does not arise from the direct relation of labour to capital. It would seem that the relation in which the same capital can repeat the process of production (creation of new value) in a given period of time is a condition not directly posited by the production process itself. Though circulation does not give rise to a moment of *value determination* itself, for this lies exclusively in the sphere of labour, the speed of circulation does determine the rate at which the process of production can be repeated, and therefore the speed with which values are created. In other words, while not creating *values,* circulation does, to a certain degree, determine the mass of values which can be created. This will be the values and surplus values posited by the process of production×the number of times the production process can be repeated in a given period of time.

When we speak of the speed of the turnover of capital, we presume that only *external barriers* obstruct the transition from one phase [of circulation] to another, not ones arising from the production process and from circulation itself (as in crises, overproduction, etc.).

Thus, in addition to the labour time realised in the product, the *circulation time* of capital comes in as a moment of value creation—of productive labour time itself. If labour time appears as the activity which posits value, the circulation time of capital appears as the *time of devaluation*. This distinction appears as follows: if we assume that the totality of labour time commanded by capital is set at its maximum, say the infinite ∞, in such a way that the necessary labour time would constitute an infinitely small part and the surplus labour time an infinitely large part of this ∞, then this would be the greatest possible valorisation of capital, and that is what it strives for. On the other hand, if we assume that the *circulation time of capital*=0, and that it traverses the various stages of its transformation as quickly in reality as it does in thought, then this would equally be the greatest possible factor by which the production process could be repeated, i.e. the greatest possible number of valorisation processes of capital which could take place in a given period of time.

The repetition of the production process would be restricted only by the duration of that process itself, the time required to transform the raw material into product. The *circulation time* is therefore not a positive value-creating element. If it were equal to 0, value creation would be at its highest level. If either surplus or necessary labour time=0, i.e. if necessary labour time absorbed all time, or if production could be carried on *without* any labour, there would be neither value nor capital, nor value creation. Hence the *circulation time* determines value only in so far as it appears as a *natural barrier* for the valorisation of labour time. Thus it is IN FACT a deduction from surplus labour time, i.e. an increase in *necessary labour time.* It is clear that necessary labour time must be paid for, whether the circulation process goes on slowly or quickly.

E.g. in industries in which specialised workers are required, who, however, can be employed for only a part of the year, perhaps because the product can only be sold during a particular SEASON, they would still have to be paid for the whole year, i.e. surplus labour time is diminished in proportion as they are underemployed during a given period of time, but still have to be paid *d'une manière ou d'une autre.* (E.g. by receiving in 4 months enough wages to subsist for a year.) If capital could employ them for 12 months, it would not pay them any more in wages, and would have gained that much [8 months'] surplus labour.

Circulation time therefore appears as a barrier to the productivity of labour=increase in necessary labour time=decrease in surplus labour time=decrease in surplus value=an obstruction, a barrier to the self-valorisation process of capital. Thus, while capital must strive on the one hand to tear down every local barrier to traffic, i.e. to exchange, and to conquer the whole world as its market, it strives on the other hand to annihilate space by means of time, i.e. to reduce to a minimum the time required for the movement [of products] from one place to another. The more capital has been developed, and the greater therefore the expansion of the market in which it circulates, which constitutes the spatial path of its circulation, the more it goes on to strive for an even greater spatial expansion of the market and for a more complete annihilation of space by means of time.

(If labour time is not considered as the working day of an individual worker but as the indefinite working day of an indefinite number of workers, all the *relations of population* come in here. The basic theories of population are therefore contained in this first chapter on capital, as are those of profit, price, credit, etc.)

The universalising tendency of capital becomes apparent here, which distinguishes it from all earlier stages of production. Although itself limited by its very nature, capital strives towards the universal development of the productive forces and thereby clears the way for a new mode of production, in which the productive forces are not developed just to reproduce a particular

situation or, at most, to extend it, but where the free, unob-
structed, progressive and universal development of the productive
forces is itself the presupposition of society and therefore of its
own reproduction; where the sole presupposition is the advance
beyond the point of departure. This tendency possessed by capital,
which simultaneously contradicts capital as a limited form of
production and hence drives it towards its dissolution, distinguishes capital from all earlier modes of production and at the
same time implies that it is posited as mere point of transition. All
previous forms of society [V-28] were destroyed by the development of wealth—or, which is the same thing, by the development
of the social productive forces. Among the ancients, who were
conscious of this fact, wealth was therefore directly denounced as
bringing about the dissolution of the community. Feudal society,
for its part, was destroyed by urban industry, trade and modern
agriculture. (Even by some inventions, e.g. gun powder and the
printing press.)

With the development of wealth—and hence also of new
[productive] forces and expanded intercourse among individuals—
the economic conditions upon which the community was based
were dissolved, as were the corresponding political relations
between the various component parts of the community: the
religion, in which it was viewed in idealised form (and both
community and religion, in turn, were rooted in a given
relationship to nature, into which all productive force resolves
itself); the character, outlook, etc., of the individuals. The
development of science alone, i.e. of the most solid form of wealth,
both product and producer of wealth, was sufficient to dissolve
this community. But the *development of science,* this notional and at
the same time practical form of wealth, is only one aspect, one
form, in which the *development of human productive powers,* i.e. of
wealth, appears.

Considered *notionally,* the dissolution of a definite form of
consciousness would be sufficient to destroy an entire epoch. In
reality, this barrier to consciousness corresponds to a *definite degree
of development of the material productive forces* and thus of wealth.
True, development not only took place on the old basis, there was
also a *development of this basis itself.* The highest development of
this *basis* itself (the flower into which it is transformed, while
remaining *this* basis, *this* plant as flower; hence withering *after*
flowering and as a result of flowering) is the point at which it is
itself worked out and developed to the form in which it becomes
compatible with the *highest degree of the development of the productive*

forces and thus also with the richest development of the individuals [possible on this basis]. As soon as this point has been reached, further development appears as a decline, and the new development begins from a new basis.

We have seen above^a that [the worker's] property in the conditions of production was posited as identical with a limited, specific form of community, a community consisting of individuals with just this kind of characteristics—limited characteristics and limited development of their productive powers. This presupposition was itself in turn the result of a restricted historical stage of development of the productive forces, of both wealth and the mode of producing it. The purpose of the community, of the individual—as well as the condition of production—was the *reproduction of these specific conditions of production* and of the individuals, both singly and in their social groups and relations— as the living carriers of these conditions.

Capital posits the *production of wealth* itself and thus the universal development of the productive forces, posits the continual overthrow of its existing presuppositions, as the presupposition of its reproduction. Value excludes no use value, i.e. includes no specific kind of consumption, etc., intercourse, etc., as absolute condition, and likewise every degree of the development of the social productive forces, of intercourse, of knowledge, etc., appears to it as a barrier which it strives to overcome. Its very presupposition—value—is posited as product, not as a higher presupposition hovering above production. The barrier to *capital* is the fact that this entire development proceeds in a contradictory way, and that the elaboration of the productive forces, of general wealth, etc., knowledge, etc., takes place in such a way that the working individual *alienates* himself; that he relates to the conditions brought out of him by his labour, not as to the conditions of *his own,* but of *alien wealth,* and of his own poverty. But this contradictory form is itself vanishing and produces the real conditions for its own transcendence.

The result is: the tendentially and δυνάμει^b universal development of the productive forces—of wealth in general—as basis, likewise the universality of intercourse, hence also the world market as basis. The basis as the possibility of the universal development of the individuals, and their actual development from this basis as constant transcendence of their *barrier,* which is

---

^a See this volume, pp. 408-20.— *Ed.*
^b Potentially.— *Ed.*

recognised as such, and is not interpreted as a *sacred limit*. The universality of the individual not as an imaginary concept, but the universality of his real and notional relations. Hence also the comprehension of his own history as a *process* and the knowledge of nature (likewise available as practical control over nature) as his real body. The process of development itself posited and known as the presupposition of the same. For this, however, necessary above all that the full development of the productive forces has become the *condition of production;* and not that particular *conditions of production* are posited as the limit to the development of the productive forces.

Let us now return to the *circulation time* of capital. Its reduction (in so far as this is not due to the development of the means of communication and transport which are necessary to bring the product to the market) is in part *creation* of a continuous market and hence of an ever expanding market; and in part development of *economic* relations, developments of forms of capital [V-29] by means of which circulation time is *artificially* reduced. *(All forms of credit.)*

⫻At this point, it may be further noted that, since only capital has the conditions of the production of capital, hence satisfies and strives to realise them, it is the general tendency of capital at all points which are presuppositions of circulation and function as the latter's productive centres, to assimilate these points to itself, i.e. to transform them into capitalising production or production of capital. This propagandistic (civilising) tendency is unique to capital—it distinguishes it from all earlier conditions of production.⫻

The modes of production in which circulation is not an immanent, dominating condition of production, naturally [do] not [have] the specific circulation needs of capital, nor, consequently, do they evolve either the economic forms or the real productive forces corresponding to them.

Production based on capital initially set out from circulation. We now see how it posits circulation as its own condition and how it likewise posits the production process in its immediacy as a moment of the process of circulation and equally posits that process as a phase of the production process in its totality.

In so far as different capitals circulate in different lengths of time (e.g. one [produces for] a more distant market, the other for one near at hand; the conversion of one capital into money is secure, that of the other hazardous; one [contains] more *capital fixe,* the other more *capital circulant*), this brings about differences among them in valorisation. But this only occurs in the secondary valorisation process. Circulation time in itself is a *barrier* to valorisation. (*Necessary labour time* is, admittedly, another barrier; but it is simultaneously an essential element, for without it there would be no value or capital.) It is a deduction from surplus labour time or an increase of the *necessary labour time* in relation to *surplus labour time.* The circulation of capital *realises value,* as living labour *produces value.* Circulation time is a barrier only to the realisation of value and to that extent to value creation. It is a barrier which does not arise from production in general but which is specific to production based on capital. Its transcendence—or the struggle against it—therefore belongs to the specific economic development of capital and provides the impulse for the development of its forms in credit, etc.//

//Capital itself is subject to the contradiction that while it constantly tries to transcend *necessary labour time* (which implies the reduction of the worker's role to a minimum, i.e. his existence as mere living labour capacity), *surplus labour time* exists only in a contradictory way, only in antithesis to necessary labour time. Consequently, capital posits necessary labour time as a *necessary* condition for its own reproduction and valorisation. A development of the material productive forces, which is at the same time the development of the forces of the working class, at a certain point *transcends capital itself.*//

//"The entrepreneur can only recommence production after he has sold the finished product and has used the price in purchasing new *matières* and new *salaires.* Hence, the more promptly circulation brings about these two effects, the more quickly is he in a position to recommence his production, and the greater the quantity of products capital produces in a given period of time" (Storch, [*Cours d'économie politique,* Vol. I, pp. 411-12,] 34).//

//"THE SPECIFIC ADVANCES OF THE CAPITALIST DO NOT CONSIST OF CLOTH, ETC., BUT OF LABOUR" (Malthus, [*The Measure of Value Stated and Illustrated,* p. 17,] IX, 26).[143]//

//"THE ACCUMULATION OF THE GENERAL CAPITAL OF THE COMMUNITY IN OTHER HANDS [than] THOSE OF THE OPERATIVE LABOURERS, NECESSARILY RETARDS THE PROGRESS OF ALL INDUSTRY SAVE THAT OF THE USUAL REMUNERATION OF CAPITAL, WHICH THE TIME AND CIRCUMSTANCES AFFORD TO THE HOLDERS OF THE CAPITAL... In the previous systems, *productive force considered IN REFERENCE TO and SUBORDINATE TO ACTUAL ACCUMULATIONS, AND TO THE PERPETUATING OF THE EXISTING MODES OF DISTRIBUTION. ACTUAL ACCUMULATION AND DISTRIBUTION ARE SUBORDINATE TO THE POWER OF PRODUCING"* (Thompson, [*An Inquiry into the Principles of the Distribution of Wealth...,* London, 1824, pp. 176, 589,] 3).[a]//

---

[a] Marx reproduces the two passages from Thompson in a free rendering, on the basis of his 1845 notebook of excerpts.— Ed.

It follows from the relationship of circulation time to the production process that the sum of values which is produced, or the total valorisation of capital in a given period of time, is determined not only by the new value which capital creates in the production process, or by the surplus time realised in that process, but also by this surplus time (surplus value) multiplied by the factor which expresses the frequency with which the production process of capital can be repeated in that period. The factor expressing this repetition can be regarded as the coefficient of the production process or of the surplus value created by it.

However, this coefficient is not positively but negatively determined by the speed of circulation. I.e. if the speed of circulation were absolute, that is to say, if the production process were not interrupted at all by circulation, this coefficient would be at its greatest. E.g. if the real conditions of wheat production in a given country allowed only one harvest a year, no speed of circulation could make that country's soil yield two harvests a year. But if circulation were obstructed, if the farmer could not sell his wheat quickly enough e.g. to hire workers again, production would be stopped. The maximum of the coefficient of the production process or process of valorisation in a given period of time is determined by the absolute time taken by the [V-30] production phase itself. Once circulation has been completed, capital can recommence its production process. If, therefore, circulation caused no delay at all, its speed would be absolute and its duration would be 0, i.e. if it were accomplished IN NO TIME, that would merely be the same as if *capital* had been able to recommence its production process just as soon as it had been completed. I.e. circulation would not have existed as a limiting barrier on production, and the repetition of the production process in a definite period of time would be absolutely dependent upon, would coincide with, the duration of the production process.

Hence, if the development of industry permitted a capital of £100 to produce x lbs of twist in 4 months, the production process could only be repeated 3 times a year with the same capital; only $3x$ lbs of twist could be produced. No speed of circulation could accelerate the reproduction of capital or rather the repetition of its valorisation process beyond this point. It could only come about in consequence of an *increase of the productive forces*. Circulation time itself is not a *productive force* of capital but a *barrier to its productive force,* arising from its nature as exchange value. The passage [of capital] through the various phases of circulation here appears as a *barrier to production,* a barrier posited by the specific nature of capital itself. An acceleration and reduction of *circulation time*—of the process of circulation—can only reduce the barrier posited by the nature of capital. The natural barriers to the repetition of the production process e.g. in agriculture, coincide with the duration of one cycle of the production phase. The barrier posited by capital is not the time which elapses between sowing and harvesting, but between harvesting and the conversion of the harvest into money and the reconversion of the money into e.g. the purchase of labour. The circulation manipulators who imagine that by accelerating circulation they can do anything other than reduce the obstacles to the reproduction of capital posited by capital itself, are on the wrong track.

(Even crazier, of course, are the circulation manipulators who imagine that credit banks and new credit devices which transcend the duration of circulation time can not only remove the delays, the interruption of production, required for the conversion of the finished product into capital, but make the capital for which the producing capital exchanges, itself superfluous, i.e. they want to continue to produce on the basis of exchange value, but at the same time to remove by some magical formula the conditions necessary for production on this basis.)

The most that credit can do in this respect, where it is a matter of *mere* circulation, is to maintain the continuity of the production process *if* all other conditions for this continuity are present, i.e. if the capital to be exchanged with actually exists, etc.

It is posited in the process of circulation that the conversion of capital into money, or the exchange of capital for capital as a barrier to the exchange of capital for labour and vice versa is posited as the condition for the valorisation of capital by production, for the exploitation of labour by capital //for from the present standpoint, we only have labour or capital at all points of circulation//.

Capital exists as capital only in so far as it passes through the phases of circulation, the different moments of its transformation, to be able to recommence the production process. These phases are themselves phases of its valorisation—but at the same time, as we have seen,[a] phases of its *devaluation*. As long as capital remains fixed in the form of finished product, it cannot be active as capital; it is *negated* capital. Its process of valorisation is held up in the same degree and its value-in-process negated. This appears as a loss for capital, a relative loss of its value, for its value consists

---

[a] See this volume, pp. 329-31.— *Ed.*

precisely in the process of valorisation. In other words, this loss [of value] of capital only means that time passes for it unutilised, time in which it could appropriate *surplus labour time,* alien labour, by exchange with living labour, if the DEADLOCK had not occurred.

Let us suppose a *large number* of capitals employed in particular branches of industry, which are all *necessary* (in the sense that if there were a massive flight of capital from one branch, the supply of products in this branch would fall below the demand, hence market price would rise above the natural price). Let us suppose further that it was necessary for capital *a* in one branch to remain longer in its devalued form, i.e. that the time it takes the capital to pass through the various phases of circulation is longer than in all other branches. This capital *a* would then consider the lesser new value it could produce to be a positive loss, just as if it had to invest so much more to produce the same value. Hence it would charge a proportionately higher exchange value for its products than the other capitals, in order to share in the same rate of profit. But IN FACT this could only happen if the loss were distributed among the other capitals. If *a* demands more exchange value for the product than is objectified in it as labour, [V-31] it can obtain this *"more"* only if the other capitals obtain less than the real value of their products. I.e. all the capitalists who exchanged with *a* would bear a fractional part of [the cost of] the less favourable conditions under which *a* had produced. In this way, an equal average profit would result. Yet the sum of surplus values produced by all the capitals taken together would be diminished precisely in proportion to the lesser valorisation of capital *a* relative to the other capitals. Only this diminution, instead of falling exclusively upon capital *a*, would be borne as a general loss shared proportionately by all the capitals.

Nothing could therefore be more ludicrous than to imagine (see e.g. Ramsay[a]) that capital can constitute an *original* source of *value creation* apart from labour, from its exploitation. For the distribution of surplus labour among the individual capitals takes place not in proportion to the surplus labour time achieved by the individual capital, but in proportion to the *total surplus labour* achieved by the totality of capitals. The *individual capital* can therefore be credited with more value creation than is directly explicable by its *particular* exploitation of labour power. But this *"more"* on the one side must be compensated for by a *"less"* on the

---

[a] G. Ramsay, *An Essay on the Distribution of Wealth,* p. 55.— *Ed.*

other. Otherwise, *average* means nothing at all. The question how the relation of capital to alien capital, i.e. the competition of capitals, distributes surplus value among them, obviously has nothing to do with the absolute amount of this surplus value. Nothing therefore more absurd than to conclude that, because a particular capital is compensated for its *exceptional* circulation time, i.e. calculates its relatively lesser valorisation as a positively higher valorisation, all the *capitals* taken together, *capital,* can make something out of nothing, turn a minus into a plus, minus-surplus labour time or minus-surplus value into plus-surplus value; to conclude, in other words, that it has a *mystical* source of value creation independent of the appropriation of alien labour.

The method of calculating the capitals' respective shares in *surplus value*—not only on the basis of the surplus labour time which they have achieved, but also in accordance with the *length of time during which their capital has been working as such,* i.e. has lain fallow, gone through the phase of devaluation—does not of course in the least affect the total amount of surplus value which they have to distribute among themselves.

This amount cannot be increased by the fact that it is smaller than it would have been if capital *a* had produced surplus value instead of lying fallow, in other words, by the fact that it has produced less surplus value in the same time than the other capitals. Capital *a* is compensated for this *lying-fallow* only in so far as it arises necessarily from the conditions of the particular branch of production, and so appears in relation to *capital* in general as an impediment to its valorisation, a *necessary barrier* to its valorisation generally. The division of labour allows us to regard this barrier only as a barrier to the production process of this particular capital. But if we regard the production process as carried on by capital in general, it constitutes a *general barrier* to its valorisation. If we regard only labour itself as productive, all larger advances which it requires during its valorisation appear as what they are— *deductions from surplus value.*

Circulation can *create value* only in so far as it requires additional employment— *of alien labour*—additional to that directly consumed in the production process. This is then the same as if more *necessary labour* were directly required in the production process. Only the real *costs of circulation* increase the *value* of the product, but they reduce surplus value.

In so far as the circulation of capital (the product, etc.) does not express merely the necessary phases [which capital must pass through] to recommence the production process, this circulation (see Storch's example[a]) does not constitute a moment of production in its totality—is not therefore circulation posited by production; and in so far as it involves costs, these are *faux frais de production*.[b] In so far as circulation costs in general, i.e. the production costs of circulation, concern the exclusively economic moments, circulation in the strict sense (bringing the product to the market gives it *new use value*), they have to be regarded as deductions from *surplus value,* i.e. as an increase of necessary labour relative to surplus labour.

The continuity of production presupposes that circulation time has been transcended. If it is not, time must elapse between the various metamorphoses through which capital must pass; its circulation time *must* appear as a deduction from its production time. On the other hand, the nature of capital presupposes that it passes through the various phases of circulation, not indeed as in the imagination, where one concept can turn into another with the speed of thought, IN NO TIME, but rather as real situations which are separated from one another in time. It must spend some time as a chrysalis before it can take wing as a butterfly. The conditions of production arising from the nature of capital itself are therefore mutually contradictory. The contradiction can be transcended and overcome//except if one were to imagine that all capitals work to order for each other, and the product is therefore always immediately money, a notion which contradicts the nature of capital and hence also the practice of large-scale industry//
[V-32] only in two ways:

Firstly, credit: A pseudo-purchaser *B*—i.e. one who really *pays* but does not really buy—mediates the transformation of capitalist *A*'s product into money. But *B* himself is only paid when capitalist *C* has purchased *A*'s product. It is immaterial whether this CREDIT-MAN *B* gives money to *A* to buy labour, or the raw material and instrument of labour, before *A* can replace them from the proceeds of the sale of his product. *Au fond,* given our premises, *B* must give him both—i.e. all the conditions of production (these, however, represent a greater value than that with which *A* embarked on the production process). In this case, capital *b* replaces capital *a*; but both are not valorised simultaneously. *B* now takes the place of *A*, i.e. his capital lies fallow until it is exchanged with capital *c*. It is fixed in the product of *A*, who has made his product liquid in capital *b*.

---

[a] H. Storch, *Cours d'économie politique,* Vol. I, pp. 404-13.— *Ed.*
[b] Overhead costs of production.— *Ed.*

[THEORIES OF SURPLUS VALUE AND PROFIT]

The absolute confusion of the economists with respect to the Ricardian determination of value by labour time—a confusion which is rooted in a fundamental defect of his own analysis—is very clearly apparent in Mr. Ramsay's work. He says, after earlier discussing the influence of the circulation time of capitals on their *relative valorisation,* i.e. on their relative share in total surplus value, and coming to the absurd conclusion that:

"This shows HOW CAPITAL MAY REGULATE VALUE INDEPENDENTLY OF LABOUR" (IX, 84. R[amsay, G., *An Essay on the Distribution of Wealth,*] 43),

or that

"CAPITAL [is] A SOURCE OF VALUE INDEPENDENT OF LABOUR" (l.c., p. 55);

literally:

"A CIRCULATING CAPITAL *(approvisionnement)* WILL ALWAYS MAINTAIN MORE LABOUR THAN THAT FORMERLY BESTOWED UPON ITSELF. BECAUSE, COULD IT EMPLOY NO MORE THAN HAD BEEN PREVIOUSLY BESTOWED UPON ITSELF, *WHICH ADVANTAGE* COULD ARISE TO THE OWNER FROM THE USE OF IT *AS SUCH?*" (l.c., p. 49). "Given two capitals of equal value, EACH PRODUCED by the labour of 100 MEN OPERATING FOR A GIVEN TIME, of which the one is entirely circulating, the other entirely FIXED, AND MAY PERHAPS CONSIST OF WINE KEPT TO IMPROVE. Now, this circulating capital, *RAISED BY THE LABOUR OF 100 MEN,* will *set into motion 150 MEN.* THEREFORE THE PRODUCT AT THE END OF THE COMING YEAR will in this case be the RESULT of the labour of 150 MEN. BUT STILL IT WILL BE OF NO MORE VALUE THAN THE WINE AT THE TERMINATION OF THE SAME PERIOD, although only 100 MEN [have been] EMPLOYED UPON THE LATTER" (50). "Or does one wish to persuade us that the QUANTITY OF LABOUR WHICH EVERY CIRCULATING CAPITAL *WILL EMPLOY* IS NO MORE THAN EQUAL TO [the labour] PREVIOUSLY BESTOWED UPON IT? That would mean THAT *THE VALUE OF THE CAPITAL EXPENDED* is equal to that of the product" (52).

There is great confusion here between the LABOUR BESTOWED UPON capital and that WHICH IT WILL EMPLOY. The capital which is exchanged for labour capacity, the *approvisionnement*—and this is what he calls *capital circulant*—can never EMPLOY more labour THAN HAS BEEN BESTOWED UPON IT. (We are not concerned here with the way in which the development of the productive forces reacts back upon existing capital.) But THERE HAS BEEN MORE LABOUR BESTOWED UPON IT THAN IT HAS PAID FOR—*SURPLUS LABOUR,* WHICH IS CONVERTED INTO *SURPLUS VALUE AND SURPLUS PRODUCE,* ENABLING THE CAPITAL TO RENEW THIS PROFITABLE BARGAIN, WHERE THE MUTUALITY IS ALL ON ONE SIDE, ON A MORE ENLARGED SCALE. IT IS ENABLED TO EMPLOY MORE NEW LIVING LABOUR, BECAUSE DURING THE PROCESS OF PRODUCTION A PORTION OF FRESH LABOUR HAS BEEN BESTOWED UPON IT BEYOND THE ACCUMULATED LABOUR OF WHICH IT CONSISTED BEFORE ENTERING THAT PROCESS.

Mr. Ramsay appears to imagine that if capital is the product of 20 working days (necessary and surplus time together), this product of 20 working days can employ 30 working days. But this is by no means the case. Say that 10 days of necessary labour and 10 days of surplus labour have been bestowed on the product. Surplus value then=10 days' surplus labour. By re-exchanging this for raw material, instrument and labour, the capitalist can set new *necessary labour* in motion again *with the surplus product.* The point is not that he would have EMPLOYED more labour time than already existed in the product, but that he re-exchanges the surplus labour time, which costs him nothing, for necessary labour time, in other words, precisely that he EMPLOYS the *whole of the labour time* BESTOWED UPON THE PRODUCE, WHILE HE HAS PAID [for] ONLY PART OF THAT LABOUR. Mr. Ramsay's conclusion is THAT if THE QUANTITY OF LABOUR WHICH EVERY CIRCULATING CAPITAL WILL EMPLOY WAS NO MORE THAN EQUAL TO THAT PREVIOUSLY BESTOWED UPON IT, THE VALUE OF THE CAPITAL EXPENDED WOULD BE EQUAL TO THAT OF THE PRODUCE, I.E. NO SURPLUS VALUE WOULD BE LEFT. This would only be correct, if the QUANTITY OF LABOUR BESTOWED UPON THE CAPITAL *had been fully paid for,* i.e. if capital had not appropriated a part of labour *without equivalent.*

These misunderstandings of *Ricardo*['s theory] obviously derive from the fact that Ricardo himself was not clear about the nature of the process [of capitalist production], nor, as a bourgeois, could he be. Insight into this process is=to the STATEMENT that capital is not merely, as A. Smith thinks, command over alien labour, in the sense in which every exchange value is that, because it provides its owner with *buying power,* but that it is the power of appropriating alien labour *without exchange, without equivalent,* but under the guise of exchange. Ricardo knows no other argument to refute A. Smith and others who fall into the same error about value AS DETERMINED BY LABOUR and value AS DETERMINED BY THE PRICE OF LABOUR (WAGES), except to say that with the product of the same quantity of labour one can sometimes set a greater quantity and sometimes a lesser quantity of living labour in motion, i.e. he regards the product of labour with respect to the worker only as *use value,* the part of the product which the worker requires to live as a worker. But it is BY NO MEANS clear to him how it comes about that the worker suddenly represents only *use value* in exchange, or that he extracts only use value from the exchange, as is already proved by his [V-33] argument against A. Smith, which is never general, but always relies on the illustration of individual examples.

How, then, does it come about that the share of the worker in the value of the product is not determined by its value but by its use value, hence not by the labour time bestowed upon it but by its quality of maintaining living labour capacity? If he tries to explain this by, say, competition among the workers, the answer would be the same as the one he himself gives to A. Smith in relation to competition among capitalists—that this competition can certainly even up and equalise the level of profit, but can in no way establish the measure of this level.[a] In the same way, competition among the workers could bring down the higher wage levels, etc., but the general standard of wages or, as Ricardo calls it, the natural price of the wages of labour, could not be explained by competition between worker and worker but only by the original relation between capital and labour. Competition in general, this essential locomotive force of the bourgeois economy, does not establish its laws but is their executor. Hence UNLIMITED COMPETITION is not the presupposition for the validity of the economic laws but the consequence—the form of appearance in which their necessity is realised. For the economists to presuppose, as Ricardo does, that UNLIMITED COMPETITION exists,[b] is to presuppose the full reality and realisation of the bourgeois relations of production in their *differentia specifica*. Competition therefore does not *explain* these laws, nor does it produce them; it lets them *become manifest*.

Ricardo also says[c] the costs of production of living labour depend on the cost of producing the values necessary to reproduce it. If previously he regarded the product with respect to the worker merely as use value, he now regards the worker with respect to the product merely as *exchange value*. He does not concern himself at all with the historical process by means of which the product and living labour enter into this relation to one another. But he is just as unclear about the way in which this relation is perpetuated. In his view, capital is the *result of saving*, which already indicates that he misunderstands its origin and process of reproduction. He therefore also believes that production cannot be carried on without capital, while he believes that capital may very well exist without ground rent. The difference between *profit* and *surplus value* does not exist for him; proof that he is not clear about the nature of either. His procedure right from the start already shows this. Initially, he lets workers

---

[a] D. Ricardo, *On the Principles of Political Economy, and Taxation*, pp. 338-39.— Ed.

[b] Ibid., p. 3.— Ed.

[c] Ibid., p. 86.— Ed.

exchange with workers—and their exchange is then determined by the equivalent, by the labour time reciprocally expended in production. Then the basic problem of his political economy emerges: he must prove that this determination of value is not changed by the accumulation of capitals—i.e. by the existence of capital.

Firstly, it does not occur to him that his first spontaneously evolved relation is only a relation which has been abstracted from production based on capital. Secondly, he assumes the [prior] existence of a *particular amount of objectified labour time,* which may of course increase, and then asks himself how it is *distributed.* But the question is RATHER how it is created, and it is precisely the specific nature of the relation of capital and labour, or the *differentia specifica* of capital, which explains this. In fact, as De Quincey puts it ([*The Logic of Political Economy,* Edinburgh, London, 1844, p. 204] X, 5), modern *(Ricardian)* political economy is only concerned with the dividends, while the total product is regarded as fixed, determined by the quantity of labour bestowed upon it—its value is estimated in accordance with that. Ricardo is therefore justifiably reproached for a lack of understanding of [the nature of] SURPLUS VALUE, although his opponents understand it even less.[a] Capital is represented as appropriating a certain part of the available value of labour (of the product); the creation of this value, which it appropriates over and above [that of] the reproduced capital, is not represented as the *source* of surplus value. The creation of this [surplus value] coincides with the appropriation of alien labour *without exchange,* and it must therefore never be clearly understood by the bourgeois economists.

Ramsay reproaches Ricardo for forgetting that *capital fixe* (which together with *approvisionnement* constitutes capital; in Ramsay's view, [circulating capital is composed of] both RAW MATERIAL and INSTRUMENT) is deducted from the sum which the capitalist and the worker have to share out among themselves.

"Ricardo overlooks the fact that the whole product is not only divided up between WAGES and PROFITS, but that a part of it is also NECESSARY FOR REPLACING FIXED CAPITAL" (IX, p. 88. R[amsay, G., op. cit.,] 174, note).

In fact, since Ricardo does not conceive the relation between objectified and living labour—which cannot be deduced from the dividends of a given amount of labour, but presupposes the

---

positing of surplus labour—in its living movement, and does not therefore grasp the relation of the different components of capital to one another, he appears to be arguing that the total product is divided into WAGES and PROFITS, so that the reproduction of capital itself is counted as part of profit.

Quincey (l.c., Notebook X, 5) analyses the Ricardian theory as follows:

"If the price is 10 shillings, then WAGES and PROFITS AS A WHOLE CANNOT EXCEED 10 SHILLINGS. BUT DO NOT THE WAGES AND PROFITS AS A WHOLE, THEMSELVES, ON THE CONTRARY, PREDETERMINE THE PRICE? NO, THAT IS THE OLD SUPERANNUATED DOCTRINE" (p. 204). "The new political economy has shown THAT ALL PRICE IS GOVERNED BY PROPORTIONAL QUANTITY OF THE PRODUCING LABOUR, AND BY THAT ONLY. BEING ITSELF ONCE SETTLED, THEN, *ipso facto*,[a] PRICE SETTLES THE FUND OUT OF WHICH BOTH WAGES AND PROFITS MUST DERIVE THEIR *SEPARATE DIVIDENDS*" (l.c., p. 204).

Capital appears here not as the positing of surplus value, i.e. surplus labour, but merely as making deductions from a given amount of labour. The fact that the instrument and raw material appropriate these *dividends* to themselves must then be explained by their *use value* in production. But this then assumes the absurdity that raw material and instrument produce use value through their *separation* from labour. For it is this *separation* which converts them into capital. Considered for themselves they are themselves labour, previous labour. Moreover, this is an affront to COMMONSENSE, since the capitalist knows very well that he counts wages and profit as part of the production costs and regulates the *necessary price* accordingly. This contradiction between the determination of [the value of] the product by relative labour time, and the limitation of the sum of profit and WAGES by the sum of this labour time, and the *real determination of price* in practice, derives simply from the failure to conceive of profit itself as a derivative, secondary form of *surplus value;* and the same applies to what the capitalist correctly regards as his *production costs.* His profit arises simply from the fact that a part of the production costs does not cost him anything, and so does not enter into *his* outlays, *his* production costs.

[VI-1][b] "ANY CHANGE THAT CAN DISTURB THE EXISTING RELATIONS BETWEEN WAGES AND PROFITS MUST ORIGINATE IN WAGES" (Quincey, l.c. (X, 5), p. 205).

---

[a] By virtue of this.— *Ed.*

[b] On the first page of this notebook Marx wrote: "Notebook VI. Chapter on Capital. London. February. 1858."— *Ed.*

But this is true only in so far as ANY VARIATIONS IN THE MASS OF SURPLU
LABOUR MUST BE DERIVED FROM A VARIATION IN THE RELATION BETWEEN NECESSAR
AND SURPLUS LABOUR. But such a variation may occur either becaus
there has been a decline in the productivity of NECESSARY LABOUR, s
that a larger part of the total labour falls to it; or because ther
has been an increase in the productivity of total labour, so tha
necessary labour time is reduced. It is NONSENSE to assert that th
productive power of labour originates from WAGES. On the contrar
the diminution of relative WAGES is its result. But it arises (1) fro
the appropriation by capital of the growth of the productive forc
resulting from the division of labour, trade, which cheapens th
raw materials, science, etc., (2) but this increase in the productiv
forces must be regarded as initiated by capital, in so far as it
realised by the employment of a greater capital, etc. Furthermor
PROFIT and WAGES, though determined by the relation of necessary
surplus labour, are not coincident with them, but mere
secondary forms of the same.

The point, however, is: the Ricardians presuppose a certa
amount of labour, which determines the price of the produc
From this price labour now draws its dividend in WAGES and capit
in PROFITS. The dividend of the worker=the price of the necessa
means of subsistence. In the "EXISTING RELATIONS BETWEEN WAGES an
PROFITS" the rate of profit is at its maximum and that of wages at
minimum. Competition between capitalists can alter only the
proportionate shares in total profit, not the relation between tot
profit and total WAGES. The GENERAL STANDARD OF PROFIT is this relation
total profit to total WAGES, and this is not altered by competitio
Where, then, does ALTERATION come from? Certainly not by
voluntary reduction in the rate of profit; and it would have to
voluntary, since competition does not have this result. So it must
by an ALTERATION in WAGES: their necessary costs may rise (cf. the theo
of the progressive deterioration of the soil through agriculture; t
theory of rent) because of a decline in the productive power
labour due to natural causes. To this, Carey, etc., rightly obje
(although he bases his objection on an incorrect analysis) that t
rate of profit falls, not because of the decrease, but because of t
increase in productive power.[a]

The solution of the whole problem is simply that the rate
profit does not orientate itself by absolute surplus value, but
surplus value in relation to the capital employed; and that t
growth of productive power is accompanied by a reduction in t

---

[a] H. C. Carey, *Principles of Political Economy*, Part I, Ch. 6, pp. 73-101.— F

part of capital representing *approvisionnement* relative to the part representing invariable capital. Hence, when the ratio of total labour to the capital which employs it declines, then the part of labour which appears as surplus labour or surplus value necessarily declines [relatively], too. This inability to explain one of the most striking phenomena of modern production, is the source of Ricardo's failure to understand his own principle. The difficulties in which he thereby involves his disciples are illustrated by this quotation, among others, from Quincey:

"IT IS THE COMMON PARALOGISM, THAT IF UPON THE SAME FARM YOU HAVE ALWAYS KEPT 5 MEN, AND IN 1800 THEIR PRODUCE WAS 25 QRS., BUT IN 1840 50 QRS., YOU ARE APT TO VIEW THE *PRODUCE ONLY AS VARIABLE,* AND THE *LABOUR AS CONSTANT;* WHEREAS *VIRTUALLY* BOTH HAVE VARIED. IN 1800 EACH QR. MUST HAVE COST $^1/_5$ PART OF A MAN; IN 1840 EACH HAS COST NO MORE THAN $^1/_{10}$ PART OF A MAN" (l.c., p. 214).

In both cases, absolute labour time was the same, 5 days; but in 1840 the productivity of labour was twice that of 1800, and the COST OF PRODUCING NECESSARY LABOUR had consequently fallen. The labour BESTOWED UPON 1 QUARTER was less, but total labour was the same. But Mr. Quincey should know from Ricardo that it is not the productivity of labour which determines the value of the product—it does determine surplus value, though not in the proportion in which productivity has increased. These contradictions [speak] *against* Ricardo, as [do] the desperate sophistries of his disciples (e.g. Mr. MacCulloch,[144] who explains by surplus labour the surplus value of old wine compared to new[a]). Nor is value determined by the labour which the UNIT has cost, i.e. the *price* of the SINGLE QUARTER. *The price multiplied by the quantity is what constitutes value.* The 50 quarters in 1840 had the *same value* as the 25 in 1800, because they objectified the same amount of labour. The price for one single quarter, the UNIT, *must* have been different [in 1800 from what it was in 1840], and *total price* (expressed in money) may have been different [in the two years] for very different reasons.

(What Quincey says about the machine is equally true of the worker:

"A machine, as soon as its secret is known, WILL NOT SELL FOR THE LABOUR PRODUCED, BUT FOR THE LABOUR PRODUCING ... IT WILL NO LONGER BE VIEWED AS *A CAUSE EQUAL TO CERTAIN EFFECTS, BUT AS AN EFFECT CERTAINLY REPRODUCIBLE BY A KNOWN CAUSE AT A KNOWN COST*" ([l.c.] pp. 84, 85).)

---

[a] J. R. MacCulloch, *The Principles of Political Economy,* p. 313.— *Ed.*

De Quincey says of Malthus:

"MALTHUS IN HIS POLITICAL ECONOMY REFUSES TO SEE, NAY HE POSITIVELY DENIES,
THAT IF 2 MEN PRODUCE A VARIABLE RESULT OF 10 AND 5, THEN IN ONE CASE EACH UNIT
OF THE RESULT HAS COST DOUBLE THE LABOUR WHICH IT HAS COST IN THE OTHER. ON
THE CONTRARY, BECAUSE THERE ARE ALWAYS 2 MEN, MR. MALTHUS OBSTINATELY INSISTS
THAT *THE COST IN LABOUR* IS CONSTANT " (l.c., p. 215, note).

IN FACT, *THE COST IN LABOUR IS CONSTANT,* because, by presupposition, just
as much labour is contained in 10 as in 5. But the *COST OF LABOUR* is
not CONSTANT, because in the first case, since the productivity of
labour has doubled, the time attributable to necessary labour is in
a certain proportion reduced.

We shall examine Malthus' views immediately after this. Now,
and before we discuss further the circulation time of capital and
its relation to labour time, is the best time to consider the whole
doctrine of Ricardo on this matter, in order to bring into sharper
relief the difference between our own conception and his. (The
quotations from Ricardo in Notebook VIII.)

His first premiss is *"competition without limitation"* and the
unlimited possibility of increasing products through industry (19.
R[icardo, D., *On the Principles of Political Economy, and Taxation,*]
3). In other words, this means nothing other than that the laws of
capital are completely realised only within UNLIMITED COMPETITION and
INDUSTRIAL PRODUCTION. Capital develops adequately [only] on the latter
productive basis and the former relation of production. [Only] on
this basis and in this relation [do] the immanent laws of capital
become complete reality. As this is so, it would be necessary to
show how UNLIMITED COMPETITION and INDUSTRIAL PRODUCTION are conditions for the realisation of capital, which it must itself produce to
an ever increasing degree. (Instead, the hypothesis here appears as
that of the mere theoretician, who places FREE COMPETITION and the
productive mode of existence of capital externally and arbitrarily
into the relation of capital to itself as capital, positing them not as
themselves developments of capital, but as imaginary presuppositions of capital for the sake of its pure form.) This is, incidentally,
the only place in Ricardo where he shows any inkling of the
historical nature of bourgeois economic laws.

On this assumption, the *relative value* of commodities ("relative"
is meaningless here, since [the concept of] absolute value is
NONSENSE) is determined by the different quantities which can be
produced in the same labour time, or in proportion to the
quantities of labour realised in the commodities. (P. 4.) (Notebook,

19.) (Henceforth the first figure for the page in the notebook [VIII], the 2nd for the page in Ricardo.)

Ricardo is not at all interested in how we get from value as equivalent, determined by labour, to the non-equivalent, or to the value which posits surplus value in exchange, i.e. from value to capital, from one determination to the apparently antithetical one. The question for him is only: how the *value relation* between the commodities can remain the same, and how it can and must be determined by the relative amount of labour, *despite the fact* that the owners of accumulated labour and those of living labour do not exchange *equivalents* in labour, i.e. despite the relation of capital and labour. It is then a very simple mathematical example to show that commodity *a* and commodity *b* may exchange in proportion to the labour realised in them, although the producers of *a* or *b* share out product *a* or product *b,* for which it is exchanged, differently. But since all *division* here takes place on the basis of exchange, it seems in fact utterly inexplicable why one exchange value—living labour—exchanges according to the labour time realised in it, [VI-2] while the other exchange value—accumulated labour, capital—does not exchange according to the same standard. In this case, the owner of the *accumulated labour* could not be exchanging as a capitalist. Bray e.g. therefore believes that only with his concept of EQUAL EXCHANGE between living and dead labour has he taken Ricardo's analysis to its proper conclusion.[a] That from the standpoint of simple EXCHANGE, the *wages of the worker* would have to be equal to the *value of the product,* i.e. that the quantity of labour in objective form received by the worker in wages would have to be equal to the quantity of labour in subjective form which he expends in labour, is so necessary a conclusion that A. Smith actually draws it.[b]

Ricardo, by contrast, avoids this fallacy, but how?

"The *value* of labour, and the quantity of commodities which a definite quantity of labour can buy, are not identical."

WHY NOT?

"*Because* the product of the worker or an equivalent for this product is not=to the remuneration of the worker."

---

[a] J. F. Bray, *Labour's Wrongs and Labour's Remedy,* Leeds, 1839, pp. 28, 31, 34, 41-43, 47-50, 52, 53-57, 59-61, 68, 81-85, 153 and 154.— *Ed.*
[b] A. Smith, *An Inquiry into the Nature and Causes of the Wealth of Nations,* Vol. I, London, 1835, pp. 100-02 and 130-31.— *Ed.*

This is to say that the identity does not exist, *because* the difference exists.

"*Therefore*" (because the identity does not exist) "it is not the value of labour which is the measure of value, but the labour bestowed upon the quantity of commodities" (19, 5).

The value of labour is not identical with the remuneration of labour. *For* they are different. *Therefore* they are not identical. This is an odd conclusion. *Au fond*, the only ground for this assertion is that the identity is *not* observed in practice. But according to [his] theory, it ought to exist. For the exchange of values is determined by the labour time realised in them. Hence equivalents are exchanged. Hence a particular amount of labour time in living form would have to exchange for the same amount of labour time in the form of past labour. What would have to be proved is precisely that the law of exchange turns into its opposite. Not even the faintest suspicion is expressed here that it does so, unless this is expressed in the frequently repeated warning against the confusion [of the amount of labour with the remuneration for that labour]. That the distinction between past and living labour cannot do the job, is readily admitted:

"The comparative quantity of commodities which a given amount of labour can produce determines their past and present value" (19, 9),

Where living labour thus even retrospectively determines the value of past labour. Thus, why is not capital also exchanged for living labour in relation to the labour realised in the capital? Why is it only an amount of living labour which is not itself=to the amount of labour in which it has objectified itself?

"Labour naturally varies in quality, and it is difficult to compare different working hours in different industries. But a scale of comparison is very quickly established in practice" (19, 13). "For short periods of time, at least from one year to another, variations in this inequality are insignificant, and are *therefore* left out of account" (19, 15).

This is nothing. If Ricardo had applied his own principle, the amounts of (simple) labour to which different *labour capacities* are reducible, the matter would have been simple. Generally, he is concerned straight away with the hours of labour. What the capitalist obtains through exchange is *labour capacity*; this is the exchange value for which he pays. Living labour is the use value which this exchange value has for him, and from this use value arises surplus value and the transcendence of exchange altogether.

By letting [the capitalist] exchange with living labour, and thus plunging straight into the process of production, Ricardo is left with an insoluble antinomy in his system, that a certain amount of living labour is not=to the commodity which it produces, in which it objectifies itself, even though the value of the commodity =the amount of labour contained in it.

"The labour necessary to bring the commodities to market is also included" in their value (19, 18).

We shall see that circulation time, in so far as it appears as determining value with Ricardo, is only the labour necessary to bring the commodities to market.

"The principle that the relative amounts of labour contained by commodities determine their value, becomes significantly modified by the application of machinery and other fixed and durable capital. A rise or fall in the wages of labour will affect differently 2 capitals, one of which is almost entirely circulating and the other almost entirely fixed; similarly the different duration of the fixed capital employed. For the *profit on the fixed capital* (interest) has to be added and also the compensation for the longer period of time which must elapse before the more valuable of the two commodities can be brought to market" (19; 25, 27, 29, 30).

This latter moment concerns only the duration of the process of production, i.e. the labour time directly employed, at least in Ricardo's example of the farmer and the baker [ibid., pp. 26, 27]. (If the former's wheat takes longer to become ready for the market than the latter's bread, then this so-called *compensation* already presupposes *interest*, as in the case of *capital fixe*; thus already something derivative, not an original determination.)

"Profit and wages are only the respective *shares* of the two classes of capitalists and workers in the original commodity, hence also in the commodity exchanged for it" (pp. 21, ⌊19-⌋20).

How much the production of *the original commodity,* its origin itself, is determined by these *shares,* how it therefore *precedes* these shares as the basis of determination, is shown by the fact that the *original commodity* would not be produced at all, if it did not contain surplus labour for the capitalist.

"Commodities upon which the same quantity of labour has been bestowed differ in relative value, if they cannot be brought to market in the same time... Also, in the case of a *greater fixed capital,* the higher value of a commodity is due to the greater length of time which must elapse before it can be brought to market... The difference in both cases arises from profits being accumulated as capital, and is only a compensation for the *time that the profits were held back*" (20, 34, 30-31, 35).

This means absolutely nothing other than that capital lying fallow *is reckoned and accounted for* as though it were not lying fallow but were being exchanged for surplus labour time. This has nothing to do with value determination; it comes under the heading of price. (In the case of fixed capital it comes into the determination of value only in so far as it is *another method* of the payment of objectified labour, abstracted from profit.)

⫽"THERE IS ANOTHER PRINCIPLE OF LABOUR WHICH NOTHING POINTS OUT TO THE ECONOMICAL INQUIRER IN OLD COUNTRIES, BUT OF WHICH EVERY COLONIAL CAPITALIST HAS BEEN MADE CONSCIOUS IN HIS OWN PERSON. BY FAR THE GREATER PART OF THE OPERATIONS OF INDUSTRY, AND ESPECIALLY THOSE OF WHICH THE *PRODUCE IS GREAT IN PROPORTION TO THE CAPITAL AND LABOUR EMPLOYED*, REQUIRE *A CONSIDERABLE TIME FOR COMPLETION*. AS TO MOST OF THEM, IT IS NOT WORTH WHILE TO MAKE A COMMENCEMENT WITHOUT THE CERTAINTY OF BEING ABLE TO CARRY THEM ON FOR SEVERAL YEARS. A LARGE PORTION OF THE CAPITAL EMPLOYED IN THEM IS *FIXED, INCONVERTIBLE, DURABLE*. IF ANYTHING HAPPENS TO STOP THE OPERATION, ALL THIS CAPITAL IS LOST. *IF THE HARVEST CANNOT BE GATHERED, THE WHOLE OUTLAY IN MAKING IT GROW* HAS BEEN THROWN AWAY... This shows that *CONSTANCY* IS A NO LESS IMPORTANT PRINCIPLE AS COMBINATION OF LABOUR. THE IMPORTANCE OF THE PRINCIPLE OF CONSTANCY IS NOT SEEN HERE, BECAUSE RARELY INDEED DOES IT HAPPEN, THAT THE LABOUR WHICH CARRIES ON A BUSINESS, IS STOPPED AGAINST THE WILL OF THE CAPITALIST... But in the *COLONIES* exactly the reverse happens. Here CAPITALISTS ARE SO MUCH AFRAID OF IT, THAT THEY AVOID ITS OCCURRENCE AS MUCH AS THEY CAN, BY AVOIDING AS MUCH AS POSSIBLE OPERATIONS WHICH REQUIRE MUCH TIME FOR THEIR COMPLETION" (Wakefield, [*A View of the Art of Colonisation*, London, 1849,] pp. 169-70, XIV [70,] 71). "THERE ARE NUMEROUS *OPERATIONS OF SO SIMPLE A KIND* AS NOT TO ADMIT *A DIVISION INTO PARTS*, WHICH CANNOT BE PERFORMED WITHOUT THE CO-OPERATION OF MANY PAIRS OF HANDS. E.G. THE LIFTING OF A LARGE TREE ONTO A WAIN, KEEPING DOWN WEEDS IN A LARGE FIELD OF GROWING CROP, SHEARING A LARGE FLOCK OF SHEEP AT THE SAME TIME, GATHERING A HARVEST OF CORN AT THE TIME WHEN IT IS RIPE ENOUGH AND NOT TOO RIPE, MOVING ANY GREAT WEIGHT; EVERYTHING, IN SHORT, WHICH CANNOT BE DONE UNLESS A GOOD MANY PAIRS OF HANDS HELP TOGETHER IN THE SAME UNDIVIDED EMPLOYMENT, AND AT THE SAME TIME" (l.c., p. 168). "*COMBINATION* AND *CONSTANCY OF LABOUR* ARE PROVIDED FOR IN OLD COUNTRIES, WITHOUT AN EFFORT OR [a] THOUGHT ON THE PART OF THE CAPITALIST, MERELY BY THE *ABUNDANCE OF LABOURERS FOR HIRE*. THE SCARCITY OF LABOURERS FOR HIRE IS THE UNIVERSAL COMPLAINT OF COLONIES" (l.c., p. 170). "Only the *CHEAPEST LAND* IN A COLONY IS THAT WHOSE PRICE AFFECTS THE *LABOUR MARKET. THE PRICE OF THIS LAND, AS OF ALL BARE LAND, AND OF EVERYTHING ELSE WHICH IT COSTS NOTHING TO PRODUCE*, DEPENDS OF COURSE ON THE *RELATION BETWEEN THE DEMAND AND THE SUPPLY*" [l.c., p. 332]. "IN ORDER THAT *THE PRICE OF WASTE LAND* SHOULD ACCOMPLISH ITS OBJECTS" (i.e. to make the worker into a *non*-proprietor of land) "IT MUST BE *SUFFICIENT* FOR THE PURPOSE. HITHERTO THE PRICE HAS BEEN EVERYWHERE INSUFFICIENT" (l.c., p. 338).

On this "SUFFICIENT" PRICE:

"IN FOUNDING A COLONY THE PRICE MIGHT BE SO LOW AS TO RENDER THE QUANTITY OF LAND APPROPRIATED BY SETTLERS PRACTICALLY UNLIMITED: IT MIGHT BE HIGH

ENOUGH TO OCCASION A PROPORTION BETWEEN LAND AND PEOPLE SIMILAR TO THAT OF OLD COUNTRIES, IN WHICH CASE, IF THIS VERY HIGH PRICE DID NOT PREVENT EMIGRATION, THE CHEAPEST LAND IN THE COLONY MIGHT BE AS DEAR, AND THE SUPERABUNDANCE OF LABOURERS AS DEPLORABLE AS IN ENGLAND: OR IT MIGHT BE A JUST MEDIUM BETWEEN THE TWO, OCCASIONING NEITHER SUPERABUNDANCE OF PEOPLE NOR SUPERABUNDANCE OF LAND, BUT SO LIMITING THE QUANTITY OF LAND, AS TO GIVE THE CHEAPEST LAND A MARKET VALUE, THAT WOULD HAVE THE EFFECT OF COMPELLING LABOURERS TO WORK SOME CONSIDERABLE TIME FOR WAGES BEFORE THEY COULD BECOME LANDOWNERS" (l.c., p. 339) (Notebook XIV, 71).

(The passage here quoted from Wakefield's *Art of Colonisation* belongs to those quoted above concerning the necessary separation of the worker from the conditions of property.)//

[VI-3] (The calculation of profit as distinct from that of the real surplus value which capital posits in its exchange with living labour, is clear e.g. in the following example.[145] It is A STATEMENT in the *First Report of the Factory Commissioners*. (Malthus, *Principles of Political Economy*, 2nd ed. [London,] 1836, [pp. 269-70] (Notebook X, p. 42).)

CAPITAL SUNK IN BUILDING AND MACHINERY	£10,000	
FLOATING CAPITAL	7,000	
£ 500 INTEREST ON £10,000 FIXED CAPITAL		
350 ....ON FLOATING CAPITAL		
150 ....RENTS, TAXES, RATES		
650 ....SINKING FUND OF 6$\frac{1}{2}$[%] FOR WEAR AND TEAR OF THE FIXED CAPITAL		
£ 1,650		
£ 1,100 CONTINGENCIES, CARRIAGE, COAL, OIL		
2,750		
2,600 WAGES AND SALARIES		
5,350		
10,000 FOR ABOUT 400,000 LBS. RAW COTTON AT 6D.		
15,350		
16,000 FOR 363,000 LBS TWIST SPUN. VALUE	£16,000	

The capital laid out on labour is 2,600; surplus value is=to 1,650 (850 INTEREST+150 RENTS, etc., making 1,000+650 profit).

But 2,600:1,650=100:63^6/$_{13}$. Hence the rate of surplus value is 63^6/$_{13}$%. If calculated in the same way as [the rate of] profit itself, the figures would be 850 INTEREST, 150 RENTS, [etc.,] and 650 profit, or 1,650:15,350; over 10.7%.

In the above example, the circulating capital is turned over $1\,^{67}/_{70}$ times a year; the fixed capital is turned over once in $15\,^{5}/_{13}$ years, once in $^{200}/_{13}$ years.[146]

Profit: 650 OR ABOUT 4.2% [on the capital of £15,350 annually employed]. The WAGES of the OPERATIVES [and salaries] $^{1}/_{6}$ [of the yearly outlay]. Profit is stated here at 4.2%; let us say it was only 4%. This 4% is calculated on an outlay of 15,350. But then we still have [to add] 5% INTEREST on £10,000 and 5% on 7,000; £850=5% on 17,000.

We must deduct from the annual ADVANCES actually MADE (1) the part of fixed capital which does not figure in the SINKING FUND; (2) that which is calculated as INTEREST. (It is possible that capitalist *B*, not capitalist *A*, pockets the interest. In any case, it is income, not capital; surplus value.) 850 must therefore be deducted from the outlays of 15,350; leaves: 14,500. Of the 2,600 for WAGES and SALARIES there were £41 $^{2}/_{3}$ in the form of SALARY; since $^{1}/_{6}$ of 15,350 is not 2,600, but 2,558 $^{1}/_{3}$.[147] This divided by 14,500 is [1:] 5 $^{205}/_{307}$, say [1:] 6.

He therefore sells the 14,500 for 16,000, giving him a profit of 1,500 or 10 $^{10}/_{29}$%. We can ignore the $^{10}/_{29}$% and take [the rate of profit as] 10%; $^{1}/_{6}$ of 100 is 16 $^{2}/_{3}$. Thus 100 [capital] would yield 83 $^{1}/_{3}$ for ADVANCES [on constant capital], 16 $^{2}/_{3}$ for wages, and profit 10. Thus:

ADVANCES	Wages	Sum	Reproduced	Profit
£ 83 $^{1}/_{3}$	16 $^{2}/_{3}$	100	110	10

10 on 16 $^{2}/_{3}$ or on $^{50}/_{3}$ is EXACTLY 60%. Therefore, if the capitalist on his own calculation is to derive an annual profit of 10% (actually, it was somewhat greater) on a capital of £17,000, wherein labour accounts for only $^{1}/_{6}$ of the annual ADVANCES of £14,500, the worker (or capital, if you prefer) must produce a surplus value of 60%. Or 62 $^{1}/_{2}$% of the total labour time is for necessary labour and 37 $^{1}/_{2}$% for surplus labour. Their ratio is 625:375 or 5:3 or 1:$^{3}/_{5}$. If, however, the ADVANCES on capital had been 50, the ADVANCES on wages also 50, then a surplus value of only 20% would have to be produced for the capitalist to derive [a profit of] 10%; 50+50+10=110. But 10:50 is 20:100 or 20%. If necessary labour posited as much surplus labour in the second CASE as in the first, the profit of the capitalist would amount to £30. On the other hand, if the rate of real value creation, of the positing of surplus labour, were only as large in the first CASE as in the second, profit would amount only to £3 $^{1}/_{3}$; and if the capitalist had to pay

5% interest to another capitalist, he would have to carry an actual LOSS.
This much arises simply from the formula: (1) that to measure the real [rate of] surplus value, one must calculate the profit on the ADVANCE made for wages; the percentage which expresses the proportion between the so-called profit and wages; (2) the relatively smaller percentage expressing the proportion between the outlay on living labour and the total outlay, presupposes a greater outlay on fixed capital, machinery, etc., a greater division of labour. Although the percentage of labour is therefore smaller than in the case of the capital working with more labour, the mass of labour it actually sets in motion must be significantly greater, i.e. a greater capital generally has to be worked with. The fractional part of labour relative to total ADVANCES is smaller; but the absolute sum of labour set in motion is greater for the individual capital, which means that this capital must itself be greater. (3) If we are dealing not with a greater quantity of machinery, etc., but with an instrument which does not set more labour in motion, and does not itself represent a great fixed capital (e.g. a manually operated lithographic press), but simply replaces labour, then the profit of one [the capitalist] using that instrument is absolutely smaller than that of one working with living labour. (But the former can make a percentage of profit higher than the latter and therefore drive him from the market.) (etc.) The examination of how far the rate of profit can decline as capital grows, in such a way that GROSS PROFIT still increases, belongs in the theory of profit (competition).

In his Principles of Political Economy, 2nd ed., [London,] 1836, Malthus has an inkling of the fact that profit, i.e. not profit but real surplus value, must be calculated not in relation to the capital advanced, but to the living labour advanced, whose value is objectively expressed in wages. But this leads him into pure trivialities, which become absurdities when he tries to use them as a basis for the determination of value or for statements concerning the relation of labour to value determination.

For if I take the total value of the finished product, then I can compare every part of the product advanced with the corresponding part of the outlays; and the percentage of profit in relation to the whole product is of course also the percentage for the fractional part of the product. Say e.g. 100 thaler yielded 110. Thus 10% on the whole product. Say that 75 thaler is for the invariable part of capital, and 25 for labour; hence $^3/_4$ [VI-4] for the former and $^1/_4$ for living labour. If I now take $^1/_4$ from the total product, i.e. from 110, I obtain $27^2/_4$ or $27^1/_2$. On an outlay of 25 for labour, the capitalist has gained $2^1/_2$, i.e. 10%. Malthus could just as well have said, if I take $^3/_4$ from the total product, i.e. 75, then these $^3/_4$ are represented in the total product by $82^1/_2$, thus $7^1/_2$ out of 75 is EXACTLY 10%. Obviously, this means nothing more than that if my profit is 10% on 100, the profit on every part of the 100 is as much as will in total add up to 10% on the overall sum. If my profit is 10 on 100, then on 2×50 my profit is 5 each time, etc. The knowledge that, if my profit is 10 on 100, it is $2^1/_2$ on $^1/_4$ of 100, and $7^1/_2$ on $^3/_4$, does not get us one step further. If my profit is 10 on 100, then what is it on $^1/_4$ of 100 or on $^3/_4$? Malthus's inspiration comes down to this sort of triviality. The advance on labour amounted to $^1/_4$ of 100, hence the profit on it was 10%, which is $2^1/_2$ on 25. Or if the capitalist's profit is 10 on 100, it is $^1/_{10}$ on each part of his capital, i.e. 10%. This does not in any way give the parts of capital any qualitative character relative to one another, and therefore this is just as true of fixed capital, etc., as it is of that advanced in labour.

Moreover, this [procedure] merely expresses the illusion that every part of capital has contributed equally to the newly created value. Not even the $^1/_4$ advanced for wages has created surplus value, but the unpaid living labour. But from the proportion of total value [outlays deducted]—in this case 10 thaler—to wages, we can ascertain what percentage of the labour has not been paid, or how much was surplus labour. In the above relation, necessary labour is objectified in 25 thaler, surplus labour in 10; hence their ratio is 25:10=100:40; 40% of labour was surplus labour or, what is the same thing, 40% of the value it created was surplus value. It is quite true that the capitalist can calculate thus: if my profit is 10 on 100, my profit on the wages of 25 is $2^1/_2$. It is not possible to see what use this calculation is supposed to be. But the purpose Malthus has in mind we shall see shortly when we go into his determination of value. That he actually believes that his simple arithmetical example contains a real determination is clear from the following:

"Suppose that capital is wholly expended in wages; £100 EXPENDED IN IMMEDIATE LABOUR. The RETURNS at the end of the year 110, 120 or 130; IT IS EVIDENT THAT IN EACH CASE THE PROFITS WILL BE DETERMINED BY THE PROPORTION OF THE *VALUE OF THE WHOLE PRODUCE* WHICH IS REQUIRED TO PAY THE LABOUR EMPLOYED. IF THE VALUE OF THE PRODUCE IN THE MARKET=110, THE PROPORTION REQUIRED TO PAY THE LABOURERS=$10/11$ of the VALUE of the PRODUCE, or PROFITS=10%" [p. 267].

(Here Mr. Malthus merely expresses the original advance, £100, as a proportion of total product. 100 is $^{10}/_{11}$ of 110. To say that my profit is 10 on 100, i.e. $^{1}/_{10}$ of 100, is the same as saying that $^{1}/_{11}$ of the 110 is profit.)

"If the value of the produce be 120, the proportion for LABOUR=$^{10}/_{12}$, and profits 20%; if 130, the PROPORTION REQUIRED TO PAY THE LABOUR=$^{10}/_{13}$, and profits=30%" [ibid.].

(Instead of saying that my profit is 10 on 100, I can also say that the advances amount to $^{10}/_{11}$ of the 110; or if my profit is 20 on 100, that the advances amount to $^{10}/_{12}$ of 120, etc. The character of these advances, whether in LABOUR or OTHERWISE, has absolutely nothing to do with this arithmetical form of expressing the matter. If a capital of 100 has only yielded 110, I can either set out from the capital and say that I have gained 10 on it; or I can set out from the product of 110 and say that I have previously advanced only $^{10}/_{11}$ of it. The relation is of course the same.)

"Now suppose that the ADVANCES of the CAPITALIST do not consist of LABOUR alone ... the capitalist *expects an equal profit upon all the parts of the capital which he advances*" [pp. 267-68].

(This only means that he attributes the profit he has made, and about whose origin he may be very much in the dark, equally to all parts of his expenses, abstracting entirely from their qualitative difference.)

"Assume that $^{1}/_{4}$ of his ADVANCES [are] for (immediate) LABOUR, and $^{3}/_{4}$ consist of ACCUMULATED LABOUR and PROFITS, with ANY ADDITIONS WHICH MAY ARISE from RENTS, TAXES or other OUTGOINGS... *Then it will be STRICTLY TRUE THAT THE PROFITS OF THE CAPITALIST WILL VARY WITH THE VARYING VALUE of this $^{1}/_{4}$ of the PRODUCE COMPARED WITH THE QUANTITY OF LABOUR EMPLOYED*" [ibid].

(Not [compared with the] QUANTITY [of labour employed], as Mr. Malthus has it, but COMPARED WITH THE WAGES PAID.)

(It is thus STRICTLY TRUE THAT HIS PROFITS WILL VARY WITH THE VARYING VALUE OF THE $^{3}/_{4}$ OF HIS PRODUCE COMPARED WITH THE ADVANCES IN ACCUMULATED LABOUR, i.e. profit relates to the total capital advanced (10:100) in the same way as each part of the total product (110) relates to the part of the ADVANCES corresponding to it.)

"As an instance let us suppose," continues Malthus, "that a FARMER employs in CULTIVATION £2,000, 1,500 of which he expends IN SEED, KEEP OF HORSES, WEAR and TEAR OF HIS FIXED CAPITAL, etc., and £500 on IMMEDIATE LABOUR; and that the RETURNS obtained at the end [of the year] are worth 2,400. His profits will be 400 on 2,000=20%. It is straight away OBVIOUS THAT IF WE TOOK $^{1}/4$ of the VALUE of the PRODUCE, namely £600, and COMPARED IT WITH THE AMOUNT PAID IN THE WAGES OF THE

IMMEDIATE LABOUR, THE RESULT WOULD SHOW EXACTLY THE SAME RATE OF PROFITS"
(l.c., pp. 267, 268. Notebook X, 41, 42).

(It is equally OBVIOUS that IF WE TOOK $^3/_4$ of the VALUE of the PRODUCE, namely 1,800, and COMPARED IT WITH THE AMOUNT PAID IN THE ADVANCES OF ACCUMULATED LABOUR, namely with 1,500, THE RESULT WOULD SHOW EXACTLY THE SAME RATE OF PROFITS. 1,800:1,500=18:15=6:5. But 6 is $^1/_5$ more than 5, hence 20%.)

(Malthus here has two different arithmetic forms in his head, and jumbles them together. *Firstly*: If my profit is 10 on 100, I have not gained 10 on each part of 100, but 10%; therefore 5 on 50, $2^1/_2$ on 25, etc.; if I make 10 on 100, I have gained $^1/_{10}$ on each part of 100, and profit must work itself out as $^1/_{10}$ profit on wages. If profit is attributed equally to all parts of the capital, I can say that the rate of profit on total capital varies with the rate of profit on each of its component parts, and thus e.g. also on that advanced in wages. *Secondly:* If I have made 10% on 100, then total product is 110. If wages were $^1/_4$ of the advances=25, they now represent only a $4^2/_5$th part of 110; i.e. a fraction which is smaller by $^2/_5$, and it will [have] to constitute a smaller part of the total product in the same proportion as the total product has increased in comparison with the original [capital]. This, again, is merely a different type of calculation. 10 is $^1/_{10}$ of 100, but only $^1/_{11}$ of 110. Therefore, I can say that in the same proportion as total product increases, each of the fractional parts of the original capital constitutes a smaller part of it. Tautology.)

In his work, *The Measure of Value Stated and Illustrated*, London, 1823, (Notebook IX), Malthus asserts that the "VALUE OF LABOUR" is "CONSTANT" and is thus the TRUE MEASURE OF VALUE GENERALLY.

"ANY GIVEN QUANTITY OF LABOUR MUST BE OF THE *SAME VALUE* AS THE WAGES WHICH COMMAND IT, OR FOR WHICH IT ACTUALLY EXCHANGES" (l.c., p. 5) (IX, 29).

He is of course referring to wage labour. The truth of the matter is rather that ANY GIVEN QUANTITY OF LABOUR IS=to the same QUANTITY OF LABOUR expressed in a product; or every product is only a particular amount of labour, objectified in the value of the product. The value of this product relative to that of others is measured by this amount. Certainly wages express the value of living labour capacity, but not at all that [VI-5] of living labour, which is expressed rather in terms of wages+profit. Wages are the price of *necessary labour*. If the worker had to work for 6 hours to live, and he produced only for himself, as a pure worker, he would obtain commodities [to the value] of 6 hours' labour, say

6d., each day. Now the capitalist sets him to work for 12 hours and pays him 6d. He pays him $^1/_2$d. per hour. I.e. A GIVEN QUANTITY OF 12 HOURS OF LABOUR HAS THE VALUE OF 12D., AND 12D. IS INDEED THE VALUE FOR WHICH THE PRODUCE EXCHANGES, WHEN IT GETS SOLD.

ON THE OTHER HAND, THE CAPITALIST COMMANDS WITH THIS VALUE, IF HE COULD REINVEST IT IN MERE LABOUR, 24 HOURS. THE WAGES COMMAND, THEREFORE, A MUCH GREATER QUANTITY OF LABOUR THAN THEY CONSIST OF, AND A GIVEN QUANTITY OF LIVING LABOUR ACTUALLY EXCHANGES FOR A MUCH SMALLER ONE OF ACCUMULATED LABOUR. THE ONLY THING THAT IS SURE IS THAT THE PRICE OF LABOUR, WAGES, MUST ALWAYS EXPRESS THE QUANTITY OF LABOUR WHICH THE LABOURERS WANT IN ORDER TO KEEP SOUL AND BODY TOGETHER. THE WAGES OF ANY QUANTITY OF LABOUR MUST BE EQUAL TO THE QUANTITY OF LABOUR WHICH THE LABOURER MUST EXPEND UPON HIS OWN REPRODUCTION. IN THE ABOVE INSTANCE A MAN WOULD SET TO WORK TWO MEN FOR 12 HOURS EACH—TOGETHER 24 HOURS—WITH THE QUANTITY OF LABOUR AFFORDED BY ONE MAN. In the above example, the product would be exchanged for another product to the value of 12d., or for 12 hours' labour, and in this way its profit of 6d. would arise (ITS SURPLUS VALUE for the capitalist).

The value of products is determined by the labour contained in them, not by that part of it which the employer pays for. *Labour performed, not labour paid for, constitutes the value of the product;* but WAGES express *only* labour *paid for,* never *the labour actually performed.* The measure of this payment itself depends on the productivity of labour, for this determines the quantity of necessary labour time; and since WAGES constitute the VALUE OF LABOUR (LABOUR itself posited as a commodity), this VALUE is continuously VARIABLE, and anything but CONSTANT. The quantity of labour actually performed by the worker is very different from the quantity which is embodied in his labour capacity, or which is necessary to reproduce his labour capacity. But as commodity he does not sell the use which is made of it; he does not sell himself as CAUSE but as EFFECT. Let us hear how Mr. Malthus exerts himself to get on top of the matter:

"THE CONDITIONS OF THE SUPPLY OF COMMODITIES DO NOT REQUIRE THAT THEY SHOULD RETAIN ALWAYS THE SAME RELATIVE VALUES; BUT THAT EACH SHOULD RETAIN ITS PROPER *NATURAL* VALUE, OR THE MEANS OF OBTAINING THOSE OBJECTS WHICH WILL CONTINUE TO THE PRODUCER *THE SAME POWER OF PRODUCTION* A N D ACCUMULATION ... PROFITS ARE CALCULATED UPON THE ADVANCES NECESSARY TO PRODUCTION ... *THE SPECIFIC ADVANCES OF CAPITALISTS DO NOT CONSIST OF CLOTH, BUT OF LABOUR*; A N D *AS NO OTHER OBJECT WHATEVER CAN REPRESENT A GIVEN QUANTITY OF LABOUR,*it is clear that it is the *QUANTITY OF LABOUR WHICH A COMMODITY WILL COMMAND*, AND NOT THE QUANTITY OF ANY OTHER COMMODITY, WHICH CAN REPRESENT THE CONDITION OF ITS SUPPLY, OR ITS *NATURAL VALUE*" (pp. 17, 18) (IX, 29).

From the fact alone that the ADVANCES of the CAPITALIST consist OF LABOUR, Malthus could see that something was wrong with this line of argument. Suppose that necessary labour time is 6 hours; A and B, two fellows both working for themselves but exchanging with one another. Let A work 6 hours, B 12 hours. If A now wishes to eat up the extra 6 hours which B has worked, wants to consume the product of the 6 surplus hours worked by B, he can do so only by giving B 6 hours of living labour, say on the next day. But B now possesses a product of 6 hours' work over and above that in A's possession. Assume now that in this situation B imagined himself as a capitalist, and stopped working altogether. On the third day, he would only have his ACCUMULATED PRODUCE of 6 hours to exchange for A's 6 hours [of living labour]; and as soon as he completed the exchange, he would have to take up working again or die of starvation. But if he continued to work 12 hours for A, and A continued to work 6 hours for himself and 6 for B, they would both exchange exactly 12 hours with one another.

The NATURAL VALUE of the COMMODITY, Malthus says, consists in its ability to return to its owner, by means of exchange, THE SAME POWER OF PRODUCTION AND ACCUMULATION. His commodity is composed of two distinct quantities of labour: one of accumulated labour, and one of IMMEDIATE labour. Hence, if he exchanges his commodity for another commodity which contains exactly the same total quantity of labour, his POWER OF PRODUCTION and ACCUMULATION is at least the same, undiminished. In fact, however, it has grown, because a part of the IMMEDIATE labour has cost him *nothing*, and yet he sells it. Malthus, however, concludes that the quantity of labour of which the commodity consists is *only* labour which has been paid for, and therefore=the sum of WAGES; or that WAGES provide the measure of the value of the commodity. If every quantity of labour contained in the commodity were paid for, Mr. Malthus's doctrine would be correct. But then it would be equally correct to say that his capitalist would not have to make any "ADVANCES OF LABOUR" and he would lose his "POWERS OF ACCUMULATION" altogether.

Where should profit come from if no gratis labour is performed? Ah, says Mr. Malthus, from the WAGES for ACCUMULATED labour. But since *labour already performed* has ceased to labour, it also ceases to draw WAGES. True, the product in which it exists could be exchanged again for living labour. But assume this product to be=to 6 hours' labour; the worker would then supply 6 hours of living labour and receive in return the ADVANCES, the 6 hours of already performed labour in the possession of the capitalist, who would have gained nothing from this transaction. Living labour would very soon be in possession of his dead labour. The reason put forward by Malthus is that, because "NO OTHER OBJECT WHATEVER CAN REPRESENT A GIVEN QUANTITY OF LABOUR", the NATURAL VALUE of a commodity consists of the "QUANTITY OF LABOUR WHICH A COMMODITY WILL COMMAND, AND NOT THE QUANTITY OF ANY OTHER COMMODITY" [ibid., p. 18], i.e. A GIVEN QUANTITY OF LABOUR can only be represented by A QUANTITY OF LIVING (IMMEDIATE) LABOUR. But far from "NO OTHER" object being able TO REPRESENT A GIVEN QUANTITY OF LABOUR, EVERY OBJECT WHATEVER CAN do so, viz. every object in which the same QUANTITY [of] LABOUR is contained. Yet Malthus wants the QUANTITY OF LABOUR contained in the commodity to be measured; in his view, it should be equal to the *quantity of paid labour* which it sets in motion, not *that of living labour* which it can set in motion.

Assume that the commodity contains 24 hours of labour. Malthus imagines that the capitalist can buy 2 days' labour with it; and if the capitalist paid for the full amount of the labour [contained in it], or if the quantity of labour already performed were=to the quantity of paid living labour, he could buy *only* 24 hours of living labour with 24 hours of labour already performed, and his "POWERS OF ACCUMULATION" WOULD HAVE GONE TO THE WALL. But the capitalist does not pay the worker for the labour time, the quantity of labour, but merely for the necessary labour time, while he compels him to work for the REST of the time free of charge. With the 24 hours' accumulated labour time, he will thus set in motion perhaps 48 hours of living labour. With one hour of accumulated labour, he therefore pays IN FACT for 2 hours of living labour, and hence gains 100% on the exchange. The value of his commodity now=48 hours; but it is in no way equal to the WAGES for which it has been exchanged, nor to the WAGES for which it is again exchanged. If he continues in the same relation, he will purchase 96 hours of living labour with 48 hours of accumulated labour.

Suppose that not a single capitalist existed, but only workers directly exchanging with one another, who worked more than was necessary to live, because they also wished to accumulate, etc. Call the part of the labour which the worker performs in order to live WAGES, and the surplus time he works in order to accumulate, *profit.* In this case, the value of his commodity would=the total quantity of labour contained in it=the total sum of living labour time; but in no way would it=the WAGES which he paid himself, or be equal to the part of the commodity which he would have to reproduce in order to live.

Because the value of a commodity is=to a certain quantity of labour, Malthus asserts that it is=to the quantity of necessary labour contained in it (i.e. the WAGES) and not to the total sum of labour contained in it; i.e. its whole is=to a fraction of it. [VI-6] Obviously, the worker's "POWERS OF ACCUMULATION" could only arise from the fact that he had worked more than was necessary to pay his WAGES to himself. If a particular quantity of living labour were=to the time for which the worker must work to live, then a particular quantity of living labour would be=to the WAGES which he produces, or the WAGES would be exactly equal to the living labour which they set in motion. If such were the case, capital would of course be impossible. If a worker cannot produce more than his WAGES in his entire labour time, he cannot with the best will in the world squeeze out a farthing for the capitalist. PROPERTY is THE OFFSPRING OF THE PRODUCTIVITY OF LABOUR.

"If one can produce only for one, everyone a worker; THERE COULD BE NO PROPERTY. WHEN ONE MAN'S LABOUR CAN MAINTAIN 5, THERE WILL BE 4 IDLE MEN FOR 1 EMPLOYED IN PRODUCTION" (Ravenstone [*Thoughts on the Funding System, and Its Effects*, p. 11]).

We have seen above how Malthus's fanciful profundity expressed itself in a purely childish kind of arithmetic. Incidentally, behind it lay the doctrine that THE VALUE OF LABOUR is constant and that WAGES constitute price. Because the rate of profit upon an entire capital can be expressed as the same rate upon the fractional part which represents WAGES, he asserts that this fractional part constitutes and determines price. Exactly the same *profundity* as here. If commodity a=an amount of x commodity, he imagines that this can only mean that commodity a=x living labour, for only labour can represent labour. From this he concludes that commodity a=the quantity of *wage labour* it can command, and that therefore the value of labour is constant, because it is always=to [that of] the commodity by which it is set in motion. The point is simply that he equates the quantity of living labour with that of wage labour, and that he believes that every fractional part of wage labour is really paid for. But x living labour can be (and as wage labour is only)=$x-y$ necessary labour (WAGES)+y surplus labour. Hence x dead labour can set in motion $x-y$ necessary labour (WAGES)+y surplus labour time, i.e. it always sets in motion as much additional living labour time as there are hours of surplus labour time over and above necessary labour time in *x* hours of labour.

Wage labour always consists of paid and unpaid labour.

To say that the VALUE *of labour* is constant therefore means nothing other than that all labour time is necessary labour time, i.e. labour time producing WAGES. There is no surplus labour time and—nevertheless there are "POWERS OF ACCUMULATION" and capital. Since WAGES are always equal to a given quantity of labour, i.e. the quantity of living labour which they set in motion, and this is the same quantity of labour which is contained in the WAGES, the *value of labour* is constant, since it is always=to the quantity of labour objectified. The fall and rise of wages thus stems from the fall and rise of the price of commodities, not of the *value of labour*. Whether a worker gets 8 or 16 shillings in silver a week, depends only on whether the price of shillings has risen or fallen, but the value of labour has remained the same. In both cases, he receives a week of accumulated labour for a week of living labour. Mr. Malthus proves this in the following way:

"If labour alone, without capital, WERE EMPLOYED IN PROCURING THE FRUITS OF THE EARTH, THE GREATER FACILITY OF PROCURING ONE SORT OF THEM COMPARED WITH ANOTHER, WOULD NOT, IT IS ACKNOWLEDGED, ALTER THE VALUE OF LABOUR, OR THE EXCHANGEABLE VALUE OF THE WHOLE PRODUCE OBTAINED BY A GIVEN QUANTITY OF EXERTION" [Th. R. Malthus, *The Measure of Value Stated and Illustrated*, p. 33].

This means nothing but that [the value of] every commodity, leaving aside its quantity, would be determined by the labour contained in it, although this labour would be expressed in a greater quantity of use values in one CASE and a lesser quantity in another, depending upon the degree of its productivity.

"*WE SHOULD, WITHOUT HESITATION, ALLOW THAT THE DIFFERENCE WAS IN THE CHEAPNESS OR DEARNESS OF THE PRODUCE, NOT OF THE LABOUR*" [ibid.].

We should say that labour is more productive in the one branch of production than in the other, or also that the product costs more or less labour. In as much as no *wage labour* existed, we could not speak of CHEAPNESS OR DEARNESS OF LABOUR. Hence an hour of immediate labour would always command an hour of objectified labour, which would not of course prevent one hour's labour being more productive than another's. Nevertheless, in so far as we distinguish the part of labour necessary for subsistence, from surplus labour—and if any hours of the day at all are worked as surplus time, it is the same as if each fractional part of labour time consisted of one part necessary and one part surplus labour—done by the IMMEDIATE LABOURERS, it could not be said that the *value of labour*, i.e. WAGES, the part of the product which is exchanged for necessary labour, or the part of total labour bestowed on the necessary product, is *constant.* The fractional part of labour time which reproduces WAGES would change with the productivity of labour. Consequently, the *value of labour*, i.e. WAGES, would constantly vary with the productivity of labour. WAGES would still be measured by a definite *use value;* and since the exchange value of this use value constantly varies with changes in the productivity of labour, WAGES or the *value of labour* would vary. The concept of the *value of labour* in any case implies that living labour is *not* equal to its product, or, what is the same thing, that it is sold not as an acting cause but as itself a produced effect. To say that the value of labour is constant means nothing but that it is constantly measured by the quantity of labour contained in it.[a]

A product may contain a greater or lesser quantity of labour. Hence at various times a greater or a lesser portion of product *a* may exchange for product *b*. But the quantity of living labour which the product purchases can never be greater or smaller than the quantity of accumulated labour it represents; for a particular quantity of labour is always a particular quantity of labour, whether it exists in the form of objectified or that of living labour. If, therefore, a greater or lesser quantity of a product is given for a certain quantity of living labour, i.e. if wages rise or fall, this does not stem from a rise or fall in the value of labour, for the value of a particular quantity of labour is always equal to the same quantity of labour. It is due rather to the fact that the products cost more or less labour, and so a greater or lesser quantity of the products represents the same quantity of labour.

The *value of labour therefore remains constant.* Only the *value of the products changes,* i.e. the productive power of labour varies, not its value. This is THE PITH OF THE THEORY OF MALTHUS, IF YOU CAN CALL SUCH A SHALLOW FALLACY A THEORY. *D'abord*, a product which costs only half a day's labour time may enable me to subsist, and thus also to work, for a whole day. Whether or not the product possesses this property does not depend on its *value*, i.e. on the labour time

---

[a] Here the following passage is crossed out in the manuscript: "In this sense, the value of every product is constant. But, Malthus says, the difference is that what measures the value of the product—namely the [living] labour bestowed on it—differs AT ALL INSTANCES from the product itself, since the latter has other properties too. The product is measured by something *distinct* from it—living labour."— *Ed.*

which is bestowed on it, but on its *use value*. And the exchange which takes place between living labour and the product of labour on this basis, is not an exchange of the two as exchange values, but their relation resides partly in the use value of the product and partly in the conditions of existence of living labour capacity.

If objectified labour is exchanged for living labour, then, according to the laws of exchange value, the product which=half a day's labour could only purchase half a day's living labour, although the worker could live a whole working day on it. And if his entire working day were to be purchased, he would have to receive a whole working day in product, on which by our assumption he could live for two working days. But on the basis of capital, living labour and accumulated labour do not exchange for one another as exchange values so that both would be identical, and the same quantity of labour in objectified form would be the *value* of, the equivalent for, the same quantity of [VI-7] labour in living form. What is exchanged, rather, is product and labour capacity, which is itself a product. Labour capacity is not=to the living labour which it can perform, i.e. the quantity of labour which it can accomplish—this is its *use value*. It is equal to the quantity of labour by which it itself *must be produced* and can be reproduced. Hence the product is not IN FACT exchanged for living labour but for objectified labour, labour objectified in the labour capacity. Living labour itself is a use value possessed by the exchange value acquired in the bargain by the owner of the product. How little or how much more of this living labour he has traded in than he has expended—in the form of the product— for the labour capacity, depends on the quantity of living labour which has been paid to the worker in the product.

If a quantity of labour exchanged for an [equal] quantity of labour, whether in the form of objectified or of living labour, every quantity of labour would of course be equal to itself, and its value would be equal to its quantity. In that case, a product of half a day's labour could only purchase half a day's labour. But then, IN FACT, there would exist neither WAGES nor *value of labour*. Labour would have no *value distinct* from its product, or from the equivalent of its product, no *specific* value, and it is precisely this specific value which constitutes the *value of labour*, WAGES.

From the fact, therefore, that a certain quantity of labour=a certain quantity of labour, or also from the fact that a certain quantity of labour=itself; from the great discovery that a certain quantity is a certain quantity, Mr. Malthus concludes that wages are constant and that the value of labour is constant, i.e. [that they both]=the same quantity of objectified labour. This *would be* correct, if living labour and accumulated labour were exchanged for one another as *exchange values*. But then neither the *value of labour* nor WAGES nor *capital* nor *wage labour*, nor Malthus's investigations, would exist. These are all based on the fact that in relation to labour accumulated in capital, living labour is *use value* and living labour capacity is *exchange value*. Malthus continues calmly:

> *"The same is true if capital and PROFITS ENTER INTO THE COMPUTATION OF VALUE and the DEMAND FOR LABOUR VARIES"* [ibid., p. 33].

Here we have the whole profundity. As soon as capital and profits enter the scene, it transpires that living labour capacity is purchased, and therefore a smaller portion of accumulated labour is exchanged for a greater portion of living labour. It is altogether characteristic of his profundity that capital, which posits wage labour and transforms labour into wage labour and labour capacity into a commodity, brings about absolutely no CHANGE in the utilisation of labour, as little as it does in that of accumulated labour. *Capital, a specific form of the relation of labour to its product and to the value of this product,* "ENTERS", *according to Malthus,* WITHOUT CHANGING ANYTHING. It is as though he recognised no change in the constitution of the Roman Republic as a result of the "ENTERING OF EMPERORS".
He continues:

> "If AN INCREASED REWARD goes to the LABOURERS without an INCREASE in the PRODUCE, this is only possible on account of a FALL OF PROFITS. TO OBTAIN ANY GIVEN PORTION OF THE PRODUCE THE SAME QUANTITY OF LABOUR IS NECESSARY AS BEFORE, BUT PROFIT BEING DIMINISHED, THE VALUE OF THE PRODUCE IS DECREASED, WHILE THIS DIMINUTION OF PROFITS IN REFERENCE TO THE VALUE OF WAGES IS JUST COUNTERBALANCED BY THE INCREASED QUANTITY OF LABOUR NECESSARY TO PROCURE THE INCREASED PRODUCE AWARDED TO THE LABOURER, LEAVING THE VALUE OF LABOUR THE SAME AS BEFORE" (l.c., pp. 33, 34, Notebook IX, 29).

By assumption, the product contains the same QUANTITY OF LABOUR [as before]. But its value is supposed to be reduced, because profits have fallen. Yet why should profits fall if the labour time contained in the product has remained the same? If wages rise, while total labour time remains the same and not because of temporary causes, such as conditions of competition being favourable to the workers—this means nothing but that the productivity of labour has fallen, that a greater quantity of time is necessary to reproduce labour capacity, i.e. that a bigger part of the living labour set in motion by capital falls to necessary time and a smaller part to surplus time. Let us leave this hair-splitting till later. For the sake of completeness, just the following conclusion:

"The converse applies in the opposite case. A SMALLER QUANTITY OF PRODUCE WOULD BE AWARDED TO THE LABOURER AND PROFITS WOULD RISE. A GIVEN QUANTITY OF PRODUCE, WHICH HAD BEEN OBTAINED BY THE SAME QUANTITY OF LABOUR AS BEFORE, WOULD RISE IN VALUE ON ACCOUNT OF THE RISE OF PROFITS; WHILE THIS RISE OF PROFITS, IN REFERENCE TO THE WAGES OF THE LABOURER, WOULD BE BALANCED BY THE SMALLER QUANTITY OF LABOUR NECESSARY TO OBTAIN THE DIMINISHED PRODUCE AWARDED TO THE LABOURER" (Malthus, p. 35) (l.c.) (IX, 29).

We shall consider later what he says on this *occasion* about the implications of his PRINCIPLE for *money prices in different countries*.

//Commodity *a* can for instance purchase one day's labour, and pays for only half a day of it (the necessary part), but exchanges for the whole day. The total quantity of labour it has purchased is then equal to necessary+surplus time. Hence, if I know that the price of necessary labour=x, the price of the entire quantity of labour would=$2x$, and I could then value the newly produced commodity in WAGES, and so calculate the prices of all commodities in wages. But this would be anything but a *constant value*. The confusion concerning the AVERAGE TIME, let us say 12 hours, which in civilised countries must indeed be worked for the prevailing wage, whatever it may be, namely as to how much of these 12 hours is necessary labour and how much surplus labour, has made even Mr. Carey, who reduces the quantity of labour to working days (and indeed they can be reduced to living working days), realise that, because the same capital costs less and less labour time to reproduce, a machine costing £100, for example, will be reduced to only £50 as a result of the progress of the productive forces during a given period of time, and will therefore be the result of half as much labour time, working days or labour hours, AS YOU LIKE. From this Mr. Carey concludes that *the worker* can buy *this machine*, acquire it for himself with half as many working days as before.[a] He commits the slight mistake of considering the growth of surplus labour time as a gain *for* the worker, while on the contrary the real result is that the worker works a smaller part of the entire working day for himself and a greater part of it for capital,

---

[a] H. C. Carey, *Principles of Political Economy*, Part I, pp. 73-80, 83-92, 99, 337 and 339-40.— *Ed.*

which means that the objective power of capital in relation to him grows rapidly and in proportion to the increase in the productive forces.

Mr. Carey lets the worker buy or borrow the machine; in short, he transforms him into a capitalist. He is supposed to achieve this greater power over capital, because the reproduction of a given amount of capital requires less necessary labour, i.e. less paid labour, in other words, because wages fall in relation to profit. In America, so long as the worker there still appropriates a part of his surplus labour himself, he may be able to accumulate enough to become e.g. a farmer (although that too is now coming to an end). Where wage labour in America can still achieve something quickly [for the worker], this occurs through the reproduction of earlier modes of production and [forms of] property on the basis of capital (e.g. of the INDEPENDENT PEASANTRY). In short, Carey regards the working days as belonging to the worker, and *instead of concluding that the worker must produce more capital to be employed for the same labour time, he concludes that he needs to work less to acquire capital* (to appropriate the conditions of production).[a]

If the worker previously produced 20 machines but can now produce 40, as a result of an increase in productivity, the individual machine does indeed become cheaper. But because a smaller part of the working day is needed to produce a given quantity of this machine, it does not follow that the product of the working day has increased for the worker. On the contrary, it means that less living labour is employed to produce a given quantity of the machine. Incidentally, Mr. Carey, who is concerned with *harmony,* has himself discovered that [even] if the rate of profit falls, GROSS PROFIT rises, because an ever larger capital is required proportionately to the living labour employed. *Therefore* it becomes ever more difficult for the worker to appropriate the requisite sum of capital, the minimum of capital required for the productive employment of labour at the new stage of production. The reproduction of a fractional part of capital requires less labour time, but a larger volume of capital is required to valorise the reduced labour time. The growth of productivity is expressed in the fact that the part of capital consisting of living labour [VI-8] constantly falls in comparison with that laid out in ADVANCES, machinery, etc.

Carey's whole argument, which is of course grist to Bastiat's mill, is based on his transforming the labour time or working days

---

a Ibid.— Ed.

necessary for production into working days *belonging* to the worker, while in reality this time belongs to capital, and relative to the increase in productivity an ever smaller portion of his labour time remains to the worker. *The less living labour time a given capital has to buy*—or the more the total sum of capital increases, and the living labour employed by it declines in proportion to its volume—the greater, according to Mr. Carey, the worker's chance of becoming an owner of capital, *because* capital is *reproduced by less living labour.* The larger the capital and the smaller the number of workers it employs in proportion to its volume, the greater these workers' chance of becoming capitalists, for is not capital now reproduced with fewer working days? Can it not, *therefore,* also be bought, acquired, with fewer working days?

Assume a capital of £100, which employs 50 in advances [on constant capital], 50 on labour and takes 50% profit. The decline in the rate of profit is Carey's chief hobby-horse and is bound up with the theory. Let each £1 in wages be equal to one working day=one worker. Then assume another capital, of £16,000, which employs £14,500 in advances [on constant capital], £1,500 in wages (also=1,500 workers) and only earns 20% profit. In the first case, the product=150; in the second case (to simplify the calculation we assume the fixed capital to turn over in a year)=19,200 (3,200 profit).

This is the most favourable CASE for Mr. Carey. The rate of profit has declined from 50 to 20%, hence by $^3/_5$ or 60%. The first capital yields a [surplus] product of 50, the result of 50 days' living labour; in the other CASE a [surplus] product of 3,200 produced by 1,500 workers. In the first case, one working day yields a [surplus] product of [£] 1; in the second, it yields a [surplus] product of [£] $2^2/_{15}$. In the second case, less than half the labour time is necessary to produce a [surplus] value of [£] 1 as compared with the first case. Now, does this mean that in the second case the worker produces [£] 1 $^1/_{15}$ for himself in half a working day, while in the first case he produced only [£] 1 in double the time, [and] that [now] he is therefore well on the way to becoming a capitalist? He would first have to acquire a capital of £16,000 and purchase alien labour, instead of working himself, if this reduction in necessary labour time were to be of any help to him.

The reduction has in fact merely created an unbridgeable gap between his labour and *the conditions* for its employment. It has reduced the rate of *necessary labour,* and has thus made redundant more than 6 times as many workers in proportion to the first relation. These workers who have been thrown into the street can now console themselves with the thought that if they enjoyed the conditions required to enable them to work independently or rather to work as capitalists, they would themselves require fewer workers. In the first CASE, the entire capital necessary is £100, and the individual worker thus has just a chance of saving up this much and, if he is exceptionally lucky, of himself becoming a *capitalist* like capitalist *A* [the owner of the capital of £100]. The time worked by the worker is the same whether he is employed by *A* or *B* [the owner of £16,000], although the total number of working days required by each of them is essentially different. For every 6 workers required by the first capitalist, the second requires less than one. Therefore the remaining ones must work just as much and more surplus time.

The fact that capital requires fewer living working days at a given stage of production in which it has increased equally with the productive forces, means according to Carey that the worker requires fewer working days to appropriate capital—presumably with the working days of the workers who are not "occupied". Because the capitalist needs fewer workers in order to valorise his immense capital, the worker he employs can appropriate more capital with less labour. SUCH IS THE LOGIC OF MR. CAREY, THE HARMONISER.//

With respect to Ricardo's theory, *Wakefield* (Notebook VII, p. 74), l.c., [Vol. I, London, 1835,] p. [230-] 231, note, observes:

"TREATING LABOUR AS A COMMODITY, AND CAPITAL, THE PRODUCE OF LABOUR, AS ANOTHER, THEN, IF THE VALUE OF THESE 2 COMMODITIES WERE REGULATED BY EQUAL QUANTITIES OF LABOUR, A GIVEN AMOUNT OF LABOUR WOULD, UNDER ALL CIR-CUMSTANCES, EXCHANGE FOR THAT QUANTITY OF CAPITAL WHICH HAD BEEN PRODUCED BY THE SAME AMOUNT OF LABOUR; *ANTECEDENT* LABOUR WOULD ALWAYS EXCHANGE FOR THE SAME AMOUNT AS *PRESENT* LABOUR. But THE VALUE OF LABOUR, IN RELATION TO OTHER COMMODITIES, IN SO FAR, AT LEAST, AS WAGES DEPEND UPON SHARE, IS DETER-MINED, NOT BY EQUAL QUANTITIES OF LABOUR, BUT BY THE PROPORTION BETWEEN SUPPLY AND DEMAND."[148]

//Bailey, *Money and Its Vicissitudes in Value etc.*, London, 1837, (Notebook V, p. 26 ff), observes that DORMANT CAPITAL may be activised by means of accelerated circulation (in his view, by means of an increase in the volume of CURRENCY; he should have said, of *money*), and seeks to demonstrate that, in general, if a country's capital were always fully employed, no INCREASE OF DEMAND could bring forth AN INCREASE OF PRODUCTION. The concept of DORMANT CAPITAL belongs to the sphere of circulation, since capital which is not in circulation is dormant. The relevant passages are:

"Much CAPITAL and PRODUCTIVE SKILL MAY EXIST IN AN INERT STATE. It is incorrect when the economists believe THAT THE NUMBER OF LABOURERS and the QUANTITY OF CAPITAL are CERTAIN DEFINITIVE POWERS which must INEVITABLY PRODUCE A DETERMINATE RESULT IN ANY COUNTRY WHERE THEY EXIST" (p. 54). "Far FROM BEING FIXED AND DETERMINED, THE AMOUNT OF COMMODITIES which the EXISTING PRODUCERS and the EXISTING CAPITAL BRING TO MARKET, IS SUBJECT TO A WIDE RANGE OF VARIATION" (p. 55). Therefore, it is "NOT ESSENTIAL TO AN INCREASE OF PRODUCTION THAT NEW CAPITAL OR NEW LABOURERS SHOULD ARISE"... (E.g. in a country where WANT OF PRECIOUS METALS) "some commodities or, what is the same thing, the POWER TO PRODUCE THEM, may at one place be in excess, OTHER COMMODITIES AT ANOTHER PLACE likewise, and the HOLDERS OF EACH WISHING TO EXCHANGE THEIR ARTICLES FOR THOSE HELD BY THE OTHER, BUT KEPT IN A STATE OF NON-INTERCOURSE FOR WANT OF A COMMON MEDIUM OF EXCHANGE, AND IN A STATE OF INACTION BECAUSE THEY HAVE NO MOTIVE FOR PRODUCTION" (pp. 55, 56).

In the circulation of capital, money makes a dual appearance. [Firstly,] as the transformation of capital into money and realisation of the price of the commodity; but in this case, the positing of price is not a formal one. The transformation of the product into money is here the reconversion of capital into *value* as such, value existing independently; capital as money or money as realised capital. Secondly, in its determination as mere means of circulation. Here it only serves to reconvert capital into the conditions of production. In this second moment, in the form of wages, a certain volume of money must be simultaneously present as means of circulation, means of payment. The fact that money now plays this dual role in the circulation of capital, makes it appear in all crises that there is a lack of money as means of circulation; whereas actually capital is lacking in value, and thus cannot *monétiser* itself. In such a crisis the volume of money in circulation may in fact increase. The new determinations of money; how it is posited as a moment of the circulation of capital, partly as its means of circulation and partly as the *realised value of capital,* as itself *capital,* will require a section of its own when we discuss interest, etc.

Bailey continues:

"The labour set in motion is not at all solely dependent upon the AVAILABLE CAPITAL of a country. It depends upon whether FOOD, TOOLS and RAW MATERIALS are distributed slowly or rapidly [VI-9] TO THOSE PARTS WHERE IT IS WANTED; whether it circulates with difficulty or not, whether it EXISTS FOR LONG INTERVALS IN INERT MASSES, and so as a result DOES NOT FURNISH SUFFICIENT EMPLOYMENT TO THE POPULATION" (pp. 56, 57).

(The example of Gallatin, l.c., p. 68,[149] of the WESTERN COUNTIES of Pennsylvania.)

"Political economists are too apt to consider a certain quantity of capital and a certain number of labourers as instruments of production of UNIFORM POWER, or

OPERATING WITH A CERTAIN UNIFORM INTENSITY... The producer, who employs a certain capital, can have his products ON HAND for a long or a short time, and while he waits for the opportunity to exchange them, HIS POWER OF PRODUCING IS STOPPED OR RETARDED, so that in a given period, for instance one year, HE MAY PRODUCE only half as much as if a PROMPT DEMAND had existed. This REMARK is EQUALLY applicable to the LABOURER, who is his instrument. The ADJUSTMENT OF THE VARIOUS OCCUPATIONS OF MEN IN SOCIETY TO EACH OTHER must be at least IMPERFECTLY EFFECTED. But if there is A WIDE DISTANCE between the stages in which [it] is effected—every EXPEDIENT which FACILITATES TRAFFIC is a STEP towards this ADJUSTMENT. THE MORE UNIMPEDED and EASY the INTERCHANGE OF COMMODITIES BECOMES, the SHORTER WILL BE THOSE UNPRODUCTIVE INTERVALS in which MEN, EAGER FOR WORK, SEEM SEPARATED BY AN IMPASSABLE BARRIER FROM THE CAPITAL ... which, although CLOSE AT HAND, is tied up IN BARREN INERTNESS" (pp. 58-60).

"The general PRINCIPLE [is] THAT A NEW DEMAND WILL BE MET BY FRESH EXERTIONS; BY THE ACTIVE EMPLOYMENT OF CAPITAL AND LABOUR BEFORE DORMANT, AND NOT BY THE DIVERSION OF PRODUCTIVE POWER FROM OTHER OBJECTS. The latter is only possible if the employment of capital and labour in a country were no longer capable of growth. The exportation OF THE GOODS perhaps does not set new labour in motion directly, but then it absorbs [them], if already existing goods [are] DEAD STOCK and SETS AT LIBERTY CAPITAL TIED UP IN AN UNPRODUCTIVE STATE" (p. 65). "Those who maintain that an influx of money cannot promote the production of other commodities, since those commodities ARE THE SOLE AGENTS OF PRODUCTION, prove that production could never be ENLARGED, for such an ENLARGEMENT requires THAT FOOD, RAW MATERIALS, AND TOOLS SHOULD BE PREVIOUSLY AUGMENTED; WHICH IS IN FACT MAINTAINING *THAT NO INCREASE OF PRODUCTION CAN TAKE PLACE WITHOUT A PREVIOUS INCREASE*" (but is that not the economic doctrine of accumulation?) "or in other words, that AN INCREASE IS IMPOSSIBLE" (p. 70).

"Now, it is said that if the purchaser goes to MARKET with an augmented QUANTITY OF MONEY and does not raise the price of the commodity which he finds there, he does not give any ADDITIONAL ENCOURAGEMENT TO PRODUCTION: [but] if he raises the price, if PRICES ARE PROPORTIONALLY ENHANCED, THE PURCHASERS HAVE NO GREATER POWER OF DEMAND THAN BEFORE" (p. 73). "It must be denied AS A GENERAL PRINCIPLE that A PURCHASER CANNOT GIVE ADDITIONAL ENCOURAGEMENT TO PRODUCTION, *UNLESS HIS DEMAND RAISE PRICES*. Apart from the circumstance that the preparation OF A LARGER QUANTITY ADMITS OF A MORE EFFECTIVE DIVISION OF LABOUR AND THE EMPLOYMENT OF SUPERIOR MACHINERY, THERE IS IN THIS MATTER THAT SORT OF LATITUDE, ARISING FROM A QUANTITY OF LABOUR AND CAPITAL LYING UNEMPLOYED, AND *READY TO FURNISH ADDITIONAL COMMODITIES AT THE SAME RATE*. So it happens that A CONSIDERABLE INCREASE OF DEMAND often TAKES PLACE without RAISING PRICES" (pp. 73-74).//

//John Wade, *History of the Middle and Working Classes, etc.*, 3rd ed., London, 1835, (Notebook, p. 20[150]):

"LABOUR IS THE AGENCY BY WHICH CAPITAL IS MADE *PRODUCTIVE OF WAGES, PROFIT, OR REVENUE*" (p. 161). "CAPITAL IS STORED UP INDUSTRY, PROVIDED TO DEVELOP ITSELF IN NEW AND EQUIVALENT FORMS; IT IS *COLLECTIVE FORCE*" (p. 162). "Capital is but another name for civilisation" (p. 164).

The association of workers—cooperation and DIVISION OF LABOUR as basic conditions of the productivity of labour—appear, like all productive forces of labour, i.e. those which determine the degree of its intensity and hence of its extensive realisation, as a *productive force of capital*. The collective power of labour, its character as social labour, is therefore the *collective power* of capital. Likewise *science* and the division of labour, which appears as the division of EMPLOYMENTS and the exchange corresponding to them. All social powers of production are productive forces of capital and consequently capital itself appears as their subject.

Hence the association of the workers as it appears in the factory is not posited by them but by capital. Their combination is not *their* being, but rather the *being* of capital. To the individual worker it appears fortuitous. He relates to his own association with other workers and to his cooperation with them as *alien,* as to modes of operation of capital. Where capital does not appear in its inadequate form—say, in that of small-scale self-employed capital—it already implies [at quite an early stage] a certain, greater or smaller, degree of concentration, both in objective form, i.e. as the concentration in the hands of one person, which here still coincides with the accumulation, of means of subsistence, raw material and instruments; or, in a word, the concentration of money as the general form of wealth, and also in subjective form, as the accumulation of the forces of labour and their concentration in one place under the command of capital. In this situation, there is not one capitalist to one worker, but a number of workers to one capitalist, not like the one or two journeymen who work for one master.

Productive capital, or the mode of production corresponding to capital, can only take two forms: manufacture or large-scale industry. In the former, the division of labour prevails; in the latter, the combination of the forces of labour (with a uniform mode of labour) and the application of scientific POWER, where the combination and, as it were, the communal spirit of labour is transferred to the machine, etc. In the first form, the number of workers (accumulated) must be large in proportion to the AMOUNT OF CAPITAL; in the second, fixed capital is large in proportion to the many associated workers. But the concentration of many workers and their allocation among the machinery as so many cogs (why in agriculture it is different, irrelevant here) is here already presupposed. Therefore we do not have to consider CASE II here in any detail, but only CASE I.

The characteristic development of manufacture is the *division of labour.* But this presupposes that a large number of workers has been (previously) assembled under one command, in just the same way as the *transformation of money into capital presupposes that a certain* AMOUNT *of means of subsistence, raw materials and instruments of labour has been set free.* Here we must also abstract from the division of labour as a later development. Certain branches of industry, e.g. mining, presuppose cooperation right from the start. As long as capital does not exist, cooperation takes place through forced labour (serf or slave labour) under an overseer. Likewise the construction of roads, etc. To undertake such activities, capital does not produce the accumulation and concentration of workers, it takes them over. This aspect is therefore not IN QUESTION.

The simplest form, and the one most independent of the division of labour, is that in which capital employs a number of hand-weavers, spinners, etc., independent of and living separately from one another. (This form still exists alongside industry.) *Therefore, at this stage, the mode of production itself is not yet determined by capital, but is found by it already in existence.* The unifying focus of these scattered workers is solely their mutual relation to capital, the fact that their product, and hence the surplus values they produce over and above their own income, are accumulated in the hands of capital. As associated labour, they exist only *in themselves,* in so far as each of them works for capital and thus possesses a centre in it, without really working together. Their association by capital is thus merely *formal,* [VI-10] and concerns only the product of labour, not labour itself. Instead of exchanging with many, they exchange with the one capitalist. Capital therefore effects a *concentration of EXCHANGES.*

Capital does not *exchange* as an individual, but as representing the consumption and the needs of many. It *no longer exchanges* as individual exchanger, but in the act of exchange represents the whole society. *Collective exchange* and *concentrating exchange* on the side of capital with individually working weavers, etc., the products of whose labour are collected and brought together by this exchange, and thus their labour is brought together, too, although they act independently of one another. The combination of their labour appears as a particular act, alongside which the independent fragmentation of their labour continues. This is the *first prerequisite* for *money* to exchange as capital with free labour.

The second prerequisite is the transcendence of the independent fragmentation of the many workers, in such a way that the *single capital* no longer appears relative to them merely as *social collective power* in the *act of exchange,* combining many exchanges in capital, but assembles them in one place under its command, in one place of work, no longer letting them continue *in the previously existing mode of production* and establishing its power on that basis, but rather creating as basis a mode of production corresponding to itself. It posits the *combination* of the workers in production, a combination which at first will be confined to a common place of work under the direction of overseers, *regimentation, greater discipline, consistency, and a* posited *dependence on capital in production itself.* With this development certain *faux frais de production*[a] are saved right away. (On this whole process, cf. *Gaskell,* which is specially concerned with the development of large-scale industry in England.[b])

Capital now appears both as the collective power of the workers, their social power, and as the unity which binds them together and thereby creates this power. Now as before, and at every stage of the development of capital, all this is mediated by the many exchanging with it as the one, so that the exchange itself is concentrated in capital. This is the social character of the exchange: capital exchanges socially with the workers, but they exchange individually with it.

With handicraft production, it is the quality of the product which matters, the particular skill of the individual labourer, and the master as master is SUPPOSED to have achieved mastery in this skill. His position as master rests not only on his ownership of the conditions of production, but also on his own skill in the particular trade. With production based on capital, right from the start it is not this half-artistic relationship which matters—a relationship which altogether corresponds [more] to the development of the use value of labour, to the development of the particular skill of immediate manual labour, to training the human hand, etc., for labour. Right from the start, capitalist production is concerned with quantity, because it is concerned with exchange value and surplus value. The developed principle of capital is precisely to render superfluous any particular skill, to render superfluous manual labour, immediate physical labour in general, both as a specialised skill and as muscular exertion, to locate all skill rather in the inanimate forces of nature.

Now, with the presupposition of the rise of manufacture as the emergence of the mode of production of capital (slaves are combined in themselves because they are under the direction of *one* master), it is presupposed that the productive power of labour to be called forth only by capital itself does not as yet exist. Hence it is presupposed that, in manufacture, necessary labour still claims a great part of all available labour time, which means that the surplus labour which can be performed by the individual worker is still relatively small.

---

[a] Overhead costs of production.— *Ed.*

[b] P. Gaskell, *Artisans and Machinery,* London, 1836, pp. 11-114 and 293-362.— *Ed.*

508 Outlines of the Critique of Political Economy

Now, this is compensated for and the progress of manufacture is accelerated by the fact that the rate of profit is larger, and hence capital is accumulated more rapidly relative to the AMOUNT of it already in existence than in large-scale industry. If 50 thaler of [an advanced capital of] 100 thaler is paid to labour, and surplus time=$^1/_5$ [of necessary time], the value created is 110, or [the rate of profit is] 10%. If only 20 thaler of [a capital of] 100 thaler is paid to labour, and surplus time=$^1/_4$ [of necessary time], the value created=105, or [the rate of profit is] 5%.

On the other hand, this greater rate of profit in manufacture can only be achieved by the simultaneous employment of many workers. The greater surplus time can only be obtained by the collection of the surplus time of many workers for the benefit of capital. Absolute, not relative, surplus time predominates in manufacture. This is even more the case originally, if the scattered independent workers still make use of part of their surplus time for themselves. For capital to exist as capital, for it to be able both to live on its profit and to accumulate, its profit must=the sum of the surplus time of many simultaneous living working days. In agriculture, the soil itself, in its chemical, etc., activity, is already a machine which makes immediate labour more productive, and it yields a surplus earlier, because it is *the first* productive activity carried on with a machine, namely a *natural* one. This is the only correct basis of the Physiocratic doctrine, which considers agriculture from this angle in relation to as yet very undeveloped manufacture. If the capitalist employed *one* worker in order to live on the surplus time worked by that worker, then it appears that he would double his profit if [instead] he worked himself and with his own funds. For apart from the surplus time, he would gain the wages paid to the worker. In fact, he would lose in the process. For either he would not yet be in the CONDITIONS enabling him to work as a capitalist, or the worker would merely be his assistant and would not yet relate to him as capitalist.

For money to be transformed into capital, it is therefore not only necessary that it should be able to set surplus labour in motion, but that it should be able to set in motion a *certain quantity of surplus labour,* the surplus labour of a certain quantity of necessary labour, i.e. *of many workers* at the same time. The combined sum must suffice for capital both to live as *capital,* i.e. to represent, in consumption, wealth as against the life of the worker, and to put aside surplus labour for accumulation. Right from the start, capital does not produce for use value, for immediate subsistence. Hence right from the start, surplus labour must be sufficiently large for a part of it to be reinvested as capital. Thus, whenever the stage is reached at which a certain quantity of social wealth is already concentrated in one hand, in an objective form, wealth which therefore as capital immediately appears as exchange with many workers and later as production by many workers, by a combination of workers, and can SIMULTANEOUSLY set TO WORK a certain quantity of living labour capacity,—when this stage is reached, production by capital begins. Right from the start, capital appears as a *collective power,* as a social power and as the transcendence of individual isolation, first of the exchange with the workers, and then of the workers themselves. The isolation of the workers still implies their relative independence. Complete dependence on capital, complete separation of the workers from the conditions of production, consequently imply their grouping around the individual capital as the sole source of their subsistence.

The result will be the same—or it is the same in another form—if we set out from the particular form of exchange which is presupposed for capital to exchange as capital, where money must already *represent many exchangers* or possess a *power of exchange* going beyond the scope of the individual and his individual surplus; no longer an individual power of exchange, but one which, though it belongs to the Individual, belongs to him as a Social function and by virtue of his exchanging as the representative· of the wealth of society. All this also arises from the conditions of *free labour.* The separation of the individual from the production conditions of labour=the assembly of many around the one capital.//

//Merchant capital also right from the start the concentration of many exchanges in one hand. It already represents a mass of exchangers both as *M* and as *C.*//

[VI-11] "This *continual progression of knowledge and experience* is our great strength," writes Babbage.[a]

This progression, this social progress, belongs to and is exploited by capital. All previous forms of property condemn the greater part of mankind, the slaves, to be mere instruments of labour. Historical development, political development, art, science, etc., are located in the higher spheres above them. But it is only capital which has subjected historical progress to the service of wealth.

---

[a] Ch. Babbage, *Traité sur l'économie des machines et des manufactures,* p. 485. Marx quotes in French.— *Ed.*

//Prior to the accumulation by capital, an accumulation is presupposed which constitutes capital and which belongs to its concept. We cannot really call it *concentration* yet, because this occurs in contradistinction to many capitals. But if one still speaks of *the* capital, concentration still coincides with accumulation or the concept of capital. In other words, concentration does not yet constitute a particular determination. But right from the start, capital does indeed exist as One or Unity, confronting the workers as Many. It thus appears as the concentration of the workers which confronts labour, [that is to say] as a unity located outside them. From this aspect, concentration is contained in the concept of capital—the concentration of many living labour capacities for a particular purpose; a concentration which initially need not by any means have been fully effected in the mode of production itself, or have permeated it. The centralising effect of capital upon labour capacities, or the positing of itself as their unity which exists independently of and outside their multiplicity.//.

//In his *Leçons d'économie politique*[a] (Notebook, p. 26), *Rossi* writes:

> "Social progress cannot consist in the dissolution of all association, but in replacing the compulsory, oppressive associations of the past by voluntary and just ones... The most extreme form of isolation is the savage state; the most extreme form of compulsory and oppressive association is barbarism. Outside these extremes, history shows us many different varieties and nuances. Perfection is found in voluntary associations which multiply strength through union, without stripping individual power of its energy, morality or responsibility" (p. 353).[b]

Under capital, the *association* of the *ouvriers*[c] is not enforced through direct physical force, compulsory, serf and slave labour; it is enforced by the circumstance that the conditions of production are alien property and are themselves present as *objective association*, which is the same as accumulation and concentration of the conditions of production.//

//The economists are led into all manner of DIFFICULTIES by their way of conceiving capital purely in its physical aspect, as instrument of production, and ignoring the economic form, which is what makes the instrument of production capital. For instance, Rossi asks (Notebook, 27):

---

[a] P. Rossi, "Cours d'économie politique. Année 1836-1837", *Cours d'économie politique,* Brussels, 1843, p. 353.— *Ed.*
[b] Marx quotes in French.— *Ed.*
[c] Workers.— *Ed.*

"Is the raw material really an instrument of production? Is it not rather an object which is acted upon by the instrument of production?" (p. 367).[a]

In this passage, Rossi merges capital completely with the instrument of production in the technological sense, and on this basis every savage is a capitalist (which Mr. Torrens in fact asserts with respect to a savage who aims a *stone* at a bird.[b]) Moreover, even from the aspect of the purely physical abstraction—i.e. the abstraction from the economic category itself—Rossi's remark is a shallow one, and only shows that he has not understood his English teacher [Torrens].

ACCUMULATED LABOUR USED AS INSTRUMENT FOR NEW PRODUCTION, or PRODUCE pure and simple APPLIED TO PRODUCTION[c]; the raw material is applied to production, i.e. subjected to an alteration of form, just as much as the instrument, which is also *produit*. The *finished result of production becomes in turn a moment of the process of production*. That is all the statement means. Within the process of production it can figure as raw material or as instrument. But it is an instrument of production, not in so far as it serves as an instrument in the direct process of production, but in so far as it is a means for the renewal of the process of production itself—one of its presuppositions.

More important and more TO THE POINT is the question whether or not the means of subsistence, i.e. wages, are part of capital, and here the whole confusion of the economists becomes evident.

"One says the remuneration of the worker is capital, because the capitalist advances it to him. If only there were families of workers who had sufficient to subsist for a year, wages would not exist. The worker could say to the capitalist: you advance the capital for the common project, I will bring the labour to it; the product will be shared among us in such and such proportions. As soon as the product has been realised, each of us will take his share" [Rossi,] (p. 369[-370]). "Then there would be no advances for the workers. Even if work were at a standstill, they would still consume. What they would [in that case] consume belongs to the consumption fund, not at all to capital. Therefore: the advances for the workers are not necessary. *Therefore wages are not a constituent element of production. They are of an accidental nature, a form arising from our social condition.* Capital, labour and land, on the other hand, are necessary for production. *Secondly:* The word 'wages' is employed in a double sense: one says that wages are a capital, but what do they represent? Labour. He who says wages says labour and vice versa. Hence, if the wages advanced constituted a part of capital, one would have to speak only of two instruments of production: capital and land" (p. 370).[d]

[a] Marx quotes in French.— *Ed.*
[b] R. Torrens, *An Essay on the Production of Wealth*, London, 1821, pp. 70-71.— *Ed.*
[c] Ibid., pp. 33-34.— *Ed.*
[d] Marx quotes in German except for a few isolated words and phrases reproduced in French.— *Ed.*

And further:

"Basically, the worker does not consume the capitalist's possessions, but his own; what is given to him as remuneration for his labour is his own fractional part of the product" (p. 370). "The capitalist's contract with *the worker is not one of the phenomena of production...* The entrepreneur goes along with this arrangement in so far as it may facilitate production. But this is nothing but *a second operation,* an operation of a quite different nature, grafted on to a productive operation. *It could disappear if labour were organised differently.* Even today there are spheres of production in which it has no place. Wages are therefore a form of the distribution of wealth, not an element of production. The part of the fund which the entrepreneur devotes to the payment of wages does not constitute a part of capital... It is a distinct operation, which undoubtedly may promote the course of production but which cannot be called a *direct* instrument of production" (p. 370).[a]

"To conceive the power of labour, while ignoring the worker's means of subsistence during the work of production, is to conceive an imagined being. He who says labour or the power of labour says worker and means of subsistence, worker and wage... *The same element reappears under the name of capital; as if the same thing could simultaneously form part of two distinct instruments of production"* (pp. 370, 371).[b]

There is much confusion here, justified only by Rossi taking the economists at their word and equating the *instrument of production* as such with capital. *D'abord,* he is quite right in arguing that wage labour is not an absolute form of labour. But he forgets that capital is just as little an absolute form of the means and materials of labour, that these two forms [wage labour and capital] are the same form in different moments, and therefore stand and fall together. Hence it is absurd of him to speak of capitalists without wage labour.

His example of families of workers who can subsist for a year without the capitalist, who therefore own the conditions of their production, and who perform their necessary labour without the permission of Mr. Capitalist, reduces the capitalist whom he lets come to them with his PROPOSAL to a producer of instruments of production. The coming to them is nothing but a division of labour mediated by exchange with the outside. Even without any arrangement—by means of simple EXCHANGES—the two share in the common product. The EXCHANGE is the sharing-out; no further arrangement is necessary. What these families of workers would be exchanging would be the absolute or relative surplus labour which the instrument would have enabled them to perform—either new labour carried on as a sideline over and above the old labour on which they were able to live from year to year before the

---

[a] Marx quotes in German except for a few isolated words and phrases reproduced in French.— *Ed.*

[b] Marx quotes in French.— *Ed.*

appearance of the capitalist, or [extra labour made possible] by the employment of this instrument in their traditional branch of work. Here Mr. Rossi transforms the worker into the owner and exchanger of his [VI-12] surplus labour, and in this way he has succeeded in removing from him the last vestige of what stamps him as a wage worker; but he has also thereby removed from the instrument of production the last vestige of what makes it capital.

It is true that the worker "basically does not consume the capitalist's possessions, but his own", however not exactly as Mr. Rossi thinks, because it is only a *fractional* part of *the* product, but because it is a fractional part of *his* product. If the semblance of exchange is stripped away, the payment consists in the fact that the worker works one part of the day for himself and another for the capitalist, but *only gets the permission to work at all* as long as his labour permits this division. As we have seen, the *act of exchange* itself is not a moment of the immediate process of production but one of its conditions. Yet within the total process of production of capital, which includes in itself the different moments of its EXCHANGES, i.e. circulation, this exchange is posited as a moment of the total process.

But, says Rossi, wages appear twice in the calculation: once as capital, the other time as labour. Hence wages represent two distinct instruments of production; and if they represent the instrument of production "labour", they cannot represent the instrument of production "capital". There is a confusion here which is likewise due to the fact that he takes the orthodox economic distinctions seriously. In production, wages figure only once, as the fund destined to be converted into wages, as *virtual* wages. As soon as they become real wages, they are paid out and now only figure in consumption as the income of the worker. What is exchanged for wages is labour capacity, and this does not figure in production at all, only the use made of it— *labour*. Labour appears as an instrument of production of value, because it is not paid for and hence is not represented by wages. As an activity producing use value, it has also nothing to do with itself as paid labour. Wages in the hands of the worker are no longer wages, but a consumption fund. Only in the hands of the capitalist are they wages, i.e. the part of capital destined to be exchanged for labour capacity. For the capitalist they have reproduced a saleable labour capacity, so that from this aspect even the consumption of the workers serves the interest of the capitalist. He does not pay anything at all for the labour itself, only for the

labour capacity. What enables him to do this is of course precisely
the efficacy of this capacity.

The double appearance of wages is not due to the fact that they
represent on two occasions two different instruments of production, but to the fact that they appear at one time under the aspect
of production and at another under that of distribution. Yet this
particular form of distribution is not any sort of arrangement that
can be altered at one's own discretion. It is posited by the form of
production itself; it is merely one of production's own moments
considered in another determination.

The value of the machine certainly constitutes a part of capital,
which is laid out in that form; but the machine as value does not
produce anything, although it makes a profit for the factory-
owner. Wages do not represent labour as an instrument of
production, as little as value represents the machine as an
instrument of production. They merely represent labour capacity,
and, since the value of that capacity exists separately from it as
capital, they are part of capital.

In as much as the capitalist appropriates *alien* labour and with
this appropriated *labour* purchases more labour, wages—i.e. the
representative of labour—appear in a dual form, if Mr. Rossi
wishes, (1) as the property of capital, (2) as representative of
labour. What really worries Rossi is that wages appear as the
representative *of two instruments of production,* of *capital* and of
labour. He forgets that labour as a productive force is embodied in
capital and that as *labour in esse,*[a] not *labour in posse,*[b] it is in no way
an *instrument of production* distinct from capital, but that, on the
contrary, it is only labour which converts capital into an
instrument of production. As for the distinction between wages as
constituting part of capital and as simultaneously the income of
the worker, we shall discuss that in the section on profit, interest,
with which we conclude this first chapter on capital.//

//*Malthus* returns to the points made in the above-mentioned
The Measure of Value etc. in his *Definitions in Political Economy, etc.,*
London, 1827. In that book he says:

"No writer that i have met with, anterior to Mr. Ricardo, ever used the
term *wages*, or real wages, as implying *proportions*. Profits, indeed, imply
proportions; and the *rate of profits* had always justly been estimated by a
percentage upon the value of the advances. But wages had uniformly been
considered as rising or falling, not *according to any proportion* which they

_____

    [a] In existence.— *Ed.*
    [b] In possibility.— *Ed.*

The sole value produced in a given production by capital, is the value added by the new quantity of labour. But this value consists of necessary labour which reproduces wages—the advances made by capital in the form of wages—, and of surplus labour, hence surplus value over and above necessary labour. The advances made in the form of material and machinery are only translated from one form into another. The instrument passes over into the product just as much as does the raw material, and its wearing out at the same time posits the form on the product. If the raw material and instrument cost nothing, as in the case of some extractive industries, where they are still almost=0 (the *raw material* always in each extractive industry, metal-mining, coal-mining, fishing, hunting, timber-cutting in primeval forests, etc.), they add absolutely nothing to the value of production. Their value is the result of previous production, not of the immediate production in which they serve as instrument and material. *Surplus value* can therefore only be estimated in relation to necessary labour. *Profit* is merely a *secondary*, derived and transformed form of surplus value, the bourgeois form in which the traces of its origin are wiped out.

Ricardo himself never understood this, (1) because he always speaks merely of the division of a *finished* quantity, never of the original positing of this distinction [between profit and wages]; (2) because an understanding of this distinction would have forced him to realise that the relation established between capital and labour differs entirely from that of exchange, and he dared not realise that the bourgeois system of equivalents turns into and is based on appropriation without an equivalent; (3) because his doctrine of PROPORTIONATE PROFITS and WAGES merely expresses the fact that, [if] a certain total value is divided into two parts, or if *any* quantity is divided into two parts, the size of the two parts is necessarily inversely related. And indeed his school subsequently reduced the matter to this commonplace.

Ricardo's purpose in putting forward the doctrine of PROPORTIONATE WAGES and PROFITS was not to discover the basis of the creation of surplus value—for he starts from the assumption that a given value must be divided between wages and profit, between labour and capital, and hence implies that this division is self-evident. His purpose was, rather, *firstly,* to assert the correct method of price determination, which he bases on value, as against the current one by showing that the limit of value itself is not affected by its distribution in various proportions between PROFITS and WAGES; *secondly,* to explain the reason for not only the transitory but the continuous fall in the rate of profit, which was inexplicable to him on the basis of the assumption that a fixed portion of value accrues to labour; *thirdly,* by explaining this fall of profits by the rise of wages, to explain this rise itself by a rise in the *value* of agricultural products, i.e. by the increasing difficulty of producing them, and thus at the same time to explain *ground rent* as not at variance with his value principle.

This also provided a polemical weapon for industrial capital against landed property, which was exploiting the progress made by industry. But at the same time, impelled by simple logic, he had thus proclaimed the contradictory nature of profit, labour and capital, [VI-13] however much he exerted himself subsequently to prove to the worker that the contradiction between profit and wages did not affect his real income, that, on the contrary, a *proportional* (not absolute) rise of wages is *undesirable,* because it impedes accumulation, and because the development of industry then benefits only the idle landowner. STILL, the contradiction was proclaimed, and Carey, who does not understand Ricardo, could therefore denounce him as the father of the communists, etc.,[a] and in a sense he is right, though he does not himself understand in what sense.

The other economists, however, who, like Malthus, want to have absolutely nothing to do with the proportional (and hence contradictory) nature of wages, *desire* on the one hand to obscure the contradiction, but on the other cling to the proposition that the worker simply exchanges a certain use value, his labour capacity, for capital, and thus renounces labour's productive power, the power of producing new value, that the worker has nothing *to do with the product,* and that consequently the exchange between capitalists and workers, wages, just like every simple EXCHANGE where economic *equivalents* are presupposed, is concerned only with *quantity,* the quantity of use value.

However correct this may be in a sense, the apparent form of BARTER and EXCHANGE prompts the worker, when competition allows him to bargain and haggle with the capitalist, to measure his

---

[a] H. C. Carey, *The Past, the Present, and the Future,* Philadelphia, 1848, pp. 74-75.— *Ed.*

claims by reference to the capitalist's profit, and to demand a certain share in the surplus value he has produced; so that the *proportion* becomes a real moment of economic life itself. Furthermore, in the struggle between the two classes—which necessarily arises with the development of the working class—the measure of the reciprocal distance between them, which is expressed precisely by wages as a proportion, becomes decisively important. The *semblance of exchange* disappears in the process of the mode of production based on capital. The process itself and its repetition now posits what is the case in itself, namely that the worker receives in his wages from the capitalist only a part of his own labour. Eventually this enters the consciousness of both the workers and the capitalists.

Actually, the only question in Ricardo is: what proportion of the total value do necessary wages constitute in the course of development? It always remains only the *necessary wages;* their proportional nature is therefore of no concern to the worker, who now as before receives the same minimum, but only to the capitalist, whose deductions from his net income vary without the workers receiving any more in terms of use value. But the fact that Ricardo formulated the contradictory nature of profit and wages, even if he was seeking to deal with quite different problems, in itself shows that in his time the mode of production based on capital had taken on a form increasingly adequate to its nature.

In the *Definitions* referred to (Notebook IX, pp. 49, 50), Malthus comments with regard to Ricardo's theory of value:

"Ricardo's assertion, that as the VALUE OF WAGES RISES PROFITS PROPORTIONALLY FALL and vice versa, can be true only on the assumption that commodities in which the same quantity of labour has been worked up are always of the same value, and this will be found to be true in one case out of five hundred; and necessarily so because the progress of civilisation and IMPROVEMENT continually increases the QUANTITY OF FIXED CAPITAL EMPLOYED and renders more VARIOUS AND UNEQUAL the TIMES OF THE RETURNS OF THE CIRCULATING CAPITAL" (l.c., pp. 31, 32).

(This relates to *prices*, not *value*.)

With respect to HIS OWN DISCOVERY OF THE TRUE STANDARD OF VALUE, Malthus remarks:

"*In the first place:* I HAD NOWHERE SEEN IT STATED, THAT THE ORDINARY *QUANTITY OF LABOUR WHICH A COMMODITY WILL COMMAND* MUST REPRESENT AND MEASURE *THE QUANTITY OF LABOUR WORKED UP IN IT, WITH THE ADDITION OF PROFITS...* BY REPRESENTING THE LABOUR WORKED UP IN A COMMODITY, WITH THE ADDITION OF PROFITS, LABOUR represents THE NATURAL AND NECESSARY CONDITIONS OF ITS SUPPLY, OR THE ELEMENTARY COSTS OF ITS PRODUCTION. *Secondly:* I HAD NOWHERE SEEN IT STATED THAT, HOWEVER THE FERTILITY OF THE SOIL MIGHT VARY, THE ELEMENTARY

COSTS OF PRODUCING THE WAGES OF A GIVEN QUANTITY OF LABOUR MUST ALWAYS
NECESSARILY BE THE SAME" (pp. 196, 197).

This only means that WAGES are always equal to the labour time
necessary for their production, which varies with the productivity
of labour. The QUANTITY OF COMMODITIES remains the same.

"If VALUE is regarded as a commodity's GENERAL POWER OF PURCHASE, this must
refer to the purchase of all commodities, the GENERAL MASS OF COMMODITIES. But
this mass is quite UNMANAGEABLE. NOW, OF ANY ONE OBJECT, IT CANNOT FOR A
MOMENT BE DENIED THAT LABOUR BEST REPRESENTS AN AVERAGE OF THE GENERAL MASS
OF PRODUCTIONS" (p. 205). "A LARGE CLASS OF COMMODITIES, such as RAW PRODUCE,
rises in the PROGRESS OF SOCIETY as compared with labour, while MANUFACTURED
ARTICLES FALL. So it is not FAR FROM THE TRUTH TO SAY that the AVERAGE MASS of
commodities which A GIVEN QUANTITY OF LABOUR WILL COMMAND IN THE SAME
COUNTRY, DURING THE COURSE OF SOME CENTURIES, MAY NOT VERY ESSENTIALLY VARY"
(p. 206). "VALUE should always be value in exchange for labour" (l.c., p. 224,
note).

In other words, [Malthus's] doctrine is that the value of a
commodity, the labour worked up in it, is represented by the
[number of] living working days which it commands, for which it
can exchange, and hence by WAGES. The living working days contain
both [necessary] time and surplus time. Let us do Malthus the
biggest possible favour. Let us assume that the proportion of
surplus labour to necessary labour, and hence the proportion of
WAGES to PROFIT, always remains constant. To begin with, the fact
that Mr. Malthus speaks of the labour worked up in the
commodity WITH THE ADDITION OF PROFITS, demonstrates his confusion,
since profits can only constitute a part of the labour worked up.
What he has in mind are the *profits* which are supposed to result
from the fixed capital, etc., *over and above the labour worked up.* But
this can only affect the distribution of total profit among the
various SHAREHOLDERS in this capital, not its total quantity. For if
everyone obtained for his commodity the labour worked up in
it+PROFITS, where do these profits come from, Mr. Malthus? If one
obtains the labour worked up in his commodity+profit, another
must obtain the labour worked up [in *his* commodity]−profit.
Profit is being considered here as greater than actual surplus value.
Hence this drops out of the calculation.

Now suppose that the labour worked up=3 working days. If the
proportion of surplus [to total] labour time is 1:2, these have been
obtained in payment for 1 1/2 working days. INDEED, the workers
worked for 3 days, but each was paid only half a day [for a full
day's labour]. Or the commodity which they received for their 3
working days had only 1 1/2 working days worked up in it. Hence,
all other things being equal, the capitalist would obtain 6 working

days for the 3 days worked up in his commodity. (This proposition is correct only because surplus labour time has been assumed as equal to necessary, so that in the second CASE *only* the first is repeated.)

(*Obviously, relative surplus value is limited not only by the above ratio* [between necessary and surplus time], *but also by the proportion in which the product enters into the consumption of the worker.* If the capitalist, through growth of the productive forces, could obtain double the number of *cashmere* SHAWLS and sell them at their *value,* he would not have created any relative surplus value, because the workers do not consume such SHAWLS, and the time necessary for the reproduction of their labour capacity would remain the same. In practice this would not be so, because in such cases the price rises above the value. But this does not yet concern us here in the theoretical section, for we are considering capital in itself, not in a particular branch.)

I.e. the capitalist will pay wages for 3 days and set the workers to work 6. With each half working day he buys a whole day; thus, with $^6/_2$ or 3 days, he buys 6 days. Therefore, to assert that the value of a commodity is expressed by the [number of] working days it commands, or the WAGES it pays, is to understand absolutely nothing about the nature of capital and wage labour. THE PITH of all value creation and capital formation is that objectified working days command a greater number of living working days. Mr. Malthus would have been correct, if he had argued that the living labour time which a commodity commands expresses the measure of its *valorisation,* the measure of the *surplus labour* which it posits. Yet this would only be the tautology that to the extent to which it posits more labour, it posits more labour, or it would express the opposite of what Malthus wants to say, namely that surplus value arises from the fact that the living labour time which a commodity commands never represents the labour time which is worked up in it.// (NOW WE HAVE FINALLY DONE WITH MALTHUS.)

[VI-14]//We have demonstrated above in the development of the concept of capital that it is value as such, i.e. *money,* which both maintains itself in circulation and grows through the exchange with living labour; that therefore the purpose of productive capital is *never use value,* but the general form of wealth as wealth. In a work which is otherwise in many ways silly and distasteful, *On Political Economy in Connexion with the Moral State and Moral Prospects of Society,* 2nd ed., London, 1832, the cleric *Thomas Chalmers* has correctly struck upon this point, and has done so

without falling into the asininity of fellows such as *Ferrier*,[a] etc.,
who confuse money as the value of capital with the metallic money
actually available. In crises, capital (as commodity) cannot be
exchanged, not because there are *too few* means of circulation; it
does not circulate because it is *not exchangeable*. The significance
which cash acquires in times of crisis arises only from the fact that,
while capital is not exchangeable for its value—and only for that
reason does its value appear to confront it fixed in the form of
money—it still has obligations to pay. Alongside the interrupted
circulation, a *forced circulation* takes place.

Chalmers writes (Notebook IX, p. 57):

"WHEN A CONSUMER REFUSES CERTAIN COMMODITIES, it is not always, as it has been
ASSUMED by the new economists, BECAUSE HE WANTS TO PURCHASE OTHERS IN
PREFERENCE—but because he WANTS TO RESERVE ENTIRE THE GENERAL POWER OF
PURCHASING. And WHEN A *MERCHANT* BRINGS COMMODITIES TO MARKET, IT IS
GENERALLY NOT IN QUEST OF OTHER COMMODITIES TO BE GIVEN IN RETURN FOR THEM ...
HE WILL EXTEND HIS *GENERAL POWER OF PURCHASE OF ALL COMMODITIES*. It is no use
saying that money, too, is a *commodity*. The REAL METALLIC MONEY FOR WHICH A
MERCHANT HAS ANY USE, DOES NOT AMOUNT TO MORE THAN A SMALL *FRACTION OF HIS
CAPITAL*, EVEN OF *HIS MONIED CAPITAL*; ALL OF WHICH, THOUGH ESTIMATED IN MONEY,
CAN BE MADE, ON THE STRENGTH OF WRITTEN CONTRACTS, TO DESCRIBE ITS ORBIT, AND
BE EFFECTIVE FOR ALL ITS PURPOSES, WITH THE *AID OF COIN AMOUNTING TO AN
INSIGNIFICANT PROPORTION OF THE WHOLE*. THE GREAT OBJECT OF THE MONIED
CAPITALIST, IN FACT, IS TO ADD TO THE *NOMINAL AMOUNT OF HIS FORTUNE*. IT IS THAT,
IF EXPRESSED PECUNIARILY THIS YEAR BY £20,000 for example, IT SHOULD BE EXPRESSED
PECUNIARILY NEXT YEAR BY £24,000. TO ADVANCE HIS CAPITAL, AS ESTIMATED IN
MONEY, IS THE ONLY WAY IN WHICH HE CAN ADVANCE HIS INTEREST AS A MERCHANT.
The IMPORTANCE of this OBJECT to him is not affected by FLUCTUATIONS IN THE
CURRENCY OR BY A CHANGE IN THE REAL VALUE OF MONEY. For instance, he may have
advanced his fortune, by the business of one year, from £20,000 to £24,000, and
yet, from a decline in the value of money, he may not HAVE INCREASED HIS
COMMAND over the COMFORTS, etc. Still it was as much his interest [to have engaged
in the business], as if money had not fallen; for else, his MONIED FORTUNE WOULD
HAVE REMAINED STATIONARY, and his REAL WEALTH WOULD HAVE DECLINED IN THE
PROPORTION OF 24 TO 20... COMMODITIES" (i.e. use value, real wealth) "are not the
TERMINATING OBJECT of the TRADING CAPITALIST"

(the illusion of the monetary system[58] lies in that it saw in REAL
METALLIC MONEY (or paper money, for that matter), in short, in the
form of value as *real* money, the *general form of wealth* and
self-enrichment; while it is precisely as *money* increases as the
accumulation of the GENERAL POWER OF PURCHASING that it declines
relatively in its particular form as means of circulation or also as
realised hoard. As *assignation* of REAL WEALTH or PRODUCTIVE POWER, it
acquires a thousand forms)

a F. L. A. Ferrier, *Du gouvernement considéré dans ses rapports avec le commerce.*—
Ed.

"*save in the spending of his revenue in purchases for the* SAKE OF CONSUMPTION. IN THE OUTLAY OF HIS CAPITAL, AND WHEN HE PURCHASES FOR THE SAKE OF PRODUCTION, MONEY IS HIS TERMINATING OBJECT" (N.B. not COIN) (pp. 164-66).

"PROFIT," says the same *Chalmers*, "HAS THE EFFECT OF ATTACHING THE SERVICES OF THE DISPOSABLE POPULATION TO OTHER MASTERS, BESIDES THE MERE LANDED PROPRIETORS, WHILE their EXPENDITURE REACHES HIGHER THAN THE NECESSARIES OF LIFE" (p. [77-]78) (Notebook IX, p. 53)./

In the book from which we have just quoted, Chalmers calls the entire *circulation process* THE ECONOMIC CYCLE:

"THE WORLD OF TRADE MAY BE CONCEIVED TO REVOLVE IN WHAT WE SHALL CALL AN ECONOMIC CYCLE, WHICH ACCOMPLISHES ONE REVOLUTION BY BUSINESS COMING ROUND AGAIN, THROUGH ITS SUCCESSIVE TRANSACTIONS, TO THE POINT FROM WHICH IT SET OUT. ITS COMMENCEMENT MAY BE DATED FROM THE POINT AT WHICH THE CAPITALIST HAS OBTAINED THOSE RETURNS BY WHICH HIS CAPITAL IS REPLACED TO HIM: WHENCE HE PROCEEDS ANEW TO ENGAGE HIS WORKMEN; TO DISTRIBUTE AMONG THEM, IN WAGES, THEIR MAINTENANCE, OR RATHER THE POWER OF LIFTING IT; TO OBTAIN FROM THEM, IN FINISHED WORK, THE ARTICLES IN WHICH HE SPECIALLY DEALS; TO BRING THESE ARTICLES TO MARKET, AND THERE TERMINATE THE ORBIT OF ONE SET OF MOVEMENTS, BY EFFECTING A SALE, AND RECEIVING IN ITS PROCEEDS A RETURN FOR THE WHOLE OUTLAYS OF THE CAPITAL. The intervention of money in no way changes the REAL character of this operation" (p. 85, l.c.) (Notebook IX, p. 54).

The difference in the RETURN [of different capitals], so far as it is dependent upon the phase of the circulation process which coincides with the immediate production process, depends not only on the *longer or shorter labour time which is necessary* for the completion of the object (e.g. canal construction, etc.), but in certain branches of industry—agriculture—also on the interruptions in labour which are inherent in the nature of the work itself, when either capital lies fallow, or labour is at a standstill. Thus the example given by A. Smith of wheat as a crop which takes a year to produce, and of oxen as one which takes five years.[a] Consequently, 5 years' labour is employed on the latter, but only 1 on the former.

Little labour is employed on e.g. cattle which grows up on the open pastures. On the other hand, in agriculture itself, little labour is employed e.g. during the winter. In agriculture (and to a greater or lesser degree in many other branches of production), there are certain interruptions, pauses in labour time, which arise from the conditions of the production process itself; work must be recommenced at a given point, to continue or to complete the process of production. Here the constancy of the production process does not coincide with the continuity of the labour

---

[a] A. Smith, *An Inquiry into the Nature and Causes of the Wealth of Nations*, Book I, Chapter XI, Part I.— *Ed.*

process. This is one moment of the difference [in the return]. *Secondly*: [In some branches] the product altogether requires a longer time to be *completed*, to be put into its FINISHED STATE [than in others]. This is the total duration of the process of production, quite apart from whether or not there are interruptions in the operations of labour; the different duration of the phase of production in general. *Thirdly*: After the product is FINISHED, it may have to lie fallow for quite a long time, during which it requires relatively little labour, in order to let natural processes work upon it, e.g. wine. (Conceptually, this is approximately the same CASE as I.) *Fourthly*: It may take a longer time to bring the product to market, because it is destined for a more distant market. (This coincides conceptually with CASE II.) *Fifthly*: The shorter or longer time involved in the total RETURN of capital (its total reproduction), so far as it is determined by the ratio of fixed to circulating capital, evidently does not relate to the duration of the *immediate process of production*, but is determined by circulation. The time for the reproduction of the total capital is determined by the total process, including circulation.

"INEQUALITY IN THE PERIODS NECESSARY FOR PRODUCTION."
"THE *DIFFERENCE OF TIME* REQUIRED TO COMPLETE THE PRODUCTS OF AGRICULTURE, AND OF OTHER SPECIES OF LABOUR, is the MAIN CAUSE of the GREAT DEPENDENCE of the AGRICULTURISTS. THEY CANNOT BRING THEIR COMMODITIES TO MARKET IN LESS TIME THAN A YEAR. FOR THAT WHOLE PERIOD they are obliged TO BORROW of the shoemaker, the TAILOR, the smith, the WHEELWRIGHT, and the VARIOUS OTHER LABOURERS, whose products they need, but which are COMPLETED IN A FEW DAYS OR WEEKS. OWING TO THIS NATURAL CIRCUMSTANCE, AND OWING TO THE MORE RAPID INCREASE OF THE WEALTH PRODUCED BY OTHER LABOUR THAN THAT OF AGRICULTURE, THE MONOPOLISERS OF ALL THE LAND, [VI-15] though they have also MONOPOLISED LEGISLATION, have not been able TO SAVE THEMSELVES AND THEIR SERVANTS, THE FARMERS, FROM BEING THE MOST DEPENDENT CLASS IN THE COMMUNITY" (Thomas Hodgskin, *Popular Political Economy. Four Lectures, etc.*, London, 1827, p. 147, note) (Notebook IX, p. 44).
"THE NATURAL CIRCUMSTANCE *OF ALL COMMODITIES BEING PRODUCED IN UNEQUAL PERIODS, WHILE* THE WANTS OF THE LABOURER MUST BE SUPPLIED DAILY... THIS INEQUALITY IN THE TIME NECESSARY TO COMPLETE DIFFERENT COMMODITIES, WOULD in the rude state of society CAUSE THE HUNTER ETC. TO HAVE A SURPLUS OF GAME ETC., BEFORE THE MAKER OF BOWS AND ARROWS ETC. HAD ANY COMMODITY COMPLETED TO GIVE FOR THE SURPLUS GAME. NO EXCHANGE COULD BE MADE; THE BOW MAKER MUST ALSO BE A HUNTER and the DIVISION OF LABOUR impossible. This DIFFICULTY led to the invention of MONEY" (pp. 179, 180) (l.c.).

//The very concept of the *free labourer* already implies that he is a *pauper*: a virtual pauper. According to his economic conditions, he is mere *living labour capacity*, and hence a bearer of the needs of life. All-round indigence, lacking the objective being to realise his labour capacity. If the capitalist has no use for his surplus labour, he cannot perform his necessary labour and thereby produce his means of subsistence. He cannot, in this case, obtain them by means of exchange. If he does obtain them, it can only be because alms accrue to him from the revenue. As a worker, he can only subsist so long as he exchanges his labour capacity for the part of capital which constitutes the wages fund. This exchange is itself tied to conditions which are *for him* accidental and indifferent vis-à-vis his *organic* being. Hence he is virtually a *pauper*.

Moreover, since the condition of production based on capital is that the worker produces an ever greater quantity of surplus labour, it follows that an ever greater quantity of *necessary labour* is set free. The chances of his sinking into pauperism therefore increase. The development of surplus labour implies that of surplus population.

In different social modes of production, there are different laws governing the growth of population and overpopulation; the latter is identical with pauperism. These different laws can simply be reduced to the different modes of relating to the conditions of production, or, in the case of the living individual, to the conditions for his reproduction as a member of society, since it is only in society that he works and appropriates. The dissolution of these [traditional] relations, with regard to the single individual or a part of the population, posits them outside the reproductive conditions of this particular basis, hence posits them as overpopulation, and not only as destitute but also as unable to appropriate means of subsistence by labour, hence as paupers.

Only in the mode of production based on capital does pauperism appear as the result of labour itself, the result of the development of the productive power of labour. What is overpopulation at one stage of social production may not be overpopulation at another stage, and its effects may be different. E.g. those sent by the ancients to the colonies constituted overpopulation, i.e. they could not continue to live in the same area on the basis of the existing material property relations, i.e. conditions of production. The number [of colonists] may appear very small when compared with the modern conditions of production. Nevertheless, they were a long way from being paupers. But the plebs in Rome with their *panis et circenses*[138] were paupers. The overpopulation which caused the great *Völkerwanderung* presupposed yet other conditions.[151]

Since in all previous forms of production the development of the productive forces is not the basis of appropriation, but the particular mode of relating to the conditions of production (forms of property) appears as a *presupposed* barrier to the productive forces, which are confined to reproduction, it follows that the growth of population, in which the development of all productive forces is subsumed, must come up even more against an *external barrier* and thus appear as something to be restricted.

The conditions of communal life are only compatible with a finite size of population. On the other hand, if the limits on population which are posited by the elasticity of the particular form of the conditions of production *change, contract or expand in accordance with the latter*—thus overpopulation among hunting peoples differed from overpopulation among the Athenians, and the latter differed from overpopulation among the Germanic tribes—the absolute rate at which population increases also changes, and thus the rate of overpopulation and population changes as well. Therefore the [level of] overpopulation which is posited on a particular basis of production is no less determinate than the [level of] sufficient population. Overpopulation and population taken together are *the* population to which a particular basis of production can give rise. How far it exceeds its barrier is determined by the barrier itself—or rather by the same factor which posits the barrier. Just as necessary labour and surplus labour taken together constitute the totality of labour on a given basis.

Malthus's theory which, incidentally, was not his own discovery, but for which he got the credit by the clerical zeal with which he proclaimed it, really only by the emphasis which he gave to it, is significant in two ways: (1) because he gave a brutal expression to the brutal view taken by capital; (2) because he *asserted* the FACT of overpopulation in all forms of society. He did not prove it, for nothing could be more uncritical than his motley, kaleidoscopic compilations[a] from historical and travel literature. His analysis is altogether wrong and childish, because

(1) he considers *overpopulation* as *of the same kind* in different historical phases of economic development, does not understand its specific differences and hence stupidly reduces those very complicated and changing relations to one relation, in which on the one hand the natural propagation of mankind, on the other the natural propagation of edible plants (or MEANS OF SUBSISTENCE) confront each other as two natural series, the one geometric and the other arithmetic in progression. In this way, he transforms

---

[a] [Th. R. Malthus,] *An Essay on the Principle of Population.*—*Ed.*

historically distinct relations into an abstract numerical relation which he simply plucks out of thin air, and which is based on neither natural nor historical laws. There is supposed to be a natural difference between the propagation of men and that of e.g. grain. The monkey here assumes that the *increase of mankind* is a purely natural process, which requires *external* RESTRAINTS, CHECKS, if it is not to proceed geometrically.

The *geometrical propagation* is [supposed to be] the natural process of human propagation. In history, he can find that population develops under widely different conditions and that overpopulation is, likewise, an historically determined relationship, and not at all determined by numbers, or by any absolute limit to the production of means of subsistence. It is always determined by limits posited by *particular conditions of production.* Limited with respect to numbers. How small do the numbers now seem to us which signified overpopulation to the Athenians! Secondly, limited with respect to character. An overpopulation of free Athenians who are transformed into colonists differs significantly from an overpopulation of workers who are transformed into INMATES OF WORKHOUSES. Similarly, the mendicant overpopulation, which consumes the surplus produce of a monastery, differs significantly from that which develops in a FACTORY. It is Malthus who abstracts from these specific historical laws of population movements, which make up the history of the nature of man, his *natural* laws. But they are the natural laws of man only at a certain level of historical development, corresponding to a certain level of development of the productive forces which is determined by his own historical process.

Malthusian man, abstracted from historically determined man, exists only in Malthus's brain; hence also the geometrical method of propagation corresponding to this natural Malthusian man. Actual history therefore appears to him in such a light that he does not conceive the propagation of his natural man as an abstraction from the historical process, from actual propagation, but, on the contrary, he conceives actual propagation as an application of the Malthusian theory. Therefore, what constitutes in history, at every stage, the immanent conditions of both population and overpopulation, appears with him as a series of *external* CHECKS, which have *prevented* population from growing in the Malthusian way. The conditions in which men historically produce and reproduce themselves, appear as *barriers* on the reproduction of Malthusian natural man, who is a pure Malthusian creation. [VI-16] On the other side, the production of the means of subsistence, as it is "CHECKED", i.e. determined by the action of men, appears as a CHECK imposed by that production itself. Ferns once covered the whole earth. Their reproduction ceased only when there was no more room for any more. It did not conform to any arithmetical proportion. It is difficult to say where Malthus discovered that the reproduction of spontaneously propagating natural products comes to a halt in response to an inner urge, without *external* CHECKS. He transforms the immanent, historically changing limits on the process of man's propagation into *external barriers*; and the *external* CHECKS acting on natural reproduction into *immanent limits* or *natural laws* of propagation.

(2) He foolishly relates a certain number of men to a certain quantity of means of subsistence. Ricardo straight away countered this by correctly pointing out that the quantity of available grain is quite immaterial for the worker if he is without *employment*; that it is therefore the MEANS OF EMPLOYMENT and not OF SUBSISTENCE which determine whether or not he belongs in the category of surplus population.[a]

But this applies more widely, and is true in general of the *social mediation* by which the individual relates to the means of his reproduction and produces them. Hence it is true of the *conditions of production* and his relation to them. For the slave in Athens, the only barrier to his multiplication was the quantity of NECESSARIES which could be produced. And we never hear that there was a *surplus of slaves* in antiquity. On the contrary, the demand for them rose. Yet there was certainly a surplus population of non-workers (in the direct sense), who were not too many with respect to the available means of subsistence, but who had lost the conditions enabling them to appropriate. The invention of surplus workers, i.e. of propertyless men who work, belongs to the epoch of capital.

The beggars who attached themselves to the monasteries, and helped them to consume their surplus product, belong to the same class as the RETAINERS of the feudal lords, and this shows that the surplus PRODUCE could not be entirely consumed by the small number of its owners. This is only another form of the RETAINERS OF OLD, or the MENIAL SERVANTS OF TODAY. Overpopulation among e.g. the HUNTING PEOPLES, which is manifested in the struggle between individual tribes, does not prove that the soil could not support the small number of people who lived on it, but rather that the conditions of their reproduction necessitated a large territory to

---

[a] D. Ricardo, *On the Principles of Political Economy, and Taxation,* pp. 493 and 495.— *Ed.*

feed a few mouths. Nowhere [overpopulation] relative to a *non-existent* absolute quantity of MEANS OF SUBSISTENCE, only relative to the conditions of reproduction, of the production of these MEANS. But this includes the *conditions of the reproduction of human beings*, of the total population, of relative SURPLUS POPULATION. This surplus purely relative: in no way related to the *means of subsistence* as such, but only to the mode of their production. Hence also a *surplus* only given this STATE OF DEVELOPMENT.

(3) What was not, properly speaking, *Malthus's* own idea at all, the bringing in of the theory of rent, [is] *au fond* only a formula expressing the fact that at the stage of industrial development familiar to Ricardo, etc., agriculture lagged behind manufacture, an aspect which, incidentally, is immanent in bourgeois production, although in varying degrees. Does not belong here.//

//Generally speaking, when we look at production based on capital, an essential condition appears to be the combination of the greatest absolute quantity of necessary labour with the greatest relative quantity of surplus labour. Hence as basic condition the greatest possible growth of population—of living labour capacities. If we further look at the conditions for the development of both productive power and exchange, we find that they are the division of labour, cooperation, observation in all directions, which can only be the work of many heads, science, as many centres of exchange as possible—and all these are identical with the growth of population.

On the other hand, it is inherent in the condition for the appropriation of alien surplus labour that necessary population—i.e. the population representing necessary labour, labour necessary for production—is matched by a *surplus population*, which does not work. In the further development of capital, we find that alongside the industrial part of this surplus population—the industrial capitalists—a purely consuming part branches off. Idlers whose business it is to consume alien products, and [who,] since crude consumption has its limits, have to have a part of these products FORWARDED to them in refined form, as luxury products.

When the economists speak of surplus population, they are not referring to this idle surplus population. On the contrary, it is precisely they, with their consumption business, who are regarded by the population fanatics as necessary population, and [if one takes their view] justly (consistently) so. The expression "surplus population" refers exclusively to labour capacities, i.e. to the *necessary population*; surplus *labour capacities.* This arises simply from the nature of capital. Labour capacity can only perform its necessary labour if its surplus labour has value for capital, if it can be valorised by capital. If there are obstacles of one kind or another to its being valorised, *labour capacity itself* (1) appears to fall *outside the conditions of reproduction of its existence*; it exists without the *conditions of its existence*, and is thus A MERE ENCUMBRANCE; it has needs and lacks the means of satisfying them. (2) Necessary labour appears superfluous, because superfluous labour is not necessary. It is necessary only in so far as it is a condition for the valorisation of capital.

Thus the relation between necessary and surplus labour, as it is posited by capital, comes to this, that a part of necessary labour—i.e. of the labour which reproduces the labour capacity— is superfluous, and this labour capacity itself is needed as a *surplus* of the necessary working population, i.e. of that part of the working population whose necessary labour is not superfluous but necessary for capital. Since the effect of the development of productive power necessarily posited by capital is to increase the ratio of surplus to necessary labour, or to reduce the amount of necessary labour required for a given quantity of surplus labour, then, in a given quantity of labour capacity, the proportion of *necessary* labour required by capital must constantly diminish, i.e. a part of these labour capacities must become superfluous, because [only] a fraction of the amount previously necessary is now sufficient to perform the given quantity of surplus labour.

Positing a certain portion of labour capacity, i.e. of the labour required to reproduce it, as superfluous, is thus a necessary consequence of the increase in the ratio of surplus to necessary labour. The relative decline of necessary labour appears as a relative increase of surplus labour capacities—i.e. as the positing of surplus population. It is maintained, not out of the wages fund, but out of the income of all classes. It is not maintained by the labour of the labour capacity itself—the worker no longer maintained by his normal reproduction as a worker; he is rather maintained as a living being, by the charity of others. He therefore becomes a derelict and a pauper; in as much as he no longer maintains himself by his necessary labour, by exchange with a part of capital, he has fallen outside the conditions of the apparent relation of exchange and independence. Secondly, society [as a whole] in various proportions takes on for Mr. Capitalist the job of maintaining his virtual instrument of labour—defraying its WEAR and TEAR—keeping it in reserve for later use by him. He passes on a part of the cost of reproducing the working class, [VI-17] and so pauperises a part of the rest of the population for his own profit.

On the other hand, since capital constantly reproduces itself as surplus capital, it tends to posit this pauperism just as much as it tends to transcend it. It acts in opposing directions, so that sometimes one tendency prevails, and sometimes the other.

Finally, positing surplus capital implies the following: (1) It needs a growing population in order to be set in motion; if the relative population it needs has diminished, it has itself grown in proportion. (2) It needs an unemployed (relatively, at least) part of the population, i.e. a relative surplus population, in order to have the population necessary for its growth immediately available. (3) At a given level of the productive forces, surplus value may already be present, but not yet to the degree and in the proportions necessary for its employment as capital. Not only is a minimum level of production posited, but of its growth as well. In this case, surplus capital and surplus population. Likewise, a surplus population may be present, but not large enough, not in the proportions required for surplus production. In all this discussion, we have purposely abstracted entirely from the vicissitudes of the market, its contraction, etc., in short from everything which presupposes the *process of many capitals.//*

//A. Smith's view that *the value of labour* never *varies*, in the sense that *for the worker a certain quantity of labour* is always a certain *quantity of labour*, i.e. in A. Smith's view, the *sacrifice* is always *quantitatively equal*. Whether I obtain much or little for one hour of work—and that depends on its productivity and on other circumstances—I have *worked* for one hour. What I had to pay for the result of my labour, for my wage, is always the same *hour of work*, no matter how its result varies.

"Equal quantities of labour, at all times and places, may be said to be of equal value to the labourer. In his ordinary state of health, strength and spirits, in the ordinary degree of his skill and dexterity, he must always lay down the *same portion* of his *ease*, his *liberty*, and his *happiness*. The *price which he pays* must always be the same, whatever may be the quantity of goods which he receives in return for it. Of these, indeed, it may sometimes purchase a greater and sometimes a smaller quantity; but it is their value which varies, not that of the labour which purchases them. Labour alone, therefore, never varies in its own value. It is the *real price* of commodities; money is their nominal price only" ([A. Smith, *Recherches sur la nature et les causes de la richesse des nations,*] ed. Garnier, Vol. I, [Paris, 1802,] pp. 64-66) (Notebook, p. 7 [152]).

Thou shalt earn thy bread in the sweat of thy brow! was the curse which Jehovah laid on Adam.[a] And so A. Smith conceives

---

[a] Genesis 3:19.— *Ed.*

labour to be a curse. To him, "rest" appears as the adequate state, as identical with "liberty" and "happiness". It does not seem remotely to occur to him that the individual "in his ordinary state of health, strength, spirits, skill, dexterity" also needs a normal portion of labour and the transcendence of "rest". Certainly, the volume of labour itself appears to be externally determined by the aim to be attained and the obstacles to its attainment which have to be overcome by labour. But equally A. Smith has no inkling that the overcoming of these obstacles is in itself a manifestation of freedom—and, moreover, that the external aims are [thereby] stripped of their character as merely external natural necessity, and become posited as aims which only the individual himself posits, that they are therefore posited as self-realisation, objectification of the subject, and thus real freedom, whose action is precisely work.

Of course, Smith is right that in its historical forms of slave labour, serf labour and wage labour, work is always repulsive and always appears as *externally imposed, forced labour*, and as against that not-work as "liberty and happiness". This holds doubly: it is true of this antagonistic work and of everything connected with it, it is true of work which has not as yet created the subjective and objective conditions (or also of the pastoral, etc., state which has lost them) for work to become *travail attractif*, to be the self-realisation of the individual, which in no way implies that work is pure fun, pure amusement, as in Fourier's childishly naive conception.[a] Really free work, e.g. the composition of music, is also the most damnably difficult, demanding the most intensive effort.

Work involved in material production can achieve this character only if (1) its social character is posited; (2) if it is of a scientific character and simultaneously general [in its application], and not the exertion of the worker as a natural force drilled in a particular way, but as a subject, which appears in the production process not in a merely natural, spontaneous form, but as an activity controlling all natural forces.

A. Smith, by the way, has only the slaves of capital in mind. E.g. not even the skilled craftsman of the Middle Ages can be subsumed under his definition. However, *our immediate concern here* is not to discuss his philosophical conception of work, but the economic aspect. If we consider work only as *sacrifice*, therefore positing value, as *price* which is paid for objects and thus endows

---

a Ch. Fourier, "Le Nouveau Monde industriel et sociétaire", *Œuvres complètes*, 3rd ed., Vol. 6, Paris, 1848, pp. 245-52.— *Ed.*

them with price according to the greater or lesser quantity of labour they cost, we confine ourselves to a purely *negative* determination of labour. On this basis Mr. *Senior* for instance could transform capital into a source of production in the same sense as labour, *sui generis*, a source of *value* creation, because the capitalist can also be said to make a *sacrifice*, the sacrifice of ABSTINENCE, in that he enriches himself instead of directly consuming his product.[a] Something that is merely negative, creates nothing. If work for instance is a source of pleasure to the worker—as Senior's *abstinence* surely is for the miser—the product does not thereby lose any of its value. Labour *alone* produces; it is the sole *substance* of products as *values*.

//How little Proudhon understands the matter is clear from his axiom that every labour leaves a surplus.[b] What he denies in the case of capital, he makes into a natural attribute of labour. The point is rather that the labour time necessary for the satisfaction of absolute needs leaves *free* time (the amount differs in different stages of the development of productive forces) and hence surplus produce can be produced if *surplus labour* is performed. The aim is to transcend the relation itself [the division of the product into necessary and surplus], so that surplus PRODUCE itself appears as necessary,[153] and so that finally material production leaves every person surplus time for other activities. There is no longer anything mystical about this. Originally, the voluntary gifts of nature abundant, or at least they only had to be appropriated. From the outset spontaneous association (family) and a corresponding division of labour and cooperation. For originally human needs also slight. They themselves grow only with the development of the productive forces.//

Its measure, labour time—assuming equal intensity of labour—is therefore the measure of values. The qualitative difference between workers, in so far as it is not natural in origin, posited by sex, age, physical strength, etc.—and thus *au fond* expresses not the qualitative value of labour but the division of labour and its differentiation—is itself an historical result and then transcended again for the great mass of labour, in that the latter is simple labour, while the qualitatively higher labour takes its measure economically from the simple.

---

[a] N. W. Senior, *Principes fondamentaux de l'économie politique*, pp. 309-35.— *Ed.*

[b] P. J. Proudhon, *Système des contradictions économiques, ou Philosophie de la misère*, Vol. I, p. 73; *Gratuité du crédit. Discussion entre M. Fr. Bastiat et M. Proudhon*, p. 200.— *Ed.*

To say that *labour time* or the quantity of labour is the measure of values, means only that the measure of labour is the measure of values. Two things can be measured in terms of the same unit only if they are *of the same nature*. Products can only be measured by the measure of labour—by labour time—because by their nature they are *labour*. They are objectified labour. As objects, they assume forms from which their being as labour may indeed be apparent (as their externally posited suitability for their purpose; though this is *not* apparent e.g. with the oxen, nor with reproduced natural products in general), but in which there is nothing else in common any more. They exist as things of the same kind [VI-18] so long as they exist as activity. This is measured by time, which therefore becomes the measure of the objectified labour. We shall examine elsewhere the extent to which this *measuring* is connected with exchange, not with organised social labour—a certain level of the social process of production.

Use value is not related to human activity as the source of the product, to its positing by human activity—but to its being for men. So far as the product has a measure for itself, it is its natural measure, its measure as a natural object, its heaviness, weight, length, spatial volume, etc. The measure of usefulness, etc. But as effect, or as inert being of the power which produced it, it is measured only by the measures of this power itself. The measure of labour is time. It is only because the products a r e *labour* that they can be measured by the measure of labour, by labour time, or by the quantity of labour consumed in them. The negation of rest, simply as negation, as ascetic sacrifice, produces nothing. *A man may mortify, torment himself, etc., the whole day long like the monks, etc., and this quantity of sacrifice which he makes will have no effect at all.* The *natural* price of things is not the sacrifice made to produce them. This is reminiscent, rather, of the pre-industrial notion of acquiring wealth by making sacrifices to the gods. Apart from the sacrifice, there must be something else. What appears as a sacrifice of rest may also be called a sacrifice of idleness, of unfreedom, of unhappiness, i.e. the negation of a negative condition.

A. Smith considers work psychologically, with respect to the pleasure or displeasure which it gives the individual. Yet it must be something else in addition to this *sentimental* relation to his activity—above all for others, since the mere sacrifice of A would be of no use to B; but also the way he himself relates to the object which he works on and to his own disposition to work. Labour is a *positive, creative activity.* Of course the measure of labour, time, does not depend on the productivity of labour; its measure is nothing but a unit of which the fractional parts of labour express a particular number. It certainly does not follow from this that the *value* of labour is constant; or this follows only in so far as equal quantities of labour are of equal measured magnitude.

If we wish to define the matter more precisely, we find that the values of products are measured not by the labour which was bestowed on them, but by the labour necessary for their production. Thus not the sacrifice but the labour as the condition of production. The equivalent expresses the condition of their reproduction as given to them by exchange, i.e. the possibility of the renewal of productive activity as posited by its own product.//

//By the way, A. Smith's *theory of sacrifice*, which actually expresses correctly the *subjective attitude of the wage worker to his own activity*, does not achieve the object of the exercise—namely the determination of value by labour time. For the worker, an hour of labour may always be an equally great sacrifice. But the value of commodities by no means depends upon his FEELINGS; nor does the value of his hour's labour. Since A. Smith admits that one may sometimes purchase this sacrifice more cheaply and sometimes more dearly, it is odd that it should always be *sold* at the same price. He is also inconsistent. For he subsequently makes wages into the measure of value, not the quantity of labour. *The sacrifice of the ox when it is slaughtered is always the same.* [But] *that does not make beef constant in value.*//

//"But though equal quantities of labour are always of equal value to the labourer, yet to the person who employs him they appear sometimes to be of greater and sometimes of smaller value. He purchases them sometimes with a greater and sometimes with a smaller quantity of goods, and to him the price of labour seems to vary like that of all other things. In reality, however, it is the goods which are cheap in the one case, and dear in the other" (A. Smith, l.c., Vol. I, p. 66) (Notebook, p. 8).//

//The way in which A. Smith explains the origin of *profit* is very naive.

"In the early and rude state of society the whole produce of labour belongs to the labourer; and the quantity" (also the greater difficulty, etc.) "of labour commonly employed in acquiring or producing any exchangeable object is the *only circumstance* which regulates the quantity of labour which it ought commonly to purchase, command, or exchange for... B u t *as soon as stock* has accumulated in the hands of *particular persons the value which the workmen add to the object resolves itself into two parts*, of which the one pays their wages, the other the profits of their employer upon the whole stock of materials and wages which he advanced. He could have *no interest* to employ them, unless he expected from the sale of their work something more than what was sufficient to replace his stock to him; and he could have no interest to employ a great stock rather than a small one, unless his profits were to bear some proportion to the extent of his stock" (l.c., pp. 96, 97) (Notebook, p. 9 [152]).

(Cf. the peculiar view of A. Smith that [in the period] *prior to the division of labour,*

"in which everyman provides everything for himself, it is not necessary that any stock should be accumulated or stored up beforehand..." [op. cit., Vol. II, pp. 191-92].

As though in this state of society, the individual, finding no stock provided by nature, would not have to find the objective conditions of life in order to be able to work. Even the savage, even animals, accumulate reserves. What Smith talks about can only apply to the state of society where nothing but immediate, momentary instinct impels men to some immediate piece of work, and in that case, the *stock* must *d'une manière* or *d'autre* be present in nature *without labour* (Notebook, p. 19). (Smith gets things confused. *Concentration of stock* in one hand not then necessary.)//

//In Vol. III of his edition of A. Smith [*An Inquiry into the Nature and Causes of the Wealth of Nations*, London, 1846], *Wakefield* remarks:

"The labour of slaves being combined, is more productive than the much divided labour of freemen. The labour of freemen is more productive than that of slaves, only when it comes to be combined *by means of greater dearness of land*, and *the system of hiring for wages*" (p. 18, note) (Notebook VIII, p. 1). "In countries where land remains very cheap, either all the people are in a state of barbarism, or some of them are in a state of slavery" (l.c.).//

//"Profit is a term signifying the increase of capital or wealth; so failing to find the laws which govern the rate of profit, is failing to find the laws of the formation of capital" (W. Atkinson, *Principles of Political Economy*, London, 1840, p. 55) (Notebook,[150] p. 2).//

//"Man is as much the *produce of labour* as any of the machines constructed by his agency; and it appears to us that in all economical investigations he ought to be considered in precisely the same point of view. Every individual who has arrived at maturity may, with perfect propriety, be viewed as a machine which it has cost 20 years of assiduous attention and the expenditure of a considerable capital to construct. And if a further sum is laid out in his education or qualification for the exercise of a business, etc., his value is proportionately increased, exactly as a machine is rendered more valuable by the expenditure of additional capital or labour in its construction, in order to give new powers to it" (MacCulloch, *The Principles of Political Economy*, Edinburgh, 1825, p. 115) (Notebook, p. 9).

"In point of fact, a commodity will always exchange for more" labour (than that with which it has been produced): "and it *is this excess that constitutes profits*" (MacCulloch, l.c., p. 221) (Notebook, p. 13).

The same worthy MacCulloch, of whom Malthus rightly says that for him the distinctive attribute of science [VI-19] is the equation of everything with everything,[a] says:

"THE PROFITS OF CAPITAL ARE ONLY ANOTHER NAME FOR THE WAGES OF ACCUMULATED LABOUR" (l.c., p. 291) (Notebook, p. 14)

and hence presumably also the WAGES OF LABOUR [are] ONLY ANOTHER NAME FOR THE PROFITS OF LIVING CAPITAL.

"WAGES ... REALLY CONSIST OF A PART OF THE PRODUCE OF THE INDUSTRY OF THE LABOURER; CONSEQUENTLY, their real value is high if the LABOURER gets a comparatively large part of the product of his industry, and conversely" (l.c., p. 295) (Notebook, p. 15).//

//Capital's positing of *surplus labour* is generally so little understood by the economists that they present individual striking phenomena in which it manifests itself as something *extraordinary*, as curiosities. *Ramsay* on night-work is an example. *John Wade*, in his *History of the Middle and Working Classes*, 3rd ed., London, 1835 (p. 240) (Notebook, p. 21), writes for instance:

"The STANDARD OF WAGES is *also* related to the hours of labour and the periods of rest. It was the policy of the MASTERS in recent years" (before 1835) "to usurp ON [THE] OPERATIVES in this RESPECT, by CUTTING [OFF] OR ABRIDGING HOLIDAYS and MEALTIMES and gradually extending the hours of labour; knowing that an INCREASE of one-quarter in labour time is equivalent to a reduction of the same extent in the AMOUNT OF WAGES."//

John Stuart Mill, *Essays on Some Unsettled Questions of Political Economy*, London, 1844. (The few original ideas of Mill junior are contained in this slim booklet, not in his voluminously pedantic *magnum opus*.[b])

"Whatever is destined to be employed reproductively, either in its existing shape, or INDIRECTLY BY A PREVIOUS (OR EVEN SUBSEQUENT) EXCHANGE, is *capital*. Suppose that I have laid out all the money I possess in wages and tools, and that the article which I produce is just COMPLETED; in the interval which elapses before I can sell the article, realise the proceeds, and lay them out again in WAGES and TOOLS, will it be said that I have *no capital*? Certainly not: I have the same capital as before, perhaps a greater, but it is locked up and is not DISPOSABLE" (p. 55) (Notebook, p. 36).
"At all times a very large proportion of the capital of a country is lying idle. The annual produce of a country is never anything approaching in magnitude to what it might be if all the resources devoted to reproduction, if all the capital, IN

[a] Th. R. Malthus, *Definitions in Political Economy*, London, 1827, pp. 69-70.—Ed.

[b] *Principles of Political Economy with some of their Applications to Social Philosophy*, in two volumes, London, 1848. Below Marx quotes from *Essays*....—Ed.

SHORT, of the country, were IN FULL EMPLOYMENT. *If every commodity on an average remained unsold for a length of time equal to that required for its production*, it is obvious that, at ANY ONE TIME, *no more than half the productive capital of the country would be really performing the FUNCTIONS of capital. The half which was in employment would be a fluctuating portion*, composed of varying parts; but the result would be, that each producer would be able to produce every year only half as large a supply of commodities, as he could produce if he were sure of selling them the moment the production was completed" (l.c., pp. 55, 56). "This, or something like it, is HOWEVER the habitual state of a very large proportion of all the capitalists in the world" (p. 56).

"The number of producers, or dealers, who turn over their capital in the shortest possible time, is VERY small. There are few who have so rapid a sale for their wares, that all the goods which their own capital, or the capital which they can borrow, enables them to supply, are *carried off* as fast as they can be supplied. The majority have not an EXTENT OF BUSINESS, AT ALL ADEQUATE TO THE AMOUNT OF THE CAPITAL THEY DISPOSE OF. It is true that, in the communities in which industry and commerce are practised with greatest success, the CONTRIVANCES OF BANKING enable the possessor of a larger capital than he can employ in his own business, to employ it productively and derive a revenue from it notwithstanding. Yet even then, there is a great quantity of capital which remains *fixed* in the shape of IMPLEMENTS, MACHINERY, BUILDINGS, etc., whether it is ONLY HALF EMPLOYED, OR IN COMPLETE EMPLOYMENT: and every DEALER keeps a STOCK IN TRADE, TO BE READY FOR A POSSIBLE SUDDEN DEMAND, though he may not be able TO DISPOSE OF IT FOR AN INDEFINITE PERIOD" (p. 56). "This *perpetual non-employment of a large proportion of capital*, is the *price we pay for the division of labour. The purchase is worth what it costs; BUT THE PRICE IS CONSIDERABLE*" (p. 56).

If I have invested 1,500 thaler in a SHOP and derive a profit of 10% on it, while 500 lies IDLE in order to decorate the SHOP, etc., it is the same as if I had invested 2,000 thaler at [a profit of] $7\frac{1}{2}$%.

"In many TRADES, there are some DEALERS who sell articles of an equal quality at a lower price than other DEALERS. This is not a voluntary sacrifice of profits: they expect by the consequent OVERFLOW of CUSTOMERS to turn over their capital more quickly, and to be gainers BY KEEPING THE WHOLE OF THEIR CAPITAL IN MORE CONSTANT EMPLOYMENT, though on any given operation their gains are less" (pp. 56, 57). "It is QUESTIONABLE whether there be any DEALERS for whom an additional purchaser is of no use; and to the great majority this hypothesis is not applicable at all. An additional customer, to most DEALERS, is equivalent to an increase of their productive capital. He enables them to convert a portion of their capital which was lying idle (and which could never have become productive in their hands until a customer was found) into WAGES and INSTRUMENTS OF PRODUCTION... The aggregate produce of the country for the succeeding year is, therefore, increased; not by the mere exchange, but BY *CALLING INTO ACTIVITY* a portion of the national capital, which, HAD IT NOT BEEN FOR THE EXCHANGE, would have remained FOR SOME TIME longer UNEMPLOYED" (pp. 57, 58).

"The benefit which a producer or DEALER derives from the acquisition of a *new customer* can be defined as follows:

"(1) If any part of his capital was locked up in the form of unsold goods, producing (for a longer or shorter period) NOTHING AT ALL; a portion of this is *called into greater activity, and becomes MORE CONSTANTLY PRODUCTIVE.*

"(2) If the ADDITIONAL DEMAND exceeds what can be supplied by setting at liberty the capital which exists in the state of unsold goods; and if the DEALER has additional resources, which were productively invested (in the public funds, for instance), but not in his own TRADE; he is enabled to obtain, ON A PORTION OF THESE, not mere interest, but profit, and so to gain that difference between the rate OF PROFIT and the rate OF INTEREST.

"(3) If all the dealer's capital is employed in his own trade, and no part of it locked up as unsold goods, he can carry on an additional business with borrowed capital, and so gain the difference between interest and profit" (p. 59).

NOTES
AND
INDEXES

NOTES

[1] The unfinished draft manuscript "Bastiat and Carey", the first of Marx's Economic Manuscripts of 1857-58, takes up the first seven pages in one of the seven notebooks containing the main manuscript of that cycle, the *Outlines of the Critique of Political Economy* (Rough Draft). However, the date, "July 1857", which Marx put on the cover of that notebook, shows that "Bastiat and Carey" was written somewhat earlier than the *Outlines.* Pages 1, 2, 3 and the upper half of page 4 contain the "Avantpropos" (Introductory Notes) to "Bastiat and Carey", the lower half of page 4 is blank, and pages 5-7 are taken up by a passage entitled "XIV. *De salaires*". From page 8 onwards, there follows the continuation of the text contained in Notebook II of the main manuscript (see page 219 of this volume). Marx marked this continuation "Notebook III" and dated it "November 29 and 30, and December 1857".

Since in the manuscript the draft bears the same subtitle as Bastiat's book, it may be assumed that Marx originally wanted to write an extensive review, but later decided that the book did not deserve detailed discussion, and therefore gave up his original intention.

The draft goes beyond the bounds of an ordinary review. In the "Avantpropos", Marx sums up the bourgeois political economy of his time and strictly delimits the era of classical political economy as beginning in the late 17th century, with the works of Petty and Boisguillebert, and ending in the first third of the 19th century, with the writings of Ricardo and Sismondi. He shows that the bourgeois economists of the subsequent period were either epigones of the classics or vulgar critics of them. The works of the Frenchman Bastiat and the American Carey, directed above all against Ricardo, were examples of that kind of criticism.

The title "Bastiat and Carey" occurs in Marx's "References to My Own Notebooks", written in the summer of 1861 (see present edition, Vol. 29). This shows that Marx himself regarded the draft as part of his Economic Manuscripts of 1857-58. He quotes from Bastiat partly in French and partly in German translation. In this volume, all quotations are in English; only foreign-language phrases in Marx's own text are given in the language of the original.

The draft was first published in the journal *Die Neue Zeit*, Vol. 2, No. 27, Stuttgart, 1903-1904. In English, it first appeared, under the title "Critique of

Bastiat and Carey", in *Marx's Grundrisse* by David McLellan, Macmillan Press Ltd., London, 1971, pp. 47-58 and in: Karl Marx, *Grundrisse. Foundations of the Critique of Political Economy (Rough Draft)*. Translated with a Foreword by Martin Nicolaus. Penguin Books in association with *New Left Review*. London, 1973, pp. 883-93.—5

2 This refers to Chapter XIV in the second edition of Bastiat's book *Harmonies économiques* (there are 25 chapters in that edition). Since this section of the draft "Bastiat and Carey" begins on page 5 of the manuscript, while half of page 4 was left blank, it may be assumed that Marx originally intended to discuss Bastiat's book in greater detail, giving, in particular, an account of the preceding 13 chapters.—11

3 According to Bastiat, "the workers' pension fund" was to be made up of contributions by the workers themselves, for thus alone the necessary degree of "stability" could be ensured (Fr. Bastiat, *Harmonies économiques*, 2nd edition, Paris, 1851, p. 395).—11

4 Marx means the philosophical and historical constructions in Proudhon's book *Système des contradictions économiques, ou Philosophie de la misère* (Paris, 1846). In 1847 Marx attacked them in *The Poverty of Philosophy. Answer to the "Philosophy of Poverty" by M. Proudhon* (see present edition, Vol. 6, pp. 105-212, particularly pp. 111-15 and 157-60).—13

5 The "supreme being" (*être suprême*) was Voltaire's designation of God, whom he, in contrast to the positive religions, described as an impersonal rational creator, who, having, laid down the laws of the world and given it an initial impulse, has refrained from any further intervention in the natural course of events.—13

6 This Introduction, prefaced by Marx to the *Outlines of the Critique of Political Economy*, the first rough draft of *Capital*, holds an important place among his Economic Manuscripts of 1857-58. It is contained in Notebook M, marked "London, 23 August '57", which is probably the day when Marx began writing the Introduction. He interrupted this work, in all likelihood, in the last days of August, leaving the Introduction unfinished.

On the cover of Notebook M, Marx listed the main items to be discussed in the Introduction. The headings of the individual sections in this table of contents differ somewhat from the corresponding headings in the text proper. Marx's list is as follows:

"Contents

"A. Introduction
"1) Production in general
"2) General relationship between production, distribution, exchange and consumption
"3) The method of political economy
"4) The means (forces) of production and production relations; production relations and relations of intercourse, etc."

As the table reflects the overall structure of the Introduction more accurately than the headings of some of the sections in the text do, one may assume that Marx wrote it *after* drafting the Introduction.

The fourth, closing section is in the form of a detailed outline. Of the subsections listed in it, only subsection 1, containing Marx's views on art, was written, and even that not in full. For instance contrary to his original intention, he did not investigate the relation of Shakespeare to the modern world. Having put to paper his views on Greek art, Marx broke off the work on the Introduction.

Later, when preparing the manuscripts for publication, he abandoned his intention to open them with an extensive introduction and confined himself to a shorter preface formulating in brief the general philosophical premises of his method of economic research (the materialist conception of history). In the Preface to Part One of *A Contribution to the Critique of Political Economy*, dated January 1859, Marx wrote: "A general introduction, which I had drafted, is omitted, since on further consideration it seems to me confusing to anticipate results which still have to be substantiated, and the reader who really wishes to follow me will have to decide to advance from the particular to the general" (see present edition, Vol. 29).

The Introduction was first published in the journal *Die Neue Zeit*, Vol. 1, Nos. 23-25, Stuttgart, 1902-1903. In English, in first appeared in *A Contribution to the Critique of Political Economy by Karl Marx*. Translated from the second German edition by N. I. Stone. With an appendix containing Marx's Introduction to the Critique recently published among his posthumous papers. Charles H. Kirr & Company, Chicago, 1904, pp. 265-312. It was also published in *Marx and Modern Economics*, ed. by D. Horowitz. Mac Gibbon & Kee, London, 1968, pp. 21-48, in *Marx's Grundrisse* by David McLellan, Macmillan Press Ltd., London, 1971, pp. 16-46, and in Karl Marx, *Grundrisse*. Translated with a Foreword by Martin Nicolaus. London, 1973, pp. 81-111.— 17

7 The heading "I. Production, Consumption, Distribution, Exchange (Circulation)" does not occur in Marx's table of contents on the cover of Notebook M and refers, strictly speaking, only to the first two sections of the Introduction, that headed "Production" (the heading in the table of contents on the cover is more accurate: "Production in general") and that headed "The General Relation of Production to Distribution, Exchange and Consumption". There are no Roman numerals in the further text of the Introduction to correspond to the figure I marking the section "Production, Consumption, Distribution, Exchange (Circulation)".— 17

8 *Contrat social*—in Rousseau's theory, the voluntary agreement entered into by primitive people—originally living in "the state of nature"—which led to the formation of the political state. The theory was set forth in Rousseau's *Du Contrat social; ou Principes du droit politique*, London, 1782.— 17

9 The term *bürgerliche Gesellschaft* (see G.W.F. Hegel, *Grundlinien der Philosophie des Rechts*, in: *Werke*, Vol. 8, Berlin, 1833, § 182, Addendum) was used by Marx, even in his early writings, in two senses: in a broader one, to denote the economic system of society regardless of the historical stage of its development, i.e. the totality of material relations determining the political institutions and ideological life; and in a narrower one, to denote the material relations of bourgeois society (later, bourgeois society as a whole), i.e. capitalism. Depending on the context, the term is translated in this edition either as "bourgeois society" or as "civil society".— 17

10 In subsequent years Marx modified his views on family relations in primitive society and the early tribal system in accordance with the latest studies in ethnography and ancient history, notably the books *Das Mutterrecht* by the Swiss historian Johann Jacob Bachofen and *Ancient Society* by the American

anthropologist Lewis Henry Morgan, published in the 1860s and 1870s. In particular, he abandoned the view, commonly held by historians in the 1840s and 1850s, asserting the primacy of the family and the secondary nature of the tribe and deriving the tribe from the developing family. The new conception of the relation between tribe and family was reflected, in particular, in Marx's synopsis of Morgan's *Ancient Society*. Frederick Engels drew on this book in writing *The Origin of the Family, Private Property and the State.*—18

11 The *zoon politicon*—literally, "political animal" or, in a broader sense, "social animal"—was Aristotle's description of man. The term occurs in Book I of his *Politica*. In a note to Chapter XIII of Vol. I of *Capital* Marx says: "Strictly, Aristotle's definition is that man is by nature a town-citizen" (see present edition, Vol. 35).—18, 420

12 *Determination is negation*—Marx quotes this thesis of Spinoza in the widely accepted interpretation given it by Hegel. In Spinoza, it means "limitation is negation" (*Epistolae doctorum quorundam virorum ad B. de Spinoza et auctoris responsiones; ad aliorum ejus operum elucidationem non parum facientes. Epistola L 2 Junii 1674*). Hegel's interpretation emphasises the element of negation inherent in any determined being, in any particular thing (see his *Wissenschaft der Logik*, Book I, Part I, Chapter 2, note on "Reality and Negation" and his *Enzyklopädie der philosophischen Wissenschaften*, Part I; *Wissenschaft der Logik*, § 91, Addendum).—28

13 Marx refers to vulgar socialists like the German "true socialists" (in particular, Karl Grün) and the French petty-bourgeois socialist Proudhon. See present edition, Vol. 5, pp. 509, 515, 518 and Vol. 6, pp. 157-58.—31

14 Marx discusses the views of Say and Storch on the relation between production and consumption in the chapter "Adam Smith" of his manuscripts of 1861-63 (see present edition, Vol. 30).—31, 339

15 Speaking of "what is called exchange between dealers and dealers", Marx has in mind Adam Smith's division of circulation into that between dealers, and that between dealers, on the one hand, and individual consumers, on the other (see Smith's *An Inquiry into the Nature and Causes of the Wealth of Nations*, Vol. II, Book II, Chapter II).—36

16 Marx drew the data on pre-Spanish Peru from the American scholar William Hickling Prescott's *History of the Conquest of Peru, with a preliminary view of the civilisation of the Incas*, in three volumes, 4th ed., London, 1850. Excerpts from Volume I of this book are contained in Marx's Notebook XIV, begun in London in 1851. That the Incas had no knowledge of money is stated on p. 147 of Volume I.—40

17 Marx expresses similar ideas in his letter to Engels of September 25, 1857: "More graphically than anything else the history of the *army* demonstrates the rightness of our views as to the connection between the productive forces and social relations. Altogether, the army is of importance in economic development. E.g. it was in the army of Antiquity that the *salaire* was first fully developed. Likewise the *peculium castrense* [personal property of soldiers in military camps] in Rome, the first legal form according recognition to the movable property of others than fathers of families. Likewise the guild system

in the corporation of the *fabri* [teams of artisans attached to the army in ancient Rome]. Here too the first use of machinery on a large scale. Even the special value of metals and their use as money would seem to have been based originally—as soon as Grimm's Stone Age was over—on their significance in war. Again, the division of labour *within* a branch was first put into practice by armies. All this, moreover, a very striking epitome of the whole history of civil societies" (see present edition, Vol. 40, p. 186).—40, 396

[18] The reference is to the *school of Ranke*, a trend in German historiography which was above all interested in political and diplomatic history, proclaimed the pre-eminence of foreign policy over domestic, ignored the history of social relations and exaggerated the part played by outstanding personalities.

The views of Leopold von Ranke (1795-1886) were formed under the influence of philosophical idealism and Protestantism. According to Ranke, religion played the key role in the life of nations, another important factor being the political idea, embodied in the state. His historical concept was Eurocentrist, with chauvinistic overtones.—46

[19] A Manchester firm which designed tools, machines and locomotives. From 1843 it was headed by Richard Roberts, the inventor of many machines, including the self-actor.—47

[20] The *Crédit Mobilier* (Société générale du Crédit mobilier) was a big French joint-stock bank founded by the Péreire brothers in 1852. It was notorious for speculation and other irregular practices. The Crédit Mobilier took an active part in railway construction and the establishment of industrial enterprises. Though closely linked with and enjoying the protection of Napoleon III's government, it went bankrupt in 1867. In 1856 and 1857, Marx wrote a series of articles about its speculative activities for the Chartist *People's Paper*, published in London, and the *New-York Daily Tribune* (see this edition, Vol. 15, pp. 8-24, 270-77, 357-60).—47, 59

[21] *Printing House Square*—a small square in London where *The Times*, the biggest British daily newspaper, had its editorial offices and printshop, famous in the mid-19th century for exemplary organisation and efficiency.—47

[22] This is the most important of Marx's Economic Manuscripts of 1857-58. Comprising seven large notebooks, numbered by Marx I-VII, it is the first rough draft of the future *Capital*. On the cover of the last, seventh notebook Marx wrote in English "Political Economy, Criticism of" and, in German, "Fortsetzung (Continuation)". This means that Notebook VII forms the continuation to the preceding six notebooks and that Marx did not consider it as the concluding one. It also implies that the words "Political Economy, Criticism of" can be regarded as the main title of the whole draft manuscript. In his letter to Engels of November 29, 1858, Marx refers to his economic manuscript of 1857-58 as a "Rohentwurf (Rough Draft)". Unfinished and breaking off in mid-sentence, it is indeed a rough draft. In a letter to Engels of May 31, 1858, Marx wrote that the manuscript was "a real hotchpotch, much of it intended for much later sections" (see present edition, Vol. 40, p. 318).

The manuscript begins with Chapter II, entitled "Chapter on Money", which is followed by the long third chapter, "Chapter on Capital". On the last page of the manuscript Marx jotted down the beginning of the missing first chapter (see present edition, Vol. 29).

Work on the manuscript apparently began at the end of 1857, as Marx's quoting, in Notebook I (p. 46), of a passage from the *Weekly Dispatch* of November 8, 1857 (this volume, p. 148) seems to suggest.

The possibility is not ruled out, however, that he began this work earlier, but interrupted it for a long time. Marx's letter to Engels of January 10, 1857, (see present edition, Vol. 40, p. 90) containing a brief analysis of Darimon's book, and the references to *The Economist* of January 24, 1857, and *The Morning Star* of February 12, 1857, on p. 18 of the manuscript (this volume, pp. 89 and 90) might be seen as pointing in this direction. At any rate, the concluding part of Notebook I could not have been written before November 8, 1857.

This edition reproduces the component parts of the economic manuscript of 1857-58 in the order given by Marx. Exceedingly long paragraphs have been broken up into shorter ones. A few passages plainly intended as addenda to earlier parts of the text have been shifted.

Where Marx, in quoting, gives references to pages of his notebooks of excerpts, these have been supplemented, in brackets, with references to the pages in the editions used by Marx. Where he merely gives the authors' names, the titles of the quoted works have been supplied (in the text or in footnotes).

This manuscript was first published in full in Karl Marx, *Grundrisse der Kritik der politischen Oekonomie (Rohentwurf). 1857-1858*, Moscow, 1939-41 (reproduced by Dietz Verlag, Berlin, in 1953).

In English, the manuscript was published in full in Karl Marx, *Grundrisse. Foundations of the Critique of Political Economy (Rough Draft)*. Translated with a Foreword by Martin Nicolaus. Penguin Books in association with *New Left Review*. London, 1973. Individual excerpts were published earlier in *Marx's Grundrisse* by David McLellan, Macmillan Press Ltd., London, 1971. A part from the "Chapter on Capital", Section Two, "Circulation Process of Capital" (pp. 399-439 in this volume) was published as a separate book under the title: Karl Marx, *Pre-capitalist Economic Formations*. Translated by Jack Cohen, edited and with an Introduction by E. J. Hobsbawm. London, 1964.—49

23 This chapter was first published—in German, with a parallel Russian translation—in the collection *Marx-Engels Archives*, Vol. IV, Moscow, 1935. Excerpts from the chapter appeared in English for the first time in *Marx's Grundrisse* by David McLellan, Macmillan Press Ltd., London, 1971, pp. 59-64, 65-69 and 70-73. The chapter was first published in English in full in Karl Marx, *Grundrisse*. Translated with a Foreword by Martin Nicolaus, London, 1973, pp. 115-238.—51

24 For an assessment of Darimon's *De la réforme des banques* see also Marx's letter to Engels of January 10, 1857 (present edition, Vol. 40, p. 90).—51

25 In the manuscript, Marx rounds off the figures cited by Darimon (the latter gives the number of centimes as well as of francs). However, some of the approximations are not quite accurate.—52

26 "La propriété c'est le vol" (Property is theft) is the main thesis of Proudhon's *Qu'est ce que la propriété?* The theory of "free credit" was expounded by Proudhon in *Gratuité du crédit. Discussion entre M. Fr. Bastiat et M. Proudhon*, Paris, 1850, pp. 66-74. For Marx's critique of this theory see the Economic Manuscripts of 1861-63, "Revenue and Its Sources" (present edition, Vol. 32).—61

[27] The Currency Act of 1844 on the Bank of England, carried through Parliament by Sir Robert Peel's government, fixed a maximum for the amount of banknotes in circulation. These were guaranteed by a special gold and silver reserve. Banknotes in excess of the fixed amount could be issued only given a proportional increase in the reserves of precious metals. The Act was repeatedly infringed by the government itself, in particular during the 1847 and 1857 monetary crises. Marx analysed its content and significance in a series of articles written for the New-York Daily Tribune in 1857 and 1858 ("The Bank Act of 1844 and the Monetary Crisis in England", "The British Revulsion", "The English Bank Act of 1844" and others, see present edition, vols. 15 and 16). Subsequently, he gave a detailed analysis of the Act in Capital, Vol. III, Ch. XXXIV (see present edition, Vol. 37).—63

[28] Collége de France—a higher educational establishment founded in Paris in 1530.—63

[29] Here and in a number of other cases the term "production costs" (Produktionskosten) is used by Marx in the sense of "the immanent production costs of the commodity, which are equal to its value", i.e., "the real production costs of the commodity itself", not the costs defrayed by the capitalist, who pays only part of the labour time contained in the commodity (see Marx's manuscripts of 1861-63, present edition, Vol. 32).—66, 241

[30] This refers to the period of operation (from 1797 onwards) of the Bank Restriction Act, which imposed a compulsory exchange rate for banknotes and cancelled their convertibility into gold. Convertibility was nominally re-established by an Act passed in 1819. Actually, it was re-introduced in 1821.—69

[31] The expropriation of the farmers by the landed aristocracy (the so-called clearing of estates) in the Scottish highlands, where survivals of the clan system lingered on for a long time, began in the mid-eighteenth century, when the clearing of estates in England had nearly been completed, and continued in the first half of the nineteenth century. Marx analysed it in the article "Elections.—Financial Clouds.—The Duchess of Sutherland and Slavery", published in the New-York Daily Tribune on February 8, 1853 (see present edition, Vol. 11), and in Capital, Vol. I, Ch. XXVII (present edition, Vol. 35).—71

[32] Wilhelm Weitling's theory of labour money is set forth in his book Garantien der Harmonie und Freiheit, Vevey, 1842, pp. 153-75. Speaking of the English supporters of this theory, Marx means John Francis Bray, Thomas Hodgskin, William Thompson and other adherents of Robert Owen, who tried to draw socialist conclusions from the economic theory of Ricardo. Marx gave a critical analysis of the views of these utopian socialists in The Poverty of Philosophy. Answer to the "Philosophy of Poverty" by M. Proudhon (see present edition, Vol. 6). Later he discussed their theory of "labour money", as propounded, e.g., by John Gray, in A Contribution to the Critique of Political Economy, Part One (see present edition, Vol. 29).—73

[33] Here as in a number of other places Marx uses the term "subject" in its pre-Kantian sense, as the bearer of predicates, properties, determinations, characteristic features, relations.—81, 124

34 An allusion to Proudhon's quasi-Hegelian arguments, in *Système des contradictions économiques, ou Philosophie de la misère*, about abstract economic categories, and his alleged discovery of their dialectical interconnection, "their serial relation in the understanding". Marx attacked this metaphysical conception of Hegelian dialectics in *The Poverty of Philosophy* (see present edition, Vol. 6, pp. 162-65).—90

35 Here Marx summarises John Locke's arguments on the fundamental difference between silver as a measure of value and standards like the ell or the quart: while the latter two may remain in the hands of the buyer or of the seller, silver coin not only measures the value of the thing bought, but always passes from the buyer to the seller (see *Further Considerations Concerning Raising the Value of Money* in *The Works of John Locke*, in four volumes, 7th ed., Vol. II, London, 1768, p. 92). Marx quotes this passage on page 34 of his seventh notebook (see present edition, Vol. 29).—91

36 Marx means Smith's arguments (in the opening part of Chapter VI, Book I, of his work) that "in that early and rude state of society which precedes both the accumulation of stock and the appropriation of land" the exchange value of commodities was determined by the amount of labour time required for their production.
   Marx uses here the term "production costs" in the sense of "the immanent production costs of the commodity" (see Note 29).—93

37 Characterising money as a "surety" or "movable surety of society" (*Pfand* or *Faustpfand der Gesellschaft*), Marx meant, first, Aristotle's words in his *Ethica Nicomachea* (Book V, Chapter 8, § 14) and, second, the definition of money given by John Bellers in his *Essays about the Poor, Manufactures, Trade, Plantations, and Immorality...* London, 1699, p. 13. Marx refers to Aristotle in his *Index to the Seven Notebooks* (see present edition, Vol. 29) and to Bellers in *Capital*, Vol. I, Chapter III (present edition, Vol. 35).
   The term "Faustpfand der Gesellschaft" occurs in J. G. Büsch's *Abhandlung von dem Geldumlauf* (Part I, 2nd ed., Hamburg and Kiel, 1800, pp. 298-99). Locke speaks of "money as a pledge". Cf. his *Some Considerations of Consequences of the Lowering of Interest, and Raising the Value of Money* (1691),(*The Works of John Locke*, Vol. II, London, 1768, p. 15).—97

38 In speaking about the Romantic embellishment of the individual's position in pre-capitalist society in contrast to capitalism. Marx is alluding to Adam Müller's *Die Elemente der Staatskunst* (Part II, Berlin, 1809. pp. 72-217), and to works by Thomas Carlyle, including his pamphlet *Chartism* (London, 1840, pp. 49-80).—99

39 According to tradition, the Roman patrician Menenius Agrippa persuaded the plebeians to return to Rome from the Holy Hill, to which they had withdrawn in 494 B.C. in protest against patrician oppression. He did so by telling them a parable about the limbs of the human body which had rebelled against the stomach. Agrippa compared society to a living organism, attributing to the plebeians the role of the hands and to the patricians that of the stomach. Refusal by the plebeians to feed the patricians, he said, was tantamount to the separation of the hands from the stomach and was bound to lead to the death of the organism, i.e. of the Roman state.—99

[40] Apparently a reference to John Francis Bray's book *Labour's Wrongs and Labour's Remedy*, Leeds, 1839, p. 141.—99

[41] James Steuart distinguishes between "agriculture exercised *as a trade*" and "agriculture exercised *as a direct means of subsisting*" (*An Inquiry into the Principles of Political Oeconomy*, Vol. I, Dublin, 1770, p. 88).—106

[42] This refers to the discovery of rich gold fields in California in 1848 and Australia in 1851. As early as January 1850, eighteen months after the Californian discovery, Marx and Engels pointed to its vast importance for the commercial and industrial development of Europe, as well as of America and Asia—in particular, as stimulating the colonisation of new territories (see present edition, Vol. 10, pp. 502-06). The Californian and Australian discoveries spurred industrial and financial activity in the capitalist countries and to a certain degree contributed to the defeat of the European revolutions of 1848 and 1849.—106, 157

[43] The *Albani*—the name given by Pliny, Strabo and other ancient writers to the inhabitants of Albania, a country in the lower reaches of the Kura and the Aras in Eastern Transcaucasia.—109

[44] In his *Système des contradictions économiques, ou Philosophie de la misère*, Proudhon claimed that the use of precious metals as money was above all due to the "sovereign consecration", the interference of sovereigns who took possession of "gold and silver and affixed their seal to them". Marx showed the fallacy of this attempt to explain the origin of money by purely political factors and to attribute to the person wielding political power the ability to lay down economic laws at will (see present edition, Vol. 6, p. 147).—110

[45] The passage is from [S. Bailey,] *Money and Its Vicissitudes in Value; as they affect national industry and pecuniary contracts: with a postscript on joint-stock banks*, London, 1837, pp. 5-6. Marx quotes in English. He also reproduces the whole passage in English in the original version of *A Contribution to the Critique of Political Economy*, Part One (see present edition, Vol. 29).—110

[46] The source of this passage, quoted in German, has not been established. Though there are no quotation marks, there is every indication that the further text, too, is an abridged excerpt from some German source.—111

[47] Marx refers to Excerpt Notebook XIV, which he compiled in London, approximately in August and September 1851.—115

[48] The *Code of Manu* (Mānava Dharma-Çāstra)—an old Hindu collection of laws and precepts, the product of an early attempt at codifying common law in accordance with the needs of the ancient Hindu state and the dogmas of Brahmanism. It is attributed to Manu ("man" in Sanskrit), the mythical progenitor of human beings. The laws and precepts making up the *Code of Manu* were accumulated over the centuries and given their more or less definitive formulation at about the beginning of the Christian era. They reflected the specific nature of the early class society in India, which was retaining many survivals of the primitive communal system.—117

[49] The data on Chinese money are from Gustav von Gülich's book *Geschichtliche Darstellung des Handels, der Gewerbe und des Ackerbaus der bedeutendsten handeltreibenden Staaten unsrer Zeit*, Vol. V, Jena, 1845, pp. 110-11, 131.—119

50 The *Punic Wars* (264-241, 218-201 and 149-146 B.C.) were fought by Rome and Carthage, the two biggest slave-owning states of antiquity, for domination in the Western Mediterranean and for the capture of new territory and slaves. They ended in the destruction of Carthage.— 119

51 This refers to the armed struggle for dictatorship between Caesar and Pompey (49-45 B.C.). It was part of the civil war in Rome at the end of the 2nd and during the 1st century B.C., which took the form of clashes between different groups of the slave-owning class, accompanied by slave uprisings and sharp conflicts between the poor sections and the landed and financial aristocracy. The civil war led to the fall of the republic and the establishment of the Empire.— 119

52 Presumably a slip of the pen, for in the next sentence Marx speaks of the relative depreciation of silver that was caused by the progress in the methods of mining and continued "until the Californian and Australian discoveries reversed this process", i.e. caused a relative depreciation of gold. In *A Contribution to the Critique of Political Economy* (Chapter Two, Section 4, "The Precious Metals"), he also points out that "the discovery of gold in Australia, California and Colombia will probably lead to another fall in the value of gold" (see present edition, Vol. 29).— 121

53 A reference to the quantitative theory of money set forth in James Mill's *Elements of Political Economy* (London, 1821), Chapter III, sections VII and VIII. Marx quoted at length from these sections and gave a critical analysis of Mill's views in *A Contribution to the Critique of Political Economy*, Part One (see present edition, Vol. 29). He took the passage showing up Mill's error from Thomas Tooke's *An Inquiry into the Currency Principle*, 2nd ed., London, 1844, p. 136.— 127

54 "Compulsory circulation" is Steuart's term for obligatory payments such as the payment of a money debt on a fixed date. In contrast to this, he calls the expenditure of money on purchases "voluntary circulation". J. Steuart, op. cit., Vol. II, p. 389.— 131

55 Marx has "ein *schlecht unendlicher Prozess*", which may be an allusion to the Hegelian term "schlechte Unendlichkeit" (bad infinity), meaning the infinite repetition of an identical situation according to the pattern: "something" becomes "something else", that "something else" is itself "something" which in turn becomes "something else", and so on *ad infinitum.*— 132

56 "*Price of production*" (*Produktionspreis*) means here the same as "the exchange value or the production costs" in the preceding sentence. As was pointed out above (see Note 29), the term "production costs" means "the immanent production costs of the commodity, which are equal to its value, i.e. to the total amount of labour time required for its production". The term *Produktionspreis* occurs in Marx's notebooks of excerpts as early as the 1840s. For instance, in one of the Brussels notebooks of 1845, containing excerpts from Louis Say's book *Principales causes de la richesse ou de la misère des peuples et des particuliers* (Paris, 1818), Marx uses it to render the words "coût de production" (page 32 of Say's book).— 135

57 The planned chapter on exchange value was not written, as Marx started from Chapter II, dealing with money. He jotted down the beginning of the chapter

on value at the end of his seventh (last) notebook of the manuscript of 1857-58 (see present edition, Vol. 29). Soon after, he decided that Chapter I should deal with the commodity, not with value. However, he realised that idea not in this manuscript, but in *A Contribution to the Critique of Political Economy*, Part One, Chapter One of which is entitled "The Commodity".— 138

58 The *monetary system,* an early form of mercantilism, consisted of a variety of economic measures applied by European states in the 17th and 18th centuries. Its advocates equated wealth with money and favoured policies designed to ensure the inflow of money into the country by maintaining an active trade balance and imposing protective tariffs.— 148, 520

59 This refers to page 2 of the excerpt notebook Marx filled in Brussels approximately in April and May 1845. The page in question contains excerpts from pages 31-73 of Ferrier's book *Du gouvernement considéré dans ses rapports avec le commerce*, Paris, 1805. Ferrier says there that silver, when mined, is a commodity, for it is the object of the direct demand of those who buy it. However, he goes on to say, "silver ceases to be a commodity as soon as it becomes money, for it turns into an indispensable mediator between production and consumption and can no longer directly satisfy any need" (p. 35).— 148

60 Page 11 of Marx's Brussels notebook of excerpts (1845).— 150

61 In the manuscript, this quotation from Ganilh, although clearly referring to the "Chapter on Money", is written in the form of a note or comment in Notebook II on the opening page of the "Chapter on Capital".— 151

62 *Nexus rerum*—"the link between things". In his excerpt notebook of 1851 entitled "The Completed System of Money Relations" Marx describes money (p. 41) as the "nexus rerum et hominum" (the link between things and people). He refers this quotation to p. 34. Unfortunately, it has been impossible to establish what work he meant. In calling money the "nexus rerum et hominum", Marx means the state of society which resulted from the disintegration of all the formerly dominant social links, patriarchal, feudal, family, religious, all of which were superseded by the rule of "cash".— 155

63 Marx wrote this chapter in late 1857, when the capitalist economy, in particular, the financial system, was beginning to experience the effects of the first world economic crisis (1857-58), which had started in the USA and spread to all large European countries.— 159

64 Here and below Marx means the "arrangement" of the material of his study first outlined at the end of section 3 of his Introduction (see this volume, p. 45).— 160

65 This passage, attributed by Marx to Malthus, is actually by the editor of the second posthumous edition of Malthus' book (1836), who tried to give a more precise formulation of Malthus' ideas.— 160, 232

66 The pages in Petty's and, further on, Misselden's book are given according to Marx's Manchester notebook of excerpts (July 1845).— 164

67 Marx is referring to a notebook he filled in Brussels in the summer of 1845
   with excerpts (on which he comments) from Boisguillebert's works, as published
   by E. Daire in a collection entitled *Économistes financiers du XVIIIe siècle* (Paris,
   1843).— 165

68 The "Chapter on Capital" forms the main content of the manuscript *Outlines of
   the Critique of Political Economy* (1857-58). It takes up the greater part of Notebook II, the whole of notebooks III to VI and 64 pages of Notebook VII.
   In Notebook II, it is entitled "The Chapter on Money as Capital", but in
   the subsequent notebooks it figures under the heading "Chapter on Capital".
   On earlier publications of this chapter see Note 22.— 171

69 The proposition that the natural content of the exchange process originally "is
   completely distinct from the economic relationship, because it still directly
   coincides with it" was developed further in Marx's *A Contribution to the Critique
   of Political Economy*. Marx says there that under the conditions of direct barter,
   the earliest form of exchange, "exchange value does not acquire an
   independent form, but is still directly tied to use value". At this stage, use
   values form the content of wealth, a content which is "indifferent" to its social
   form. "Use value in this indifference to the determined economic form lies
   outside the sphere of investigation of political economy" (see present edition,
   Vol. 29).— 173

70 Under the conditions of a simple commodity economy, to which this refers, the
   exchange value of labour and the value of the products of labour coincide (at
   this stage Marx still speaks of the value of labour rather than that of labour
   power). In *A Contribution to the Critique of Political Economy* he points out that
   the study of the higher, capitalist stage of commodity production should provide
   the answer to the question: "how does production on the basis of exchange value
   solely determined by labour time lead to the result that the exchange value of
   labour is less than the exchange value of its product?" (see present edition,
   Vol. 29).— 175

71 This refers to Bastiat's attempt wholly to reduce the exchange of commodities,
   both under the conditions of barter and under commodity-money circulation,
   to an exchange of "services" between farmers, bakers, shoe-makers, weavers,
   machine builders, teachers, physicians, lawyers, etc. See Fr. Bastiat, *Harmonies
   économiques*, 2nd ed., Paris, 1851, pp. 87-169.
   The theory of services, which Bastiat and other vulgar economists opposed
   to the labour theory of value, was meant to gloss over the capitalists'
   appropriation of the surplus value produced by wage labourers, and demonstrate the "harmony" of economic interests under capitalism. Marx wrote:
   "Because therefore in the purchase of *services* the specific relation between
   labour and capital is in no way involved, being either completely obliterated or
   altogether absent, it is naturally the favourite form used by Say, Bastiat and
   their consorts to express the *relation between capital and labour*" (see present
   edition, Vol. 34).— 175

72 "Self-reflection" is a Hegelian term denoting the reflection of a conceptual
   determination back into itself.— 176

73 One of the four parts of the *Corpus iuris civilis*, a code of Roman civil law
   compiled under the Byzantine Emperor Justinian between 529 and 534. The
   four parts are: a collection of legal decrees, a collection of pronouncements by

Roman lawyers (*Digesta* or *Pandectae*), a rambling survey of law (*Institutiones*), and a collection of additional constitutional acts (*Novellae*). Marx refers to the 1815 stereotyped edition of the *Institutiones.*—177

[74] Marx means such opponents of Bastiat as Proudhon and the Proudhonist Chevé. In 1849 and 1850, the two polemised against Bastiat in seven letters published in a pamphlet entitled *Gratuité du crédit. Discussion entre M. Fr. Bastiat et M. Proudhon*, Paris, 1850, which also contained seven letters by Bastiat written in reply.—181

[75] Marx means the page number in his 1846 notebook of excerpts entitled *Geschichte der Nationalökonomie*; *b* indicates the column.—190

[76] The page number refers to the 1844 notebook of excerpts.—192

[77] The Roman numeral indicates the page number in a notebook which has not reached us.—192

[78] J. B. Say's theory of utility, set forth in his *Traité d'économie politique*, was a vulgarisation of Adam Smith's labour theory of value. By reducing value to use value and equating the latter with utility, Say sought to prove that utility resulted from the harmonious interaction of human industry, nature and capital.—198

[79] This refers to the critique of Proudhon's views on the origin and relation of use value and exchange value Marx gave in *The Poverty of Philosophy*, Chapter I, § 1. Proudhon considered the problem in isolation from the specific historical conditions of the development of commodity and capitalist production, basing his analysis on an arbitrary contraposition of the abstract concepts of abundance and scarcity, and utility and estimation (see present edition, Vol. 6, pp. 111-20).—198

[80] In an excerpt notebook compiled in Brussels approximately in March and April 1845 and containing passages from Storch's *Cours d'économie politique*, Vol. I, Paris, 1823, Marx has the following summary of a passage occurring on p. 154 of Storch's book: "Human industry is only productive if it produces a value sufficient to replace the production costs ... actually, that reproduction is not enough: it ought to produce a certain value over and above that".—201

[81] Marx means Storch's assertion that "non-material labour"—the labour of doctors, teachers, artists and the like—is productive (*Cours d'économie politique*), and Senior's attributing of productivity to all functions useful to the bourgeoisie and the bourgeois state (*Principes fondamentaux de l'économie politique*, Paris, 1836). This theory, like many others, differed from the views of Adam Smith who, albeit inconsistently, distinguished between productive labour, i.e. labour creating surplus value, and all other kinds of labour, unproductive from the standpoint of bourgeois relations.

Marx gave a detailed analysis of Smith's views on productive and unproductive labour and a critique of the relevant theories of Storch, Senior and others in his manuscripts of 1861-63 (see present edition, Vol. 31).—203

[82] Marx gave a broad analysis of productive and unproductive labour later, in his manuscripts of 1861-63 (see present edition, vols. 31 and 34).—204

⁸³ Marx discusses Wakefield's theory of colonisation in detail in *Capital,* Vol. I, Ch. XXXIII. In conclusion he points out that this theory confirms the laws governing the rise and development of capitalist production. "...The capitalist mode of production and accumulation, and therefore capitalist private property, have for their fundamental condition the annihilation of self-earned private property; in other words, the expropriation of the labourer" (see present edition, Vol. 35).—208

⁸⁴ Market reports on the listed commodities were published regularly in *The Economist* in 1850-57. Quotations from the journal in Marx's notebooks of excerpts and his frequent references to *The Economist* in his newspaper articles show that he followed these reports regularly.—211

⁸⁵ Here Marx has "Arbeitsvermögen" (labour capacity). In his manuscripts of 1857-58 he as a rule uses this term in place of "Arbeitskraft" (labour power), which occurs once in his earlier economic work, *Wage Labour and Capital* (see present edition, Vol. 9, p. 214) and several times in his manuscripts of 1861-63. In Volume I of *Capital* he treats the two terms as identical: "By labour-power or capacity for labour is to be understood the aggregate of those mental and physical capabilities existing in a human being, which he exercises whenever he produces a use-value of any description" (see present edition, Vol. 35).—212

⁸⁶ Linguet's views are discussed in the manuscripts of 1861-63 (see present edition, Vol. 31).—218

⁸⁷ The text beginning on page 8 of Notebook III is the continuation of the text of Notebook II. The beginning of the sentence opening page 8 was on page 29—which has not reached us—of Notebook II and was reconstructed, together with the continuation, on the basis of the economic manuscripts of 1861-63. The first seven pages of Notebook III contain an unfinished critique of Bastiat and Carey, written several months earlier (see this volume, pp. 5-16).—219

⁸⁸ Britain's working class had fought for a legal limitation of the working day to ten hours from the late 18th century, the struggle assuming a mass character in the 1830s. The Ten Hours' Bill, passed by Parliament on June 8, 1847, applied only to women and "young persons". Marx discusses the British workers' struggle for a normal working day in detail in *Capital,* Vol. I, Ch. X (see present edition, Vol. 35).—220, 361

⁸⁹ *Existing for itself* may be an allusion to the Hegelian term "Fürsichsein", which denotes the condition of an attribute regarded in its fixity or relative self-containment.—228

⁹⁰ This refers to the British Owenites John Francis Bray, John Gray, Thomas Hodgskin, William Thompson and others who drew socialist conclusions from Ricardo's theory (see Note 32). Marx discussed their views in the manuscripts of 1861-63, in connection with the pamphlet *Labour Defended against the Claims of Capital* (London, 1825), published anonymously by Thomas Hodgskin. He examined the tendency, common to all these socialists, to regard capital not as a social relation but as a sum of objects and explain the misery of the working people by the estranged form in which these objects appear in the hands of the capitalists (see present edition, Vol. 32).—229, 436

91 Marx refers, in particular, to the pamphlet *Labour Defended against the Claims of Capital* (see previous note).—231

92 Marx discussed this example in greater detail in the manuscripts of 1861-63, where he writes: "...The workman employed by a piano maker is a productive labourer... But assume on the contrary that I buy all the materials required for a piano (or for all it matters the labourer himself may possess them), and that instead of buying the piano in a shop I have it made for me in my house. The workman who makes the piano is now an unproductive labourer, because his labour is exchanged directly against my revenue" (see present edition, Vol. 31).

Marx also showed that "a singer who sells her song for her own account is an *unproductive labourer*. But the same singer commissioned by an entrepreneur to sing in order to make money for him is a *productive labourer*; for she produces capital" (see present edition, Vol. 34). "*The same* kind of labour," Marx concludes, "may be *productive* or *unproductive*".—231

93 In Kantian terminology, an analytical proposition is one in which the predicate merely explains the content of the subject, as distinct from synthetic propositions, in which the predicate adds to the subject an attribute not inherent in it.—239

94 "Price of production" (*Produktionspreis*) means here the same as, in the preceding paragraph and elsewhere in this manuscript, "production costs" or "the necessary price of the commodity" (see Note 56). In his manuscript of 1857-58 Marx did not yet make a clear distinction between value and the price of production.—241

95 This is the first time Marx uses the term "surplus value" (*Mehrwert*) to denote that surplus over and above the advanced value which is appropriated by the capitalist without compensation. Further in the text he frequently uses the combination "Surplus-wert" for surplus value.

The term "surplus value" also occurs in *An Inquiry into the Principles of the Distribution of Wealth Most Conducive to Human Happiness* (London, 1824, pp. 167, 169) by the English socialist William Thompson, who based his conclusions on the theory of Ricardo. However, as Engels showed, Thompson meant by it the extra profit obtained by the capitalist employing machinery over and above the profit of the manual artisan. Thompson also used the term "additional value", to designate all newly created value (the value of the expended part of constant capital and the surplus value) ($v + s$). Apart from this, as Engels noted in his article "Juridical Socialism", "in the daily business life of France the term *plus-value* has been commonly used since time immemorial to denote any increase in value which involves no expense for the owner of the commodity" (see present edition, Vol. 27).

In one of his early articles (written in October 1842) Marx used the term "Mehrwert" several times for the extra value received by forest owners in the form of fines imposed for the theft of wood (see present edition, Vol. 1, pp. 250-51, 254-55). This had no relation to his later use of the word "Mehrwert" in the analysis of the capitalist exploitation of wage labourers.—241

96 This refers to Marx's notebook of excerpts from and critical commentaries on Ricardo (Notebook VIII).—242

97 Marx also analysed Proudhon's views on interest in the manuscripts of 1861-63 (see present edition, Vol. 32).—245

98 This is the first time Marx uses the term "surplus labour" in this work.—250

99 In his synopsis of Ricardo's book *On the Principles of Political Economy, and Taxation* (April 1851, Excerpt Notebook VIII), Marx says: "Most of Ricardo's opponents, like e.g. Wakefield, assert that he cannot explain what the surplus is. Thus suppose that a manufacturer lays out £30 for raw material, £20 for machinery, and £50 for wages. A total of £100. He sells his commodity for £110. Where does the £10 come from?"
    Ricardo's failure to analyse the source of surplus value is also noted by Marx in the manuscripts of 1861-63 (see present edition, Vol. 32).—252

100 A detailed analysis of Malthus' theory of value and, in particular, of his critique of Ricardo is given in Marx's manuscripts of 1861-63 (see present edition, Vol. 32).—252

101 Marx discusses the Physiocrats' role as the "fathers of modern political economy" in the manuscripts of 1861-63 (see present edition, Vol. 30).—253

102 This is the first time ever that Marx uses the term "necessary labour".—260

103 In *Capital,* Vol. I, chapters IX, X and XI Marx analysed in detail the capitalists' tendency to prolong the working day beyond all reasonable limits. He discussed the history of English factory legislation, in particular the struggles over the Ten Hours' Bill (see Note 88). In describing the condition of the English working class, he made extensive use of the reports of Factory Inspector Leonard Horner, who upheld the workers' interests (*Reports of the Inspectors of Factories to Her Majesty's Principal Secretary of State for the Home Department,* 1847-56).
    In his reports, Horner cited numerous infringements of the Ten Hours' Bill by factory owners, expressed, in particular, in the introduction of the so-called Relay System, which included night work and led to the prolongation of the working day.—261

104 This is the first time ever that Marx uses the term "relative surplus value".—262

105 This example can be presented as follows:
    Before the doubling of productivity, a working day of, say, 8 hours fell into 2 hours of necessary labour and 6 hours of surplus labour. After the doubling, it falls into 1 hour of necessary labour and 7 hours of surplus labour.—264

106 This refers to the 3rd edition of Ricardo's *On the Principles of Political Economy, and Taxation,* London, 1821, pp. 325-26.—266

107 Marx gives a detailed analysis of Ricardo's views on the accumulation of capital in the manuscripts of 1861-63 (see present edition, Vol. 32).—271

108 Marx means his Notebook VIII of excerpts on political economy (1851). It includes, in particular, a synopsis of Ricardo's *On the Principles of Political Economy, and Taxation* (see Note 99) with Marx's commentaries. On pp. 35-37 he

has an abstract of Chapter XX ("Value and Riches, Their Distinctive Properties") of Ricardo's book. He is referring to this chapter.—274

[109] Ricardo had "production".—276

[110] Marx is referring to his abstract, in Excerpt Notebook VIII, of the opening part of Chapter VII ("On Foreign Trade") of Ricardo's book.—276

[111] Marx gives a detailed critique of Malthus' views on value and surplus value in the manuscripts of 1861-63 (see present edition, Vol. 32).—279

[112] This refers to G. Ramsay (who writes in *An Essay on the Distribution of Wealth,* Edinburgh, London, 1836, p. 55: "Capital is a source of value independent of labour") and particularly to N. W. Senior (see his *Letters on the Factory Act,* London, 1837, pp. 12-13).—282

[113] Here Marx proceeds from the assumption that the capitalised surplus value is wholly spent on the purchase of new labour power—"an impossible assumption", as he says himself a few lines further.—294

[114] In the manuscript, there follow the words: "sind erst $^1/_5$ vom 100 und $^{11}/_{12}$ vom 100 zuviel gerechnet; $^1/_5$ vom 100=20%, $^{11}/_{12}$ vom 100 $8^4/_{12}$% oder $8\ ^1/_3$%."—295

[115] There follows a blank space in the manuscript, presumably for calculations referring to the second case.—295

[116] On the confusion of the rate of surplus value with the rate of profit by Carey and other bourgeois economists see *Capital,* Vol. I, Ch. IX and Vol. III, Ch. VIII (present edition, vols. 35 and 37).—296

[117] In 1786, the government of William Pitt, Jr., set up a special sinking fund to repay the growing national debt by means of taxes. The project, based on recommendations by Dr. Richard Price, provided for the government to draw loans on simple interest and grant credits on compound interest. Far from alleviating the financial difficulties, the operation of the fund caused serious complications in the sphere of government credit. In 1825 the fund was practically liquidated. For details see *Capital,* Vol. III, Chapter XXIV, and Marx's article "Mr. Disraeli's Budget", written in April 1858 (present edition, vols. 37 and 15).—298

[118] On the *qualitative limit* to the accumulation of capital see Marx's manuscripts of 1861-63 (present edition, vols. 32 and 34).—298

[119] Marx assumes here that the rate of surplus value after the rise in the price of labour power remains unchanged (25% for capital I and $33^1/_3$% for capital II). This is only possible given a corresponding lengthening of the working day.—308

[120] This is the first time ever that Marx uses these terms to denote the two different components of capital.—314

[121] This refers to Excerpt Notebook XII (July 1851).—324

122 The last sentence is Marx's rendering of the following passage from Ravenstone's *Thoughts on the Funding System, and Its Effects,* London, 1824, p. 46: "Where the labour of nine is required for the maintenance of ten, only one-tenth of the gross produce can be given to rent. Where one man's labour is sufficient for the maintenance of five, four-fifths will go to rent, or the other charges of the state, which can only be provided for out of the surplus produce of industry. The first proportion seems to have prevailed in England at the time of the Conquest, the last is that which actually takes place. As only one-fifth part of the people are now employed in the cultivation of the land..." (Marx refers to his Excerpt Notebook IX).— 325

123 Marx means James Mill's proposition that there exists a permanent and necessary equilibrium between production and consumption, between supply and demand, and between the sum-total of purchases and the sum-total of sales. First put forward in Mill's pamphlet *Commerce Defended* (London, 1808), it was seconded by Say. Marx discusses this proposition in greater detail in *A Contribution to the Critique of Political Economy,* Part One, Chapter Two, 2 (see present edition, Vol. 29) and in the manuscripts of 1861-63.— 338

124 Marx means the "little shilling men", the Birmingham school of political economy initiated by the English banker Thomas Attwood. Its views were put forth in *The Currency Question. The Gemini Letters,* a book published anonymously in London in 1844 by Thomas Wright and John Harlow, who called themselves the Gemini.— 339

125 The last sentence is a summary of the following passage in Hodgskin's book (pp. 245-46): "When the capitalist, being the owner of all the produce, will allow labourers neither to make nor use instruments, unless *he* obtains a profit over and above the subsistence of the labourer, it is plain the bounds are set to productive labour much within what Nature prescribes. In proportion as capital in the hands of a third party is accumulated, so the whole amount of profit required by the capitalist increases, and so there arises an artificial check to production and population."— 343

126 The page numbers refer to Marx's London Excerpt Notebook XII.— 344

127 Should be: 45.— 344

128 The presuppositions being what they are, the value newly added by living labour (10 thaler) would actually constitute $1/9$, not $1/10$, of the total value of the product, as the value of the lb. of twist has decreased from 5 thaler to $4 1/2$ thaler and the total value of 20 lbs of twist has, accordingly, declined from 100 to 90 thaler.— 360

129 Marx examines the effect of changes in the organic composition of capital on the size of surplus value in *Capital,* Vol. I, Chapter XXIV (see present edition, Vol. 35).— 361

130 The figures in this calculation should be as follows: the worker would obtain each pound of twist at a discount of $1/20$ thaler, and since he would now get, altogether, $4 4/99$ lbs, or $400/99$ lbs, his gain would be $\frac{1\times400}{20\times99}$ thaler, i.e. $20/99$ thaler, not $20/100$ thaler, as Marx assumes to simplify the calculation.— 364

[131] The figures in this calculation should be as follows: before the rise in wages the value of the 40 lbs of twist fell into 160 c (constant capital) + 20 v (variable capital)+20s (surplus value). Now it falls into $160c+22v+18s$. Formerly, the rate of profit was $^{20}/_{180}$, i.e. $11\,^{1}/_{9}\%$, now it is $^{18}/_{182}$, i.e. $9\,^{81}/_{91}\%$.—367

[132] In working on this manuscript, Marx attached great importance to the logical and methodological aspects of economic research. In this connection, he repeatedly had recourse to Hegel's *Wissenschaft der Logik* and even conceived the idea of writing a special work comparing his own materialist method with Hegel's idealist method and bringing out the rational features of Hegel's dialectics. On January 16, 1858, he wrote to Engels: "I should very much like to write 2 or 3 sheets making accessible to the common reader the *rational* aspect of the method which Hegel not only discovered but also mystified" (see present edition, Vol. 40, p. 249). In 1860, Marx copied out a number of passages from *Wissenschaft der Logik* in one of his notebooks. He never wrote a special work on Hegel's method, but he did compare that method with his own, in his Afterword to the second German edition of Volume I of *Capital* (1873).—379

[133] This section of the 1857-58 manuscript takes up pages 50-53 of Notebook IV and pages 1-15 of Notebook V. The title, "Forms Preceding Capitalist Production", is from Marx's *References to My Own Notebooks* (see present edition, Vol. 29). Pages 1-15 of Notebook V are entitled in the *References* "Continuation on the Process Preceding the Formation of the Capitalist Relationship or Primitive Accumulation". For details concerning earlier publications of this section see Note 22.—399

[134] The term "Stamm", translated here as "tribe", was used in the middle of the 19th century in a broader sense than today and denoted all people descended from a common ancestor, thus covering the modern concept of the "gens" as well as that of the "tribe". A precise definition and differentiation of these concepts was given by the American ethnographer and historian Lewis Henry Morgan. In his *Ancient Society* (1877), he brought out the importance of the gens as the basic unit of the primitive communal system and thus laid the scientific foundation for the study of the history of primitive society as a whole. Marx and Engels saw in Morgan's discoveries confirmation of their proposition—put forward by them in *The German Ideology,* and elaborated by Marx in the present manuscript and by Engels in his studies on the history of Ireland (1869-70)—that tribal relations constituted a stage common to the development of all peoples. (See also Note 10.)—400

[135] *Demotes*—a commoner assigned to a *deme,* a unit of local government in Attica (district of ancient Greece). Several demes constituted a *phyle.* Under the administrative reform of Cleisthenes (6th century B.C.) there were 10 phyles in Attica.—406

[136] *Dithmarschen*—a region in North Germany. Inhabited in the Middle Ages by East Saxons and Franks, Dithmarschen was a stronghold of the free peasantry, who for a long time retained the communal system and staunchly resisted the attempts by German and Danish feudal lords to subjugate them. The communal system survived even after the conquest of Dithmarschen, in 1559, by the King of Denmark.—406

137 *Gaels*—the indigenous population of the mountain regions of Northern and Western Scotland, descendants of the Celts.—406

138 *"Panis et circenses"*—"bread and circuses". Marx means the heyday of the Roman slave-holding state, when the lower strata of the urban population, the *plebs,* were excluded from production and lived largely on sops from the State and rich slave-holders, who granted "bread and circuses" to them (Juvenal, *Satires,* X, 81).—424, 523

139 This refers to the laws against vagabonds and beggars introduced in England under the first Tudors (Henry VII and Henry VIII) and in later years. They envisaged cruel corporal punishment (branding, maiming) and slavery, in some cases even execution, for able-bodied persons accused of vagabondage and beggary. On the part played by this legislation in turning the expropriated population into wage labourers see *Capital,* Vol. I, Chapter XXXVIII (present edition, Vol. 35).—431

140 The insertion "(Wrong!)", added by Marx later, refers to the sentence immediately preceding it. In the course of his further work on the manuscript, Marx demonstrated that the duration of the production process depended on a number of circumstances (see, e.g., this volume, pp. 521-22).—441

141 The Liverpool and Manchester Railway was opened on September 15, 1830. Built under the direction of George Stephenson, it was the first line fully served by locomotives. Earlier-built lines, including the 21-kilometre Stockton and Darlington Railway (opened in 1825), on which Stephenson's locomotive was first employed, partly used horse traction.—454

142 The Roman numeral refers to an undiscovered notebook of Marx's filled between 1844 and 1847.—461

143 For Marx's comments on this proposition of Malthus' see the manuscripts of 1861-63 (present edition, Vol. 32).—467

144 McCulloch's unjustified extension of the concept of labour to the processes of Nature was discussed by Marx in detail in the manuscripts of 1861-63 (see present edition, Vol. 32).—479

145 Marx uses the same example to illustrate the calculation of profit in a letter to Engels written about a month later, on March 5, 1858 (see present edition, Vol. 40, p. 283).—485

146 To calculate the turnover of the *fixed* capital (£10,000) Marx divides it by the sinking fund (£650); to calculate the turnover of the *circulating* capital, he divides the contingencies (£1,100), the wages (£2,600) and the cost of the raw materials (£10,000)—£13,700 in all—by the circulating capital (£7,000).—486

147 In his letter to Engels of March 5, 1858, Marx adduces this example of profit calculation and remarks: "It is a great pity that the above statement does not show the *number* of operatives, or the proportion of actual *wages* to what appears as *salaries*" (see present edition, Vol. 40, p. 283). In this passage of his manuscript Marx assumes that wages account for exactly $1/6$ of the annual outlays, while the rest of the £2,600 goes for salaries.—486

¹⁴⁸ For Marx's comments on this proposition of Wakefield's see the manuscripts of 1861-63 (present edition, Vol. 32).—502

¹⁴⁹ This refers to a quotation in Bailey's book (pp. 57-58) from Albert Gallatin's *Considerations on the Currency and Banking System of the United States*, Philadelphia, 1831, p. 68.—503

¹⁵⁰ Marx means his Manchester notebook of excerpts of 1845.—504, 534

¹⁵¹ For the colonies of antiquity and the *Völkerwanderung* see Marx's article of March 4, 1853 for the *New-York Daily Tribune*, "Forced Emigration.—Kossuth and Mazzini.—The Refugee Question.—Election Bribery in England.—Mr. Cobden" (present edition, Vol. 11).—523

¹⁵² Marx is referring to his Paris notebook of 1844.—529, 534

¹⁵³ Concerning the transformation of surplus labour into necessary labour under communism, Marx says the following in *Capital*, Vol. I (present edition, Vol. 35): "Only by suppressing the capitalist form of production could the length of the working day be reduced to the necessary labour-time. But, even in that case, the latter would extend its limits. On the one hand, because the notion of 'means of subsistence' would considerably expand, and the labourer would lay claim to an altogether different standard of life. On the other hand, because a part of what is now surplus labour, would then count as necessary labour; I mean the labour of forming a fund for reserve and accumulation."—531

NAME INDEX

theory of the harmony of class interests in capitalist society.—5-11, 18, 23, 180, 296, 478, 499-502, 516

Cato, Marcus Porcius (the Elder) (234-149 B.C.)—Roman politician and writer, author of the treatise *Agriculture.*— 411

Cervantes Saavedra, Miguel de (1547-1616)—Spanish writer.— 14

Chalmers, Thomas (1780-1847) — Scottish Protestant theologian, economist, follower of Malthus.—5, 519-21

Cherbuliez, Antoine Elesée (Elisée) (1797-1869)—Swiss economist, tried to combine Sismondi's theory with elements of Ricardo's theory.—226, 234, 461

Chevalier, Michel (1806-1879)—French engineer, economist and writer, follower of Saint-Simon in the 1830s, later a Free Trader.—63

Cicero, Marcus Tullius (106-43 B.C.)—Roman orator and statesman.—406

Cleisthenes (6th cent. B.C.)—Athenian politician.—406

D

Daire, Louis François Eugène (1798-1847)—French economist, publisher of works on political economy.—271

Darimon, Louis Alfred (1819-1902)—French politician, writer and historian, follower of Proudhon.—51, 52, 55-59, 61-65, 71-72

Darius the Great (c. 550-486 B.C.) — King of Persia (c. 522-486 B.C.).—116

Defoe, Daniel (1660-1731)—English writer.— 17

De Quincey, Thomas (1785-1859)—English writer and economist; commentator of Ricardo's works.—476-80

Dionysius Halicarnassensis ("of Halicarnassus") (second half of the 1st cent. B.C.)—Greek historian and teacher of rhetoric.—405

Du Cange, Charles du Fresne, sieur (1610-1688)—French historian and philologist.—437

Dureau de la Malle, Adolphe Jules César Auguste (1777-1857)—French poet and historian.— 115-20

E

Euclid (late 4th-early 3rd cent. B.C.)—Greek mathematician.— 119

F

Ferrier, François Louis Auguste (1777-1861)—French economist, epigone of mercantilism.— 148-49, 520

Fourier, François Marie Charles (1772-1837)—French utopian socialist.—530

G

Gallatin, Albert (1761-1849)—American statesman and economist, author of works on finance and on money circulation.— 503

Ganilh, Charles (1758-1836)—French politician and economist, epigone of mercantilism.— 151, 190

Garnier, Germain, marquis (1754-1821)—French economist and politician, follower of the Physiocrats, translator and critic of Adam Smith.— 118, 121, 126, 529

Gaskell, Peter (first half of the 19th cent.)—English physician and journalist, liberal.— 507

Girardin, Émile de (1806-1881)—French journalist and politician; editor of *La Presse*; notorious for his lack of principles in politics.— 71

Goethe, Johann Wolfgang von (1749-1832)—German poet.— 58

Gray, John (1798-1850)—English economist, utopian socialist.— 74, 90, 340

Grimm, Jacob Ludwig Carl (1785-1863)—German philologist, professor of Berlin University.— 115

Gülich, Gustav von (1791-1847)—German economist and historian; author of several works on the history of national economy; protectionist.—5, 119

H

Harlow, John (mid-19th cent.)—British economist of the Birmingham school, known as the "little shilling men". He and his fellow-thinker Wright wrote under the pseudonym of Gemini.—339

Hegel, Georg Wilhelm Friedrich (1770-1831)—German philosopher.—38, 39, 75, 110

Henry VII (1457-1509)—King of England (1485-1509).—431

Henry VIII (1491-1547)—King of England (1509-1547).—431

Herodotus (c. 484-c. 425 B.C.)—Greek historian.—116, 117

Hesiod (c. 8th cent. B.C.)—Greek poet.—117, 127

Hobbes, Thomas (1588-1679)—English philosopher.—93

Hodgskin, Thomas (1787-1869)—English economist and writer, utopian socialist.—343, 344-45, 350, 522

Homer—semi-legendary Greek epic poet, author of the Iliad and the Odyssey.—110, 117, 127

Honorius (384-423)—Emperor of the Western Roman Empire (395-423).—119-20

Horner, Leonard (1785-1864)—English geologist and public figure; factory inspector (1833-56), upheld the workers' interests.—261

Hubbard, John Gellibrand (1805-1889)—British politician, Conservative; M.P. (1859-68 and 1874-87); a director of the Bank of England (1838).—128

Humboldt, Alexander (Friedrich Heinrich Alexander), Baron von (1769-1859)—German naturalist and traveller.—117

J

Jacob, William (c. 1762-1851)—English businessman; author of several works on economics.—80, 103, 116, 117, 118, 127, 128, 163

L

Lauderdale, James Maitland, 8th Earl of (1759-1839)—British politician and economist, criticised Adam Smith's theory.—150, 316

Letronne, Jean Antoine (1787-1848)—French archaeologist and philologist.—116

Linguet, Simon Nicolas Henri (1736-1794)—French lawyer, writer, historian and economist; adherent of absolutism; critic of the Physiocrats' theories and bourgeois views of freedom and property.—218

Locke, John (1632-1704)—English dualist philosopher and economist.—91

Loyd, Samuel Jones, first Baron Overstone (1796-1883)—English banker and economist; a theoretician of money circulation.—375-76

Lucretius (Titus Lucretius Carus) (c. 99-c. 55 B.C.)—Roman philosopher and poet.—117

M

M(a)cCulloch, John Ramsay (1789-1864)—Scottish economist who vulgarised Ricardo's teaching; developed theories which justified capitalist exploitation.—5, 338, 479, 534-35

Malthus, Thomas Robert (1766-1834)—English clergyman and economist.—5, 160, 232, 252, 279, 328, 339-40, 344, 346, 467, 480, 485, 487-99, 514-19, 524-27, 535

Menenius, Agrippa (d. 493 B.C.)—Roman patrician.—99

Mill, James (1773-1836)—British historian, economist and positivist philosopher, follower of Ricardo's theory, who tried to remove its contradictions by a formal logical method.—127, 338, 352

Mill, John Stuart (1806-1873)—British positivist philosopher and economist; son of James Mill; epigone of classical political economy.—5, 24, 25, 535-37

Mirabeau, Victor Riqueti, marquis de (1715-1789)—French economist,

INDEX OF LITERARY AND MYTHOLOGICAL NAMES

INDEX OF QUOTED
AND MENTIONED LITERATURE

WORKS BY KARL MARX

The Poverty of Philosophy. Answer to the "Philosophy of Poverty" by M. Proudhon (present edition, Vol. 6)
— *Misère de la philosophie. Réponse à la philosophie de la misère de M. Proudhon.* Paris-Bruxelles, 1847.—75, 90, 198, 412

WORKS BY DIFFERENT AUTHORS

Aristoteles. *Ethica Nicomachea.*—97
— *Metaphysica.*—72
— *Politica.*—18, 420

Atkinson, W. *Principles of Political Economy; or, the laws of the formation of national wealth: developed by means of the Christian Law of government; being the substance of a case delivered to the hand-loom weavers commission.* London, 1840.—534

Babbage, Ch. *Traité sur l'économie des machines et des manufactures.* Traduit de l'anglais sur la troisième édition. Paris, 1833.—269, 307, 509

[Bailey, S.] *Money and Its Vicissitudes in Value; as they affect national industry and pecuniary contracts; with a postscript on joint-stock banks.* London, 1837.—110, 168, 169, 502-04

Bastiat, Fr. *Gratuité du crédit. Discussion entre M. Fr. Bastiat et M. Proudhon.* Paris, 1850.—61, 181, 195, 196, 237, 244, 311, 352, 354, 360
— *Harmonies économiques.* 2-me édition, augmentée des manuscrits laissés par l'auteur. Paris, 1851.—5-16, 175, 181, 248

Bellers, J. *Essays about the Poor, Manufactures, Trade, Plantations, and Immorality...,* London, 1699.—97

Bible
  The Old Testament
    Genesis.—165, 529

The New Testament
    Matthew.—164
    Revelation.—169

Böckh, A. *Die Staatshaushaltung der Athener.* Bd. 1-2. Berlin, 1817.—116

Boisguillebert, P. *Dissertation sur la nature des richesses, de l'argent et des tributs...* In: *Économistes financiers du XVIIIᵉ siècle.* Précédés de notices historiques sur chaque auteur, et accompagnés de commentaires et de notes explicatives, par M. Eugène Daire. Paris, 1843.—133-34, 153, 165, 201

Bray, J. F. *Labour's Wrongs and Labour's Remedy; or, the Age of Might and the Age of Right.* Leeds, 1839.—229, 436, 481

Büsch, J. G. *Abhandlung von dem Geldumlauf in anhaltender Rücksicht auf die Staatswirtschaft und Handlung.* Th. 1-2. Hamburg, Kiel, 1800.—97

Carey, H. C. *The Past, the Present, and the Future.* Philadelphia, 1848.—516
— *Principles of Political Economy.* Part the first. Philadelphia, 1837.—296, 478, 499, 502

Cervantes Saavedra, M. de. *Don Quixote.*—14

Chalmers, Th. *On Political Economy in Connexion with the Moral State and Moral Prospects of Society.* Second edition. Glasgow, Edinburgh, Dublin and London, 1832.—519-21

Cherbuliez, A. *Richesse ou pauvreté.* Paris, 1841. The first edition appeared in Paris and Geneva in 1840 under the title *Riche ou pauvre.*—226, 234, 461

Darimon, A. *De la réforme des banques.* Paris, 1856.—51-65, 71-72

De Quincey, Th. *The Logic of Political Economy.* Edinburgh, London, 1844.—476-80

Dionysius Halicarnassensis. *Antiquitates Romanae.* In: Niebuhr, B. G. *Römische Geschichte.* 2. Ausg., Th. 1. Berlin, 1827.—405

Du Cange, Ch. D. *Glossarium mediae et infimae latinitatis conditum a Carolo Dufresne Domino Du Cange.* Tomus secundus. Parisiis, 1842.—437

Dureau de la Malle, A. J. *Économie politique des Romains.* Tomes 1-2. Paris, 1840.—115-20

Ferrier, F. L. A. *Du gouvernement considéré dans ses rapports avec le commerce.* Paris, 1805.—148-49, 520

Fourier, Ch. *Le Nouveau Monde industriel et sociétaire.* Paris, 1848 (Œuvres complètes. 3ᵉ éd. T. 6).—530

Gallatin, A. *Considerations on the Currency and Banking System of the United States.* Philadelphia, 1831. Quoted from Bailey, S. *Money and Its Vicissitudes in Value...* London, 1837.—503

Ganilh, Ch. *Des systèmes d'économie politique, de leurs inconvéniens, de leurs avantages, et de la doctrine la plus favorable aux progrès de la richesse des nations.* Tomes I-II. Paris, 1809.—151, 189-90

Garnier, G. *Histoire de la monnaie, depuis les temps de la plus haute antiquité, jusqu'au règne de Charlemagne.* Tomes I-II. Paris, 1819.—118, 121, 126

Gaskell, P. *Artisans and Machinery: the moral and physical condition of the manufacturing population considered with reference to mechanical substitutes for human labour.* London, 1836.—507

Girardin, É. de. *Introduction.* In: Darimon, A. *De la réforme des banques.* Paris, 1856.—71

Goethe, J. W. von. *Egmont.*—58

Gray, J. *Lectures on the Nature and Use of Money.* Edinburgh, 1848.—90, 340

Grimm, J. *Geschichte der deutschen Sprache.* Erster Band. Leipzig, 1853.—115

Gülich, G. von. *Geschichtliche Darstellung des Handels, der Gewerbe und des Ackerbaus der bedeutendsten handeltreibenden Staaten unsrer Zeit.* Band V. Jena, 1845.—119

Hegel, G. W. F. *Grundlinien der Philosophie des Rechts, oder Naturrecht und Staatswissenschaft im Grundrisse.* Berlin, 1833.—17, 39
— *Wissenschaft der Logik.* Berlin, 1834 (*Werke.* Bd. 4).—75

Hesiod. *Works and Days.*—117

Hobbes, Th. *De cive* (1642). In: *Thomae Hobbes opera philosophica.* Tomus I. Amstelodami, 1668.—93
— *Leviathan, sive de materia, forma, et potestate civitatis ecclesiasticae et civilis* (1651). In: *Thomae Hobbes opera philosophica.* Tomus II. Amstelodami, 1668.—93

[Hodgskin, Th.] *Labour Defended against the Claims of Capital. Or the Unproductiveness of Capital proved with Reference to the Present Combinations amongst Journeymen.* London, 1825.—231, 345
— *Popular Political Economy. Four Lectures delivered at the London Mechanics' Institution.* London, 1827.—343, 344, 350, 522

Homer. *The Iliad.*—47, 110, 127

Hubbard, J. G. *The Currency and the Country.* London, 1843.—128

An Inquiry into those Principles, respecting the Nature of Demand and the Necessity of Consumption, lately advocated by Mr. Malthus, from which it is concluded, that taxation and the maintenance of unproductive consumers can be conducive to the progress of wealth. London, 1821.—344

Jacob, W. *An Historical Inquiry into the Production and Consumption of the Precious Metals.* In two volumes. London, 1831. Quoted from Dureau de la Malle, A. J.

Économie politique des Romains. T. 1. Paris, 1840.—80, 103, 116, 118, 127, 128, 163

Juvenalis. *Satirae.*—424

Lauderdale, J. *Recherches sur la nature et l'origine de la richesse publique, et sur les moyens et les causes qui concourent à son accroissement.* Traduit de l'anglais, par E. Lagentie de Lavaïsse. Paris, 1808. The English edition appeared in Edinburgh in 1804.—150, 316

Lectures on Gold for the Instruction of Emigrants about to Proceed to Australia. Delivered at the Museum of Practical Geology. London, 1852.—113-15

Letronne, A. J. *Considérations générales sur l'évaluation des monnaies grecques et romaines, et sur la valeur de l'or et de l'argent avant la découverte de l'Amérique.* Paris, 1817.—116

[Linguet, S. N. H.] *Théorie des loix civiles, ou Principes fondamentaux de la société.* T. I-II. Londres, 1767.—218

Locke, J. *Further Considerations Concerning Raising the Value of Money* (1695). In: *The Works of John Locke* in four volumes. The seventh edition. Volume II. London, 1768.—91

Lucretius. *De rerum natura.* In: Dureau de la Malle, A. J. *Économie politique des Romains.* T. 1. Paris, 1840.—117

MacCulloch, J. R. *The Principles of Political Economy: with a sketch of the rise and progress of the science.* Edinburgh, London, 1825.—338, 479, 534

Malthus, Th. R. *Definitions in Political Economy, preceded by an inquiry into the rules which ought to guide political economists in the definition and use of their terms; with remarks on the deviation from these rules in their writings.* London, 1827.—514-15, 517-18

— (anon.) *An Essay on the Principle of Population as it affects the future improvement of society with remarks on the speculations of Mr. Godwin, M. Condorcet, and other writers.* London, 1798.—524
— *The Measure of Value Stated and Illustrated, with an application of it to the alterations in the value of the English currency since 1790.* London, 1823.—252, 279, 467, 476, 490-92, 495, 498, 499, 514
— *Principles of Political Economy considered with a view to their practical application.* London, 1820.—480
— *Idem.* Second edition with considerable additions from the author's own manuscript and an original memoir. London, 1836.—160, 232, 328, 340, 344-46, 485, 487-89, 490

Mill, James. *Commerce Defended. An answer to the arguments by which Mr. Spence, Mr. Cobbett, and others, have attempted to prove that commerce is not a source of national wealth.* 2nd ed. London, 1808.—338, 352
— *Élemens d'économie politique.* Trad. de l'anglais par J. T. Parisot. Paris, 1823.—338, 352

— *Elements of Political Economy.* London, 1821. Quoted from Tooke, Th. *An Inquiry into the Currency Principle...* Second edition. London, 1844.— 127

Mill, John Stuart. *Essays on Some Unsettled Questions of Political Economy.* London, 1844.—535-37
— *Principles of Political Economy with some of their Applications to Social Philosophy.* In two volumes. London, 1848.—5, 24, 25, 535

[Misselden, E.] *Free Trade. Or, the Meanes to Make Trade Florish.* London, 1622.— 161, 164, 165

Müller, A. H. *Die Elemente der Staatskunst.* Erster Theil. Berlin, 1809.—437

Niebuhr, B. G. *Römische Geschichte.* Erster Theil. Zweyte, völlig umgearbeitete, Ausgabe. Berlin, 1827.—404-06, 425

Petty, W. *Several Essays in Political Arithmetick.* London, 1699.—106, 164

Plinius. *Historia naturalis.*Quoted from Dureau de la Malle, A. J. *Économie politique des Romains.* T. 1. Paris, 1840.— 118

Prescott, W. H. *History of the Conquest of Peru, with a preliminary view of the civilisation of the Incas.* Fourth edition. In three volumes. London, 1850.—40

Price, R. *An Appeal to the Public, on the Subject of the National Debt.* 2nd ed. London, 1772.— 298
— *Observations on Reversionary Payments; on schemes for providing annuities for widows, and for persons in old age; on the method of calculating the values of assurances on lives; and on the national debt.* 2nd ed. London, 1772.— 298

Proudhon, P. J. *Gratuité du crédit*—see Bastiat, Fr. *Gratuité du crédit. Discussion entre M. Fr. Bastiat et M. Proudhon*
— *Qu'est-ce que la propriété? ou Recherches sur le principe du droit et du gouvernement.* Paris, 1841.—61, 352
— *Système des contradictions économiques, ou Philosophie de la misère.* Tomes I-II. Paris, 1846.— 13, 18, 44, 68, 90, 236, 412, 531

Ramsay, G. *An Essay on the Distribution of Wealth.* Edinburgh, London, 1836.—241, 470, 473-74, 476

Ravenstone, P. *Thoughts on the Funding System, and Its Effects.* London, 1824.—169, 325, 494

Reitemeier, J. F. *Geschichte des Bergbaues und Hüttenwesens bey den alten Völkern.* Göttingen, 1785.—118

Ricardo, D. *The High Price of Bullion a Proof of the Depreciation of Bank-Notes.* London, 1810. Quoted from Darimon, A. *De la réforme des banques.* Paris, 1856.— 64
— *On the Principles of Political Economy, and Taxation.* Third edition. London,

1821. The first edition appeared in London in 1817.—17, 33, 188, 235, 236, 242, 252, 271, 273-78, 311, 313, 340, 378, 475, 480-83, 526

Rossi, P. *Cours d'économie politique. Année 1836-1837*. In: *Cours d'économie politique*. Bruxelles, 1843.—510, 514

Rousseau, J. J. *Du Contrat social; ou Principes du droit politique*. Londres, 1782.— 17

Say, J. B. *Traité d'économie politique, ou simple exposition de la manière dont se forment, se distribuent et se consomment les richesses*. Troisième édition. Tomes I-II. Paris, 1817.—31, 148, 182, 192, 235, 352
— Idem. Quatrième édition. Paris, 1819. Quoted from Storch, H. *Considérations sur la nature du revenu national*. Paris, 1824.—31, 339

[Senior, N. W.] *Principes fondamentaux de l'économie politique, tirés de leçons édites et inédites de Mr. N.-W. Senior, par le c-te Jean Arrivabene*. Paris, 1836.—168, 231, 531

— *Three Lectures on the Cost of Obtaining Money, and on some effects of private and government paper money; delivered before the University of Oxford, in Trinity term, 1829*. London, 1830.—124

Shakespeare, W. *Timon of Athens*.—100

Sismondi, J. C. L. Simonde de. *Études sur l'économie politique*. Tomes I-II. Bruxelles, 1837-1838.—127, 152, 235, 339-40
— *Nouveaux principes d'économie politique, ou De la richesse dans ses rapports avec la population*. Seconde édition. Tomes I-II. Paris, 1827.—192, 234, 461

Smith, A. *An Inquiry into the Nature and Causes of the Wealth of Nations*. In two volumes. London, 1776.—36, 432, 521
— *An Inquiry into the Nature and Causes of the Wealth of Nations*. With a commentary, by the author of *England and America* [E. G. Wakefield]. In six volumes. [Vols. I-IV.] London, 1835-1839.—17, 24, 36, 93, 121, 149, 231, 254, 398, 502, 534
— *Recherches sur la nature et les causes de la richesse des nations*. Traduction nouvelle, avec des notes et observations, par Germain Garnier. Tomes I-V. Paris, 1802.—104, 106, 107, 529, 533, 534

Solly, E. *The Present Distress, in relation to the Theory of Money*. London, 1830.—149-50

The Source and Remedy of the National Difficulties, deduced from principles of political economy, in a letter to Lord John Russell. London, 1821.—324, 344

Spinoza, B. *Epistolae*.—28

Steuart, J. *An Inquiry into the Principles of Political Oeconomy: being an essay on the science of domestic policy in free nations*. In three volumes. Dublin, 1770.—106, 128, 131, 139, 158, 159, 206, 395

Storch, H. *Considérations sur la nature du revenu national*. Paris, 1824.—31, 339
— *Cours d'économie politique, ou Exposition des principes qui déterminent la prospérité des nations*. Avec des notes explicatives et critiques par J. B. Say. Tomes I-IV. Paris, 1823.—127, 160-61, 168, 170, 201, 467, 472

Strabo. *Rerum geographicarum libri XVII.* Tomus II. Quoted from Dureau de la Malle, A. J. *Économie politique des romains.* T. 1. Paris, 1840.— 109-10, 116

Taylor, J. *A View of the Money System of England, from the Conquest; with proposals for establishing a secure and equable credit currency.* London, 1828.— 151

Thompson, W. *An Inquiry into the Principles of the Distribution of Wealth Most Conducive to Human Happiness; applied to the newly proposed system of voluntary equality of wealth.* London, 1824.— 467

Tooke, Th. *A History of Prices, and of the State of the Circulation.* Volumes I-VI. London, 1838-1857.— 5
— *An Inquiry into the Currency Principle; the connection of the currency with prices, and the expediency of a separation of issue from banking.* Second edition. London, 1844.— 127

Torrens, R. *An Essay on the Production of Wealth; with an appendix, in which the principles of political economy are applied to the actual circumstances of this country.* London, 1821.— 511

Urquhart, D. *Familiar Words as ˙ Affecting England and the English.* London, 1856.— 80

Virgil. *Aeneid.*— 100, 155

Wade, J. *History of the Middle and Working Classes; with a popular exposition of the economical and political principles which have influenced the past and present condition of the industrious orders.* Third edition. London, 1835.— 504, 535

[Wakefield E. G. A commentary to A. Smith's *Wealth of Nations*.] In: Smith, A. *An Inquiry into the Nature and Causes of the Wealth of Nations.* London, 1835-1839.— 340, 502, 534
— *A View of the Art of Colonization, with present reference to the British Empire; in letters between a statesman and a colonist.* London, 1849.— 484-85

Weitling, W. *Garantien der Harmonie und Freiheit.* Vivis, 1842.— 73

Wirth, J. G. A. *Die Geschichte der Deutschen.* Zweite durchaus verbesserte Auflage. Bd. 1. Stuttgart, 1846.— 127

[Wright, T. B. and Harlow, J.] *The Currency Question. The Gemini Letters.* London, 1844.— 339

Xenophon. *De vectigalibus.*— 106

DOCUMENTS

Factories Inquiry Commission. First Report of the Central Board of His Majesty's Commissioners. Ordered, by the House of Commons, to be printed, 28 June 1833.

Quoted from Malthus, Th. R. *Principles of Political Economy...* Second edition. London, 1836.—485

Justiniani, D. *Corpus iuris civilis.*
— *Institutiones.*—177
— *Digesta.*—393

Reports of the Inspectors of Factories to Her Majesty's Principal Secretary of State for the Home Department, for the half year ending 30th April 1849. London, 1849.—261

ANONYMOUS ARTICLES AND REPORTS
PUBLISHED IN PERIODIC EDITIONS

The Economist, No. 700, January 24, 1857: *Trade of 1856.—Decrease of Consumption.*—89
— No. 700, January 24, 1857, supplement: *The Double Standard in France.*—90

The Morning Star, No. 286, February 12, 1857: *Paris, Feb. 10. ('France').*—89

The Times, No. 22844, November 21, 1857: *Negroes and the Slave Trade. To the Editor of 'The Times'.*—251

Weekly Dispatch, No. 139, November 8, 1857: *The Panic and the People.*—148

INDEX OF PERIODICALS

SUBJECT INDEX

A

Abstraction—37-45, 75, 80-81, 101, 107-09, 153-55, 157-58, 166, 179-81, 222-23, 229-30, 232, 253, 256, 284, 334, 353-54, 362, 412
— economic category as an abstract form of real relations—8, 9, 38-45, 165, 179-80, 256, 354-55, 413
— abstract determinations—223, 334
— abstract and concrete—37-42
Accountancy and book-keeping—80, 90, 93, 96
Accumulation of capital—165-66, 205, 245, 268, 271, 273, 292, 298, 299, 313, 319, 320, 321, 345, 361, 373, 430, 431, 455-56, 508-10
— in the form of money—73, 100, 118, 134, 151, 162-66, 178, 182, 184, 214, 388, 427-28, 436
— in the form of commodities—165
— and surplus value—370-72
— and production—372, 373
— primitive—245, 388, 427-28
— bourgeois economists on—271, 274, 276-78, 296, 298, 427
Advanced capital—306, 313, 314, 316, 319-22, 356, 357, 455
Agriculture—43-44, 106, 188, 206-09, 225, 253-54, 287, 399, 400, 402, 405, 409, 412-16, 417, 418, 432, 450-52, 468-69, 508, 521-22
Alienation—87, 97-98, 158, 233, 235,

248, 381, 382-83, 389-90, 412, 438, 439, 465
America—35, 112, 120, 159, 208, 415
See also *United States of America, the*
Anatomy—42
Antiquity—40, 46-48, 94-96, 109-10, 127, 155-57, 158, 162-63, 176-77, 362, 401-04, 405-07, 410-11, 417, 418, 425, 435, 452-53, 523, 526
See also *Rome, Ancient; Community, commune; Greece, ancient; Slavery; Tribal system*
Army—15-16, 40, 45, 84, 116, 117, 119, 156, 395-96, 453
See also *War*
Art—30, 38, 46-48, 109, 163, 212, 231, 328
Asia—116, 120, 159, 161, 163, 213, 406, 414, 455
Australia—120-21, 208

B

Banknotes—51, 56-60, 63-65, 69-71, 73, 90-92, 163
Banks—51-52, 55-60, 62-64, 68-71, 96, 121, 130, 163, 210, 216-17, 257-58, 378
Barter—80, 86, 87, 103, 110, 116, 127, 132-33, 135, 139-40, 149, 158, 237
Basis and superstructure—45-48, 391, 464
See also *Law, legislation; Relations of production; Religion; State, the*

Joint-stock (share) capital; Money as a form of capital; Organic composition of capital; Reproduction; Technical composition of capital; Variable capital; Wealth
"Capital in general"—236, 272, 334, 378, 443, 444
Capitalist relations of production—see Capital; Relations of production
Caucasus—109
Chemistry—237, 286, 451
China—10, 59, 119, 120, 445
Circuit of capital—439, 440, 460-61
Circulation—131-32, 136-37, 138, 143, 184, 245, 448, 458, 460
— conditions of—123, 457, 458
— simple (of commodities and money)—51-52, 56-57, 61, 64, 70, 121-23, 128-33, 135-37, 143, 148-54, 156, 157-58, 160-63, 165-70, 172-74, 177-78, 179, 184-86, 189-93, 196-97, 198-99, 203-05, 212-14, 227, 237-38, 241, 242, 244-46, 271, 272, 291, 329, 330, 333, 334, 393-96, 439-41, 445, 460
— of capital—152, 166, 168, 184-85, 190-93, 198, 237-38, 244, 245-46, 291, 329-31, 332, 333, 338, 428, 439-43, 461, 462, 463, 466-70, 472, 502, 503, 522
— and production—152, 167, 168, 186-88, 331, 333, 335, 341, 379, 391, 435-45, 447, 458, 459, 466, 469, 470, 472, 513
— and relations of production—60, 61, 172-76, 178-80, 447, 448
— and exchange—36,44,151-52, 333
— circulation time and labour time—457, 462-63, 466-70, 471, 472, 480
— and value—167-68, 187, 193-94, 196-97, 233, 241-42, 440, 443, 460, 461-63, 470, 471
— and surplus value—246, 334, 463, 468, 470-72
— and circulation (turnover) of capital, circulating capital—441, 445, 460, 522
— and credit—52, 447, 459, 466, 467, 469
Circulation of capital—439, 440, 441, 442, 443, 445, 462, 521, 522

Civil society—17, 18, 45
See also Society, bourgeois
Classes—45, 71, 96, 101, 195, 217, 249, 328, 345, 362, 396, 425, 467, 516, 517
See also Working class
Classical bourgeois political economy—6, 34, 175, 251-53, 256, 258, 259, 274-78, 279, 473, 474, 476-84, 515-17
See also Bourgeois political economy
Coin—69, 89, 90, 121, 137, 159-60, 161, 162, 169, 171, 199, 214, 268-70, 274, 278-80, 334, 357, 359, 361-66, 367-68, 374, 377
Colonisation—157, 208, 484
Commodity—78-84, 87-88, 90-91, 102-07, 109, 110, 132, 143, 148-54, 157-59, 161, 163-66, 168, 191-92, 197-99, 202, 204-05, 227, 246, 331, 333, 445, 446, 458-60, 461
See also Realisation
Communism (socio-economic formation)
— presuppositions of—95-96, 108-09, 250-51, 337, 389, 390, 464, 466
— necessity of socialist revolution—60, 72, 96, 101, 160, 337
— social relations—95, 96, 98
— character and organisation of production and labour—90, 92-93, 95, 108-09, 149, 250-51, 433-34, 530
— absence of money relationships—90, 149
— law of economy of time—109
— development of the productive forces—439, 464, 466
— reproduction process—250, 298
— wealth—250, 411
— science under—250
— consumption—108, 251
— development of the individual—131-32, 251, 411, 439, 465
Community, commune—13, 18, 25, 41, 43, 94, 96, 106-07, 139, 159, 184, 333, 393, 399-411, 414-21, 423-24, 426, 433, 448-49
Competition—8, 10, 17, 93, 96, 138, 173, 212, 265, 349, 361, 363, 364, 376, 444, 454, 457, 471, 475, 478, 480, 487, 499
See also Reproduction

— determination of, by labour time—66, 72-73, 74, 76, 77, 78, 97, 104-06, 109, 112, 139-40, 141-42, 152, 186, 194, 197, 202, 224-25, 229, 233, 243-44, 270, 290, 375, 438, 449, 456, 462, 471, 479, 490, 491, 495, 531, 533
— and contradictions of bourgeois society—97, 171-72, 178-79
— as a social relationship—78, 94
— evolution of—139-40, 179, 431-33
— as a basis of bourgeois society— 93-96, 277, 433, 438, 448, 469
— and development of productive forces—77, 273-75, 310, 311
— and division of labour—179, 450, 471
— and price—74-78, 124-28, 139, 141, 142, 240-41, 271, 272, 353-54, 361-62, 363-65, 375, 395, 479
— and money—82-83, 88, 90-91, 94, 97, 102-03, 123-25, 134, 147, 149, 152-54, 155, 177, 185, 193, 196, 198, 199, 227, 257, 274, 377, 379
— and capital—158, 168, 180, 181, 182, 183, 185, 189-91, 193, 196-99, 201, 205, 224, 229, 232, 233, 235-39, 242-44, 249, 253, 257, 264-67, 272, 278, 283, 284, 289, 292, 311, 312, 315-22, 326, 330-32, 334, 350, 351, 376, 436, 455, 458, 460-63, 465, 468-71, 528
— and capitalist production—186-88, 238-42, 379, 433, 448
— and surplus value, and profit— 246, 250, 273, 326, 355-57, 359, 480, 481
— real and nominal—70, 75-77
— average—74-76, 129
— expression of—93, 95, 128, 140-41
— rarity as an element of—112
— law of—75, 124
— and use value—199, 200, 237, 241, 331, 334, 342, 343, 352, 376, 457, 460, 465
— and exchange, and circulation— 139, 167-68, 186-87, 193-94, 196-97, 233, 241-42, 275, 352, 376, 440, 442-43, 451, 458-60, 462-63, 470-72

Variable capital—246-47, 316

Vulgar bourgeois political economy—6-15, 18, 23

W

Wage labour—13-14, 15, 61, 84, 156, 157, 158, 180, 206-09, 248-49, 251, 252, 253, 255, 292, 328, 331, 333, 391, 393, 394-95, 396, 397, 399, 412-13, 422, 426, 427, 430, 431, 434, 435, 436, 453, 456, 459, 495, 498, 509-10, 512, 530
Wages
— level of—15, 212, 215-16, 266, 354-55
— and exchange between labour and capital—220-21, 354-55, 491
— military pay—15, 45, 84, 395-96
— and value of the product—244, 356-57
— and prices—353-55
— and demand and supply—15, 368
— and capital—511, 513, 514
— and production—461-62, 513
— and productive forces—479, 491, 496, 497, 498-99, 518
— reproduction of—283, 291, 299, 300
— and labour capacity (power)—15, 215-17, 279, 352, 354, 490, 498, 513, 514
— and necessary labour—342, 353, 478, 487, 490, 491, 495, 496
— and profit—353-55, 365-68, 478, 479, 500, 516, 517
— and consumption—290, 513
— bourgeois theories of—11-16, 181, 255, 256, 278, 515-17
Wages fund—316, 317, 318, 323
Wales—414
War—66, 163, 401, 402, 404, 406, 408, 411, 414, 415, 417-18
See also *Army*
Wealth—156, 411
— and capital (exchange value)— 222, 251, 253, 332-33, 342, 376-78, 384, 427-30, 454, 456, 465, 466, 509, 510
— social form and material content of—103, 154, 274, 411, 451
— production and distribution of— 342, 465

— concentration and accumulation of—162-63, 165-66, 454, 508
— monetary—133-34, 137, 138, 141-42, 144, 145, 149-69, 171, 178, 185, 190-91, 200-02, 214, 226, 253, 259, 271-74, 277, 292, 428-32, 435, 436, 505, 509, 520
— in the form of gold and silver—106, 113, 162-65
— and labour—222, 233, 381-84, 386-87, 389, 433
— and productive forces—275, 277, 464, 465
— as mediator between use value and exchange value—257, 275
— under communism—250, 411
— in pre-capitalist socio-economic formations—253, 254, 411, 412, 431-32, 464

— quest for enrichment—155-57, 162-64, 199-200, 250, 251, 253, 266
— bourgeois concept of—251-52, 256, 258, 259, 274, 276-78

Worker—15, 158, 197, 204, 212-18, 219-21, 223, 226, 229-30, 232-36, 243, 247-50, 283, 299, 345, 346, 349-51, 353-54, 355-59, 361, 364-66, 368-72, 381, 392, 398, 399, 412, 420, 422, 425-32, 434, 435, 438, 439, 457, 463, 475, 499-502, 508, 513, 518, 522, 526, 528, 533
See also *Working class*
Working class—249, 467, 517, 528
See also *Worker*
Working day—220, 259-68, 269, 279-81, 283, 284, 297, 326, 327, 361
World market—8-10, 66-67, 96, 97-98, 159, 160, 210, 335, 436, 451, 465